The Translator and Editors

WALTER BLANCO is Professor of English at the City University of New York. He is the translator and co-editor of the Norton Critical Edition of Herodotus's *The Histories*.

JENNIFER TOLBERT ROBERTS is Professor of Classics and History at the City College of New York and the CUNY Graduate Center. Her books include *Accountability in Athenian Government* and *Athens on Trial: The Antidemocratic Tradition in Western Thought*. Together with Walter Blanco she co-edited the Norton Critical Edition of Herodotus's *The Histories*.

THE PELOPONNESIAN WAR

A NEW TRANSLATION
BACKGROUNDS AND CONTEXTS
INTERPRETATIONS

NORTON CRITICAL EDITIONS IN THE
HISTORY OF IDEAS

AQUINAS • ST. THOMAS AQUINAS ON POLITICS AND ETHICS
translated and edited by Paul E. Sigmund

DARWIN • DARWIN
selected and edited by Philip Appleman (Third Edition)

ERASMUS • THE PRAISE OF FOLLY AND OTHER WRITINGS
translated and edited by Robert M. Adams

HERODOTUS • THE HISTORIES
*translated by Walter E. Blanco, edited by Walter E.
Blanco and Jennifer Tolbert Roberts*

HOBBES • LEVIATHAN
edited by Richard E. Flathman and David Johnston

MACHIAVELLI • THE PRINCE
translated and edited by Robert M. Adams (Second Edition)

MALTHUS • AN ESSAY ON THE PRINCIPLE OF POPULATION
edited by Philip Appleman

MARX • THE COMMUNIST MANIFESTO
edited by Frederic L. Bender

MILL • MILL: THE SPIRIT OF THE AGE, ON LIBERTY,
THE SUBJECTION OF WOMEN
edited by Alan Ryan

MORE • UTOPIA
translated and edited by Robert M. Adams (Second Edition)

NEWMAN • APOLOGIA PRO VITA SUA
edited by David J. DeLaura

NEWTON • NEWTON
selected and edited by I. Bernard Cohen and Richard S. Westfall

ROUSSEAU • ROUSSEAU'S POLITICAL WRITINGS
translated by Julia Conaway Bondanella, edited by Alan Ritter

ST. PAUL • THE WRITINGS OF ST. PAUL
edited by Wayne A. Meeks

THOREAU • WALDEN AND RESISTANCE TO CIVIL GOVERNMENT
edited by William Rossi (Second Edition)

THUCYDIDES • THE PELOPONNESIAN WAR
*translated by Walter E. Blanco, edited by Walter E. Blanco
and Jennifer Tolbert Roberts*

WATSON • THE DOUBLE HELIX: A PERSONAL ACCOUNT
OF THE DISCOVERY OF THE STRUCTURE OF DNA
edited by Gunther S. Stent

WOLLSTONECRAFT • A VINDICATION OF THE RIGHTS OF WOMAN
edited by Carol H. Poston (Second Edition)

FOR A COMPLETE LIST OF NORTON CRITICAL EDITIONS, VISIT
www.wwnorton.com/college/english/nce.welcome.htm

A NORTON CRITICAL EDITION

Thucydides
THE PELOPONNESIAN WAR

A NEW TRANSLATION
BACKGROUNDS
INTERPRETATIONS

Translated by

WALTER BLANCO

Edited by

WALTER BLANCO   JENNIFER TOLBERT ROBERTS

BOTH OF THE CITY UNIVERSITY OF NEW YORK

W • W • NORTON & COMPANY • *New York* • *London*

The text of this book is composed in Electra
with the display set in Bernhard
Composition by Publishing Synthesis
Manufacturing by Courier Companies

Library of Congress Cataloging-in-Publication Data
Thucydides.
[History of the Peloponnesian War. English]
The Peloponnesian War : a new translation, backgrounds and
contexts, interpretations / Thucydides ; translated by Walter Blanco
; edited by Walter Blanco and Jennifer Tolbert Roberts.
p.   cm. — (Norton critical edition)
Includes bibliographical references.

ISBN 0-393-97167-8 (pbk.)

1. Greece—History—Peloponnesian War, 431–404 B.C.
2. Thucydides—Criticism and interpretation. I. Blanco, Walter.
II. Roberts, Jennifer Tolbert, 1947-   .   III. Title.
DF229.T55B56 1998
938'.05—dc21 97-30006

W. W. Norton & Company, Inc., 500 Fifth Avenue, New York, N.Y. 10110
http://www.wwnorton.com

W. W. Norton & Company Ltd., Castle House, 75/76 Wells Street, London W1T 3QT

2 3 4 5 6 7 8 9 0

Contents

List of Maps

Translator's Note

I have tried to make a translation of Thucydides' famously difficult text that would be accessible to students and general readers. To do so, I have relaxed the compressed, often crabbed, syntax of the speeches and have adopted a relatively colloquial vocabulary for them and for the narrative as a whole. I offer no apologies. A strict rendering of Thucydides' speeches would make them seem as artificial to modern readers as Sidney's Arcadia or Lyly's Euphues, and would, as a result, deprive the history of the utility Thucydides himself desired for it as a work of permanent value. I will be very pleased if this text engages readers in one of the greatest histories ever written and enables them to follow some of the scholarly debate that surrounds it.

I want to thank some of those who have helped and encouraged me over the four years it has taken to complete this task. Walter Dubler has been the ideal general reader of early drafts of this translation. Professor Mireille Azzoug, Director of the Institut des Etudes Européens of the University of Paris coddled me with a teaching schedule that made long hours of translation possible during my year as Visiting Professor. Arthur Brimberg, M.D., kindly read the description of the plague and correctly diagnosed it as essentially undiagnosable. Stuart D. Warner patiently won me over to his views on the meaning of *syngraphein*, and James Romm and other members of the Fordham University Department of Classics made valuable comments on the translation during a talk I gave there last fall. Many thanks to Carol Bemis, our editor at Norton, for the thorough professionalism with which she has led this book from proposal to publication, and especial thanks to Dr. Robert Lejeune, who was endlessly generous with his time in helping us solve all manner of computer and word processor problems. Thanks also to Dr. Judith Esterquest and to Dr. Mark Nevins for the enthusiasm they have always shown for this project. I also wish to acknowledge my indebtedness to the many commentators—Andrewes, Dover, Gomme, Hornblower, and Lamberton, among others—who have led me through the Scylla and Charybdis of this text. My final and greatest debt is of course to my wife, Ingrid, for her loving support and clear-eyed common sense.

WALTER BLANCO
February, 1998

Introduction

Twenty-five hundred years ago, there was no sovereign nation known to the world as Greece. Throughout the region of the Aegean, the Mediterranean, and the Black Sea, dozens of towns whose inhabitants spoke primarily Greek exchanged goods, fought wars, and shared in assorted religious and athletic festivals such as the Olympic games. The primary political unit was the polis, or city-state, an urban center linked to its surrounding countryside. Some of the squabbling city-states were allied with the powerful polis of Sparta, but it never occurred to any of them to form a single Greek nation.

Shortly after 500 B.C.,[1] a terrifying threat from Persia galvanized the Greeks' sense of a common culture. Although Persian designs on Greece ultimately proved fruitless, it would be impossible to overestimate their consequences for world history. For when Darius, the intelligent and ambitious king of Persia, attacked the area around Athens at the beginning of the fifth century, Athens, Sparta, and other Greek states united to protect the civilization of what they were coming to call Hellas (the modern Greek name for Greece) from absorption into the Persian empire. In 490, Darius's expeditionary force was defeated by a small Greek army at the battle of Marathon northeast of Athens (see map, p. 34). Darius planned to avenge this defeat with a full-scale invasion, and when he died a few years later, the war against the Greeks was taken up by his son Xerxes. In 481, many Greek city-states formed an alliance known as the Hellenic League to counter Xerxes, and by 479 they had they succeeded in expelling the Persians from the Greek mainland.

The unity inspired by the Persian threat was short-lived, however. Though the Greeks had come to view their civilization as a cohesive entity that required protection from external enemies, still they chose not to band together in a political unit larger than the polis (plural, poleis). They sought safety against the Persians in alliances rather than political unity. Apprehensive about another invasion, many of the Greek city-states nearest Persia joined together in a powerful maritime organization designed to keep the Persians in check. Originally the Greek states looked to Spartan leadership for this alliance, but in time they settled on the Athenians, and as the years passed, the Greek world came to be divided into two spheres of influence, one Spartan and one Athenian: the Spartans led a loose association of mainland states known to historians as the Peloponnesian League, while the Athenians stood at the head of the maritime organization which came to be known as the Delian League, because its treasury was kept on the Aegean island of Delos. To some extent, this breakdown corresponded to different ethnic and linguistic groups among the Greeks, the Athenians and their allies in the Ionian group and the Spartans and theirs in the Dorian group. (Very broadly speaking, Ionian culture was more easygoing, Dorian culture more austere.)

As the danger of a third invasion appeared to recede, however, the autonomous city-states of the Greek world reverted to their customary quarreling,

---

1. Unless otherwise noted, all dates in the Introduction and in the notes to *The Peloponnesian War* are B.C.

and ironically, the very project that had brought the Greeks together proved to contain within it the seeds of a new struggle. For the large role played by the Athenian navy in defeating the Persians caused a significant shift in the balance of power among the Greek states. Sparta, once the undisputed military leader of the Greek world, now would have to share that leadership with Athens. Some Spartans accepted this change graciously, but others were apprehensive about the growth in Athens' influence and prestige.

Greek civilization thrived during the decades that followed the Persian Wars, and because the Athenians collected tribute from their allies in exchange for policing the seas, the prosperity of Athens was particularly noticeable. Under the leadership of the charismatic statesman Pericles, beautiful temples were built to adorn the Athenian acropolis. Drama flourished, inspired by the astonishing victory of the tiny coalition of Greek states over the monolithic Persian empire. Nevertheless, throughout the 470s and 460s, there were some in both Athens and Sparta who sought to cripple their rivals, and in fact an undeclared war—the so-called "First Peloponnesian War"—broke out between the Athenian alliance and Sparta's Peloponnesian League in 461.

The terms of the Thirty Years' Peace that ended the war in 446 at first seemed to offer the two leagues the prospect of amicable coexistence. Athens and Sparta each agreed to respect the other's sphere of influence. No state could be compelled to join either alliance; neutrals were free to join either side; and disputes were to be submitted to arbitration. But the Thirty Years' Peace lasted only fourteen years. The reasons for this are several. First, inevitable ambiguities in the treaty combined with the complexities of the international situation to leave the door open to further conflict. Second, even after 446 there continued to be factions in both Athens and Sparta whose members were eager for war. Third, Athens' great commercial rival, Corinth, was a key member of the Peloponnesian League and continued to regard the Athenians with suspicion.

Corinth and Athens had enjoyed friendly relations for many years when, in 461, the Corinthians became involved in a bitter border dispute with their neighbors the Megarians. Megara, lying between Corinth and Athens on the narrow isthmus that separated mainland Greece from the Peloponnese, decided to defect from the Peloponnesian League and ally with Athens instead; it was Athens' acceptance of this decision that prompted the First Peloponnesian War, and the Corinthians never forgot the slight. Years later, when the Thirty Years' Peace had been in force for a little more than a decade, tensions between Athens and Corinth erupted again, and this time the consequences were still more serious.

In 433 conflict developed between Corinth and its colony Corcyra. Although Greek colonies were politically independent from their mother states, sentimental ties generally bound them together. Corinth and Corcyra, however, had been hostile to one another for years. When Corcyra, a neutral power, sought to ally with the Athenians, everyone in Greece understood that it was because the Corcyraeans anticipated a Corinthian attack. The projected alliance, therefore, was highly problematic. The Athenians understood that accepting Corcyra into their naval confederacy would increase the likelihood of war with the Peloponnesian League. Leaving Corcyra undefended before the onslaught of the powerful Corinthian navy, however, presented a different set of problems, for the Corcyraean navy, though smaller than that of Corinth, was large enough so that Corinth's conquest of Corcyra would tip the balance of Greek naval power in favor of the Peloponnesian League. The Athenians decided to make an alliance with Corcyra. Though they were careful to define the alliance as defensive only, this fine point was of little significance in view of the impending Corinthian attack, and in the conflict that ensued, Athenians and Corinthians found themselves fighting hand to hand.

Because their relations with Corinth had grown hostile, the Athenians became uncomfortable at the large role Corinthian magistrates played in the government of the northern Greek city of Potidaea, which was in the uncomfortable position of being both a Corinthian colony and a member of the Athenian confederacy. Athens' neighbor Megara also played a major role in the escalation of hostility between the Athenians and the Peloponnesian League, to which Megara had returned by the terms of the Thirty Years' Peace. The chronology of this friction is somewhat uncertain, but around 432 the Athenians, angry with the Megarians over assorted disputes that had arisen as a result of the border they shared, passed a series of decrees barring the Megarians from trading in the ports of the Athenian confederacy. Since nearly all ports of significance in the Greek world were in this confederacy, this constituted a stranglehold on Megarian trade. The Athenians insisted they were acting in keeping with the terms of the Thirty Years' Peace and were merely regulating trade within their league; the Megarians—and the Spartans—saw things differently.

Such in brief were the long- and short-term causes of the brutal and debilitating war that consumed the Greek world for over a quarter of a century. The feelings of Panhellenism and mutual goodwill that had burst forth in the wake of Persia's defeat did not endure, and by the end of the period known as the "Pentecontaetia"—the era of (almost) fifty years between 479 and 431—the Greek poleis had embarked on a war that would alter definitively the course of Greek civilization.

Many opposed the war. Though the Spartans and their allies declared war in 432, fighting did not actually break out for a year, so great was the ambivalence on both sides. The embassies the two sides anxiously exchanged, however, served only to delay open hostilities, not to prevent them. Finally, in March 431, the Spartans' ally Thebes attacked Athens' ally Plataea by night. This action was a clear breach of the Thirty Years' Peace. Both sides made final preparations for war, and in May the Peloponnesians invaded Attica.

Both sides expected to win the war; indeed, optimists in both Athens and Sparta believed that matters could be resolved within one or two campaigning seasons. Greeks generally fought in the warmer weather and took a break in winter, though these niceties would not always be observed during the Peloponnesian War, and what had passed for "wars" in previous decades—even, in fact, the chilling war with the Persians—had generally been decided in a few decisive engagements. The strengths of the two alliances that faced one another in this war were radically different, and the difference facilitated dramatically divergent forecasts of the future. With the fruits of their far-flung commerce and the tribute from their empire—for the Delian League had evolved unmistakably into an Athenian empire—the Athenians had much more money than the Peloponnesians, and at sea they held the undisputed advantage. Athens alone possessed over 300 ships, and about a hundred more could be expected from its allies Chios, Lesbos, and of course Corcyra. The Peloponnesians—principally Corinth—could not expect to muster much more than 100 ships, and their crews were not nearly so well trained as those of the Athenians. By land, on the other hand, all Greece was agreed that no polis was a match for Spartan troops, who spent their whole lives in daily preparation for the hour of battle. If the Spartans could do one thing, it was fight infantry battles. At a local level, moreover, the Athenians were outnumbered on land. Pericles reassured his con-

stituency that they could put 13,000 men in the field and count on 16,000 others—the very young, the very old, and the resident aliens known as metics—to
defend the city walls of Athens, its port the Piraeus, and the Long Walls that had
been built to connect them (see map p. 37). He also listed 1,200 cavalry, some
of them mounted archers, and 1,600 bowmen on foot. But the army that invaded Attica in 431 included at least 30,000 fully armed soldiers from the Peloponnesus and Boeotia, and perhaps as many as 50,000.

Traditionally, conflicts between Greek states had been decided primarily
on land by combat between the heavily armed infantrymen known as hoplites.
Although the mountainous topography of Greece might seem to dictate the use
of fast-moving, light-armed soldiers, nonetheless hoplites (so-called from the
round shield known as a hoplon that they carried) had formed the core of the
Athenian and Peloponnesian infantry since well before the Persian Wars. Indeed, Greek states continued to rely primarily on hoplites even after the impressive success of the fourth-century commander Iphicrates in using
light-armed troops. Though lightly armed soldiers played some role in the Peloponnesian War—as, for example, under Demosthenes at Sphacteria—the bulk
of the fighting fell to hoplites. Outfitting themselves at their own expense with
shield (about three feet in diameter, made of wood fortified by metal), helmet,
shin guards, a spear some six feet long, and a sword of about two feet, hoplites
came from the Greek middle class. They moved in densely packed units known
as phalanxes. A hoplite phalanx was at least eight men deep, and sometimes
much deeper. Each man relied for protection on the shield of his comrade to
the right. A solid line of overlapping shields indeed provided a formidable defense, although the man at the right end of every line remained vulnerable, and
for this reason, as Thucydides tells us, a phalanx tended to shift to the right. Periodically the ranks of hoplites were eked out by mercenaries, and in an emergency by slaves. The same was true of rowers in the navy, who were ordinarily
drawn from the lowest class of citizens because those who could afford a set of
hoplite armor chose to serve in the infantry. Nevertheless, rowers played a crucial role in warfare.

The Athenian and Peloponnesian navies consisted of ships known as
triremes. Invented at some point during the seventh century to improve on the
power of the already existing two-banked model known as the penteconter, the
trireme with its three banks of oars was more expensive to build. Experience
showed, however, that the increased power of the vessel made it a worthwhile investment. Archeologists examining the remains of triremes have concluded that
they must have been at least 100 feet long, under twenty feet wide, and under
eight feet high. Each was propelled by a complement of 170 men; plainly these
sailors operated under oppressively cramped conditions, though the arrangement of rowers in three tiers reduced crowding somewhat. The 170 sailors were
accompanied by thirty additional men—ten infantrymen, four archers, and sixteen assorted others, including a helmsman, a boatswain, and a pipe player.

Practice was essential, and it went on throughout the war. Thucydides reports that the Athenians manned forty ships to send to Sicily in 426—not the
year of the famous and disastrous Sicilian expedition, but eleven years earlier—
in part because they needed to keep the navy in shape, and a later historian,
Diodorus of Sicily (first century), reported that the Spartan admiral Mindarus
spent five days training and exercising his men while preparing to fight the Athenians off the Ionian coast in 411. Triremes were fitted with rams of timber cased
in bronze, useful for pounding enemy ships to loosen their seams, and practice
included work on ramming maneuvers.

The finest triremes of the fifth century belonged to the Athenians. Pericles' strategy for winning the war was grounded in his keen awareness of Athenian strengths and weaknesses. The Athenians, he proposed, should abandon the countryside to the enemy, whom they stood little chance of defeating in a pitched battle, and retreat behind the Long Walls. A steady supply of foodstuffs from the cities of the empire would be guided safely into port by the Athenian navy, cutting off the possibility of a siege. Meanwhile the powerful Athenian fleet would harass the enemy's coasts. Two things were essential for the strategy: Athens had to refrain from trying to expand its empire and to make peace as soon as Sparta was willing to accept the status quo. Pericles' plan had much to recommend it, but it did not take into account either a foreseeable difficulty—the natural urge to fight that would come over the average soldier when he saw his land being ravaged—or an unforeseeable one, the dreadful plague that entered the city and spread quickly in the unsanitary and overcrowded urban area. The populace was so frustrated by Pericles' policies that they deposed him in the summer of 430; they re-elected him in the next elections, but he promptly died of the plague. After his death, the Athenians did choose to march out and meet the Spartans in battle.

The Peloponnesian War gets its name because the primary source for it has been the history written by Thucydides, an Athenian general. Obviously the Spartans must have called it the Athenian war, but it has been known to history as the Peloponnesian War. This first phase of the Peloponnesian War, the ten years known as the Archidamian War (431–421, named after the Spartan king Archidamus), was perceived by some contemporaries as a war in itself. It was Thucydides who enshrined the view that these ten years were in fact part of a longer war that heated up again after 421 and then continued until 404. In any event, fighting did cease for a few years after the Peace of Nicias ended the Archidamian War in 421, but the international scene was extremely tense—Spartans and Athenians actually faced one another in battle at Mantinea in the Peloponnesus in 418—and by 415 it was clear that the war was back on.

In June of 415, a huge Athenian armament set sail against Syracuse in Sicily, ostensibly in response to an appeal from Athens' Sicilian ally Egesta, but in reality to expand the Athenian empire to include this very fertile island. Pericles would not have approved, although given the restless adventurism of the Athenian people, the desire for this kind of enterprise might also have been foreseen. The expedition had been encouraged by Pericles' young and hot-headed ward Alcibiades, whose good looks and showy lifestyle charmed the populace. Nicias, the conservative older general who had helped negotiate the Peace of 421, opposed the expedition; nevertheless, the Athenians sent him as Alcibiades' colleague. The Peloponnesians threw their support to Syracuse, and the adventure ended in disaster for Athens. Nicias was put to death, thousands of his fellow soldiers were killed or enslaved, and the huge fleet was lost.

By this time Alcibiades, under suspicion at home for scoffing at time-honored religious customs, had defected to the Spartans, who at his instigation had fortified a post at Decelea in Attic territory. The Peloponnesians also rose to the naval challenge and built a sizable fleet. The Athenians struggled on, however, and it was not so much the resourcefulness of Sparta that determined the outcome of the war as the intervention of Persia. Beginning in 412, the Persians consented to back Sparta financially, in exchange for the promise that the victorious Peloponnesians would return the Greek cities on the western coast of what is now Turkey to Persian rule.

After over two decades of fighting, in 405 the Persian-backed Spartans defeated the Athenians decisively in the battle of Aegospotami, and by 404 the war was formally brought to an end. Sparta had won; but what, really, had the Spartans gained by the painful loss of life among their fighting men? Some advocated obliterating Athens from the face of the earth, but cooler heads prevailed and the city was spared. A puppet government of thirty pro-Spartan oligarchs was set up in Athens—the so-called "Thirty Tyrants"—but this bloody regime proved so unpopular that when the Athenian democrats organized to overthrow it, they received some support from Pausanias, the young king of Sparta. Fearing the alliance of the murderous oligarchs with Sparta's successful general Lysander, architect of the victory at Aegospotami, Pausanias helped arrange an agreement among the various factions. Democracy was restored at Athens, the oligarchy overthrown, and the first recorded amnesty in history ratified by both parties.

Nor did Sparta retain hegemony in Greece throughout the decades that followed. In the 390s, Sparta alienated its allies one by one, with the result that by 395 Corinth and Thebes joined with the Athenians, who had shown great determination in rebuilding their economy, in making war on the Spartans. Although the peace treaty of 404 stipulated the end of the naval confederacy and thus signaled the end of the Athenian empire, by 377 Athens inaugurated a new naval alliance known today as the Second Athenian Confederacy, organized on a more egalitarian basis than the earlier fifth-century league. By the 360s, Thebes occupied the most prominent position in Greek intercity politics. Finally, in 338 the crafty Macedonian king Philip II defeated a hastily formed coalition of Greek states at Chaeronea in Boeotia and brought the freedom of the poleis to an end. Assassinated two years later, he was succeeded by his son Alexander, whose conquest of large chunks of western Asia, as well as Egypt, earned him the surname "the Great." With the death of Alexander in 323, the classical Greek world came to an end. Alexander's empire was divided among various generals, and throughout the Mediterranean world a new composite culture came into being, to which historians have given the name Hellenistic, meaning Greek-like but not entirely Greek. In this world there was no longer room for the polis that was a sovereign nation, whose citizens argued passionately about matters of war and peace, of right and wrong, and listened to the kinds of speeches we read in Thucydides' history. By 300, the world of the Peloponnesian War was very much a thing of the past.

No historian can be certain which changes in the Greek world of the fourth century can confidently be ascribed to the long war of 431–404, or just how the debilitating effects of that war contributed to Philip's success in conquering Greece. It is clear, however, that the prolonged war accounted for the decline of Corinth as a major power. Together with the plague, moreover, the war took a considerable bite out of the Athenian population. As many as 50,000 men, women, and children probably died in the epidemic. War casualties were never added up by the Athenians as far as we know, but they seem to have included at least 5,000 hoplite soldiers and 12,000 sailors (including some 3,000 executed by Lysander after Aegospotami). This was a huge number when one bears in mind Athens' male citizen population in 431, probably about 43,000. Contemporary sources, moreover, claimed that the Thirty Tyrants of 404–403 killed 1,500 citizens. It seems safe to say that the number of adult male citizens in 403 was half what it had been in 431. Where were women to find husbands?

In Sparta, depopulation within the citizen class was also problematic; when women began maintaining the population by conceiving children with

non-citizen fathers, a whole new class was created, fostering social change—
something Spartans feared even more than most Greeks. Though radically different from Athens, the social, political, and economic structures of Sparta were
not any better able to protect the state in a long war. In order to appreciate the
particular kinds of strains posed by this war, it is necessary to understand some
basic facts of Greek life that Thucydides does not tell us, because he imagines
that we know. For all his claims of creating a *ktēma eis aiei*, a "possession for all
time," Thucydides assumes a contemporary Greek readership for his work. He
expects his readers to know the Homeric epics, the *Iliad* and the *Odyssey*, and
Herodotus' *Histories* of the Persian Wars, and he assumes a general knowledge
of the Greek polis and the Greek lifestyle.

As Greek poleis, Athens and Sparta had much in common. In both states
people spoke Greek, worshipped the traditional Olympian gods, valued a government based on law, and cherished their independence. Slave labor formed
an important part of both states' economies, and in neither Athens nor Sparta
could women participate in government. All able-bodied male citizens were expected to serve in the army. In other respects, however, the states were very different. The Spartans prized martial valor above all else and had organized their
state to promote military strength. At birth, Spartan infant boys were presented
for inspection to state officials who decided whether they were sturdy enough
to be raised. (Weaklings could be disposed of in Athens too, but there the decision lay with the father alone.) Spartan males were separated from their mothers at the age of seven so they could be raised by soldiers. They remained among
men at least until the age of thirty, and even if they were married, men under
thirty could not live with their wives on a regular basis. The unusual social and
economic system of classical Sparta was made possible in part by an exceptionally high ratio of slave to free citizen. The adult male citizens of Sparta—a
few thousand strong—were able to live in barracks and share common meals
because the land was worked by a large population of state serf-slaves called
helots. Handicraft occupations were relegated to a third class, the perioikoi (literally, the "the people who lived in the vicinity"), who were neither citizens nor
slaves. Helots and perioikoi had no civic rights. Members of both groups might
serve in the Peloponnesian land or naval forces, though the Spartans were understandably skittish about placing weapons in helot hands. Among the male
citizens—who were assigned equal plots of land by the state—authority was al-
lotted as follows: two men, one from the family of the Agiads and another from
that of the Eurypontids, served concurrently as kings. The power was passed
down in each family, usually from father to son. Keeping some kind of check
on royal power were five ephors, literally "overseers," who were elected from a
limited number of prestigious families, and twenty-eight men over sixty years of
age who comprised the council of elders, the gerousia. Periodically the army
met as an assembly, the apella, which could vote—by banging on shields—after
hearing speeches by prominent men. This assembly, however, did not debate.

Most power at Sparta lay not in the apella but in smaller bodies of government. At Athens, by contrast, where the assembly debated loudly and long,
power truly lay with the adult male citizenry, who had the authority to impeach
any magistrate or general whose conduct had displeased them. By the time of
the Persian Wars, the Spartan state had already been organized for quite some
time along the principles outlined above, but in Athens, the state was still evolving. Early in its history, the state of Athens had come to include all the little
towns on the peninsula of Attica, a territory of about 1,000 square miles. Tradition ascribed the unification of Attica to the legendary king Theseus. As in most

parts of the Greek world, kingship failed to endure in Athens, and with the passing of time, the political base of government gradually broadened. The duties of the king came to be performed by three officials known as archons. At first these served life terms. During the eighth century, the term of the three archons was shortened to ten years; by around 650 we see nine archons serving for a single year. Continuing social and economic unrest led the Athenians to appoint a lawgiver, Draco, to formulate a written code of law. His harsh code—later described as written in blood rather than in ink—failed to put an end to tensions within the state, and shortly after 600, Solon was asked to arbitrate among the various classes. Solon established a sliding scale of privilege among the various classes that made up the Attic citizenry, dividing Athenians into four groups based on income. Only the highest class was eligible for election to the position of archon, but the middle two classes could hold lower offices, and everyone was eligible to participate in the assembly of citizens and serve on juries.

In 560 the energetic and ambitious Peisistratus set himself up as tyrannos of Athens by a military coup. Inevitably translated by the English word "tyrant," a tyrannos was originally just a strongman who came to power outside traditional legal channels; often his regime fostered the general welfare and was affectionately regarded. Peisistratus' sons, however, were unable to retain popular support. Hipparchus was assassinated in 514 and Hippias driven into exile in 510. Popular perceptions of the Peisistratids were of great interest to Thucydides, and he discussed them at length in Book 6 in the context of the religious scandals of the year 415.

Shortly after the end of the Peisistratid era, a reformer from the celebrated family of the Alcmaeonids (to which Pericles also belonged) reorganized the Athenian citizenry into ten tribes, breaking down the tribal loyalties among aristocrats that had been making life difficult for ordinary people. Under Cleisthenes' system, each tribe chose by lot fifty councillors to serve on the boule (Council of 500) and elected one strategos. Most often translated as "general," a strategos (plural, strategoi) also had considerable political influence, and had the right to summon the assembly and to address it before others could speak. The term of strategos was only one year long, but it could be, and often was, renewed at the next election. The painful experience of the Persian Wars suggested to the Athenians that the job of strategos was the really significant one, and that it would be a safe democratic measure to begin selecting the archons by lot. Combined with terms of a single year, the use of the lot to select officials was to become one of the most important devices by which the Athenians blocked the development of a self-interested political elite. A check on individual ambitions was also provided by the curious procedure known as ostracism, named for the broken piece of pottery that the Athenians used as a ballot to determine if any citizen should be banished to preserve order in the state. The man with the most votes against him would be compelled to leave Attica for ten years. He did not stand accused of any crime, and when the ten years were up, he was free to return and resume his civic and property rights. By this inverse popularity contest, the Athenians sought to prevent another tyranny and provided redress other than civil war for those occasions when two or more men locked horns over the best policy for the state.

The first ostracisms took place in the context of the Persian Wars, when Aristides, who would later carry out the assessment of the various members of the Delian League, lost out to his rival Themistocles. Having received the greatest number of votes, Aristides was banished for ten years, though under the stress of the war, the Athenians decided to recall him before this term was up. Themistocles himself was a later victim of the procedure. In the conflicts over Athenian imperialism during the Pentecontaetia, ostracism befell Thucydides, the son of Melesias, a relative of the historian (Thucydides, son of Olorus.)

Around 460 the Athenian constitution received additional fine-tuning at the hands of one Ephialtes, who transferred most trials to the jurisdiction of the people, undermining the authority of the august Council of the Areopagus, which had previously heard many cases. After effecting this democratic reform, Ephialtes died under mysterious circumstances and the leadership of the democratic party fell to his associate Pericles. A few years later, the historian Thucydides was born into this proud imperial and democratic state. (We must always bear in mind that "democracy" to Greeks meant equal opportunity for rich and poor male citizens to participate in government, rather than in the modern sense that accords civic rights to both sexes and outlaws slavery. Slavery existed in all Greek states, and women voted nowhere. The belief in the superiority of male citizens to slaves, women, children, and non-Greeks, i.e., the lack of any concept of universal human dignity, may have contributed to the Greeks' eventual ability to make war brutally and indiscriminately on other Greek males as well.)

Thucydides was born into a wealthy family around 460, and like other Greek aristocrats, he probably never had to support himself by working. Almost nothing is known about him beyond the details that can be inferred from his writing; it is fitting that so little is known of the personal life of this man who was determined to excise all such details from his history. From his account of the Peloponnesian War, we learn that his family owned gold mines in Thrace and that it was for a military failure in Thrace, where he served as strategos during the Peloponnesian War, that he was exiled from Athens in 423. The two may be connected; it is possible that Thucydides was devoting too much attention during his generalship to family business and not enough to state business, and that genuine laxness led to his failure to prevent the key post of Amphipolis from falling into Spartan hands. On the other hand, Thucydides and his colleague in the Thracian region, Eucles, had the misfortune to be pitted against the eloquent and enterprising Spartan commander Brasidas, a formidable opponent. Thucydides' exile deprived him of the opportunity to see political developments in Athens at first hand, but he had many informants for Athenian affairs, and it may have done his history more good than harm. Leisure for travel and writing fostered the development of his work, and he plainly profited from conversations with soldiers on the Peloponnesian side—quite possibly with central figures such as Brasidas himself, about whose motives he seems strikingly well informed. The combination in a single person of the citizen's passionate involvement with the exile's special perspective is only one of many parallels between Thucydides and Machiavelli.

Though he did not complete his narrative, Thucydides lived to see the end of the war and probably died around 400, perhaps violently: several sources report that he was murdered. One tradition maintained that his unfinished manuscript survived because his daughter preserved it. The text breaks off while he is recounting the events of 411, and it remained for his younger contemporary Xenophon, also an Athenian, to tell the story of the war's last years and the final Spartan victory. (Xenophon's account appears on pp. 353–77 in this edition.) It is possible that Thucydides would have broadened the scope of his history had he lived to complete and revise it. The role of Persia, for example, which became increasingly prominent during the years after 411, might have been re-examined and explored more deeply. It seems likely, however, that the essential focus of the manuscript as it now stands is an accurate indicator of his priorities as a historian. Much that another writer might have chosen to stress was de-emphasized in his work, and much was left out entirely. Foremost among Thucydides' omissions is the role played by economic considerations in the international conflicts of the fifth century. Attica was not rich in natural resources, and we would like to know more about how the Athenians financed this war: it is only from other sources that we know the imperial tribute was raised in 425. The land of Attica was suited to the olive tree; it also provided clay, marble, and—fortunately for the Athenians—silver, without which it is difficult to see how they could have built the fleet that had defeated Xerxes at Salamis. Timber and grain, however, were conspicuously lacking. Ancient historians are notorious for giving economic factors short shrift in their writings, but the Athenians were no fools, and they felt their dependence on foreign markets for vital imports quite keenly. Grain was necessary to stay alive, and timber to build ships. These needs explain in part the watchful eye the Athenians kept on the Black Sea area and on the world of the western Greeks in Sicily and southern Italy. In addition, the trade rivalry between Athens and the Isthmian city of Corinth was central to tensions between Athens and the Peloponnesian League.

Nor is Thucydides the most useful source for the bitterness with which some Athenians plainly regarded the war. From Thucydides, we learn that both sides included some who supported entry into the war and some who opposed it; he also reports a speech by Pericles chastising Athenians who were sending embassies to the Spartans seeking to make peace. His treatment of Pericles' deposition in 430, however, ascribes the Athenians' action largely to emotion. He does not give the names of the politicians who agitated for Pericles' removal, nor the speeches they gave, nor the strategies they wished to deploy in place of his. Nowhere, moreover, does he mention the powerful anti-war plays that were produced in Athens.

The comic dramatist Aristophanes had much to say about the war, none of it laudatory: the *Acharnians* highlights the economic deprivation it brought about. Euripides' exquisitely painful *Trojan Women*, though ostensibly about the sufferings entailed by the Greek victory at Troy, plainly sought to focus the Athenian audience's attention on the horrors of war in general, and perhaps on the recent destruction the Athenians had visited on the people of Melos in particular: the play was produced in the spring of 416, just after the grisly events on Melos narrated by Thucydides in Book 5, and there is no reason to doubt that the audience included men who had taken part in the killing. We learn more about the sufferings of noncombatants from Athenian drama—even when that drama is comedy of the most fanciful and fantastic nature—than we do from Thucydides' detailed narrative of the war. Thucydides' account sheds no light on women's experience during the twenty-seven miserable years from 431 to 404—on the responsibilities they were forced to assume in men's absence, on the impact of the shrinking marriage pool, and on the measures the dearth of citizen husbands forced them to consider. This stunning omission reveals much of what Thucydides thought history was all about. If Thucydides surpassed Herodotus in tough-minded analytical capacity, Herodotus eclipsed him in his grasp of history's richness and breadth.

Thucydides makes plain his familiarity with Herodotus' work. He is open about his wish to distinguish his kind of history from that of his renowned predecessor, remarking pointedly in Book 1 (22) that his work lacks the romantic, fantastical elements that make for good entertainment but is substantial enough to last forever. So much for the charming tales with which Herodotus had built up to the sober accounts of battles and campaigns—anecdotes featuring children raised among sheep, kings who fathered lion cubs, and dolphins who carried famous singers to land. In fact Thucydides was profoundly indebted to Herodotus. What he did for the Peloponnesian War was not entirely different from what Herodotus had done for the Persian Wars; together with Herodotus, Thucydides enshrined the war monograph as an important branch of the genre of history writing, one that is still very much alive today. Like Herodotus, he assembled facts primarily through living informants—what we would call "oral history"—gathering as much data as his lifespan would allow and shaping it into a coherent story of a war and its causes. He also entrenched the convention, conspicuous in Herodotus' work, of reporting verbatim speeches he could not possibly have heard—a custom that may have its origins in Homeric epic, where speeches figure prominently. To twentieth-century readers, this habit of Greek and Roman historians appears peculiar; today it marks a work as historical fiction—or as history written for children. Ancient readers thought differently. They knew perfectly well that the words they encountered in these speeches were not likely to be the actual words spoken, even in those rare cases where the historian was actually present (as Thucydides surely was, for example, at many speeches given in Athens prior to his exile). By the insertion of speeches in dramatic form, Thucydides and other ancient historians were able to give their text a transparent feel, breaking down the barriers that divided their readers from the actual events described. Readers "listening" to the speeches of politicians addressing the Athenian assembly or generals offering encouragement to their troops were able to enter into the minds of those who had lived the experience the historian sought to bring alive. They also give meaning to and create a context for the torrent of events described in the narrative. Thucydides sets forth his guidelines for composing the speeches in Chapter 22 of Book 1:

> As to the speeches of the participants, either when they were about to enter the war or after they were already in it, it has been difficult for me and for those who reported to me to remember exactly what was said. I have, therefore, written what I thought the speakers must have said given the situations they were in, while keeping as close as possible to the gist of what was actually said.

Thucydides was careful to distinguish between his effort to convey what was said—a project in which imagination as well as the thirst for accuracy played a role—and his attempts to discover what actually happened:

> As to the events of the war, I have not written them down as I heard them from just anybody, nor as I thought they must have occurred, but have consistently described what I myself saw or have been able to learn from others after going over each event in as much detail as possible. I have found this task to be extremely arduous, since those who were present at these actions gave varying reports on the same event, depending on their sympathies and their memories.

Thucydides expressed serious reservations about Herodotus' belief in the value of research into the past. At first glance, this seems puzzling; is not history, by definition, about the past? In a culture that was just becoming literate, however—in which extensive written sources for knowing about what happened outside one's own presence were just coming into being—ascertaining and analyzing the facts about events before the birth of any possible informant was extraordinarily difficult. And in fact it might be more honest for historians of our own day to recognize that we can "know" the factors at work in the decision-making of Lyndon Johnson differently from the way in which we can "know" the factors at work in the decision-making of Pericles—that the work of a historian of ancient Greece is radically different from the work of a historian of the Vietnam War. Thucydides believed that only contemporary history could really be written. It is an interesting idea, and not very popular today, when historians are likely to point to the lack of perspective that undermines the work of those who live too close to the events they seek to analyze. We might also want to consider the possibility that some of what Thucydides says in comparing himself to his illustrious predecessor was simply a product of professional rivalry, as when he boasts that "his" war was bigger and longer and more complex than the one Herodotus had treated.

Herodotus aside, it is difficult to trace direct influence on Thucydides. In attempting to ascertain both the facts and their significance, Thucydides certainly shows an affinity with the growing enthusiasm for medical research in fifth-century Greece. In Ionia during Thucydides' lifetime, the physician Hippocrates (c. 460–377) and his followers were compiling detailed case histories from which they made general inferences about diseases. The scientific method plainly struck a responsive chord in Thucydides. We see this not only in his tireless determination to ferret out information and subject it to analysis, but also in his very specific interest in the plague that struck Athens in 430, an epidemic he describes in meticulous detail so that, he says, "should the disease ever strike again, someone who gives an examination may have some prior knowledge of it and not fail to recognize it" (2.48).

Whether Thucydides was actually influenced by the writings of the Hippocratics is uncertain; it may be that he simply evolved similar interests as a consequence of living at the same time. Much the same can be said about the impact of other schools of thought and literary genres. Certainly many aspects of Thucydides' work—most conspicuously the account of the Athenian expedition against Sicily—show thought patterns similar to those of the great tragedies composed in the fifth century by Aeschylus (525–456, older than Thucydides) and by his contemporaries Sophocles (c. 496–406) and Euripides (c. 485–c. 406). The dramatic portrayal of discovery and recognition and of the sudden reversal of fortune provides another parallel. This need not mean, however, that Thucydides was influenced by the tragic dramatists nor they by him. Thucydides' contemporaries also included the itinerant intellectuals known as sophists, non-Athenian Greek teachers and rhetoricians who haunted Athens in the later fifth century, instructing young men in the art of persuasive speaking and evolving theories about social structure and power relations. Several of Plato's dialogues depict Socrates' encounters with sophists (Hippias of Elis and Protagoras of Abdera, to name just two) and their followers. Socrates and Thucydides were contemporaries, and may even have died in the same year. The presentation of two sides of an argument apparent in the paired speeches of Thucydides' history may well reflect the increasing popularity of verbal sparring.

The history of the Peloponnesian War can and must be eked out from other sources besides Thucydides. A variety of inscriptions from the fifth century shed light on the internal politics of many of the city-states involved, particularly on those of Athens. Archeology has also proved a useful tool, particularly in the reconstruction of battles and fortifications. Tragedy and comedy, as we have seen, offer a window into the lives of noncombatants and the concerns of Athenian intellectuals, and the last years of the war were recounted by Xenophon. Some material on these years can also be extracted from the manuscript known as the Oxyrhynchus papyri, named for the site in Egypt where they were found in A.D. 1906; but though the so-called Oxyrhynchus historian seems a more astute observer and analyst than Xenophon, many of the nine hundred or so lines of his text that survive deal with the period shortly after the war. Speeches by fourth-century orators such as Lysias and Aeschines often make reference to the events of the war, and Andocides' speech *On the Mysteries* is a useful addition to Thucydides' account of the religious scandals of 415.

The workings of democracy are also illuminated in two different works both called *The Constitution of the Athenians*. One is a diatribe whose unknown author is sometimes called the Old Oligarch. Formerly he was called pseudo-Xenophon, and at one time historians thought he was Xenophon himself, with whose writings the little pamphlet had come to be classed. Hostile to Athenian democracy (unless he is writing tongue in cheek, which is a possibility), the author seeks to lay bare the calculated way in which the Athenian demos ("people") retains power in its own hands and keeps the rich—or, as he calls them, the better people—in check. The document makes an interesting contrast with the view of Athenian democracy put forward in Pericles' funeral oration in Book 2 of Thucydides' work. The other *Constitution of the Athenians* is much longer and contains a wealth of information about the machinery of Athenian government. It is classed with the works of Aristotle, though it may have been written by one of his students. The first part treats the evolution of the democracy; the second discusses in detail the functioning of the constitution at the time it was written, perhaps around 330.

Other sources add to our knowledge of the war. The *World History* of Diodorus of Sicily, written in the first century, discussed fifth-century Greece in detail. Plutarch, who wrote around A.D. 100, composed biographies of several important statesmen who were active during the war and the years that led up to it—mostly Athenians, such as Aristides, Themistocles, Cimon, Pericles, Nicias, and Alcibiades, but also the Spartan Lysander. Both Diodorus and Plutarch were able to make use of valuable sources that no longer survive. These lost sources include the fourth-century historians Theopompus and Ephorus, as well as Timaeus, who lived around 300, and Philistus, who had been a boy in Syracuse at the time of the Athenian siege.

Our ability to understand the war fully is compromised severely by the lack of authentic Spartan sources. It is not just a cliché that Spartans neglected the intellectual and verbal side of life; they truly chose not to leave written records of their actions or concerns, thus leaving themselves vulnerable to a wide variety of misinterpretations and misunderstandings.

Though Thucydides' history should be fleshed out from other sources, his compelling narrative will always remain our primary avenue to understanding this devastating war. Thucydides is often described as the first "objective" or "scientific" historian. If that were true, it would be astonishing, since history is, by definition, neither objective nor scientific. Thucydides' history of the Peloponnesian War was conceived in passion and patriotism, circumstances from which it derives much of its vigor. Thucydides' great strengths were three. He had a masterful understanding of human psychology, keen powers of analysis, and tremendous narrative power. Working together, these skills make his account of the war both gripping and thought-provoking.

Thucydides' gifts have won him an extraordinary reputation in the West, beginning with the translation of his text into Latin by Lorenzo Valla in the fifteenth century. Alfonso V of Aragon (A.D. 1416–1458) frequently copied the text by his own hand, and Emperor Charles V (A.D. 1500–1558) was said to have carried Thucydides' history with him when he traveled. Readers of Thucydides have conceived his view of the world in a wide variety of ways (frequently corresponding to their own constructions of the human condition). Hobbes translated Thucydides into English in the 1620s and was convinced he had been a supporter of monarchy. During the French Revolution era of the 1790s, opponents of popular government believed that the sins of democracy leapt from the pages of Thucydides, who, they believed, had been prescient in foreseeing the awful events of their own day. Also at this time a distinguished member of the British Parliament claimed there was no question with which he was compelled to deal in debate on which Thucydides did not afford guidance. During the Victorian era, the notes to Thomas Arnold's edition of Thucydides were laced with modern parallels. Ancient history, Arnold maintained, was in reality "a living picture of things present" and hence ideal reading for statesman and citizen alike.[2] During World War I, quotations from Pericles' Funeral Oration were placed in buses in London to hearten passengers and confirm their belief that they were fighting for something precious.

Similar convictions of Thucydides' relevance to modern life have been apparent on the other side of the Atlantic as well. In A.D. 1777 the future president John Adams wrote to his wife that he sometimes felt inclined to write a history of the American Revolution in imitation of Thucydides, since he saw striking resemblances between the revolution and the Peloponnesian War. In A.D. 1897 Basil Gildersleeve, the founder of the discipline of classics in American universities, published an essay in the *Atlantic* comparing the anguish of the Civil War with that experienced in fifth-century Greece and bearing the thought-provoking title "A Southerner in the Peloponnesian War." The wars of the twentieth century have spawned similar parallels. During World War II, the editors of the *Saturday Review* labeled Thucydides "required reading" for those who wished to understand what was at stake. Speaking at Princeton University in A.D. 1947, General George C. Marshall observed that he doubted "whether a man can think with full wisdom and with deep convictions regarding certain of the basic international issues of today who has not at least reviewed in his mind the period of the Peloponnesian War and the fall of Athens."[3] Several years later *Life* magazine carried Thucydides into the cold war era, running a series of articles cautioning Americans about the disasters that might attend on ignoring the lessons of the Greek past. Robert Campbell's "How a Democracy Died," published during the fighting in Korea, was designed for high drama. "The world," Campbell began,

> was divided, the combat was mortal and the issue in deep doubt. While the soldiers fought back and forth in savage seesaw across the 38th parallel, most of the world's lesser states—although proclaiming with stubborn solemnity their sovereignty and independence—clustered in fear around one or the other of the two great powers. Of these two, one was a great democracy: rich in freedom, its citizenry proud to rule themselves. The other was a police state: compact, powerful, mobilized within and insulated against the outer world. Each so dedicated and so divided, their conflict far transcended a mere power war between nations. Riot and revolution, contemptuous of the state frontiers, blazed through the world. Neutrals fretted futilely as the flames licked near—and were consumed. This was humanity's great civil war.

---

2. Thomas Arnold, *The History of the Peloponnesian War by Thucydides,* 3.xiv.
3. Quoted in M. Wight, *Power Politics,* introduction by H. Bull and C. Holbraad, eds. (New York, 1979), 24–25.

Campbell conceded that the world of A.D. 1950 could be so described, but he went on to reveal that he was in fact speaking of the Peloponnesian War, whose "graph of disaster" was recorded in meticulous detail by "a historian named Thucydides." While conceding that "history does not consist of a series of pat and perfect analogies," Campbell maintained nonetheless that when reading Thucydides "a deadly parallel leaps to the mind," for there one finds portrayed "two states, the most powerful in the world, which were not unlike the great protagonists of the mid-20th Century world."[4]

American involvement in Vietnam also brought Thucydides' somber work before many minds: did not the failure of Athens' efforts in Sicily caution against this sort of adventure? When Congressman Wyche Fowler, Jr. of Georgia read from Thucydides' account of the Sicilian expedition during the congressional debate over military action in the Persian Gulf in January 1990, some classicists were moved; others were bemused at the echo of the 1960s and 70s. Recently a group of ancient and modern scholars met at the Woodrow Wilson Center in Washington, D.C., for two days to explore parallels between the Peloponnesian War and the Korean War. The undying fame of the Peloponnesian War is owing to the historian who gave it its identity; Thucydides' text, we discover, is hardy and susceptible to a wide spectrum of interpretations.

The questions Thucydides' history presents are many. Some can be answered only by evaluating his work in the light of other data on the Peloponnesian War—questions such as whether his writing contains factual errors, or whether he suppressed evidence that undermined his interpretations. Certain difficulties can never be resolved, such as the relationship of the speeches in the history to the words actually spoken. Some readers would say the text alone is sufficient to judge whether, say, the Athenian expedition against Sicily had a good chance of success, or whether the decision-making that led up to the Peace of Nicias in 421 was prudent or irresponsible; others would bring external evidence to bear on these questions. But many of the most intriguing questions raised by Thucydides' work are internal to the text. Did Thucydides believe that international relations could or should be governed by laws of morality? Did Thucydides expect his book to enable people to change the course of history by avoiding mistakes, or did he simply want to provide the intellectual satisfaction of understanding historical processes? What did Thucydides think about political forms in general and Athenian democracy in particular? How did Thucydides compose his history—did he really write the thoughtful, analytical prose we have today year by year as the events were fresh in his mind, or, working with extensive notes, did he shape his account of the war with the benefit of hindsight? Does the text reflect changes in interpretation as the war progressed? Did Thucydides hope for his native Athens to win the war? Did he expect it? Plainly Thucydides saw the dark side of human nature, and he has often been compared to Hobbes; but was Thucydides a pessimist? Did he or did he not believe people had what we today would call free will? What, according to Thucydides, made history turn out the way it did? To what degree did Thucydides believe it was possible to know the truth about history? Individual readers have come to widely differing conclusions in grappling with these questions, and they will continue to do so as long as Thucydides' text is read.

JENNIFER TOLBERT ROBERTS

4. *Life* 30 (January 1, 1951): 96.

The Text of
THE PELOPONNESIAN WAR

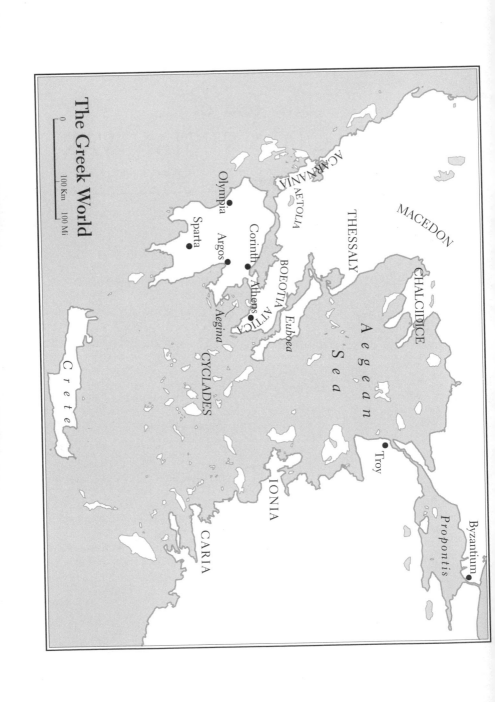

The Greek World

0

100 Km

100 Mi

Olympia

Sparta

Argos

Corinth

Athens

Aegina

ATTICA

BOEOTIA

Euboea

AETOLIA

ACARNANIA

THESSALY

MACEDON

CHALCIDICE

CYCLADES

Crete

Aegean Sea

IONIA

CARIA

Troy

Propontis

Byzantium

Book 1

Book 1 is the only book in *The Peloponnesian War* devoted to events that preceded the outbreak of the war of 431 to 404. Because the events are presented thematically rather than in chronological order, readers may wish to consult the chronology on pp. 523–26.

In this book Thucydides begins to develop several of the themes that will be important in his work, such as the nature of naval power and of leadership. He begins with a statement (1) of the war's historical significance; after a digression on early Greek history (2–19), he discusses the problems that hinder an accurate understanding of historical fact (20–21), explains his methodology as a historian (including his approach to speeches delivered before and during the war) (22), and returns to expand his claim about the importance of the Peloponnesian War, comparing it to the wars with Persia (23). At the close of chapter 23 he identifies what, in his view, was the most accurate explanation for the outbreak of the war: the growth of Athenian power and the Spartans' attendant fear. He then proceeds to detail the crises that led up to the outbreak of the war, beginning with the civil strife at Epidamnus and the resulting clash between Corcyra, a neutral state, and Corinth, an important member of the Peloponnesian League (24–31). The first speeches of the history appear in 32–43: Corcyra seeks to join the Athenian alliance, arguing that its navy will be important for the Athenians in the event of war with the Peloponnesian League. Corinth predictably tries to dissuade the Athenians from making the alliance, maintaining that war can be avoided. Chapters 44–55 concern the new phase of conflict initiated by the Athenians' decision to make a defensive alliance with Corcyra. Chapters 56–66 treat the escalation of tensions as the Athenians move against the northern Greek city of Potidaea, originally a Corinthian colony but for some years a member of the Athenian alliance. In chapters 67–88, Thucydides describes the congress that took place at Sparta to debate the need for war with the Athenians, including several long speeches.

Chapter 89 begins the section known as the Pentecontaetia, the "period of fifty years" (roughly speaking) that separated the Persian Wars from the Peloponnesian War, and it continues through Chapter 118. This gallop through a rich and conflict-ridden half-century is the closest thing historians possess to a contemporary account of this pivotal era. At 119–125, Thucydides describes the second congress at Sparta, the one that issued a declaration of war on the Athenians. Chapters 126–146 are devoted to the negotiations that occupied the prospective belligerents for the seven months or so that divided the declaration of war from the actual fighting. The issues raised in the course of these negotiations move Thucydides to include in his discussion a long digression on events involving the Athenian Themistocles and the Spartan Pausanias during the years after the Persian Wars.

Thucydides places comparatively little emphasis on the Athenian economic sanctions against the small Isthmian state of Megara as factors in bringing on the war. Many modern historians have seen these as more important and have explored the references to the decrees against Megara in the writings of Aristophanes (*Acharnians*, lines 524–39 and *Peace*, lines 606–609 and 615–618). The Megarian episode is also discussed in chapter 30 of Plutarch's *Life of Pericles*.

Book 1

1. I, Thucydides of Athens, prepared a written account of the war that was fought between the Peloponnesians and the Athenians. I began writing as soon as the war broke out, in the belief that it would be more important and more interesting than any war that had gone before it. I reached this conclusion because both sides were at the highest state of readiness in every way, and because I saw the whole Greek world joining one side or the other, some immediately, and some planning to do so eventually. This was the greatest ferment ever to sweep the Greeks and many of the barbarians[1] — in other words, the majority of the human race.

Because of the amount of time that has gone by, I have been unable to obtain accurate information about the period that preceded the war or about epochs in the still more distant past; but on the basis of the most reliable evidence I could find after the most painstaking examination, I do not consider those times to have been very important as far as either war or anything else is concerned.

2. The reason for this is that what is now called Hellas[2] does not seem to have been stably settled in the past; rather, there were continual migrations and, after constantly being forced out by larger groups, people learned to abandon their land with little ado. There was no maritime trade and people could not safely have contact with each other either by land or sea. They occupied only as much territory as they needed to live on, and they neither planted trees nor accumulated excess wealth, because they never knew when someone would attack their unwalled settlements and take away their property. Because they believed they could satisfy their basic daily needs anywhere, they were able to pull up stakes and move away without difficulty, and as a result they never gained power through the strength of their cities or through their military might. The settlers always migrated into the best land: what is now called Thessaly, Boeotia, most of the Peloponnese except Arcadia, and the best parts of other places. Communities were torn apart by civil strife because some men had grown more powerful than others through ownership of the richest land, while at the same time foreigners plotted ways to take such land for themselves. Thus Attica[3] enjoyed civil peace because of its thin topsoil and has kept its indigenous population from the beginning. Attica proves my point that the rest of Greece grew unevenly due to constant migration, because wealthy people, uprooted from other parts of Greece by war or civil strife, moved to Athens for its security. They started becoming citizens from antiquity on and kept increasing the population of the city — so much so that the Athenians later sent colonists to Ionia[4] because Attica was no longer big enough for its population.

3. The weakness of the ancients is also proved to me by the fact that Hellas did not accomplish anything through a concerted effort before the Trojan War. Indeed, I am inclined to think that the whole country was not even called by the name of "Hellas." The appellation did not even exist before Hellen, son of Deucalion. Instead, each tribe gave its territory its own eponymous designa-

---

1. Like other Greeks, Thucydides uses the word "barbarians" to denote people who do not speak Greek. The word may derive from the Greek belief that other languages just sounded like "bar, bar, bar." It does not always imply a lack of civilization, although it often does, and it frequently indicates the Persians, whom many Greeks did consider to be a refined people.
2. Greece. This translation uses the terms "Hellas" and "Greece" interchangeably.
3. The peninsula on which Athens is located.
4. Ionia was on the west coast of Asia Minor, the modern Turkey. Because of the tradition that it had been settled by people from Athens, the Athenians felt a strong sense of kinship with Ionia.

tion, with "Pelasgian" predominating. When Hellen and his sons became powerful in Phthiotis and other cities called on him for help, they each came to be called "Hellenic" by association, though it took a long time for the name to win out over all of them. The best witness is Homer, because although he lived many years after the Trojan War, he nowhere calls all the Greeks "Hellenes"—only those who came from Phthiotis with Achilles, since they were the first Hellenes. He calls all the rest Danaans, Argives, and Achaeans in his epics. In my opinion, Homer did not even refer to "barbarians" because the Hellenes had not yet been differentiated from them by one name. Thus cities that spoke the same language, and that all came later, one by one, to be called "Hellenic," accomplished nothing jointly before the Trojan War because of weakness and lack of communication among themselves. Indeed, they were able to set out in this campaign together only because they had by then gained enough experience at sea.

4. We know through oral tradition that Minos was the earliest man to build a navy, and that he controlled most of what is now called the Greek Sea.[5] He also ruled over the Cyclades Islands and became the first colonizer of most of them after driving out the Carians and setting up his own sons in power.[6] It is likely that Minos rid the sea of piracy to the extent that he could in order to safeguard his maritime revenues.

5. In antiquity, the Greeks and the barbarians who either lived along the mainland coast or on islands turned to piracy as soon as they started crossing back and forth to one another in ships. The pirate ships were commanded by the most powerful men, as much for their own gain as to provide a livelihood for the poor. They would attack and plunder unwalled and loosely federated villages, and for the most part, they made their living in this way. This sort of work did not entail the slightest shame; on the contrary, it brought great renown, as is made clear by some mainlanders for whom piracy remains an honorable activity to this very day. Furthermore, in the ancient poets, when newly arrived mariners, come from far and wide, were asked whether they were pirates, they would never disavow their work, while those who did the asking would never censure it.

They also raided each other on land, and even now this ancient system prevails in much of Greece, as for example in Western Locris,[7] Aetolia, Acarnania, and the rest of the mainland in that region. Because of those ancient raids, it has remained the practice of these mainlanders to carry weapons.

6. Indeed, all Greeks used to go armed. Their homesteads were unfenced and contact with others was dangerous, and so they made it their habit to live their lives with their armor on, just like barbarians. The fact that people still carry weapons in that part of Greece indicates that it used to be the practice everywhere.

The Athenians were the first to lay down their arms and to switch to a more relaxed and gracious way of life, and it has not been long since old men of the upper classes with a taste for self-indulgence stopped wearing linen tunics or doing up their hair in buns and fastening it with gold cricket-shaped barrettes.

5. The Aegean Sea.
6. According to Greek tradition, King Minos had ruled at Cnossus in Crete during the distant past. It was this Minos who was reputed to have kept the half-human, half-bull creature known as the Minotaur in the middle of a great labyrinth.
7. Two groups of Locrians inhabited mainland Greece. Although the Western (Ozolian) Locrians lived closer to Sparta, on the north shore of the Gulf of Corinth near Naupactus, they were not usually allied with Sparta, whereas the Eastern (Opuntian) Locrians, who faced Euboea, were.
There was also a Locrian colony in Italy known as Epizephyrian, or Italian, Locri.

Because of Ionia's kinship with Athens, even the older Ionians wore this outfit for a long time. The more moderate fashion of the present day was first adopted by the Spartans, whose rich people also adopted a way of life in other ways as much like that of the common people as possible. Their athletes were the first to undress in public and work out naked and to rub their bodies with olive oil after exercise. In antiquity, athletes used to compete with supporters around their genitals even at the Olympic games, and it has not been many years since they stopped doing so. Even now, there are some barbarians—especially Asians[8]—who wear supporters during their boxing and wrestling matches. Indeed, there are many other ways in which one could show that the ancient Greeks led a life similar to that of the modern barbarians.

7. With increasing safety of navigation, people could build new cities right on the coast and use their growing surplus wealth to construct protective walls. Isthmuses were occupied too, both for the sake of maritime trade and as strong points against neighbors. Because of widespread piracy, on the other hand, the old cities on both the islands and the mainland were built away from the sea, since pirate states plundered not only one another but also low-lying nonmaritime towns. These inland cities remain inhabited to this day.

8. The islanders were even more piratical than the mainlanders. After all, they were Carians and Phoenicians, for those were the people who had settled most of the islands. (A proof of their origins is that when the Athenians purified Delos during the present war, and removed all the corpses on the island from their graves, over half of them were found to be Carians.[9] They could be recognized by the design of the armor that was buried along with them and by the method of burial, which they still use.) The rise of Minos' navy, however, made navigation safer, because he colonized most of the islands and forced out the criminal element. The people who lived on the coast now began to live in greater security and acquire more wealth. Some even used their ever-increasing riches to build walls around themselves. In their desire for gain, the weaker cities put up with being subject to the stronger, while the stronger cities with surplus wealth brought the weaker cities over to servitude. This was more or less the state of Greek society when they later made war on Troy.

9. In my opinion, Agamemnon was able to raise his army not so much because the suitors of Helen were bound by their oath to Tyndareus as because he was the most powerful man of his time.[1] The Peloponnesians who preserve the best traditions that have come down from their forebears say that Pelops, with his vast wealth, first came among their poverty-stricken people from Asia, and that after acquiring power, he gave his name to the country even though he was an immigrant. Later his descendants became even more powerful when Eurystheus, king of Mycenae, was killed by the sons of Heracles while campaigning in Attica. Before going off to war, Eurystheus had entrusted the administration of Mycenae to the son of Pelops—his maternal uncle, Atreus, whom Pelops had banished because of the murder of Chrysippus. Eurystheus, however, never returned, and the Mycenaeans lived in fear of the sons of Heracles. With the consent of the Mycenaean people, who thought him to be powerful and whom he had courted, Atreus took over Eurystheus' kingship and his domains, thus making the sons of Pelops more powerful than the sons of

---

8. By "Asia," Thucydides always means Asia Minor (the modern Turkey).
9. On the purification of Delos, see Herodotus 1.64 and Thucydides 3.104.
1. Tradition told that the competition to marry Helen was so intense that her suitors promised her father, Tyndareus, to come to her aid if anyone snatched her from the man who succeeded in becoming her husband. Helen married Menelaus, whose brother Agamemnon became the leader of the Greek army.

Perseus. Agamemnon inherited this kingdom and commanded, as well, a more powerful navy than did other states; therefore, the army he gathered was, in my opinion, based less on goodwill than on fear. If we can accept the evidence of Homer, Agamemnon reached Troy with the greatest number of ships and supplied the Arcadians with a navy. Also, in the scene in which Agamemnon receives the scepter, Homer says that he is the "lord of many islands and of all Argos."[2] Now as a mainlander, Agamemnon could not have controlled any but neighboring islands (of which there are not "many") unless he also had a substantial navy. We can also infer from Agamemnon's armada what previous expeditions must have been like.

10. The fact that Mycenae was small, or that none of the cities of that time was notable by present-day standards, is no reason to doubt that the expedition was as large as the poets say or as popular opinion maintains. If, for example, Sparta were deserted, with nothing left but the temples and the foundations of buildings, I imagine that people in the distant future would seriously doubt that Sparta's power ever approached its fame. Its power would appear to have been less, because although the Spartans occupy two-fifths of the Peloponnese, and have hegemony over all of it as well as over many allies outside it, they never developed one metropolitan area or built lavish temples and buildings, but rather live in unfederated towns in the old-fashioned Greek way. If the same thing were to happen to Athens, however, its power would be put at double what it is because of the visual impression its ruins would make. It is not fair, therefore, to base our judgments on the appearance of cities instead of on their military forces. If we can trust the evidence of Homer—which, considering that he was a poet, was probably exaggerated—we must conclude that the expedition against Troy was the greatest of any that had gone before it, though it was clearly smaller than those of the present day. Homer puts the number of ships at twelve hundred. The Boeotian ships had crews of one hundred and twenty men each, and Philoctetes' ships had crews of fifty each, thus marking, in my view, the largest and smallest contingents. At any rate, no other numbers are mentioned in the Catalog of Ships.[3] Homer makes it clear in the description of Philoctetes' ships that all the crews served as both rowers and soldiers when he says that all the rowers were archers. It is unlikely that there were any passengers on board aside from the kings and their highest officers, especially since they were crossing the open sea carrying military equipment in ships without decks and outfitted like ancient pirate vessels. Taking the average of the largest and smallest ships, therefore, and considering that contingents came from all of Greece, it does not appear that many men went to Troy.

11. The reason was not so much lack of men as lack of money. Because of the difficulty of obtaining supplies, the Greeks took a small army—one they hoped would be able to live off the land they were fighting in. After they arrived and won some battles (as they clearly did, otherwise they would not have been able to build a wall around their beachhead), they do not seem even then to have used all their forces. For want of food, some men were driven to farming the Chersonese or to pillaging. This scattering of the Greek forces enabled the Trojans to withstand ten years of war because they were always a match for the men who were left behind. The Greeks would easily have taken Troy by force if they had arrived with surpluses of food and had continuously fought the war in full strength, without having to resort to farming and pillaging. Since they

2. *Iliad*, 2.108.
3. In the *Iliad*, 2. 484–759.

proved able to hold on with only a fraction of their forces, they would surely have captured Troy with less trouble and in less time if they had dug in and besieged the city in strength. Previous campaigns had been weak for want of funds, and so, too, was this, the most famous of all. It is clear, though, that its deeds did not match its fame or the now-prevalent tradition that the poets have established.

12. Even after the Trojan War, Greece continued to undergo migration and colonization and thus lacked the tranquillity necessary for growth. The return of the Greeks from Troy after such a long absence resulted in political changes. In general, there was civil strife in the cities, thus creating exiles who founded yet other cities. The present-day Boeotians, for example, were forced out of Arne by the Thessalians sixty years after the fall of Troy and founded what is now Boeotia in the former Cadmeian territory. (There had already been a Boeotian subgroup in this territory, and some of them had gone off to fight in the Trojan War.) Furthermore, the Dorians, along with the Heraclids, captured the Peloponnese eighty years after the war.[4] After a long time, and with great difficulty, Greece achieved a secure peace and sent forth not forced migrants any longer, but colonists. The Athenians settled Ionia and most of the islands, whereas the Peloponnesians settled most of Italy and Sicily and places here and there in Greece. All of these colonies were founded after the Trojan War.

13. As Greece became more powerful and amassed ever greater quantities of wealth, tyrannies came to be established in most of the cities.[5] (Formerly, there had been patrilineal kingships with specified prerogatives.) As revenues increased, Greece began to outfit navies and to take increasingly to the sea. They say that the Corinthians came closest to conducting naval operations in the modern way, and that the first Greek triremes were built in Corinth.[6] It is known that the Corinthian shipbuilder Ameinocles built four ships for the Samians, and Ameinocles went to Samos about three hundred years before the end of the present war. The oldest naval battle we know of was fought between the Corcyraeans and the Corinthians, and this happened about two hundred and sixty years before the same date.

Because of its location on the Isthmus, Corinth has been a commercial center from the first. In antiquity, more business was conducted by land than by sea, and most Greeks, both inside and outside the Peloponnese, had to travel through Corinthian territory to trade with one another. Their wealth made them powerful, as the ancient poets make clear: after all, their epithet for Corinth was "rich." As the Greeks took more and more to the sea, the Corinthians built a navy and rid the seas of piracy, and their markets brought economic power to the city through both maritime and overland revenue.

Later the Ionians also became an important naval power in the reigns of Cyrus, first King of the Persians, and of his son Cambyses; and during their war with Cyrus, the Ionians gained control over their own territorial waters for a time.[7] Polycrates, who was the tyrant in Samos in the time of Cambyses, used

---

4. The Dorians were an ethnically and dialectically distinct group of Greeks who settled in the Peloponnese and elsewhere; the most prominent Dorian Greeks were the Spartans, but there were also Dorians in Crete and even Asia Minor. The so-called Heraclids (descendants of the hero Heracles) figured large as Dorians in Peloponnesian legend.

5. The men the Greeks called "tyrants" (*tyrannoi*) were strongmen who took power by force rather than constitutionally. Their rule was not always harsh; in fact, it was often quite popular. In mainland Greece, tyranny disappeared after 500, but it continued in Sicily.

6. By Thucydides' time, the trireme was the mainstay of Greek navies. It was a sleek, light, easily maneuverable ship about one hundred feet in length, which took its name from its three banks of oars.

7. Cyrus founded the Persian empire during the second half of the sixth century. Upon his death in 530, he was succeeded by his son Cambyses. The Ionian Greeks first became subjects of Persia under Cyrus.

his fleet to conquer other islands and make them subject to him. He also captured Rhenea and dedicated it to the Delian Apollo. The Phocaeans also defeated the Carthaginians in a naval battle while founding Massalia.[8]

14. These navies, then, which arose many generations after the Trojan War, were the most powerful, and it seems that even these were using few triremes. They continued to outfit penteconters and long boats just as in the earlier conflict.[9] Shortly before the Persian Wars and the death of Darius, who ruled Persia after Cambyses, triremes were used in strength by the tyrants in Sicily and by the Corcyraeans.[1] These were the only fleets in Greece worth mentioning before the expedition of Xerxes. Aegina, Athens, and perhaps a few other states had paltry navies made up mostly of penteconters. It was only recently, when Athens was at war with Aegina and expecting the barbarian invasion, that Themistocles persuaded the Athenians to build the ships with which they fought the Persians—and even these were not yet fully equipped with decks fore and aft.

15. Such were the inadequacies of the Greek navies, both those of antiquity and those that arose later. Nevertheless, the states that turned their energies to the sea were assured of power in the form of revenue and hegemony over others. For naval powers, and especially those that did not have enough land for their own needs, attacked the islands and conquered them. As to land wars, there were none that resulted in the acquisition of any power. What wars there were, were all against neighboring states: the Greeks did not send armies far from their own borders on wars of conquest. Small states did not gravitate toward the greater powers as subjects, nor did they contribute as equals to the creation of allied armies. Instead, neighboring cities just made war on each other. It was only in the ancient war between the Chalcidians and the Eretrians that the rest of Greece formed alliances and took sides.[2]

16. Different states met different obstacles to their growth. Thus when Ionia was achieving great success, Cyrus and the Persian empire overthrew Croesus, invaded Ionian territory on this side of the Halys River as far as the sea, and enslaved the cities on the mainland.[3] Later, with the help of the Phoenician navy, Darius gained control over the islands also.

17. In the Greek cities, the tyrants looked out only for themselves—for their own safety and for the growth of their personal households—and they governed their cities to ensure as much security as possible. Nothing they did is worth mentioning, except for some military exploits against their neighbors—although the Sicilian tyrants did very greatly advance their power through this means. Thus a situation long prevailed throughout Greece in which they accomplished nothing remarkable in common and in which individual cities were even less enterprising.

18. The tyrannies that had long prevailed in Athens and even longer in the rest of Greece were finally put down by the Spartans—except for those in Sicily. (After it was occupied by the Dorians who now inhabit it, Sparta experienced the longest period of turmoil we know of. Nevertheless, it has been well governed since antiquity and has never had a tyrant. Reckoning from the end of the recent war, Sparta has had the same form of government for somewhat

---

8. Massalia (the modern Marseilles) was founded around 600. This battle is otherwise unknown, and Thucydides may be confusing these events with a battle between the Phocaeans and the Carthaginians off Alalia in Corsica in 546.
9. The penteconter was a fifty-oared ship. In time it was replaced as a warship by the trireme.
1. The Persian Wars were fought from 490 to 479; Darius died in 486 and was succeeded by his son, Xerxes.
2. This was the so-called Lelantine War, which occurred perhaps c. 700.
3. See Herodotus 1.46–91.

more than four hundred years, and this has given it the strength to put the affairs of other states in order.) Not many years after the dissolution of the tyrannies in Greece, the battle between the Greeks and the Persians at Marathon took place.[4] Ten years later the barbarian returned at the head of a large army with the aim of enslaving Greece. With the gravest danger hanging over Greece, the Spartans, as the foremost power, led the Greek alliance. Faced with a Persian attack, the Athenians decided to abandon their city. They packed off their possessions, boarded their ships, and became a naval power. The Greeks, acting together, repelled the barbarian, but not much later both the allies in the war and those who had revolted from the King gravitated towards either the Athenians or the Spartans, for these two had proved themselves to be the most powerful states, the one on land and the other at sea. The alliance between Athens and Sparta lasted but a short time, whereupon they quarreled and, with their respective allies, made war on each other. Meanwhile, any Greek states that were at odds with one another took sides with either the Athenians or the Spartans. Thus from the end of the Persian Wars to the beginning of this one, Athens and Sparta were always fighting or making treaties, either with each other or with their own rebellious allies, thereby perfecting their fighting skills and gaining ever more experience as they conducted their military exercises in a climate of actual danger.

19. The Spartans led their allies without making them pay tribute. Instead, they set up puppet oligarchies so that states would be governed in Sparta's interests. Over time, the Athenians had taken over the navies of their allies (except those of Chios and Lesbos) and required all of them to pay tribute. Thus Athens and Sparta were individually at greater strength for this war than they had been at their peak as one undivided allied force during the Persian Wars.

20. This, then, is what I have been able to find out about the more remote past, given the difficulty of trusting every bit of evidence. People, you see, unquestioningly accept the legends handed down by their forebears even when those legends relate to their own native history. Why, most Athenians even believe that Hipparchus was the tyrant in Athens when he was assassinated by Harmodius and Aristogeiton. They do not know that Hippias, as the oldest son, had succeeded Peisistratus—his brothers being Hipparchus and Thessalus—and that on the very day set for the assassination of Hippias, Harmodius and Aristogeiton decided on the spur of the moment to refrain from killing him, because they suspected that they had been betrayed by their co-conspirators and that Hippias had advance knowledge of the plot. Nevertheless, Harmodius and Aristogeiton were determined to do something audacious before they were captured, so they killed Hipparchus when they came upon him forming up the Panathenaic procession at what is known as the temple of the Daughters of Leos.[5] Other Greeks, indeed, even have inaccurate opinions about many contemporary facts, facts which have not been obscured by time, such as the belief that the kings of Sparta cast two votes apiece instead of one, or that the Spartans have a "Pitanate Battalion," when there has never been any such thing. Thus most people expend very little effort on the search for truth and prefer to rely on ready-made answers.

---

4. The battle of Marathon was fought in 490.
5. Thucydides makes frequent reference to Peisistratus and his sons; see the digression on the assassination of Hipparchus at 6.54–59.
   The Panathenaic festival was a festival held in Athens to honor Athena. It featured a great procession, athletic and musical competitions, and sacrifices.

21. Nevertheless, one will not go wrong if he accepts the inferences I have drawn from the facts as I have related them, and not as they are sung by the poets—who embellish and exaggerate them—or as they are strung together by popular historians with a view to making them not more truthful, but more attractive to their audiences; and considering that we are dealing with ancient history, whose unverified events have, over the course of time, made their way into the incredible realms of mythology, one will find that my conclusions, derived as they are from the best available evidence, are accurate enough.

Even though people always think that the war they are fighting is the greatest there ever was, and then return to marveling at ancient wars once theirs has ended, it will be clear, after we examine the events themselves, that this war between Athens and Sparta actually was the greatest war there has ever been.

22. As to the speeches of the participants, either when they were about to enter the war or after they were already in it, it has been difficult for me and for those who reported to me to remember exactly what was said. I have, therefore, written what I thought the speakers needed to say given the situations they were in, while keeping as close as possible to the gist of what was actually said. As to the events of the war, I have not written them down as I heard them from just anybody, nor as I thought they must have occurred, but have consistently described what I myself saw or have been able to learn from others after going over each event in as much detail as possible. I have found this task to be extremely arduous, since those who were present at these actions gave varying reports on the same event, depending on their sympathies and their memories.

My narrative, perhaps, will fail to please some listeners because it lacks an element of fiction. Those, however, who want to see things clearly as they were and, given human nature, as they will one day be again, more or less, may find this book a useful basis for judgment. My work was composed not as a prizewinning exercise in elocution, to be heard and then forgotten, but as a work of permanent value.

23. The Persian Wars were the greatest event of the past. Nevertheless, they were quickly decided by two battles on land and two at sea. In contrast, the recent war was of long duration and brought such suffering to Greece as had never before been seen in a comparable period of time. Never before had so many cities been captured and depopulated, either by barbarians or by Greeks at war with each other, and then, in some cases, resettled by new inhabitants. Never before had there been so many exiles and so much killing, some brought about by the war itself and some by civil strife. Ancient events that were better established in legend than in experience now seemed less incredible, for there were now violent earthquakes spread through much of the world; eclipses of the sun, which now occurred much more frequently than ever before in memory; terrible regional droughts and the famines they caused; and last but not least, the plague, which caused great harm and great loss of life. All of these things were associated with this war.

The Athenians and the Peloponnesians began the war after breaking the thirty-year truce they had made after the capture of Euboea.[6] In order to make it perfectly clear how a war of this magnitude broke out among the Greeks, I have begun by describing the grievances and quarrels between the two sides that led to the rupture of the truce. I believe, though, that the truest explanation for the war is that Sparta was forced into it because of her apprehensions

---

6. The optimistically named Thirty Years' Peace was signed in 445. The Spartans declared war on Athens in 432; their allies the Thebans began the fighting in 431.

over the growing power of Athens—although this is not obvious from the statements they made. The following, however, are the openly avowed reasons why they broke the truce and entered into a state of war.

24. The city of Epidamnus is on your right as you sail into the Ionian Gulf. Non–Greek-speaking Taulantians—an Illyrian people—live nearby. The Corcyraeans colonized the city, although the founding father, summoned according to the ancient custom from their mother city, was a Corinthian—Phalius, son of Eratocleides, a descendant from the line of Heracles.[7] Some Corinthians and other Dorians joined in the settlement. The power and the population of the Epidamnians grew great over the course of time, although it is said that they were depleted after a war with the surrounding barbarians, and that they then fought among themselves and lost most of their power. The result was that before the outbreak of the present war, the masses expelled the ruling families, who later returned with the barbarians to raid the urban populace by land and sea. The Epidamnians in the city, now hard pressed, sent ambassadors to their mother city of Corcyra begging them not to look away as they died, but rather to negotiate a reconciliation between them and the exiles and to bring the war with the barbarians to an end. Although they made these requests as suppliants sitting in the temple of Hera, the Corcyraeans still did not accept the supplication and dismissed the ambassadors, who had not accomplished anything.[8]

25. When the Epidamnians realized that there would be no help from the Corcyraeans, they did not know what to do, so they sent ambassadors to Delphi and asked the god whether it would be permissible to give the city to their founding fathers, the Corinthians, and to ask them for some help.

He ordained that they give the leadership to the Corinthians.

In keeping with the oracle, the Epidamnians went to Corinth and gave them the colony. They pointed out that their founding father had been from Corinth; they showed them the oracle; and they begged them not to look away as they died, but to come to their aid.

The Corinthians accepted the obligation to establish their rights, because they believed that the colony belonged to them no less than to the Corcyraeans—but also out of hatred for the Corcyraeans, who slighted Corinth, though they were themselves Corinthian colonists. They did this in a number of ways: by failing to pay the customary respects at intercity festivals; by not serving the choicest cuts from the sacrificial animals to the Corinthian representative, as the other colonists did; by looking down on Corinth from a position of wealth equal at that time to the richest of the Greeks; by being more powerful, too, in their military equipment, and particularly in the superiority of their navy. At times they even exulted in their nautical reputation because the Phaeacians had previously inhabited Corcyra![9] (And in fact, the Corcyraeans had outfitted a powerful navy and were not inexpert seamen. After all, they had one hundred and twenty triremes when they began the war.)

26. What with all of these grievances, the Corinthians gladly sent aid to Epidamnus and called for any colonists willing to accompany their detachment of Ambraciot, Leucadian, and Corinthian guardsmen. These forces made their way on foot to the Corinthian colony of Apollonia, fearful lest they be blockaded by the Corcyraeans as they crossed the sea.

7. When a Greek "mother city" (metropolis) sent out a colony, that colony became independent. If that colony in turn wished to found its own colony (as was the case when Corinth's colony Corcyra decided to found Epidamnus), it took a "founding father" from the original mother city.
8. Greek suppliants customarily sat in a temple with olive branches in their hands.
9. The Phaeacians were the most famous seafarers from the early days of Greek antiquity and played a large role in the *Odyssey*, in which Odysseus spends time on their island, Scheria.

The Corcyraeans were furious when they learned that the colonists and guardsmen had arrived at Epidamnus, and that the colony had been handed over to the Corinthians, so they set sail with twenty-five ships right away and with another contingent later, and they insultingly demanded that the Epidamnians restore their exiles and expel the guards and colonists the Corinthians had sent. (You see, the Epidamnian exiles had gone to Corcyra, pointing out gravesites and claiming ancestral ties that they used as arguments in their request to be restored to power in Epidamnus.) The Epidamnians complied with none of this, so the Corcyraeans attacked them with forty ships, carrying the exiles who were to be restored and taking along a force of Illyrians. They took up a position in front of the city and announced that any Epidamnian or foreigner who wished to do so could leave unharmed—otherwise, they would be treated as enemies. When this proved fruitless, the Corcyraeans besieged this city, which is located on an isthmus.

27. When messengers arrived at Corinth with the news that Epidamnus was besieged, the Corinthians levied an army and sent out heralds to announce that full citizenship would be extended to anyone who wanted to join their colony at Epidamnus. If anyone did not want to join in the expedition immediately, but still wanted a share in the colony, he could deposit fifty Corinthian drachmas and stay behind. Although many paid the silver coin, many also sailed away. They asked the Megarians for some ships to sail ahead with them, just in case their passage should be blocked by the Corcyraeans, and the Megarians outfitted eight ships to accompany them. Pale, on Cephallenia, sent four. They also asked the Epidaurians, who supplied five ships. Hermione sent one, the Troezenians two, the Leucadians ten, and the Ambraciots eight. They asked the Thebans and Phliasians for money and the Eleans for money and unmanned ships. The Corinthians themselves outfitted thirty ships and three thousand hoplites.

28. As soon as the Corcyraeans learned of these preparations, they went to Corinth with some Lacedaemonian[1] and Sicyonian ambassadors and called on the Corinthians to withdraw the Corinthian guardsmen and the colonists from Epidamnus, since they had no claim to it. If Corinth did have some claims, however, Corcyra was willing to submit the matter to arbitration by Peloponnesian cities agreeable to both sides. Whichever of the two cities it was adjudged the colony belonged to, that one would rule. They were also willing to turn the matter over to the oracle at Delphi. They advised Corinth not to wage war, but if war it was to be, and if they were forced into it by Corinthian pressure, they said that they would, out of necessity, make unwanted alliances with other cities than the ones they had now.

The Corinthians answered that if Corcyra withdrew the ships and the barbarians from Epidamnus, they would think about it. Otherwise, it wouldn't do for Epidamnus to be besieged while they went to court.

The Corcyreaeans replied that if the Corinthians, too, withdrew their forces from Epidamnus, they would do the same; but they were also prepared to have both sides remain in place and to arrange a cease-fire until a ruling should be given.

29. The Corinthians would hear none of this, and as soon as their ships were ready and their allies had arrived, they sent a herald ahead to declare war on Corcyra, and then set out with seventy-five ships and two thousand hoplites to do battle with the Corcyraeans besieging Epidamnus. In command of the ships were Aristeus, son of Pellichus; Callicrates, son of Callias; and Timanor,

---

1. Lacedaemon was another name for Sparta.

son of Timanthes. Archetimus, son of Eurytimus, and Isarchidas, son of Is-
archus, commanded the infantry. When they reached Actium in the territory of
Anactorium, where the temple of Apollo stands at the mouth of the Ambracian
Gulf, the Corcyraeans sent out a herald in a small boat with a warning not to
sail against them. At the same time, the Corcyraeans manned their ships, after
strengthening the old ones with thwarts to make them seaworthy and repairing
the rest. By the time the herald returned without a message of peace from the
Corinthians, eighty Corcyraean ships had been fully manned. (Of their one
hundred twenty ships, forty were blockading Epidamnus.) The Corcyraeans put
to sea against the Corinthians, took up their positions, and won an overwhelming victory, destroying fifteen Corinthian ships. It happened that on the same
day the besiegers persuaded Epidamnus to terms of surrender by which the Epidamnians would give up the foreigners unconditionally and hold the Corinthians in irons pending a further decision.

30. After the naval battle, the Corcyraeans set up a victory marker[2] on the
Corcyraean promontory of Leucimme, held the Corinthians in chains, and
killed the other prisoners of war. Later, after the defeated Corinthians and their
allies had returned home in their ships, thus leaving the Corcyraeans in control of the sea around all of that region, Corcyra sailed to the Corinthian colony
of Leucas and destroyed its crops. They also burned the Elean port of Cyllene
because the Eleans had supplied Corinth with ships and money. They spent
most of their time after the battle tightening their control of the sea and attacking and plundering Corinth's allies. The following summer, Corinth, her allies
exhausted, sent an army and a fleet to Actium and the area around the Thes-
protian headland at Cheimerium in order to protect Leucas and all the other
cities that were friendly to her. The Corycyraeans countered with ships and infantry opposite them at Leucimme. They maintained their standoff through the
summer, with neither side sailing against the other, and returned to their homes
that winter.

31. For a full year after the battle, and for another year after that, the
Corinthians sustained a war frenzy against the Corcyraeans, building ships and
doing their utmost to create a great armada and, with promises of pay, recruiting oarsmen from the Peloponnese and from the rest of Greece. The Corcyraeans grew fearful when they learned of these preparations. They had no
alliances with any Greek state and had not signed on to either the Delian
League or the Spartan alliance, so they decided to go to Athens, become their
allies, and try to get some help from them. When the Corinthians found out
about this, they went to Athens to engage in diplomacy to keep Athens from
adding its naval strength to that of Corcyra and thus prevent Corinth from carrying on the war according to plan.

After an assembly was called,[3] they entered into debate, and the Corcyraeans spoke as follows:

32. Men of Athens! When those who have neither performed great
services nor earned the debt of an alliance come asking their neighbors for
help, as we do now, it is only right that they first demonstrate, preferably,
that what they want is advantageous — or failing that, at least not harmful —
and then that they will preserve a steadfast gratitude. If they aren't able to

---

2. A victory marker, sometimes called a trophy, was made of crossed wooden poles on which were hung
   shields and other enemy weaponry. It was dedicated to Zeus as the god of battles and it usually marked
   the point at which the enemy fled the field.
3. The principal organ of Athenian government was the assembly of adult male citizens. It met several times
   a month on the hill known as the Pnyx.

establish any of these things, they ought not to be angry if they don't get what they want. The Corcyraeans have sent us to you to ask for an alliance, confident in the belief that they can make these representations.

It happens, though, that our very own policy works against us from your point of view and puts us in an awkward position in the present circumstances. You see, we never willingly became anyone's ally before, yet here we are now, seeking an alliance with others just because our policy has isolated us in this war with the Corinthians. It turns out that what seemed to be our prudence in not risking involvement in the plans of others by avoiding foreign alliances now looks like weakness and folly. It is true that we repelled the Corinthians in the recent naval battle all by ourselves, but they are now about to set forth against us with a much greater force from the Peloponnese and from the rest of Greece, and we do not see how we will be able to survive with only our own resources. It would be fatal if we were subjected to them, so we have no choice but to ask for help from you and everyone else and for your understanding that we, less from cowardice than from disappointment, risk a departure from our former isolationist neutrality.

33. Things have worked out in such a way that you will greatly benefit if you grant our request. In the first place, you will be giving aid to the injured party and not to the one who is injuring others; and secondly, by admitting into your alliance a people who are in danger of losing everything, you will lay up a store of gratitude to be witnessed in everlasting memory.—And besides, we have built up the largest navy after yours.

And consider this. What triumph could be rarer for you or more painful to your enemies than for a power you would have paid great sums in wealth and gratitude to acquire, for that power now to present itself to you of its own free will, to surrender itself without your risking or spending anything—and not only that, but to carry with it honor for your people, gratitude from us whom you defend, and power for yourselves. In all of time, the conjunction of all these things has come to very few, and few have been those who have come forward to request an alliance with no less to offer in the way of security and honor than they stand to receive. Because the war in which we will be useful to you is coming, and if any of you thinks it isn't, he is seriously mistaken. He does not see that the Spartans, out of fear of your empire, can't wait to make war, and that the Corinthians, who are your enemies and who deeply influence the Spartans, are attempting to subdue us now in preparation for an attack on you by making sure they either cripple our fleet or add it to theirs, so that you and we will not be able to stand together in our common hatred of them. Our task is to beat them to it, we by offering an alliance and you by accepting it, and to plan our strategy against them rather than to react to their strategy against us.

34. If they should say that it is illegal for you to accept their colonists, let them know that every colony honors its mother city when it is treated well and grows apart when it is treated unjustly. After all, colonists are not sent out to be the slaves but the equals of those they leave behind. And it is clear that they have done wrong. Offered the chance to submit the matter of Epidamnus to arbitration, they decided to resolve their complaints on the battlefield rather than in the lawcourts.[4] Let the way they treat us, their kinsmen, be a warning to you. Don't be led astray by their guile, and don't help them when they ask you for something outright. He who has the fewest regrets over obliging his enemies will have lived the safest life.

4. See 1.29.

35. You do not even break your treaty with the Spartans by accepting us into your alliance, because we are allied to neither the Spartans nor the Corinthians. The treaty says: "It is permissible for any unallied Greek city to enter, as it may please, into an alliance with either party."[5] It would be really strange if they were allowed to recruit their sailors not only from their allies but from the rest of Greece (and not least from your subjects), while we are excluded from an alliance that is natural for us and denied help from anywhere. And then they cry foul if you grant our request! Why, we would have much more to blame you for if we failed to persuade you! You would be rejecting us when we are not your enemies and when we are in danger. You would not only not be hindering your enemies and attackers, but you would be turning a blind eye on them when they gather forces from your own empire!

This is not just. Either forbid the mercenaries from your empire to join them; or send the mercenaries to us, in numbers as you shall decide; or, best of all, openly accept us into your alliance and come to our aid. We began by saying that we could show many advantages in this. The greatest advantage is that the Corinthians are our enemies too, which guarantees our loyalty. And they are by no means weak, but quite able to hurt breakaway states. Furthermore, since what is being offered is a naval and not a land alliance, this is not just any defection. If it is in your power, you must not allow anyone at all to build a navy; if it is not, make the strongest naval alliances you can.

36. Now if some of you agree that the alliance would be advantageous but fear that entering it would mean breaking the treaty, they should know that worried though they may be, if they have power they really frighten their enemies, while if they reject the alliance they will be weaker in the face of powerful enemies, no matter how confident they feel. They are deliberating as much about Athens now as about Corcyra, and they are not making the best plans for her when, in the coming and all-but-present war, they survey what's here and now and doubt whether to annex a territory that is befriended or antagonized with critical consequences. (We are within easy sailing distance to Italy and Sicily, by the way, and can prevent their ships from traveling to the Peloponnese and Peloponnesian ships from going along the coast to Italy and Sicily—so this is another great advantage, along with all the others.)

To sum up, the long and the short of why you should not reject us is that there are three navies worth mentioning in Greece: ours, yours, and Corinth's. If you look on while Corinth incorporates our navy into hers, you will end up by fighting at sea with both the Corcyraeans and the Peloponnesians, but if you accept us into your alliance, you will have our ships as well as yours to fight them with.

That is what the Corcyraeans said. After them, the Corinthians spoke as follows:

37. These Corcyraeans have not only framed an argument about accepting them into your alliance, but have gone on to say that we are the wrongdoers whereas they are the victims of our aggression. We must address these last two issues first and then move on to the argument about the first issue so that you will have the merit of our claim firmly in mind when, with good reason, you deny the necessity of theirs.

---

5. The two parties meant here are Athens and Sparta.

They say prudence kept them from making alliances with others, but this was their policy out of criminality and not moral virtue. They didn't want any partners in crime—or witnesses either, who would shame them when called into court. Because they hardly ever export their goods, but instead receive others whom trade compels to anchor at their shores, their city is a self-sufficient outpost that lets them be the judges of their own crimes rather than live by international agreements. They have pleaded this modest neutrality of theirs not so that they could avoid joining in the crimes of others, but so that they could commit their crimes alone. It allows them to engage in outright expropriation where they hold sway, increase whatever they can get away with by stealth, and never have to be ashamed of their ill-gotten gains. But if they were honest men, as they say, the more invulnerable they were to their neighbors, the more possible it would have been to make their honor plain by accepting the rule of law.

38. But they are not honest, either with others or with us. Though they are our colonists, they have always been rebellious, and now they are bearing arms against us, arguing that they were not sent out to be treated badly. For our part, we say that we did not found this colony to be insulted by these people but to be their leaders and to be shown due respect. Our other colonists honor us. Why, we are the most beloved of all the mother cities. So it is obvious that since we are acceptable to the others, there is no good reason why we should be unacceptable to these Corcyraeans, and it is also obvious that we are not preparing to attack them without reason, but because we have been grievously wronged. And even if we were mistaken, the handsome thing for them to do would be to give way to our anger, whereupon it would be shameful for us to answer their moderation with force. Instead, they have insolently flaunted their wealth before us and crossed us in all sorts of other ways, and when they refused to recognize Epidamnus—which is in distress, and which is ours—and we came to her aid, they then took it and held it by force.

39. They actually say that they wanted to submit the matter to arbitration, although this is not an offer that should be made by one who securely holds the upper hand. It should be made before fighting breaks out by one whose deeds match his words. Instead, it was only when these Corcyraeans besieged Epidamnus and realized that we would not put up with it that they gave way to the proprieties of the law. And now, not satisfied with their misdeeds at Epidamnus, they have come here entreating you to join them, not as allies but as accomplices, and to accept them because of your differences with us. They ought to have done this when they were most secure, and not at a time when we have been wronged and when they are in danger, and certainly not when you would be giving them help without ever having shared their power and when you, though distant from their crimes, would have to bear an equal part of our censure. You ought to have shared power in the past if you are to share in the consequences now.

40. We have proved that we have come with just complaints and that these Corcyraeans are avaricious bullies. It remains for you to understand that you would wrongfully accept them into your alliance. Granted that the treaty states that any of the unsigned cities may join either of the two alliances, the article does not apply to those who join in order to harm others, but rather to whoever seeks security without depriving any other state of its allegiance, and to whoever brings peace and not war to the alliance—to the prudent alliance—that accepts it. And war is what you would get if you do not listen to us. You would

not just become their allies, you would become our enemies because the treaty would have been broken. We would be forced, if you joined them, to defend ourselves against both you and them. The right thing for you to do is to stay clear of both of us, or if not that, to join us against them (after all, you have a treaty with us Corinthians, and have never had any sort of agreement at all with the Corcyraeans) and avoid setting the precedent of accepting cities that have revolted from either alliance. We did not cast the deciding vote against you when Samos revolted from you and when the Peloponnesians were evenly divided over whether to help them.[6] We openly opposed it, saying that any city could punish its own allies. If, however, you accept and aid outlaw cities, it will be clear that your cities can also come over to our side and that you will be setting a precedent against yourselves rather than against us.

41. These claims on you are good and sufficient in Greek custom, but we can also claim a favor, and as people who are neither enemies out to hurt you nor friends who maintain regular relations, we can say that this is the situation in which you ought to repay it. Before the Persian Wars, when you needed long boats in your war with Aegina, you borrowed twenty ships from us Corinthians. This favor enabled you to capture Aegina, just as we enabled you to punish the Samians when we prevented the Peloponnesians from going to their aid. Our help came at those critical moments when people who are at war with their enemies are going all-out for victory. At such times they consider those who help them to be their friends, even if they had formerly been enemies, and their enemies to be those who oppose them, even if they were friends only a moment before, because they put no value on what is closest to them in their eagerness for immediate victory.

42. Bear this history in mind, and let your young men learn it from their elders. Decide to repay us with like for like, and don't think that ours is merely the rhetoric of justice whereas your advantage, if you go to war, will be elsewhere. Advantage follows you along the path on which you least go astray. The "future war" with which the Corcyraeans are trying to frighten you as they call on you to do wrong is not yet on the horizon, and it wouldn't be worth it to get all stirred up about it now only to gain the present—not the future—hatred of the Corinthians. Instead, it would be prudent of you gradually to remove some of the suspicions we still have about Megara. If it is timely, the most recent favor you do, though it be a little one, is able to undo a bigger grievance. And as to the argument that they will give you a great naval alliance—don't be led along by that. There is a more secure strength in not wronging your peers than in being goaded by the illusion of the moment into a risky expansionism.

43. Now that we find ourselves in the same situation as the one we defended at Sparta when we argued that every city should be allowed to punish its own allies, we expect the same defense from you, and not for you to harm us with your vote after having benefited from ours. Give back like for like. Understand that this is the critical moment in which he who helps you is your best friend and he who stands against you is your worst enemy. Do not harm us by accepting these Corcyraeans into your alliance, and do not abet their crimes. Do as we ask and you will be doing the right thing as well as deciding in your own best interests.

That is what the Corinthians said.

---

6. The revolt of Samos took place in 440.

44. After listening to both sides, the Athenians were slightly inclined to accept the arguments of the Corinthians in the first of two meetings of the assembly. In the second they changed their minds. They decided not to make a full offensive and defensive alliance with the Corcyraeans, one in which the friends and enemies of either would be the friends and enemies of both, because if the Corcyraeans called on them to join in a naval assault against Corinth, they would have to break their treaty with the Peloponnesians. Instead, they made a mutual defense treaty requiring each to help the other in the event that anyone should attack Corcyra, Athens, or any of their allies. Because the prevailing opinion was that there would be war with the Peloponnese, the Athenians would not permit the loss of Corcyra and its large navy to Corinth. Instead, they would let them fight it out among themselves so that Corinth and the other naval powers would be weaker if it came to war. They also took into consideration that the island lay within easy sailing distance along the coast to Italy and Sicily.

45. This was the Athenian thinking when they undertook an alliance with Corcyra. The Corinthians left, and not long afterwards Athens sent ten ships to aid Corcyra. They were commanded by Lacedaemonius, son of Cimon; Diotimus, son of Strombichus; and Proteas, son of Epicles, whose orders were not to engage the Corinthians in a naval battle unless the Corinthians sailed on Corcyra or its surrounding territory with intent to make a landing, in which case they should do everything in their power to prevent it. These orders were intended to avoid a breach of the peace treaty.

46. The Corinthians, their fleet ready, set sail for Corcyra with one hundred and fifty ships after the Athenians had already arrived there. They were: from Elis, ten ships; from Megara, twelve; from Leucas, ten; from Ambracia, twenty-seven; from Anactorium, one; and from Corinth itself, ninety. Each city sent its own commander. Xenocleides, son of Euthycles, was the Corinthian commander, along with four others. When they reached the mainland opposite Corcyra, after sailing from Leucas, they anchored in Cheimerium in Thesprotia. Cheimerium is only a harbor, but there is a city, Ephyra, which lies above it and away from the sea in the Elean part of Thesprotia. Near Ephyra, Lake Acherusia flows into the sea. The river Acheron, from which the lake takes its name, empties into it after flowing through Thesprotia. There is another river, the Thyamis, which forms the border between Thesprotia and Cestrina. The headland of Cheimerium juts out between these two rivers, and it was at that point on the mainland that the Corinthians anchored and set up a camp.

47. When the Corcyraeans learned that the Corinthians had sailed, they manned one hundred and ten ships under the command of Miciades, Aesimides, and Eurybatus, and set up a camp on one of the Sybota Islands. The ten Athenian ships accompanied them. The Corcyraean infantry, along with one thousand Zacynthian hoplite reinforcements, was on the promontory at Leucimme. Meanwhile, on the mainland, many of the barbarians had gone to the aid of the Corinthians, the mainlanders in these parts having always been friendly with them.

48. When the Corinthians were ready, they took a three-day supply of food, and, by night, they put out to sea from Cheimerium looking for a naval battle. At dawn, they saw the Corcyraean ships coming at them from the open sea. As soon as they saw each other, both sides went into their respective battle formations. The Athenian ships were off the right flank of the Corcyraean formation, which was made up of three divisions, each of which was commanded

by one of their three admirals. That was how the Corcyraeans had drawn up. As to the Corinthian ships, the Megarians and Ambraciots held the right flank. The other allies formed the center, and the Corinthians themselves, in their best ships, took the left flank opposite the Athenians and the right flank of the Corcyraean fleet.

49. After the signals were raised on both sides, the battle was joined. Inexperienced in modern naval warfare, both sides were arrayed in the old-fashioned way, with many hoplites on deck, along with many archers and javelin men. The battle was hard—though not skillfully fought, and was more like a land battle, because after they had rammed into each other, it wasn't easy to disengage, what with the crush and number of the ships, so they relied for their victory on the hoplites who stood and fought on the decks of immobilized ships. There was no maneuvering, and they fought with courage and brawn rather than with intelligence. It was a battle of tumult and disorder everywhere, in which the Attic ships supported the Corcyraeans when they were hard pressed; but though the Athenians struck terror into the enemy, their commanders did not start any fights for fear of disobeying orders. The Corinthian right flank suffered the most, because twenty Corcyraean ships turned them back and pursued them helter-skelter onto the shore, and then sailed right up to their camp, landed, and burned their empty tents and plundered their goods. On the right flank, then, the Corinthians and their allies were defeated and the Corcyraeans prevailed, but on the left flank, where the Corinthians themselves were, they won decisively because the twenty Corcyraean ships—out of an already outnumbered fleet—were pursuing the enemy and were not available. When the Athenians saw the Corcyraeans in distress, they openly came to the rescue—although they held off from ramming anyone at first. When the rout became obvious, though, and the Corinthians were really laying it on, why then everything happened so fast that distinctions were no longer made and it inevitably came about that the Corinthians and the Athenians were fighting with each other.

50. After the rout had taken place, the Corinthians did not tow away the ships they had sunk to the waterline. Instead, they rowed through the wreckage, intent on killing men rather than taking them alive, and, not knowing that their allies on the right wing had been defeated, they unwittingly killed their own friends. For there had been a great many ships on both sides on a wide expanse of sea when they clashed, and the Corinthians couldn't easily distinguish the victors from the vanquished. In terms of the number of ships, in fact, this battle was the largest that had ever been fought between Greek and Greek.

After the Corinthians had run the Corcyraeans onto the shore, they turned their attention to their own corpses and wrecked ships. They secured most of these and towed the ships to Sybota where the barbarian infantry had come to their support. (Sybota is a deserted harbor in Thesprotia.) After doing this, they regrouped and again sailed out against the Corcyraeans. Fearful lest the Corinthians attempt to land on their territory, the Corcyraeans set out to oppose them with the Athenian ships, with their seaworthy battleships, and with whatever other reserve ships they had. It was late afternoon; the battle hymn had been sung to signal the attack; but the Corinthians suddenly backed water when, in the distance, they saw bearing down on them twenty Athenian ships that the Athenians had sent out to aid the original ten for fear (which proved justified) that the Corcyraeans would be defeated and that their own ten ships would be too few to help.

51. So the Corinthians saw these ships from a distance and withdrew, suspecting that they were from Athens and that there were more than met the eye.

The Athenians, meanwhile, sailed toward the Corcyraeans, who couldn't see them from where they were. The Corcyraeans were wondering why the Corinthians were backing water until some lookouts said that these other ships were coming at them. It was growing quite dark by now and the Corcyraeans also withdrew—whereupon the Corinthians brought about a cessation of hostilities when they turned and sailed away. Thus a disengagement was effected on both sides, and the battle ended with nightfall. Not long after they were spotted, these same twenty Athenian ships, commanded by Glaucon, son of Leagrus, and by Andocides, son of Leogoras, made their way through the corpses and wrecked ships and sailed to the Corcyraeans who were encamped on Leucimme.[7] The Corcyraeans were afraid that they were enemy ships (for it was night by now) but then they recognized them, and so the Athenians dropped anchor.

52. The next day, wanting to see whether the Corinthians would fight, the thirty Athenian ships and such Corcyraean ships as were seaworthy put out to sea and set sail for the harbor at Sybota where the Corinthians had anchored. The Corinthians, for their part, dragged their ships off the beach and took no action after forming up at sea. They had no mind to initiate a battle when they saw the fresh ships from Athens arrayed before them and when they thought about the many disadvantages that they were under, what with the prisoners of war they were guarding on board and their inability to repair their ships in such a desert place. On the contrary, they were looking for some way they could arrange to return home; for they feared that the Athenians would regard the treaty as broken—on the grounds that they had come to blows—and not let them sail away.

53. They therefore decided to put some men aboard a fast vessel without a herald's wand and to send them to the Athenians to see what they could do.[8] The men were despatched and spoke as follows.

"You Athenians are in violation. You are breaking the treaty and starting a war. You stood in our way and raised your weapons against us as we were retaliating against our enemies. If it is your intent to prevent us from sailing against Corcyra or anywhere else we please, why then just break the treaty, treat us as enemies, and take us as your first prisoners."

After they said this, the men on the Corcyraean side who could hear them immediately began to shout out that the Athenians should take them and kill them. But the Athenians answered as follows.

"We are neither starting a war nor breaking the treaty. We are here to help our Corcyraean allies. If you want to sail somewhere else, we won't stop you, but if you sail against Corcyra or any part of her territory, we will use force to prevent it."

54. After the Athenians gave them this answer, the Corinthians set up a victory marker on the Sybotan mainland and began to prepare for their voyage home. The Corcyraeans gathered the wreckage and the corpses that had been carried their way after having been scattered in every direction by the overnight winds and tides, and then they erected a victory marker of their own on Sybota Island.

---

7. This is probably a mistake. Andocides, the son of Leogoras, who was implicated in the religious scandals of 415 and wrote about them in his speech *On the Mysteries*, was born too late to be general by this time, and his grandfather by the same name was born too early.

8. The herald's wand was a wooden staff carried by the messengers of warring parties. To have given the men a wand would have meant that the Corinthians thought they were at war with the Athenians—something they were not yet willing to do.

This is what both sides were thinking when they made their claims to victory:

The Corinthians set up a marker because they had the upper hand in the battle until nightfall—enough so that they could bring back the most shipwrecks and corpses—and they also had captured no fewer than one thousand prisoners of war and had sunk around seventy ships.

The Corcyraeans erected a marker because they had destroyed almost thirty ships and had been able to collect the wrecks and corpses in their vicinity after the Athenians arrived. Also, on the day before, the Corinthians had backed water and withdrawn when they saw the Athenian ships, and then—after the Athenians arrived—they did not sail out of Sybota to engage them.

Thus each side declared victory.

55. On their homeward voyage, the Corinthians used treachery to capture Anactorium, which is at the mouth of the Ambracian Gulf, and which they had administered with the Corcyraeans. They settled Corinthian colonists there and returned home. They sold eight hundred of the Corcyraeans who were slaves. They kept two hundred and fifty Corcyraeans under close guard, but treated them very well so that they might win Corcyra over to the Corinthian side when they returned. Most of them happened to be the most powerful leaders of the city. Thus Corcyra survived the war with Corinth, and the Athenian ships withdrew from the city. For the Corinthians, this became the first of the causes for war with Athens: that while the treaty was in effect, the Athenians, with the Corcyraeans, engaged in a naval battle against them.

56. Immediately after this, the following dispute became a cause for war between the Athenians and the Peloponnesians. Because the Corinthians kept scheming to get even with them, the Athenians became very apprehensive about their hatred. So they ordered the Potidaeans (who live on the isthmus of Pallene, and who, though originally Corinthian colonists, were Athenian allies subject to Athenian taxes) to tear down their city wall on the Pallene side and to give hostages to Athens. They also ordered that the annually appointed magistrates from Corinth be expelled and that no more be accepted in the future. The Athenians took these actions for fear that Perdiccas and Corinth might persuade the Potidaeans to revolt and bring the rest of the Athenian allies in the vicinity of Thrace into revolt along with them.

57. The Athenians took these precautionary measures against Potidaea right after the naval battle off Corcyra. By now, the Corinthians were openly hostile, and Perdiccas, son of Alexander and king of Macedonia, was at war with Athens although he had formerly been a friend and ally. He had gone to war because Athens had made an alliance with Derdas and with his brother Philip, who were united in opposition to him.[9] Frightened of Athens, he began negotiations with Sparta to bring about a war between Athens and the Peloponnesians, and he also tried to win Corinth over to the cause of a revolt in Potidaea. He advanced arguments to the Chalcidians in Thrace and to the Bottiaeans that they should join in revolt in the belief that if he had an alliance with all of these neighboring territories, it would be easier for him to wage a war with Athens. The Athenians learned of these events and were eager to stifle the revolt of the cities. They were about to send thirty ships and one thousand hoplites against Perdiccas's domain under Archestratus, son of Lycomedes, along with two others, when they ordered the commanders to also seize the Potidaean hostages, tear down the wall, and make sure that the nearby cities did not revolt.

9. It is not clear just who Derdas was; he may have been Perdiccas' nephew.

58. The Potidaeans sent ambassadors to Athens to see whether they could persuade them not to adopt any drastic new policies toward Potidaea, but they also sent ambassadors, along with some Corinthians, to Sparta to arrange for help should it be needed. After lengthy negotiations, they had not only not obtained a satisfactory answer from Athens, but the ships bound for Macedonia were now also sailing against them. Meanwhile, the Spartan authorities promised that if the Athenians attacked Potidaea, they would invade Attica; so the Potidaeans swore binding oaths with the Chalcidians and the Bottiaeans, and together they seized that opportunity to revolt.

Meanwhile, Perdiccas persuaded the Chalcidians to abandon and destroy their coastal towns and to resettle upcountry in Olynthus, which they would convert into one fortified city. He also gave these migrants some of his own Mygdonian territories around Lake Bolbe to cultivate while the war with Athens lasted. And so they tore down their cities, moved upcountry, and prepared for war.

59. When the thirty Athenian ships arrived in the Thracian region, they found that Potidaea and the other cities had already revolted. The commanders decided, however, that they would be unable to make war on both Perdiccas and the rebellious territories with the forces available to them; so they turned to Macedonia, which was their primary objective, joined forces with Philip and the brothers of Derdas, who had invaded with an army from the west, and carried on the war against Perdiccas.

60. At this point, with Potidaea in rebellion and the Athenian ships off Macedonia, the Corinthians grew apprehensive about the whole region and regarded the danger as really to themselves. Accordingly, they dispatched a total of sixteen hundred hoplites and four hundred light-armed troops, all made up of Corinthian volunteers and Peloponnesian mercenaries. Their commander was Aristeus, son of Adeimantus, and most of the Corinthians joined the expedition out of affection for him; he, for his part, had always been friendly toward the Potidaeans. This force arrived in Thrace forty days after Potidaea revolted.

61. Athens, too, quickly got the news that the cities had revolted, and when they learned that Aristeus' forces were also on the way, they sent two thousand of their own hoplites in forty ships against the rebels, with Callias, son of Calliades, in command along with four others. They went to Macedonia first, and found that their original one thousand hoplites had just captured Therme and were starting to besiege Pydna, so they also took up positions in front of Pydna and joined in the siege. But the arrival of Aristeus and the pressing situation in Potidaea forced them to come to terms with Perdiccas and patch together a treaty with him, whereupon they left Macedonia and went to Beroea. From there, the Athenians went to Strepsa and, after attacking the place and failing to take it, they made their way by land to Potidaea. They had three thousand of their own hoplites, not counting many from their allies, and six hundred Macedonian cavalry under Philip and Pausanias. In addition, there were seventy ships hugging the shore along their route. They advanced slowly, and on the third day reached Gigonus, where they set up camp.

62. In anticipation of the Athenians, the Potidaeans and the Peloponnesians with Aristeus encamped in front of Olynthus on the isthmus; they also set up a market outside of Potidaea. The allied rebels elected Aristeus the commander of the combined infantry and Perdiccas of the cavalry. (What had happened was that he had immediately rebelled against the Athenians again and joined forces with the Potidaeans, after appointing Iolaus to take his place with the expedition.) Aristeus' strategy was to stay on the isthmus with his army in readiness for an Athenian attack. Meanwhile, the Chalcidians and the allies

from outside the isthmus, along with Perdiccas' two hundred cavalry, were to be stationed in Olynthus so that they could come at the Athenians from the rear when they attacked Aristeus and thus trap the Athenians between them.

The Athenian general Callias and his co-commanders, however, sent their Macedonian cavalry and some of their allies against Olynthus, to prevent an attack from there while they struck camp and moved against Potidaea. When they reached the isthmus and saw their opponents prepared for battle, they too took up their positions and came to blows not much later. Aristeus' wing and whatever Corinthian and other picked troops surrounded him turned back their attackers and chased them for some distance. The remaining army of Potidaeans and Peloponnesians was defeated by the Athenians and fled behind the city wall.

63. When Aristeus returned from the chase and saw the other part of his army in defeat, he couldn't decide whether it would be riskier to go to Olynthus or to Potidaea. He finally decided to bunch his men and to force his way on the run into Potidaea through the beach along the seawall. He was heavily bombarded by spears and arrows but though he lost a few men, he saved most of them.

Olynthus is about seven miles from Potidaea and is clearly visible from there. When the battle began and the signals were raised, the reserves from Olynthus advanced a little way toward Potidaea before the Macedonian cavalry moved into position to stop them from joining in the battle. Since the Athenians achieved a quick victory, however, and the signals were taken down, the reserves returned to the city wall and the Macedonians returned to the Athenian forces. Thus the cavalry of neither side took part in the battle. After the battle, the Athenians set up a victory marker and, under a truce, returned the dead to the Potidaeans. A little less than three hundred Potidaeans and their allies died; for the Athenians, it was one hundred fifty, including their commander, Callias.[1]

64. The Athenians immediately built and garrisoned a wall running out of the isthmus. The route into Pallene was not walled off, though, because they did not think there were enough of them to both stand guard at the isthmus and to go over to Pallene and build a wall: they were afraid that the Potidaeans and their allies would attack them if they split up their men. It was learned at Athens that Pallene was not walled off, so they later sent sixteen hundred of their own hoplites there under the command of Phormio, son of Asopius. After reaching Pallene, he set out from his base at Aphytis and led his army to Potidaea, advancing slowly and deforesting the land along the way. Since no one came out to fight, he walled off the way out of Pallene. Thus Potidaea was completely besieged on both sides as well as blockaded by ships at sea.

65. With the city walled off, Aristeus had no hope of rescue unless help arrived from the Peloponnese or from some other, unexpected, place. To conserve food, he suggested waiting for a strong wind and having all but five hundred men sail away, with him among those staying behind. But he failed to persuade them, and so, wanting to arrange help for the city and to maintain the best possible situation outside it, he sailed away unnoticed through the Athenian blockade. He remained in Chalcidice and joined in the fighting here and there, including ambushing and killing a large number of Sermylians near their city. He also negotiated with the Peloponnesians to find some way to arrange for help. After walling off Potidaea, Phormio took his sixteen hundred hoplites and ravaged Chalcidice and Bottice and captured a few villages.

1. This was also the battle at which Socrates saved the life of Alcibiades; Plato refers to this in the *Symposium*, 220E.

66. The following grievances between the Athenians and the Pelopon-nesians were born of these events: for the Corinthians, that Athens besieged their colony of Potidaea while Corinthian and Peloponnesian men were in it; for the Athenians, that a city allied to them and subject to their taxation had been led to revolt by Peloponnesians who then went there and openly fought against them with the Potidaeans. War did not break out, however. There was still an armistice because the Corinthians had so far acted alone.[2]

67. With Potidaea under siege, though, the Corinthians could not rest. Their own citizens were in the city, and they were also apprehensive about the whole region. They immediately appealed to their allies to come to Sparta, where they railed against Athens for breaking the treaty and for wronging the Peloponnese. Fearful of the Athenians, the Aeginetans did not openly send en-voys, but they nonetheless secretly joined with the Corinthians in fomenting war and complained that they had been denied the autonomy granted by the treaty. The Spartans invited not only the allies but any other states that said they had been treated unjustly by Athens, and then called a regular meeting of their own assembly and urged everyone to speak. Numerous envoys attended and voiced their grievances. These included the Megarians, who detailed a good many complaints, especially being barred—in violation of the treaty—from har-bors in the Athenian empire and from the Athenian agora.[3] After first letting the others rile up the Spartans, the Corinthians finally came forward and spoke as follows.

68. Men of Sparta. Your clannish trust in your public and private dealings among yourselves makes you suspicious of others when we have something to say. You get your prudence from it, but it makes you ignorant of what goes on outside Sparta. We, your allies, have frequently warned you of how we were about to be injured by the Athenians, but you never learned the lesson we tried to teach. Instead, you distrusted the speakers as referring to private quarrels that concerned only themselves. As a result, you did not bring us, your allies, here before we were hurt, but waited until now when we are actually suffering. And it is fitting that we Corinthians, more than any others, should speak, for we are the most aggrieved in hav-ing been both abused by the Athenians and neglected by you.

If Athens had wronged Greece invisibly somehow, you would be ig-norant and need instruction. But as things are, why should we lecture you when you can see both those they have already enslaved and the others they are plotting against—especially our allies—and see, too, that they have been making long-range plans for future aggression. They would not have taken Corcyra away from us by force or besieged Potidaea if the latter did not give them the most strategic base of operations in Thrace and the for-mer were not going to provide the Peloponnese with its largest fleet of ships.

69. You are responsible for all this. You let them fortify their city after the Persian Wars in the first place, and then later you let them build their Long Walls, thus effectively depriving not only their slaves of their free-dom, but your allies as well. For the truth is that slavery is not brought about by the slaveholder, but by the one who has the power to stop it yet looks the other way—especially when he has a reputation for excellence as "the liberator of Greece."[4]

---

2. Note the clear parallels between the events in Potidaea and those in Corcyra.
3. The agora of a Greek city combined the functions of marketplace and civic center. To be cut off from the agora was effectively to be excluded from trade.
4. Sparta had this reputation because it was nominally the leader of the alliance of Greek states that de-feated the forces of the Persian king Xerxes in 480–479.

But it has still been hard to get a meeting with you, and even now we do not have a clear agenda, because it is no longer necessary to consider whether we have been wronged. We must now consider how we are going to defend ourselves, because the Athenians are men of action with well-laid plans, in contrast with people who haven't yet made up their minds, and they aren't *going* to come—they're coming. We know the road they take and how they move, step by step, against their neighbors. They are less bold now because they think they have to sneak past your obliviousness, but they will come on in force when they realize that you knowingly look away. For you alone among the Greeks, O men of Sparta, you alone still bide your time! You alone defend yourselves not with power, but with delay, and do not nip the growth of your enemies in the bud, but only when the stem has doubled in its length! They always said you could be counted on, but your reputation is stronger than your deeds.

We know that the Persian had to come from the ends of the earth and attack the Peloponnese before you sent out a force adequate to meet him; but now the Athenians are near, and instead of going forth to defend yourselves, you would rather wait for the attack and leave things to chance by taking a stand in a battle with men who are growing increasingly powerful, though you know that the barbarian kept tripping over himself and that even against the Athenians, we have often only survived because of their mistakes and not because of any help from you. Indeed, trust in you, and being unprepared because of that trust, has already been the ruin of some cities.[5]

But let none of you think that these things are said more in a spirit of enmity than of reproach: a denunciation is appropriate for the outlaws we hate; but a reproach is for dear friends who have gone astray.

70. We believe, furthermore, that if anyone has the right to censure their neighbors, we do—especially when you seem to us so ignorant of the great issues at stake, and when you have never thought through the kind of people the Athenians are, compared to you, or how great the struggle will be with people so totally different from yourselves. They are innovators, quick to formulate plans and to put those plans into practice. You want to preserve things as they are, to invent nothing, and to forego even minimal gains. They in turn are bold beyond their strength, daring beyond their better judgment, and optimistic in the direst straits. As for you, you fall short of doing what is in your power, mistrustful even of what you know for sure—and as to straits, you think you'll never get out of them. They are impetuous where you procrastinate, and they are explorers where you are homebodies, because they think they might get something out of going abroad whereas you think that moving will threaten what you already have. They press their advantage when they are stronger than their enemies and retreat as little as possible in defeat. When they act on behalf of their city, their minds are their own, but they sacrifice their bodies as though they belonged to others; and if they fail to achieve their goal, they consider that they have lost what already belonged to them, whereas if they go after it and get it, they treat it like a trifle in comparison with what is to come. If they try and fail, they hope something will turn up to satisfy their needs. They are the only people on earth for whom achieving what they have in mind and hoping for it are virtually the same, because of the speed with which they attempt whatever they decide to do. And they toil for all this with pain and trouble their whole life long, enjoying little of what they

---

5. As in Potidaea, for example. See 1.58.

have because they are always getting something new, and thinking that simply doing their duty is a holiday, and that a quiet idleness is no less a chore than boring work. In brief, the truth is that Athenians were born not to have peace and not to let anyone else have it, either.

71. Yet you Spartans constantly delay in the face of this city so opposed to you in every way, and you think that it is not enough in the long run to achieve peace by using one's armed forces justly and by having a clear policy of not allowing oneself to be wronged. Instead, you place an equal value on not hurting others and on taking no risks, even in self-defense. It would have been hard to achieve this even if you lived next to a city just like yours, but as it is, and as we have now made clear, your ways are outmoded compared with theirs. In politics as in any skill, it is always necessary to keep up with new developments, and though it is best for a city at peace to preserve its customs, that city needs a great deal of flexibility when it is forced to deal with changing circumstances. Because of its varied experience, Athens has reformed its government much more than you.

So put an end to your sluggishness as of now. Come now to the aid of Potidaea and the other cities, as you are obligated to do, and swiftly invade Attica so as not to lose your friends and your kin to their most hated enemies and so as not to force us, out of sheer demoralization, into a different alliance.[6] If we were to do that, we would be doing nothing wrong either in the eyes of the gods who guarantee our oaths or of the men who observe our deeds. After all, those who have been abandoned do not break treaties when they go over to others; treaties are broken by those who do not help the cities with whom they have sworn alliances. If you decide to move, we will stay with you, for then it would be a sacrilegious violation of our oaths to change our allegiance—and besides, we could not find allies more like ourselves than you. Make the right decision and try not to lead a Peloponnese that is less powerful than the one your fathers left you.

72. That is what the Corinthians said.

Meanwhile, there happened to be a group of Athenian ambassadors in Sparta. They were there about another matter, but after hearing the debate, they thought they should go before the Spartan assembly—not to defend themselves in any way against the accusations the cities were making, but to give the Spartans a clear, overall view of why this was a question they should consider at length and not one they should decide quickly. The Athenians wanted to indicate how great the power of their own city was, reminding the older generation of what it already knew and giving the younger generation a lesson about things of which it had no experience. They thought their speech might turn the Spartans onto the path of peace and away from war. Thus they approached the Spartans and said that unless there was some objection, they would also like to address the assembly. The Spartans invited the Athenians to come forward, which they did, and spoke as follows.

73. Our mission here was not to refute your allies, but to attend to the business of our city. When we learned, though, that there was a considerable outcry against us, we came forward. We do so not to answer the complaints of the cities (for, after all, neither our speeches nor those of these envoys will have been made as though you were judges), but so that you will not lightly make ill-advised decisions about weighty matters under the influence of your allies. We also want to show, from the perspective of

---

6. Corinth may be threatening here to make an alliance with Argos.

a clear, overall view of our generally accepted history, that we do not improperly hold what we have and that our city is to be taken seriously.

As to the events of the distant past, what is the point of talking about them when you know of this history through hearsay and not through experience? It is, however, necessary to speak of the Persian Wars and other events you do know about, even though it may be rather boring to have them always cited at you. We took our actions, and our risks, for the common good; you had your share of the profit, so let us not be totally deprived of the renown, for what it's worth. Our speech will be given not as an apology, though, but as evidence and proof of the kind of city this struggle will be with if you do not make the right decision. For we maintain that we alone, at Marathon, braved the first fight with the barbarian, and that when he later returned, the whole Athenian people, incapable of defending themselves by land, boarded their ships to join the battle at Salamis, which kept the barbarian from sailing to the Peloponnese and sacking city after city unable to defend each other against so many of their ships.[7] Xerxes himself gave the greatest proof of this, because when he was defeated by our navy and his forces were no longer what they had been, he quickly retreated with most of his army.

74. That is what happened, and it clearly showed that the outcome of the war depended on the Greek navy, to which we made the three most important contributions: the most ships, the smartest general, and our unhesitating courage. Nearly two-thirds of the almost four hundred ships![8] The commander, Themistocles—who was most responsible for fighting in the narrows, which brilliantly ensured the outcome, and for which you honored him more than any other noncitizen who ever visited you. And we showed the boldest courage by far—we who, when no one came to our aid by land, and when everyone beyond our borders had been enslaved— we who decided to abandon our city and destroy our homes, and we who still did not forsake the common cause of our remaining allies or scatter ineffectually away from them, but boarded our ships, risking all and not showing any anger that you had so far done nothing to help us.

We maintain, then, that we helped you no less than you helped us. After all, you were nowhere to be seen when our city was in danger, and you only left cities that were inhabited then and that would be inhabited in the future and came to help when you were more afraid for yourselves than for us. We set forth from a city that no longer existed and, putting ourselves at risk when it had scant hope of ever existing again, we saved ourselves and, in part, you. If in fear for our land, we had first gone over to the Persian, as others had done, or if we, a ruined people, had not dared to embark upon our ships, it would not have been necessary for you to give battle with your inadequate navy. Things would have come to Xerxes just the way he wanted them.[9]

75. So then, you men of Sparta, don't our courage and intelligent strategy in those days entitle us not to be treated with such resentment by the Greeks just because of our present empire? Why, we didn't even grab this empire by force! You didn't want to stay and confront what was left of the barbarians, so the allies approached us and we became their leader at their request. Because of that act we were constrained

---

7. Their successes in the land battle at Marathon in 490 and the sea battle at Salamis in 480 were crucial to the Greeks' victory in the Persian Wars. Marathon was indeed won by the Athenians, and Athens under Themistocles also took the lead at Salamis.
8. There is some disagreement about these numbers.
9. Xerxes and his father Darius were the two Persian kings who had attacked Greece. Compare this passage with Herodotus 7.139.

from the beginning to develop the empire into what it is today, under the influence, first, of fear; then of the desire for respect; and finally of gain. It also didn't seem safe to risk relinquishing our empire when most people hated us, when some rebellious cities had already been quashed, and when you were no longer the friends you once were, but had turned querulous and suspicious. And the rebel cities would have gone over to you, wouldn't they?

76. Faced with the greatest dangers, no one can be reproached for managing his interests well. After all, you Spartans led the cities of the Peloponnese after organizing them to your advantage. And we know perfectly well that if you had persevered against the Persians, and your leadership, like ours, had come to be hated, you, no less than we, would have been compelled either to rule your grudging allies by force or to put yourselves in danger. So we did nothing in the least unusual or beyond the pale of human nature if we accepted the empire that was offered to us and didn't let it go—subject as we were to the most powerful drives of fear, the desire for respect, and gain. Nor are we the first for whom this is so. It is an eternal law that the strong shall rule the weak. And we are deservedly strong, in our opinion—and in yours, too, at least before you mated expediency with a rhetoric of justice. Justice never kept anyone who was handed the chance to get something by force from getting more. The ones who deserve to be praised are those who, after succumbing to human nature by ruling over others, are more just than they have to be in view of their strength. We think that others who took what we have would show how moderate we are; but our very reasonableness has brought us more unreasoning slander than praise.

77. We are thought to be litigious, for example, even though we lose in binding arbitration between ourselves and our allies, as well as in the impartial courts in which we try the cases. And yet none of the allies looks at any states that have empires elsewhere and are less moderate towards their subjects than we are and blames them for *that*! After all, nobody has to go to court, but everybody will use force if they can. Our allies are used to associating with us on a basis of equality, and if they are overruled for reasons of state in even the least little way contrary to what they think is necessary on matters of opinion or of power, why, they aren't grateful that they haven't been deprived of more, but carry on about their diminished status more than they would have if we had openly set all law aside and claimed the lion's share from the first. They wouldn't have answered then that the weak ought not to give way to the strong! It seems that people get angrier when they are the victims of injustice than of aggression. In the case of injustice, it's thought to be self-aggrandizement at the expense of equals; in the case of aggression, it's being overpowered by a stronger force. When they were subject to the Persians, they suffered worse than this and put up with it. But our rule seems hard. Naturally. Subjects always find their present masters overbearing. If you Spartans were to rule after overthrowing us, you just might lose the good will you've gained from those who fear us—if, that is, you had a mind now to exercise the authority you briefly showed when you were the leaders against the Persians. Your ways are uncongenial to others, after all—and besides when any one of you leaves home, he doesn't obey the laws of Sparta or the laws of the rest of Greece either![1]

---

1. The speaker may be referring to the behavior of Pausanias. See 1.95 and 128.

78. Deliberate slowly, then, for this is no trivial matter, and do not, persuaded by the opinions and complaints of others, bring trouble on your own house. Assess before you are actually in it how great is the incalculable element of war, how it tends to degenerate into a gamble the longer it lasts. We are only at the start, but which way it will go is a stab in the dark. When people go to war, they do first what should be done last by going into action. Then, when they have setbacks, they grope for talks. As far as we can see, neither you nor we has made that mistake yet, and so we say to you that for so long as good sense is still an option, we should not break the treaty or violate our oaths but resolve our differences at law according to our agreement. Otherwise, we call the gods who guarantee oaths to witness that we will defend ourselves against you, the aggressors, wherever you may strike.

79. That is what the Athenians said. After hearing both the complaints of the allies against the Athenians as well as what the Athenians said, the Spartans asked everyone to leave the assembly and deliberated about the situation among themselves. The opinion of the majority tended to be the same: the Athenians were in the wrong and the Spartans ought to go to war quickly. But Archidamus, who was their king and who was considered to be a prudent and intelligent man, came forward and spoke as follows.

80. I am a veteran of many wars, my fellow Spartans, and I can see that, unlike most, those of you who are the same age as me are not overeager for this business, and do not think that it is either a good thing or a sure thing. And you may find that the particular war you are now considering, if you think it through prudently, could turn out to be the worst of our wars by far. Firstly, the might opposed to us Peloponnesians and our neighbors is almost equal to our own and is able to come against each of us by short marches. Secondly, the Athenians are men who hold distant territories and have command of the sea. And more than that, they are equipped with the best of everything—with private and public wealth, with ships and cavalry and heavy infantry, and with a larger population than is to be found in any one place elsewhere in Greece. And more even than that, they have many allies subject to taxes. So just how are we going to make war easily against them, and what will we rely on to sustain the war, unprepared as we are? On our ships? But we are outnumbered, and it will take quite some time if we delay the war to build a navy to match theirs. On our money then? But we are in even shorter supply of that. We don't have it in the public treasury and we are unwilling to tax our private wealth.

81. There are some of you, perhaps, who will be encouraged by the fact that we are superior to the Athenians in the number of our hoplites and that this will enable us to go around ravaging their land. But they have dominion over a great deal of land and they will be able to import what they need by sea. If, then, we try to foment revolution among their allies, we would also need to come to the aid of those allies with ships, since most of them are islanders.

So what kind of war would this be for us? Because if we cannot defeat them with our navy, or at least intercept the tribute payments with which they support their fleet, we will be hurt badly, and when that has happened, disengaging will not be an attractive possibility—especially if we are thought to have been the ones who began the fight. Oh, and let us not be uplifted by the hope that the war will be ended quickly, once we begin to ravage their land. What I'm really afraid of is that we will pass this war on to our children—that's how unlikely it is that Athenian planning will be enslaved to their land, or that, like fresh recruits, they will be dumbstruck by war.

82. Not that I obliviously urge you to let them harm our allies or to avoid exposing them in the act when they are hatching their plans—just not to take up arms quite yet, but to send ambassadors with our allegations, neither threatening war too plainly nor indicating that we will endure aggression under any circumstances. Meanwhile, we must make our own preparations and cultivate allies both Greek and barbarian who can give us either naval or financial strength. (Since the Athenians are plotting against us, no one could blame us for making alliances in self-defense with barbarians and not just with Greeks.) At the same time, we must continue to be self-reliant.

It would be best if they listened to our ambassadors. If not, after two—or better still, three—years have passed, we can attack them from a totally fortified position, should we decide to do so. And maybe they will be more inclined to give way once they see that our words and our preparations are sending the same signals while their land is still unharmed and they are making decisions about real and intact goods. Because you must not think of their land as anything other than a hostage—all the more so the better it has been cultivated. It needs to be spared as long as possible so as not to push them into a desperate frame of mind that will make them that much less accessible. Beware, for if we, impelled by the complaints of the allies, rush prematurely into destroying their crops and trees, we may bring even more disgrace and difficulty on the Peloponnese. It is always possible to resolve the complaints of private citizens and individual cities, but when a whole alliance declares war on behalf of private interests—war, whose direction is impossible to predict—it is not easy to come to terms without a loss of face.

83. And let no one think it cowardice that many cities do not swiftly attack that one city. For they have no fewer tax-paying allies than we, and war is a matter not so much of weaponry as of finance, which pays for weaponry, especially when the war is between mainlanders and seafarers. Let's build up our money supply first, before we get excited over the arguments of the allies. We are going to have most of the responsibility for the outcome one way or the other, so let us try calmly to foresee that outcome.

84. As to the slowness and delay we are always being reproached with, don't be ashamed of that. Otherwise, you'll go to war quickly and have to get out of it slowly because you will have undertaken it without being ready. We have always lived in a free and highly respected city, where prudence means keeping our heads. This makes us the only ones who don't become arrogant in prosperity and who don't give way as much as others to misfortune. We are not titillated by flatterers who incite us to dangerous, ill-advised acts, and we aren't goaded into going along if somebody provokes us with denunciations instead. Good government makes us both warlike and judicious—warlike, because honor is the better part of prudence and courage is the better part of honor; judicious because we have been educated to be ignorant of contempt for the laws and punished into being more sensible than to disobey them. And we're not so good at idle speculation as to critique the preparations of our enemies with well-reasoned speeches and then to attack them with half-baked tactics. We think our neighbors' plans are about equal to ours and that the accidents of chance cannot be logically analyzed. We always prepare for action against opponents as if they planned well, so that it isn't necessary to pin our hopes

on their mistakes because we ourselves will have carefully planned ahead. Bear in mind that one man doesn't differ much from another; the strongest is the one who is educated in the toughest school.

85. These are the lessons our forefathers handed down to us, and let's not forget them after having benefited from them for so long. Let's also not fix on the short space of a day to decide about so many lives and cities, about so much treasure and honor. Let's take our time. Our strength makes this more possible for us than for others. Send ambassadors to Athens about Potidaea. Send to them concerning the matters in which the allies say they have been wronged, especially since the Athenians are prepared to go to arbitration. After all, it isn't customary to attack a defendant as if he were already convicted. Meanwhile, prepare for war. This is the strongest decision you can make for yourselves, and the most intimidating to your enemies.[2]

That is what Archidamus said.
Finally, Sthenelaidas, who was one of the ephors at that time, said this:[3]

86. I don't understand all of the arguments of the Athenians. They congratulated themselves a lot but they didn't deny that they wronged our allies and the Peloponnese. Besides, if they behaved nobly towards the Persians then and basely towards us now, they deserve a twofold punishment for having gone from good to bad. We are the same now as then, and if we are prudent we will neither look the other way when our allies are wronged nor delay about coming to their aid. Their suffering is not being delayed. Others have lots of money and ships and horses; we have trusty allies who must not be betrayed to the Athenians or have to endure lawsuits and speeches, when it is not by speeches that they are being harmed. We must help them quickly and with all our strength. And let no one teach us that we should deliberate when we have been wronged; instead, let those who plan to do wrong take a long time to deliberate. So vote for a war worthy of Sparta, you men of Lacedaemon! Do not allow the Athenians to become even more powerful and do not sell out our allies, but with the help of the gods let us go forth against these criminals!

87. After saying this, Sthenelaidas, who was the ephor, put the question to the Spartan assembly. They have a voice vote and not a ballot, and he said that he could not tell which side was louder. Because he really wanted them to show their opinion openly so as to incite them all the more to war, he said, "Whichever of you men of Sparta think the treaty has been broken and that the Athenians are the wrongdoers should stand over there," and he pointed out a spot to them. "Whoever doesn't think so, go to the other side." They stood up and took their positions opposite each other, and the larger number by far were those who thought the treaty had been broken. Then the Spartans summoned the allies and said that they had decided that the Athenians had broken the law, but that they wanted to take a vote with all the allies present so that they could make war, if that should be their decision, after reaching a consensus.

---

2. Throughout this speech, Archidamus has been playing with words the Corinthian speaker has used in his speech. For example, "ignorance" in chapter 68 and "denunciation" in 69 are both used in chapter 84, and the word "prudence" is played with throughout. Archidamus also echoes the Corinthian references to going to school and learning lessons. Fifth-century audiences were accustomed to paying close attention to long speeches and appreciated well-phrased rhetoric and subtle distinctions in the meanings of words.

3. Spartan government included five important officials known as ephors ("overseers").

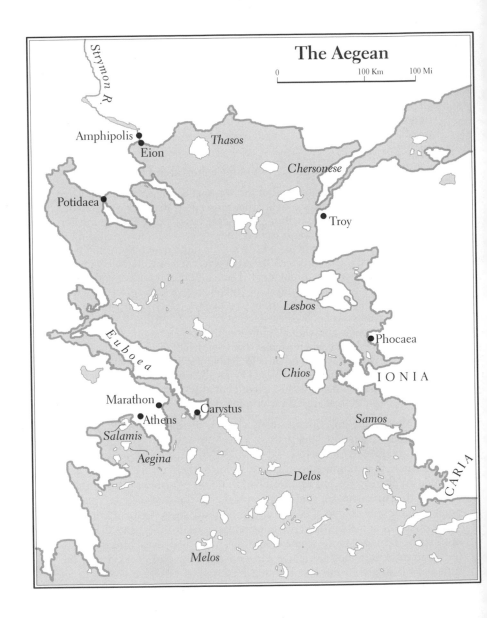

The Aegean

0   100 Km   100 Mi

Strymon R.

Amphipolis

Thasos

Eion

Chersonese

Potidaea

Troy

Lesbos

Phocaea

Euboea

Chios

IONIA

Marathon

Carystus

Samos

Athens

Salamis

Aegina

Delos

CARIA

Melos

Having brought about this result, the allies departed for home; the Athenian ambassadors left later, after transacting their business. This resolution of the assembly that the treaty had been broken took place in the fourteenth year of the thirty-year truce that went into effect after the events at Euboea.[4]

88. The Spartans voted that the treaty had been broken and that they should go to war not so much because they were persuaded by the arguments of the allies as because they feared that Athenian power would grow even greater in view of the fact that most of Greece was already in Athenian hands.

89. The following are the events that led to the growth of Athenian power.[5] The Persians had withdrawn from Europe, their infantry and their navy defeated by the Greeks, the fleeing remnant of their armada destroyed at Mycale.[6] Leotychides, the king of Sparta and the man who had led the Greeks at Mycale, returned home with his Peloponnesian allies. Meanwhile, the Athenians and their allies from Ionia and the Hellespont who had now rebelled against the King stayed behind to besiege Sestos, which was still in Persian hands. They maintained the siege through the winter, captured the city after the barbarians abandoned it, and then sailed away from the Hellespont to their respective cities. Once the barbarians had left their land, the men of Athens immediately brought their wives, children, and remaining possessions back from their hiding places and prepared to rebuild their city and its walls. Only short stretches of wall were still standing and most of the houses were in ruins; the few that survived were those in which the Persian commanders had been quartered.

90. When the Spartans learned of what was happening, they sent a delegation to Athens, partly because they would have preferred to see neither the Athenians nor anyone else with a walled city, but mostly because they had been egged on by allies frightened by the size of the Athenian navy, which had not been so formidable in the past, and by the daring the Athenians had shown in the war. The Spartans urged the Athenians not to rebuild their walls and to join them instead in demolishing the walls in cities outside the Peloponnese. They did not disclose their true desires or their suspicions of the Athenians, but argued instead that if the barbarians should come again, they would not have a stronghold in Athens from which to operate, as they had just had in Thebes.[7] The Spartans said, in addition, that the whole Peloponnese was military base and shelter enough. On the advice of Themistocles, the Athenians managed to get rid of the Spartans by responding that they would dispatch ambassadors to Sparta to discuss the matter. Themistocles then urged the Athenians to send him off to Sparta right away and to select other ambassadors besides him, whom they should hold off on sending until the wall was just high enough to fight from. Meanwhile, the whole population of the city—men, women, and children—should work on the wall, sparing neither private nor public buildings that might be of use. Everything should be torn down for the project. Having given these instructions and indicating that he would take care of things in Sparta, Themistocles left. When he reached Sparta, he did not go directly to the magistrates, but delayed and made excuses; and whenever one of the authorities asked him why he did not go before the assembly, he said that he was waiting for his fellow ambassadors, who had stayed behind on important busi-

---

4. 445.
5. Thucydides here begins the digression known as the Pentecontaetia, the half-century beginning with the end of the Persian Wars, and traces the growth of Athenian power.
6. This took place in 479.
7. The fact that the Thebans "medized" (i.e., went over to the Persians) was a sore point among the Greek states, but the Spartans' argument that walls around Athens would be dangerous in the event of Persian invasion is bizarre.

ness. He was expecting them to arrive at any moment, and was astonished that they were not there yet.

91. At first, the Spartans believed Themistocles out of their high regard for him, but it became impossible for them to doubt others who arrived from Athens and said flatly that the wall was being built and that it was already quite high. Aware of their suspicions, Themistocles urged the Spartans not to be influenced by hearsay, but to send some reliable men of their own to study the situation and return with a report they could trust. The Spartans did so, but Themistocles sent a secret message ordering the Athenians to detain the Spartan envoys discreetly and not to release them until he and the others had returned. (In fact, his fellow ambassadors, Habronichus, son of Lysicles, and Aristides, son of Lysimachus, had arrived by now.) They had brought the message that the wall was now high enough, and Themistocles feared that the Spartans would not release him and his colleagues once they had heard the truth. As ordered, the Athenians detained the envoys, and Themistocles went before the Spartans and openly declared that his city had been walled sufficiently to protect its inhabitants. If the Spartans or their allies wanted to negotiate with them, he said, from now on it would be with people who knew what was in their own interests and in those of the alliance.[8] When the Athenians had made the bold decision that it would be best to abandon their city and to take to their ships, they did so without consulting their allies; and when, later, they deliberated with those allies, their opinion proved to be second to none. They had now decided that it would be best for their city to be fortified with a wall. This would be advantageous for the individual citizens of Athens as well as for the allies, because a state's counsel in joint deliberations could not carry equal weight unless all states were on the same footing. He said that either everyone in the alliance should have an unfortified city or acknowledge that the Athenians had acted fairly.

92. When the Spartans heard this, they showed no open anger toward the Athenians—after all, they said, they had sent their ambassadors to the Athenian assembly merely to express an opinion, not to forbid them to build a wall; and besides, they felt an especial friendship toward Athens because of their zeal in fighting the Persian foe. Nevertheless, the Spartans were secretly vexed over the failure of their policy. The envoys from both sides then returned home without formal charges being made against them.

93. In this way, the Athenians built a wall around their city in a very short time. And even now it is quite clear that the wall was hastily built. The foundation is made of different kinds of stones, unsquared here and there and laid down as they came to hand. Many gravestones and bits of sculpture were also built into it. The circumference of the wall everywhere exceeded the size of the city, so they had to put everything they could move to use. Themistocles also persuaded them to finish fortifying the Piraeus, something he had begun during his year as archon. He thought the location, with its three natural harbors, was excellent, and that the harbor would contribute greatly to the growth of their power now that they were a maritime nation. He had been, after all, the first man bold enough to say the Athenians must take to the sea, and with the fortification of the Piraeus, he helped to prepare the way for the Athenian empire.

---

8. Themistocles refers here to the alliance the Greeks had made with one another against the Persians, the so-called Hellenic League.

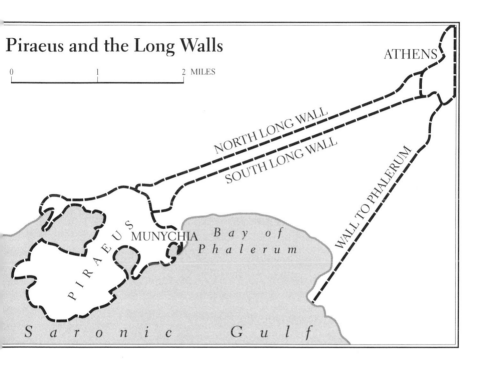

Piraeus and the Long Walls

0   1   2 MILES

ATHENS

NORTH LONG WALL

SOUTH LONG WALL

WALL TO PHALERUM

PIRAEUS

MUNYCHIA

Bay of Phalerum

S a r o n i c   G u l f

In keeping with his plan, the wall was made wide enough so that two wagons abreast could carry building stones atop it. The space between the outer blocks was not filled in with either gravel or clay. Instead, huge hewn stones were fitted together throughout and secured on the outside by iron and lead clamps. The height of the wall, however, was only half what Themistocles had intended. He had wanted its sheer height and width to deter enemy aggression, and he believed that a few of the least combat-worthy men would be able to defend it while the rest of the armed forces would man the fleet. In my opinion, he inclined so much toward naval power because he saw that the King's attack force could make its approach more easily by sea than by land. He believed that Piraeus to be more valuable than the upper city, and he frequently urged the Athenians to go down to it if they were ever attacked by land and take on all comers in their ships.

In this way, then, the Athenians constructed their walls and rebuilt the rest of their city after the retreat of the Persians.

94. At this time, Pausanias, son of Cleombrotus, was dispatched from Sparta in command of the Greek forces.[9] He had twenty ships from the Peloponnese and was accompanied by thirty Athenian ships and by a number of ships from the other allies. They attacked Cyprus and conquered most of it. Later, still under the command of Pausanias, they attacked and besieged Byzantium, which was held by the Persians.

95. Pausanias had by this time become excessively authoritarian. The Greeks were irked by him, especially the Ionians and others who had recently been liberated from the King. They approached the Athenians and asked them to assume the leadership over them on the basis of their kinship, and to protect them if Pausanias tried to use force against them. The Athenians assented to their request. They were determined not to put up with the high-handedness of Pausanias and to manage things from then on as they thought best. Meanwhile, the Spartans recalled Pausanias for questioning about the reports they had been getting. He had been accused of all sorts of wrongdoing by Greeks who had come to Sparta, and he seemed to be behaving more like a tyrant than a general. His recall happened to come at the same time that the allies, with the exception of the Peloponnesian soldiers, went over to Athens out of hatred for him. When Pausanias arrived in Sparta, he was held accountable for any crimes he personally had committed against individuals, but he was acquitted of the most serious charges. The worst of these was that he had collaborated with the Persians, for which there seemed to be a clear-cut case. The Spartans no longer sent Pausanias out as a commander. Instead, they sent Dorcis and others with a small force. The allies, however, no longer acknowledged their authority, and Dorcis left when he saw how things stood. The Spartans did not dispatch any other commanders later, for fear that they would become as corrupt as they had seen Pausanias to be. The Spartans wanted no further part in the war with Persia. They believed that the Athenians were perfectly capable of leading the fight, and that they were, at that time, loyal to Sparta.

96. Thus the Athenians assumed the leadership with the full consent of the allies, who hated Pausanias. They determined which cities should contribute money to fight the barbarians and which should contribute ships, with the avowed intention of plundering the King's territory to get back what they

---

9. King Cleombrotus of Sparta died in 480. Pausanias, who was serving as regent for the underage Pleistarchus, had commanded the combined Greek land forces at Plataea in 479.

had lost. Athens now created the office of "Greek Treasurer." These officials received the "tribute," which was the name given to the cash payments from the
allies. At first, the allies were required to pay a tribute of four hundred and sixty
talents. Delos served as the Greek treasury, and the allies held their meetings in
the temple.

97. At first, the Athenians led independent allies who engaged in joint deliberations,[1] and in the administration of that alliance as well as in their military campaigns, they made huge gains between the Persian War and the present
war, over the barbarians, their own rebellious allies, and the Peloponnesian
states they had dealings with from time to time. I have recorded these events
and inserted this digression here because this period has been omitted in all previous histories, which narrated either the events that occurred before the Persian War or the events of the Persian War itself—although Hellanicus does
touch on the subject in his history of Attica, albeit sketchily and with inaccurate dates.[2] I am also interested in showing how the Athenian empire was established.

98. First, with Cimon, son of Miltiades, in command, the Athenians besieged and captured Eion, on the Strymon River, which was in the hands of the
Persians, and sold its people into slavery. They enslaved the Dolopians, who inhabited the Aegean island of Scyros, which the Athenians then colonized themselves. In addition, a war broke out between the Athenians and the Carystians—
though not with the other Euboeans—which was eventually resolved through
negotiations. Next, they made war on rebellious Naxians and set up a siege. This
was the first allied city to be subjugated in violation of the terms of the alliance.
It later happened to the other cities for one reason or another.

99. There were numerous causes for rebellion, but the main causes were
shortfalls in tribute and ship production and, in some cases, refusal to serve in
the army. The Athenians were strict and demanding taskmasters, and they dealt
harshly with those who were neither willing nor accustomed to making sacrifices. For various reasons, then, the Athenian leadership was no longer as agreeable as it had once been, but since they provided most of the forces in every
campaign, it was easy for them to reduce rebel cities to subjection. The allies
themselves were to blame for this. Because most of them did not want to be away
from home, they were reluctant to serve in the armed forces; so instead of supplying ships and crews, they had agreed to pay enough money to defray their
cost. The Athenians spent this money to improve their navy, and the allies rendered themselves inexperienced and unprepared for war when they tried to
break away.

100. Next, there was a battle on land and sea at the Eurymedon River in
Pamphylia between the Athenians and their allies and the Persians.[3] The Athenians and their allies, with Cimon, son of Miltiades, in command, won both
battles on the same day, capturing and destroying all two hundred Phoenician

1. From this point onward, Thucydides' references to Athens' "allies" are to members of this newly founded
   Delian League, not to the previous alliance of assorted Greek states (including Sparta) against the Persians that was known as the Hellenic League. The original alliance, however, remained in force, and the
   Spartans would appeal to it when seeking Athenian assistance against the rebellious helots (1.102,
   below).
2. A somewhat older contemporary of Thucydides, Hellanicus of Lesbos (c. 480–395) was an important historian, but his work is almost entirely lost. He shared Herodotus' interest in local customs and folklore
   and wrote several ethnographic studies; he also sought to integrate the assorted myths of Greek tradition
   into a coherent historical framework. His interest in establishing a chronology for Greek history was reflected in his *Universal Chronicle* and in the work to which Thucydides refers here, his local history of
   Attica.
3. This battle took place sometime in the early 460s, perhaps 467.

triremes. Later the Thasians tried to break away from Athens in disputes over the markets on the opposite shore in Thrace as well as over their gold mine. The Athenians brought a fleet against the Thasians, defeated them in a naval battle, and went ashore. At about the same time, the Athenians sent ten thousand of their own and their allies' colonists to the Strymon River to colonize what was then known as the Nine Roads, although it is now called Amphipolis. They gained control of the Nine Roads, which had been held by the Edonians, but then, after advancing into the interior of Thrace, they were wiped out at Edonian Drabescus by a combined force of Thracians who considered the colonization of the territory to be an act of war.

101. Defeated in battle and under siege, the Thasians called on the Spartans to help them by invading Attica. Unbeknownst to the Athenians, the Spartans agreed and were about to invade when they were deterred by the great earthquake, after which the helots and the neighboring Thuriatae and Aethaeae rebelled and took Ithome.[4] Most of the helots were the descendants of the Messenians, who had been enslaved in antiquity. For this reason, all the rebels were called Messenians. Because the Spartans were preoccupied with the war against the rebels in Ithome, the Thasians came to terms with the Athenians in the third year of the siege. They agreed to tear down their wall and surrender their ships. They raised the money they owed and paid it immediately, and agreed to pay their share in the future. They also gave up their claim to the mainland markets and to the mine.

102. Because the war at Ithome dragged on, the Spartans called on various allies, including the Athenians, for help.[5] The Athenians came with a large force under the command of Cimon. They were called in especially because they were thought to be skilled in siege warfare, and the long siege had clearly found the Spartans wanting in this respect. Otherwise, they would have taken the place by storm. This campaign led to the first open breach between the Spartans and the Athenians. They still could not take the place by storm, and the Spartans grew afraid that the bold, revolutionary Athenians, who were also of a different race from themselves, would fall under the influence of the rebels and change sides. They therefore dismissed the Athenians, and only the Athenians, though without disclosing their suspicions. The Spartans said, instead, that they did not need their help any longer. The Athenians realized that this was not the real reason—that it was because they were not trusted—and took great offense, feeling that they did not deserve to suffer this indignity at the hands of the Spartans. As soon as they returned to Athens, they broke their existing alliance with Sparta against Persia and made an alliance with Sparta's enemies, the Argives. At the same time, the Athenians and the Argives became bound by the same oaths of alliance to the Thessalians.

103. In the fifth year of the siege, the rebels in Ithome were unable to hold out any longer and came to an agreement with the Spartans by which they would leave the Peloponnese under a truce and never return to it again. If anyone was captured doing so, he would become the slave of his captor. (Long before, incidentally, the Spartans had received an oracle from Delphi commanding them to "release the suppliant of Ithomaean Zeus.") The rebels left with their women and children, and the Athenians accepted them out of what was by now their hostility toward the Spartans. They sent them to colonize

4. The helots were the state workers of Sparta. Essentially enslaved, they worked the land while the male Spartan citizens trained in barracks. The fact that they outnumbered the citizens by about ten to one made their masters very nervous.
5. The Athenians and Spartans were still allied through the Hellenic League.

Naupactus, which they had recently captured from the Western Locrians. And now the Megarians approached the Athenians about an alliance, after revolting from the Peloponnesian League because the Corinthians were making war on them over a border dispute. The Athenians accepted Megara and Pegae in alliance and built the Megarians a long wall, which they garrisoned themselves, from the city to Nisaea. This was the beginning of the intense hatred the Corinthians felt for the Athenians.

104. Meanwhile Inaros, son of Psammetichus, a Libyan and king of the Libyans who bordered on Egypt, set out from the town of Marea, south of the city of Pharos, and incited most of Egypt to rebel against King Artaxerxes.[6] After taking power, Inaros asked the Athenians for help. They and their allies were at that time campaigning in Cyprus with two hundred ships. They abandoned Cyprus and, sailing up the Nile from the sea, gained control of the river as well as of two-thirds of the province of Memphis. They attacked the last third, the so-called White Fortress, where Persians and Medes had taken refuge along with Egyptians who had not cooperated in the rebellion.

105. The Athenians launched an amphibious assault on the Corinthians and Epidaurians at Halieis. The Corinthians won the battle. Later the Athenians engaged in a naval battle with Peloponnesian ships off Cecryphalia, which the Athenians won. Next, war broke out between the Athenians and the Aeginetans, and there was a large naval battle off Aegina, in which the allies of Athens and Aegina took part. The Athenians won the battle, capturing seventy ships, and then, under the command of Leocrates, son of Stroebus, went ashore to besiege the city. The Peloponnesians, wanting to assist the Aeginetans, landed on Aegina with three hundred hoplites who had previously been serving with the Corinthians and Epidaurians. The Corinthians took the heights at Geraneia and then descended into the Megarid with their allies, in the belief that the Athenians would be unable to help the Megarians while so much of their army was away in Aegina and Egypt; and if they did help, they would have to withdraw from Aegina. The Athenians did not, however, move the army attacking Aegina. Instead, their oldest and youngest men, who had been left behind in Athens, went to Megara under the command of Myronides. They fought the Corinthians to a standstill before the two sides separated, and both sides felt that they had won. The Athenians, who had in fact had the better of it, set up a victory marker when the Corinthians left. About twelve days later, after enduring insults from the elders of their city, the Corinthians made their preparations and went forth to set up a victory marker of their own. The Athenians then sortied[7] out from Megara, killed the men who were setting up the marker, and went on to defeat their companions in battle.

106. The beaten Corinthians retreated, but a large contingent of them, hard pressed by the enemy, lost their way and wandered into some private property that was surrounded by a ditch from which there was no escape. When the Athenians saw this, they blocked off the front of the area with their hoplites and then, stationing lightly armed troops around the ditch, stoned to death all the Corinthians who were inside. The Corinthians suffered a terrible loss, but most of their army made its way back home.

107. At about this time, the Athenians began to build their Long Walls down to the sea—one to Phalerum and one to the Piraeus. The Phocians also attacked Doris, the original homeland of the Spartans. Doris contained the

---

6. Artaxerxes became king of Persia after the death of his father Xerxes in 465.
7. A sortie is a sudden attack from a usually defensive position.

towns of Boeum, Cytinium, and Erineum, and after the Phocians had captured one of them, the Spartans came to the relief of the Dorians with fifteen hundred of their own hoplites and ten thousand belonging to their allies. Nicomedes, son of Cleombrotus, was in command because King Pleistoanax, son of Pausanias, was still a minor. The Spartans forced the Phocians to come to terms and to restore the town, and then they began to withdraw their force. Athenian ships, however, were patrolling the Crisaean Gulf and would stop them should they try to cross the sea. Meanwhile, it did not seem safe to go over Mount Geraneia, since the Athenians held Megara and Pegae. The road over Geraneia was rough, in any case, and now constantly guarded by the Athenians, and the Spartans had learned that the Athenians intended to stop anyone from taking it this time. They decided, therefore, to stay in Boeotia and to consider the best way to return home. Another factor in their decision was that some Athenians had been secretly urging them to adopt this course in hopes of tearing down both the Athenian democracy and the Long Walls. The Athenians then attacked the Spartans in full strength, along with one thousand Argives and contingents from their other allies. There were fourteen thousand men in all. They made this attack because they believed the Spartans had no way out and because they suspected the plot to undo their democracy. In keeping with the terms of the alliance, a troop of Thessalian cavalry came with the Athenians, but they deserted to the Spartans in the heat of the battle.

108. They fought in Tanagra, in Boeotia. The Spartans and their allies won, with great carnage on both sides. The Spartans next went into Megara, destroyed its crops, and returned home via Geraneia and the Isthmus. Sixty-two days after the battle, the Athenians, with Myronides in command, marched into Boeotia. In a battle at Oenophyta, they defeated the Boeotians and gained control of Boeotia and Phocis. They tore down the fortifications at Tanagra and took hostage one hundred of the richest Eastern Locrians. Later the Athenians finished building their own Long Walls. After this, the Aeginetans made a treaty with the Athenians whereby they would demolish their walls, surrender their ships, and pay tribute in the future. Also, under the command of Tolmides, son of Tolmaeus, the Athenians sailed around the Peloponnese, burned the Spartan shipyard, captured the Corinthian town of Chalcis, and defeated the Sicyonians after an amphibious assault.

109. The Athenians and their allies remained in Egypt, saw many kinds of warfare, and experienced all its changing fortunes. At first, the Athenians controlled Egypt, and the King sent Megabazus the Persian to Sparta with money, in hopes of bribing them to invade Attica so as to draw Athenian troops out of Egypt. The plan met with no success, and money was being spent to no purpose, so Megabazus made his way back to Asia with what was left of it. Then the King sent another Persian, Megabyzus, son of Zopyrus, to Egypt with a large army. He marched overland and defeated the Egyptians and their allies in battle. He drove the Greeks out of Memphis and ended up by isolating them on Prosopitis Island, where he besieged them for eighteen months. Finally, Megabyzus diverted the water from the channels around the island and dried them up. The island was now joined to the mainland for the most part, and the Greek ships were high and dry, so he crossed the channel and took the island with infantry.

110. Thus the Greek expedition to Egypt was destroyed after six years of fighting. A few of the many men who took part in it made their way through Libya to Cyrene and were saved; but most were killed. Egypt reverted to the King, except for the marsh country, which was ruled by King

Amyrtaeus. It was not possible to capture him because of the extent of the marshes, and besides, the marsh-dwellers are the most warlike of the Egyptians. Inaros, king of Libya, who was responsible for what took place in Egypt, was betrayed and abandoned and later impaled on a stake. Meanwhile, a relief force of fifty Athenian and allied triremes sailed to Egypt and put in at the Mendesian mouth of the Nile without knowing anything about what had happened. They were attacked by land-based troops and by a Phoenician fleet, and most of the ships were destroyed, though a few were able to escape. This, then, was how the great expedition of Athens and her allies against Egypt came to an end.

111. At about this time, Orestes, the exiled son of King Echecrates of Thessaly, persuaded the Athenians to restore him to power. The Athenians enlisted the help of the Boeotians and the Phocians, who were now their allies, and attacked Pharsalus, in Thessaly. Though they were able to control the country near their camp, the Thessalian cavalry prevented them from venturing very far. They were not, however, able to capture the city or to achieve any of the objectives they came for. They returned, unsuccessful, with Orestes. Not much later, one thousand Athenians took ship in Pegae (which they now controlled) and sailed along the coast to Sicyon under the command of Pericles, son of Xanthippus. After landing, they defeated the defending Sicyonians in battle. They then immediately embarked an Achaean force and sailed across to Acarnania, where they attacked and besieged Oeniadae. They failed to take it, however, and returned home.

112. After an interval of three years, the Peloponnesians and the Athenians agreed to a five-year truce. The Athenians, now barred from a Hellenic war, attacked Cyprus with two hundred of their own and their allies' ships under the command of Cimon. At the request of Amyrtaeus, king of the marsh country, sixty of the ships sailed to Egypt. The rest besieged Citium. Cimon died there, however, and they ran out of food, so the fleet withdrew from Citium, and as they were sailing off Cyprian Salamis, they fought battles on land and sea against Phoenicians, Cyprians, and Cilicians. After winning both battles, the Athenians returned home along with the ships that had by now returned from Egypt. Next, the Spartans fought the so-called Holy War. They gained control of the temple of Delphi and turned it over to the Delphians. Immediately after their withdrawal, though, the Athenians attacked and captured the temple and turned it back over to the Phocians.

113. Some time afterwards, with Boeotian exiles holding Orchomenus, Chaeronea, and other areas of Boeotia, the Athenians, under the command of Tolmides, son of Tolmaeus, attacked this now-hostile territory with one thousand of their own hoplites and with some of the allied forces. They captured Chaeronea, enslaved the population, and withdrew after leaving a detachment to garrison the place. Then, as they were passing through Coronea, they were attacked by the Boeotian exiles from Orchomenus along with the exiles from Euboea. There were also Eastern Locrians and others who shared their views. These forces defeated the Athenians in battle, killing many and taking many others prisoner. The Athenians then agreed to a treaty whereby they abandoned all of Boeotia in return for their men. The exiled Boeotians returned to power, and all the rest of Boeotia regained its independence.

114. Not much later, Euboea revolted from Athens. Pericles then went to Euboea with an army, but he withdrew his army on the double when he received a message from Athens saying that Megara had also rebelled, that the Peloponnesians were about to invade Attica, and that, except for those who had

been able to escape to Nisaea, the Athenian garrison had been wiped out by the Megarians. The Megarians had brought in Corinthians, Sicyonians, and Epidaurians to help them carry out their rebellion.

The Peloponnesians then attacked and plundered Attica as far as Eleusis and Thria under the command of the Spartan king Pleistoanax, son of Pausanias. They returned home without penetrating farther. Then the Athenians again crossed over to Euboea under the command of Pericles and subdued all of it. They settled matters with the Euboeans by treaty, except for driving the Histiaeans out of their homeland and occupying it themselves.

115. Not long after they withdrew from Euboea, the Athenians made a thirty-year truce with the Spartans and their allies, by which they returned Nisaea, Pegae, Troezen, and Achaea, the places they held in the Peloponnese.

In the sixth year of the truce, war broke out between the Samians and the Milesians over Priene. When the Milesians were defeated in the war, they went to Athens to denounce the Samians. They were joined along the way by some private citizens from Samos itself who wanted to overthrow the government. The Athenians then sent forty ships to Samos and set up a democracy. They also took hostage fifty Samian boys and an equal number of men and deposited them on Lemnos. Then they stationed a garrison on Samos and left. There were some Samians, however, who had fled the island for the mainland. They formed an alliance with some of the most powerful people in Samos, as well as with Pissuthnes, son of Hystaspes, who was the satrap of Lydia at that time.[8] The exiles put together a force of seven hundred mercenaries and crossed over to Samos by night. They first attacked the democrats, detained most of them, and rescued the hostages from Lemnos. Then they declared their independence from Athens. They turned over to Pissuthnes the Athenian garrison and the officers who were with them and immediately prepared to attack Miletus. The Byzantines joined the Samians in revolt.

116. When the Athenians learned of the revolt, they sent sixty ships to Samos. Sixteen of the ships had been detached, some to go to Caria to reconnoiter the Phoenician fleet, and others to Chios and Lesbos to call on them for help; but with the forty-four remaining ships, under the command of Pericles and nine others, they engaged seventy Samian ships returning from Miletus (of which twenty were troop ships) and defeated them in battle off the island of Tragia. They were later reinforced by forty ships from Athens and by twenty-five from Chios and Lesbos. They then landed their troops on Samos, where their infantry took control on the ground and built three walls with which to besiege the city. At the same time, the ships blockaded the island by sea.

Pericles then detached sixty ships from the blockading force and hurriedly sailed to Caunus and Caria after receiving news that a Phoenician fleet was about to attack them. What had happened was that Stesagoras and others had left Samos with five ships to call in the Phoenicians.

117. While Pericles was gone, the Samians suddenly sailed out to the attack. They fell on the undefended Athenian beachhead, destroyed the sentry ships, defeated the vessels that came up to oppose them, and controlled their own waters for over fourteen days, bringing supplies in and out at will. When Pericles returned, he resumed the naval blockade. His fleet was later reinforced

---

8. The Persian empire was divided into provinces known as satrapies, each governed by a royally appointed satrap.

from Athens by forty ships commanded by Thucydides,[9] Hagnon, Phormio, as well as by twenty under the command of Tlepolemus and Anticles, and another thirty from Chios and Lesbos. The Samians put up a brief struggle at sea, but they were unable to hold out against the siege and were forced to come to terms nine months later. They agreed to tear down their city wall, give hostages, surrender their fleet, and pay war reparations to Athens in installments over time. The Byzantines also agreed to return to their former subject status.

118. Not many years afterwards, the events in Corcyra and Potidaea, which I have already narrated, provided the immediate causes for the present war. All the abovementioned actions that the Greeks took against each other and the barbarians occurred in the fifty years between the retreat of Xerxes and the beginning of the present war. During this time, the Athenians increasingly strengthened their empire and greatly enlarged their power. The Spartans saw this but made only sporadic attempts to stop it. They held their peace for most of those years since they had traditionally been slow to go to war unless they were forced to; and besides, they were prevented from intervening by local wars. But now the power of Athens had risen to an unmistakable height and had begun to impinge on Sparta's allies. The strength of Athens then became unendurable to them, and having decided that they must try with all their might to destroy it, if they could, they started this war.

The Spartans had decided that the treaty had been broken and that the Athenians were in the wrong, but they nevertheless sent envoys to Delphi to ask the god whether the best course would be to go to war. He answered, it is said, that victory would be theirs if they fought with all their might and that he would help them whether they called on him or not.

119. Moreover, the Spartans summoned the allies again because they wanted to take a vote on whether they should go to war.[1] The ambassadors from the allied states arrived, and an assembly took place in which various speakers said their piece, with most denouncing Athens and demanding war. The Corinthians, for fear lest Potidaea be destroyed before war began, had earlier privately urged each city to vote for war. They were also present on this occasion, and coming forward last, they spoke as follows.

120. We can no longer, fellow allies, blame the Spartans for not having committed themselves to war since they have gathered us together now to do just that. Leaders do, after all, enjoy precedence over everyone else in all sorts of ways, so they must look out for the common good and not give greatest weight to their own interests.[2] Those of us who have already had dealings with the Athenians don't need to be taught that we must guard against them. Those who live inland and not on the trade routes need to know that if they do not defend the coastal cities, it will be harder for them to export their harvests and to import the goods that come to the mainland from the sea, and that they should not be carping critics of this speech as irrelevant to them, but rather accept the fact that if they abandon the coast, the danger will reach their doorstep, and that they are now

9. The identity of this Thucydides is uncertain. If, as is remotely possible, the historian is referring to himself here, he must have been older than has generally been imagined. Thirty was the minimum age for a generalship, and Thucydides is believed by most people to have been born around 460, only twenty years before the Samian revolt.
1. This chapter returns to the eve of the war (432), where Thucydides interrupted it at chapter 88 to relate the history of Athens' growth in the fifty years after the Persian Wars.
2. The Corinthians seem here to be patching up their differences with the Spartans and persuading reluctant Peloponnesian cities, and perhaps dissident Spartans, to go along with them and with most Spartans in a vote for war. The following arguments make sense in this context, because if the Corinthians were addressing the Spartans, they would be exhorting them to do what they had already decided to do.

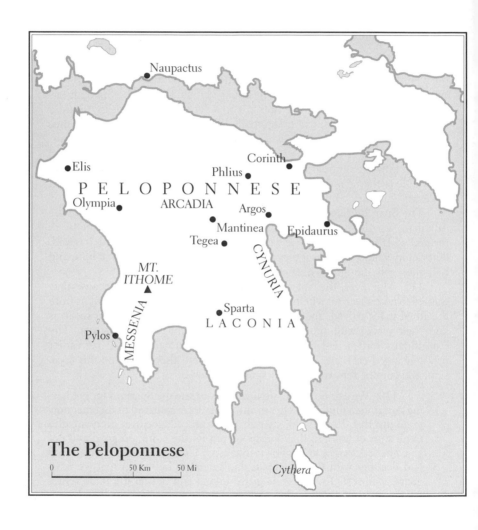

The Peloponnese

Naupactus

Elis

Corinth

Phlius

P E L O P O N N E S E

Olympia

ARCADIA

Argos

Mantinea

Epidaurus

Tegea

CYNURIA

MT.
ITHOME

MESSENIA

Sparta

L A C O N I A

Pylos

0   50 Km   50 Mi

Cythera

making decisions as much about themselves as about us. They must therefore not shrink from the necessity of choosing war over peace. Prudent men hold their peace for so long as they are not wronged, but when brave men are wronged, they must give up peace for war and make peace again when the time is right. They must not be emboldened by good fortune in war, and they must not allow themselves to be wronged because they enjoy the tranquillity of peace. He who flinches because of this pleasure and chooses peace is most likely to be kept from enjoying the indolence that makes him flinch; he who overreaches because of success in war is unaware that he is emboldened by a treacherous audacity. A lot of things that are badly planned turn out well because the enemy has planned even worse, and still more things that seem to have been planned well turn out terribly. Because we reach our decisions in safety but fall short, through fear, in the act, what we confidently plan is not what we accomplish in practice.

121. We, the injured parties, now begin the war with sufficient cause, and after we have beaten the Athenians back, we will find the right time to make peace. There is every likelihood that we will prevail. First, there is our numerical superiority and our military experience. Next, we will all be marching with the same agenda. As to a navy, in which they are superior, we will build one from our own resources and from the treasuries of Delphi and Olympia. After we have borrowed the money, we will be able to hire their foreign sailors by offering higher pay. Athenian power is mercenary more than homegrown. Ours suffers less from this disadvantage: our strength is in our fighting men and not in our money. We will most likely destroy them with one naval victory, but if they hold out, we will have that much more time to practice our seamanship, and once we have established our equality in skills, why then we will win because of our courage. For we are courageous by nature; they can't go to school for that. They are pre-eminent sailors through skill, which we can achieve with practice. We will supply the money to reach these goals. It would really be strange if their allies do not refuse to pay for their own enslavement while we refused to spend our money to save ourselves and avenge our enemies, thereby preventing that wealth from being robbed and used to destroy us!

122. We can also make war on the Athenians in other ways: fomenting revolt among their allies, thereby stripping them of the taxes on which their strength depends; building strongholds on their territory, and other things that no one can now foresee. War is the last thing to follow a stated plan. It improvises itself for the most part out of chance material as it goes along. Safest is the one who wages it with a cool head; the one who is flustered by it will stumble and fall.

Let us bear in mind that we could go it alone if these were quarrels we were having with a rival city over boundaries; but as it is, Athens is a match for all of us combined and is that much more of a match for any one of us. Thus if we are divided and do not defend ourselves together, as one people and with one common purpose, Athens will easily overpower us all. And however terrible it may be to hear it, you must know that defeat will carry with it nothing other than outright enslavement. It is a disgrace to the Peloponnese that this should even be a question for debate, or that one city might oppress so many others. If we were enslaved, others would think that we deserved our sufferings or that we endured them out of cowardice. We would be seen as inferior to our fathers—our fathers, who freed Greece, while we could not even secure freedom for ourselves!—and we would be allowing one city to set itself up as a tyrant, we who have put

down one-man rule everywhere it has appeared. I fail to see how this behavior can be acquitted of one of the three greatest faults: stupidity, weakness, or neglect. For surely you have not avoided these faults by falling prey
to a far more harmful thing: disdain for your enemy, which changes its
name to its opposite, folly, after repeated defeats.

123. But why go on complaining about the past except to the extent
that it bears directly on the present? You must redouble your efforts for the
future by attending to things right now. You have a long tradition of achieving your prosperity through hard work. You must not change your ways just
because you have a slight temporary advantage in wealth and surpluses.
(Anyway, it wouldn't be right if you lost in plenty what you gained in want!)
Take heart and go to war with all your strength. The god has spoken and
has promised to take your side, and all the rest of Greece will be fighting
along with you—some from fear and some for gain. You will not be breaking the treaty first. Why, even the god thinks it has been infringed since he
has commanded you to go to war! Rather, you will be helping those who
have been wronged, for the transgressors are not those who come to the
rescue, but those who attack first.

124. Thus the prospects for war are good for you in every way, and
we advise this course in the common interest—if, that is, it is true that for
states, as for individuals, the safest course is based on an identity of interests. So waste no time in coming to the aid of the Potidaeans. They are Dorians besieged by Ionians—the other way around from the way it used to
be in the past. Strive also to win the freedom of the other states. It is no
longer acceptable for us to stand by when some states have already been
destroyed and when others will suffer the same fate as soon as it becomes
known that we have met but have not dared to take action. You must realize, my fellow allies, that we are all up against it now and that we Corinthians are advising you for the best. Vote for war, unafraid of its immediate
dangers and eager for the lasting peace that it will yield. For peace is more
secure when it is the outcome of a war; it is much more risky when it results from an inaction that will not fight. We have decided that the entrenched tyrant city of Greece wants to establish its tyranny over all alike,
with designs on those she has not already conquered. Let us attack and subdue her; let us pass the rest of our days in safety; and let us free those Greeks
who are now enslaved!

That is what the Corinthians said.

125. After the Spartans had listened to all the opinions, they put the question, in turn, to all the allies who were present, to cities large and small. The
majority voted for war. They decided, though, that they were unprepared to attack immediately; but they also decided that each city should supply itself with
what it needed and that there should be no delay. Nevertheless, they spent
nearly a full year in making preparations before they invaded Attica and openly
made war.

126. During this time, the Peloponnesians kept sending ambassadors to
Athens to lodge complaints, so that they would have the strongest grounds for
war should the Athenians refuse to listen. First, the Spartans sent ambassadors
demanding that the Athenians drive out the "curse of the goddess." The "curse"
was as follows. Cylon was an Athenian from the old days, a well-born, powerful
Olympic champion who had married the daughter of Theagenes the Megarian, at that time the tyrant in Megara. After Cylon consulted the oracle at Delphi, the god answered that he should seize the Athenian acropolis during the

greatest of the festivals of Zeus. Cylon persuaded his friends to join him and also took a contingent of men from Theagenes, and when the Olympic games came around in the Peloponnese, Cylon seized the acropolis with intent to set up a tyranny. He regarded the Olympic games as the greatest festival of Zeus, and they had special meaning for him as an Olympic champion. Cylon did not stop to consider, and the oracle did not make clear, whether it meant the greatest festival in Attica or somewhere else. (You see, the Athenians also observe the Diasia, which is held outside the city and which is called the greatest festival of the Kindly Zeus, and during which all the people of Attica sacrifice not animals but animal-shaped cakes peculiar to the country). In the belief, though, that he had understood the oracle correctly, Cylon seized the acropolis. When the Athenians heard the news, they came en masse from the fields, took up positions around the acropolis, and besieged it. As time went by, though, the Athenians tired of the siege and most of them left after turning over the guard to the nine archons, giving them full power to dispose of the matter in any way they thought best. (At that time, the nine archons conducted most of the affairs of government.) Cylon and his besieged followers grew weak for lack of food and water. Cylon then ran away, along with his brother, and since the others were totally hard pressed—with some even dying of starvation—they went as suppliants to sit on the altar of the acropolis. When the Athenians who had been entrusted with the guard saw that these men were dying in the temple, they made them get up, and after promising not to do anything bad to them, they led them out and killed them. They even killed some who had gone to sit on the altars of the Furies while walking past them. Because of this act, the killers and all their descendants have been called cursed and sinners against the goddess. The Athenians banished these accursed men. Later, in a time of civil strife, there was another expulsion, when Cleomenes the Spartan and his Athenian supporters banished their living descendants and dug up the bones of the accursed dead and cast them out of the city. Descendants later returned, however, and their offspring are still living in Athens.[3]

127. The Spartans demanded that this curse be expunged, ostensibly because they cared first and foremost about avenging the gods, but really because they knew that Pericles, son of Xanthippus, was tainted by it on his mother's side and because they believed that if he was banished, they would be far more successful in their dealings with Athens.[4] They didn't so much expect that this would actually happen to him as that they would slander him in the city and make this taint the cause of the war. For Pericles was the most powerful man of his generation and totally opposed the Spartans in his administration of the government; he would permit no retreat and urged the Athenians to war.

128. The Athenians made the counterdemand that the Spartans drive out the curse of Taenarus. The reason for this was that the Spartans had once made some helot suppliants get up from the temple of Poseidon in Taenarus and then led them away and killed them, as a result of which the Spartans themselves believe that the great earthquake took place in Sparta.[5] The Athenians also demanded that they drive out the curse of the Goddess of the Brass House, which came about in the following way.

3. The family in question is the Alcmaeonids. Numerous prominent Athenians belonged to this family, including Cleisthenes, the political reformer of the late sixth century, and Pericles. In the sixth century, Cleomenes and the Athenians working with him had called for the expulsion of the Alcmaeonids because Cleisthenes, who was agitating for reforms at that time, could thus be gotten rid of. Cleisthenes returned after Cleomenes was forced out of Athens.
4. I.e., Pericles' mother was an Alcmaeonid.
5. See glossary on the state slaves known as helots.

After Pausanias was first recalled by the Spartans from his command in the Hellespont,[6] and after he was tried and acquitted of wrongdoing, he was no longer sent abroad on public business. He did, however, go to the Hellespont without Spartan authorization in a trireme that he had obtained as a private citizen from the town of Hermione. He said that he was going to participate in the Greek war against Persia; but he was really going to work on behalf of the King, as he had been doing from the beginning, in order to fulfill his ambition to be Persian viceroy over all of Greece. He had first won the King's gratitude and created the groundwork for the whole enterprise on his first posting, after his return from Cyprus, when he captured Byzantium.[7] The place was held by the Persians and by some friends and relations of the King who were also captured. Pausanias then sent his prisoners to the King unbeknownst to the rest of the allies and made up the story that they had escaped from him. He did this with Gongylus the Eretrian, to whom he had entrusted Byzantium and the prisoners. He also sent a letter to the King, which Gongylus carried. As was later discovered, this is what he had written:

> The Spartan chief, Pausanias, wishing to oblige you, returns these, the captives of his spear, and, if it seems fitting to you, I suggest that I marry your daughter and deliver Sparta and the rest of Greece into your hands. I consider myself able to do this in cooperation with you. If any of this should please you, send a trustworthy man to the coast through whom we can negotiate in the future.

129. Thus much was committed to writing.

Xerxes was delighted with the letter and sent Artabazus, son of Pharnaces, to the coast with orders to take over the satrapy of Dascylium from Megabates, its former satrap.[8] He also gave Artabazus a letter to forward to Pausanias at Byzantium as quickly as possible. He was also to show Pausanias the King's seal and was instructed to carry out confidentially and fully whatever Pausanias might order him to do in the King's interest. When Artabazus arrived, he carried out the orders which had been given to him and sent on the letter. The King had written the following reply:

> Thus saith King Xerxes unto Pausanias. Not only shall those men whom you have spared for me beyond the sea in Byzantium be inscribed on thy behalf as a benefaction unto the house of Xerxes for all time, but I am also well pleased with thy reasons. Let not the night nor the day stay thee from performing any of those things that thou hast promised me, nor be not hindered by the expense of gold or silver nor by the need to levy armies, wheresoe'er their presence shall become needful; but with the worthy Artabazus, whom I have sent unto thee, work with stout heart thy will and mine in such wise that they result most fairly and nobly for us both.

130. Pausanias was already held in high regard by the Greeks because of his command at Plataea, but these words were enough to puff him up so much that he could no longer endure his normal way of life. He wore Persian clothes whenever he marched out of Byzantium, and when he traveled through Thrace he was preceded by spear-carrying Persian and Egyptian guards. He held elaborate Persian banquets and could not keep his thoughts in check, and in minor

6. In 478. Thucydides here picks up the story of Pausanias' misadventures from where he had left off in 1.95.
7. Cf. 1.94.
8. Cf. Herodotus 3.89.

acts signaled what he intended to do later on a larger scale. He limited access to himself and had such a stern manner towards all alike that no one could approach him. It was in no small part because of this behavior that the alliance shifted in favor of the Athenians.

131. It was for just this sort of thing that the Spartans recalled him when they found out about it the first time. When he appeared to be doing it again after his second, this time unauthorized, voyage on the ship from Hermione; when he had been forced out of Byzantium by the Athenians; when he did not then return to Sparta, but instead set up headquarters in Colonae in the Troad and was reported to be conspiring with the barbarians and using his stay to make trouble; why, at that point the Spartans held off no longer. The ephors sent a herald with a scytale to him and told him to return with the herald[9]; if he did not, the Spartans would proclaim him an enemy of the people. Wanting to be under as little suspicion as possible, and believing that he could buy his way out of the prosecution, Pausanias returned to Sparta for the second time. At first, he was thrown in jail by the ephors, who have the power to do this to a king, but he later got himself out and submitted himself to a trial brought by anyone who sought to prove the charges against him.

132. The Spartans, though—not just his enemies but the whole city—had no clear evidence whatever by which they could without a shadow of a doubt execute a man of the royal line who had the high rank he held at that time. (You see, as the nephew of Leonidas, he governed in the place of Pleistarchus, son of Leonidas, who was still a boy.) Still, his breaks with custom and his love of barbarian ways gave grounds to suspect that he aimed to tamper with the status quo, so they also scrutinized his other actions, to see whether he had ever veered from established customs—as, for example, when the Greeks dedicated the victory offering of a tripod at Delphi after the Persian Wars and he arrogantly and at his own expense had the following inscription etched on it:

CHIEFTAIN OF THE GREEKS WHEN HE DESTROYED THE PERSIAN ARMY
PAUSANIAS HAS DEDICATED THIS MEMORIAL TO PHOEBUS APOLLO

At the time, indeed, the Spartans immediately erased the inscription from the tripod and etched over it the names of each of the cities that had joined together to defeat the barbarian and that had made the offering.[1] Even then this was thought to be a wrongful act on Pausanias' part, but considering the situation he was in now, it seemed to have been of a piece with his present state of mind. The Spartans also heard that he was even conspiring with the helots—and so he was, for he had promised them freedom and citizenship if they would all rise up in rebellion and join him in realizing all his plans. Yet even so, the Spartans refused to believe any of the helot informers, and decided not to take drastic action against him. They thus observed their usual practice when it came to themselves, which was to avoid pronouncing speedy death sentences on a Spartan male without absolutely indisputable evidence. The story goes that it did not happen until Pausanias' then lover and most trusted slave became an informer. He was an Argilian who was going to deliver Pausanias' most recent

---

9. Spartans frequently coded dispatches by the use of a baton or staff known as a scytale. The message would be written crosswise on a strip of leather that had been wound carefully around a scytale, then the unwound leather strip would be delivered to the recipient of the message, a Spartan official abroad who would possess a baton of identical shape. Only when rewound around the matching scytale could the message be read.

1. The remains of the tripod can be seen standing in Istanbul today in the square known as the Hippodrome.

letters to the King via Artabazus, but he became frightened because he had noticed that none of the messengers who preceded him had ever returned. He
counterfeited the seal, in case his hunch was mistaken and so Pausanias
wouldn't find out in the event that he wanted to make some revisions. Then he
opened the letters, and just where he had suspected some such thing would be
appended, he found written instructions that he himself should be killed.

133. After he had shown them the letters, the ephors began to be convinced, but they still wanted to hear Pausanias say something himself, so they
struck a deal whereby the man went to Taenarus as a suppliant and built himself a hut with a false wall behind which he concealed some of the ephors.
When Pausanias came to see him and asked why he had taken refuge, the
ephors heard everything clearly: the man's accusations over what had been written concerning him, along with all his other revelations in detail, such as that
he had never, ever, betrayed Pausanias' services to the King, yet that he had nevertheless been rewarded with a death sentence along with many other messengers; and then Pausanias admitting it, and pleading with the man not to be angry
over what had happened, and guaranteeing his safety if he gave up his sanctuary, and asking him to make the journey as quickly as possible and not hinder
the conspiracy.

134. The ephors heard it word for word, and although they left at the
time, they now had certain knowledge and intended to make the arrest in
the city. The story continues that as Pausanias was about to be arrested on
the street, he saw the expression on the face of one of the ephors coming
toward him and knew why they were coming, while another, sympathetic,
ephor gave it away with a slight nod. He then escaped to safety by running
to the temple of the Goddess of the Brass House, the grounds of which were
nearby. To avoid exposure to the weather, he went into a small building that
formed a part of the temple and stayed there. The ephors were too late to
catch him just then, but they afterward tore the roof off the building and,
making sure that he was inside, they removed the doors, walled him in, encircled the place, and proceeded to starve him to death. When they found
out that he was about to die in that room, they started to lead him out of
the temple while there was still some breath in him. As soon as he was out,
he died. They were going to throw him into the Caeadas[2] along with the
other criminals, but then they decided to bury him somewhere nearby. The
god at Delphi later commanded the Spartans to move his grave to where he
had died (it is at the entry to the temple grounds to this day, as the engraved
stelae indicate). The god also commanded them to requite two bodies for
one to the Goddess of the Brass House, since their deed was a curse unto
them. The Spartans, therefore, sculpted two bronze statues to take the place
of Pausanias and dedicated them in the temple. Since even the god had adjudged that there was a curse, the Athenians tasked the Spartans, in their
turn, to drive it out.[3]

135. In connection with Pausanias' collaboration with the Persians, the
Spartans sent ambassadors to Athens to condemn Themistocles: they said that
they had found in their investigations of Pausanias that Themistocles should be
punished for the same crimes. The Athenians believed them—after all,
Themistocles had been ostracized and was living in Argos, although he traveled
around the rest of the Peloponnese.[4] So they sent some men along with the

2. The Caeadas was a pit or underground cavern into which the Spartan state threw criminals.
3. For Herodotus on Pausanias, see Herodotus 5.32; 9.64; 9.78–82.
4. See glossary on the institution of ostracism.

Spartans, who were only too willing to follow, with orders to bring Themistocles back from wherever they found him.

136. Themistocles, though, got wind of what was happening and fled from the Peloponnese to Corcyra, where he was a public benefactor. The Corcyraeans told him that they feared keeping him lest they incur the anger of the Spartans and the Athenians, so he was shipped over to the mainland opposite. Pursued by the officers wherever they learned he was, he was forced, in one emergency, to flee to the palace of Admetus, king of the Molossians, a man who was not his friend. Admetus happened to be away from home, so Themistocles supplicated his wife, who told him to take their son and sit on the hearth. When Admetus returned a little later, Themistocles revealed who he was and said that he, a refugee, should not be punished just because he had once opposed a request Admetus had made of the Athenians. After all, he said, though Themistocles, who was much weaker in the present circumstances, might be made to suffer by Admetus, the noble thing would be for Admetus to punish his equals on a level of equality. Furthermore, he had opposed Admetus on some matter of business and not on a matter of life and death (and here Themistocles explained who was chasing him and why), while Admetus would be depriving him of his life if he gave him up.

137. When Admetus heard this, he helped Themistocles up, along with his son, whom Themistocles held as he sat on the hearth, for this was the most solemn form of supplication. When the Spartans and Athenians arrived not much later, he would not give up Themistocles no matter what they said, but sent him off, according to his wishes, to make his way overland along the Thermaic Gulf to Pydna in the kingdom of Alexander. There Themistocles chanced on a merchant vessel making its way to Ionia. He boarded her but was driven by storms toward the Athenian camp besieging Naxos. Themistocles' identity was unknown to the ship's crew, but he grew frightened and told the captain who he was and why he was in flight, and said that if the captain did not save him, he would claim that the captain had been bribed to take him aboard. He said that the safest thing would be for no one to leave the ship until they could get under way, and that if the captain trusted him, he would remember it with a generous gift. And that is what the captain did. He rode at anchor off the fleet for a day and a night and then later put in at Ephesus. Then, when Themistocles received the money that he had stashed in Argos and with his friends in Athens, he rewarded the captain with a gift in cash. He then made his way upcountry with one of the Persians who lived on the coast and sent a letter to King Artaxerxes, son of Xerxes, who had recently become king. The letter said

> I, Themistocles have come to you, I who, more than any other Greek, worked the greatest evils on your house during the time your father attacked me and forced me to defend myself, but who also worked far more good when I was in safety and he, in danger, made his retreat. A reward for my services is owing to me (and here he wrote of his warning about the Greek withdrawal from Salamis and his warning about the bridges, for which he falsely took credit, since he had nothing to do with the failure to destroy them).[5] Now, having done these great services, I am here, pursued by the Greeks because of my love for you. I request that I may wait a year before I, in person, explain to you why I have come.

5. Cf. Herodotus 8.75 and 108ff.

138. It is said that the King was amazed at the workings of his mind and told him to do as he had asked. During this waiting period, Themistocles learned as much as he could of the Persian language and of the customs of the country. When he went before the King after a year, he had more influence with him than any Greek ever because of the reputation that preceded him; because of the King's hopes over Greece, which Themistocles promised to enslave for him; but especially because of the intelligence that shone forth every time it was put to the test. For Themistocles was a man who consistently showed the strengths of his nature, and it is for this that he deserves to be admired more than any other man. He had an innate intelligence that needed neither coaching nor hindsight. He was better than anyone at forming an opinion on the spot with the least deliberation and had a broader picture of what would actually take place in the future; he could explain whatever he had set his hand to and did not shrink from forming adequate judgments out of inexperience: he was always able to foresee what it was better or worse to do. In brief, because of the power of his nature, because of the quickness of his study, the man was indeed the best at improvising what had to be done.

Themistocles developed an illness and died, though some say that he poisoned himself because he decided that he was unable to bring about what he had promised the King. There is a monument to him in the agora of Magnesia in Asia, which he governed. The King had given him Magnesia for bread, which yielded him fifty talents a year, and Lampsacus for wine (which was thought to produce more wine than any other place at that time), and Myus for meat.[6] His family says that at his request, his bones were brought home and buried, unbeknownst to the Athenians, in Attica. It was illegal to bury him because he was a fugitive from a charge of treason.

Thus ends the tale of Pausanias the Spartan and of Themistocles the Athenian, the two most illustrious Greeks of their time.

139. This then is what the Spartans commanded and what was, in turn, demanded of them on their first embassy concerning the expulsion of the accursed ones. They came to Athens repeatedly, insisting that the Athenians withdraw from Potidaea and that they grant independence to Aegina. Above all, and in the clearest terms, they warned that if there was not to be war, Athens must rescind the Megarian decree, which said that the Megarians were prohibited from trading in the agora in Attica and in any port in the Athenian empire. The Athenians neither gave in to any of the other demands nor rescinded the decree, accusing the Megarians of border violations, of farming on sacred ground, and of sheltering runaway slaves. Finally, the last of the ambassadors arrived from Sparta—Rhamphias, Melesippus, and Agesander. They made none of the usual statements, only this: that "the Spartans want peace, but on condition that you grant independence to the Greeks."

The citizens of Athens called an assembly, had a discussion, and decided to deliberate about all these matters and make a decision once and for all. Many were present and spoke on both sides, giving their views either that they had to go to war or that the decree ought not to be an obstacle to peace and should be rescinded. Then Pericles, son of Xanthippus, came forward. He was the foremost Athenian of that time, and the most powerful—as both speaker and man of action. He spoke as follows.

140. Men of Athens. I have always held to the same policy—not to give in to the Spartans—though I know that people do not have the same

---

6. The talent was a substantial weight of silver; see glossary under *currency, Athenian.*

feelings when they are persuaded to go to war as when they are actually engaged in it, and change their resolve with changing events. But I see that I must once again give the same, or similar, advice, and I think it only right that those who come to see the merit of what I say then support the majority opinion, even if we falter—either that or claim no share in our brilliance if we succeed. The vagaries of events are probably no less wayward than the minds of men, and it is for this reason that we tend to blame chance whenever anything unexpected comes to pass.

Clearly, the Spartans were plotting against us in the beginning no less than they are now. The treaty says that we must submit to and accept arbitration of the differences between us, but they have neither asked for arbitration nor accepted our offers to submit to it. They want to settle their complaints by war and not by reason, and they are no longer coming before us to make allegations but to give orders. They demand that we withdraw from Potidaea, that we grant Aegina its independence, and that we rescind the Megarian decree, and these last envoys come here and publicly command us to give the Greeks their independence! Let none of you think that we would be going to war over a trifle if we refused to rescind the Megarian decree, though they make a point of dangling before us the proposition that if we rescinded it, there would be no war. And let there be no trace of the self-reproach that you went to war over a minor matter, for this seeming trifle comprises the whole test and confirmation of your resolve, and if you yield to them, you will immediately be ordered to do something bigger on the grounds that you gave in over this trifle because of fear. But if you flatly refuse, it will be clearly established that they can only deal with you on the basis of equality.

141. So decide right now to either give in before you get hurt, or, if we do go to war—as I, for one, think we should—not to yield over issues large or small and not to hold on timorously to what we have acquired. The biggest and the smallest claims amount to the same kind of slavery when they are given as orders by equals to their neighbors without a judgment in a court of law.

Listen carefully so you will know in detail that we will not be weaker than they in our respective war-making capabilities. The Peloponnesians are farmers and have no money either in private hands or in the public treasuries. Thus they have no experience of extended or overseas warfare because, being poor, they carry out limited operations only against each other. Such people will be unable to man navies or to regularly send out armies, because they can't be away from their land and spending their own money at the same time; meanwhile, we will be cutting them off from the sea. Furthermore, wars are better financed with savings than with compulsory taxes on property, and farmers are more willing to fight wars with their bodies than with their money, because they have confidence that their bodies will survive the danger but they aren't at all sure that they won't use up all their money—especially if the war (as usual!) does the unexpected and drags out on them. The Peloponnesians and their allies are able to hold off all of Greece for one battle, but they are unable to carry on a war against an enemy unlike themselves because they don't have a single council to give orders quickly in emergencies. Also, each city has an equal vote, and they are not all of the same racial stock, so each pushes its own interests. As a result, nothing ever gets done. One group wants to punish an enemy as much as possible; another group wants to lose as little as possible. They meet rarely, tend to consider just a small part of the common interest, and for the most part go about their own business. Thus no one thinks he is being harmed by his own slackness, since it's up to everyone else to watch out for him. And so, because each one has the same idea about all the others—without noticing it—they all go down to defeat together!

142. Their biggest problem, then, is that they will be hampered by a lack of money, because the slowness with which they collect it will cause delays, and because the opportunities in war don't wait.

Furthermore, their navy and the forts they may build on our frontiers are nothing to be feared. It's hard to maintain a fortress against an evenly matched city even in peacetime, and that much harder in wartime when we can just as easily build fortresses as they. They may well build little outposts so that they can destroy patches of territory and bring about desertions with hit-and-run raids, but they won't be able to prevent us from sailing to their shores, building forts, and supporting them with our ships, which are our strength.

Our experience at sea has made us better at fighting on land than their experience on land has made them at naval warfare. And they won't easily come by a knowledge of seamanship. Why, even you, who have been practicing it since just after the Persian Wars, haven't got it completely right yet—so how can they, landlubbers and not seafarers, ever do anything much, especially when they will be prevented from getting complete training because they will be constantly blockaded by us and our many ships? They might, emboldened by ignorance, risk a battle in strength against a small blockading force. But they'll stay put when they're checked by a large fleet, which in turn will make them less skilled from lack of practice—which will make them even more reluctant to fight. Seamanship, more than most things, is a skill, and it isn't possible to work at it as a pastime whenever you have the chance, because it doesn't let you have any pastimes.

143. If they were to remove the treasuries from Olympia and Delphi and try to lure away our foreign sailors with higher pay, and we and our metics[7] were not equal to manning our ships, why, that would be frightening. But equal to it we are, and best of all, we have more and better citizen pilots and crews than all the rest of Greece. Besides, none of the foreigners would risk exile to fight along with the Peloponnesians for a few days' extra pay in a less than promising cause.

It seems to me, at least, that this is more or less the situation in the Peloponnese. We are free of the faults I found in them, and we have other great advantages. If they attack our territory by land, we will invade theirs by sea, and it won't be the same thing even for all of Attica to be destroyed as for a part of the Peloponnese, because they don't have any other land they can take without a struggle, while we have a lot of land both in the islands and on the mainland. Sea power is a great thing! Think about it. If we were islanders, who could be more invulnerable? And we have to imagine that we are as close to being islanders as possible.

Give up your homes and your farms! Guard your city and the sea! Do not, enraged over the loss of your property, fight it out on land with the far larger forces of the Peloponnese. Even if we won, we would not fight with fewer enemies the second time, and if we lost, we would also lose control over our allies—and that is our strength—because they would not keep still if we were unable to attack them. Do not mourn

---

7. On the resident aliens known as metics, see the glossary.

the loss of your homes and your land, but the loss of your bodies; for the land does not own men, men own the land. If I thought I could persuade you, I would ask you to destroy your property yourselves to show the Peloponnesians that it was not for those things that you refused to obey them!

144. I have many other reasons for believing that we will prevail, provided you refrain from adding to our empire while we are at war and from running unnecessary risks. I am much more worried about your own flaws than about the plots of our enemies . . . but all that will be made clearer in another speech when we are at war. For now, let us give these ambassadors our answer and send them away. Let us tell them that we will allow the Megarians to trade in our market and in our ports if the Spartans do not enact exclusionary laws against foreigners in order to keep us and our allies out—after all, the treaty neither proscribes such laws nor prohibits our decree. Let us tell them that we will grant our cities independence if they were independent when we made the treaty, and that we will do it when the Spartans, too, grant their allies the right to act in a way that is best not for Sparta, but in accordance with their own wishes. Let us tell them that we call for arbitration according to the articles of the treaty, and that we will not start a war, but that we will defend ourselves against those who do. This is the right and fitting answer for a city such as ours to give.

You must know that we will have to go to war, and the more willing we are to accept that fact, the less aggressive our enemies will be. Also, the greatest honor accrues to the citizen and the city that face the greatest dangers. After all, our fathers stood up to the Persians, and they set out from a city nothing like the one you see before you now. But they abandoned their property, and with planning more than luck, with boldness more than strength, they repelled the barbarian and led the city to its present greatness. We must not fail our fathers, and we must by any and all means defend ourselves against our enemies and try not to leave a diminished city to those who come after us.

145. That is what Pericles said.

The Athenians decided that he had given them the best advice and voted to do as he asked. Their answer to the Spartans conformed to his thinking as he had expressed it in general and in detail: they would do none of what they had been ordered to do, and they were prepared to go to court, according to the articles of the treaty, to resolve the Spartan claims on a level basis of equality. The ambassadors went home and came on no more missions thereafter.

146. These, then, were the accusations and disagreements that arose between both sides before the war, beginning right after the events at Epidamnus and Corcyra. They nevertheless continued to have dealings with each other in the midst of these differences without heralds—but not without distrust, because the events of this period initiated the breakdown of the treaty and the search for pretexts for war.

Book 2

Book 2 deals with the earliest stages of the war and highlights the statesmanship of Pericles. Having announced that he has recorded the events of the war in the order of their occurrence, Thucydides first shows his narrative powers in the account of the Theban attack on Plataea (2–6). He then turns to an important discussion of the general preparedness of both sides (7–17). This discussion includes: the strong statement that on the whole the Greeks were rooting for Sparta (8); a list of the allies on each side (9); an exhortation by King Archidamus of Sparta (11); the memorable statement of the spurned Spartan envoy Melesippus, "This day will mark the beginning of evils for the Greeks" (12); Pericles' statement of the strategy he proposes for the Athenians (13–14); a digression on the social organization of Attica (15); and an account of the painful migration to the city (16–17). The narrative of the war then resumes as Thucydides recounts the events of 431: the Peloponnesians invade Attica under Archidamus (18–24), and the Athenians harass the Peloponnese (25–31).

Some of the most famous passages in Thucydides' history are in Book 2. One is the Funeral Oration (35–46), which Thucydides contends was given by Pericles in 430. We will never know who wrote this speech—Pericles, Thucydides, or someone else. This speech has stood throughout history as a defense of democratic civilization.

The funeral speech is followed immediately by Thucydides' account of the plague (47–54), which ultimately claimed Pericles' life. Thucydides' description of the disease's symptoms illustrates his passionate commitment to a meticulous exposition of carefully gathered evidence, and his astute analysis of the psychology of fear and suffering shows him at his best. Already in antiquity the segment on the plague was admired, and it is the model for the poetic portrait of the plague that appears at the end of the long Latin epic of the Epicurean philosopher Lucretius, *On the Nature of Things*, written during the first century B.C. as the Roman republic was collapsing.

Chapters 55–64 deal with the Peloponnesian invasion of Attica and Pericles' difficulties convincing the Athenians of the wisdom of his policy. Chapter 65 contains Thucydides' account of Pericles' fining, deposition, and reinstatement as well as his famous assessment of Pericles' statesmanship and his theory about why and how Athens lost the war under Pericles' successors. The next chapters treat the fighting in central Greece, including the surrender of Potidaea (70), the Spartans' siege of Plataea (71–78), and the naval operations of the Athenian strategos, Phormio in the Gulf of Corinth (83–92). After a brief description of an abortive Peloponnesian raid on the Piraeus (94), Thucydides describes the empire of Sitalces in Thrace and its conflict with Macedonia (95–101). The book ends with the further exploits of Phormio and his return to Athens (102–103).

Book 2

1. From this point[1] begins the war between the Athenians and the Peloponnesians and their respective allies. They fought continually once they started and had no contact with each other except through heralds during the whole war. The events of the war have been recorded as they occurred chronologically from summer to winter.

2. The thirty-year peace treaty that went into effect after the recovery of Euboea had thus lasted fourteen years. In the fifteenth year, during the forty-eighth year of the priestesshood of Chrysis in Argos; when Aenesius was the eponymous ephor in Sparta; with two months left in the archonship of Pythodorus in Athens; six months after the battle at Potidaea, at the beginning of spring, at midnight, a little more than three hundred heavily armed Thebans under the command of the boeotarchs Pythangelus, son of Phyleides, and Diemporus, son of Onetorides, entered Boeotian Plataea, an ally of Athens.[2] Naucleides and his followers—Plataean citizens—had opened the gates for the Thebans and brought them in as protectors, because they wanted power for themselves and because they wanted to kill the citizens who opposed them and to align the city with Thebes. Naucleides had arranged for this in a deal with one of the most powerful men in Thebes, Eurymachus, son of Leontiades.[3] The Thebans, foreseeing that the war was sure to come, wanted to take their perennial antagonist, Plataea, by surprise while there was still a peace and while the war had not yet openly begun. They easily got into the city without being noticed, because under the circumstances no sentries had been posted. After halting at arms in the agora, though, the Thebans did not obey their collaborators and go right to work by breaking into the homes of the opposition, but decided instead to make a friendly announcement and to take over the city on amicable terms. Thus, because the Thebans believed that it was the easiest way to make the city support them, the herald announced that if anyone wanted to join them in fighting, according to the ancestral traditions of the whole body of Boeotians, he should take his place at arms beside them.

3. The Plataeans were panic-stricken when they learned that the Thebans were inside the walls and that the city had been so suddenly captured. Because they could not see that night, the Plataeans thought that many more had gotten in, so they accepted the terms, came to an agreement, and held still, especially since the Thebans did not take harsh measures against anyone. While they went about reaching this agreement, though, they noticed that there were not many Thebans and concluded that they could easily attack and overpower them. (The fact is that the majority of the Plataean people did not want to revolt from Athens.) So they decided to give it a try. They gathered by breaking holes through the common walls of each other's houses so that they would not be conspicuous by going through the streets, and then they positioned unhitched wagons in the streets to serve as barricades and got everything else ready

1. I.e., the vote of the Athenian assembly.
2. This happened in the spring of 431. The effort Thucydides has to expend in explaining the date in terms everyone will understand reveals the problems occasioned by the Greek states' lack of a common dating system. The "eponymous" ephor was the Spartan official who gave his name to the year; similarly the Athenians had an "eponymous" archon.
  Boeotarchs were magistrates of the territory of Boeotia. The organization of Boeotia was rather fluid, since the claims to primacy of its principal city, Thebes, were not always recognized by other Boeotians. During the Peloponnesian War, Boeotia had a federal constitution to which (beginning in 427) eleven units provided one boeotarch each.
3. Leontiades was the man who had commanded the Theban forces that deserted Leonidas at Thermopylae. See Herodotus 7.233.

in ways that seemed most useful for the operation. When the Plataeans had prepared everything as best they could, they left their houses to attack the Thebans, having waited until the darkness before the dawn so that they would not be hitting them in the daylight, when they would be more confident and more equally matched, and so that, being more frightened at night, they could be defeated by the Plataeans' knowledge of the layout of the city. They attacked immediately and were quickly fighting hand to hand.

4. When the Thebans realized that they had been completely deceived, they closed ranks and repelled the attacks wherever they were made. They pushed back two or three waves, but then in the confusion of charging Plataeans and of women and house slaves screeching, screaming, and throwing stones and rooftiles down on them, and what with heavy rain the whole night through, the Thebans panicked, turned tail, and fled through the city. Most of them did not know, in the mud and darkness, the roads they needed to take to save their lives, and since all this happened on a moonless night, and they had pursuers who knew the ways to keep them from escaping, most of them were killed. A Plataean locked the gate they had entered (and the only one that was open) by jamming a bronze spear butt into the sliding bar in place of the locking pin, so that the Thebans no longer had even this exit.

And so, pursued through the city, some climbed the wall and jumped, with most killing themselves in the process; some found an unguarded gate and got away unnoticed, after smashing the bolt with an axe a woman had given them—but not many, for this was quickly discovered; others were killed as they scattered here and there throughout the town. Most of the Thebans had kept together, though, and burst into a large building adjoining the city wall whose doors happened to be open. They thought the doors of the building were gates leading straight out through the wall. When the Plataeans saw that the Thebans were trapped, they had to decide whether to set fire to the building and burn them alive on the spot or whether to do something else with them. Finally, these men and whatever other Theban survivors happened to be roaming around the city agreed with the Plataeans to unconditionally surrender themselves and their weapons.

That is what was happening inside Plataea.

5. Meanwhile, the rest of the Theban army had orders to stand by in full strength while it was still dark, just in case things did not go according to plan with the men who had gone in. They were on the road and rushed to help as soon as they heard news of what had happened, but Plataea is eight miles from Thebes and the rain that had fallen overnight slowed their march, because the Asopus River was in full flood and not easily crossed. After crossing the river with great difficulty and making the rest of the way in the rain, they arrived too late: the men had already been killed or captured. When the Thebans learned what had happened, they thought about going after the Plataeans outside the city walls because, since this trouble came unexpectedly in peacetime, there were both people and property in the fields. They wanted anyone they might capture to be available to them to trade for the men inside—if, that is, any of them had been spared. The Thebans mulled this over, but while they were still making plans the Plataeans suspected some such thing would happen, and fearing for those outside the city, sent a herald to the Thebans to say that there could be no sanction for what they had done in trying to capture their city in peacetime, and to tell them not to harm the people and property outside the city; otherwise, they would kill the men they had taken alive. Once the Thebans had withdrawn from Plataean territory, though, they would return their men. This,

at least, is what the Thebans say, adding that the Plataeans swore to it. The Plataeans, on the other hand, do not agree that they promised to return the men immediately. They would first have had talks to see whether they could come to terms, they say, and they deny that they took an oath. In any case, the Thebans withdrew without further lawlessness, while the Plataeans hurriedly brought their people and property back from the fields and then immediately killed the prisoners. There were one hundred and eighty of them, including Eurymachus, the man with whom the traitors had conspired.[4] After the executions, they sent a messenger to Athens. Then they returned the dead to the Thebans under a flag of truce and set about organizing things in the city as they thought best in view of the current situation.

6. The events in Plataea had been reported to the Athenian people at once. They immediately arrested any Boeotians who were in Attica and sent a herald to Plataea with orders to announce that they take no hostile action against the Thebans they held until Athens too could join in the deliberations concerning them. They did so because they had not gotten the news that the men were dead. The first Plataean messenger had left right after the entry of the Thebans, and the second after they had been defeated and rounded up. Athens knew nothing of what happened after that. Thus Athens had sent its message in ignorance of the facts, and when the herald arrived, he found the men already dead. After this, Athens sent a force to Plataea. They brought food, stationed a joint garrison there, and brought out the women and children under escort, along with the men who were unfit for military service.

7. Now that this fighting had occurred in Plataea, and now that the treaty had clearly been broken, the Athenians prepared for war. So did the Spartans and their allies. Both sides planned to send ambassadors to the King and elsewhere in the non-Greek world, in the hope of getting whatever help they could, and they also tried to form alliances with cities outside their normal spheres of influence. Also the Spartans ordered their allies in Italy and Sicily to build ships, in accordance with the size of their cities, to be added to the fleet in the Peloponnese so as eventually to bring the total number up to five hundred. They were also ordered to collect a designated sum of money, but otherwise to remain neutral and to allow only one Athenian ship at a time into their harbors until the orders were carried out.[5] Athens also reviewed its existing alliances and made a point of sending embassies to the states surrounding the Peloponnese. Their eyes were especially on Corcyra, Cephallenia, Acarnania, and Zacynthus to see whether those alliances were secure, since Athens planned to harry the Peloponnese from its perimeters.

8. Everyone was thinking big on both sides and felt enthusiastic about the war. Quite naturally. People always get excited when taking on something new, and at that time, with a large younger generation in the Peloponnese and a large one in Athens as well, inexperience made them quite willing to latch onto the war with both hands. Meanwhile, all the rest of Greece was in suspense over the clash of the foremost cities, and many prophecies were uttered, many old oracles intoned by soothsayers, both in the cities that were about to go to war and in the others. Why, even Delos had an earthquake before the war, when there had never been so much as a tremor there for as long as Greeks could remember. It was said, and indeed it was believed to be, a sign of things to come.

---

4. Cf. 2.3.
5. In wartime, admitting only one ship of a belligerent at a time was a state's way of indicating its neutrality.

And if some other such event happened to occur, every possible meaning was thoroughly scrutinized.

Popular opinion shaped up in favor of the Spartans by far, especially since they had proclaimed that they were going to liberate Greece.[6] Everywhere, city and citizen alike were eager, if at all possible, to join with them in word and deed, and everyone felt that any plan would come to a standstill if he himself could not take part in it. That is how angry most people were at Athens—some because they wanted to rid themselves of Athenian rule, and others because they were frightened lest they fall under that rule.

9. Such, then, was their state of mind and their degree of preparedness when they set out. These are the cities each side had in its alliance when the war began. The Spartan allies comprised all the Peloponnesians inside the Isthmus, except Argos and Achaea, which were friendly with both sides. (Pellene alone among the Achaeans joined the Spartans from the first, though all of them did later.)[7] Outside the Peloponnese, there were Megara, Boeotia, Eastern Locris,[8] Phocis, Ambracia, Leucas, and Anactorium. Corinth, Megara, Sicyon, Pellene, Elis, Ambracia, and Leucas provided ships, while Boeotia, Phocis, and Locris provided cavalry. The other cities provided infantry.

That was the Spartan alliance. For the Athenians, there were the Chians, the Lesbians, the Plataeans, the Messenians in Naupactus, most of the Acarnanians, the Corcyraeans, the Zacynthians, as well as other cities that were subject to taxes in the following regions: coastal Caria and its Dorian neighbors, Ionia, the Hellespont, Thrace, the islands to the east of the Peloponnese and Crete, and all the Cyclades except Melos and Thera. Of these states, ships were provided by the Chians, Lesbians, and Corcyraeans, and infantry and money by the others.

These were the alliances and the equipment that each side brought to the war.

10. Immediately after the events in Plataea, the Spartans sent out orders to their allies both in the Peloponnese and beyond to prepare their armies and to furnish them with enough supplies for a lengthy foreign campaign. Their objective was the invasion of Attica. When everything was ready, at the appointed time, two-thirds of the forces from each city gathered at the Isthmus of Corinth. After the whole allied army had been assembled, the commander of the expedition, Archidamus, king of the Spartans, convened the generals from all the cities, along with public officials worthy of attendance, and spoke as follows.

11. Men of the Peloponnese! Allies! Our forefathers in and outside the Peloponnese fought many campaigns, and we of the older generation are also experienced in war, though none of us has ever set forth with a larger force than this. Now we march at our most numerous and best against a very powerful city, and it is only right that we not show ourselves as inferior to our ancestors nor as falling short of our own reputation. For all of Greece has been uplifted by this enterprise and, out of its hatred for Athens, turns its thoughts toward us, hoping that we achieve our aims. Thus though it may seem to some of you that we are attacking in strength with a fair certainty that our enemies will not come out to meet us in battle, we must not for that reason march in careless disarray. Every general, every soldier from every city, must always expect to be personally in dan-

---

6. The liberation of Greece—a fervent wish during the Persian Wars—increasingly became a slogan to justify an expansionism that culminated in the empire of Alexander the Great.
7. Cf. 5.82. Probably 417, though possibly earlier.
8. The Eastern (Opuntian) Locrians were allied with the Spartans.

ger. War is unpredictable. Attacks usually come fiercely and suddenly, and often a smaller force defends itself better out of fear than a larger one that is unprepared out of overconfidence. In enemy territory, we must always march out confident in our strategy and nervous about our readiness for battle. Thus we will be coolest when we attack our enemies and safest when they attack us. And we are not going up against a city incapable of defending itself, but against one that is well prepared in every way. We must anticipate that they will, in fact, come out to meet us in battle, if not now, before we have reached their territory, then when they see us slashing and burning their fields and destroying their property. A rage comes over people when they see themselves having to put up in actuality with injuries they are not used to, and they swing into action with the least forethought and the most heat. The Athenians are more likely than others to behave in this way, they who think they have a right to rule over others and who are more accustomed to attack and ravage the property of their neighbors than to see it happen to their own. Follow, then, wherever we lead as we march against this mighty city, bearing before us—for good or ill, depending on the outcome—our own high reputation and that of our ancestors. And above all, maintain a wary discipline and swiftly obey our orders, for the bravest and the safest course is to seem to be one, though we are many.

12. The first thing Archidamus did after making this speech and adjourning the meeting was to despatch a Spartan citizen, Melesippus, son of Diacritus, to Athens just in case they were willing to make any concessions in view of the fact that the Peloponnesians were already on the way.[9] The Athenians not only did not send him before the people, but did not so much as admit him into the city. Pericles' strategy had prevailed—not to admit Spartan heralds or ambassadors while their army was on the march. They sent him away without a hearing, with orders to be across the border by sundown. Thereafter, if the Peloponnesians wanted to send ambassadors, it should be only after they had withdrawn to their own cities. They also sent an escort along with Melesippus so that he would not be able to communicate with anyone. When they reached the border and were about to part, Melesippus crossed over saying only, "This day will mark the beginning of evils for the Greeks."

When Melesippus reached the Spartan army and Archidamus learned that the Athenians would make no concessions whatsoever, he finally broke camp and advanced into their territory. The Boeotians left two-thirds of their army and their contingent of cavalry to accompany the Peloponnesians and made their way with the rest of their forces to Plataea, ravaging the land as they went.

13. While the Peloponnesians were still gathering at the Isthmus, or else were on the way—but before they invaded Attica—Pericles, son of Xanthippus, and a general in the Athenian army along with nine others, gave notice to the Athenian assembly that Archidamus was a friend of his, but that the friendship had not been to the detriment of Athens.[1] Pericles realized that the invasion was about to take place and suspected that, as his friend, Archidamus might pass over his lands and not deforest them, either because he personally wanted to please Pericles or because the Spartans had

---

9. Melesippus had also been the envoy sent on the last diplomatic mission. Cf. 1.139.
1. The Greek word here translated as "friend" is "xenos." There is no satisfactory English equivalent for this word. It denoted friendship in the usual modern sense, but it also meant "guest," as well as a quasi-official relationship between two people who extended hospitality to one another when they visited each other's cities.

ordered him to do so out of a desire to discredit Pericles—just as it had been because of him that they demanded that the curse be driven out.[2] He said that if the enemy should happen not to destroy his property in the same way as they did everyone else's, he thereby relinquished it to the state—so let no suspicion fall on him on that account.

His advice in the current situation was what it had been all along: to prepare for war; to bring their movable property in from the fields; not to go out and give battle, but to stand guard behind the city walls; to equip their navy, which was their strength; to control their allies—and here he reminded them that tax revenues were the advantage they got from their allies, and that, in general, wars were won by a combination of sound strategy and surplus wealth.[3] He told them to be encouraged by the fact that, on average, six hundred talents flowed into the city from the allies every year, not counting other revenue, and that, to date, they still had six thousand talents' worth of silver coins in the acropolis. (At its greatest, that amount had been ninety-seven hundred, before the expenditures for the propylaea and the buildings on the acropolis as well as for the siege of Potidaea.) This was not counting the unminted gold and silver in the private and public offerings, along with sacred paraphernalia for processions and athletic contests, as well as the spoils of the Persian Wars and the like, all of which amounted to no less than five hundred talents. To all this he added the not-inconsiderable sums available to them in the other temples, and, as an absolute last resort, the inlaid gold in the statue of the goddess herself.[4] He revealed that the statue contained forty talents in refined gold, all of it removable. He said that it could be used in life-or-death situations provided it was not replaced by less than had been taken.

In this way, then, Pericles bucked them up with an accounting of their finances and with the number of their hoplites—thirteen thousand, not counting the sixteen thousand in the fortresses in Attica and on the walls around Athens. (At the beginning of the war, these troops defended the walls whenever the enemy invaded and were made up of old men, boys, and metic hoplites. The wall to Phalerum from the city wall was four miles long, and there were about five guarded miles of the wall around the city itself. Some of it—the stretch between the Long Walls to the Piraeus and the wall to Phalerum—was unguarded. The Long Walls—of which only the outer wall was guarded—were nearly five miles long, and the walls around the Piraeus, along with the wall to Munychia, were over seven miles around, all told, although only half that length was guarded.)

Pericles went on to say that they had twelve hundred cavalrymen, including mounted archers, sixteen hundred archers, and three hundred triremes that were ready for service. These resources, at least, were available to the Athenians just before the first Peloponnesian invasion at the onset of the war. Pericles also made his usual statements to prove that they would win the war.[5]

14. The Athenians gave this speech a careful hearing and followed his leadership. They brought their women, children, and household belongings in from their farms and even stripped the woodwork from their homes. They shipped their flocks and yoke-oxen to Euboea and to the offshore islands. This

---

2. Cf. 1.127ff.
3. Cf. 1.141 and 143.
4. Pericles referred to the gold on the statue of Athena in the Parthenon. The huge statue, which had been made of wood by the sculptor Phidias, was inlaid with panels of gold and ivory.
5. This schematic, indirect account of Pericles' speech may comprise Thucydides' notes on a speech he intended to work into full rhetorical form in a final revision.

Attica and Environs

0   50 Km   50 Mi

E u b o e a

Chaeronea

Coronea

Thebes   Tanagra   Delium

Asopus River

Plataea

Panactum

Pegae   Thria   Decelea   Marathon

Eleusis   Acharnae

Megara   Athens

Nisaea   Piraeus

Carystus

ATTICA

LAURIUM

Cape
Sunium

Athens

Piraeus

Bay of
Phalerum

Phalerum

Eetionia
(moles or breakwaters)

65

uprooting was a great hardship for them because most people had been accustomed to living in the countryside from time immemorial.

15. This way of life had especially characterized the Athenians since deep-
est antiquity. From the time of Cecrops and the first kings until the reign of Theseus, Attica had always been organized, politically, as distinct cities.[6] Each had
its own prytanies and archons, and only when they were threatened would they
band together and consult with the king. Otherwise, they governed themselves
and passed their own laws, and some even went to war against the king, as when
the Eleusinians went to war with Eumolpus against Erechtheus. When Theseus (who combined intelligence with power) became king, however, he
changed the political alignments, dissolved the deliberative bodies and magis-
tracies of all the cities besides those of what is now Athens, and created one
council and one prytany,[7] uniting all the cities into one state. Although everyone managed his own property, as in the past, Theseus required them to do so
under the authority of one state, which grew powerful (and whose power he
handed down to succeeding generations) because of the taxes paid by all the
members of a single community. From his time to the present day, Athenians
have celebrated their political unification with a publicly financed festival to
the goddess Athena. Before that time, the present-day acropolis was but one of
the cities, along with some of the land below it to the south. This is proved by
the fact that the temples and shrines of Athena and of other gods are on the
acropolis, while those that are not in the acropolis tend to be in the southern
region of the city. These include the temples of Olympian Zeus, of Pythian
Apollo, of Mother Earth, and of Dionysus of the Marshes, to whom the older
of the two festivals of Dionysus is held on the twelfth day of the month of Anthesterion—as is still the custom among the Ionians who are descended from
the ancient Athenians.[8] There are also other ancient shrines in this area. Furthermore, the fountain that the tyrants built, and which we now call Nine-
spouts, was an open spring called Lovelyflow in antiquity.[9] Because it was
nearby, people in those days used the spring on the most important occasions,
and because of its antiquity, it is still the custom to use its water before marriages
and other rituals.[1] Because of the ancient settlement there, the acropolis is
called "the city" to this day by the Athenians.

16. Thus Athenians for the most part belonged to independent homesteads
throughout the countryside despite having united into a single city; and because
the ancients and their descendants had this ethos—lasting right up to the present
war—of living all their lives on their lands, it was not easy for them to uproot their
households, especially since they had recently finished restoring their property
after the Persian Wars. They took it very hard and were deeply saddened to abandon the homes and family shrines that had been theirs since before the union of
the Attican cities, and to be faced with giving up their way of life, and with having, each and every one, to forsake nothing less than his native city.

17. When they arrived in Athens, only a few had homes of their own or a
refuge with family or friends, so most of them lived in the undeveloped parts of

6. Cecrops, Theseus, and Erechtheus were believed to be early kings of Athens; Theseus, who was consid-
    ered to have lived later than the others, was credited with unifying all the towns of Attica into one polit-
    ical body, Athens.
7. The Athenian Council of 500 was made up of fifty members from each of Athens' ten tribes. Since the
    Athenian year had ten months, one tribe served as chair each month; its councillors were known for that
    period as prytaneis (singular prytanis).
8. Anthesterion was the eighth Attic month and lasted from late February to late March.
9. The tyrants were Peisistratus and his sons, who governed Athens in the sixth century. Thucydides dis-
    cusses the tyranny in a digression at 6.54–59.
1. Athenian brides, for example, were bathed in water from this spring on their wedding day.

the city and in all the monuments and temples, except on the acropolis, in the Eleusinium,[2] or anywhere else that was securely locked. Even the area on either side of the so-called Pelasgic wall—the one below the acropolis—was filled with squatters in the present emergency, in spite of the curse on those who lived there and of the tag-end of some Delphic oracle that prohibited it, saying ". . . better for the Pelasgic wall to be unused."[3] (It seems to me, though, that the oracle turned out in a way opposite to what people expected. Calamity didn't come to the city because of the unlawful occupation; rather, the need to occupy the area arose because of the war, which the oracle does not specifically identify, but which it foresaw as the baleful cause of the area's habitation.) Many people also set themselves up in the towers of the city wall and wherever else they could, because the city could not hold the incoming population—and in fact the people later settled along the Long Walls and divided up most of the Piraeus. At the same time, the Athenians prepared for war, marshaling their allies and outfitting a hundred ships for the attack on the Peloponnese.

18. While the Athenians were in this stage of their preparations, the advancing Peloponnesian army first reached the fortress of Oenoe in Attica, from which they planned to launch their invasion.[4] After taking up their positions, they prepared for an assault on the walls of the fortress with siege engines and by other means. (Oenoe was a walled fortress on the Attic–Boeotian border, and the Athenians used the stronghold whenever war broke out.) The Peloponnesians, though, wasted a lot of time getting ready for the assault, and Archidamus received no little censure because of it. Failing to urge war wholeheartedly, he had already been regarded as weak in mobilizing for the war and as soft on the Athenians. The waiting around at the Isthmus after the army had been assembled and the leisurely pace on the march—but especially the standstill at Oenoe—made him unpopular because the Athenians were taking shelter during this time and the Peloponnesians believed that but for his inaction they could have advanced swiftly and captured everything while it was still outside the walls of Athens. Though this was the hostile attitude of the army towards Archidamus while they were encamped at Oenoe, there were those who said that he held off because he expected the Athenians to give way a bit while their land was still unharmed and to shrink from having to stand by and watch it being deforested.

19. They did make an assault on Oenoe, and tried without success to take it by every manner of means; but the Athenians still refused to negotiate. So, about eighty days after the events in Plataea, when the summer and the grain were at their height, the Peloponnesians set off from Oenoe and invaded Attica. Their commander was Archidamus, son of Zeuxidamus and king of the Spartans. They camped and destroyed crops in Eleusis and the plain of Thria first, meanwhile turning back some Athenian cavalry in a skirmish around the so-called Streams. They then advanced through Cropia, keeping Mount Aegaleus on the right until they came into Acharnae, the largest of what are called the "demes" of Attica.[5] They stopped and set up a camp there, and stayed for a long time deforesting the land.[6]

---

2. A temple to Demeter northeast of the acropolis.
3. The Pelasgic wall was the oldest of the walls around the acropolis.
4. By going to Oenoe, Archidamus took a long detour to the northeast, avoiding the direct southerly road to Athens.
5. Attica was composed of one hundred and thirty-nine "demes" or districts. These varied enormously in size and functioned not only as voting precincts, but as centers of civic life. Citizenship was signaled by formal enrollment in a deme. Conglomerations of demes made up the ten tribes of Attica.
6. By following this route, Archidamus again took the long way around and avoided entering the Attic plain near Athens.

20. They say that the strategy Archidamus adopted at Acharnae was to remain in battle formation without going down into the Attic plain during that invasion. He hoped, they say, that Athens, at the height of its power, with a large younger generation, and prepared for war as never before, might come out to give battle and not look away as its land was being destroyed. Thus when the Athenians did not oppose him at Eleusis and the plain of Thria, he camped in Acharnae and probed to see whether they would come out there. Partly, of course, the terrain seemed suitable for an encampment, but he also thought that since Acharnae, with its three thousand hoplites, constituted a large part of Athens, the Acharnians would not ignore the destruction of their property but would urge everyone to battle. If, on the other hand, the Athenians did not come out during that invasion, he could the more fearlessly ravage the plain on the next invasion and even approach the city itself, because the Acharnians, bereft of their own land, would not be very eager to take risks over anyone else's. Dissension would have crept into the Athenian populace. This, then, was Archidamus's thinking during his operations in Acharnae.

21. While the army was in Eleusis and the plain of Thria, the Athenians continued to have some hope that they would not come any closer. They remembered when Pleistoanax, son of Pausanias and king of Sparta, invaded Attica past Eleusis and almost to Thria fourteen years before this war with a Peloponnesian army; but he withdrew without advancing any further, for which he was exiled from Sparta on an accusation of bribery. Therefore, when they saw an army operating in Acharnae, seven miles from the city, they could no longer endure it. Their land was being destroyed before their very eyes—a thing that the younger ones had never seen before, nor the older ones either, except during the Persian Wars. It terrified them and they—especially the young—naturally wanted to march out and to stop just looking on. They gathered in knots, quarreling furiously, some for going out and others not allowing it. Soothsayers chanted all manner of oracles, and everyone heard only the ones he wanted to. The Acharnians, especially, urged going out. In their view, they were not the smallest segment of the Athenian population and it was their land that was being destroyed. The city was in total ferment and, remembering none of his earlier advice, people were enraged with Pericles, branding him a coward because he was a general who would not lead them out to fight and making him the cause of all their suffering.

22. Seeing that the people were angry about the situation and not thinking clearly, and believing that he was right not to march out, Pericles called neither a formal assembly of the citizens nor any meeting at all, lest they gather more in anger than in reason and make a serious mistake. He continued to ensure that the city was well protected and kept it as calm as he could. He did, however, constantly despatch cavalry to prevent advance Peloponnesian horsemen from falling on the fields near the city and destroying them. There was a minor cavalry skirmish at Phrygia[7] between one of the Athenian squadrons (which was accompanied by some Thessalians) and the Boeotian cavalry. The Athenians and the Thessalians were more than holding their own until hoplites came to the aid of the Boeotians, whereupon the Athenians and Thessalians retreated with the loss of a few men. They were, however, able to recover the bodies the same day without obtaining a truce. The Peloponnesians stood a victory marker there the next day. (The Thessalians provided this assistance to the Athenians in keeping with their long-standing alliance.[8] They were accompa-

---

7. A place northeast of Athens and southeast of Acharnae.
8. Cf. 1.102 and 107.

nied by Larissans, Pharsalians, Crannonians, Pyrasians, Gyrtonians, and Pheraeans. From Larissa, the commanders were Polymedes and Aristonus, each representing his own faction, and Menon was the commander from Pharsalus. The other cities also had their own generals.)[9]

23. Since the Athenians did not come out to meet them in battle, the Peloponnesians left Acharnae and ravaged some of the demes between Mount Pentelicon and Mount Parnes. While the Peloponnesians were operating on land, the Athenians sent the hundred ships they had been outfitting to the Peloponnese. There were a thousand hoplites and four hundred archers aboard. They were commanded by Carcinus, son of Xenotimus; Proteas, son of Epicles; and Socrates,[1] son of Antigenes. After this fleet set sail on its expedition around the Peloponnese, the Peloponnesians, who stayed in Attica for as long as their provisions lasted, returned home through Boeotia and not via the route by which they had invaded. They did, however, pass through Oropus and waste the territory known as Graice, which is occupied by Oropian subjects of Athens. After returning to the Peloponnese, they disbanded and returned to their cities.

24. After the Peloponnesians had withdrawn, the Athenians posted coast guards and inland lookouts, just as they were to do throughout the war. They also voted to set aside a reserve fund of one thousand talents from the money in the acropolis. It was not to be spent, and the war was to be funded with the remaining monies. They imposed a penalty of death on any of themselves who so much as moved or put to a vote that this fund be used for any reason other than to repel an enemy actually bearing down on the city with a "maritime force." They also created a naval reserve to be composed of the hundred best triremes of any given year, complete with trierarchs.[2] These ships too were to be used only in an emergency, along with the reserve fund, if need be.

25. The Athenians in their hundred ships, along with the Corcyraeans in their fifty ships and the other western allies who had come to help, did damage as they sailed around the Peloponnese. Among other things, they landed and attacked the weak and undefended fortification at Methone in Laconia.[3] It happened, though, that a Spartan citizen, Brasidas, son of Tellis, was in the area with a small mobile force, and when he learned of the attack, he came to the relief of the people of Methone with a hundred hoplites. He ran through the Athenian line, which had been thinly spread over the terrain and which was concentrating on the fortress, and rushed into Methone. He lost a few of the men who were with him in this onrush, but he saved the city, and for this act of daring, he became the first officer in the war to receive the thanks of the state at Sparta.

The Athenians decamped and continued to sail along the coast, landing at Pheia, in Elis, where they slashed and burned the land for two days and won a battle against three hundred picked men, who had rushed to the rescue from the Elis Valley along with natives from the surrounding area. A high wind began to blow, however, and since they were caught in a storm in a place without a harbor, most of the men boarded the ships, rounded the so-called "Cape Fish," and sailed into the harbor at Pheia. The Messenians and some others who could not get aboard made their way by land and captured Pheia. Later they abandoned Pheia when the ships sailed around, picked them up, and put out to sea.

---

9. These cities were members of the Thessalian League.
1. Not the famous Socrates but another Athenian of the same name.
2. The trierarchy was one of the so-called "liturgies" that marked the Athenian social and economic system. According to this scheme, the richest citizens were called upon to perform a variety of public services, such as training a chorus for a dramatic festival or hosting a large banquet. Trierarchs were in charge of commanding triremes and of maintaining them at their own expense.
3. Laconia was the territory around Sparta.

By then, most of the Elean army had come to the relief of the city. The Athenians continued to sail along the coast ravaging other areas.

26. At around the same time, Athens dispatched thirty ships to sail around Eastern Locris and to keep an eye on Euboea. Cleopompus, son of Clinias, was in command. He made some landings, ravaging the coast here and there, and captured Thronium. He took some hostages and then, in a battle at Alope, he defeated the Eastern Locrians who had come to help the Thronians.

27. That same summer, the Athenians also drove the Aeginetans—men, women, and children—out of Aegina, accusing them of having been one of the main causes of the war. It also seemed safer, since the island lies close to the Peloponnese, to hold it by sending settlers of their own; and indeed they did send colonists there not much later. The Spartans gave the outcast Aeginetans Thyrea and its countryside to live in and cultivate, because of their hostility to Athens and for having helped Sparta during the earthquake and the uprising of the helots.[4] Thyrea is the country that slopes down to the sea between Sparta and the Argolid, and some of the Aeginetans did in fact settle there, though others dispersed throughout Greece.

28. That summer also, at the new moon according to the lunar calendar (which is the only time this seems to be possible), the sun was eclipsed in the afternoon and later returned to fullness after it became crescent-shaped and some stars began to shine.[5]

29. That summer also, the Athenians sent for the son of Pythes, Nymphodorus the Abderite, whom they had once regarded as their enemy, and appointed him their proxenus[6] in Thrace, because he had great influence over Sitalces, who was married to his sister. Their aim was to make an alliance with Sitalces, son of Teres and king of Thrace.

Now this Teres, the father of Sitalces, was the first to extend the great kingdom of the Odrysians over most of Thrace, although much of Thrace remains autonomous. This Teres was not connected by blood with the Tereus who married Procne the daughter of Pandion the Athenian—they didn't even come from the same "Thrace." Tereus lived in Daulis, in what we now call Phocis—although at that time it was being settled by Thracians—and it was there that the women murdered Itys. (Indeed, many poets who have wanted an epithet for a nightingale have called it "Daulian.") This is obvious: the mutually advantageous marriage connection Pandion made through his daughter would be with neighbors and would not involve as many days' travel as it did to the Odrysians. Teres (even the name isn't the same) was the first king to come to power over the Odrysians, and it was with *his* son that the Athenians made an alliance, because they wanted him to help them subdue Perdiccas and the Chalcidic peninsula.[7]

---

4. Thucydides discusses the earthquake and the attendant helot revolt in 1.101–3. Probably these events happened around 465.
5. This eclipse took place on August 3, 431.
6. A proxenus was a citizen of one state who undertook to represent the interests of another state there. In this case, the Athenians agreed with Nymphodorus, a Thracian, that he would look after Athenian interests in Thrace. A proxenus also provided hospitality and services for visitors from the state with whom he had this special tie. Famous proxeni included Cimon, who was the Spartans' proxenus in Athens, i.e., a pro-Spartan Athenian on whom the Spartans could count to represent Spartan interests.
7. This fussily written passage has all the earmarks of a Thucydides who wants to set the historical record straight and detach history from myth. He may also have wanted to distinguish between the mythological figure Tereus and the historical king Teres in order to justify an Athenian alliance with Thrace. The myth Athenians seem to have been confusing with the historical reality went like this: Tereus married Pandion's daughter, Procne, who bore Tereus a son, Itys. Later Tereus raped Procne's sister, Philomela, and cut out her tongue to keep her from telling the tale. The two women avenged this act by killing Itys and feeding him to his father. Zeus then transformed Procne into a nightingale and Philomela into a sparrow, although the Romans got it the other way around, with Philomela becoming the nightingale. What may be most interesting is that the passage of two generations sufficed to jumble history and myth in the minds of many Athenians.

Nymphodorus came to Athens and arranged to make Sitalces an ally and Sitalces' son, Sadocus, a citizen of Athens; he also undertook to end the war in the Chalcidic peninsula by persuading Sitalces to send a force of cavalry and light troops to Athens. Nymphodorus also reconciled Perdiccas to the Athenians and persuaded them to restore Therme to him, whereupon Perdiccas immediately joined forces with Phormio and his Athenian army against Chalcidice. In this way, Sitalces, son of Teres and king of Thrace, and Perdiccas, son of Alexander and king of Macedonia, became Athenian allies.

30. The hundred Athenian ships that were still off the Peloponnese captured the Corinthian town of Sollium and ceded it to the Acarnanian people of Palaira to be the sole inhabitants of the city and cultivators of the land. They also took Astacus, which had Evarchus as its tyrant. They expelled him after an all-out fight and brought the region into their alliance. They sailed to the island of Cephallenia and took it without a struggle. Cephallenia is near Acarnania and Leucas and is made up of the four towns of Pale, Crane, Same, and Pronnaea. Not much later, the ships began to make their way back to Athens.

31. Towards the end of that summer, the whole Athenian army—citizen and metic alike—invaded the Megarid with Pericles, son of Xanthippus, in command. The Athenians aboard the hundred ships that had been detailed to the Peloponnese had by now reached Aegina on their homeward voyage, and when they learned that the army had left Athens in full strength and was in the Megarid, they sailed their way and joined forces with them. Athens was still at the height of its power, and not yet stricken with the plague, and this was the largest combined military force in Athenian history. There were no fewer than ten thousand Athenian hoplites, not counting the three thousand at Potidaea; and the metics who joined in the invasion numbered no fewer than three thousand hoplites; there was also an extremely large throng of lightly armed troops. They ravaged most of the land and withdrew. Every year thereafter, there were Athenian invasions of the Megarid by either the full army or the cavalry until Nisaea was captured by the Athenians.[8]

32. At the end of that summer, Atalanta, a once-desert island off Eastern Locris, was made into a walled fort by the Athenians to keep pirates from sailing from Opus and elsewhere in Locris to harry Euboea.

These, then, were the events that took place that summer, after the Peloponnesian withdrawal from Attica.

33. The following winter, Evarchus the Acarnanian, wanting to return to Astacus,[9] persuaded the Corinthians to set sail with forty ships and fifteen hundred hoplites to restore him to power. He himself hired some mercenary soldiers, and Euphamidas, son of Aristonymus; Timoxenus, son of Timocrates; and Eumachus, son of Chrysis, were in command of the whole expedition. They did set sail and they did restore him. They also wanted to procure other Acarnanian territory here and there on or near the coast, but they made for home after trying without success to do so. As they made their way along the coast, they stopped at Cephallenia and landed at Crane. They reached some sort of agreement with the Cranians, who used it to trick them. They lost some of their men after the Cranians attacked them unawares, and they were only able to put out to sea and return home after a considerable struggle.

34. That same winter, the Athenians observed an ancestral custom and arranged for the funeral, at the public expense, of the first men to die in the war.

8. In 424. Cf. 4.66–69.
9. Cf. 2.30.

They always did it in the following way. Two days beforehand, they would build a tent and lay out the bones and ashes of the dead, and everyone would make whatever offerings he wished to his kin.[1] On the day of the funeral procession, wagons brought in cypress coffins, one for each tribe, with every man's bones to be in the coffin of his tribe.[2] There was one empty bier spread with a coverlet for the missing, the men who could not be found and carried away. Any man, citizen or stranger, could attend the funeral; women who were related to the dead were also present, mourning the dead right up to the grave. The soldiers were buried in the national cemetery, which is in the most beautiful suburb of the city. Those who die in war are always buried there, except for those who died at Marathon, for the Athenians decided that they had shown surpassing courage and buried them right on the battlefield in Marathon. When the coffins are covered with earth, a man who has been chosen by the city for his outstanding reputation and exceptional wisdom delivers a fitting eulogy over the dead. After this, they all depart. Thus are the dead buried, and the custom was observed throughout the whole war whenever it was necessary to do so. Now Pericles, son of Xanthippus, had been chosen to speak over these very first dead, and at the appropriate time, he stepped forward from the gravesite and up onto a podium built high enough so that the largest number of the audience could hear, and spoke as follows.

35. Most of those who have spoken in this place have praised the man who added this speech to our funeral customs. It was good, they said, for there to be an oration over the fallen men we honor with these rites. As for me, it would have seemed enough to show our respect for brave men who fell in action *with* action—like the one you see us publicly performing here, now, at this national gravesite—and not to risk letting the reputation for courage of so many depend on whether one man speaks well or poorly. For it is hard to say the right thing when people barely agree as to the truth of it. The sympathetic, knowledgeable listener might, perhaps, think that what is said falls short of what he knows and wants to hear. Those who do not know the facts might, from envy, think some things exaggerated if they sound like more than they themselves can do, for praise of others is bearable only insofar as each man thinks he is capable of doing what he hears praised. They therefore begrudge and disbelieve in men who surpass their own abilities.

Nevertheless, since our forefathers thought fit that this should be so, I must observe our customs and try as best I can to satisfy your wishes and your expectations.

36. I will begin with our ancestors. It is both fitting and right on such an occasion as this to pay them the due regard of memory, because through their courage, they bequeathed this land they always occupied as a free state from one generation to the next down to the present day. They deserve our praise, but our fathers deserve even more because they, with great effort, added the empire we now possess to their inheritance and left it as a legacy for us, the living. We, who are still more or less in the prime of our lives, have enlarged most of that empire and have made our city self-sufficient both for war and peace. I will not go on at length about the things we did in our wars, through which each gain was made; or how our fathers or we ourselves readily defended ourselves against the attacks of hostile

1. The bodies of soldiers who died abroad were burned and their remains sent to Athens. The first to die were honored in this way, but all were buried alike.
2. Since the reforms of Cleisthenes shortly before 500, Athenians were grouped in ten tribes. This system provided the base of ten from which the generals and members of the council were chosen.

Greeks and barbarians alike. You know all that; let it go. But the way of life that brought us to our present state—the constitution, the customs, through which it has become great—these things I will first set forth before going on to the eulogy of these men, because I think it fitting that they be said on this occasion, and right for all this throng of citizens and noncitizens to give them heed.

37. We practice a politics that does not emulate the customs of our neighbors. On the contrary, we are the models, not the imitators, of others. Because we are governed for the many and not for the few, we go by the name of a democracy. As far as private interests are concerned, everyone has equal access to the law; but you are distinguished in society and chosen for public service not so much by lot as because of your individual merit. Furthermore, your poverty will not keep you in obscurity if you can do something worthwhile for the city. We are generous towards one another in our public affairs; and though we keep a watchful eye on each other as we go about our daily business, we don't get angry at our neighbor if he does as he pleases, and we don't give him dirty looks, which are painful though they do not kill. Painless as our private lives may be, we are terrified of breaking the laws. We obey them as they are administered by whoever is in power, especially the laws meant to relieve victims of oppression, whether they have been enacted by statute or whether they are the unwritten laws that carry the undisputed penalty of shame.

38. In addition, we give our minds many a respite from their toils with games and festivals all year long and with the handsome private furnishings whose daily enjoyment dispels the cares of life. Because of its size, all sorts of merchandise comes pouring into our city from all over the world, and foreign goods are no less ours to enjoy than those that are produced right here.

39. Our approach to military training differs from that of our Spartan opponents in the following ways. We have an open city and do not, by periodically expelling foreigners, keep them from seeing and learning things lest some enemy benefit from what is open to his view. We trust less to our equipment and our guile than to our personal courage in action. When it comes to education, Spartans no sooner reach boyhood than they painfully train to become men, whereas we, who live a more relaxed life, will nevertheless advance to meet the same dangers as they. The proof is that while the Spartans will not march into our land on their own but only with all their allies, we, by ourselves, attacking on foreign soil, usually gain easy victories over men defending their homes. Because we send our own citizens on numerous expeditions by land while simultaneously conducting naval operations, not a single enemy has ever engaged with our whole combined force. Nevertheless, if they should meet with a contingent of our armed forces and defeat some of them somewhere, they boast that they have repelled us all; but if they lose, it is by all of us that they have been vanquished. And since we prefer to run risks with ease of mind rather than with harmful exercise, and with an ingrained rather than an enforced manliness, we do not worry about hardships to come and go to meet them no less boldly than do those who drill incessantly.

40. This city of ours is amazing for these reasons, but for others as well. In the first place, we love nobility without ostentation and we have a virile love of knowledge. Furthermore, wealth is for us something to use, not something to brag about. And as to poverty, there is no shame in admitting to it—the real shame is in not taking action to escape from it. Finally, while there are those who manage both the city and their own private

business, there are others who, though wrapped up in their work, nevertheless have a thorough knowledge of public affairs. For we are the only people who regard a man who takes no interest in politics to be leading not a quiet life, but a useless one. We are also the only ones who either make governmental decisions or at least frame the issues correctly, because we do not think that action is hampered by public discourse, but by failure to learn enough in advance, through discourse, about what action we need to take. We are especially daring in our analysis and performance of whatever we undertake, whereas for others, ignorance is confidence and reason a drag on action. The bravest men are rightly regarded as those who have the clearest knowledge of pleasure and pain but who do not shrink from danger because of it.

We are also markedly different from most others when it comes to doing good, because we make friends not by receiving favors, but by doing them. The one who does the favor is the firmer friend because his kindness towards the recipient keeps the debt of gratitude unpaid; but the friendship of the debtor has a duller edge because he knows that he reciprocates friendship not by doing favors, but by owing gratitude. And so we alone will also fearlessly help others, not from a calculation of advantage but from the confidence that comes from our freedom.

41. To sum up, I tell you that this city, taken all in all, is the school of Greece, and as far as I am concerned, any man among us will exhibit a more fully developed personality than men elsewhere and will be able to take care of himself more gracefully and with the quickest of wit. The very strength our city has acquired through our way of life shows that this is not just a speechifying boast for this occasion, but the truth in action. Alone among today's cities, Athens proves stronger than its reputation, and no attacking enemy need be chagrined that he dies at the hands of an inferior, just as no subject state need censure our unworthiness to rule over it. Our power has not gone unnoticed, as you know only too well, and we have given great proofs to those who are living and yet to come as to why we should be the objects of their admiration. We need no more, not a Homer to sing our praises nor any other poet to please us with verses whose plots and fictions are hobbled by the truth. We have forced the earth and all its seas to make way before our daring, establishing an eternal memory everywhere of the vengeance we have taken and the good that we have done, and it was because they could not bear to think of losing such a city as this that these noble men fought and died, and it is fitting that each and every one of us who remain continue the struggle on her behalf.

42. This is why I have gone on for so long about our city—to teach the lesson that this struggle means more for us than for those who do not have our advantages, and to establish a foundation in fact for the eulogy I will now deliver. . . . But most of it has already been spoken, for the qualities I have extolled in the city were adorned by the valor of these men and of men like them, and it would be true of very few Greeks that words and deeds are so perfectly balanced as it is for these. For me, the end that came to these men makes plain a man's true worth, whether it came as the first sign or as the final confirmation of that worth. These men had human frailties, but it is only right that we emphasize their courage against the enemy in the defense of their fatherland. Their valor for the common good erased any harm done by their private faults. None of these men put off the day of reckoning because, like a coward, he preferred to enjoy the pleasures of his wealth or because he hoped, being poor, that he might yet escape poverty and become rich. They yearned more to take vengeance on their

enemies than they did for these things, whatever the danger, and believing that of all the dangers this was the noblest, they chose to punish their foes and relinquish the world, committing their hopes to an uncertain success and relying on themselves alone to enter the action they saw before them. They chose to save themselves by suffering and struggle but never by surrender, to flee disgrace and to withstand the battle with their bodies, and in that brief crisis of chance, at the height not of fear but of glory, they took their leave of us.

43. These were men worthy of their city! The rest of us must pray that our resolve against the enemy is safer, but we must be determined to be just as courageous. No one needs to harangue you, who know it so well, about how valor consists in driving off our enemies, but you must remember that the greatest gift to the city is not in public speeches but in daily beholding her power in action, in being like lovers to her. Thus when she is great in her glory, you will take it to heart that men knowingly, daringly, reverently built her power by doing what needed to be done, and that even when they perished in one of her enterprises, they did not think that the city was being deprived of their valor, but that they had freely made the handsomest possible investment in her. They offered up their bodies for the common good and took for themselves that undying praise and that most distinctive tomb—not the one in which they lie, but the one in which their fame remains to be eternally remembered in word and deed on every fitting occasion. The whole world is the tomb of famous men. Not just an inscribed tablet in their homeland commemorates them, but an unwritten memorial that lives on not in a monument, but in the minds even of strangers. You must now imitate these men. Think of happiness as freedom and freedom as courage, and do not worry over the dangers of war. It is not the wretched of the earth, for whom there is no hope of improvement, who have reason to be reckless with their lives, but those for whom a change for the worse is a risk they must run for as long as they live and for whom the contrast would be the greatest if they faltered. To a thoughtful man, the knowledge that he is miserable after having proved himself a coward is more painful than a death he hardly feels in strength and comradeship.

44. Thus, you parents who are here now, I will not weep for you, only console you. You know that you have lived in troubled times. Lucky men, like these here, who have won the handsomest of deaths—for you, a proud grief—have lived for as long as they have been happy. I know it is hard to persuade you of this when you will often be reminded of your sons by the good fortune of others—good fortune in which you yourselves used to exult. And we feel grief not for the deprivation of the good things we have never known, but for what we had grown used to before it was snatched away.

Those who are still of child-bearing age must endure their sorrow in the hope of other children. For them, personally, a new generation will be a way to forget those who are gone; and it will carry the two benefits for the city of preventing underpopulation and of providing security. Those who do not expose their children to the risk of danger along with everyone else are not able to make decisions about equality and justice. To those of you who are past your prime, think of that larger part of your lives in which you were happy as profit. What follows will be short and eased by the good repute of these men. Only the love of honor never grows old, and it is not making money, as some people say, that pleases us most in our useless old age, but the esteem of others.

45. As to you, the sons and brothers of these men, I foresee that you will have a formidable task before you, because everyone praises those who have passed away, and it will be hard enough for you to be thought of as having fallen just short of their high valor, much less as having equaled it. You see, envy for the living derives from competition, but those who are no longer with us are honored with an unchallengeable good will.

And since I must also make some mention of womanly virtue to those who will now be widows, I will define it in this brief admonition: your greatest fame consists in being no worse than your natures, and in having the least possible reputation among males for good or ill.

46. I have spoken, in my turn, and according to our custom, what words I could for this occasion, and those who are interred have here been honored, for now, with our deeds. From this day on, the city will rear their children at public expense until they come of age, thus offering a tangible prize to these men and their survivors for their struggle. After all, the people who institute the greatest rewards for excellence will have the best citizens. And now that each of you has mourned your kin to the full, go on your way.

47. These funeral rites were celebrated that winter, after which the first year of the war came to an end. As soon as the summer began, the Peloponnesians and their allies—with two-thirds of their total force, as in the first year—invaded Attica under the command of Archidamus, son of Zeuxidamus and king of Sparta. They took up their positions and proceeded to scorch the earth. They had not been in Attica for very many days before the plague broke out in Athens for the first time. They say that it had already struck far and wide, including at Lemnos and elsewhere, although there is no mention that it was a disease of such magnitude or that it caused such loss of life anywhere else. Physicians were the first to treat the disease, but they did so in ignorance of its nature and were no match for it. They died in large numbers, in direct proportion as they treated it. No other human skill did any good, either, and as to supplications in temples, consultations of oracles, and such like, these too were all to no avail. In the end, people gave up on all these things, defeated by the illness.

48. They say that the disease first began south of Egypt, in Ethiopia, and then descended into Egypt, Libya, and most of the King of Persia's domains. It attacked Athens suddenly, getting its grip, at first, on the people of the Piraeus, who said that the Peloponnesians had poisoned their cisterns—for there were not yet any wells in the Piraeus. It later advanced up into the city of Athens proper, and the deaths became much more numerous as a result. Let others, physician and layman alike, say what they know about the probable origin of the disease and about what they think enabled it to spread so far and to bring about so many violent changes. I will say what it was like and how, should the disease ever strike again, someone who gives an examination may have some prior knowledge of it and not fail to recognize it. I give this description having been sick myself and having myself seen others who suffered from the disease.

49. Everyone agrees that it was an unusually disease-free year with respect to other illnesses, and if anyone did have a prior condition, it always developed into this one. Other, healthy people were suddenly and for no discernible reason gripped first by severe feverish sensations in the head and by redness and inflammation of the eyes. Inside the head, the throat and tongue were swollen with blood, and breathing was irregular and foul-smelling. These symptoms were followed by sneezing and hoarseness, after which the affliction descended into the chest, accompanied by severe coughing. When the disease took hold

in the stomach, there ensued heaving and the vomiting of every bilious substance ever given a name by physicians, and all this with terrible distress. In
most people, there ensued a dry retching that gave way to severe convulsions,
in some cases right after the retching abated and in others much later. The skin
was not particularly hot to the touch, nor was it pale; it was a reddish blue and
was broken out in small pimples and sores. Their innards, however, burned so
much that they could not endure having the thinnest garments or linens thrown
on them, nor anything but to be completely naked, and what they wanted most
was to throw themselves into cold water. And indeed many of those who were
unattended ran off to wells and cisterns and actually did so, in the grip of an un-
quenchable thirst. Their condition remained the same, however, no matter how
much or how little they drank. In addition, they were beset by continual in-
somnia and restlessness. The body did not waste away during the time that the
disease was at its height; on the contrary, it unexpectedly withstood the ordeal,
with most people dying on the sixth or the eighth day as a result of the internal
fever, even though they still retained some strength. If they escaped death then,
though, the disease descended into the bowels, where it produced severe ul-
cerations followed by a liquid diarrhea, which so weakened them that most later
died from it. Thus the disease ran its course through the whole body after beginning at the top and firmly planting its illness first in the head, and if anyone
survived the most serious stages, it still left its mark by spreading to the body's
extremities, attacking the genitals, fingers, and toes. Many of those who survived
lost these, and some also lost their eyes.[3]

50. As soon as they recovered, some were afflicted with a total amnesia
and failed to recognize either their friends or themselves. You see, the shapes
the plague took were greater than the mind could frame. Not only did it attack
each person with symptoms more powerful than the human constitution could
endure, but in this respect in particular it showed that it was a different kind of
thing from any ordinary disease: many bodies were left unburied, but the birds
and four-footed animals that feed on human corpses either did not approach the
bodies or died if they did eat them. The proof of this is that there was a notable
absence of carrion-eating birds: they were nowhere to be seen, not around the
corpses or anywhere else. Dogs, however, who live among people, provided a
better chance to see what happened to animals that ate the dead.

51. On the whole, then, this was the course of the disease, though I have
omitted many peculiarities that may have occurred from case to case. During
this time, none of the usual illnesses troubled people, and if it did, it developed
into this one.[4]

Some died in neglect, others while being fully cared for. There was not a
single remedy to speak of that could be applied to bring relief, because what
helped some, harmed others. No body type, whether weak or strong, stood out
for its ability to withstand it; the disease carried off all alike regardless of the reg-
imen they followed. The most awful thing of all was the despair of those who
realized that they were sick, because their attitudes immediately became hopeless. They stopped resisting and were much more inclined to give themselves
up for lost. Furthermore, when people attended to each other, they became infected and died like cattle. This is what did the greatest damage. Either people
stayed away from one another out of fear and perished alone (and many house-

---

3. It is not clear how these were "lost"—perhaps by amputation, even self-mutilation.
4. This disease has been identified as smallpox, plague, and typhus, all of which have symptoms resembling
those described by Thucydides. It is most likely, though, that the agent that caused the illness has either
significantly mutated or disappeared in the past 2,400 years.

holds were left empty for want of any one to care for the sick) or they consorted with each other and died, especially those who made some claim to merit. These people were too embarrassed not to expose themselves by visiting their friends, since in the end even relatives were exhausted by the constant laments for the dying and were defeated by all the woe. Those who had escaped the disease, however, had the most pity on those who were suffering and dying, because they knew what the pain was like and because they were now full of confidence.[5] You see, the disease did not attack the same person twice, at least not so as to kill him. So these people were congratulated by the others, and in the jubilance of the moment held the vain belief that they would never die from any other disease in the future either.

52. The basic calamity of the disease itself was aggravated by the crowding of people from the country into the city—especially the newcomers. It was summer, they lived in stifling huts because they had no homes of their own, and the death rate was completely out of control. The dead had fallen on top of one another in their death-throes, after rolling around half-dead in the streets and near every spring in their desperate desire for water. The temples, in which they had pitched tents, were full of corpses because they died even there. Not knowing what was to become of them and completely overwhelmed by the illness, people lost respect for the sacred and the secular alike. All the burial customs they used to observe were thrown into confusion and they buried their dead as best they could. Many resorted to sacrilegious burial methods for want of appropriate ones, because of the many who had already died in their families. For example, they got a head start on people who had built funeral pyres by lighting them and piling on their own dead first, or they would throw the corpse they were carrying onto one that was already burning and go away.

53. In addition to this, the plague initiated a more general lawlessness in the city. People dared to indulge more openly in their secret pleasures when they saw the swift change from well-being to sudden death, and from not having anything to immediately inheriting the property of the dead. As a result, they decided to go for instant gratifications that tended to sensuality because they regarded themselves and their property as equally short-lived. No one was willing to persevere in received ideas about "the good" because they were uncertain whether they would die before achieving it. Whatever was pleasurable, and whatever contributed to pleasure, wherever it came from, that was now the good and the useful. Fear of the gods? The laws of man? No one held back, concluding that as to the gods, it made no difference whether you worshipped or not since they saw that all alike were dying; and as to breaking the law, no one expected to live long enough to go to court and pay his penalty. The far more terrible verdict that had already been delivered against them was hanging over their heads—so it was only natural to enjoy life a little before it came down.

54. Into this misery the Athenians had fallen, and in it they suffered, with people dying inside the walls and the land outside being laid waste. In the midst of this affliction, the older men naturally remembered the following verse, which, they alleged, used to be chanted in the old days: "A Dorian war will come, and with it, plague." People argued, however, over whether the ancients had specified "plague" in the verse or "famine," but under the circumstances, "plague" of course won out. People shaped their memories to their suffering. I suspect, though, that if there is ever another Dorian war after this one and there

---

5. The implication is that their pity was genuine because it was untinged by embarrassment or shame.

happens to be a famine, they will most likely be chanting it that way.[6] Those who knew it also remembered the Spartan oracle, in which the god answered in response to the question whether they should go to war, that victory would be theirs if they fought with all their might, and that he himself would take their side.[7] People compared the facts with the oracle and found them to agree: the plague began right after the Peloponnesians had invaded; the plague did not penetrate the Peloponnese in any way worth mentioning; it spread through Athens especially and then through the most populous areas of other regions. These, then, were the things that happened during the plague.

55. After the Peloponnesians had deforested the plain, they advanced into the coastal area known as the Paralus as far as Laurium, where the Athenian silver mines are. They first slashed and burned the part of this region that faces the Peloponnese and then the part that faces Euboea and Andros. Pericles, who was still general, implemented the same strategy as he had during the first invasion, of not letting the Athenian army march out to meet them.[8]

56. While the Peloponnesians were still in the plain, and before they entered the coastal region, Pericles began to prepare an attack force of a hundred ships against the Peloponnese, and it set off as soon as it was ready. He had brought four thousand Athenian hoplites and three hundred cavalry in horse transports converted, for the first time, from old ships.[9] They were accompanied by Chians and Lesbians in fifty ships. When this Athenian force set out, it left the Peloponnesians behind in the coastal region of Attica. When they reached Epidaurus in the Peloponnese, they slashed and burned much of the land and then attacked the city. They had brief hopes of capturing it, but without success. They withdrew from Epidaurus and devastated Troezen, Halieis, and Hermione, all on the Peloponnesian coast. After leaving those places, they went to Prasiae, a fortified Laconian coastal town, scorched the earth around it, and then captured and plundered the town. After completing these actions, they returned home. On arrival, they found that the Peloponnesians had withdrawn and were no longer in Attica.

57. For as long as the Peloponnesians were on Athenian soil and the Athenian fleet was cruising, the plague continued to kill Athenians in both the army and the city; and it has even been said that the Peloponnesians, for fear of the illness, left the region sooner than planned when they learned from deserters that it was in the city. (They could verify this by the smoke from the funeral pyres.) Nevertheless, they remained for the longest time ever on this invasion and devastated land throughout the region. They were in Attica for approximately forty days.

58. That same summer, Hagnon, son of Nicias, and Cleopompus, son of Clinias, who had been elected generals along with Pericles, relieved Pericles of the force he had just commanded and immediately advanced on the Chalcidians near Thrace and on Potidaea, which was still under siege. When they arrived at Potidaea, they brought siege engines against it and tried to take it by every means possible. They were, however, unable to achieve the capture of the town or do anything else worthy of the forces they had at their disposal. This was

---

6. The Greek words for "plague" and "famine" are *loimos* and *limos*, respectively.
7. See 1.88. Apollo, the god in question, would have played his part by inflicting the plague on Sparta's enemies. See also the first book of Homer's *Iliad*, in which Apollo afflicts the Greeks at Troy with a plague because the Greek commander Agamemnon has insulted one of his priests.
8. The second Spartan invasion was more thorough than the first. This time, the army entered the Athenian plain, as they had not in the first invasion, and by advancing toward Laurium, they threatened the silver mines that were a major source of Athens' wealth.
9. Aristophanes makes comic capital of the notion of horses on shipboard in *Knights* 595–610.

because the plague broke out there too, completely overwhelming the Athenians and devastating the army. Even the force already in place, which had formerly been healthy, caught the disease from the Athenians in Hagnon's command. (Phormio and his sixteen hundred men were no longer around Chalcidice.) Hagnon returned to Athens with his ships, having lost one thousand and fifty of his four thousand hoplites to the plague in approximately forty days. The original army remained in place and continued to besiege Potidaea.

59. After the second Peloponnesian invasion, the Athenians, their land ravaged for the second time and beset by both war and plague, had a change of heart. They blamed Pericles for persuading them to go to war and for bringing these hardships on them. They were eager to come to terms with the Spartans and even sent some ambassadors to Sparta, but to no avail. And now, desperate, they put tremendous pressure on Pericles. He saw how furious they were over their situation and how they were behaving in every way as he had expected, and since he was still a general, he called for a meeting of the assembly. He wanted to rally them, to soften their angry feelings, and to make them less afraid. He came forward and spoke as follows.

60. I expected that these signs of your anger would be directed against me, and I know the reasons for them.[1] That is why I have called for this assembly—to refresh your memories and to reproach *you* should it turn out that you are misguided in being angry at me or in giving way to your misfortunes. I believe that a city that is on the whole well governed benefits individual citizens more than one in which individual citizens do well while the city collectively staggers and falls. A man who does very well for himself will ultimately be ruined by the destruction of his city; but he has a much better chance of surviving his own bad luck in a successful city. Since, then, a city is able to carry individual misfortunes—something a single individual cannot do for the city—wouldn't it be better for all of us to defend her instead of what you are doing now? For, driven to distraction by the calamities in your homes, you are casting aside the safety of the whole and are holding me, who counseled war, and yourselves, who agreed with me, responsible. When you get angry at me, it is at the sort of man who, as well as any other, knows what must be done and how to put it into words, a man who is both patriotic and uninterested in money. The man who has ideas but can't teach them might as well not have any at all. The one who has both abilities but is disloyal won't say what is good for the city. If he is also patriotic but can be bought off, he will sell it all for the right price. So if you considered me to have these abilities to even a slightly greater degree than others when you were persuaded to go to war, it would be unfair for me now to bear the blame for having done you wrong.

61. It is, surely, folly for those who have a choice and who are in other respects well off to go to war. If, however, they either had to immediately give in and submit to their neighbors or prevail by taking risks, then the one who fled danger is more blameworthy than the one who stood his ground. I remain the same; I have not changed my position.[2] It is you who have changed. What has happened is that you listened to me when you were unharmed and have changed your minds now that you are in a bad way. Your irresolution makes the policy I advocated seem wrong, because grief has taken hold of your objectivity and you are yet to see the realization of its benefits, and because the great change that has befallen you in

1. Cf. 1.140.
2. Cf. 1.140 and 2.13.

a short time has weakened your determination to persevere in your decision. The will is enslaved by sudden and unexpected events, events completely beyond our calculation. More than anything else, the plague has
done this to you. Nevertheless, you live in a great city and have been
brought up with habits corresponding to its greatness. You must willingly
hold out in the greatest misfortunes and not tarnish the city's reputation.
(After all, people think it is equally right to condemn whoever falls short
of his reputation out of cowardice and to hate whoever reaches for a reputation he doesn't deserve out of arrogance.) You must put aside your private sorrow and strive to save the state.

62. Now as to the war effort, that it would be onerous and that we
would still not win—you must be satisfied from the speeches I frequently
gave on other occasions that your fears about that were unfounded. But I
want to make this clear too. It has to do with the greatness of your empire.
I think you never had any idea of it before, and I never revealed it in my
previous speeches. Nor would I now, since it involves a claim that is a bit
boastful, if I didn't see you so unreasonably frightened out of your wits. You
see, you think that you just rule over your allies. But I tell you that of the
two realms open to man's use, the land and the sea, you are the lords and
masters of all of the latter—of as much as you now control and of as much
more as you may want, because given your current naval resources, there
is no one, not the Great King or any other people on earth, who can stop
you from sailing where you please. Thus this sea power is a far greater thing
than your lands and your farms, whose loss you think is so terrible. We
ought not to trouble ourselves about them or take them any more seriously
than gardens or the ornaments of wealth in comparison with this power.
And freedom—we must know that if we cling to our freedom and win
through to safety, we will easily recover these trifles, but that if you submit
to others, even what you already have will tend to wither away. We must
not be inferior to our fathers in both realms, land and sea—our fathers,
who did not inherit them from others but who took them, won through,
and handed them down to you. It is more disgraceful to be stripped of what
you have than to be unlucky about getting what you want, so go and grap-
ple with your enemies not just with spirit, but with a spirit of contempt. A
lucky stupidity breeds boastfulness in cowards; contempt belongs to those
who can trust in their strategy to triumph over their enemies, as you can.
When the chances are even on both sides, intelligence makes for a surer
daring when combined with a sense of superiority. Intelligence trusts less
to hope, which is powerful only in desperate straits, than to a strategy based
on facts, and this is the source of a firm foreknowledge.

63. It is right that you uphold the honor the city gets from its empire—honor in which we all take pride—and that you either not run away
from the effort involved or stop pursuing the honor. You must also stop
thinking that you are fighting about just one thing: freedom versus slavery.
It is also about the loss of the empire and about the danger you are in from
being hated because of that empire. You can no longer detach yourselves
from it, just in case anyone, from fear of the present crisis, makes a manly
virtue of staying home and minding his own business. You hold your empire like a tyranny by now. Taking it is thought to have been criminal; letting it go would be extremely dangerous. The do-nothings I referred to
would quickly destroy a city, either by influencing others or by somehow
going off and living on their own. An easygoing man is only protected if he
marches beside a man of action. The safety of slavery is convenient in a
subject city, but not in an imperial one.

64. Don't be led astray by these citizens, and don't be angry with me, with whom you joined in voting for war, just because our enemies attacked and did what they naturally would when you refused to submit to them. Over and above what we foresaw has come this plague, the only thing that has occurred that has been, in fact, beyond our expectation. I know that it is largely because of this that I am hated, unjustly I believe—unless, of course, you have an equally unexpected success and then give me credit for it. No, we must bear acts of god with fortitude and acts of war with courage. This attitude used to be part of the ethos of this city; don't let it come to an end in you. Bear in mind that we have the highest reputation in the whole world for not giving in to misfortune, for having lost the greatest number of lives and endured the greatest hardships in war, and for having acquired the greatest power so far. And even if we eventually have to relinquish some of that power (for after all, there is a natural tendency for all things to decay), we will have left behind the memory that we were the Greeks who ruled over the greatest number of Greeks, that we fought the greatest wars against enemies coming singly and together, and that we inhabited what was in every way the greatest and the richest city on earth. True enough, the do-nothing will disapprove of this; but the man of action will want to emulate it, and those who do not equal our achievements will envy us. To be hated and envied for a time is the lot of everyone who dares to rule over others, but whoever incurs envy in a great cause has made the right choice. Hatred can't survive for long, and present splendor is passed on as eternally remembered fame. It is your duty to throw yourselves into achieving the glory to come and avoiding disgrace in the here and now. Do not negotiate with the Spartans. Do not show that you are disheartened by your present suffering. For city and citizen alike, those whose minds are least saddened by misfortune, and who take action against it, are the strongest.

65. With these words, Pericles tried to deflect the Athenians' anger from himself and to divert their minds from their fears. For their part, they took his advice as far as public policy was concerned. They no longer sent ambassadors to Sparta, and they redirected their energies to the war. Privately, they constantly felt the pain of their sufferings, the common people because they were being stripped of the little they had to begin with, and the rich and powerful because their fine country property, their houses and expensive belongings, were being destroyed. Worst of all, they were not at peace, but at war. And in fact the people did not abate their anger towards Pericles before they levied a monetary fine on him.[3] As the masses have a way of doing, though, they not much later re-elected him general and entrusted the leadership of the government to him. They did so because everyone was by now becoming inured to his personal pain, and because they thought that Pericles was the ablest man for what the city as a whole needed. For as long as he led the city in peacetime, he governed it with moderation and unfailingly maintained its security. Athens was at its greatest in his time. After the war broke out, he showed himself here too to be

3. Although Thucydides does not say so explicitly, plainly Pericles was removed from office. Athenians had no qualms about deposing officials who had displeased them. No formal charge was necessary; such removal could be accomplished by a simple vote of no confidence. Normally, removed officials were then tried on criminal charges. Frequently, as in the case of Pericles, these attacks were politically motivated. During the Peloponnesian War, complete or abortive impeachments are reported by Thucydides for Xenophon, Hestiodorus, and Phanomachus, who accepted the surrender of Potidaea in 430/29; Sophocles, Pythodorus, and Eurymedon, who returned unsuccessful from Sicily in 424; Thucydides himself in 423 after the loss of Amphipolis; Alcibiades in the religious scandals of 415; and several people in the civil strife of 411/410. Xenophon reports additional cases, one involving Alcibiades and one entailing the eight generals in command at Arginusae in 406.

a good judge of the city's power. He lived for another two and a half years, and after he died,[4] his prescience about the war was even more fully understood. He had said that they would prevail by being patient, by building their navy, by not trying to expand their empire during the war, and by not putting the city in jeopardy. In every respect, however, the Athenians did just the opposite, and in matters that seemed to be unrelated to the war, they followed a policy that was advantageous to private interests and ambitions but harmful to the city and its allies. When it worked, it brought prestige and profit to private citizens; when it failed, it damaged the city and the war effort. The reason for the change is that when Pericles was in power, his popularity, his intellect, his conspicuous imperviousness to bribes gave him free rein to bridle the majority. He was not led by it, he led it, because he was not always trying to acquire power improperly, by saying just anything to please the people; he could contradict them and even make them angry, because his prestige gave him power. Indeed, whenever he saw that they were rashly about to do something flagrantly premature, he would give a speech and whip them into a panic; but then when they were irrationally frightened, he would restore their confidence. In its rhetoric, Athens was becoming a democracy; in practice it was the domain of its foremost man. Its later leaders, all on an equal footing with one another, yet each striving to be pre-eminent, began to surrender even policy-making to the whims of the people. As a result, a great many things went wrong, as they would in a powerful city with an empire. The biggest mistake, the Sicilian expedition, was not so much an error of judgment about those whom they were attacking, as the failure of those who ordered the expedition to make the right additional decisions to support their men abroad. Instead, in their personal machinations for the leadership of the people, they blunted the edge of the fighting force and introduced civil strife by quarreling among themselves. After the disaster in Sicily, involving the loss of the subsequent reinforcements and of most of the navy, and with the city by now in turmoil, the Athenians nevertheless held out for three years[5] against not only their original enemies but also against the Sicilians who were now allied with them; against their own allies, most of whom had rebelled; and later against the King's son, Cyrus, who gave the Peloponnesians money for a navy. Furthermore, they did not surrender until they had succumbed to their private quarrels and destroyed themselves. That is how much reason Pericles had for predicting that Athens would easily defeat the unaided Peloponnesians in the war.

66. That same summer,[6] the Spartans and their allies sent a fleet of one hundred ships against the island of Zacynthus, which lies off Elis. The Zacynthians are Achaean colonists from the Peloponnese and had joined in the fighting on Athens' side. There were one thousand Spartan hoplites aboard, with Cnemus, a Spartan admiral, in command. They made a landing and ravaged most of the land. They returned home when the Zacynthians would not come to terms.

67. At the end of that summer Aristeus, a Corinthian, and the Spartan ambassadors Aneristus, Nicolaus, and Pratodamus, along with Timagoras, a Tegean, and Pollis, an Argive acting on his own, were traveling through Asia to see the King about whether they could persuade him to provide them with money and to join the war on their side.[7] They went, first, to the court of Sital-

---

4. Pericles died of the plague in the summer of 429.
5. This number has been emended to "six" or "eight" by most editors, depending on their views about the order of the composition of the history and about how this passage should be read. If it is taken as meaning that the Athenians held out for three years after the intervention of Cyrus, it may be correct.
6. I.e., 430.
7. This story is told by Herodotus 7.137.

ces, son of Teres, in Thrace, aiming to persuade him, if they could, to break away from the Athenian alliance and to relieve Potidaea, which was being besieged by an Athenian army. From Thrace they intended, with Sitalces' help, to make their way across the Hellespont to Pharnaces, son of Pharnabazus, who was going to send them on to the King.[8] As it happened, the Athenian ambassadors Learchus, son of Callimachus, and Ameiniades, son of Philemon, were also visiting Sitalces, and they urged his son, Sadocus, who had become an Athenian citizen,[9] to turn the Peloponnesians over to them, to prevent them from making their way to the King and thereby doing great harm to his adoptive city. Sadocus agreed and had the Peloponnesians arrested as they were making their way through Thrace to the ship in which they intended to cross the Hellespont. They were taken before they could get aboard by some men Sadocus had sent along with Learchus and Ameiniades, and in accordance with Sadocus' orders, they handed them over to the Athenians. The Athenians took them into custody and brought them to Athens. When they arrived, the Athenians feared that Aristeus might escape and do them yet more harm. After all, it had been he who had brought about all the earlier events in Potidaea and the Chalcidic peninsula.[1] And so, without a trial (though there were some things the prisoners wanted to say), the Athenians killed all of them on that same day and threw their bodies into a ravine. They thought that it was right to protect their interests with the same kind of action the Spartans had initiated, when they seized Athenian and allied merchants as they sailed their trading vessels around the Peloponnese and then killed them and threw them into ravines. At the beginning of the war, the Spartans killed as enemies whoever they captured at sea, whether they were neutrals or fighting for Athens.

68. At about the same time at the end of that summer, the Ambraciots raised a large force of barbarians and campaigned with them against Amphilochian Argos[2] and the rest of Amphilochia. Their hatred of the Argives began in the following way: Amphilochus, son of Amphiareus, founded Amphilochian Argos and the rest of Amphilochia (which are around the Ambracian Gulf) after he returned home from the Trojan War and was dissatisfied with conditions in Argos. He named it after his homeland, Argos. This city was the largest in Amphilochia and had the most powerful settlers. Hard-pressed during a troubled period many generations later, the Argives brought their neighbors, the Ambraciots, into Argos as co-colonists. Their present language began to be Hellenized as a result of this political union with the Ambraciots. The other Amphilochians are barbarians: they do not speak Greek.[3] In time, the Ambraciots expelled the Argives and took control of the city. After this happened, the Amphilochians submitted to the authority of the Acarnanians, and together they called in the Athenians, who sent them thirty ships under the command of Phormio. After Phormio arrived, they captured Argos in very hard fighting and sold the Ambraciots into slavery, whereupon Amphilochians and Acarnanians jointly settled the city. After this, the alliance between the Acarnanians and the Athenians was begun.[4] The hatred of the Ambraciots for the Argives began with the enslavement of their people. Later, in the present war, they

---

8. Pharnabazus was the Persian satrap (governor) for the Hellespontine region.
9. Cf. 2.29, also Aristophanes, *Acharnians*, 145–7.
1. See 1.60–65.
2. The reader should bear in mind that Amphilochian Argos was in northwest Greece. It is different from the more powerful and better-known Argos of the Peloponnese.
3. This more than implies that Thucydides believed that the "Argives" who fought in the Trojan War did not speak Greek, and that they later learned Greek from Dorians like the Ambraciots.
4. These events may have taken place in the 450s or 440s.

formed the abovementioned army made up of themselves, Chaonians, and some of their other barbarian neighbors.[5] They marched on Argos, took control of the countryside, and attacked but were unable to capture the city. They returned home and disbanded into their respective tribes.

These are the events that took place that summer.

69. The following winter, the Athenians sent twenty ships around the Peloponnese with Phormio in command. He headquartered at Naupactus and set up a blockade to prevent anyone from sailing either into or out of Corinth and the Crisaean Gulf.[6] They sent another six ships to Caria and Lycia with Melesander in command to levy money and to keep Peloponnesian pirates from setting out from there to destroy merchant shipping from Phaselis, Phoenicia, and the mainland thereabouts. While going upcountry into Lycia with an army made up of Athenians from the ship's crews and of allied forces, Melesander was killed and a portion of his army wiped out after being defeated in battle.

70. That same winter, the besieged Potidaeans were able to hold out no longer. The Peloponnesian invasion of Attica had failed to draw the Athenians away from the siege. The food in Potidaea had run out and on top of everything else, the want of food had forced some of them even to eat each other. As a result, they proposed talks about surrender to Xenophon, son of Euripides[7]; Hestiodorus, son of Aristocleides; and Phanomachus, son of Callimachus, the Athenian generals assigned to the siege. They accepted, in view of the hardships their army suffered in that wintry place and of the cost, by now, to Athens of two thousand talents for the siege. The Potidaeans agreed to the following terms. They, their women, their children, and their allies would be allowed to leave with one outer garment—the women with two—and with a stipulated amount of silver for traveling expenses. The Potidaeans left under a truce and went to Chalcidice or wherever they could, but the Athenians faulted the generals for coming to terms without their authorization, thinking that they could have taken the city on whatever terms they wished. Later the Athenians sent their own colonists to Potidaea and settled the place. These are the events that occurred that winter, and the second year of the war that I, Thucydides, wrote down came to an end.

71. The following summer, the Peloponnesians and their allies did not invade Attica. Instead, they attacked Plataea under the command of Archidamus, son of Zeuxidamus and king of Sparta. They took up their positions and were about to ravage the land, but the Plataeans immediately sent envoys to Archidamus saying: "Archidamus! Men of Sparta! What you are doing by invading Plataean soil is unjust, and unworthy of you and of the fathers who begot you. When Pausanias the Spartan, son of Cleombrotus, freed Greece from the Persians with the Greeks who willingly shared with him the danger of the battle that took place on our land, he performed sacrifices to Zeus the Emancipator in the agora of Plataea. He convened all the allies and restored autonomy to the Plataeans on their lands and in their city.[8] No one would be allowed to attack us, certainly not to enslave us. If they did, all the allies present would defend us with all their power. Your fathers promised this to us because of our courage and our zeal in those perilous times. But now you are doing just the opposite! For you and our worst enemies, the Thebans, have come here to enslave us! We call on the gods who witnessed those oaths, on the gods of your fathers, on the gods of our

---

5. The summer of 430.
6. Thucydides' regular name for the Gulf of Corinth. Naupactus is at the entrance to the gulf.
7. Not the playwright Euripides but another Athenian of the same name.
8. This is the Pausanias discussed by Thucydides at 1.94–96 and 1.128–34.

homeland, and say to you: do not violate Plataean soil and break your oaths. Allow us to live in freedom in accordance with the declaration of Pausanias."

72. After they said this, Archidamus summarily replied: "What you Plataeans say is just, but your deeds must conform to your words. That is, according to what Pausanias granted you, you should govern yourselves and join us in freeing the others who, though sharing the dangers of that time and taking that oath with you, are now subject to the Athenians. This army exists and this war is taking place to free them and the other Greeks. It would be best if you shared in that effort and abided by the oaths yourselves. If not, do as we proposed earlier and be on neither side. Receive both sides in friendship into your city and be at war with neither. That would be enough for us."[9]

That is what Archidamus said. The Plataean envoys heard him out and returned to the city, where they made known to the people what he had said. Then they answered Archidamus that because their wives and children were in Athens, it was impossible for them to do as he had earlier proposed without first consulting with the Athenians. They were also afraid for their city, because after the Spartans withdrew, the Athenians might come and refuse to permit their neutrality. Either that, or the Thebans, who would be included in the oath "to receive both sides," would once again attempt to capture the city.[1]

Archidamus reassured them in this regard and said: "Surrender the city and your homes to us Spartans. Show us the boundaries of your land. Count up your fruit trees and, as far as possible, make an inventory of everything else you own. Then withdraw to wherever you like for as long as the war lasts. When it is over, we will give you back what we have taken. Until then, we will keep it in trust, working your land and making whatever payments you deem appropriate."

73. The envoys heard him out and once again returned to the city, and after consulting with the people, they answered that they wanted to inform the Athenians of his offer. If they could persuade the Athenians, they would do it. Until then, they called on the Spartans to enter a truce with them and not ravage their land. Archidamus agreed to a truce to last enough days for them to travel back and forth, and he did not ravage the land. The envoys went to Athens, and after deliberations with them, returned to deliver the following message to the people in the city: "The Athenians say that in the time we have been allies, they have never in any way allowed you to be wronged and that they will not permit it now. They will support us with all their strength. They enjoin you, by the oaths our fathers swore, not to make any changes in our alliance."

74. After the ambassadors relayed this message, the Plataeans decided not to betray the Athenians, but to endure the sight of their land being ravaged, if necessary, and whatever other sufferings might befall them. No one was to leave the city; they were to answer from the city wall that it was not possible for them to comply with the Spartan offer. After they gave this answer, the first thing King Archidamus did was to then and there call the local gods and heroes[2] to witness, saying: "O you gods and heroes who protect Plataean soil, be witnesses that it is not unjustly but only after the Plataeans first forsook our sworn confederacy that we have come upon this soil on which our fathers, invoking you, defeated Persia, and which you vouchsafed to the Greeks as a propitious battlefield. Nor

---

9. Thucydides never mentions when Archidamus made his previous offer.
1. Cf. 2.2–7.
2. In addition to a variety of gods, Greeks also worshiped figures they called heroes, who occupied a status somewhere between human and divine. Men (and sometimes women) who were believed to have performed great services to a particular state in the (usually distant) past were frequently revered as benefactors and granted sanctuaries and sacrifices similar to those accorded to gods.

shall we be doing wrong now if we take action, for we have made many reasonable offers without success. Be disposed to sanction the punishment of those who first began the crime and the receipt of retribution for those who inflict that punishment lawfully."

75. After this invocation of the gods, Archidamus put troops into action and, so that the Plataeans could not get out, built a palisade around the town with the fruit trees he had cut down. He then began to pile a ramp up against the city wall, expecting that he would quickly capture the town with an army the size of his at work. Then, with the wood they cut down from Mount Cithaeron, they started to build a structure on both sides of the ramp by placing wood in a latticework to serve as a reinforcement and to keep the earth from sliding down its sides. They piled brushwood, stones, and earth onto the ramp and anything else that would do the job. They piled up this ramp for seventy days and nights continuously, working in shifts so that while some carried material, others ate and slept.[3] Spartan commanders set over troops from each of the cities forced the men on. The Plataeans saw that the ramp was rising and built a wooden framework and set it up on their wall where the attack ramp was being built. Then they filled in the framework with bricks taken from nearby houses. The wooden framework held the structure snug so that it would not weaken as it was built higher, and a covering of raw and tanned hides was hung in front of it to keep the workers and the wood from being struck by burning arrows. The wall kept getting higher, but the ramp went up just as fast. Then the Plataeans got the idea of breaking through the city wall where the ramp abutted it and sapping the earth out from within the ramp.

76. When the Peloponnesians realized what was happening, they wrapped mud up in reed mats and threw them into the hole so that they could not be carried away, as the earth had been, to produce a cave-in. Stymied, the Plataeans ended this operation and after making careful calculations, began to dig a tunnel under the city wall and the ramp and then, tunneling up, once again started carrying earth out of the ramp and into the city. The Spartans did not notice this for quite some time, so that though they kept piling earth onto the ramp, they made little progress because the ramp was being excavated out from under them and kept subsiding into the cavity. The Plataeans were still afraid that this would not be enough to allow them, who were so few, to hold out against so many, so they took this additional measure: they stopped work on the large structure opposite the ramp and began to build a crescent-shaped wall extending into the city from both sides of the ramp and beginning inside the city wall where it was at its lower height. Thus if the great wall was captured, they could hold the crescent wall and force their opponents to build another ramp and have the same problem all over again while trying this time to advance under attack from two sides.

In addition to building the ramp, the Peloponnesians brought battering rams against the city. One of them was moved up the ramp to the wall opposite and terrified the Plataeans when it knocked down a large part of it. Others battered the wall in other places, but the Plataeans threw lassoes around the front ends of the rams and yanked them up. The Plataeans also fashioned huge beams with long iron chains attached to either end. Then they fastened the chains to two other beams leaning against the walls, projecting beyond them like antennae, and pulled the first beam up to the top

---

3. Editors consider seventy days far too long. Thucydides said in 2.57 that forty days was the longest campaign in Attica. Suggested emendations have been nine days and seventeen days.

of the wall, between the projecting beams and transverse to the ram. Whenever the ram was about to strike the wall, they released the chains holding up the transverse beam, which then fell down onto the tip of the ram with such force that it broke it off.

77. Since the battering rams did no good and the ramp was neutralized by the opposite wall, the Peloponnesians at length decided that it was impossible to capture the city by these tactical methods. So they prepared for circumvallation and siege. First, though, they decided to see whether they could burn down the city, which was not very large, once the wind rose. They were trying to think of every way possible to take the city without the expense of a siege. First they carried bundles of brushwood up the ramp and threw them side by side into the space between the ramp and the wall. So many men were used that this space quickly filled up, and then they made more piles over as much of the rest of the city as they could reach from that height. Then they threw lighted torches, along with sulphur and pitch, on top of the bundles to set them on fire. This was the biggest man-made fire that anyone had ever seen up to that time, although in the mountains, of course, branches rubbed together by the wind have caught fire spontaneously and flamed up. But this was a huge fire, and the Plataeans, who had managed to escape from everything else, came within an inch of destruction. A large area within the city was unapproachable, and if a wind had risen and carried the flames into the city, as their enemies hoped, the Plataeans would not have escaped. It is now said that this also took place: it began to thunder and rain heavily, which extinguished the fire and thus put an end to the danger.

78. When this too failed, the Peloponnesians dismissed most of their army and began to build a circular wall around the city with the force that remained behind, dividing the work on the sections of the wall by city. There were trenches on either side of the wall, from which they made bricks. When everything was finished, at about the time of the rising of Arcturus,[4] they left sentries to guard half the wall (the other half was guarded by the Boeotians), and the army returned home and disbanded to their respective cities. The Plataean women, children, and elderly, as well as the rest of their population that was not fit for military service, had already been taken to Athens. Four hundred Plataean men had been left behind to endure the siege, along with eighty Athenians and one hundred ten women to bake and cook. This was the total when the siege began: there was no one else within the walls, slave or free.

That is how the siege of Plataea came about.

79. That same summer, at the same time as the attack on Plataea, when the grain was almost ripe, the Athenians attacked the Thracian Chalcidians and the Bottiaeans with two thousand of their own hoplites and two hundred cavalry. Xenophon, son of Euripides, was in command along with two other generals. When they reached Spartolus in Bottiaea, they destroyed the grain. They had thought that the city would be surrendered by agents working inside it, but opponents of surrender had sent to Olynthus for help, and a military force accompanied by hoplites arrived to guard the city. They marched out of Spartolus and fought the Athenians right in front of the city wall. The Chalcidian hoplites and some allies who were with them were defeated by the Athenians and withdrew into Spartolus, but the Chalcidian cavalry and light-armed troops defeated the Athenian light-armed troops and cavalry. Some peltasts, though not many, from the territory known as Crousis,

---

4. I.e., when Arcturus is visible before sunrise. This is about September 15.

were also involved in the fighting.[5] The battle had just ended when some peltasts from Olynthus came to the aid of the Spartolans. When the light-armed Spartolans saw them, they were greatly encouraged, as they were by their previous victory, and along with the Chalcidian cavalry and their new reinforcements, they once again attacked the Athenians, who fell back on the two companies they had left behind with the pack animals. Thereafter, whenever the Athenians attacked, the Chalcidians gave ground, and when-ever they withdrew, the Chalcidians bore down on them and pelted them with javelins. The Chalcidian cavalry charged and attacked them at will, and were absolutely terrifying, routing the Athenians and then pursuing them over a considerable distance. The Athenians fled to Potidaea and after later collecting their dead under a truce, they returned to Athens with their sur-viving army, having lost four hundred thirty men and all their generals. The Chalcidians and Bottiaeans erected a victory marker and dispersed to their cities after gathering their dead.

80. That same summer, not much later than the events described above, the Ambraciots and Chaonians, wanting to subdue all of Acarnania and wrest it from Athens, persuaded the Spartans to gather a naval force from its allies and to send one thousand hoplites against Acarnania.[6] They said that if they were supported by ships and infantry, they could keep the Acarnanians from sending aid inland from the coast, easily gain control of Acarnania, and then go on to conquer Zacynthus and Cephallenia. Furthermore, it wouldn't be as easy for the Athenians to sail around the Peloponnese; why, it might even be possible to capture Naupactus. The Spartans were persuaded and immediately sent Cne-mus, who was still admiral, and the hoplites in a few ships. They sent out word to ready the ships as quickly as possible and to sail to Leucas. The Corinthians especially shared in the enthusiasm of their colonists, the Ambraciots. The por-tion of the fleet that was to come from Corinth, Sicyon, and that region was in preparation; the portion from Leucas, Anactorium, and Ambracia reached Leu-cas and waited there. Unbeknownst to Phormio, who commanded the twenty Athenian ships that stood guard at Naupactus, Cnemus and the thousand ho-plites who were with him had made their way across and had immediately begun to prepare for the campaign on land. The Greeks who were with Cne-mus were Ambraciots, Leucadians, Anactorians, and the thousand Pelopon-nesians he himself had brought. There were a thousand Chaonian barbarians, who were not governed by a king but by Photys and Nicanor, members of the ruling family, who were governing as presidents for a term of one year. Thes-protians, who also have no king, joined the Chaonians in the campaign. The Molossians and Atintanians were led by Sabylinthus, regent for King Tharyps, who was still a child; and the Paravaeans were led by King Oroedus. There were one thousand Orestians, whose king was Antiochus. He had entrusted their command to Oroedus and they marched with the Paravaeans. Without the Athenians knowing it, Perdiccas also sent a thousand Macedonians, but they ar-rived too late.[7] Cnemus set out with this army without waiting for the ships from Corinth. They made their way through the Argive territory and plundered the unwalled town of Limnaea. They got as far as Stratus, the largest city in Acar-nania, and decided that if they took this city first, all the other towns would soon come over to their side.

---

5. Peltasts were lightly armed soldiers who could move quickly and were good for skirmishing.
6. See 2.68.
7. Perdiccas was supposed to be Athens' ally. See 2.29.

81. The Acarnanians saw that an army had invaded much of their land and knew that it was to be followed by a naval force. They did not, however, join in a common defense of Stratus. Instead, each region set up its own defense and sent word to Phormio demanding that he come to their aid. He said that he couldn't leave Naupactus undefended with a fleet about to set sail from Corinth. The Peloponnesians and their allies formed themselves into three divisions and advanced on Stratus with the aim of setting up camps near the city, so that they could go into action and attack the walls if negotiations failed. The Chaonians and the other barbarians approached the city at the center of the line. On their right were the Leucadians, Anactorians, and those who were with them, and on their left were Cnemus and his Peloponnesians, along with the Ambraciots. They were widely separated and sometimes couldn't even see each other. The Greeks approached in a defensive formation until they camped on favorable ground. The Chaonians, who were reputed by the mainlanders thereabouts to be the most warlike, were full of self-confidence and had no intention of joining the Peloponnesian camp. They thought that they and the other barbarians could rush forward, take the city by storm, and claim the victory for themselves. The Stratians saw that the Chaonians were still advancing and decided that if they could defeat the overexposed barbarians, the Greeks would not be as likely to attack them; so they laid ambushes around the city and when the barbarians were close enough, they charged out of the city and engaged them in hand-to-hand combat and fell on them from their ambushes. Many of the Chaonians were slaughtered in the ensuing panic, and when the other barbarians saw them giving up, they backed off and ran away. Neither of the Greek camps knew of the battle because the barbarians had pushed so far ahead; they thought the barbarians had hurried forward to set up camp. When the fleeing barbarians fell back on them, though, they took them in, drew the divisions together, and stayed put for the rest of the day. The Stratians did not advance and come to close quarters with them because the other Acarnanians had not yet sent aid. The Greeks were helpless because the Stratians, who are thought to be the best at this, used slings on them from a distance and it was impossible to move without armor.

82. Once night fell, Cnemus withdrew with his army on the double to the Anapus River, which is ten miles from Stratus. The next day, he gathered up his dead under a truce. The Oeniadae, who were friendly, came to his aid, and he retreated to their town before the Acarnanian reinforcements arrived. From there, the Peloponnesians all returned home. The Stratians set up a victory marker to commemorate their battle with the barbarians.

83. The fleet in the Crisaean Gulf from Corinth and the other allies, which was supposed to back up Cnemus and prevent aid from the coastal Acarnanians to the inlanders, did not, in fact, do so. On or about the day of the battle at Stratus, the fleet had been forced into a naval engagement with Phormio and his twenty Athenian ships standing guard off Naupactus. Phormio spotted them hugging the shore as they sailed out of the gulf, but waited to attack them in the open sea. The Corinthians and the other allies were not sailing in battle formation; they were equipped more like troop transports en route to Acarnania, and it never occurred to them that the Athenians, with twenty ships, would dare to give battle to their own forty-seven. But they saw that the Athenians were keeping pace with them along the opposite shore as they made headway on their side. They were also unable to slip their moorings unnoticed before dawn, when they started crossing over to the mainland opposite from Achaean Patras in the direction of Acarnania. Now they saw the Athenians coming at them from

Chalcis and the Evenus River, and by that time they had no choice but to fight in the middle of their passage. Their commanders came from the cities that had readied the ships; the Corinthian commanders were Machaon, Isocrates, and Agatharchidas. The Peloponnesians adopted a wheel-like formation, prows outward, sterns in, keeping as wide a space as possible between the ships without giving the enemy room to sail through. At the hub of the wheel were their accompanying small craft and their five fastest ships, at the ready so they could quickly sail out to wherever the enemy might approach.

84. The Athenians formed up in single file and kept rowing around them in a circle, gradually tightening the circle and shaving them ever closer as they gave the impression that they were about to ram them. Phormio had, however, given his men prior instructions that they were not to attack until he gave the signal. He expected that the Peloponnesians would not be able to remain in formation the way infantry can on land, but that the ships would drift into one another and the small craft would cause confusion; and if, as tended to happen at dawn, the wind were to rise and blow out of the gulf (which he was waiting for as he kept rowing in circles), the Peloponnesian formation would collapse in no time. He thought that the timing of the attack was up to him. He could make it whenever he wanted to because he had the better-manned, better-built ships, and the best time would be when the wind blew up.

The wind did in fact start to blow, and what with the small craft and the gusting winds, the Peloponnesian ships, already at close quarters, fell foul of each other. As sailors tried to push the colliding ships apart with boat hooks, shouting curses and warnings that nobody could hear any more than they could hear their coxswains or their orders from ship to ship, and as unskilled oarsmen—unable to lift their oars above the choppy waters—made their craft unresponsive to the helmsmen, at precisely that moment Phormio gave the signal and the Athenians attacked, first sinking one of the command ships and then destroying others wherever they went. Because of this confusion, the Peloponnesians were unable to put up any sort of fight at all and fled to Patras and Dyme in Achaea. The Athenians pursued them and captured twelve ships, taking most of their men prisoner, and then sailed to Molycrium. They erected a victory marker at Rhium and dedicated a ship to Poseidon, and then they returned to Naupactus. The Peloponnesians hurriedly sailed along the coast with the remainder of their ships from Dyme and Patras to the Elean dockyard at Cyllene. Cnemus and the ships from Leucas, which were supposed to rendezvous with the ships from Corinth, also made their way to Cyllene after the battle at Stratus.

85. The Spartans sent Timocrates, Brasidas, and Lycophron to Cnemus to advise him about the fleet and ordered them to prepare for another, more successful, battle and not to allow themselves to be kept off the sea by so few ships. Especially because it was the first naval battle of the war, this effort seemed to the Spartans extremely out of keeping with what they might reasonably expect. They did not believe their navy fell so far short of the Athenians'; there must have been cowardice. They failed to weigh Athens' long experience against their recent drills, and they were furious when they sent the advisers.[8] When the advisers reached Cnemus, they sent word to all the cities that they wanted more ships and then began to outfit the ones they had for a naval battle. Phormio sent messengers to Athens to brief them about the Peloponnesian

8. Cf. the contrasting views of the Corinthians and Pericles on the Peloponnesian and the Athenian navies at 1.121 and 1.142.

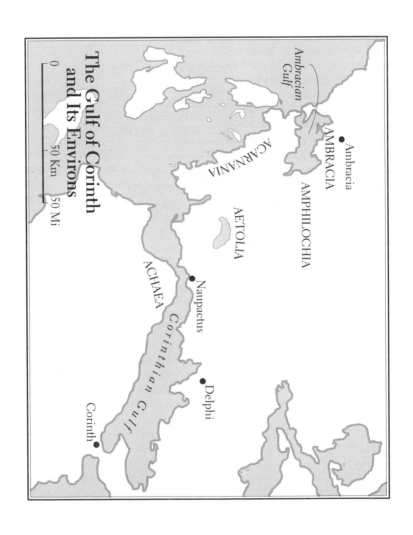

The Gulf of Corinth and Its Environs

0

50 Km

50 Mi

Ambracian Gulf

ACARNANIA

AMBRACIA

●Ambracia

AMPHILOCHIA

AETOLIA

ACHAEA

Naupactus●

Corinthian Gulf

●Delphi

Corinth●

preparations and to describe the battle they had won. He also urged them quickly to send him as many ships as possible, since he expected another battle from one day to the next. They sent him twenty ships, but they ordered their commander to go to Crete first. They did so because Nicias, a Cretan from Gortynia who was the Athenian proxenus there, had persuaded them to send a fleet against the hostile city of Cydonia by promising to win it over to their side. Nicias did this to oblige the Polichnitans, who bordered the Cydonians. So the commander took the ships, went to Crete, and, with the Polichnitans, ravaged the land of the Cydonians. But then he was prevented from sailing by adverse winds and lost a great deal of time.

86. While the Athenians were delayed at Crete, the Peloponnesians at Cyllene, having prepared their ships for warfare, coasted towards Panormus in Achaea where the Peloponnesian infantry had come up in support. Phormio was also sailing along the coast, to the headland of Rhium at Moly-crium, and he anchored off it with twenty ships—the same twenty with which he had just done battle. This Rhium was friendly to Athens; the other Rhium is on the opposite shore, in the Peloponnese. It is at the mouth of the Crisaean Gulf, and the two points are separated from each other by about a mile of water. When they saw the Athenians, the Peloponnesians also dropped anchor—at the Achaean Rhium, not far from Panormus, where their infantry was waiting for them. They had seventy-seven ships. They moored opposite each other for six or seven days, exercising and preparing for battle. The Peloponnesians, still fearful after their earlier disaster, were determined not to sail beyond Rhium into open water; the Athenians planned to avoid sailing into the narrows, thinking that fighting in a small space favored their opponents. At the end of this time, Cnemus, Brasidas, and the other Peloponnesian generals wanted to have the battle immediately, before any reinforcements arrived from Athens; so they called their troops together and, seeing that they were frightened and dispirited after their earlier defeat, they encouraged them and addressed them as follows:

87. Men of the Peloponnese! If any of you is afraid of the battle to come because of the one just past, that battle isn't really cause for fear. As you know, we were poorly equipped and we weren't sailing as a battle fleet but as a convoy. We also had a lot of bad luck going against us and maybe even some inexperience tripped us up here and there in our first naval battle. So we weren't defeated because of any cowardice, and it wouldn't be right for your courage to lose its edge when you weren't defeated in an all-out fight, but merely by the way things happened to develop.

You still have something to prove! You have to think that luck makes it possible for men to fail even while their spirits are always those of true men. And when the courage is there, it's not likely that anyone will use inexperience as an excuse to be a coward. You don't fall short in experience as much as you excel in daring. Their skill—which is what you're mostly afraid of—will do what it has been trained to do if it is coupled with courage and memory. But without courage, no skill can conquer danger. Fear blacks out memory and skill is useless without guts. Set your boldness against their experience. Set unlucky rigging as troop transports against any fear on account of that defeat. You have plenty of ships left over to fight with and hoplites to back you up on your home soil. Victory goes to the larger and better-prepared force most of the time. We can't find a single reason to think that we could fail, and even the mistakes we made then will work to our advantage as a lesson now.

So cheer up! You steersmen and you sailors, do your duty! Don't desert the posts that you have been assigned to! We have planned the attack a little better than your former commanders and haven't left anybody any room for cowardice. But if anybody wants it that way, he'll be punished accordingly, and the brave will be honored with the usual rewards for merit.

88. That is how their commanders exhorted the Peloponnesians. Phormio, too, was worried about the anxiety of his men, and when he saw that they were standing around in groups fearful of the number of Peloponnesian ships, he decided to call them together, build their confidence, and advise them about their situation. In the past, he had always told them, and prepared their minds to believe, that they could stand up to any such number of ships if it attacked them; and for the most part, it was an integral part of their self-esteem that they, as Athenians, would never give way before any rabble of Peloponnesian ships. This time, though, he saw that their spirits were sagging at the sight before them, and he wanted to remind them of their previous confidence. So he called the Athenians together and spoke as follows:

89. I have called you men together because I see that you are terrified of our enemies' numbers, and don't think that you should dread what isn't scary. In the first place, they have readied this hugely disproportionate number of ships because they have already been beaten and don't think they're your equals. Furthermore, as to their assumption that they are naturally courageous when they attack, the only grounds for their confidence is the fact that their skill as infantrymen lets them win most of the time. They think that same skill will have the same importance at sea, but if they possess skill on land, it rightly belongs to us here, and since they are in no way more courageous than we, we are stronger because we have more experience at sea than they do. The Spartans are in command because of their reputation, but they are leading the Peloponnesians into danger against their wills, since they wouldn't otherwise try another naval battle after having been so badly beaten. So don't you be afraid of this "boldness" of theirs. You give them much more and much better reason to be afraid because first, they've already been beaten, and second, they think you would not oppose them unless you were going to do something to offset their superior numbers. Most fighting men, like these here, attack with more confidence in their strength than in their strategy. When the outnumbered side fights without having to, they dare to stand up against the enemy because they trust their intelligence. The Spartans are trying to figure out what doesn't make sense to them, and this scares them more than if we were evenly matched! Many an army has been defeated by smaller ones because they weren't experienced enough. And some because they weren't bold enough! We are both bold and experienced. I won't fight the battle in the gulf if I can help it. I won't even sail into it. Don't worry. I know that the narrows isn't the right place for a few highly maneuverable ships with experienced crews to fight a lot of ships that don't know what they're doing. You wouldn't be able to ram them the way you had to if you couldn't see them all from a distance, and you wouldn't be able to back water when you were in trouble. You couldn't cut between them and wheel around, which is what highly maneuverable ships do. Instead, you'd have to turn your naval battle into a land battle, and in that kind of fight numerical superiority *is* better. I'll keep all this in mind as much as I can. You stand smartly by your ships on the beach and look sharp to obey your orders, especially since we'll be casting off soon. Most important—when

we're in battle, maintain good discipline and keep quiet. That's usually a good idea in any kind of battle, but especially in naval battles. And then let's beat them back the way we did before! This is an important battle for us. We'll either crush Sparta's hopes for a navy or bring closer to Athens the fear of what might come from the sea. Again, I remind you that you've already beaten most of these men, and that beaten men do not face the same danger with their former resolve.

90. That is how Phormio rallied his men.

When the Athenians did not sail into either the gulf or the narrows, the Peloponnesians decided to draw them in against their will. They cast off at dawn, sailing four abreast into the gulf along their own shore. They were arrayed just as they had lain at anchor, and their right wing led the way. The twenty fastest ships were positioned on the right, so that if Phormio thought that they were heading for Naupactus and should himself sail along the coast to its defense, the right wing could surround him and prevent him from sailing past them and escaping attack. As the Peloponnesians had expected, Phormio was alarmed when he saw that they were heading towards Naupactus, because the place was undefended. Against his will, he hastily manned his ships and sailed along the coast while the Messenian infantry kept pace beside him in support.[9] When the Peloponnesians saw that the Athenians were sailing in single file along the coast and that they were by now well within the gulf and close to shore, which is what they wanted above all, the signal was given and they suddenly turned and sailed, line abreast, straight at the Athenians as fast as they could, in the hope of capturing all the ships. The first eleven Athenian ships, however, slipped out into open sea and past the turning Peloponnesian right wing. The Spartans overtook the others as they tried to escape, though, and pushed them back against the shore and destroyed them. They killed all the Athenians who were not able to swim to safety. They attached ropes to some of the ships and began to tow them away empty (though one had been captured crew and all), but some of the supporting Messenians ran into the water with their armor on and boarded the ships. Fighting from the decks, they were able to recapture some ships that were already in tow.

91. The Peloponnesians, then, were victorious in this action and destroyed the Athenian ships. The twenty ships on the right wing, however, had started to pursue the eleven Athenian ships that had slipped out ahead of their turning maneuver into the open sea. All but one of the Athenian ships got ahead of them and escaped to safety at Naupactus. There they lined up near the temple of Apollo, bows facing the Peloponnesians, and prepared for defense in case they should sail towards shore against them. The Spartans soon approached and began to chant a song of victory as though they had already won. The single Athenian ship that had been left behind, however, was being pursued by a Leucadian ship far ahead of the others. By chance, there was a merchant ship anchored in the open water. The Athenian ship reached it first, rowed around it, rammed the middle of the pursuing Leucadian ship, and sank it. After this unexpected, incalculable event took place, panic gripped the Peloponnesians.

---

9. Phormio's plan had been based on the belief that the Peloponnesians wanted to sail through the narrows, out of the gulf, and towards Acarnania. Brasidas surprised him by heading for Naupactus, on the northeast coast *inside* the gulf. Phormio had to defend Naupactus, his main base, which meant sailing deeper into the gulf whether he wanted to or not. The Spartan plan, however, was not to actually attack Naupactus, but to lure Phormio in that direction and then to turn suddenly, trapping Phormio between the coast and their much larger number of ships. It was crucial for the Spartan right wing (right with respect to the Athenians, *not* the Spartans), to be fast enough to sail in front of Phormio, thus cutting him off and preventing his escape. As to the Messenian infantry, Thucydides has failed to mention them until now.

Also, because they had the upper hand, they had been pursuing the Athenians without any formation, and some of them dropped their oars into the water, wanting to slow their progress and wait for the others. This was a mistake, given the attackers nearby. Meanwhile, from inexperience, some of their ships ran aground in shallow water.[1]

92. The courage of the Athenians revived when they saw these events, and after hearing a single command, they started yelling and attacked the Spartans. Having made so many mistakes, and being all out of formation, the Peloponnesians did not wait long before turning towards their embarkation point at Panormus. The Athenians gave chase and captured the six closest ships and recovered the ships these had earlier disabled off the coast, tied up, and towed away. They killed some of the crews and held others for ransom. Aboard the sinking Leucadian ship that had been rammed near the merchantman, Timocrates, the Spartan captain, cut his own throat and washed ashore in Naupactus harbor. The Athenians withdrew and erected a victory marker at the spot from which they had set off to victory, and then they recovered the dead and the wreckage that were near their ships and returned what belonged to their enemies under a truce. The Peloponnesians also erected a victory marker, because they had been victorious in the turning maneuver by which they disabled the ships. Near the marker, they also dedicated the one ship they had captured at Rhium in Achaea. After this, for fear of the reinforcements from Athens, they all (except for the Leucadians) sailed back into the Crisaean Gulf and to Corinth under cover of darkness. The Athenians from Crete—with the twenty ships with which they should have joined Phormio before the battle—arrived at Naupactus not long after the retreat of these ships; and the summer came to an end.

93. At the beginning of winter,[2] before disbanding the fleet that had withdrawn to Corinth and the Crisaean Gulf, Cnemus, Brasidas, and the other Peloponnesian commanders decided, at the instigation of the Megarians, to make a bold attack on the Athenian port at Piraeus. The port was open and unguarded, understandably enough, given the overwhelming superiority of the Athenian navy. It was decided that each sailor should take his own oar, rower's mat, and oar-loop, and travel on foot from Corinth to the Athenian side of the Isthmus of Corinth. From there, they were to proceed on the double to Megara, launch forty ships that happened to be at the Megarian dockyards at Nisaea, and immediately set sail for the Piraeus. There were no ships on guard in it, since the Athenians never expected that the enemy would suddenly attack it in this way. They thought the Peloponnesians would not dare to launch an open attack. Also, if the enemy ever did take such an idea into their heads, their ships could not possibly go unnoticed. The Spartans acted on their decision immediately. They reached Nisaea at night, launched their ships, and set sail—but not for the Piraeus, as they had planned. They had become afraid of the danger, and it is also said that they were prevented from doing so by "adverse winds." Instead, they headed for the promontory on Salamis that faces Megara. There was a fort there and a guard of three ships to prevent anyone from sailing into or out of Megara. They made an assault on the fortress and towed away the triremes without their crews. Then they carried out a surprise attack on Salamis, which they plundered.

94. Warning fires were lit, and when they were seen at Athens, they caused a panic like no other in the whole war. People in the city thought

---

1. In this passage, Thucydides exemplifies chance, overconfidence, inexperience, and courage, all of which are the themes of the speeches that have gone before.
2. 429–428.

the enemy had already sailed into the Piraeus, while people in the Piraeus thought that Salamis had been captured and that they themselves were about to be attacked—which could very easily have happened if the Spartans had not shrunk from the danger, and no wind would have prevented it, either. Instead, at daybreak the Athenians reached the Piraeus en masse, hastily launched and manned the ships, and with much confusion set sail for Salamis. The infantry was ordered to stand guard at the Piraeus. When the Peloponnesians learned that help was on the way, they quickly sailed back to Nisaea after having rampaged through most of Salamis, capturing people and booty along with the three ships from the fortress at Budorum. They were also somewhat worried about their ships, which were no longer water-tight after having been beached for a long time before being launched. They did reach Megara, however, and made their way back to Corinth on foot. The Athenians, unable to catch them at Salamis, also sailed home. There-after they always maintained a guard at the Piraeus. They also closed off the harbor and took other necessary precautions.

95. At about the same time at the beginning of that winter, the Odrysian king of Thrace, Sitalces, son of Teres, attacked both the king of Macedonia, Perdiccas, son of Alexander, as well as the Thracian Chalcidians. He did it to collect on one promise and to keep another. Perdiccas had made him a promise on condition that he, Sitalces, make peace between him and the Athenians when he was hard pressed at the beginning of the war, and that Sitalces also not restore Perdiccas' hostile brother, Philip, to the throne. Perdiccas did not keep the promise.[3] As to the second promise, when Sitalces made his alliance with Athens, he agreed to put an end to the Thracian Chalcidians' hostilities against Athens. It was for these two reasons, then, that he launched his campaign. He brought along Amyntas, son of Philip, with the intent of making him king of Macedonia. He also brought some Athenian ambassadors who were with him concerning this very business, and he brought Hagnon as military adviser.[4] The Athenians were committed to accompany him against the Chalcidians with as many ships and men as possible.

96. Beginning with the Odrysians, Sitalces called up all the Thracians whom he ruled from the Haemus and Rhodope mountains seaward to the Eu-xine and the Hellespont. Next he levied the Getae and the other groups who are settled beyond the Haemus range in the regions south of the Ister towards the Euxine Sea. These people and the Getae border on the Scythians and they are similarly equipped: they are all mounted archers. He also called up many of the self-governing, mountain-dwelling and saber-carrying Thracians, most of whom live on the Rhodope Mountains and who are called the Dii. He per-suaded some of these people to come for pay; others followed him voluntarily. He also conscripted the Agrianians, the Laeaians, and whatever other Paeonian tribes he ruled over. These are the last of the peoples in his domains. His em-pire is bounded here by the Laeaian Paeonians and the Strymon River, which flows from Mount Scombrus through Agriania and Laeaea. Beyond that live the Paeonians, who are independent of his rule. In the direction of the Triballi, who are also independent, the Tilataeans and the Treres formed his boundary. These people live north of Mount Scombrus and extend westward as far as the Oscius River, which flows out of the same mountains as the Nestus and Hebrus

3. Thucydides does not say what the promise was. Cf. also 1.57, 2.29, and 2.100 below.
4. Cf. 2.58.

rivers. This is an uninhabited and extensive mountain range of which the Rhodope Mountains are a part.[5]

97. The Odrysian empire stretched along the seacoast from Abdera to the Euxine Sea as far as the Ister River. Following the shortest route, if the wind is always at your back, this voyage takes four days and nights in a round-bottomed merchant ship. It takes a man in good condition eleven days to travel the shortest road from Abdera to the mouth of the Ister. That was the extent of the coastline. Going overland from Byzantium to Laeaea and the Strymon, which was the farthest inland the empire reached from the sea, it took a man in good condition thirteen days to complete the trip. In the reign of Seuthes, who became king after Sitalces, and under whom the amount was greatest, the tribute collected from all the barbarian territories and Greek cities had a value of about four hundred talents in gold and silver coin. Gold and silver gifts were also brought that had no less value, not counting plain and embroidered fabrics and other things — and these were not just for the king, but for his vassals and other high-born Odrysians. For them, as for the other Thracians, the custom was different from that of the Persian kingdom. It was to take rather than to give, and it was more shameful to be asked and not to give than to ask and not receive. Because of their power, the Odrysians made the most extensive use of the custom, and it was impossible to accomplish anything without giving gifts. As a result, the kingdom became even more powerful, and was, in fact, the greatest European nation between the Ionian Gulf and the Euxine Sea in terms of revenues and other indicators of prosperity, although in the size of its armed forces and in its fighting strength, it was a far second to the Scythians. Indeed, not only are there no states in Europe that can rival the power of the Scythians, but even in Asia there is no nation that can stand up to them when they band together. This is not to say, however, that they come anywhere near others in applying intelligence and common sense to improve their standard of living.[6]

98. This, then, was the extent of Sitalces' kingdom when he raised his army. When everything was ready, he broke camp and headed for Macedonia, travelling first through his own kingdom and then over the uninhabited Mount Cercine, which is on the border between the Sinti and the Paeonians. He went that way along the road he had earlier cut through the forest when he attacked the Paeonians. As they came down the mountain and out of Odrysian territory, they kept the Paeonians on the right and the Sinti and Maedi on the left. Leaving the mountain behind, they came to Doberus in Paeonia. Sitalces lost none of his army on the march except through illness; on the contrary, his army grew, because many autonomous Thracians followed along voluntarily in search of plunder. It is said that the total number of the army was no less than one hundred fifty thousand men, most of whom were infantrymen, although about a third were cavalrymen. The Odrysians themselves supplied most of the cavalry, followed by the Getae. The most ferocious foot soldiers were the independent saber men who came down from Mount Rhodope, whereas the remaining disorganized throng that followed was frightening mostly because of its size.

---

5. The region Thucydides describes here includes what is now northeast Greece and much of Bulgaria and Turkey. The Euxine Sea is the present-day Black Sea, and the Ister is the Danube river. The river Strymon formed the western boundary of Sitalces' empire; the Black Sea and the Aegean the eastern and southern boundaries respectively; the northern boundary was the Danube. Very little is known about the people Thucydides mentions. They were considered outlandishly barbarian in Thucydides' day (although the Scythians, probably because of their savage reputations, were employed as policemen in Athens), and the comedians especially enjoyed ridiculing their tribal names and their attempts to speak Greek.

6. The Scythians occupied some regions of what is now Russia.

99. They gathered at Doberus and prepared to come down from the high ground into the region of Macedonia ruled by Perdiccas. (The Macedonians also comprise the Lyncestians, Elimiots, and other tribes in the interior, who are allied with and subject to Perdiccas' Macedonians, but who have their own kings.) The present-day coastal Macedonia was conquered by Perdiccas' father, Alexander, and by his ancestors, who were originally from Argos and were descendants of Temenos.[7] They ruled after driving the Pierians out of Pieria by force. The Pierians later settled beyond the Strymon River in Phagres and other places at the foot of Mount Pangaeus, and to this day the land below Mount Pangaeus that slopes toward the sea is called the Pierian Valley. They also drove the Bottiaeans out of what is known as Bottiaea, and these people now live on the border of Chalcidice. They also conquered a narrow strip of land along the Axius River in Paeonia, which stretches down from the highlands as far as Pella and the sea; and, after driving out the Edonians, they occupied what is now called Mygdonia, between the Axius and the Strymon rivers. From what is now known as Eordia, they also expelled the Eordians, most of whom perished, although a remnant of them settled the area around Physca; and from Almopia, they expelled the Almopians. These coastal Macedonians conquered and to this day control land taken from other tribes: Anthemus, Grestonia, Bisaltia, and much of what belonged to the original Macedonians. The whole region is now called Macedonia, however, and Perdiccas, son of Alexander, was their king when Sitalces attacked.

100. The Macedonians were unable to resist the invasion of such a large force and took shelter in what fortresses and natural defenses there were in their country. These were few, but later, when Archelaus, son of Perdiccas, became king, he built the strongholds that are in the country now. He also cut straight roads and made other improvements. In addition, he strengthened the cavalry, the hoplite force, and other armaments more than all the other eight kings who had gone before him.

The Thracian army came down from Doberus and began by invading what had formerly been Philip's kingdom. They took Idomene by storm. Then Gortynia, Atalanta, and several other places capitulated, brought over by their friendship for Amyntas, son of Philip, who was with Sitalces. They besieged Europus but were unable to capture it. Then they penetrated into the rest of Macedonia to the left of Pella and Cyrrhus. They plundered Mygdonia, Grestonia, and Anthemus, but they did not go as far south as Bottiaea and Pieria. The Macedonians did not even consider defending themselves with infantry, although they did send for cavalry from their allies from the northeast, which, though greatly outnumbered, charged the Thracian army wherever they could. When they did attack, no one was able to withstand these brave mounted men protected with breastplates; but since they were placing themselves in danger, surrounded by a force so many times larger than they, they finally held back, deciding there were not enough of them to take risks against such large numbers.

101. Sitalces began to negotiate with Perdiccas over the grievances for which he had invaded. The Athenians, not believing that Sitalces would invade, did not come with the ships. They did send him gifts and ambassadors, however, so he sent a part of his army against the Chalcidians and Bottiaeans and ravaged their land after driving them behind their walls. While he was camped in this region, the people to the south—Thessalians, Magnesians, and other Thessalian subjects, along with the Greeks as far as Thermopylae—be-

7. Cf. Herodotus 8.137–139.

came afraid that the army would attack them and were on high alert. Also alarmed were the Thracians who lived in the plains beyond the Strymon to the north—the Panaeans, Odomantians, Droans, and Dersaeans, all of whom are independent. There even arose a rumor among the Greek enemies of Athens that Sitalces' troops would, under the terms of his alliance with Athens, be brought in to attack them. Sitalces, however, only overran and plundered Chalcidice, Bottice, and Macedonia, and was unable to obtain any of the objectives for which he had invaded. His army was also running short of food and was beginning to feel the hardships of the winter weather, so he was induced to retreat as quickly as possible by his nephew Seuthes, son of Sparadocus, whose influence was second only to his. Seuthes, however, had been secretly won over by Perdiccas, who had promised him his sister in marriage and a sum of money along with her. Thus Sitalces quickly returned home with his army after a total of thirty days, of which eight were spent in Chalcidice. Later, as promised, Perdiccas gave his sister, Stratonice, to Seuthes. These were the events connected with the campaign of Sitalces.

102. That same winter, after the Peloponnesian navy disbanded, the Athenians at Naupactus, with Phormio in command, sailed along the coast to Astacus, where they made a landing and marched into the interior of Acarnania with four hundred Athenian hoplites from their ships and four hundred Messenian hoplites. After driving into exile men who were thought to be untrustworthy from Stratus, Corus, and elsewhere, and restoring Cynes, son of Theolytes, to power in Coronta, they returned to their ships. Because it was winter, they decided that it was impossible to attack the Oeniadae, the only Acarnanians who were unremittingly hostile. The reason was that the Achelous River, which flows out of Mount Pindus and through Dolopia, the Agraean and Amphilochian territories, and then through the Acarnanian plain and down along Stratus, flows into the sea at Oeniadae, surrounding the city with water. It is impossible to conduct military operations there because of the winter flooding. Most of the Echinades Islands lie opposite Oeniadae, right at the mouth of the Achelous, and they make this powerful river constantly silt up.[8] Some of the islands have become part of the mainland, and it is expected that this will happen to all of them in a very short time, for the flow is wide, muddy, and swift, and the islands act as catchment areas for the silt because they are close set, arranged not in succession but in uneven rows, and thus prevent the water from flowing through straight lanes between them to the sea. These islands are small and uninhabited.

It is said that when Alcmaeon, son of Amphiaraus, was wandering as an outcast after he had murdered his mother, Apollo decreed in an oracle that he should live in this region, adding that there would be no release from his terrors until he had found a place to settle that had never been seen by the sun and that was not even a part of the earth when he killed his mother. The rest of the world would be accursed to him. They say that he was at a loss for what to do until he finally noticed this silting up of the Achelous, and it seemed to him that enough land would have been created in the long time he had wandered since killing his mother to make him self-sufficient. So he settled in and ruled over the area around Oeniadae, naming the country after his son, Acarnan. This is the oral tradition which has come down to us about Alcmaeon.

8. Cf. Herodotus 2.10.

103. Phormio and the Athenians left Acarnania, arriving at Naupactus at the beginning of spring, and then continued on to Athens, bringing the ships they had captured and the freeborn men they had taken prisoner in their naval battles. They were released in a man-for-man exchange. Thus that winter came to an end, and with it also ended the third year of this war that I, Thucydides, wrote down.

Book 3

In Book 3, Thucydides displays the hurtfulness of Greek to Greek in all its horror. The book begins by interweaving the story of the Spartans' destruction of Plataea with that of the Athenians' treatment of Mytilene. Each painful tale reaches a climax in direct discourse—the Mytilenean affair in the opposing speeches of Cleon and Diodotus (37–48), the end of Plataea in the paired speeches of the Plataeans and the Thebans at 53–67, followed by the nonconversations in 68, in which the Spartans are depicted asking each individual Plataean what he had done to help Sparta before leading him off to execution. Cleon is introduced at 36; we will meet him again and again and come to know that Thucydides despises him. Diodotus is an unknown quantity; his name appears nowhere else in Greek literature. The speeches at Plataea, in contrast to those at Athens, are ascribed simply to "the Plataeans" and "the Thebans."

Events at Corcyra do nothing to restore faith in humanity. Thucydides' tortured account of the brutal developments there (70–85), accompanied by an analysis of how people behave when civil strife breeds polarization, is one of the most frequently quoted sections of his work and, coupled with the discussion of the plague in Book 2, has often been cited in modern times by writers seeking to understand and explain the depths to which people can sink under stress. To many writers working around A.D. 1800, it seemed an apt description of revolutionary France.

After a brief discussion (86–90) of the beginnings of Athenian involvement in Sicily, to which he returns at 103 and 115, Thucydides details the campaigns of Demosthenes towards the west. His account (91–114) includes a conversation between an Athenian and a herald from Ambracia (113) an exception that highlights the rules by which Thucydides' normally terse, spare narrative proceeds: the picture of two individuals engaged in an actual conversation, while a common event in both war and peace, is not one we ordinarily see in Thucydides, who on the whole excises ordinary speech from his work and allows us to hear only formal presentations.

The events of this book raise interesting questions. One wonders just why the Athenians did not come to the Plataeans' aid; no matter how busy they were with the revolt on Lesbos, Plataea was an ally of long standing, and the privileged status traditionally accorded to Plataea as the site of the Greek victory over Persia in 479 gave the Peloponnesians' attack on it special significance. The revolt on Lesbos is of particular interest to historians because of its pertinence to the debate over the popularity of the Athenian empire.

Book 3

1. The following summer, when the grain was high, the Peloponnesians and their allies invaded Attica. They were led by Archidamus, son of Zeuxidamus, king of Sparta, and after setting up camp, they began to slash and burn the earth. As usual, there were Athenian cavalry attacks wherever the opportunity arose, which prevented the large number of lightly armed troops from venturing out of the camp and harming the area near the city. The Peloponnesians stayed until their supplies ran out and then withdrew and disbanded to their respective cities.

2. Immediately after the invasion of the Peloponnesians, all of Lesbos except Methymna revolted from Athens. They had been wanting to do so since even before the war, but the Spartans would not guarantee aid. They were now forced to act, and staged the revolution before they had intended to. They were still busy fetching various supplies and were waiting for the harbor to be blockaded, the walls to be erected, and the ships to be built, and for the archers and food they needed from the Pontus to arrive; but the people of Tenedos and Methymna were at odds with them and even some Mytileneans were inclined to dissent for their own personal reasons. The latter were Athenian proxeni, and, turning informer, they told Athens that Mytilene aimed to force the unification of the Lesbian states under a central Mytilenean government, and that with the aid of the Spartans and the Boeotians (who were their blood kin), they were pushing ahead with all the preparations for a rebellion. If the Athenians didn't put a stop to it, and quickly, they warned, Athens would lose Lesbos.

3. The Athenians were hard pressed by the plague and by what was developing into a full-scale war, and they thought that it would be a huge undertaking to also go to war with Lesbos, which had undiluted energy—and a navy. At first, they would not accept the intelligence reports and inclined heavily to wishing they were not true. When, however, they had sent ambassadors to Mytilene and failed to persuade them to give up their preparations for war and their plans for unification, they became alarmed and decided on a pre-emptive strike. They immediately dispatched forty ships that had been readied to sail around the Peloponnese. Cleippides, son of Deinias, was in command with two other generals. The Athenians had been informed that there was to be a festival of Apollo of the Apple Country. It was to be held outside the city, all the Mytileneans would celebrate it, and the hope was to advance rapidly and attack suddenly. If it worked . . . but if not, the generals were to tell the Mytileneans to hand over their navy and tear down their city walls and to say that if they refused, it meant war.

The fleet left.

Meanwhile, the Athenians seized ten Mytilenean triremes, which happened to be serving at Athens as an auxiliary force under the terms of the alliance, and put their crews under guard; but a man crossed from Athens to Euboea, sped on foot to Geraestus, hopped a merchantman just as it was casting off, caught a current, reached Mytilene two days after leaving Athens, and told the Mytileneans of the oncoming fleet. As a result, the Mytileneans did not make a procession to the temple of Apollo at Malea, but patched up the half-finished walls and harbor and kept watch.

4. Not much later, the Athenians arrived and saw how things stood. The generals then delivered their message. When the Mytileneans refused to obey, the generals went into action. The Mytileneans were unprepared, but they were

forced to hurry up and fight, and they sailed a little way out of their harbor and put up some token resistance. Then, after being chased back by the Athenian ships, they held talks with the generals, wanting, if possible, to rid themselves of the ships for the time being through some sort of face-saving agreement. The Athenian generals were inclined to listen because they too were afraid—afraid that their force was not adequate to make war on all of Lesbos. After negotiating a cease-fire, the Mytileneans sent a group, including one of the informers (who had by now changed his mind), to Athens to see whether they could persuade the Athenians that they no longer contemplated revolution and that the ships should be withdrawn. At the same time, a trireme with ambassadors bound for Sparta slipped past the Athenian fleet, which was anchored at Malea to the north of the city. Clearly, the Mytileneans did not believe that the representations they made at Athens would succeed. The ambassadors reached Sparta after sailing, with great difficulty, over open sea and negotiated with them about getting some sort of aid for Mytilene.

5. The ambassadors to Athens returned empty-handed, and so the Mytileneans and other Lesbians, except Methymna, were again at war with Athens. The Methymnians had come to the aid of the Athenians, along with the Imbrians, Lemnians, and a few of the other allies. The Mytileneans left the city and attacked the Athenian camp in full strength. There was a battle, and the Mytileneans had the best of it, but lacking self-confidence, they retreated behind their walls and did not encamp in the field. They took no further action, wanting to run risks only after making further preparations and in the event that the Spartans sent help. Because by now, Meleas, a Spartan, and Hermaeondas, a Theban, had arrived. They had been sent in advance of the rebellion, but had not been able to get ahead of the Athenian task force. They secretly sailed into the harbor in a trireme after the battle and advised sending another trireme, along with some ambassadors, to accompany them back to Sparta. The Mytileneans did so.

6. The Athenians, much encouraged by the Mytileneans' inaction, called in their allies, who came all the faster when they saw that the Lesbians weren't putting up a fight. The Athenians brought their ships around to anchor to the south of the city, fortified two camps on either side of it, and set up blockades of both harbors. Thus the Mytileneans were denied access to the sea; the island itself was under the control of the Mytileneans and the other Lesbians who had by now come to their aid; the Athenians held a little of the area around their camps; they had an anchorage rather than a harbor for their ships; and Malea was their market and supply base.[1] That, then, was the combat situation on the ground at Mytilene.

7. At the same time that summer, the Athenians sent thirty ships around the Peloponnese with Asopius, son of Phormio, in command, because the Acarnanians had asked them to send a commander who was related to Phormio, whether a son or other relative.[2] The ships sailed along the Laconian coast and plundered coastal towns. Then Asopius sent most of the ships back home while he continued on to Naupactus with twelve of them. Later he mobilized the Acarnanians and attacked Oeniadae in full strength, he and his ships sailing up the Achelous while the infantry slashed and burned the ground.[3] Since the Oeniadae did not capitulate, he dismissed the infantry, sailed to Leucas, and made

---

1. Greek troops were not always given their food. They had to buy it at markets set up near their bases of operations.
2. Thucydides does not say why Phormio was unavailable; probably he had died.
3. Cf. 2.102.

a landing at Nericus. While he was returning to his ships, he and a part of his army were killed by natives who came out to fight him, supported by a few Peloponnesian guards. The Athenians sailed away, after recovering the bodies from the Leucadians under a truce.

8. The ambassadors who had been sent by the Mytileneans on the first ship had gone on to Olympia, after the Spartans told them to attend the Olympic games so that their allies could also hear them out and come to a decision. This was the Olympiad in which Dorieus of Rhodes was the winner for the second time. When they got down to talking after the games were held, the Mytileneans spoke as follows.

9. Spartans. Allies. We know the deep-rooted Greek attitude. To the extent that it is beneficial, states are pleased to make alliances with breakaway states who abandon their old allies in wartime; but they also have contempt for them as traitors to their former friends. And this judgment is not unjust when the rebels and the state with which they may differ share a good will, a cast of mind, and are evenly matched in power and resources. Then, of course, there are no reasonable grounds whatever for secession. But this was not the case between Athens and us. Nor should we be regarded with contempt if, honored by them in peacetime, we separate from them in war.

10. We will talk first about justice and honesty, especially because we are asking you for an alliance, and because we know that neither private friendships nor intercity associations amount to anything unless they are conducted with manifest honesty and have a shared cultural basis in other respects. Different ways of thinking lead to differences in behavior. Our alliance with Athens began when you withdrew from the scene after the Persian Wars and they remained to perform the mopping-up operations.[4] We did not, however, become Athens' allies in order to enslave the Greeks to Athens, but in order to free them from the Persians. For so long as they led everyone as equals, we eagerly followed; but when we saw them abating their hatred for the Persians and contriving to enslave their allies, we no longer felt so secure. Individual states were unable to defend themselves because they were always being outvoted by the others, until all except us and the Chians were enslaved. We, free and independent in name only, fought beside Athens. But we reasoned from previous examples and no longer trusted our Athenian leaders. It seemed unlikely that they would enslave some of those they had made allies with our help, and then refrain from doing the same thing to the rest of us if they could.

11. If we were all still independent, we could have been surer that the Athenians would not radically change their policy towards us; but when most of the allies were under their thumb while we associated with them on a basis of equality, it naturally got harder for them to put up with us in the face of a subservient majority—especially since they kept getting stronger and stronger and we became more and more isolated in our equality of rights. Mutual fear is the only guarantee an alliance has. Whoever wanted to step over the line would be deterred by his lack of superior force. We have been allowed to remain independent only because it seemed to the Athenians that their imperialist goals were more attainable through the plausibility of their policies and arguments than through the application of brute force. Whenever they vi-

4. The Mytilenaeans are referring to the formation of the Delian League of 478–477. The "enslavement" of which they speak began with the transfer of the League's treasury to Athens in 454/53 and with the formation of the Athenian empire. Cf. Thucydides 1.95 and Herodotus 9.106. Cf. also Thucydides 1.75.

olated the rights of those they attacked, they used us as proof that their equal partners did not march along with them unwillingly. At the same time, they led their most powerful allies against their weaker ones first, leaving the powerful ones weaker in the end, so that they could take care of them after the others had been disposed of. If they had begun with us when all the allies had their own resources and a cause to fight for, the Athenians would not have subdued them so easily. Our navy also generated some fear that it might, by acting in unison with yours or someone else's, pose a danger to them. In part, too, we saved ourselves by paying court to the Athenian people and whatever leaders were in power.[5] But judging by the example of the other states, we would not have been able to last much longer if this war had not broken out.

12. What kind of reliable friendship or freedom was peace becoming when we dealt with one another so insincerely? Athens courted us in this war out of fear and we did the same to them in peacetime. For other people, good will strengthens trust; with us, fear made for security, and we were held in the alliance more by fear than by friendship. Whichever of us first gained the confidence of safety would be the first to violate our agreements. Thus if anyone thinks we do wrong by rebelling in anticipation of the terrible things the Athenians have been waiting to do to us, instead of waiting ourselves to be sure whether they *are* planning to do something, that person isn't looking at things correctly. If we were able, as equals, to make our own plans and to see how things turned out, why should we, their equals, be in their power? No, they have always had the advantage of the initiative, and we have always been forced to defend ourselves.

13. These then are our grounds, Spartans, allies, these our motives for secession. They are clear enough for those who hear to recognize that we acted properly, and they were sufficient to frighten us into seeking some security. We sought it in the past, when we sent ambassadors to you in peacetime to discuss our withdrawal from the League, and you prevented it by refusing to guarantee aid. Now, however, the Boeotians have invited us and we have immediately responded.[6] We intend to secede from the league in two senses: *from* doing the Greeks harm *with* the Athenians, but instead joining *with* the Greeks in their own liberation; *from* the Athenians by making the first move now and avoiding being destroyed by them later. This secession, though, has been hurried and unprepared. All the more reason why you must accept us in your alliance and quickly send help: to show yourselves as helping those you should, while harming your enemies at the same time. This is an opportunity like none before. The Athenians are wasting away from plague and from the expense of the war. Some of their ships are sailing off your coasts; others have been assigned to ours. It isn't likely that they have a surplus of ships, so if you were to invade them by land and sea for a second time this summer, they would either be unable to defend themselves by sailing against you, or they would have to withdraw from both fronts. And let no one think that he is running a risk at home for the sake of a foreign land, for though you may think Lesbos is far away, the advantage it offers is right next door—because the war won't be in Attica, as one might think, but in the sources of Attica's strength. Their taxes come from the treasuries of their allies, and those revenues will grow even greater if they bring us into subjection. No one else

---

5. See Aristophanes, *Acharnians*, 633–45.
6. The speaker may be referring to the invitation of Hermaeondas the Theban, who was mentioned at 3.5.

will break away; they will add our wealth to theirs; and we would suffer far worse than those they have previously enslaved. But if you come energetically to our aid, you will add to your alliance a city that has a large navy—something you badly need—and you will more easily destroy Athens by pulling their allies out from under them, for every one of them will be more emboldened to defect. You will also shed your reputation for not helping rebel states. If others actually see you as liberators, you will be more assured of victory in this war.

14. Do not bring shame on the hopes Greeks have in you and on the Olympian Zeus, into whose precinct we have come almost as suppliants. Help the Mytileneans. Become our allies and do not forsake us to risk our lives alone. We will confer a benefit on all Greeks if we succeed, but the harm will be even more widespread if you do not do as we ask and we fail. Be such men as the Greeks think you are and as we in our danger and dread need you to be.

15. That is what the Mytileneans said. When the Spartans and their allies had finished listening, they accepted their arguments and formed an alliance with the Lesbians. Orders were given for an invasion of Attica, and the allies who were present were told to proceed to the Isthmus with two-thirds of their forces to carry it out. The Spartans arrived first and readied the pulleys and rollers with which to drag ships overland from Corinth across the Isthmus to the Saronic Gulf for an assault by land and sea. The Spartans readily performed this duty, but the other allies mustered more slowly because they were harvesting their crops and were sick of fighting.

16. The Athenians saw that the Peloponnesians were making these preparations out of an underestimation of their strength, and they wanted to make it very clear that the Peloponnesians had made the wrong decision and that they could easily defend themselves against the Peloponnesian attack without budging their fleet at Lesbos. Except for the cavalry class and the owners of the most productive land,[7] all Athenian citizens and metics manned one hundred ships and made a show of strength as they sailed along the Isthmus and landed at will on the Peloponnese. When the Spartans saw how badly they had miscalculated, they decided that the Lesbians' arguments had been false. They also realized that they were at an impasse, because their allies had not arrived and they had received messages that the hundred Athenian ships off the Peloponnese were plundering the countryside near Sparta. And so they returned home. (Later they made preparations for a task force to be sent to Lesbos. They sent word to the allies to ready forty ships in all, and they appointed as admiral Alcidas, who stood by for the attack.) The Athenians and their hundred ships also left when they saw the Spartans do so.

17. [During the time that these ships were at sea, the Athenians had their largest number of fast ships fit for active duty, although there were at least as many—indeed, there were even more—at the beginning of the war. One hundred were on guard duty at Attica, Euboea, and Salamis. There were one hun-

---

7. These were the two highest classes that Solon had created in his social reforms at the beginning of the sixth century. The cavalry class was the second-richest class of the four Solon had marked out. They were the men who could afford horses. Above them was the top class, the pentacosiomedimni, the very wealthy whose land produced more than five hundred medimni (bushels) of grain annually. Below them were two more classes: the next lowest was made up of those who owned a yoke of oxen, and after these came the poorest farmers, who were not always much better off than slaves. The point the Athenians are making here is that they remain strong enough, despite the plague and the expense of the war, not only to continue their other military operations, but to man an additional one hundred ships without calling on their upper classes.

dred off the Peloponnese, not counting the ships at Potidaea and elsewhere, so that altogether there were two hundred and fifty in that particular summer. This fleet, along with the siege at Potidaea, constituted Athens' greatest expense. It cost two drachmas per day for a hoplite to guard Potidaea (one for the hoplite and one for his servant.)[8] Three thousand hoplites began the siege; at least that number continued it; and then there were the sixteen hundred who left early with Phormio. The pay for all the ships' crews was the same. That, then, was the expense early on in the war, and that the greatest number of ships that had been manned.][9]

18. While the Spartans were at the Isthmus, the Mytileneans and their allies attacked Methymna by land, in the belief that traitors within would turn it over to them. They attacked the city, but when things did not go according to plan, they withdrew to Antissa, Pyrrha, and Eresus. They posted garrisons and strengthened the walls in these towns and quickly returned home. After the Mytileneans had left, the Methymnians attacked Antissa, but the Antissans and their allies rushed out to meet them and overwhelmingly defeated them; many were killed, and the survivors hurriedly retreated. When the Athenians heard that the Mytileneans had control of the ground and that their troops were inadequate to stop them, they despatched one thousand of their own hoplites at the beginning of the autumn under the command of Paches, son of Epicurus. These hoplites rowed their ships themselves, and when they arrived, they built a single circular wall all around Mytilene and also erected forts at strong points within the wall. Thus with winter coming on, Mytilene was blockaded, in strength, on both sides, by land and sea.

19. To mount this siege, the Athenians needed more money, so for the first time, they levied on themselves a property tax of two hundred talents and sent out twelve ships to levy taxes on the allies, with Lysicles and four others in command.[1] He sailed here and there collecting taxes until, going upcountry in Caria from Myus through the plain of the Meander as far as Sandius Hill, he and a large number of his troops were killed in an attack by the Carians and the people of Anaea.

20. That same winter, still besieged by the Peloponnesians and the Boeotians, suffering from food shortages and with no hope whatever of help or rescue from Athens or anywhere else, the Plataeans and the Athenians who were under siege with them came up with a preliminary plan for all of them to break out of the city and over the enemy's walls. The plan was suggested to them by their seer, Theaenetus, son of Tolmides, and by one of their generals, Eupompides, son of Daimachus. Later, half of them shrank from the danger, leaving about two hundred twenty volunteers who stuck with the escape, which they performed in the following way. They began by building ladders equal to the height of the enemy's wall, getting the right measurements from the layers of bricks wherever they happened not to be covered with whitewash on the side facing them. Many of them counted the layers together, and though some got the wrong number, most got it right, especially since they counted often and were not far from the wall and could easily look down to whatever part of it they wished. Thus by determining the likely width of the bricks, they got the right height for the ladders.

---

8. On Athenian currency, see glossary under *currency, Athenian*.
9. Many editors reject this section as spurious, garbled, or misplaced. Others accept it, though with many reservations too numerous to mention here.
1. Thucydides probably means that this tax was levied for the first time during the war. There are records of its having been levied on extraordinary occasions before the war.

21. The Peloponnesian wall was constructed as a double wall, one wall facing Plataea, with another outer wall, in case a force should attack from Athens. The two walls were separated from each other by about sixteen feet. This intervening space was built to form living quarters distributed among the garrison. These quarters were attached, so that there appeared to be one thick wall with parapets on either side. At every tenth parapet, there was a large tower that equaled the breadth of the walls, extending from the inner face of the inner wall to the outer face of the outer wall. Thus you could not walk alongside the tower, but had to go under the middle of it. At night, when the weather blew up wet, the guard left the parapet and kept watch from the towers, which were not far apart and which had roofs over them. That is what the wall by which the Plataeans were surrounded was like.

22. When everything was ready, the Plataeans watched and waited for a stormy, moonless night of wind and rain. They were led by the men who had formed the plan. First they crossed the surrounding ditch. Then, unbeknownst to the guards, they reached the enemy wall. The guards did not catch sight of them in the darkness, and they did not hear the noise of the advancing Plataeans because of the howling wind. Also, the Plataeans kept a wide distance apart, so that they wouldn't give themselves away by banging into each other's armor. They were lightly armed and wore a sandal on the left foot only, for a safer foothold in the mud. Knowing that parapets would be unmanned, they broached the wall at the parapets between the towers. First came the men carrying the ladders, who put them in position. Then twelve men lightly armed with breastplates and daggers went up, commanded by Ammeas, son of Coroebus, who mounted first. After him came others, making six to each of the towers. Then other light-armed men with spears went up to join them. So that these men could ascend more easily, their shields were carried by the others who followed and were to be given to them when they engaged with the enemy. When most of them were up, they were discovered by the sentries in the towers because one of the Plataeans, taking hold of a parapet, threw down a tile that made a noise as it fell. A shout went out immediately and the garrison hurried up the wall, though in the stormy night they didn't know just what the trouble was. At the same time, the Plataeans who had been left behind in the city came out and, to distract the Peloponnesians' attention, attacked the Peloponnesian wall opposite to where their men had mounted. The confused Peloponnesians stayed put, no one daring, in his inability to understand what was going on, to leave his own post and go to another. Three hundred Peloponnesians, who had been detailed as a reserve force to assist wherever needed, ran outside the wall towards the noise. Warning torches were raised towards Thebes, but the Plataeans in the city also raised torches they had prepared in advance for this very purpose. The point was to make the signals meaningless, so that their Theban enemies, not knowing what was going on, would not send help until the Plataeans had escaped and gotten to safety.

23. To return to the Plataeans who were going over the wall. The advance group, which had already mounted, had killed the sentries and taken control of both towers. They stood guard at the passageways of the towers to prevent enemy troops from coming through. They also leaned ladders against the towers from the walls and sent up more men, holding off enemy reinforcements with missiles from above and below. Meanwhile, the main body of Plataeans leaned a great many ladders against the wall between the towers, climbed up, pushed down the parapets, and went over the other side. Whoever had gotten over stood on the rim of the ditch, shooting arrows or throwing spears from there at any de-

fender who might come along the wall and try to prevent their buddies from crossing the ditch. When everyone had gotten over, the last men from the towers climbed down with great difficulty and were making their way across the ditch. At this point, the three hundred reserves, carrying torches, bore down on them. But the Plataeans, standing on the rim of the ditch, had the better view of them from out of the darkness and shot arrows and threw spears at the exposed parts of their bodies. The enemy, surrounded by blankness, were blinded by the light of their own torches, so that the last Plataeans got ahead of them and crossed the ditch, albeit after a hard struggle. The reason it was so difficult is that there was ice in the ditch, though it had not frozen solid enough to support them. Instead, it was mushy, the way it is with a northeast wind. During that snowy night, with that wind, a great deal of slush had built up in the ditch, and the men could barely keep their heads above it while crossing over. On the other hand, their escape was only made possible by the intensity of the storm.

24. The Plataeans set off from the ditch and, keeping the shrine of the hero Androcrates on the right, made their way together along the road leading to Thebes. Their thinking was that no one would suspect them of following the very road that led to their enemies. As they went, in fact, they saw the Peloponnesians, torches in hand, chasing up the road that led to Athens via Cithaeron and Oak Head. They followed the road to Thebes for about three-quarters of a mile and then, doubling back to the mountain road through Erythrae and Hysiae, they escaped over the mountains to Athens. There were two hundred and twelve of them. There had been more, but some had turned back to the city before going over the wall, and one, an archer, had been captured at the outer ditch.

The Peloponnesians gave up and returned to their reserve positions; the Plataeans in the city knew nothing of how things had turned out, since those who came back had reported that no one had gotten away. They sent out a herald as soon as it was day to obtain a truce to gather their dead, but they came back as soon as they learned the truth.

That, then, was how the men from Plataea got over the wall and escaped to safety.

25. At the end of that winter, Salaethus, a Spartan, was sent from Sparta to Mytilene by trireme. He sailed to Pyrrha and went from there on foot through a ravine, from which, going unnoticed up over the siege wall, he made his way into Mytilene, where he told the city's presiding officers that there would be an invasion of Attica timed to coincide with the arrival of the forty ships they needed for their relief.[2] He told them that he had been sent on ahead to inform them of this and to take charge of operations; whereupon the Mytileneans plucked up their courage and became less inclined to come to an agreement with the Athenians.

That winter ended, then, and with it ended the fourth year of this war that I, Thucydides, wrote down.

26. The following summer,[3] after sending the forty-two ships to Mytilene and putting their admiral, Alcidas, in command, the Peloponnesians and their allies invaded Attica so that the Athenians, harried on two fronts, would be less inclined to send help against the ships bearing down on Mytilene. This invasion was led by Cleomenes, on behalf of his fraternal nephew Pleistoanax, son of Pausanias, who, though king, was still a minor. They destroyed anything that

2. Cf. 3.15.
3. 427.

was growing back in the parts of Attica they had previously deforested, and anything they had overlooked in their other invasions. After the second one, this was the invasion the Athenians felt most severely. The Peloponnesians stayed on, destroying everything in sight wherever they went and constantly awaiting news from Lesbos about their fleet, which should have gotten there by then; but when nothing went according to their expectations and their food had run out, they withdrew and dispersed to their respective cities.

27. As for the Mytileneans, they too had run out of food. Time passed and still the ships from the Peloponnese did not arrive, so they were forced to come to terms with the Athenians. It happened in the following way. Even Salaethus no longer expected the ships, so he outfitted the previously light-armed populace with armor for an attack on the Athenians. As soon as the people were armed, however, they stopped obeying their leaders. They held meetings and demanded that those in power bring the food supply to a public place and distribute it to everyone—either that, they said, or they would reach an agreement with the Athenians to hand over the city.

28. The government officials realized that they were powerless to stop this, and that they would be in danger if they were excluded from an accord, so in conjunction with the people, they framed an agreement with Paches and the army whereby Athens could do as it pleased with the Mytileneans. The army would be allowed into the city, but the Mytileneans could send a delegation to Athens on their own behalf. Until it returned, Paches must not imprison, enslave, or kill a single Mytilenean. In spite of this agreement, those Mytileneans who had worked most closely with the Spartans were absolutely terrified, and as soon as the army entered the city, they couldn't stand it any more and became suppliants at the temples. Paches, however, removed them without violence and put them on Tenedos until the Athenians came to a decision. He also sent triremes to Antissa and gained control of the place and did whatever else he thought needed to be done on behalf of his army.

29. The Peloponnesians in the forty ships—the ones that were supposed to arrive in Mytilene immediately—had taken their time about sailing up the Peloponnesian coast. Then they took a leisurely route across the Aegean, thus managing to avoid being reported to the authorities at Athens. They finally reached Delos, but by the time they got from there to Icarus and Myconos, they heard that Mytilene had been taken. Wanting to verify the story, they sailed to Embatum, in Erythrae. They reached Embatum about seven days after the fall of Mytilene. After learning the full story, they had a meeting to discuss the situation, and an Elean, Teutiaplus, spoke to them as follows.

30. Alcidas and you other Peloponnesian commanders here present. It seems to me that we ought to attack Mytilene with what we've got before they find out that we're here. The Athenians have just captured the city, and it's likely that we'll catch them pretty much off guard there—and totally off guard at sea, where they will least expect any hostile force to come at them and where, for a change, our strength happens to be. It's also likely that their infantry, relaxed after their victory, has scattered to their quarters. So then. If we fall on them, suddenly and by night, and if there is anybody left who still likes us, I imagine that there's a chance the city can be taken. Let's not back away from the danger. Hitting the enemy when his defenses are down is precisely what makes for surprise in warfare, and a general will win most often if he guards himself against surprise while taking advantage of the chance to use it against his enemies.

31. This speech did not persuade Alcidas. Some Ionian exiles, along with the Lesbians who had joined the mission, recommended that, since he was afraid of this danger, he should capture one of the cities in Ionia—either that, or Aeolian Cyme—so that he could foment revolt in Ionia with a city as a base of operations. There was some hope of success in this. After all, they hadn't been unwelcome anywhere yet. This way, they could seize Athens' greatest source of revenue, while also being a cause of expense if the Athenians should attack them. Why, there was reason to think they might even persuade Pissuthnes[4] to join them in the fighting! But Alcidas was not receptive even to this. All his thinking inclined towards going back to the Peloponnese as fast as possible, now that he had been late in getting to Mytilene.

32. He set off, sailing along the coast from Embatum. He landed at Myonnesus in Teios and cut the throats of most of the prisoners he had taken on his voyage. He also brought his fleet into the harbor at Ephesus, where some envoys from the Samians of Anaea visited him with the message that he was not going about this so-called liberation of Greece the right way if he killed men who had not raised a hand against him and who were not his enemies, but who were only allied with Athens by constraint. If he didn't stop, he would turn very few of his enemies into friends and many more of his friends into enemies. This persuaded him, and he released the Chians he still had, along with some others. (These people had not fled at the sight of Alcidas' ships. On the contrary, they went over to them in the assumption that they were Attic ships, never in the least expecting, given Athens' command of the sea, that Peloponnesian vessels would venture into Ionia.)

33. Alcidas quickly sailed out of Ephesus and made a run for it. He had been seen by the *Salaminia* and the *Paralus*[5] while they were still anchored near Clarus, where they had arrived after a journey from Athens. Fearing pursuit, he sailed across the open sea, unwilling to land on any but Peloponnesian soil.

The news reached Paches and the Athenians from Erythrae—although it kept coming in from all sides. They feared that the Peloponnesians might sail along the coast of an unwalled Ionia. Even if they didn't intend to stay, they could attack and plunder the cities. The crews of the *Paralus* and the *Salaminia* said that they had seen Alcidas with their own eyes at Clarus. Paches pursued him eagerly as far as the island of Patmos, but when it seemed no longer possible to catch up with him, Paches turned back. Since he had not come across them on the open sea, Paches thought it a net gain that he had not caught the Peloponnesians in a tight place, where they would have been forced to set up a camp and where he would have had to blockade and guard them.

34. As he made his way back along the coast, Paches also stopped at the Colophonian port city of Notium. It had been inhabited by Colophonians after the upper city, which was back from the sea, had been seized by Itamenes and the barbarians who had been brought in as a result of internal strife. The city had been seized at about the time of the second Peloponnesian invasion of Attica. The exiles who settled at Notium resumed their dissensions there, however. One group, along with Arcadian and barbarian mercenaries they got from Pissuthnes, occupied a fortress. They formed a government after being joined

---

4. The satrap of Lydia.
5. Cf. 3.33. These two ships were the pride of the Athenian navy and were used to showcase Athenian power on important diplomatic and religious missions, as well as in reconnoitering operations and actual combat.

by medizing Colophonians from the upper city.[6] The other group escaped into exile and called in Paches. He invited Hippias, the leader of the Arcadians in the fortress, to hold talks with him, promising to bring him safe and sound back behind the wall if their talks proved unsatisfactory. Hippias came out to meet him, but Paches put him under guard, though not in chains. Paches then suddenly and unexpectedly attacked and took the fortress and killed the Arcadians, along with whatever barbarians were inside. Later, as promised, he conducted Hippias back, and as soon as he was inside, Paches arrested him and had him shot to death with arrows. He then handed Notium over to the Colophonians, though not to the ones who collaborated with the Persians. Later, after bringing together every Colophonian from the neighboring cities, the Athenians sent commissioners to govern Notium according to Athenian law.

35. After returning to Mytilene, Paches conquered Pyrrha and Eresus and sent Salaethus the Spartan to Athens, after finding him hiding in Mytilene. He also sent the Mytileneans he had put on Tenedos and anyone else he believed to have been responsible for the rebellion. He dismissed most of his army and remained with the men who were left to make what were, in his judgment, the best arrangements for Mytilene and the rest of Lesbos.

36. When Salaethus and the Mytileneans arrived in Athens, the Athenians immediately executed Salaethus even though he offered, among other things, to withdraw the Peloponnesians from Plataea, which was still under siege. The Athenians had a debate about the Mytileneans and angrily decided to kill not just the men who were there, but all Mytilenean males above the age of puberty, and to sell all the women and children into slavery. They cited the fact that the Mytileneans had revolted even though they were not governed like the other allies; but what most contributed to their impulsiveness was the Peloponnesian fleet's startling audacity in coming to Ionia in aid of Mytilene. It made them quite sure that the revolt did not happen on the spur of the moment. They therefore immediately sent a trireme to Paches to announce their decision: his orders were to annihilate the Mytileneans.

The very next morning the Athenians were seized by regrets and second thoughts. They realized that the decision to destroy a whole city rather than just the guilty parties had been sweeping and cruel. When the Mytilenean ambassadors who were present learned of this, they, in conjunction with cooperative Athenians, got the authorities to bring the matter up for discussion again. They were easily persuaded, especially since it was obvious to them, too, that the majority of the citizens wanted someone to authorize them to reconsider the matter. An assembly was immediately convened and various opinions from several speakers were delivered. Cleon, son of Cleaenetus, who was by far the most hot-tempered of citizens—and by far the most trusted by the people in those days—had won the first debate with the decision to kill everyone. He now came forward once again and spoke as follows.

37. I, for my part, have often noticed before that democracies cannot rule over others, but I see it especially now in these regrets of yours about Mytilene. You go fearlessly along from day to day without suspecting each other, and you have the same attitude towards your allies, and whenever you make a mistake because you've been convinced by their arguments or given in to them out of pity, you never think that you have dangerously weakened your position without creating any grat-

itude in them. You don't understand that you hold your empire as a tyranny and that your subjects are schemers who are governed unwillingly. They won't obey you because of the good you do them to your own hurt; you will prevail because of your strength and not because of their high opinion of you. Worst of all would be not making your decisions stick and not knowing that it is better for a state to enforce bad laws that are always obeyed than to have good ones that go unenforced. Ignorance combined with prudence has advantages over cleverness combined with intemperance. Thus ordinary people run their cities far better than intelligent ones, for these want to seem wiser than the laws and to outdo whatever nonsense is spoken in public assemblies, as though they couldn't possibly be talking about anything more important. Intelligent people are the downfall of cities because of this sort of thing. Ordinary people don't believe in their own intelligence, and they regard themselves as less learned than the laws. They are less able to dissect arguments than those who speak well. They are judges who are equal to each other, not competitors, and they get things right, for the most part. And that is how we speakers must be today, not carried away in a battle of wits to give wrong-headed advice to the majority.

38. I, for one, have not changed my mind, and I am astonished at those who have foisted this waste of time on us and proposed that we debate about Mytilene again. This can only benefit the criminal, because the victim now goes after him with an anger that has lost its edge—whereas the closer the pain is, the more tightly the punishment fits the crime. I will also be astonished when whoever speaks in rebuttal has the nerve to represent Mytilenean crimes as beneficial to us and our misfortunes as painful to our allies. It is obvious that, confident of his rhetorical power, he will try mightily to prove that you didn't decide what you in fact did decide once and for all, or that, his pockets bulging with bribes, he will labor to lead you astray with specious logic.

With contests like these, the city shoulders all the risks and gives its prizes to others. And you are to blame. You are wrong to make a game of this. You like to watch debates and hear about actions. Skillful speakers make you think that what *can* happen will happen, and as to what already *has* happened, you don't believe your eyes about it so much as your ears when smart critics censure it in their speeches. No one is better at being deceived by new turns of phrase, and you won't pay attention to what's tried and true. You are slaves to the improbable and flouters of the customary, and what each of you wants most of all is to be able to give speeches himself. If you can't do that, though, you vie with your favorite speakers by being the first to follow their arguments. So you get the idea of a clever phrase and applaud it in advance. You're eager to catch on to what's about to be said, but slow to foresee the consequences of those words. You want experiences that this life does not have to offer and you don't take enough thought about the way things really are. You have given yourselves up completely to the pleasure of listening, and you are more like an audience sitting at a theater of sophists than like citizens deliberating about politics.

39. I'll try and steer you away from all that by showing you that no one city has wronged you more than Mytilene. I can understand people who can't bear your rule or who are forced into rebellion by our enemies. But for people who live on an island, with walls around their cities, with nothing to fear but naval attacks from our enemies and with plenty of triremes with which to ward them off—for people who are self-governing

and whom we honored above all others—for them to carry out something like this! What is this but treachery, what but war! Not rebellion, which is the act of those who have been oppressed, but war. They tried, standing shoulder to shoulder with our worst enemies, to destroy us—which, come to think of it, is more horrifying than if they had merely waged war against us on their own to build up their power.

They learned nothing from the sufferings of their neighbors who rebelled and were then taken firmly in hand; nor did their prosperity make them shrink from this danger. No, they became cocky about the future, and with hopes beyond their power but still short of their real ambitions, they made war on us, deciding to place force above justice and attacking us without provocation just at a time when they thought they were most likely to get away with it. When success comes too quickly and unexpectedly to a city, it tends to skip along the path of hubris. In general, the most secure good fortune comes not as a surprise, but from sound planning, and it seems to be easier for people to fend off failure than to hold on to prosperity. The Mytileneans would not have become so high and mighty if you had treated them the same as the others from the first. By nature, men have contempt for those who court them and stand in awe of those who will not yield. So let them all now be punished, and punished severely, for their crimes. Don't fix guilt on the few and acquit the populace. All of them attacked you alike, including those who could have come over to us and been full citizens of Mytilene again, but who decided that the safer risk lay with joining the oligarchs in rebellion.

Think about it. If you administer the same punishment to those who rebel of their own free will as you do to the allies who are forced into rebellion by the enemy, who do you think won't rebel on some slim pretext when it means freedom if he succeeds and no great harm if he fails? As for us, we will have had to risk our money and our lives against each and every city. If we win, we get back some ruined city and are thus deprived, from then on, of the revenues that keep us strong, whereas if we fail, we get more enemies added to the ones we already have and we spend the time in which we should be opposing our long-standing enemies on fighting with our very own allies.

40. It is imperative, therefore, that you not extend the hope, whether secured by sophistry or bought with bribes, that the Mytileneans will find grounds for pardon in human error. Pardon is for unwilling accomplices. They knowingly made their plans; they willingly did their harm. I fought for it the first time, and I'm fighting for it again now. Don't reconsider what you've already decided, and don't make the three worst mistakes there are for an empire: pity, pleasure in disputation, and leniency.

It's right to requite like-minded people with pity, but not those who wouldn't show pity in their turn and who are necessarily our inveterate enemies.

Let the politicians who love to give speeches have contests about other, lesser matters, but not about matters that the city may briefly enjoy but pays dearly for, while those same politicians get to live well in exchange for speaking well.

Leniency is best shown to those who will be friendly now and into the distant future and not to those who are hostile now and are likely to stay that way.

To sum up. If you listen to me, you will be doing the right and the expedient thing with the Mytileneans. If you decide otherwise, you won't win their gratitude and you will be convicting yourselves, because if they were right in rebelling, you had no business ruling over them. Even if you shouldn't have an empire, yet persist in having it anyway, then they damn well need to be punished whether it's fair or not. Either that or give up your empire and practice the manly virtues where it's nice and safe. Decide on the same punishment you voted yesterday and don't show yourselves to be less ruthless than those who plotted against you just because you got away safely. Bear in mind what they would probably have done if they had beaten you, especially since they were the ones who broke the law first. Those who do wrong without cause are most likely to go out and kill everyone. They keep a stealthy eye on the menace of the surviving enemy, because a man who has suffered for no reason is more dangerous when he escapes than an enemy who has fought in equal combat.

Don't become traitors to yourselves. Get closer to your state of mind when you were aggrieved, when you would have given anything to destroy them. Pay them back now. Don't weaken in the passing moment, and don't forget the danger that hung over you then. Punish them as they deserve and set this example for the other allies: the punishment for rebellion is death. The better they know that, the less you will be distracted from your enemies to fight with your allies.

41. That is what Cleon said. After him Diodotus, son of Eucrates, who was especially vehement in the first assembly in speaking against killing the Mytileneans, came forward this time too and spoke as follows.

42. I neither blame those who reintroduced the resolution about the Mytileneans, nor praise those who find fault with frequently deliberating the greatest questions. I believe that two things most opposed to good counsel are anger and haste. The first has a way of consorting with recklessness and the second with ignorance and shallow thinking. Whoever does battle against debate as the schoolteacher of government is either stupid or has a private agenda—stupid if he thinks it is otherwise possible to plan for an uncertain future; and self-interested if he wants to argue for something shameful, yet knows that he cannot give honest speeches in a bad cause, and so bullies his opponents and his listeners with skillful abuse. The toughest such speakers are those who add the accusation that a point is being made "for the money." If they would only accuse you of ignorance! Then the one who failed to persuade would walk away feeling more stupid than criminal. But when the accusation is one of wrongdoing, you are suspect if you win and not only stupid but criminal if you lose!

The city does not benefit from this sort of thing. It is deprived of good counsel by fear. It would be better off by far if such citizens were prevented from speaking, because then, when the people were persuaded to do something, they would be least likely to make a mistake. The good citizen must not intimidate opposing voices; he must, on a level playing field, clearly have the better argument. And the prudent city must not give extra rewards to the citizen who gives good advice most often—just never diminish the rewards that already exist. It must also neither punish nor despise the citizen whose opinion does not prevail. In this way, speakers whose views are accepted would then not go on to speak against their better judgment, currying favor in order to be ever more popular; and the speaker whose views are rejected would not then strive to please by the same means so that he too could win over the majority.

43. But we do just the opposite. Furthermore, if someone is so much as suspected of profiting from his speeches, even if he gives the best advice, we deprive the city of its obvious advantage out of resentment over the un-

certain appearance of gain. It has come to the point that plainspoken good is no less suspect than just plain bad, so that it's not only necessary for someone who wants to convince the public of the most dreadful things to win it over by deceit, but for someone speaking in a better cause to become credible by telling lies. Since everybody here is so very smart, this is the only city where it is impossible to do good openly and without lying all the time. And the man who openly does good is rewarded with the suspicion that he will secretly be getting a payoff from somewhere. You must decide, you whose time for reflection is short, that where vital interests are at stake—in circumstances such as these—we speakers have taken thought for the consequences of what we say, especially since *we* are held responsible for our advice, while you are not held responsible for listening to it. If the one who gives the advice and the one who follows it were punished equally, you would be more prudent in making your decisions; but as it is now, there are times when things go wrong and, according to your feelings at the moment, you punish the lone advisor for his opinion and not yourselves for your own part in the failure—especially when a large number of you joined in making the mistake.

44. I have come forward neither to rebut arguments about Mytilene nor to denounce anyone. If we look at it prudently, this debate is not about the wrongdoings of the Mytileneans, but about the wisdom of our judgments. Even if I were to demonstrate that the Mytileneans were utterly and completely criminal, I would not for that reason call on you to execute them *unless it was expedient to do so*. If, on the other hand, there were some reason to pardon them, why then, let them be, unless *that* did not seem like the best course for the city. In my opinion, we are making a decision more about the future than about the present. Cleon keeps insisting that it will be better for you if you impose the death sentence because it will result in fewer rebellions, but I, who also have a view to what is best for the future, know, and also insist, that the opposite is true, and I do not believe that you should brush aside the practical value of my argument in favor of the apparent logic of his. Given your present angry mood toward the Mytileneans, the greater justice of his argument might attract you. But there is no need for justice because we are not here to put them on trial; we are deliberating about what to do with them, about how they can be most useful to us.

45. In all cities, there are many crimes that are punishable by death—and they are lesser crimes, not comparable to this. Nevertheless, people take the risk, egged on by hope. No one has ever committed a crime unless he thought he could get away with it. Likewise, what rebellious city ever thought itself too weak to rebel with its own forces or in alliance with others? Everyone, individually or collectively, is naturally inclined to go wrong, and there is no law that can prevent them from doing so. Indeed, people have exhausted every punishment, constantly adding one to another, in the hope of reducing the harm done by criminals. It's likely that in the distant past, punishments for even the gravest crimes were weaker than they are now, and that most of them evolved into the death penalty as people just kept on breaking the law. And capital crimes, too, will keep on being committed. So a more terrifying terror than death has to be found, for this penalty won't prevent anything either. Poverty, with its want, will give people the audacity; and plenty, with its arrogance and presumption, will give them the greed. The other conditions of life combined with the drives of men, as each feels them with overwhelming force, all lead us into the thrills of risk. Desire and hope do the greatest harm by far, the one

leading and the other following after, the one thinking out the plan, the other whispering that everything is possible; and since they are invisible, hope and desire are more powerful than the punishments we can see. Last but not least, luck plays its part in urging us on. It unexpectedly becomes our best friend, and, though we know we don't have the resources, it provokes us to take the gamble. And to the extent that the issues are about the greatest things, freedom or dominion over others, what I have said applies above all to cities, where, impelled by the crowd, each man irrationally imagines himself to be greater than he is. Simply put, when human nature itself is eagerly rushing forward to do something, only a fool would think that it is possible for the force of the law or any other bugbear to stop it.

46. It is imperative, therefore, that you not make bad decisions because you have put your trust in the security of the death penalty, and that you also avoid driving rebels past the point of no return by making it impossible for them to change their minds and quickly make up for their mistake. Think about it. As it is now, a rebellious city, realizing that it will not survive, can come to terms while it still has the resources to pay reparations and can then go on to pay its taxes in the future. The other way, do you think there is any city at all that wouldn't make even better preparations than it does now and drag the siege out to the bitter end, if it amounted to the same thing whether it capitulated in haste or at leisure? And as for us, how can it not be harmful to our interests to spend our money during the standoff of a siege and then, if we conquer the place, to assume control of a wasteland only to be deprived, from then on, of its revenues? It is through those, after all, that we prevail over our enemies.[7] We ought not, by acting like hanging judges, to harm ourselves more than those who have done the wrong. We ought, rather, to see how, by executing moderate punishments, we can from now on control strong cities that we can list on the tax rolls; and we should understand that we do not make ourselves secure by the perils of the law but by the diligent performance of our duty. We are doing just the opposite now, for if we subdue a free man who is ruled by force and who has revolted, as he naturally would, in order to govern himself, we think we are obliged to inflict a harsh punishment on him. But we must not excessively punish free men who have rebelled; we must keep a careful watch to prevent rebellion and to prevent the idea of it from so much as entering their minds, and then, when we do use force, to prosecute as few of them as possible.

47. Think about another big mistake you would make if you listened to Cleon. So far, the populace in all of the cities is well inclined toward you. Either they do not join in rebellion with the oligarchs, or, if they are forced to do so, they quickly turn against them. Thus when you go to war, you have the populace of the city you are attacking on your side. If you kill the Mytilenean people, who took no part in the rebellion, and who willingly handed the city over to you as soon as they had access to weapons, you will be wrongfully killing your benefactors. You will also be giving the powerful few what they most want, because after you have shown that the same punishment applies to those who do wrong as to those who don't, they will immediately have the people as their ally when they foment rebellion in their cities. Even if the people *were* guilty, you shouldn't make an issue of it, so as not to make an enemy of the only friend you still have. I regard this as by far the more expedient way to hold on to your empire:

---

7. Here, as elsewhere in his speech, Diodotus uses Cleon's own words against him. Cf., for example, 3.39.

to allow yourself to be wronged before you rightfully kill people you don't need to kill.

Thus as to Cleon's equation of justice with expedience in his call for revenge, we have found that it is not possible to have both in this case.

48. Follow my advice, then, in the knowledge that mine is the better course, dispensing neither pity nor leniency—for I, too, would not have you embracing either—but based only on the argument I have made. In due course, try the alleged Mytilenean wrongdoers Paches has sent and let the others stay where they are. This is a sound policy for the future and a frightening one for our enemies now, because whoever adopts a well-considered policy towards his opponents is stronger than someone who recklessly rushes forward with brute force.

49. That is what Diodotus said. After these remarkably evenly matched opinions were delivered, the Athenians were of two minds before the vote. The show of hands was nearly equal, but Diodotus' counsel nonetheless prevailed. Another trireme was at once ordered to set off on the double, so that the first ship, which had almost a day and a night's head start, would not arrive first and the second arrive to find an annihilated city. The Mytilenaean ambassadors provided the ship with wine and barley and promised the men large rewards if they got there first. The crew was in such a hurry that they rowed and at the same time ate barley cakes mixed with wine and olive oil; also the men took turns, some catching their sleep while the others rowed on. Luckily, there was no wind in their faces and the first ship was in no great hurry to perform its unpalatable duty. The first ship got there far enough ahead so that Paches had read the decree and was about to carry out the order, but the second, after pushing itself in this way, arrived close enough in its wake to prevent the slaughter of the population. That is how close Mytilene came to extinction.

50. On a motion of Cleon, though, the Athenians executed the men Paches had sent as most responsible for the revolt. There were somewhat more than one thousand of them. The Athenians also tore down the walls of Mytilene and seized its navy. Thereafter, instead of taxing the Lesbians, they divided the island (except for Methymna) into three thousand parcels of land, with three hundred to be set aside as precincts for the gods and the rest to be distributed, by lottery, to Athenian citizens, who were sent to Lesbos to cultivate them without loss of Athenian citizenship. The Lesbians were then charged an annual fee of two silver mnae per parcel to work the land.[8] The Athenians also seized the fortified towns on the mainland that Mytilene had controlled, and these too became subject to Athens.

That, then, was how events unfolded in Lesbos.

51. That same summer, after recovering Lesbos, the Athenians, with Nicias, son of Niceratus, in command, attacked the island of Minoa, which lies off Nisaea, the port of Megara. The Megarians had built a fort there and used the island as a garrison. Nicias wanted Athens' lookout here, rather than at Budorum on Salamis, because it was closer to Athens and because he wanted to prevent the Peloponnesians from secretly launching triremes and pirate expeditions from the place, as they had previously done. From here, they would also be able to keep anything from sailing into Megara. Nicias attacked by sea and, using scaling ladders, first captured two offshore towers on the side of the island opposite Nisaea, thus freeing a way into the middle of the island. Then he walled off the part of the island facing the mainland, which was not distant and

---

8. On the mna, see glossary under *currency, Athenian.*

which could send relief to the island via a causeway over the shallow water. It took a few days to perform these operations, after which Nicias, leaving a garrison and a wall on the island, withdrew with his army.

52. At around the same time that summer, the Plataeans, with no food left and unable to withstand the siege, came to terms with the Peloponnesians in the following way. The Peloponnesians had attacked the wall and the Plataeans were unable to defend it. The Spartan commander, however, though fully aware of their weakness, did not want to take the city by force. He had received word from Sparta that should there ever be a truce with Athens, and should they reach an agreement whereby each side must surrender the territory it had captured in war, Plataea would not have to be given up provided the Plataeans themselves had gone over to the Spartans of their own free will. He therefore sent a herald over to them, saying that if they wished, they could willingly hand over the city to Sparta and appoint them as judges to punish the guilty, but no one without just cause. The herald delivered his message and the Plataeans, who were by now completely exhausted, handed over the city. The Peloponnesians fed the Plataeans for a number of days, during which the five judges made their way from Sparta. After they arrived, no charges whatever were brought. Instead, the Plataeans were summoned before the judges and asked only whether they had done the Spartans and their allies any good turns in the present war. They asked to be allowed to speak at greater length, and appointed Astymachus, son of Asopolaus, and Lacon, son of Aeimnestus (the Spartan proxenus at Plataea), as their spokesmen.[9] These two came forward and spoke as follows.

53. We handed the city over to you Spartans because we trusted you, never thinking that we would have to submit to such a trial as this, but to something more traditional, and because we thought that by choosing you as our judges, as we have, we would have the best chance of getting a fair trial. Now, though, we fear that we have been mistaken on both counts. We suspect, with good reason, that this trial will be for life or death and that you will not prove impartial, and we cite as evidence for this suspicion the fact that no formal charges have been brought forward to which we are required to make answer. On the contrary, we ourselves have pleaded for the chance to speak. Also your question is curt, and answering with the truth would be self-incriminating, while a lie would be immediately refuted. We have no way out, and we are forced to risk an unsolicited statement. Indeed, that seems the safest way. For people in our position, the unspoken speech might lead to the reproach that if it had been spoken, it might have saved us.

And how can we ever persuade you? If we did not know each other, we might have brought in evidence that you didn't know about and that might have helped us. As it is, everything will have to be said to people who already know the facts, and what we are afraid of is not that we stand accused because of the prejudice that we are worse people than you, but rather that the verdict has already been reached in order to please others.

54. We will, nevertheless, set forth the merits of our case both with respect to our differences with Thebes, and with respect to you and the rest of Greece. We will remind you of services we have performed and do what we can to persuade you.

---

9. "Lacon" in fact means "Spartan" (Laconian). In view of the short memory the Spartans demonstrate here of Greek history and of the agreement that Plataea would remain inviolate because of her role in the Persian Wars, it is ironic that Lacon's father's name (Aeimnestus) means "always remembered."

To your short question, whether we have done you and your allies any good turns in this war, we say that if you ask us as your enemies, you were not wronged if you were not treated well; but if you regard us as your friends, then the ones who did wrong were those who attacked us. Now, we have been loyal in peace and in the war with the Persians. We were not the first to violate the peace; and in the war, we alone among the Boeotians joined in the liberation of Greece. Furthermore, we who are mainlanders took part in the naval battle at Artemisium, and when battle came to our soil, we stood beside you and Pausanias; and if any other great danger threatened the Greeks in those days, we shared in it beyond our strength.[1] And as for you Spartans in particular, when the helots rebelled after the earthquake and took Ithome, and Sparta was gripped by the greatest panic ever, we sent a third of our own citizens to help you.[2] Or is it possible that you have forgotten?

55. In the old days, the greatest days, those were the men we took pride in being. Only later did we become your enemies, and it was your own fault. When the Thebans were about to crush us and we needed allies, you spurned us, saying that you lived too far away, and told us to turn to the Athenians, who were closer; and yet in this war you neither suffered nor were about to suffer anything out of the ordinary at our hands. We did no wrong if we didn't want to revolt from the Athenians at your request. After all, they helped us against the Thebans after you had shrunk from doing so. It would have been dishonorable to abandon them then, especially since we ourselves had asked them to be our allies and had been treated well, enjoying joint citizenship. No, it was only right to carry out their orders energetically. You and Athens gave the orders to your allies, and it is not those who followed them who are to blame if anything wrong was done, but you, the leaders, for giving wrongful orders.

56. The Thebans have wronged us in all sorts of ways. You are well aware of the last wrong they did, the one that has brought us to this pass. They tried to seize our city when the treaty was in effect—and on a holy day at that!—and we rightfully punished them, according to the established custom among all people that you have a right to defend yourself against an aggressor. So it would be very wrong if we now came to harm because of them. If you form a judgment as to the rights of our case based on your present advantage and their enmity, you will show yourselves to be the handmaidens of expediency and not true judges of the law.

But if the Thebans seem to be useful to you now, how much more useful were we and the other Greeks then, when you were in greater danger. Now, though, it is you who are feared, for you invade others; but in that crisis, when the barbarian tried to impose slavery on everyone, these Thebans were with him. It is only fair to set our present mistakes—if, indeed, there are mistakes—against our readiness to help in those days. You will find that you are setting less against more, and more in a crisis in which Greek courage to stand up and fight the power of Xerxes was hard to come by, when Greeks were praised not for seeking safety in expediency against their onslaught, but for willingly daring to be brave in the face of danger. And we *were* brave, and we *were* among the foremost to be honored; but now, for those very same qualities, we are afraid lest we be killed for loyally choosing the Athenians instead of cunningly choosing you. But you must recognize like for like when you see it, and you must think of true expedi-

---

1. The Greeks and the Persians fought a naval battle at Artemisium in 480 B.C.
2. See 1.101 and 2.27.

ency as nothing other than preserving your immediate interest by the constancy of your gratitude toward allies who have deserved it by their valor.

57. Look to the future! You aren't making this decision unobserved. You are now thought to be an example of upright conduct for most Greeks, but if you, who are so praised, make an unjust decision about us, whom no one blames, you will see that they will not accept an iniquitous verdict against good men based on your superior virtue any more than they will allow spoils taken from us, the benefactors of Greece, to be dedicated in the sacred shrines common to us all. What a terrible reputation! The Spartans who sacked Plataea! You, whose fathers inscribed the name of our city on the tripod at Delphi because of its courage, and you, who erased the city itself, buildings and all, from the whole Greek world because of some Thebans. That it should come to this! That we, who were all but destroyed when we were overpowered by the Persians, stand now defeated by our once best friends on behalf of the Thebans, and having to endure the two worst ordeals—death by starvation if we didn't surrender the city a few days back, and death by process of law now. Shoved aside by everyone. Plataeans, who fought for Greece. . . . Loyally! . . . Beyond our strength! . . . Abandoned and disgraced. . . . None of the allies of those old days to help us now, and you, O men of Sparta, our only hope, we fear that you too are untrue.

58. And yet we appeal to you, by the gods who once ratified our alliance and by our services to Greece, to relent and to reconsider whatever you were persuaded to do by the Thebans. Take back the promise you made and do not kill those it is unseemly for you to kill. Trade shame for prudence and win the prize of gratitude, and do not, by giving satisfaction to others, take infamy for yourselves. You can make short work of our bodies, but it will be hard labor to live down the ill repute of it, for you would not be taking a proper vengeance on enemies, but on people who are well-disposed toward you and who fought you out of necessity. So if you made us unafraid for our lives, you would be reaching an upright verdict and taking into consideration that we surrendered willingly and with outstretched hands, and that it is the custom among the Greeks not to kill such prisoners. Moreover, we have always helped you in your troubles. Just look at the graves of your fathers, who were killed by the Persians and were buried in our soil and whom we annually honor at the public expense with offerings of shrouds and other customary rituals, bringing the first fruits yielded by our land in season, kindly from the friendly fields, allies still to the comrades we once had.[3]

You would violate all this with a corrupt verdict. Just think: Pausanias found your fathers a burial ground in the belief that he was laying them in friendly soil among friendly men; but if you kill us and transform Plataean into Theban land, what would you be doing but abandoning your fathers and your kindred on enemy ground to the men who slew them, stripped of the gifts of honor they now receive. Then too you will enslave the land on which the Greeks won their freedom; you will desolate the shrines of the gods to whom they prayed before defeating the Persians and tear away the ancestral offerings from those who founded them.

59. It would not, O men of Sparta, redound to your fame either to offend against the common laws of Greece and against your own forebears, or to kill us, your benefactors, in order to satisfy hatreds that are not yours,

---

3. The Plataeans wish to underscore the role of Plataea in the Persian Wars in part because mention of the Persians calls to mind the way the Thebans "medized" (went over to Persia) in that crisis.

when you yourselves have not been wronged. Spare us instead and prudently bend your judgments toward pity. Reflect not only on the terrible things we would suffer, but on how little we would deserve such suffering, and reflect, too, on the uncertainty of fate, which may undeservedly befall anyone. Impelled by custom and by need, we implore you, invoking the common altars of the Greek gods, to heed us. We invoke the oaths your fathers swore and call on you not to forget them, and, suppliants on the graves of your fathers, we pray that those dead not fall to the Thebans, and that we, their best friends, not be given over to their most hated foes. We call to mind those days when we performed the most illustrious deeds with them, whereas here, now, we are in danger of suffering deeds most foul. It is necessary, though very difficult, for men in our situation to bring this speech to an end, because it may mean bringing an end to our lives. But as we come to a close, we remind you that we did not hand over the city to the Thebans. Before we did that, we would have preferred to die by starvation, the most wretched of deaths. We trusted you and we surrendered to you, and it would be only just, if we fail to persuade you, for you to allow us to return to our previous condition so that we ourselves may choose our fate. We beg though that we Plataeans, we suppliants, the most loyal of the Greeks, not be taken from your hands, your promise of security, and given to our most hated enemies, the Thebans. Be our saviors, and do not destroy us while you are liberating the rest of Greece.

60. That is what the Plataeans said. The Thebans, afraid that the Spartans might give in to their argument, came forward and said that they, too, wanted to speak, since against their better judgment the Plataeans had been allowed a longer speech than they needed to answer the question. The judges so ordered, and they spoke as follows.

61. We would not have asked to say these words if the Plataeans had only given short answers to the question instead of turning against us with denunciations and irrelevantly going on about themselves, with explanations for what hasn't been alleged and praise for what hasn't been blamed. Now, though, we must contradict their denunciations and refute their explanations, so that they won't be helped by our bad name or by their famous one, and so that you can form a judgment as to the truth about both.

We first fell out with them because, although we founded the rest of Boeotia and then Plataea, along with other regions that we captured after driving out a mixed population, these Plataeans did not deign to be led by us as had been agreed from the beginning. Instead, they seceded from the rest of Boeotia and broke with ancestral custom, and when an attempt was made to force their compliance, they turned to Athens, with whom they did us a great deal of harm, and for which they were harmed in return.

62. Next, they say that after the barbarian attacked Greece, they were the only Boeotians who did not collaborate with the Persians, and with this fact they are especially fond of exalting themselves and reviling us. We, however, say that they did not collaborate with the Persians only because the Athenians didn't. By the same token, though, when the Athenians later attacked the Greeks, the Plataeans were the only Boeotians who collaborated with the Athenians. Consider also the condition we were in as we did what we did. At that time, our city was governed neither as a democracy nor as an oligarchy in which every citizen was equal before the law. Instead, a small dynasty controlled the government, and from the point of view of law, this is the opposite of truly prudent government—the closest

thing to tyranny. This group, hoping to extend its private power if Persia prevailed, kept the people down by force and invited the barbarian in. The whole city had to do this because it did not have control over its own affairs; so it is not fair to reproach it for the mistakes it made when it was not governed by the rule of law. And consider this. After the Persian left and Thebes adopted constitutional government, the Athenians later went on the attack and tried to put us and the rest of Greece in subjection to them. They had acquired most of our territory by fomenting insurrection, but we fought them and defeated them at Coronea and then went on to liberate Boeotia.[4] And we are now—loyally—joining in the liberation of the other cities by providing more cavalry and other equipment than any of the other allies.

63. That is what we have to say on the matter of collaboration. We will now go on to show that it is really you Plataeans who have wronged the Greeks and that you deserve whatever punishment you receive. You yourselves say that you became Athenian allies and citizens in order to take your revenge on us. It follows, then, that you should have led them only against us and not gone on the attack with them against others. It was surely possible for you not to, because if you were in any way unwilling to be led by Athens, there was still the alliance you had made against the Persians with these Spartans here. You certainly refer to it often enough. It would have been sufficient to turn us back, and what is more important, to plan your own course in safety. But no. You willingly and without restraint preferred the Athenian alliance. You also say that it would have been shameful to forsake your benefactors, but it was much more shameful and unjust to betray all of Greece, with whom you had sworn an alliance, than the Athenians only, when the Athenians were subjecting Greece to slavery and the others were trying to liberate it. The gratitude with which you repaid the Athenians went beyond the favors you received and does not expunge your shame because, as you yourselves say, you brought the Athenians in because you had been wronged, but then you became their accomplices in doing wrong to others. The fact is that it is shameful not to repay kindness for kindness except when the debt that is justly incurred is repaid in the service of injustice.

64. You have made it quite clear that it was not because of Greece that you were the only ones who didn't collaborate with the Persians then, but because of the Athenians. You wanted to do the same as the Athenians, the opposite of the rest of Greece. And now you expect to benefit from the good qualities you only displayed on account of others. Well, it won't work. You chose the Athenians—now suffer their fate, and don't bring up the old alliance as a reason why you should be spared now. You abandoned it and then you betrayed it by joining in, and not trying to stop, the subjugation of Aegina and some of its other members, and you did this willingly, with the same government you have always had, and with nobody to force you, unlike us. You even rejected neutrality, our final offer of peace before you were besieged. Who then is more deserving than you to be hated by the Greeks, you who flaunt your manly virtues in the service of their destruction? You have just shown that the virtues you say you had then didn't come naturally. You have been shown up for what you really are, and for what you always wanted, because you were fellow travelers with the Athenians as they went down the path of injustice.

---

4. The battle of Coronea took place in 447. Cf. 1.113.

65. So much for our forced collaboration with Persia and your willing collaboration with Athens. As to the last allegation of wrongdoing—that we unlawfully entered your city on a holy day while the treaty was in force—we don't think that we are any more at fault than you even in this, because if we, on our own, as your enemies, had made war on you by entering your city and ravaging your fields, why then we would have done you wrong; but if your foremost men, men distinguished by their wealth and birth, wanting to bring an end to your foreign alliances and wanting to restore your city to its common Boeotian heritage, freely invited us in, then what wrong did we do? After all, "Those who lead break the law, not those who follow."[5] In our judgment, though, they did no wrong and we did none. They were citizens just like you, only with more at stake. They opened their own gates and escorted us in—friends, not enemies—wanting to keep those of you who were bad from becoming worse and to help those of you who were better to get their due. They were there to discipline not your bodies, but your minds, and they were there not to turn the city over to strangers, but to restore it to its rightful home and kin, and to establish it as the enemy of none, with all alike at peace.

66. The proof that we did not act out of hostility is that we harmed no one and announced that anyone wishing to run the government according to the ancient traditions of Boeotia should come over to our side. You readily did so and kept the peace for a time after we reached an agreement. Later, though, you noticed that there were very few of us, whereupon your behavior was in no way consonant with our own (even allowing that we acted somewhat inappropriately in entering your city without the knowledge of the majority.) Instead of trying to talk us into leaving, you broke our agreement, resorted to violence, and attacked us. You killed some of our men in the fighting, which we do not feel so deeply, because after all there was some rough justice in that. But the men with outstretched hands, whom you took alive and later promised us not to kill, though you did, lawlessly, murder them—how can you say that was not a terrible act? Here were three crimes committed in a short time: the breach of the agreement, the subsequent murder of the men, and the false promise you made us not to kill them, provided we did you no injury in your fields. And yet you say that it was we who broke the law, and you claim that you should not have to incur any punishment! No, if these judges reach the right verdict, you shall be punished for all these things.

67. And that, men of Sparta, is why, on your behalf and our own, we have gone through this bill of particulars. It is so that you know that you have the right to condemn them and so that we may know that we are all the more righteously avenged. Don't let the recitation of past virtues—if, that is, there ever were any—move you to pity. Those virtues should be mitigating factors in the case of those who are wronged, but in the case of those who have committed heinous crimes, they call for a double punishment, because such crimes are far from what we have a right to expect from such a history. And don't let pitiful whining help them either—all this business of the graves of your fathers and their own desolation. After all, we can show that we suffer far worse from their murder of our young men, some of whose fathers died before your eyes as they led Boeotia at Coronea, while other old men, now left alone in desolate homes, make much more righteous supplication that these men be punished. People who suffer wrongful pain are worthy of pity, but we should *enjoy* the sufferings of those who, like these, really get what they deserve.

5. Cf. 3.55.

Their present isolation is their own fault, because they willingly pushed aside the superior alliance. They broke the law; they were not the first to suffer; and they did not suffer on our account. And even now, after having preferred hatred to justice, they won't be repaid with an equal retribution because they will be punished according to law, not after coming out of battle with their hands up, as they say, but after reaching an agreement to undergo a trial. Men of Sparta, uphold the laws of Greece these men have broken and return to us, who suffered the crime, just thanks for our zeal on your behalf. Don't shove us away in favor of these men's speeches. Set an example for the Greeks of giving prizes not for contests of words but of deeds, for which, when they are good, a brief report suffices, but which, when they are criminal, need a mask of arguments heavily made up with words. If only leaders came straight to the point before passing sentence—as you have done with your brief question to all these men—there would be less seeking after pretty speeches to explain unjust acts.

68. That is what the Thebans said. The Spartan judges decided that the question, whether they had ever been done a good turn by the Plataeans in the war, was justified. After all, the Spartans had all along been asking the Plataeans to keep the peace under the old treaty of Pausanias after the Persian Wars (or so they said), and the Plataeans had rejected the offer of neutrality before the siege under that treaty. The Spartans decided that justice served their purposes, that they were not bound by any treaties, and that they had been victims of Plataean criminality. So they again had the Plataeans brought before them one by one, and asked them the same question. Had they ever done the Spartans or their allies any good turns in the war? When the Plataeans said no, the Spartans had them taken away and killed without exception. They executed no fewer than two hundred Plataeans, along with twenty-five Athenians who had endured the siege with them. They sold the women as slaves. For about a year, they allowed the city to be occupied by whatever surviving Plataeans shared their way of thinking and by some Megarians who had been exiled during civil strife. Later, though, they razed the whole city to the ground and used the foundation stones of the houses to build an inn in front of the temple of Hera. The inn was two hundred feet in circumference, with rooms on the first and second floors. They used Plataean roofing and doors in the construction, and they used whatever brass and iron furniture they found inside the town to make couches, which they dedicated to Hera. They also built her a stone temple one hundred feet to a side. The land was removed from private ownership and rented to the Thebans for ten-year periods. Practically everything the Spartans did in utterly turning their backs on Plataea was done on account of Thebes, which the Spartans considered to be useful at that point in the war. That is how events turned out in Plataea, ninety-three years after it became an ally of Athens.

69. After fleeing the pursuing Athenians across the open sea, and then being driven by storms off Crete and scattered toward the Peloponnese, the forty ships that had gone to the aid of the Lesbians fell in with thirteen Leucadian and Ambraciot triremes at Cyllene, along with Brasidas, son of Tellis, who had come to advise Alcidas. After their failure at Lesbos, the Spartans wanted to strengthen the fleet and send it to Corcyra, which was having a civil war. There were only twelve Athenian ships at Naupactus, and Brasidas and Alcidas needed to make their preparations for the voyage and to set out before more ships arrived from Athens.

70. The Corcyraeans had been in turmoil ever since the prisoners of war who had been captured in the naval battles off Epidamnus had been released by the Corinthians and returned home.[6] The official version was that the men had been ransomed for eight hundred talents, which had been deposited with their proxeni at Corinth; in reality, they had been persuaded to win Corcyra over for Corinth. And they went from one citizen to another, incessantly working to bring about a secession of the city from the Athenian alliance. An Attic and a Corinthian ship arrived with ambassadors, speeches were given, and the Corcyraeans voted to remain allied to Athens under the already existing terms of their agreement,[7] but also to renew their original friendship with the Peloponnesians.

Now there was a certain Peithias, who was a self-appointed proxenus of the Athenians and a leader of the common people, and these former prisoners of war pressed charges against him on the grounds that he wanted to bring about the subjugation of Corcyra to Athens. He was acquitted and brought counter-charges against his five richest opponents, accusing them of habitually cutting down vine poles in the sacred precincts of Zeus and of Alcinous. The judges levied a fine of one stater per pole. Because of the size of the fine, the debtors went to the temples, where they sat as suppliants in hopes of paying off the fine in installments, but Peithias, who happened to be a member of the council, prevailed on the court to impose the full penalty of the law. Precluded from any legal recourse and learning that Peithias, for the rest of his term as councilman, aimed to persuade the populace to enter an offensive as well as a defensive alliance with Athens, these men banded together, armed themselves with daggers, broke suddenly into the council, and killed Peithias and up to sixty councilmen and private citizens. A few men who were of the same mind as Peithias escaped to the Athenian trireme, which was still there.

71. After taking these actions, the conspirators called the Corcyraeans together and announced that this had been the best course and would be least likely to lead to enslavement by Athens. They would maintain a peaceable neutrality, allowing only one ship into their harbor from either side at a time, and regarding more than that as hostile. Then, virtually as they spoke, they used force to make the people adopt their proposal. They also immediately dispatched envoys to Athens to give them whatever explanation of events seemed best and to persuade the exiles who were there not to take any action prejudicial to Corcyraean interests, lest there be Athenian reprisals.

72. When the envoys arrived, though, the Athenians arrested them and any refugees they had persuaded to join their side and held them on Aegina.

While this was going on, a Corinthian ship with Spartan envoys arrived at Corcyra, whereupon the men who controlled the government attacked the leadership of the people and defeated them after a struggle. When night fell, the people fled to and occupied the acropolis and the high ground of the city, along with the harbor at Hyllaicus. The oligarchs seized the agora, where most of them lived, along with the adjacent harbor that faced the mainland.

73. The next day, they fought each other at a distance with spears, arrows, and stones for a while, and then both sides sent messengers around to the fields, calling out to the slaves and promising them freedom. Most of the slaves allied themselves with the people, though eight hundred mercenaries from the mainland joined the other side.

---

6. Cf. 1.54, 55.
7. Cf. 1.44. This was a defensive alliance only. It prevented Corcyra from giving Athens such help as described in 2.25. In practice, of course, it was impossible to be allied to Athens and friendly with Sparta, but the vote represented a concession to the Corinthian interest.

74. Two days later, another battle took place, which the people won due to their numbers and the strength of their position. Their women also boldly took part in the fighting, hurling pottery from their houses and withstanding the tumult of battle in a way women cannot normally do. The oligarchs turned and ran in the late afternoon and became terrified that the people would take control of the arsenal with a rush and kill them all. So to prevent an onslaught, they set fire to the private and multiple dwellings that ringed the agora, sparing neither their own nor those of others, with the result that a great deal of commercial stock was consumed by flames, and the whole city would have been destroyed if a wind had blown up to carry the fire in its direction.

Both sides now stopped fighting and, staying where they were, kept a careful watch as they rested through the night. Once the people had won, the Corinthian ship slipped secretly out to sea and most of the mercenaries made their way unnoticed back to the mainland.

75. The next day, the Athenian general Nicostratus, son of Diitrephes, arrived from Naupactus with twelve ships and five hundred Messenian hoplites to help. He worked to arrange an agreement and persuaded the Corcyraeans to come to terms whereby ten of the most responsible (who had already left) would stand trial while everyone else would return to normal life after making peace with each other and entering an offensive and defensive alliance with Athens. Nicostratus prepared to set sail after bringing about this agreement, but the leaders of the people persuaded him to leave five of his ships behind with them, so that the opposition would be less inclined to unrest. In return, they would man five of their own ships and send them with him. He agreed, and they drafted their enemies for duty on the ships. These men, fearing that they were being sent to Athens, took refuge in the temple of the Dioscuri.[8] Nicostratus reassured them and tried to get them to leave the temple. When he couldn't talk them into it, the people armed themselves on the grounds that the oligarchs' unwillingness to sail must be a sign of evil intent. The people also confiscated the weapons in their opponents' homes, and would have killed some of the men they came across had not Nicostratus prevented it. When the other oligarchs saw what was happening, they sat down as suppliants in the temple of Hera. There were at least four hundred of them. The people, fearing that they might resort to violence, persuaded them to leave the temple and took them over to the island opposite the temple, to which they also sent over supplies.

76. At this point in the civil war, on the fourth or fifth day after the transfer of the men to the island, the fifty-three Peloponnesian ships that had anchored at Cyllene after the voyage to Ionia arrived on the scene. As before, they were commanded by Alcidas, though Brasidas was aboard as an advisor. After anchoring off the mainland, at Sybota harbor, they set out for Corcyra at dawn.

77. The tumultuous conditions, the situation in the city and the onset of the Peloponnesian fleet, had thrown people into a panic. Nevertheless they readied their sixty ships, which they sent out as fast as they were manned, despite the Athenian request to be allowed to sail out first with the whole Corcyraean fleet joining them later. Thus the Corcyraean ships were scattered helter-skelter before the enemy. Two ships immediately deserted; on others, the crews fell to fighting among themselves; it was a completely chaotic operation. When they saw this confusion, the Peloponnesians detached twenty ships to go

---

8. The Dioscuri were Castor and Pollux, Greek heroes generally believed to have been sons of Zeus and brothers of Helen of Troy. They had cults in several Greek states, including Athens.

against the Corcyraeans and sent the rest against the twelve Athenian ships, of
which two were the *Salaminia* and the *Paralus*.

78. The Corcyraeans, undisciplined and engaging the enemy in small
numbers, were being beaten at their end of the battle. Because of the number
of enemy ships, the Athenians feared encirclement and so attacked the enemy
squadron neither in its entirety nor at its center. Instead, they hit them on one
flank, sinking a ship. After that, the Peloponnesians formed themselves in a circle, whereupon the Athenians started rowing around them in an attempt to
throw them into confusion.[9] When the Peloponnesians fighting the Corcyraeans saw this, they feared a repetition of what had happened at Naupactus,
so they came to the rescue, joined forces, and bore down on the Athenians, who
began to back water and withdraw, hoping that the Corcyraeans would escape
to safety while they slowly retreated before an enemy that was concentrating its
forces on them.

79. This battle, such as it was, ended at sunset. Fearful that the victorious enemy might set sail to the city, or pick up the men on the island, or
stir up some other trouble, the Corcyraeans brought the men back from the
island to the temple of Hera and put the city under guard. The Peloponnesians, though victorious in the naval battle, did not venture to attack the
city and instead sailed back to their base on the mainland with thirteen Corcyraean ships they had captured. They didn't sail against the city the next
day either, although the Corcyraeans were frightened and in disarray, and
although it is said that Brasidas urged Alcidas (with whom he did not have
an equal vote) to do so. Instead, they made a landing at the promontory at
Leucimme and ravaged the fields.

80. During this time, the Corcyraean populace was in absolute terror that
the ships would attack them, so they held talks with the suppliants and the other
oligarchs on how to save the city. They even persuaded some of them to board
the ships, managing to man thirty of them in anticipation of a naval assault. The
Peloponnesians, however, ravaged the countryside until noon and sailed away.
That night, they learned from signal fires at Leucas that sixty Athenian ships
were headed their way. (They had been sent, with Eurymedon, son of Thucles,
in command, when Athens got news of the civil war and of the impending assault of Alcidas' ships on Corcyra.)

81. Accordingly, that very night, the Peloponnesians hurriedly made their
way home, hugging the shore. They carried their ships over the Isthmus of Leucas, so as not to be seen sailing around the peninsula, and escaped. When the
Corcyraeans learned that the Athenian ships were approaching and that the
enemy was leaving, they took the Messenian hoplites, who had been outside the
city, and brought them inside. Next they ordered the ships they had manned to
sail around to the Hyllaic harbor, and then, while the ships were going around,
the populace killed all of their enemies that they could find. Then, at the harbor, they disembarked the oligarchs they had persuaded to board the ships and
killed them; and then they went to the temple of Hera, persuaded some fifty of
the suppliants to stand trial, and imposed the death penalty on the spot. Most
of them had not been talked into the trial, and when they saw what was happening, they killed each other right there in the temple or hanged themselves
from trees. Others killed themselves in any way they could. Eurymedon remained at Corcyra for seven days with his sixty ships, during which Corcyraeans
ceaselessly slaughtered those among them whom they thought to be enemies.

9. Cf. Phormio's tactics at the first battle off Naupactus (2.84).

They were accused of seeking to dissolve the democracy, but some died because of private feuds, and others because their captors owed them money. One saw every imaginable kind of death, and everything that is likely to take place in situations like this did, in fact, take place—and even more. For example, fathers killed their sons; people were dragged from the temples and slaughtered in front of them; some were even walled up in the temple of Dionysus and left to die.

82. That was the kind of brutality the civil war led to, though it seemed even worse, because it was the first in this war. Later virtually all of Greece was in a frenzy, with dissension everywhere, with the leaders of the people trying to bring in the Athenians, and the oligarchs the Spartans. In peacetime, there would have been neither pretext nor inclination for inviting their intervention; but in war, where alliances are at one and the same time a way to hurt your enemies and gain something for yourself, inducements came easily to those who wanted radical change. Events struck these strife-torn cities (as they always do and always will for so long as human nature remains the same) hard and fast with more or less violence, quickly changing shape as change kept pace with happenstance. In times of peace and prosperity, both cities and individuals can have lofty ideals because they have not fallen before the force of overwhelming necessity. War, however, which robs us of our daily needs, is a harsh teacher and absorbs most people's passions in the here and now.

But to resume. Once civil war had broken out in the cities, latecomers to the phenomenon learned about what had already happened elsewhere and went even further in rethinking accepted ideas about taking power, which became ever more cunning, and about taking revenge, which became ever more cruel. People even changed the accepted meanings of words as they saw fit. "Foolish boldness" came to be considered a "courageous devotion to the cause"; "watchful waiting" became "an excuse for cowardice." "Prudence" was a "mask for unmanliness," and "a jack of all trades" was "a master of none." Being "beside yourself with rage" was posited as "part of the human condition," and "thinking things over" to "be on the safe side" was "a glib excuse for a cop-out." The lover of violence was "semper fi,"[1] and the man who challenged him a "subversive." If you plotted against someone and got away with it, you were "smart," and you were even more "brilliant" if you saw plots coming. But if you planned ahead so as to have no fear of plots and counterplots, you were a "traitor to the party" and "panicked by the opposition." In other words, you were praised for beating someone to it in doing harm and for egging on those who meant no harm at all.

Even relatives were rejected in favor of fellow party members, who were less likely to need a good reason to take risks. These parties did not operate in the service of legitimate interests according to established custom, but outside the rules for selfish gain, and mutual trust was not enforced by the invocation of the gods, but by complicity in crime. A fair proposal from the opposition was accepted by the party in power with safeguards for implementation and not in a spirit of well-bred liberality. People were willing to get hurt provided they were able to get even. If they ever took oaths of reconciliation, they did so in an emergency on the spur of the moment, and their promises derived no binding strength from anywhere else; but then, given the opportunity, the first side that was able to mobilize itself and to see an opening took greater pleasure in clan-

---

1. The Greek here, *pistos aiei*, which means "always faithful," translates literally into the Latin *"semper fidelis."* Semper fidelis became the motto of the United States Marine Corps, which often abbreviates it to *"semper fi."*

destine than in open revenge because of the trust of the other side, and figured not only that they would more safely win by deceit, but that they would gain kudos for having been smart. Your average ignoramus would prefer to be called a smart criminal than an honest man, and besides, "honest" makes him cringe while "smart" makes him proud.

The cause of all this was power pursued for the sake of greed and personal ambition, which led in turn to the entrenchment of a zealous partisanship. The leadership in the cities on both sides advanced high-sounding phrases like "The equality of free men before the law," or "A prudent aristocracy," but while serving the public interest in their speeches, they created a spoils system. Struggling with one another for supremacy in every way they could, they kept committing the most horrible crimes and escalated to ever greater revenges, never to promote justice and the best interests of the city, but—constantly setting the limit at whatever most pleased each side at any given moment—they were always prepared to sate their partisanship either by rigging votes or by seizing power with their bare hands. Thus neither side observed the rules of piety: they were more respected for the high words with which they got away with performing their base actions. As for the citizens who tried to be neutral, they were killed by both sides, either because they did not join in the fighting, or out of envy because they were managing to survive.

83. Thus the civil wars led to every sort of depravity imaginable in Greece, and openness, which is the better part of liberality, disappeared in utter ridicule. Ideological strife produced distrust everywhere, and nothing—no binding word or awe-inspiring oath—could end it, because when any one side had the upper hand, they were incapable of trusting others and made sure to provide against attack, convinced that they could not hope for security.

Lesser intellects fared best, on the whole, because their apprehensions about their own shortcomings and their opponents' intelligence, ability to manipulate ideas, and win debates, led them to get a head start in hatching plots, which they then moved boldly to execute. The more intelligent, disdainfully thinking that they would know about such things in time, and that they did not have to take by force what it was possible to achieve by policy, were often caught off guard and slaughtered.

84. [Corcyra was the place where most of these things first occurred. People did just what they would do when they had been governed more by caprice than by prudence and when, offered a chance for revenge, they could finally get even. Some who coveted their neighbors' property sought freedom from their lifelong poverty by going outside the law—especially when it was poverty coupled with oppression. Others, not actuated by greed but carried away by ignorant rage, attacked their equals with an implacable savagery. As people's lives kept pace with the tumultuous changes in the city, human nature came to predominate over the laws; human nature, which habitually breaks laws anyway, showed itself in its purest form as eager to be above the law, as the enemy of all authority. If it were not, if people were not insane with malice, they would not have placed revenge above piety and self-interest above justice. In taking their revenge on others, people annul the common laws of mankind, which are the hope of everyone who falters and would find safety, leaving nothing behind for the time when they are themselves in danger and have need of them.][2]

85. Thus the Corcyraeans in the city unleashed these passions—the first of their kind—on each other, after which Eurymedon and the Athenians sailed

2. Many editors consider this passage to be spurious.

away in their ships. Now five hundred Corcyraeans had managed to escape, and these exiles later captured some fortresses on the mainland, thus gaining control of Corcyraean territory opposite the island, and using that as its base of operations did a great deal of harm as they raided and plundered the inhabitants of the island. The result was a severe famine in the city. The exiles also sent envoys to Sparta and Corinth to discuss returning them to power, but nothing came of the negotiations. Some time later, they got together some ships and mercenaries and made a landing on the island. There were about six hundred of them in all. They burned their boats so that their only hope would lie in gaining control of the island. After climbing Mount Istone and building a fortress there, they proceeded to raid the city and to solidify their control of the countryside.

86. At the end of that same summer,[3] Athens sent twenty ships to Sicily, with Laches, son of Melanopus, and Charoeades, son of Euphiletus, in joint command. The reason was that war had broken out between Syracuse and Leontini. Except for Camarina, the other Dorian cities were allied with Syracuse. At the beginning of the war between Athens and Sparta, these cities had lined up as allies of Sparta, although they did not join in the fighting. On the other side, the Chalcidian cities and Camarina were allied with Leontini. As to Italy, the Locrians were with Syracuse and Rhegium was with Leontini because of bonds of kinship. On the basis of their ancient alliance and their Ionian heritage, the allies of Leontini sent envoys to Athens to persuade the Athenians to send ships. They were, they said, being blockaded on land and sea by the Syracusans. The Athenians did send the ships, allegedly because of their long-standing relationship, but really because they wanted to keep grain from reaching the Peloponnese from that region and to feel out whether it would be possible to take control of things in Sicily. Accordingly, they set up a base at Rhegium, in Italy, and began, along with their allies, to take part in the war. And the summer came to an end.

87. The next winter, the plague fell on Athens for the second time. It had never entirely gone away, although there had been some breaks in it. The first epidemic had lasted two years, the second lasted at least one, and nothing demoralized the Athenians and weakened their fighting power so much as this plague. From the hoplite ranks, no fewer than forty-four hundred men died, along with three hundred cavalry and an indeterminable number of the general population. This was also the time of the frequent famous earthquakes in Athens, Euboea, and Boeotia, but especially in Boeotian Orchomenus.

88. That same winter, the Athenians on Sicily and the Rhegians invaded the so-called Isles of Aeolus with thirty ships. These islands are invulnerable to attack in the summer because of the lack of water. The Liparians, who are Cnidian colonists, occupy the islands, although they mainly live on one of them, a not particularly large island called Lipara. They set out from this island to the others—Didyme, Strongyle, and Hiera—where they farm. The people who live there believe that Hephaestus keeps his forge on Hiera because they see great flames shooting up from the place at night and smoke during the day. These islands lie off Sicel and Messanian[4] territory and are allied with the Syracusans. When the Liparians gave them no support, the Athenians slashed and burned the land and sailed back to Rhegium.

---

3. The summer of 427.
4. Readers should not confuse Messana, in Sicily, with Messenia in the Peloponnese.

Sicily and Southern Italy

Thus the winter came to an end, and along with it the fifth year of this war that I, Thucydides wrote down.

89. The following summer, the Peloponnesians and their allies got as far as the Isthmus of Corinth for an invasion of Attica, with Agis, son of Archidamus and king of Sparta, in command;[5] but they turned back after a long series of seismic shocks and there was no invasion that year.[6]

At around the time that all the earthquakes were taking place, the sea pulled back from the shore at Orobiae in Euboea, formed a wave, and washed up over part of the city. It receded from some of this land, but left the rest completely under water, so that what was once dry land is now a part of the sea. The flood drowned everyone who was unable to run up to the high ground ahead of its onrush.

There was a similar flood at Atalanta, the island off the coast of Eastern Locris. It swept away some of the Athenian garrison there and shattered one of two boats it threw up on shore.

There was a receding and rising wave at Peparethus, although there was no flood. An earthquake did, however, shake down part of the wall, the town hall, and a few houses.

In my opinion, the reason for these events was that wherever the earthquake was at its most violent, it drew back the sea and then sent the flood all the more forcefully forward. I do not think these events would have taken place without the earthquake.

90. There was other fighting in Sicily that summer as the occasion arose. Sicilians made war on each other, while the Athenians campaigned with their allies. From now on, I will include only the most noteworthy actions in Sicily that the Athenians and their allies undertook and that their opponents took against them. The Athenian general Charoeades having by now been killed by the Syracusans in the fighting, Laches took sole command of the fleet and launched a campaign with the allies against Mylae, in Messana. Two Messanian tribes happened to be defending Mylae, and they had set an ambush for the troops who disembarked from the ships. The Athenians and their allies fought off their attackers and killed a great many of them. They then stormed the bulwarks and forced the defenders to come to an agreement whereby they would hand over the acropolis and join in the attack on Messana. Later, at the approach of the Athenians and their allies, the Messanians also came to terms, giving up hostages and making the usual pledges.

91. That same summer, the Athenians sent thirty ships around the Peloponnese, with Demosthenes, son of Alcisthenes, and Procles, son of Theodorus, in command. They also sent sixty ships and two thousand hoplites against Melos, with Nicias, son of Niceratus, in command. Their aim was to bring over the Melians, who, though islanders, would not accede to Athens and join in the Athenian alliance. They ravaged the country, but the Melians would still not submit, so they left Melos and went to Oropus in the Graean territory. They made a night landing, and the hoplites immediately made their way from the ships on foot to Tanagra in Boeotia. Meanwhile, the whole Athenian army had left Athens, with Hipponicus, son of Callias, and Eurymedon, son of Thucles, in command, and when the signal was given, they went overland to meet the hoplite force. They took up a position in Tanagra that day, ransacked the coun-

5. Though Thucydides has not mentioned this, Archidamus has apparently died.
6. The shocks and their aftereffects would have been a deterrent to an invasion, but they would also have been seen as a very bad omen and might have made the Spartans turn back even had there been fewer of them.

try, and bivouacked overnight. The next day, they defeated a force of Tanagrans who came out of the city, along with some Thebans who had come to their aid. The Athenians gathered the spoils of battle, set up a victory marker, and then broke camp and withdrew, the army to the city and the hoplites to their ships. Then Nicias sailed along the coast of the Eastern Locrians with his sixty ships, deforesting coastal areas here and there as he made his way back home.

92. At around the same time, the Spartans founded their colony of Heraclea in Trachinia. Their strategy was as follows. The Malians comprise three groups: the Paralians, the Hiereans, and the Trachinians. Of these, the Trachinians had been decimated in a war with their neighbors, the Oetaeans. At first, they intended to form an alliance with Athens, but they feared that Athens would not prove to be a reliable ally, so they sent instead to Sparta and chose Tisamenus as their ambassador. Doris, the mother city of Sparta, whose people had the same needs, joined in this diplomatic mission, for they too were being worn down by the Oetaeans. The Spartans heard out the ambassadors and decided to send the colonists. They wanted to avenge the Trachinians and the Dorians, but they also thought the city would be well placed for them in their war with Athens. A fleet could be built there for an attack on Euboea, which was just a short crossing away, and it would also provide easy access to Thrace. For every reason, therefore, they were eager to colonize the place. The first thing they did was to consult the god at Delphi, and at his command, they sent out colonists from Sparta and from neighboring cities. They also called on volunteers from the rest of Greece to join in, except for Ionians, Achaeans, and certain other peoples. Three Spartans—Leon, Alcidas, and Damagon—led the colony. They decided on a place and built a walled city from scratch. It is now called Heraclea, and it is about five miles from Thermopylae and two and a half miles from the sea. They also built a dockyard and walled off Thermopylae at the pass itself to make the city even easier to defend.

93. When this town was founded by settlers from different regions, the Athenians were at first alarmed. They believed that its position made it a threat, especially against Euboea, because of the short crossing to Cenaeum in Euboea. But things later turned out very differently, because the town came to pose no threat whatever. The reason was that the Thessalians held sway over the region where the town was built. At first, the place was extremely populous, because all sorts of people enthusiastically moved there in the belief that with Spartan founders, the city was safe; but the Thessalians, fearing such a large force dwelling nearby, made unremitting war on these newly arrived people until they completely wore them down by attrition. Worst of all were the governors the Spartans themselves sent out from time to time. These men ruined everything and brought about a reduction of the population by scaring away most of the people with their harsh and at times inept administration, thus making it all the easier for their neighbors to overpower them.

94. That same summer, at about the same time the Athenians were on Melos, the first action of the Athenian troops from the thirty ships that had been sent around the Peloponnese[7] was to ambush and kill some of the garrison in Ellomenus, in the territory of Leucas. Next they went to the city of Leucas with a much larger force, consisting of the Acarnanian army (all of which had followed them, except for the Oeniadae), the Zacynthians, the Cephallenians, and fifteen Corcyraean ships. The Leucadians held still in the face of a superior force that ravaged the fields outside the isthmus as well as inside it, where the

7. Cf. 3.91.

city and the temple of Apollo are. The Acarnanians asked the Athenian general, Demosthenes, to wall off the Leucadians, thinking that they could easily force them to surrender and thus get rid of a city that had always been their enemy. At the time, however, the Messenians were winning Demosthenes over to the view that such a large combined force offered him an excellent opportunity to attack the Aetolians. They were hostile to Naupactus, and if he defeated them, he could easily subject the other mainlanders in the region to Athens. The Messenians said that the Aetolian people were numerous and good fighters, but that they lived in unwalled villages that were widely dispersed. They were also lightly armed, so it would be easy to crush them before they could gather their forces. The Messenians urged Demosthenes to attack the Apodotians first, then the Ophionians, and after them the Eurytanians, the largest of the Aetolian tribes. (It is said that the Eurytanians speak an incomprehensible dialect of Greek and that they eat their meat raw.) Once they were conquered, however, the other mainlanders in the region would quickly come over to him.

95. Demosthenes was persuaded to follow this course partly as a favor to the Messenians, but mostly because control of Aetolia would enable him and his mainland allies to take an overland route in an attack on Boeotia without additional forces from Athens. He would be able to pass through Western Locris and into Dorian Cytinium, keeping Mount Parnassus on his right, to the east, until he descended into Phocis. The Phocians would probably join forces with him willingly because of their long-standing friendship with Athens, but they could be brought over by force, if need be. And there, just across the Phocian border, was Boeotia.

Therefore, much against the wishes of the Acarnanians, Demosthenes set sail from Leucas with his whole army and hugged the shore until he came to Sollium. He then made his plan known to the Acarnanians, but they would not go along with it because he had not walled off Leucas. So he began his campaign against the Aetolians with the rest of the army: the Cephallenians, Messenians, Zacynthians, and (since the fifteen Corcyraean ships had left) with three hundred Athenian marines from Athenian ships. He made Oeneon, in Western Locris, his base of operations and started out from there. Now these Western Locrians were allies and were supposed to join up in full strength with the Athenians in the interior. Their participation in the expedition was considered a great advantage because they bordered on the Aetolians, used the same type of equipment, and were familiar with both their terrain and their style of fighting.

96. Demosthenes and his army camped overnight at the temple of Nemean Zeus, where it is said that the poet Hesiod was killed by the people of that region, it having been prophesied that he would be killed "in Nemea." At dawn, Demosthenes broke camp and made his way into Aetolia. On the first day there he captured Potidania, on the second Crocyleum, and on the third Teichium. He stayed there and sent all his booty back to Eupalium, in Western Locris. His plan was to go on in this way, conquering everything as far as the Ophionians; if they would not come to terms, he would withdraw to Naupactus and launch another campaign against them later.

From the very first, this army and its aims were well known to the Aetolians, and once it had invaded, all the Aetolians came to the defense in great numbers. Even the most distant Ophionians, the Bomians and Callians who are spread as far as the Malian Gulf, came to help.

97. The Messenians repeated the advice they had given Demosthenes at first, when they told him that it would be easy to conquer Aetolia. They told him not to wait until the combined forces of the Aetolians could take up positions

against him, but to move as fast as possible against the villages and try to capture everything in his path. No one had stood up to him yet, so buoyed by success, he followed their advice. He did not wait for the Western Locrians who were to have joined him, and whose lightly armed javelin men he badly needed. He marched up to Aegitium, attacked it, and took it by storm. He was able to do this because its people had slipped away and taken up positions on top of the hills above the town. (The place was in high country about ten miles from the sea.) The other Aetolians, who had by now come to the relief of Aegitium, ran down from the hills on all sides and attacked the Athenians and their allies, hurling javelins. They gave ground when the Athenian army counterattacked and pressed forward when they withdrew. For the most part that was what the battle was like—chase and retreat, retreat and chase—and the Athenians were at a disadvantage in both.

98. The Athenians could hold out for as long as their archers had arrows and were able to shoot them, because the lightly armored Aetolians would pull back out of range, but the archers broke ranks after the captain of the archery company was killed, and then, exhausted from the long, repetitive struggle against Aetolians who constantly pressed forward, constantly hurling javelins at them, the others just turned and ran, falling into blind gulches and unfamiliar terrain where they were destroyed. To make matters worse, Chromon, their Messenian guide through that country, had been killed.

Continuously hurling javelins, the lightly armed, swift-footed Aetolians outran and caught many fleeing soldiers and killed them on the spot. Most lost their way and were driven into the pathless forest, whereupon the Aetolians brought fire and torched the woods around them. The rout and destruction of the Athenian army took every conceivable form, and the survivors were barely able to get back to the sea and their base at Oeneon, in Western Locris. Many allied troops were killed, along with over one hundred twenty Athenian hoplites. This was the largest number of men to die from the same age group up to this point in the war, and they came from the finest families in Athens. Procles, the other general, was also killed. Under a truce, the Athenians gathered their dead from the Aetolians, withdrew to Naupactus, and later made their way back to Athens in their ships. Demosthenes stayed behind at Naupactus and its environs, frightened of what the Athenians might do to him.

99. At about the same time, the Athenians who had been operating off Sicily had also sailed to Italian Locri, where they overwhelmed the Locrian defenders and captured a small fort on the Halex River.[8]

100. That same summer, the Aetolians had at first sent envoys to Corinth and Sparta. They were Tolophus the Ophionian, Boriades the Eurytanian, and Tisander the Apodotian, and their mission was to persuade Corinth and Sparta, in view of the Messenian invitation to Athens, to send them an army for an attack on Naupactus. Accordingly, the Spartans that autumn despatched three thousand of the allies' hoplites. Five hundred of these came from the newly founded city of Heraclea, in Trachinia. Eurylochus, a Spartan, commanded the army in conjunction with two other Spartans, Macarius and Menedaius.

101. After the army gathered at Delphi, Eurylochus sent an embassy to the Western Locrians because the road to Naupactus ran through their territory, but also because he wanted to induce them to break away from the Athenians.

---

8. This Locri is different from the Western Locris in the region north of the Corinthian Gulf where Demosthenes and his men had established a base, and different from the area of Euboea that Nicias ravaged, though the residents of all are called Locrians.

Of the Locrians, the Amphissans were most willing to cooperate with him, frightened on account of the hated Phocians.[9] The Amphissans were the first to surrender hostages, and they persuaded the Locrians, who were afraid of the approaching army, to do the same. The Myonians, who hold the most difficult part of the road into Western Locris, surrendered hostages, then the Hypneans, Messapians, Tritaeans, Chalaeans, Tolphonians, Isians, and Oeantheans. All of these peoples also joined the Spartan campaign. The Olpaeans surrendered hostages, but did not join, and the Hyaeans did not surrender any hostages until one of their villages was captured—a place by the name of Polis.

102. After everything was ready and the hostages were transferred to Cytinium, in Doris, Eurylochus marched his army toward Naupactus through Western Locrian territory, taking the Locrian towns of Oeneon and Eupalium on the way, since they had not capitulated. By the time he reached the area around Naupactus, the Aetolians had joined in the operation. They rampaged through the countryside and captured the unwalled suburbs; they also attacked and captured Molycrium, which was subject to Athens although it had been a Corinthian colony. After the events in Aetolia, Demosthenes the Athenian was still in the area around Naupactus. He had gotten news of the approaching armies and became alarmed for the city, so he went to the Acarnanians and persuaded them to come to the relief of Naupactus. This was difficult to do after the withdrawal from Leucas, but they sent a thousand hoplites aboard his ships, and when they reached the city, they began to strengthen the defenses of the place. The wall was long, the defenders were few, and there had been great concern that they would not be able to hold out. When Eurylochus and his men learned that the army was now in the city and that it could no longer be taken by storm, they withdrew—not to the Peloponnese, but to what we now call Aeolis, to Calydon and Pleuron—and to the area thereabouts. He also went to Proschium in Aetolia. The reason he went to these places was that the Ambraciots had approached him and prevailed on him to join them in an attack on Amphilochian Argos as well as on the rest of Amphilochia and Acarnania. They had told him that if he gained control of these people, he could bring that whole region of the mainland into the Spartan alliance.[1] Eurylochus, persuaded, dismissed the Aetolians and took no further action with his army in those parts until the time came to join forces with the Ambraciots, when they began their campaign against Amphilochian Argos.

And so that summer came to an end.

103. The following winter, the Athenians in Sicily went on the move with their Greek allies and some Sicel allies who had revolted from an authoritarian Syracusan rule. They went against the Sicel city of Inessa, whose acropolis was held by Syracusans. They attacked the place but were unable to take it, so they withdrew. The Syracusans then left their fortifications, fell on the rear guard of the retreating Athenian allies, and routed a part of the army, killing not a few of them. After this action, Laches and his Athenians staged some amphibious landings at the Caicinus River in Italian Locri, where they defeated some three hundred defenders under Proxenus, son of Capaton, and then sailed away with the booty they had captured.

9. In 2.9 we were told that the Phocians were allies of Sparta, but in 3.95 Thucydides speaks of their long-standing friendship with Athens. In that passage, though, he says that Demosthenes thinks he might have to bring them over by force. Here the Amphissans fear them as allies of Sparta. The Phocians, like some other remote peoples (cf. the many shifts of Perdiccas) seem to have been adept at changing sides.
1. Compare these with the promises made to Demosthenes at 3.94.

104. That same winter, the Athenians also purified Delos because of some oracle or other.[2] The tyrant Peisistratus had already purified the island—not all of it, but as much of it as could be seen from the temple. This time, though, the whole island was purified in the following way: the Athenians carried away all of the tombs of the dead on Delos and proclaimed that from then on people must not be allowed to die or give birth on the island, but must be taken over to Rhenea. (Rhenea is so close to Delos that when Polycrates, the tyrant of Samos, had naval superiority for a time and ruled over the other islands, he captured Rhenea and dedicated it to the Delian Apollo by attaching it to Delos with a chain.) After the purification, the Athenians restored the Delian games, thereafter to be held every five years. In the past, there were great gatherings on Delos by the Ionians and the neighboring islanders. They went to the festival with their wives and children, just as the Ionians now go to the festival of Ephesus. Both gymnastic and musical competitions were held, and the city-states organized choruses. Homer makes it clear that this was so in these verses from the *Hymn to Apollo*:

> It was Delos that most delighted your heart, O Apollo,
> Delos where the long-robed Ionians gathered
> With their wives and children on your streets.
> There, commemorating you with boxing, dance, and song,
> They gave you pleasure whenever they held their games.

In the same hymn, Homer shows that there was also a musical competition that attracted singers, for, after celebrating the Delian women's dance, he ends his praise with these verses, in which he also mentions himself:

> So then, girls, farewell to you all, and Apollo be gracious,
> And Artemis, too. Think of me, though, from time to time,
> Whenever some other long-suffering stranger
> Arrives hereabouts and asks,
> "Girls, which of the singers who frequents these parts
> Is sweetest to you, the one you delighted in most?"
> Let every one of you then answer politely,
> "A blind man, but he lives in rocky Chios."

In this way, Homer bears witness that, even in antiquity, there was a large gathering and festival on Delos. Later the islanders and the Athenians sent choruses along with animal sacrifices. Most of the pageantry surrounding the competitions was abandoned, though, probably because the region had fallen on hard times, until the Athenians instituted the new games, which included horse races, a thing unknown in the past.

105. That same winter, the Ambraciots kept the promise by which they had induced Eurylochus to stay in the Aeolid with his army and marched out against Amphilochian Argos with three thousand hoplites. They invaded the Argive territory and captured Olpae, a well-defended fort on a hilltop near the sea, which the Acarnanians had fortified long before and used as a courthouse common to all the states of Acarnania. It is about three miles from Amphilochian Argos, which is also on the coast. Some of the Acarnanians went to the aid of Argos, but others went to a place in those parts called "the Springs," where they set up camp

---

2. See 1.8 and Herodotus 1.64. The purification of Delos may have been undertaken to appease Apollo after the second onset of the plague. (See 3.87 and, for Apollo as the bringer of plague, the *Iliad*, Book 1.)

and stood guard to keep the Peloponnesians from passing through unnoticed to the Ambraciots. They also sent to Demosthenes (who had led the Aetolian campaign), asking him to be their commander, and to the fleet of twenty Athenian ships that were at the time off the Peloponnese under the command of Aristotle,[3] son of Timocrates, and of Hierophon, son of Antimnestus. Meanwhile, the Ambraciots at Olpae sent a message to Ambracia ordering them to come to their aid in full strength, because they had become afraid that the troops with Eurylochus would not be able to break through the Acarnanian line and that they would either have to fight it out alone or attempt a dangerous retreat.

106. When they found out that the Ambraciots had reached Olpae, the Peloponnesians with Eurylochus struck camp at Proschium and went to their aid on the double. They forded the Achelous River and marched through Acarnania, which was deserted because everyone had gone to help Argos. They kept the city of Stratus, with its garrison, on the right and the rest of Acarnania on the left. After crossing Stratian territory, they marched past Phytia, along the outer border of Medeon, and then through Limnaea. They left Acarnania and entered Agraea, which was a friendly territory. They took the road to Mount Thyamus, which is in Agraean territory, marched over it, and descended into Argive territory after night had already fallen. They then slipped unnoticed between Argos and the Acarnanian guard at the Springs and joined forces with the Ambraciots at Olpae.

107. After teaming up, they positioned themselves, come daybreak, at a place called Metropolis, where they made an encampment. Not much later, the Athenians with their twenty ships reached the Ambracian Gulf in relief of Argos. Aboard them were Demosthenes with two hundred Messenian hoplites and sixty Athenian archers.

The ships blockaded the ridge of Olpae from the sea. Meanwhile, the Acarnanians and those few Amphilochians who were not pinned down by the Ambraciots had come up to Argos and prepared to fight the enemy. They also chose Demosthenes to command the allies in conjunction with their own generals. He then led them close to Olpae and camped where a wide ravine separated the two sides. They remained there for five days; on the sixth, both sides positioned themselves for battle. Now the Peloponnesians had a larger army, which outflanked the enemy, so Demosthenes, fearing encirclement, stationed up to four hundred light- and heavy-armed troops at an ambush in a bushy hollow on the road, so that when the armies clashed and the enemy performed its flanking maneuver, these troops could come out of hiding and be behind them. When preparations had been made on both sides, they began to approach each other. Demosthenes commanded the right wing, consisting of Messenians and a few Athenians. On the other flank, the Acarnanians moved forward arrayed by tribes, along with what Amphilochian javelin men were on hand. The Peloponnesians and the Ambraciots were arrayed in no particular order, except for the Mantineans. These were clustered on the left wing, though not at its end, which was held by Eurylochus and his men, opposite Demosthenes and the Messenians.

108. When they had come to hand-to-hand combat, the Peloponnesians outflanked and began to encircle the right wing of their opponents, whereupon the Acarnanians came out of their hiding place and routed them after falling on them from behind. These troops did not so much as stand and fight, and their panic caused most of the army to run away, utterly terrified at the sight of Eu-

---

3. Not the philosopher, who lived in the fourth century and was not an Athenian citizen.

rylochus and the most powerful contingent of their army being destroyed. In this area of battle, the Messenians with Demosthenes had the best of it by far. The Ambraciots and the troops on the right wing defeated their opponents, however, and chased them back to Argos, but then they are the fiercest fighters of all the peoples in that region. They were hard pressed by the remaining Acarnanians, however, when they returned and saw that most of the army had been thoroughly defeated. With great difficulty, they found safety at Olpae, although many of them were killed as they raced forward out of formation, with no discipline whatever—all but the Mantineans, who, out of the whole army, maintained cohesion in their retreat.

The battle ended at nightfall.

109. Eurylochus and Macarius had been killed in battle, so on the next day Menedaius assumed sole command. Given this great defeat, he did not know how, besieged by land and blockaded by Athenian ships at sea, he could either stay where he was or make a safe retreat. So he proposed talks to Demosthenes and the Acarnanian generals about gathering up the dead, but also about a retreat under a truce. The Athenians set up a victory marker and returned the dead—also collecting some three hundred of their own dead—but they would not openly agree to the withdrawal of all the troops. But Demosthenes and his fellow generals from Acarnania secretly agreed to allow the Mantineans and Menedaius, with the other Peloponnesian commanders and notables among them, to withdraw quickly. They wanted to isolate the Ambraciots and their troops of mercenaries, but most of all they wanted to vilify the Spartans and Peloponnesians among the Greeks in that region as ready to leave them in the lurch if it served their own interests. The Peloponnesians gathered their dead, hurriedly buried them as well as they could, and secretly prepared for the withdrawal of those to whom it had been promised.

110. Meanwhile, Demosthenes and the Acarnanians received a message that the Ambraciots, acting on the first news from Olpae, and knowing nothing of what had happened, had marched out of their city in full strength and were making their way through Amphilochian territory with the intention of joining forces with the defenders at Olpae. Demosthenes immediately detached a part of his army to set ambushes and secure the strong points along the way and then readied the rest of the army to join in the assault.

111. While this was going on, the Mantineans and others who were part of the secret truce left camp in small groups, ostensibly to gather herbs and firewood, which in fact they did; but then, when they had gotten a good distance from Olpae, they quickly picked up their pace. When the Ambraciots and the others, who were not in this large group of soldiers leaving the camp, realized that they were running away, they too took off at a run in order to catch up with them. At the same time, the Acarnanian troops at first thought that the whole camp at Olpae was trying to get away without a truce and also began to go after the Peloponnesians, but they were stopped by their very own generals, who explained that a truce had been made. At this point, one of the men, believing that they had been betrayed by their officers, threw his spear at the generals. Nevertheless, they thereafter let the Peloponnesians and Mantineans go and began to kill the Ambraciots, although there was a great deal of disagreement and uncertainty about whether someone was Peloponnesian or Ambraciot. They killed some two hundred of these men; the rest got away to the neighboring Agraean territory, where they were received by the Agraean king, Salynthius, who was their friend.

112. Meanwhile, the Ambraciots from the city had reached Idomene, which is made up of two high ridges. After dark, Demosthenes' advance forces,

unnoticed, took up positions on the higher of the two and bivouacked there; the Ambraciots had already gone up the lower ridge. After dinner, just as night fell, Demosthenes moved out with the remaining portion of his army, himself taking the pass between the ridges with half of it, while the rest positioned itself throughout the Amphilochian mountains.

At dawn, he hit the Ambraciots while they were still in their bedding and had no advance warning of what was happening; on the contrary, they thought the attackers were their own men. Demosthenes sent in the Messenians first, for the good reason that they spoke a Dorian dialect. It was still dark, and they could not be recognized; so he ordered them to greet the Ambraciot sentries and gain their confidence. As a result, when they attacked the Ambraciot army, they completely routed them, killing a great many of them on the spot while the rest ran down the mountain. But the roads had been occupied in advance, and besides, the Amphilochians knew their own terrain and were lightly armed, as opposed to the heavily armed hoplites who did not know the area and had no idea where to turn, and who were destroyed when they dashed into the ravines and into the preset ambushes. Trying every which way to escape, some even ran for the beach, which was not far off. Then, when they saw the Athenian ships that chanced to be off the coast just when the fighting began, they began to swim towards them, thinking, in the panic of the moment, that if they had to die, it would be better for them to be killed by the men on the ships than by the detested barbarian Amphilochians. The Ambraciot troops were slaughtered and very few were able to escape to their city.

The Acarnanians then stripped the corpses, set up a victory marker, and withdrew to Argos.

113. The next day a herald from the Ambraciots, who had escaped to Agraean territory from Olpae, arrived in order to request the corpses of those who were killed after the first battle, when they left without a truce in the wake of the Mantineans and others with whom a truce had been made. When the herald saw the armor of the Ambraciots from the city, he was amazed at the quantity of it. You see, he did not know about the disaster and thought it belonged to men he had been with. Someone then asked him why he was amazed, and how many of his men had died. (He, for his part, thought the herald had come from the troops on Idomene.) The herald said two hundred at most. The other retorted by saying,

"Doesn't look like it from this armor. It looks more like a thousand."

And the herald said, "Then it doesn't come from the men who did our fighting."

"It does if you fought at Idomene yesterday," answered the other.

"There's no way we fought yesterday. It was the day before, during the retreat."

"All I know is that we had a battle with these reinforcements from Ambracia yesterday."

When the herald heard this and realized that the reinforcements from the city had been wiped out, he shrieked, beside himself at the magnitude of the catastrophe that had occurred, and then immediately left without getting what he came for, without so much as asking for the bodies.

This was the greatest disaster to befall any one Greek city in this number of days during the present war. I have not even written down the number of dead, because they say that the amount lost is incredible in proportion to the size of the city. I know, though, that if the Acarnanians and Amphilochians had decided to heed Demosthenes and the Athenians and to capture Ambracia, they would have met with no resistance at all. The fact is, they were afraid that if the Athenians had Ambracia, they would be more troublesome neighbors than the Ambraciots.

114. After the battle, a third of the spoils was distributed to Athens and the rest among the other cities. The Athenian share was captured on their sea voyage. The portion that is now on deposit in the Athenian temples is the three hundred full sets of armor, which were set aside for Demosthenes and which he sailed home with. One of the benefits of this campaign for him was that his return home was less worrisome after the Aetolian disaster.

The Athenians on the twenty ships returned to Naupactus. After the departure of Demosthenes and the Athenians, the Acarnanians and the Amphilochians made a truce with the Ambraciots and Peloponnesians who had escaped to Salynthius and the Agraeans, whereby they would be allowed to withdraw from Oeniadae, to which they had gone after leaving Salynthius. As to the future, the Acarnanians and Amphilochians made a one-hundred-year treaty of alliance with the Ambraciots on the following terms: the Ambraciots would not join with the Acarnanians in an attack on the Peloponnesians nor would the Acarnanians join the Ambraciots in attacking the Athenians. They would come to each other's aid and the Ambraciots would return whatever Amphilochian land or hostages they held. The Ambraciots would also not aid the Anactorians, who were the enemies of the Acarnanians. After agreeing to these terms, they ended their war. After these events took place, the Corinthians sent a garrison of their own men to Ambracia. It consisted of three hundred hoplites with Xenocleides, son of Euthycles, in command, and it arrived after a difficult overland journey.

That is how the events at Ambracia unfolded.

115. That same winter, the Athenians in Sicily made an amphibious landing at Himera while the inland Sicels, who were acting with the Athenians, invaded Himera's outer borders. Next, they sailed against the Isles of Aeolus. Returning to Rhegium, they found on arrival that the Athenian general Pythodorus, son of Isolochus, had succeeded Laches in command of the ships. The reason was that the Sicilian allies had sailed to Athens and persuaded the Athenians to aid them with more ships. The Syracusans controlled their land and blockaded them with a few ships at sea. The allies wanted to resist and were putting a navy together. The Athenians outfitted forty ships to send them, partly because they thought that doing so might end the war more quickly, partly because they wanted to sharpen the fleet's naval skills. They sent one general, Pythodorus, with a few ships and intended to send Sophocles,[4] son of Sostratides, and Eurymedon, son of Thucles, with the rest. Pythodorus had by now assumed Laches' command, and as the winter came to an end, he sailed for the garrison of the Italian Locrians that Laches had captured earlier, but he withdrew after the Locrians defeated him in battle.

116. At about the beginning of that spring, as there had been in the past, there was an eruption of lava from Mount Etna. It destroyed some of the fields of the Catanaeans, who live below Etna, the highest mountain in Sicily. They say that fifty years had elapsed since the last eruption, and that there had been three eruptions in all since Sicily was colonized by Greeks.

These are the events that took place that winter, and the sixth year of this war that I, Thucydides, wrote down came to an end.

---

4. Not the playwright.

Book 4

Book 4 deals with the events of 425–423, opening with the extraordinary forti-fication of Pylos in the Peloponnese by the Athenians and the subsequent military operations that culminated in the capture of nearly three hundred Spartan soldiers, an event that Thucydides says (40), caused more surprise among the Greeks than anything else that happened during the war. Thucydides' discussion of the Pylos af-fair places Cleon in a consistently bad light, denying him credit for the Athenians' success. After a brief discussion of Athenian successes near Corinth (42–45), Thucy-dides returns to the chilling denouement of the civil war at Corcyra (46–48), where butchery was carried out with the tacit consent of the Athenian generals Eurymedon and Sophocles (not the author of *Oedipus*, but another Athenian of the same name). Having recorded the Athenian capture of Cythera (53–57), Thucydides turns his at-tention to Sicily, where the Athenians had sailed under Pythodorus, Sophocles, and Eurymedon to render aid to their allies. Thucydides' account includes a long speech (59–64) by which the Syracusan Hermocrates persuaded the Sicilians to set aside their differences and unite to prevent intervention from outsiders (such as the Athe-nians). When the three generals returned home, the Athenians banished two of them and fined the third. The formal charge against them was the taking of bribes, but in reality the Athenians were displeased that they had failed to prevent the Si-cilians from uniting against them. Thucydides criticizes the Athenians for their treat-ment of the generals, ascribing it to an inflated sense of Athenian possibilities after their success at Pylos (65).

Immediately afterwards Thucydides turns his attention to the operations of the charismatic Spartan Brasidas—first in Megara (discussed in 66–73) and subse-quently in far northern Greece (78–88, 102–135), taking time out to recount the events at Delium in central Greece (76–77, 89–101), where the Athenians had cho-sen to depart radically from Pericles' strategy and meet the Spartans in pitched bat-tle; he also records the death of Sitalces, king of the Odrysians (101), who was succeeded by his nephew Seuthes. Brasidas' successful speech rousing the people of Acanthus to revolt is rendered at 85–87. Brasidas, Thucydides reports, "wasn't an ineffective speaker, for a Spartan"; in fact his skills as a diplomat and a general played an important role in western history and historiography. Not only did Brasi-das enable Sparta to hold its own against Athens on land, but by his capture of Am-phipolis (102–107) he also sparked the exile of Thucydides, who was serving in Thrace as strategos and was blamed by the Athenians for the loss of the key outpost. There is no question that Thucydides' exile changed the kinds of sources to which he had access, providing some and depriving him of others. It may also have done much to internationalize his perspective on the war. Book 4 also includes (118) the text of the armistice signed between Athens and Sparta in 423 but disregarded by Brasidas.

Characteristically, Thucydides says little here about the sufferings on the home front; Aristophanes' *Acharnians*, produced in 425, gives some sense of the depriva-tions the war entailed.

Book 4

1. The following spring, when the grain was ripening, ten Syracusan and an equal number of ships from Italian Locri set sail and captured Messana, in Sicily. The Messanians, who had themselves instigated this action, then broke away from Athens. The Syracusans were the ones who were most eager for this operation, because they saw that Messana was a foothold in Sicily and because they feared that the Athenians would one day use it as a base from which to attack them with a larger force. The Locrians participated out of hatred for the Rhegians, whom they wanted to wear down with a war on two fronts. Accordingly, the Locrians simultaneously invaded Rhegium in full strength to prevent the city from sending a force to Messana. The Locrians, for their part, were accompanied by Rhegian exiles who had been living among them. Rhegium had for some time been experiencing civil strife and was, under the circumstances, unable to resist the Locrians — all the more reason for the Locrian invasion. The Locrian infantry ransacked the country and withdrew; their ships, however, remained to protect Messana. Meanwhile, the Syracusans and Locrians were manning other ships that would be based at Messana and that would carry on the war from there.

2. At about the same time that spring, before the grain had reached full height, the Peloponnesians and their allies invaded Attica, led by Agis, son of Archidamus and king of Sparta. They took up their positions and deforested the fields. As soon as the forty ships were ready,[1] the Athenians sent them off to Sicily along with Eurymedon and Sophocles, the two generals who had remained behind. The third general, Pythodorus, had already gone ahead to Sicily. Eurymedon and Sophocles were ordered to follow the coast and to help the Corcyraeans in the city, who were constantly being raided by the exiles in the mountains. There was a serious famine in the city, and the Peloponnesians had already gone up the coast with sixty ships to support the exiles in the belief that they could easily take control of the government. The Athenians ordered Demosthenes, who at his own request had remained a private citizen after the retreat from Acarnania, to take command of the fleet, if he wished, as it went around the Peloponnese.

3. While they were sailing down the coast of Laconia, they learned that the Peloponnesian ships were already in Corcyra. Eurymedon and Sophocles were for hurrying there, but Demosthenes ordered them to put in at Pylos and to continue with the voyage after he had carried out his mission. They opposed this, but chance intervened and a storm blew up and carried the fleet to Pylos. Demosthenes immediately urged them to fortify the place, as this was, in fact, the real reason he had gone along on the voyage. He pointed out that there was an abundance of timber and stones, that it was a natural stronghold, and that it was undefended, as was a considerable part of that region. Pylos is about fifty miles from Sparta, in what used to be Messenian territory, and the Spartans call it Coryphasium. The other generals said that there were lots of other undefended points on the Peloponnese he could capture if he wanted to add to the financial drain on Athens. To Demosthenes, however, this place seemed rather different from the others. It had a harbor, and because it had been inhabited since antiquity by Messenians who spoke the same dialect as the Spartans, they could do the

---

1. See 3.115.

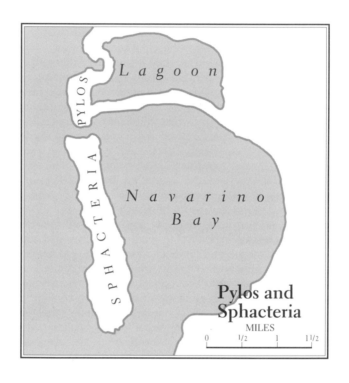

Pylos and
Sphacteria

most damage by using it as their base. Also the Messenians would prove to be trustworthy guardians of the place.

4. Demosthenes failed to persuade either the generals or the men to fortify Pylos, despite later involving their squadron leaders; but after sitting idle during a calm in which they could not sail, the men themselves felt a burst of energy and they began to wall off the open spaces in the terrain. Though they had no stonemason's tools, they set their hands to work, bringing stones as they picked them out and placing them wherever they happened to fit. When they needed mortar, they carried it on their backs for want of pots, bent over so the mortar would lie still and wreathing their hands behind them to keep it from falling. They did everything they could to hurry up and wall off the most vulnerable points before the Spartans could come and try to stop them. The place itself was a stronghold for the most part and needed no walls.

5. As for the Spartans, they were observing a festival at the time, and besides, they made light of the matter when they learned of it. After all, when they did march out, the Athenians either would not stay to fight them, or they would be able to take the place by storm; then, too, they were restrained by the fact that their army was still in Attica.

After spending six days fortifying the terrain that fronted the mainland and other spots as needed, the Athenians left Demosthenes on guard there with five ships and hurried away on the voyage to Corcyra and Sicily with the rest of the fleet.

6. As soon as the Peloponnesians in Attica learned that Pylos had been captured, they returned home on the double, partly because King Agis and his Spartans regarded the area around Pylos as home soil, but also because they had invaded too early, while the grain was still green, and most of the troops were on short rations. Also, the army had been hit hard by unusually bad weather for that time of year. For many reasons, then, it served their purposes to withdraw quickly, making this the shortest of the invasions: all told, they had been in Attica for fifteen days.

7. At about the same time, the Athenian general Simonides captured Eion, in Thrace.[2] Though it had been a colony of Mende, it had become an enemy of Athens, and Simonides assembled a few Athenians from the fortresses in the region and a large number of allies from those parts and took the place, which had been betrayed from within. The Chalcidians and Bottiaeans immediately came to the rescue and Simonides was beaten off with the loss of many of his troops.

8. After the Peloponnesian withdrawal from Attica, the Spartans and their closest neighbors immediately set off to recapture Pylos. Other Lacedaemonians were slower to set out, having just returned from another campaign. They put word out throughout the Peloponnese to go to the relief of Pylos as quickly as possible, and they also sent for their sixty ships at Corcyra. These arrived at Pylos after being carried over the Leucadian isthmus and slipping past the Athenian ships at Zacynthus. The Spartan infantry had already arrived. While the Peloponnesian fleet was still on the way, Demosthenes managed to get off two ships to tell Eurymedon and the Athenians in the fleet at Zacynthus to come back, since the island was in danger. On Demosthenes' orders, the fleet immediately set sail. The Spartans prepared to attack the wall by land and sea, expecting that they would easily capture a structure so quickly built and held by so few men. But they bore in mind the coming help from the Attic ships at

2. This is not the same place as Eion on the Strymon River, which is also in Thrace.

Zacynthus, and just in case they did not take the place on the first assault, they planned to block off the entrances to the harbor to make it impossible for the Athenians to anchor there. You see, the island known as Sphacteria stretches out along the harbor, close enough to give it shelter and to create narrow entrances—two ships wide on one side along the Athenian wall and Pylos and eight or nine ships wide between the island and the mainland at the other end. The whole island was wooded, completely pathless (since it is uninhabited), and is about two miles wide.[3] The Spartans therefore intended to close off the entrances by packing them with ships, prows out, but they became afraid that the Athenians would make war on them from the island itself, so they landed some hoplites on it and positioned others along the coast on the mainland. Thus both the island and the mainland would be hostile to the Athenians, and they would have nowhere to land, because the part of Pylos facing the sea outside the entrances has no harbors they could use as a base from which to support their troops. To the Spartans, it looked like they would force the place to surrender without a naval battle, without any risk at all, since it was without supplies and had been taken with little provision made for its occupation. With this in mind, they brought the hoplites over to the island, after selecting them by lot from all the companies of the army. Men were rotated in and out. Four hundred twenty men, the last to go, ended up being trapped there, not counting the helots who attended them. Their commander was Epitadas, son of Molobrus.

9. When Demosthenes saw that the Spartans were about to attack with ships and infantry, he too made his preparations. He hauled his remaining ships (out of the five that had been detached from the fleet) up under the wall and built a fence of wooden stakes in front of them. Then he armed the sailors with, for the most part, flimsy wicker shields, since there was no armor to be had in such a remote place—and even this stuff was taken from a thirty-oared Messenian pirate ship and from a fast, light ship, both of which had just arrived. There were forty hoplites among these Messenians and they were pressed into service along with the others. Demosthenes positioned most of his men, armored and unarmored alike, primarily on the walls and on easily defended terrain facing the mainland, with orders to fight off the infantry if it attacked. He selected sixty hoplites and a few archers from the whole force and moved outside the walls to the point on the shore where he most expected the enemy to attempt a landing. It was rugged, rocky ground facing the sea, and he thought that they would be keen to force that point because the wall was weakest there. They had not strongly fortified the place, never expecting that the Spartans would have superior seapower; but if they could force a landing, the point could be captured. Demosthenes therefore marched over this ground right to the edge of the sea, positioned the hoplites to prevent a landing, if possible, and then exhorted his men as follows.

> 10. We are all in this together. It won't do any of you any good to try to be smart in a pinch like this by adding up all the terrors around us. You'll survive if you look straight ahead and attack the enemy up close with high hopes. When you are up against it, like now, calculation is the last thing you want—you want the danger to just come quickly. I think the odds are on our side if we stand our ground and do not throw away our advantages by panicking over the number of our enemies. I think the difficulty of landing on this beach counts for us. If we stand and fight, the ground will be

---

3. Probably Thucydides was a little off in his calculations; the length of the island seems to have been closer to three miles.

an ally; if we run for it, their landing will be difficult, but they'll manage it because no one will be stopping them. We are going to have a tougher enemy because it won't be easy for him to retreat even if we do beat him. We can defend against him well enough when he's in his ships, but once he lands, it's man to man.

And we needn't fear his numbers too much. Only a few can fight at a time because of the difficulty of landing, and their army will not be on solid ground, where they would outnumber us and the situation would be the same for both of us. They are coming off ships, where everything has to go just right at sea. I think our numbers are offset by their problems, and I also think that you, who are Athenians and have experience in amphibious landings against others, know that a man will never be beaten if he stands his ground and doesn't run away in fear of the breaking waves and the terrifying onslaught of ships. So it is up to you to stand and fight right here on this rocky shore and to save us and our position.

11. After Demosthenes spoke these words, the Athenians plucked up their courage and took up positions right down on the beach. Next the Spartans went into action, simultaneously attacking the wall with infantry and ships, of which there were forty-three, under the command of the Spartan Thrasymelidas, son of Cratesicles. The ships attacked just where Demosthenes had expected them to. The Athenians went on the defensive on two fronts, land and sea. The Peloponnesians had divided their ships into small squadrons, because they could not land with larger ones, and then took turns attacking and resting, all the while urging and cheering each other on in hopes of pushing back the Athenians and taking the walls.

The most conspicuous of all the Spartans was Brasidas. He was the captain of a trireme, and when he saw other captains and pilots hanging back because of the rugged terrain and taking care lest their ships collide even where it looked like it might be possible to land, he shouted out that it didn't make sense to worry about their ships' timber when their enemies had built walls on their soil. He told them to break their ships to pieces and force a landing, and he called on the allies not to pull back, but to donate their ships to Sparta in return for all her favors, to run aground and land any way they could and take the point and the men on it.

12. Brasidas made his own pilot run their ship aground after prodding the others in this way, and then he began to climb down the ship's ladder; but when he tried to get off, he was beaten back by the Athenians. Badly wounded, he lost consciousness and fell onto an outrigger after his shield slipped off his arm into the sea. When it was washed up onto the beach, the Athenians took it, later using it in the victory marker they set up to commemorate the battle. The other Peloponnesians were game enough, but they were unable to disembark, because of the ruggedness of the terrain and because the Athenians stood their ground and would not give way.

Thus happenstance had brought about a reversal whereby the Athenians were defending themselves on land—and Spartan land at that—against Spartans bearing down on them in ships, while the Spartans were trying to make a landing, against Athenians, from ships, on their own now-hostile soil! So completely had opinion in those days come to regard the one side as landlubbers pre-eminent with infantry and the other as seafarers, peerless in their ships!

13. After making repeated attacks all that day and part of the next, the Spartans stopped. On day three, they sent some of their ships to Asine for wood to make rams and enginery. They hoped to use these to take the wall along the

harbor. This wall was high, but they could at least make a landing there. At this point, the Athenian ships arrived from Zacynthus—forty of them, because they had been reinforced by some ships from the base at Naupactus and by four from Chios. When they saw that both the mainland and the island were packed with hoplites, that the Peloponnesian fleet was in the harbor and not about to sail out, and that there was nothing they could use as a base, they headed for the island of Prote, which was not far off and uninhabited, and spent the night there. The next day, they set out after preparing themselves for a naval battle. It would be in the open sea if the Spartans chose to sail out to meet them there. If not, they would sail into the harbor and get them. For their part, the Spartans neither set out to meet them nor did what they had planned to do—block up the entrances. Instead, while holding their position on land, they were manning and readying their ships for a battle in their very large harbor in the event that anyone should sail in.

14. The Athenians noticed this and attacked them via both entrances to the harbor. Most of the Peloponnesian ships were on the water, bearing straight ahead, when the Athenians came on them and put them to flight. The Athenians pursued them and, because of the short distance between the enemy and the shore, were able to damage many of them, capturing five, one with its entire crew. They rammed the rest, which had already run themselves to ground, and hit some that were still being boarded in preparation for casting off. They were even towing away some that they had secured with ropes and that were unmanned after their crews had run away. When the Spartans saw this, they were aghast. This defeat meant that their men were trapped on the island, and they rushed to rescue their ships. They ran down into the sea with their armor on, got hold of the ships, and engaged in a tug-of-war over them. It was an action in which everyone thought everything depended on himself alone.[4] There was a huge din, and there was also a reversal of their usual roles in fighting for those ships. The Spartans, under the influence, so to speak, of a stunned eagerness, engaged in nothing less than a naval battle from the shore, while the Athenians, who had the upper hand and who wanted to press their luck to the maximum, fought a land battle from their ships. The two sides inflicted a great deal of damage on each other and disengaged with many casualties, though the Spartans saved all the unmanned ships except for those that were first captured. Both sides returned to their original positions, whereupon the Athenians set up a victory marker, returned the dead, and took possession of ships' wreckage. They also immediately began to sail continuously around the island, keeping the men trapped on it under guard. The Peloponnesians on the mainland, by now reinforced from all sides, remained in place at Pylos.

15. When the events at Pylos were reported at Sparta, they decided that it was a disaster great enough to warrant their chief magistrates' going down to the camp to inspect the situation on the ground and consider what ought to be done. They saw that it was impossible to help their men and, not wanting to risk letting them starve or be overpowered by the strength of numbers, they decided, if the Athenian generals were willing, to call a halt to the fighting at Pylos and to send a delegation to Athens to negotiate an agreement by which they could remove the men as quickly as possible.

16. The generals accepted the proposal and a truce was made on these terms: the Spartans would bring to Pylos all the ships on which they had just

---

4. Thucydides uses almost identical language at 2.8.

fought, as well as all the longboats in Laconia, and hand them over to the Athenians. The Spartans would not bring weaponry to bear on the fortifications either by land or by sea. The Athenians would allow the Spartans on the mainland to send their men on the island a fixed quantity of ready-kneaded dough, consisting of two Attic liters of barley per man, along with a half-liter of wine and a ration of meat. Each servant was to get half this amount. This was to be sent in under Athenian inspection, and no vessel whatever was to sail in secretly. The Athenians would still guard the island, though not land on it and not bring weaponry to bear on the Peloponnesian army, either by land or by sea. The truce would be broken by whoever violated its terms in any way whatsoever and it would remain in effect until the Spartan ambassadors returned from Athens. The Athenians would also take them to, and bring them back from, Athens in a trireme. Once they returned, the truce would be dissolved and the Athenians would return the ships in the condition in which they were received.

The truce was made on those terms, the ships—over sixty of them—were surrendered, and the ambassadors were sent off. When they reached Athens, they spoke as follows:

17. Men of Athens. The Spartans have sent us to negotiate about the men on the island and to persuade you, perhaps, that this event offers the same opportunity to you as to us by giving us a chance to bring stability out of the present situation. If we speak at length, it will not be contrary to our normal practice. It is our way not to use many words when few will do, and to use more words when it is vital for us to explain something important about what must be done. Don't take them ill, or as though we considered you to be stupid schoolboys in need of a lesson; take them rather as words to the wise about the best way to think things through.

We say this because it is possible for you to achieve a desirable result from your present good fortune while keeping what you now control and gaining honor and glory without suffering the usual fate of those who unexpectedly get hold of a good thing. They always reach out in hopes of more, you see, because of their uncommon good luck of the moment. But those who have most often seen luck change are rightly suspicious of success, and this is what experience has surely taught your city and ours.

18. Learn a lesson from studying our present misfortunes, we who have the highest reputation among the Greeks, and who now stand before you asking for what we used to think we had the power to grant. We do not have to endure this because of any loss of military strength or out of an arrogant overreaching; no, we made a decision based on the facts, and we went wrong, and that is the way things will always be, for everyone. So it would be a mistake for you to think that because of your city's present military might, or because of the gains that you have made, luck will also always go your way. Prudent men preserve their gains with a view to the uncertainty of the future, and this makes them able to deal with disaster more intelligently when it comes. They realize that war does not remain within the range in which we would like to wage it, but that it follows wherever chance may lead. These people are least likely to falter, because they never trust war to go according to plan and never get excited when it does, but are more likely to quit while they are ahead. To quit while you are ahead, men of Athens, is the opportunity we now offer you. If you reject us and then stumble (which is entirely possible), it will later be thought that the victories that are now coming your way were merely due to luck. Instead, it is now possible for you to leave to the future an unassailable reputation for intelligence and strength.

19. Sparta invites you to conclude a solemn treaty and end the war. They offer peace, an alliance, and such friendly relations as would amount to kinship. In return, we ask for the men on the island, in the belief that it would be better for both sides to avoid risk: for you, the risk that our men will force an escape if the chance arises; for us, that they will be captured after a long siege. We believe that great hatreds are most securely resolved not when one party is bent on vengeance, gains the advantage, and then compels his enemy to accept an agreement enforced by binding oaths, but when, it being in his power to do this after having defeated his enemy far beyond his expectations, he effects a measured, equitable reconciliation worthy of his own honor and dignity. That way, the enemy does not feel obliged to take revenge after suffering a humiliating defeat, but to return generosity in kind, and he is all the readier to abide by the terms he agreed to for shame of transgressing them. People are more likely to respond to their worst enemies in this way than to those with whom they have trivial differences. They are naturally happy to yield to those who have willingly given way themselves, whereas they will run reckless risks against the acts of overweening pride.

20. Now, if ever, is the right time for us to make peace, before some incurable wound is inflicted in the meanwhile that keeps us both from doing so, and forces us to hate you, privately and publicly, forever, or that strips you of the advantage that has brought us to make this offer. Let us come together and reach a sensible settlement over the disaster on the island while the issue is still unresolved, before we are disgraced, and while you still have your glory and we still have some feelings of friendship for you. Let us choose peace instead of war and give a respite from their troubles to the rest of Greece, for which they will give more of the credit to you. They are fighting without knowing which of us started the war; once there is peace—which is now mostly up to you—they will thank you for it. If you make this decision, the Spartans will be able to become your firm friends, gratified that you accepted their invitation before they were forced to accept your dictation. And just think of what the inherent benefits of this course are likely to be, for if we and you speak with one voice, you must know that the rest of Greece, our subject states, will honor us with the greatest respect.

21. That is all the Spartans said, thinking that since the Athenians had, at one time, wanted a truce that Sparta had opposed and denied,[5] the Athenians would be happy to accept a Spartan offer of peace and to return the men. The Athenians, for their part, thinking that because they had the men on the island, they could make a treaty with Sparta whenever they wanted to, reached for more. They were incited mostly by Cleon, son of Cleaenetus, the most trusted populist leader of the time.[6] He persuaded the people to respond that the Spartans on the island must surrender themselves and their weapons and be brought to Athens, and that once the men arrived, Sparta must return Nisaea, Pegae, Troezen, and Achaea, which they had not captured in the war, but which had been surrendered under a former treaty to which the Athenians had consented at a time when it was they who most needed a truce.[7] At that point, the men would be returned and a treaty concluded for as long as both sides would agree.

22. The Spartans said nothing to this response. Instead, they asked that a committee be selected that would, undisturbed, hear arguments, engage in dis-

5. See 2.59.
6. See 3.36ff.
7. See 1.115.

cussions on each point, and reach a settlement about whatever matters they could. Cleon, however, vigorously objected to this, saying that he had always known that Sparta's intentions were not honorable, but that this was perfectly clear now. These were men who didn't have anything to say to the people; they wanted to get together with a chosen few. He called on the Spartans, if they had any sound proposals to make, to address them to everyone. The Spartans saw that it wasn't possible for them to speak in plenary session because if, under pressure, they were perceived to give way on any point, they would be denounced to their allies as having failed in their negotiations. They also saw that the Athenians were not inclined to take a moderate view of any of their proposals, so they left Athens empty-handed.

23. When they returned, the truce at Pylos immediately became void and the Spartans asked for their ships back, as had been agreed. The Athenians, however, refused to return them, protesting that there had been an assault on the fortifications in violation of the truce, along with other complaints the Spartans considered trivial. The Athenians insisted that the treaty specifically stated that it would be null if it was violated in any way whatever. Denying the charge and protesting the illegality of keeping the ships, the Spartans left and took up their battle positions. Both sides went all-out in the battle of Pylos. The Athenians kept two ships continuously sailing around the island from opposite directions all day, and at night the whole fleet would anchor off it, except for the seaward shore when a wind blew up. In addition, twenty ships arrived from Athens to join the guard, making seventy ships in all. The Peloponnesians encamped on the mainland and continued their assaults on the wall, while always looking out for a chance to save their men.

24. In the meanwhile, on Sicily, the Syracusans and their allies continued the war from Messana, after bringing the other fleet they had outfitted over to the ships guarding the place. They were egged on in this mostly by the Italian Locrians, who hated the Rhegians and who had already invaded their territory in full strength.[8] The Syracusans, who saw the few Athenian ships that were at Rhegium, and who had learned that the large number that was expected to arrive was involved in the siege of Sphacteria, were eager to try their hand at a naval battle. If they won a victory at sea, they expected to capture Rhegium easily with a combined naval and land blockade, and this would then put them in a very strong position, because the extreme points of Italy and Sicily—Rhegium and Messana—are very close to each other, and the Athenians would be unable to anchor off Rhegium and control the strait of Messana. This strait is the water between Rhegium and Messana, from which Sicily is least distant from the mainland; it is what has come to be called "Charybdis," and through it Odysseus is said to have sailed.[9] Because of its narrowness, and because the waters flowing into it come from large seas—the Tyrrhenian and the Sicilian—it has many currents, which were naturally regarded as very treacherous.

25. Late one afternoon, the Syracusans and their allies were forced to fight in this strait with somewhat more than thirty ships to rescue a merchantman sailing through. They put out to sea against sixteen Athenian and eight Rhegian warships. They were quickly defeated by the Athenians, and then both sides sailed as best they could back to their home bases at Messana and Rhegium. The Syracusans had lost one ship when night fell on the battle.

8. See 4.1.
9. In Homer's *Odyssey*, 12.234–59.

After this, the Locrians withdrew from Rhegium. The ships of Syracuse and her allies gathered at Peloris, in Messana, where they anchored and where their infantry was. The Athenians and Rhegians sailed their way and started to ram them, once they noticed that the crews were not aboard. They lost one ship when the men dived off it and swam away after it was hooked by a grappling iron. After this, the Syracusans boarded their ships and were being tugged along the shore toward Messana, when the Athenians again started to ram them. The Syracusans, however, turned their sterns toward the Athenians and backed water into their prows, sinking another ship. Both in the maneuvers along the shore and in the naval battle, such as it was, the Syracusans more than held their own and finally made their way into the harbor at Messana.

The Athenians set sail for Camarina when they got news from there that it would be betrayed to the Syracusans by Archias and his followers. Meanwhile, the Messanians attacked their neighbor, Chalcidian Naxos, in full strength by land and sea. They placed Naxos under siege on the first day and then set about deforesting their fields. The next day, the fleet sailed around to the region near the Acesines River and again wasted the fields there while their infantry attacked the city. While this was going on, a large force of Sicels came over the highlands and down to the aid of the Naxians against the Messanians. The Naxians revived when they saw them and, shouting encouragement to each other that the Leontines and their other Greek allies were coming to their rescue, they suddenly rushed out of the city and fell on the Messanians. The Naxians turned them back, killing over a thousand of them, while the rest suffered a torturous retreat homeward as the barbarians attacked and killed most of them on the road. Their ships put into Messana and later dispersed to their cities. The Leontines and their allies, along with some Athenians, now advanced on a much-weakened Messana. The Athenians probed the harbor for an attack with their ships; the infantry attacked the city; but the Messanians and some Locrians under Demoteles, who had been left to stand guard in the city after the disaster, suddenly rushed out, then fell on and routed most of the Leontine army, killing many of them. The Athenians saw this, disembarked from their ships, and came to the rescue. The Messanians were in disarray when the Athenians came on them, and they were chased back into the city. After setting up a victory marker, the Athenians returned to Rhegium. After this, the Greeks in Sicily continued to make war on each other by land, but without the help of the Athenians.

26. At Pylos, the Athenians were still blockading the Spartans on the island while the Peloponnesian encampment bided its time, in strength, on the mainland. For the Athenians, however, the blockade had become burdensome because of the unavailability of food and water. There was only one spring, which was not very large, on the acropolis at Pylos, and most of the men had to scrape away the gravel on the beach to get their drinking water, such as it was. They were bivouacked in cramped quarters on a small space, and since their ships had no harbor, crew members took turns landing and eating their meals while the others rode at anchor on the open sea. Time wrought the greatest demoralization, as it unexpectedly dragged on for men who had thought they would, in a few days, starve out enemies on a desert island who had nothing to drink but salty water. The reason this had not happened was that the Spartans had offered volunteers a very high price to bring in ground grain, wine, cheese, and all kinds of other food needful to men under siege. They also promised freedom to any helot willing to bring in food.

And bring it in they did. Many ran the risk, but especially the helots, setting out from wherever they happened to be on the Peloponnese and sailing down under cover of night toward the part of the island facing the sea. They kept a sharp lookout for a wind to carry them in, because it was easier to slip past the blockading triremes when the wind blew in off the sea. At such times, the triremes couldn't lie at anchor around the island, whereas the blockade runners had been paid in advance for their ships and would recklessly drive them ashore as the hoplites stood guard at the island's landing places. Whoever risked making the run in calm weather was caught. Also, from the harbor side, divers swam underwater to the island, towing by thin cords winesacks filled with honeyed poppyseed and crushed linseed. These divers went unnoticed at first, but the Athenians guarded against them later. Thus each side used every trick it could think of, the one side to get the supplies in, the other to catch them in the act.

27. The Athenians didn't know what to do when they found out that their army was in dire straits, while food was getting in to the men on the island. They became afraid that winter would overtake their garrison, seeing that it would no longer be possible to get the supply shipments around the Peloponnese. Remember, the men were in a desolate spot, and it wasn't possible to ship enough food around even in summer; and there could be no winter blockade in territory where there was no harbor. So either they would lift their blockade and the Spartans would survive, or the men would watch for stormy weather and sail away on the ships that had brought them their food. Above all, the Athenians had become afraid that the Spartans, who no longer wanted to negotiate, had good reasons for confidence, and they regretted not having accepted the treaty.

Cleon, sensing the ill will people bore him, personally, because he had foiled the agreement, said that the messengers were not telling the truth. The men who had returned from the front said that if the people didn't believe them, they should send some fact-finders, whereupon the Athenians chose to send him—Cleon—and Theagenes. Realizing that he would be forced either to agree with the men he had accused of lying or to contradict them and be shown up as a liar himself, and seeing that people were determined to continue the campaign, Cleon told the Athenians that they shouldn't be sending fact-finders or wasting time and letting opportunities slip by. No, if they thought the messages were true, they should set sail for the men on the island. Then he pointed his finger at Nicias, son of Niceratus, who was a general and who was his enemy, and said scornfully that if the generals were real men, they could easily set out with an armada and capture the troops on the island. If he were in command, he continued, that was what he would do.

28. When the Athenians excitedly encouraged Cleon to sail immediately, if he thought it would be so easy, Nicias reacted to Cleon's rebuke by telling him that as far as the generals were concerned, he could take whatever force he wanted and give it a try. Thinking, at first, that Nicias was just saying that he would relinquish command, Cleon declared that he was ready; but when he realized that Nicias really was handing over power, he backed off in alarm and said that not he, but Nicias, should lead the campaign. He had never thought that Nicias would go so far as to yield the command to him, but Nicias repeated his demand. He then resigned his command at Pylos, and he called on the Athenians to witness his act. They behaved as crowds will, and the more Cleon tried to back out of what he had said and avoid sailing, the more they urged Nicias to hand over his command and called on Cleon to sail. Not having any way to free himself from his own words, Cleon reluctantly took on the expedi-

tion, and coming before the people, he said that he was not afraid of the Spartans. He would set sail without taking any Athenian citizens, only the Lemnians and Imbrians who were on hand, along with the lightly armed troops who had come to help from Aenus and four hundred archers from various regions. With this force plus the Athenian troops at Pylos, he said, he would either bring the Spartans back alive in twenty days or kill them right there. The bombast of the man struck the Athenians as funny, but the most prudent people were quite pleased with it. They figured that this was a no-lose situation. They would either be rid of Cleon — which is what they expected to happen — or, if they were mistaken in their opinion, he would defeat the Spartans for them.

29. After he arranged everything in the assembly and the Athenians had voted to give him the expedition, Cleon chose one of the generals at Pylos, Demosthenes, to join him in command, and then prepared to put quickly out to sea. He chose Demosthenes when he learned that Demosthenes had been planning a landing on the island. You see, Demosthenes' troops had been suffering under the hardships of the place and, feeling more like the besieged than like the besiegers, they were eager to risk it. Then a fire on the island gave him all the encouragement he needed. Because it had never been inhabited, most of the island had been heavily wooded and pathless before the fire, and Demosthenes had feared that conditions would favor the enemy if he landed. A large army attacked from deep cover as it was landing could be badly hurt. Neither the position nor the mistakes of the enemy would be clear to them because of the woods, whereas every wrong move in their camp would be clear as day, and the enemy could surprise them wherever he pleased. The advantage would be with him. Also, Demosthenes thought that if he was forced to fight up close in thick brush, the enemy's smaller army, which knew the terrain, would prove stronger than his larger one, which did not. His own large army wouldn't know where they were and would be slaughtered, because there would be no way to see in advance where they had to protect each other.

30. These factors had made a big impression on him because of the Aetolian disaster, which was caused, for the most part, by the presence of a forest.[1] Because of their cramped space, however, some of the Athenian troops had to land on the far side of the island in order to take their morning meal under guard, and when a wind blew up after one of the men unintentionally set fire to a bit of the brush, most of it had burnt down practically before they knew it. As a result, Demosthenes could see that there were rather more Spartans on the island than he had thought during the truce, when he suspected the Spartans of sending in food for a smaller number than they said.[2] He also saw that it would now be easier to make a landing, so he decided that it was worth it for the Athenians to make the attempt with all possible speed. He made preparations accordingly, getting everything ready and sending for troops from allies nearby. Also, Cleon now arrived at Pylos, having sent Demosthenes word that he was coming with the army Demosthenes had requested. As soon as they arrived, Cleon and Demosthenes despatched a herald to the Spartan camp on the mainland, inviting them, if they so wished, to surrender themselves, their weapons, and their men on the island without prejudice, to be kept under a light guard until such time as a general agreement could be reached.

31. When the Spartans refused, the Athenians waited a day and set out late the following night with all their hoplites aboard a few ships. Just before

1. See 3.97–98.
2. See 4.16.

dawn, about eight hundred hoplites landed on two sides of the island, off the sea and towards the harbor, and ran towards the first guard post on the island as fast as they could. This is how the enemy was positioned: there were about thirty hoplites at this first post, while most of the Spartans, under the command of Epitadas, held the levelest ground around the well in the middle of the island. A small force guarded the extreme end of the island opposite Pylos. This point rose sharply from the sea and was hardest to attack from the land side, because there was an ancient wall made of gathered stones, which the Spartans thought would be a good fallback for them if they were ever forced to retreat. That, then, is how the Spartans were positioned.

32. The Athenians overran and slaughtered the Spartan advance guard in their bedding while they were still reaching for their weapons. They had landed unnoticed: the Spartans had thought the Athenians were sailing to their night moorings, as usual. At dawn the rest of the Athenian army landed from somewhat more than seventy ships. Not counting the lowest-ranking oarsmen, this force consisted of the whole army in diverse battle gear—eight hundred archers and at least as many lightly armed troops, the Messenian reinforcements, and all the other men stationed at Pylos except those left to guard the walls. Demosthenes had ordered the men to be divided into companies of two hundred, more or less. They seized the highest ground to maximize the disadvantage to a completely surrounded enemy, by denying them any ground on which to take up a position and by exposing them to attack in strength from all sides. If the Spartans attacked their enemy in front, they were shot at from the rear; if they turned against the troops on one flank, they were hit by those positioned on the other. Wherever the Spartans turned, their lightly armed enemies would always be at their backs. These are the hardest troops to cope with because they are able to strike their targets from a distance with arrows, spears, stones, and slings. It was impossible to come to grips with them because they had the upper hand even when they fled; and when the Spartans retreated, they pressed the attack. This is the strategy Demosthenes originally conceived of and which his men were now positioned to carry out.

33. When the men with Epitadas, who made up the main body of Spartans on the island, saw that the first guard had been wiped out and that an army was advancing against them, they formed their line of battle and attacked the Athenian hoplites with the intention of coming to hand-to-hand combat. The Athenian hoplites had been positioned in front of them, with the lightly armed troops on their flanks and at their rear. The Spartans were not able, however, to make the best use of their military skill and to come to grips with the hoplites. They were frustrated by the constant bombardment from both sides by the light-armed forces. The Athenians' hoplites, meanwhile, did not step up to meet them but held their ground. Whenever the light-armed troops charged and engaged them, the Spartans forced them to turn and run, but then they would turn around again and resume fighting. Their light equipment enabled them to get a head start in rough, difficult, terrain that had never been inhabited, and the Spartans were unable to pursue them over it in their heavy armor.

34. They skirmished with one another in this way for a short time. The Spartans, however, soon became unable to sharply counter where they were attacked, and the light troops saw that they had become slower on the defensive. They were especially encouraged by seeing that they far outnumbered the Spartans, and by getting increasingly used to the fact that the Spartans were not so terrifying to them any more. They had not suffered anything like what they had expected beforehand, because when they first landed, they had been enslaved

to the dread idea that they were going against Spartans; but now they had contempt for them and together they rushed the Spartans with a shout, hurling stones, arrows, spears—whatever they could get their hands on. The combined shouting and charging panicked men unaccustomed to this kind of warfare. Also, the ashes from the recently burnt timber rose very high in the air, and it was impossible for a man to see in front of himself on account of the arrows and stones of so many men coming out of the dust. And now the fighting became hard and bitter for the Spartans. Their helmets couldn't keep the arrows off, and when they were hit with spears, the broken tips stuck in their armor. Deprived of the ability to see in front of them, and unable to hear their orders for the shouting of the enemy, there was nothing they could do to help themselves. There was danger everywhere and they had no hope of fighting back and saving themselves.

35. Finally, badly mauled from constantly regrouping under the same battle conditions, the Spartans closed ranks and moved towards their own garrison at their last defense on the island. It was not very far away, but as they gave ground, the light-armed troops were all the more encouraged and immediately pressed them with louder shouts than ever. The Spartans who were captured in the retreat were killed, but most escaped to the wall and its garrison and took up positions all along it, to defend it wherever it might come under attack. The Athenians were close behind, but were unable to encircle and surround them because of the strength of the position, so they kept advancing and tried to push them back by a frontal assault. Both sides struggled for a long time—indeed for most of the day—holding out against the battle, the thirst, the sun, with one side trying to take the high ground and the other refusing to give way. The Spartans were able to defend themselves more easily than they had before, because there was no way to get past their flanks and surround them.

36. After they had reached a standstill, the Messenian commander came up to Cleon and Demosthenes and told them that they were laboring in vain. If they would give him some of the archers and some of the lightly armed troops, he thought that he could find a way to slip around behind the Spartans' backs and force a breakthrough. Taking the men he had asked for, he set off from where the Spartans could not see him and made his way along the steepest cliffs of the island where, trusting to the natural strength of the position, the Spartans had not posted guards. With great difficulty, he just barely made it around unobserved, and then, out of the high ground, he suddenly appeared at their backs. The unexpectedness of it scared the Spartans out of their wits, and the sight of what they were waiting for gave the Athenians that much more fighting spirit. The Spartans, who were taking hits from both sides, found themselves in the same predicament (to compare small things with great ones) as the men at Thermopylae. Those men were annihilated when the Persians went around by that famous path; these, attacked on two sides, could hold out no longer.[3] Few against many, their bodies weakened from want of food, they gave way and the Athenians became the masters of the position.

37. Cleon and Demosthenes realized, however, that if the Spartans yielded even slightly more ground, they would be utterly destroyed by the Athenian army, so they restrained their own men and called a halt to the fighting. They wanted to bring the Spartans back to Athens alive—if, that is, by of-

---

3. On the battle at Thermopylae, see Herodotus 7.213ff. The heroism of the Greeks who fought at Thermopylae was famous. There, in 480, the Spartans held a Greek force in place for several days to keep the Persians at bay, buying time for the rest of Greece even though they knew their cause was doomed. The Greek soldiers all died fighting.

fering terms they could somehow induce them to give way to the terrors of the moment and, their resolve shattered, surrender their weapons. So they sent over a herald to announce that if they wished, they could surrender their weapons and themselves to the Athenians unconditionally.

38. After listening to the announcement, most of the Spartans indicated that they submitted to the terms by dropping their shields and waving their hands over their heads. Later, after an armistice was reached, Cleon and Demosthenes and, for the Spartans, Styphon, son of Pharax, held talks. Of the original commanders, Epitadas, the first in command, was dead. Hippagretas, the man who had been chosen to succeed him, was still alive but had been given up for dead and was lying among the corpses. Styphon was the third in command, having been designated the leader by law in case anything should happen to the others. Styphon and his officers said that they wanted to send a herald over to the Spartans on the mainland for instructions as to what they should do. Although the Athenians wouldn't let a Spartan go, they themselves called for heralds from the mainland and after two or three consultations, the last Spartan who sailed over from the mainland brought the message that "the Spartans order you to make your own decisions provided you do nothing to disgrace yourselves." After talking it over in private, the Spartans decided to surrender themselves and their weapons.

The Athenians held the men under guard that day and night. The next day, the Athenians erected a victory marker on the island and prepared to cast off. They transferred the prisoners to the custody of the trierarchs, and the Spartans brought over their dead after sending a herald. The men taken alive and the men who died on the island were as follows. In all, four hundred and twenty Spartan hoplites had landed there. Two hundred and ninety-two of these were taken away alive; the rest were killed. About one hundred and twenty of the living were Spartans of the citizen class. Not many Athenians lost their lives: it had never come to all-out hand-to-hand combat.

39. The total time during which the men were besieged—from the naval battle to the battle on the island—was seventy-two days. During this time, the men were given their food for about twenty days while their ambassadors were in Athens trying to negotiate a truce; for the rest of the time, they were provisioned by the clandestine shipments. And indeed, there was even some grain and other food captured on the island because the commander, Epitadas, had distributed less to each man than was available. Both the Athenians and the Peloponnesians left Pylos with their armies and returned home; and Cleon's promise—crazy as it was—came true, for he brought the men back within twenty days, just as he had said he would.

40. To the Greeks, this was the most unexpected of all the things that had happened in the war. They had always thought that Spartans would never be forced by either hunger or any other necessity to surrender their weapons; for as long as they were armed, they would go on fighting with all their strength to the death. People wouldn't believe that the men who surrendered were the social equals of those who died, and some time later one of the Athenian allies spitefully asked a prisoner from the island whether their dead had been from the upper classes. The man answered that it would be a very valuable spindle—which is Spartan for "arrow"—that could single out aristocrats. The point he was making was that stones and arrows kill whomever they happen to hit.

41. After the men were brought to Athens, the Athenians decided to keep them in irons until an agreement of some sort was reached, but to lead them out and kill them if the Peloponnesians should invade their land before that

time. They also stationed a garrison at Pylos, and the Messenians from Naupactus, who considered Pylos to be their homeland (since Pylos had been a part of what was once Messenia), sent over some of their best forces. These men raided Laconia and were able to do a great deal of damage, since they spoke the same Greek dialect as the Spartans. The Spartans had at no time in the past ever suffered this sort of guerilla warfare. In addition, their helots were deserting them, and they couldn't stand their growing fear that even greater changes would take place in their land. Thus, although they did not want it to be generally known among the Athenians, they repeatedly sent ambassadors to Athens in an effort to get Pylos and their men back. The Athenians, however, held out for more and sent them away empty-handed as often as they came.

These, then, were the events that took place at Pylos.

42. That same summer, right after these events, the Athenians invaded the territory of Corinth with eighty ships, two thousand of their own hoplites, and two hundred cavalry in horse transports. They were accompanied by their Milesian, Andrian, and Carystian allies with Nicias, son of Niceratus, and two others in command. Sailing until dawn, they put in on the coast between the Chersonese and Rheitus in the country below the hill of Solygia, on which in antiquity the Dorians had set up their base of operations in their war against the Aeolian inhabitants of the city of Corinth. There is still a village, called Solygia, on the hill, one and a half miles from the beach where the ships put in; Corinth is seven and a half, and the Isthmus two and a half, miles from the beach.

The Corinthians had learned in advance from Argos that the Athenian army was coming and had brought all the forces they could mobilize (except for those northeast of Isthmia) to the Isthmus. Five hundred of their guardsmen were also posted in Ambracia and the Leucadian territory[4]; but all the rest of their force were keeping a lookout to see where the Athenians would land. The Athenians, however, eluded them by sailing down at night, and when this was signaled to them, they left half of their men behind at Cenchreae, in case the Athenians moved against Crommyon, and marched towards the Athenian landing site on the double.

43. Now Battus was the second of the two Corinthian generals who were present at this battle. He took a battalion and went up to guard the unwalled village of Solygia, while Lycophron attacked the Athenians with the rest of the men. They hit the Athenian right wing first, just after they had finished disembarking at the Chersonese; then they were pitted against the rest of the army. The whole battle consisted of brutal, hand-to-hand combat. The right wing of Athenians and Carystians (who had been positioned next to the Athenians at the end of the line) withstood the Corinthian charge and just barely managed to push them back. The Corinthians retreated to a terracing wall (all the land was very steep there, you see), threw stones down at the Athenians from the high ground, and then, beating their drums, they charged again. The Athenians stood their ground and they returned to hand-to-hand combat. Then a company of Corinthians came to the aid of their left wing, turned back the Athenian right wing, and chased them down to the sea. Both the Athenians and the Carystians, though, rallied at the ships and drove them back. The rest of both armies had been fighting nonstop, especially the Corinthian right wing where Lycophron fought the Athenian left wing, in the belief that the Athenians would make an attempt on Solygia.

4. See 3.114.

They held out for a long time, neither side giving way. Then (and here the cavalry, which had joined the fighting, came in handy for the Athenians, since the other side had no horses) the Corinthians turned tail and retreated to the hill, where they joined forces with the others and stayed put without going back down. It was in this rout of their right wing that most of the Corinthians died, including their general, Lycophron. The rest of the army was likewise forced back, not with hot pursuit and swift flight, but in a steady retreat to the high ground where they dug in. Since the Corinthians no longer came down to meet them in battle, the Athenians stripped the Corinthian dead and collected their own corpses; they also immediately erected a victory marker.

The half of the Corinthian army that was standing guard at Cenchreae lest the Athenians sail against Crommyon was prevented by Mount Oneion from seeing that there was a battle going on. They realized it when they saw a dust cloud, however, and immediately ran to the rescue. The older men of Corinth also went to the rescue when they learned what had happened. Seeing all of these men bearing down on them, and thinking that the nearby Peloponnesian neighbors were coming to help, the Athenians quickly withdrew to their ships, taking their spoils and all their dead but two, whom they abandoned when they could not find them. They boarded their ships and made their way to the off-shore islands, from which they sent a herald who made a truce and recovered the bodies they had abandoned. Two hundred and twelve Corinthians and a little less than fifty Athenians died in the battle.

45. The Athenians set off from the islands that same day and sailed to Crommyon in the territory of Corinth. It is fifteen miles from the city of Corinth. After anchoring in its harbor, they ransacked its fields and bivouacked there for the night. The next day, they sailed along the coast, first to the territory of Epidaurus where they sent out a landing party, and then continuing to Methana, between Epidaurus and Troezen. They built a wall across the isthmus, cutting off the peninsula on which Methana stands, and established a garrison there from which they were to raid the territory of Halieis, Epidaurus, and the fields of Troezen for some time to come. When they finished walling off the isthmus, they sailed for home in their ships.

46. At about the same time as these events were taking place, both Eurymedon and Sophocles, after leaving Pylos for Sicily with the Athenian fleet, reached Corcyra and joined with the city-dwellers in an assault on the Corcyraeans who had become entrenched on Mount Istone—the ones who crossed over from the mainland after the civil war, took control of the countryside, and generally wreaked havoc.[5] The combined Athenian and Corcyraean forces attacked and captured their fortifications, whereupon the men fled in a body to a mountain peak and came to an agreement whereby they would give up their mercenaries while they, though surrendering their weapons, would be judged by the Athenian people. Protected by this truce, they were taken by the generals to the island of Ptychia, to be safeguarded until such time as they could be sent to Athens, on condition that if anyone should be caught trying to escape, the truce would be broken for all of them. The leaders of the Corcyraean populace, fearing that the Athenians would not kill the men when they arrived in Athens, came up with the following plan, with which they managed to trick a few of the men on Ptychia. They secretly sent over some friends of the prisoners after rehearsing them to say, as if they really meant it, that the best thing would be for the prisoners to run away as fast as they could. The reason, they

5. See 3.85.

said, was that the Athenian generals were about to turn them over to the Corcyraean mob. They added that they would provide some sort of transport.

47. They won them over and jury-rigged a ship for them, but the men were caught as they were sailing away from the island. The truce had now been broken, and all the men were handed over to the Corcyraeans. What most contributed to making this trick work and to inducing its inventors try it out with confidence was that the Athenian generals had made it perfectly obvious that they did not want the men to be brought to Athens by others, who would get all the credit, while they sailed off to Sicily.

The Corcyraeans took the men into custody and locked them up in a large building. Later, they led out twenty of them at a time and drove them through two lines of hoplites standing opposite each other. The men were tied together and beaten and stabbed by anyone in the lines who happened to see one of his enemies. There were also men with whips on hand to hurry on his way anyone who took his time before running the gauntlet.

48. The Corcyraeans had managed to lead sixty men out of the building and kill them before any of the others realized what was going on. They had thought that the men were being taken out for transfer to some other place. Eventually, though, they grew suspicious, and when someone told them the truth, they appealed to the Athenians, demanding that if they wanted them killed, they do it themselves. They also said that they would no longer willingly leave the building and that they would do everything in their power to prevent anyone from entering it.

The Corcyraeans, though, had no intention whatsoever of forcing their way through the doors. Instead, they climbed up to the roof of the building, and after tearing through the ceiling, they started throwing roof tiles and shooting arrows down into the crowd. The men inside tried to protect themselves as best they could, but most had already begun to commit suicide. They took the arrows the Corcyraeans had shot and shoved them down into their own throats and strangled each other with ropes from beds that happened to be inside and with strips of cloth torn from their own clothes. Night had fallen on their sufferings, and they spent most of it killing themselves any way they could and being killed by objects striking them from above, until they were all dead. When day broke, the Corcyraeans dumped their bodies crosswise into wagons and drove them outside the city. As for the women who had been captured at the mountain fortification, they used them as their slaves. That is how the Corcyraeans from the mountain were killed by the people, and with this event the long-lasting civil strife in Corcyra came to an end—at least as far as this war was concerned. After all, there was no longer any opposition worth mentioning. The Athenians sailed away to Sicily, where they had been going in the first place, and joined their allies there in the fighting.[6]

49. As the summer came to an end, the Athenians and Acarnanians at Naupactus, in a joint operation, captured the Corinthian city of Anactorium at the mouth of the Ambracian Gulf after it had been betrayed from within. The Acarnanians despatched colonists from all of their cities and took possession of the place. And that summer came to an end.

50. The following winter, Aristides, son of Archippus, one of the captains of the Athenian tribute ships that had been sent out to collect taxes from the allies, captured Artaphernes at Eion on the Strymon River. He was a Persian who

---

6. This was the second time that Eurymedon stood by at Corcyra during the commission of atrocities. See 3.81.

was traveling on a mission from the King to Sparta. He was brought to Athens, where the Athenians translated from the Assyrian the despatches he was carrying and read them. There was a great deal of verbiage about all sorts of things in them, but the gist of it was directed toward the Spartans and said in effect that the King did not know what the Spartans wanted. A great many ambassadors had come, the despatches said, though none had said the same thing. If they wished to deliver a clear message, therefore, they should send him ambassadors with the Persian, Artaphernes. It was the Athenians, however, who later sent Artaphernes to Ephesus along with some ambassadors. There they learned that Artaxerxes, son of Xerxes, had recently died (and indeed he had been near death throughout that period), so they returned home.[7]

51. That same winter, the Chians tore down their newly built wall on orders from Athens, which suspected them of plotting a revolt of some sort. The Chians, for their part, obtained assurances and guarantees that the Athenians, insofar as possible, would make no drastic changes with respect to them.

That winter then ended, as did the seventh year of the war that I, Thucydides, wrote down.

52. At the very beginning of the following spring, on the first of the month, there was a partial eclipse of the sun; and, early that month, there was also an earthquake.[8]

Most of the exiles from Mytilene and the rest of Lesbos were using the mainland as a base of operations. They had hired a mercenary force from the Peloponnese and recruited men on the spot, and they had proceeded to capture Rhoeteum. They returned the town unharmed, however, on receipt of two thousand Phocaean staters. After this, they led an expedition against Antandros and captured the city after it was betrayed from within. Their aim was to free the other so-called Actaean cities, which had formerly been governed by the Mytileneans but which were now held by Athens.[9] Their main objective, though, was Antandros. After gaining control of Antandros, they would have the material with which to build ships, because of the proximity of Mount Ida with its abundance of timber, and they would also be able to obtain all the other tackle they needed. They could also easily use Antandros as a base from which to harry nearby Lesbos and to conquer the Aeolian cities on the mainland. This, in any case, was the exiles' overall strategy.

53. That same summer, the Athenians, with sixty ships, two thousand hoplites, a small contingent of cavalry, and accompanied by some of their Milesian and other allies, led a campaign against Cythera. Nicias, son of Niceratus; Nicostratus, son of Diitrephes; and Autocles, son of Tolmaeus, were in command. Cythera is an island off Cape Malea, in Laconia. Its inhabitants are dependents of Sparta, and a Spartan magistrate went there annually to administer the place as the judge of Cythera. A hoplite garrison was regularly rotated in and out, and the Spartans kept it under tight security. It was their port of call for Egyptian and Libyan merchant ships and a barrier for Laconia against raiders from the sea, which was the only way it was vulnerable to depredation, since the whole of the Peloponnese projects into the Sicilian and Cretan seas.

---

7. Artaxerxes was succeeded by Darius II, who ruled until 404.
8. This eclipse took place on March 21, 424, which implies that for Thucydides summer begins with the vernal equinox. Thucydides divides the year into two seasons, summer and winter. Spring is the first part of summer and autumn the first part of winter.
9. See 3.50.

54. After the Athenian armada arrived, they captured the coastal city of Scandea with a detachment of ten ships and two thousand Milesian hoplites.[1] They landed with the rest of the army on the part of the island facing Malea and marched against the Cytherian capital city, where they found that all its inhabitants had immediately taken the field in full strength. A battle took place in which the Cytherians stood their ground for a short time before they turned and fled to their upper city. Later they came to terms with Nicias and his fellow commanders, whereby they would leave it up to the Athenians to decide what to do with them, provided they were not put to death. (There had been previous talks between Nicias and some of the Cytherians, and these had led to speedy agreements on favorable terms both on this occasion and in the future.) Ordinarily, the Athenians would have driven the Cytherians off the island: after all, they were Spartans, and their island lay off the Laconian coast. After the agreement was reached, the Athenians took possession of the fortress of Scandea at the harbor, placed a garrison in the city of Cythera, and then set sail for Asine, Helus, and most of the other towns on the coast, making landings, bivouacking wherever the opportunity offered itself, and pillaging the land for about a week.

55. The Spartans, seeing that the Athenians held Cythera and expecting that they would continue to make landings of this sort on their soil, nowhere opposed them in full strength. Instead, they dispersed hoplite garrisons throughout their territory where and as they were needed and kept everything else under tight security. After the great unexpected disaster on the island, with Pylos and Cythera in enemy hands, and ringed around by an enemy waging swift, unpredictable war, they were deeply afraid that some new change for the worse might affect the very foundations of their government. Thus going against their normal practice, they built a force of four hundred cavalry and archers, and believe it or not, they became even more reluctant to engage in active warfare than they had ever been. Contrary to the basic structure of their military, they were involved in a conflict at sea, and with the Athenians at that, people for whom not to attempt something was to disappoint their expectations for themselves. Also, the many sudden reversals of fortune had thrown the Spartans into a great panic, and they were terrified that another disaster might befall them like the one on the island. This made them all the more timid about going into battle, and having lost the security of self-confidence in their first experience of failure, they thought that all their initiatives would go wrong.

56. Demoralized, Spartan garrisons seldom took action against the Athenians when they raided the coastal towns. Whenever a landing took place near them, they were convinced that they were outnumbered. One garrison, however, that stood guard near Cotyrta and Aphrodisia, did make a run at a scattered throng of lightly armed troops and scared them off, but then retreated before hoplite resistance. A few of their men were killed and some of their armor was captured, and the Athenians sailed off to Cythera after setting up a victory marker. From there, they sailed around to attack Epidaurus Limera. After ravaging a part of that territory, they went to Thyrea, which forms a part of the so-called Cynurian territory at the border between Laconia and Argolis. The Spartans owned the place but had given it to the exiled Aeginetans to occupy, because the Aeginetans had helped the Spartans in the aftermath of their earth-

---

1. This number had been questioned as far too high. It was probably more like a few hundred hoplites, and the number two thousand was probably erroneously carried down by a copyist from the previous paragraph.

quake and during the helot revolt, and because the Aeginetans had always taken their side, though subject to the Athenians.[2]

57. The Aeginetans happened to be building fortifications on the beach as the Athenians were sailing in, but they abandoned them and withdrew about a mile and a quarter from the sea to their upper city, where they lived. The Aeginetans asked one of the regional Spartan garrisons, which had been helping them to construct the fortifications, to accompany them behind their city wall, but the Spartans refused because they thought it would be dangerous to be pent up behind it; instead, in the belief that they were no match for the Athenians, they retreated to the highlands and stayed there. While this was going on, the Athenians landed, quickly went on the march with their whole army, and captured all of Thyrea. They burned down the city, plundered everything inside, and brought to Athens the Aeginetans who had not immediately died at their hands, along with Tantalus, son of Patrocles, a Spartan overseer who was with the Aeginetans and who had been wounded and taken alive. They also brought a few men from Cythera who they thought should be removed for security reasons. The Athenians decided to settle them in the islands and to impose a tax of four talents on the other Cytherians, who were to remain on their own soil. They also decided, from inveterate hatred, to execute all the Aeginetans who had been captured and to put Tantalus in prison with the Spartans from Sphacteria.

58. On Sicily that same summer, the Camarinaeans and Geloans made a truce. At first, it was only with each other, but thereafter all the other Sicilian cities sent ambassadors to Gela, where they held talks to see whether they could come to terms. All sorts of opinions were delivered on both sides, pro and con, depending on how each party considered itself to have been injured. Then a Syracusan, Hermocrates, son of Hermon, came before the assembled delegates and delivered the decisive speech. His words were to this effect.

59. My fellow Sicilians. My city is far from being the least powerful in Sicily, and it is not especially suffering in this war, but I give this speech in the common interest, spelling out what seems to me to be the best policy for all of Sicily. I will not go on at length listing the horrors of war—you know all about them. No one is forced to fight a war by ignorance, and no one is deterred by fear if he thinks he has something to gain. The truth is that the gains seem greater to the aggressor than the perils, while those who are attacked prefer to face danger rather than suffer the slightest immediate loss. But when both sides drag on the war without achieving their objectives, they can be helped by those who counsel peace. That is the situation you are in now, and heeding that counsel is our best course. No doubt each of us went to war, at first, intending to settle things in his own best interests; now, through a mutual process of give and take, let us try to make peace, and if it turns out that not all of us can leave here with a share exactly equal to everyone else's, why then we can all go back to making war again.

60. We must realize, however, if we are prudent, that this meeting won't be about our private interests alone, but about whether we will be able to keep ourselves intact—if, as I believe to be the case, all Sicily is in danger from the Athenians. We must regard the Athenians as far more exigent mediators of these matters than my words. They have the greatest military force in all of Greece, and they are here with a few ships keeping an

2. See 2.27.

eye out for our mistakes. Nominally the "lawful allies" of states "hostile by nature" to others, they find a cover for arranging things to their own advantage.[3] We have started a war and brought the Athenians in, men who make war even when they are not invited, and we have harmed ourselves and strained our own resources to promote their empire. When they see that we have completely worn ourselves out, they will surely come with a much greater armada and try to subject the whole island to themselves.

61. If we were prudent, however, each of us would be taking chances and bringing in allies in order to gain new resources rather than to destroy those we have. And we should bear in mind that civil strife is destroying Sicily and its cities—Sicily, whose people are under attack and which we have rent asunder into opposing states. We must understand this, and reconcile individual with individual and city with city, and try, together, to save all of Sicily. So let no one think that it is the Dorians among us who are the enemies of the Athenians, whereas the Chalcidians are safe because of their Ionian kinship. The Athenians are not attacking because we are divided into two races, one of which they hate, but because Athens longs for the goods of Sicily, which we have all acquired together. They have just shown as much by accepting the appeal on behalf of the Chalcidian race.[4] They eagerly granted the "just claim," and more, of their treaty with the Chalcidians to a people that has never yet helped them under the terms of that treaty. And it is quite understandable that the Athenians make these provisions and seek these gains. I don't blame those who want to rule over others. I blame those who are more than ready to submit, because although it is human nature everywhere to dominate those who give way, it is also in our nature to defend ourselves against attack. We who know this will be making a mistake if we do not plan for the future, or if we have come here with the thought that there is anything more important than for all of us to avert this common danger together. We will be rid of it all the sooner if we come to terms with one another, because the Athenians are not operating from their own territory, but from that of the people who invited them over. We can avoid the futile round of ending one war only to begin another and of breaking the peace only to renew our strife, and the outside interventionists who came with such fine excuses for doing wrong will have a fine reason to depart without having accomplished anything.

62. That will be found to be the benefit of coming to the right decision with respect to the Athenians. And this thing—peace—that everyone agrees is the greatest good, should we not make it among ourselves? Don't you think that if something is good for one of you and bad for another, you can end the bad and save the good in peace rather than in war? Don't you think that peace offers safer splendors and honors and other advantages, which one could go on about in long speeches just as one can go on about the glories of war? Think about what I am telling you and don't look down on my words. Look into them instead, and find your own safety there, however you may understand it. And if anyone thought he could achieve security either through force or the letter of the law, he should not be too disappointed. He should be aware that there have been many by now who have sought to take vengeance on wrongdoers, while others have hoped to advance their ambitions by

---

3. The Sicilian cities were "hostile by nature" because they were Dorian cities, and the Athenians, as the original Ionians, were the "lawful" allies of all the Ionians. The Spartans were likewise the lawful allies of any Dorians.
4. See 3.86.

force. The former not only did not get revenge, but couldn't even save themselves; the latter, instead of acquiring more, abandoned on the battlefield what they already had. A just revenge doesn't succeed simply because someone has been wronged, and might is not secure because it is confident. What holds sway over the future is uncertainty, for the most part, and though that uncertainty is the slipperiest of things, it is nevertheless clearly the most beneficial, because it forces us to go up against each other warily, with advance preparation on a level playing field.

63. We are baffled for two reasons. First, because we cannot see the future, and second, because of the terrifying presence of the Athenians. We also know that these obstacles have prevented us from achieving our goals. We must therefore lead these enemies out of our land and come to terms with one another, preferably for all time, but if not, for a time that is so long that we can put off our private differences indefinitely. In short, you must know that if you listen to me, each of you will preserve a free city, from which, fully independent, you will be able as equals to give high-born requital to those who do you right and those who do you wrong. If you do not heed me and instead subject yourselves to others, you will, of necessity, not really be taking vengeance on anyone—especially if you are too successful. Instead you will be forced to befriend your worst enemies and to make enemies of your true friends.

64. As I began by saying, I represent the largest city here and one that would be on the attack and not on the defensive. Foreseeing the dangers I have mentioned, however, I am resolved to seek reconciliation and to neither hurt my opponents so badly that I hurt myself more, nor delude myself in the folly of political rivalry into believing that I am as much the master of chance as I am of my own principles. I will, instead, compromise as much as possible. And I think it right that others do the same as I, enduring compromise with each other and not with our enemies. There is no shame in family giving way to family, or Dorian to Dorian, or Chalcidian to his kin, when we are all neighbors, dwelling together in one seagirt land and calling ourselves by one name—Sicilians. I know that we will fight each other when it must be so and that we will again reach agreement among ourselves, but that we will always defend ourselves as one, if we are prudent, against the alien invader. Otherwise, even if only one of us is attacked at a time, we are all in danger of harm, and we will nevermore, in the future, be able to bring in either allies or arbitrators.

If we do as I urge, we will gain two advantages for Sicily. We will rid ourselves of the Athenians and of civil war, and we will govern ourselves from now on in freedom and be less subject to the machinations of others.

65. That is what Hermocrates said. The Sicilians took his advice and decided among themselves to end their war provided that each party hold on to what it had, except that Morgantina would go to the Camarinaeans, who were to pay a stated amount of money to the Syracusans. The allies of the Athenians sent for the Athenian commanders and told them that they were about to conclude an agreement and that Athens could also take part in it. The Athenians assented, and the Sicilians framed an agreement, after which the Athenian ships left Sicily. When the generals returned, the Athenians in the city sentenced Pythodorus and Sophocles to exile and imposed a monetary fine on Eurymedon, on the grounds that it had been possible for them to conquer Sicily but that they had been influenced to leave by bribes. For as a consequence of the good luck they had been enjoying, the Athenians thought there should be

no obstacles to their success. They were convinced that they could achieve the possible and the impossible alike, whether they were well or ill prepared, for the reason that the unexpected success of most of their initiatives gave an underlying impetus to all their hopes.

66. That same summer, the Megarians in the city were being ground down in their war with the Athenians, who had been invading their territory twice a year, every year, in full strength.[5] They were also being severely harried by their own exiles at Pegae, who had staged an insurrection and who had been expelled by the majority of the people. As a result, the people began to debate among themselves whether to seek a reconciliation with the exiles, in order to eliminate one of the two enemies who were destroying the city. The friends of the exiles, getting wind of this talk, also decided to be more open then they had been in urging a debate. The leaders of the people's party now realized that their hard-pressed supporters would not be able to hold out under their leadership. They grew alarmed and held talks with the Athenian generals Hippocrates, son of Ariphron, and Demosthenes, son of Alcisthenes: they wanted to surrender the city to the Athenians in the belief that they would thereby be in less danger than if the men they had exiled were restored. They agreed that the Athenians should first seize the long walls, so that the Peloponnesians would not be able to bring up support from Nisaea. (The walls were about a mile long from the city to the Megarian harbor of Nisaea, which the Peloponnesians alone guarded to ensure the safety of Megara.) They would then attempt to surrender the upper city, which the people would more readily go along with after the seizure of the walls had taken place.

67. Plans were concerted on both sides, and the Athenians, under cover of night, sailed into the Megarian island of Minoa with six hundred hoplites commanded by Hippocrates. They took up positions in a trench not far off from which soil had been taken to make bricks for the walls. Troops under the other general, Demosthenes, along with light-armed Plataeans and various other special forces, set up an ambush at the temple of Ares the Warlike, which is even closer to the walls. The only men who knew of the operation that night were the ones who were supposed to know. Just before daybreak, the men who would betray Megara carried out their plan. Long before, they had bribed the captain of the guard to make sure that the gates would be opened for them. They routinely put a light rowboat they said they used for piracy onto a wagon and brought it over the trench and down to the beach, where they would shove off. Before dawn, they would bring the boat back on the wagon to the walls and take it through the gates. This way, they said, the Athenian watch at Minoa would have no clue as to what they were doing, because there would be no vessel of any kind visible in the harbor. That night, too, the wagon was just in front of the gate, which was being opened, as usual, to let in the boat. When the Athenians saw this, they rushed out of their hiding place according to plan, to get to the gates before they were closed again and while the wagon was still going through and keeping them from being shut. Meanwhile, their Megarian collaborators were killing the guards at the gates. First, the Plataeans and the special forces with Demosthenes rushed in from the point where the victory marker now is. Once inside the gates, the Plataeans did battle with the Peloponnesian reinforcements, who were the closest to the action and who had come up when they saw what was happening. The Plataeans overpowered them and

secured the gates for the Athenian hoplites who were charging in. Then, as soon as he got inside, every Athenian made for the wall.

68. A few of the Peloponnesian guards put up a fight at first, and some of them were killed, but most ran away in terror. It was night; the enemy was suddenly attacking; treacherous Megarians were fighting against them; and the Peloponnesians thought that all the Megarians had betrayed them. You see, acting on his own recognizance, the Athenian herald just then called out for every Megarian to voluntarily join forces with the Athenians, and when the Peloponnesians heard that, they no longer stood their ground. Thinking that this was a joint Athenian–Megarian attack, they made a run for Nisaea.

By dawn, the walls had already been taken and the Megarians in the city were in chaos. The men who had been conspiring with the Athenians, along with a number of others who were in the know, said that they had to open the gates and go out to fight the Athenians, it having been preconcerted that as soon as the gates were opened, the Athenians would rush in. The conspirators were to have rubbed their bodies with oil, so as to be clearly recognizable, and left unharmed. It would also be that much safer for them to open the gates now because, by agreement, the four thousand Athenian hoplites and six hundred cavalry from Eleusis had traveled overnight and were on the scene. The conspirators had smeared themselves with olive oil and were already at the gates when one of them betrayed the plot to the other side, who then closed ranks and said that they didn't have to march out. After all, they said, they had not gone out even when they were stronger and they should not now expose the city to such clear and present danger. If anyone didn't agree, the battle would begin right there. They gave no sign that they knew what was going on; they just insisted that what they had decided was for the best and stood guard at the gates making it impossible for the conspirators to put their plans into effect.

69. The Athenian generals, realizing that there had been a hitch and that they would not be able to take the city by storm, immediately began to wall off Nisaea. Their thinking was that if they could neutralize Nisaea before anyone could come up to stop them, Megara would be all the more quickly forced to capitulate. Iron was quickly brought from Athens, along with stonemasons and everything else they needed. They began with the wall they held and built across to the other of the long walls fronting Megara. From there, the army divided their labor and formed work gangs to extend a ditch and a wall on either side of Nisaea to the sea, using bricks and stones they got on the outskirts of town. They also cut down fruit trees and lumber and built fences where needed. The very houses in the suburbs were provided with parapets and themselves became a part of the fortifications. The army worked that whole day, and by dusk of the next day, the wall was all but finished. The people in Nisaea panicked. They had no food, because they used to get it every day from the upper city; they did not think the Peloponnesians would come to their relief fast enough; and they regarded the Megarians as hostile. So they agreed with the Athenians that every man was to go free after surrendering his weapons and paying a fixed amount of money, but that as to the Spartans—the commander and any others at the garrison—the Athenians could do with them as they pleased. They left Nisaea after agreeing to these terms, whereupon the Athenians made a breach in the long walls, severing them from Megara, and secured their position after taking control of Nisaea.

70. Brasidas, son of Tellis, a Spartan, happened at this time to be in the vicinity of Sicyon and Corinth preparing for a campaign against Thrace. When he learned of the capture of the long walls, he feared for the Peloponnesians at

Nisaea and also worried that Megara might be captured, and immediately sent orders to the Boeotians that they come up on the double with an army and meet him at Tripodiscus. (The Megarian village of this name is in the foothills of Mount Geraneia.) Brasidas, thinking that he might reach Nisaea before it was captured, arrived at Tripodiscus with twenty-seven hundred hoplites from Corinth, four hundred from Phlius, six hundred from Sicyon, and as many as had previously been enrolled under his command. He had set out for Tripodiscus at night in the belief that Nisaea had not been captured, but when he got the news of Nisaea's capture, he selected three hundred men from the army, and before word of his movements could spread, he advanced on the city of Megara unbeknownst to the Athenians, who were on the coast. He planned to tell the Megarians that he wanted to attack Nisaea—and he really would have, if he could have—but the most important thing was to get into and secure Megara. He therefore demanded that the Megarians let him in, saying that he had hopes of recovering Nisaea.

71. The respective Megarian parties were wary, however. They denied him entry, one side fearing that he would bring in the exiles and throw themselves out; the other side that the people, fearing just that, would attack them, and that between civil war and the Athenians couched nearby, the city would be destroyed. Both sides decided to hold their peace and see what happened, because each expected that there would be a battle between the Athenians and the relief column. It would be safer not to join the side one favored until it won. Brasidas, unable to persuade them, went back to the main body of his army.

72. The Boeotians arrived at dawn, having intended even before Brasidas sent for them to go to the relief of Megara, on the grounds that the danger there threatened Boeotian interests. They had, in fact, already gathered in full strength at Plataea. Thus when Brasidas' messenger arrived, the Boeotians were relieved that Brasidas was on the scene. They despatched twenty-two hundred hoplites and six hundred cavalry and returned home with the bulk of their forces.

Brasidas's whole army of at least six thousand hoplites was now in the field and the Athenian hoplites were in formation around Nisaea and along the shore. Their light-armed forces were scattered throughout the plain, however, and they were not expecting it when the Boeotian cavalry fell on them and drove them toward the sea, because never before had there arrived any help whatever for the Megarians from anywhere. When the Athenian cavalry rode out to oppose the Boeotians, they came to close quarters, and there ensued a wide-ranging cavalry battle in which each side thought it at least held its own. The Athenians charged the Boeotian cavalry near the walls of Nisaea and killed their commander and a few others, whose weapons they stripped. They took possession of the corpses and then, under a truce, returned them and set up a victory marker. In the entire action, however, neither side was able to finish off the other decisively, so they disengaged, the Boeotians to their positions and the Athenians to Nisaea.

73. After this action, Brasidas and his army moved closer to the sea and the city of Megara, occupied a favorable field position, drew up their battle lines and stood firm. They believed that the Athenians would not initiate an attack, and they knew that the Megarians were looking to see which way the victory would go. They therefore thought they had the best of both worlds. They didn't have to start the attack or run any risks. Nevertheless, they had plainly shown that they were ready to defend themselves. They could justly claim a victory without so much as kicking up a dust cloud. By the same token,

things would work out well with the Megarians. The Peloponnesians would have been out of luck if they had not made a demonstration in plain sight. That would have been tantamount to a defeat, and they would have lost the city. But if the Athenians did, in fact, refuse to fight, they would get what they had come for without a struggle.

And that is just what happened.

The Megarians held their breaths while the Athenians came out and took up their position along the long walls. But the Athenians were not about to attack if the Peloponnesians did not. The Athenian generals reasoned that it wasn't worth the risk of initiating a battle against a larger force, when winning meant conquering Megara and losing meant destroying the flower of their hoplite army, especially since most of this campaign had gone the Athenians' way. Also, each enemy company was made up of detachments from all the Peloponnesian forces and was naturally willing to face any danger.

They waited for a time, but when nothing was attempted by either side, the Athenians withdrew first, to Nisaea, and then the Peloponnesians returned to their starting point. Thus with the Athenians no longer willing to fight, the Megarian friends of the exiles were encouraged to open the gates and accept Brasidas personally as the victor, along with the commanders from the other cities, and to enter into negotiations with him. Meanwhile, those who had collaborated with the Athenians were reduced to utter terror.

74. Later, after the allies had dispersed to their cities, Brasidas returned to Corinth and prepared for the campaign against Thrace, his original destination. After the Athenians too went home, the Megarians who had taken the greatest part in collaborating with them, realizing that they had been found out, quickly slipped away. The rest of the Megarians reached an understanding with the friends of the exiles whereby the exiles would be brought back from Pegae. They swore solemn oaths that no one would dredge up the evils of the past, and that from now on they would think only of what was best for the city. When the exiles were in power, however, they held a review of the troops, detached the various companies from each other, and segregated out around a hundred of their enemies who had seemed to be most closely working with the Athenians. They then compelled the popular assembly to try them on an open ballot and, when they were convicted, executed them. They then turned the city into a radical oligarchy, which it remained for longer than any government ever brought about by a counter-revolution achieved by so few after a civil war.

75. That same summer, the Mytilenean exiles were going to carry out their plan to fortify Antandros.[6] Demodocus and Aristides, the commanders of the Athenian tax-collection ships, were in the region of the Hellespont—the third commander, Lamachus, had already sailed into the Pontus with ten ships. When they learned of the preparations that were being made on the place, they decided that it might become as dangerous to Lesbos as Anaea was to Samos. For the Samian exiles had entrenched themselves at Anaea and were using it to help the Peloponnesians, by sending pilots to their navy, by stirring up trouble with the urban populace at Samos, and by taking in refugees.[7] They therefore set sail after gathering an army from their allies, defeated in battle the men who marched out against them from Antandros, and regained control of the place. Not much later, after Lamachus had sailed into the Pontus and anchored at the river Calex, in the territory of Heraclea, he lost his ships in a flash flood that

6. See 4.52.
7. See 3.19 and 32.

came down after a rainstorm upcountry. He and his army reached Chalcedon, the Megarian colony at the mouth of the Pontus, after traveling on foot through the territory of the Bithynian Thracians who live on the other side, in Asia.

76. During the same summer, the Athenian general Demosthenes arrived at Naupactus with forty ships immediately after the withdrawal from the Megarid. There he and Hippocrates had talks with some men from the cities who wanted to change the government and turn it into a democracy on the Athenian model. Ptoeodoros, an exile from Thebes, took the lead, and the following plan was developed. One group was to betray Siphae, the Siphians being a coastal people in the territory of Thespiae on the Crisaean Gulf. Others from Orchomenus were to give up Chaeronea, which belongs to what was formerly called Minyan Orchomenus, but which is now Boeotian Orchomenus. The Orchomenian exiles were especially active in bringing this about and were hiring Peloponnesian mercenaries. Chaeronea is on the Boeotian frontier near Phocian Phanotis, and some Phocians also took part. It was imperative that the Athenians secure Delium, the sacred precinct of Apollo, which faces Euboea in the Tanagran territory, and that these actions take place on the same day so that the Boeotians could not come to the aid of Delium together, but would instead move toward centers of agitation within their own territory. If the action was successful and Delium could be fortified, the Athenians thought it would be easy to make Boeotian governments amenable to their will even if there were not an immediate Boeotian political revolution, because they would be in control of this region, would be able to conduct raids from it, and would offer an easily accessible refuge for revolutionaries. Governments would not remain stable, because over time the Athenians would be able to aid the rebels and the Boeotians would not be able to gather a unified force.

77. A plan was readied along these lines. When the time came, Hippocrates himself was to lead a force from Athens in the campaign against Boeotia. He had sent Demosthenes ahead to Naupactus with the forty ships, to gather an army from the Acarnanians and the other allies and then sail against Siphae, which was to be given up to them. They agreed on a day on which these joint actions were to be carried out. Demosthenes learned on arrival that Oeniadae had been forced into the Athenian alliance by the whole Acarnanian people. He called up all the allies in the region, first campaigning against and winning over Salynthius and Agraea, and then making his preparations to rendezvous at Siphae at the appointed time.

78. At about the same time that summer, Brasidas made his way to the Thracian region with seventeen hundred hoplites. When he reached Heraclea, in Trachis, he sent a messenger ahead to friends in Pharsalus asking them to accompany him and his army through the country. Panaerus, Dorus, Hippolochidas, Torylaus, and Strophacus, the Chalcidian proxenus, went to meet him at Achaean Melitia, from which he continued his march. There were other Thessalians who also escorted him and, from Larissa, Niconidas, a friend of Perdiccas. Thessaly was a difficult country to cross without an escort—especially if you were an armed force! And indeed it used to arouse suspicion everywhere in Greece to pass through a neighbor's territory without his consent. In addition, the majority of Thessalian citizens had always been well disposed towards the Athenians. Thus Brasidas would not have gotten very far had not Thessaly been ruled by its customary cliques rather than as a government of laws, since even now he was met and stopped at the Enipeus River by opponents of the ruling class, who said that he was violating the law by traveling without the consent of all the people. His escorts said that they would not lead him

through the land of anyone who did not give their consent, it was just that they were his hosts, he had arrived suddenly, and they were keeping him company. For his part, Brasidas said that he was traveling as a friend to them and to the land of Thessaly, and that he was bearing arms not against them, but against the Athenians, who were at war with Sparta. He did not know of any enmity between the Spartans and the Thessalians to prevent their access to each other's territory, and he would not now proceed any further if they didn't want him to (not that he could have), though he didn't think it right that he should be prevented from doing so. The Thessalians left after hearing this, and Brasidas, at the insistence of his escorts, kept marching without a halt, on the double, before a larger force could assemble to stop him. On the very same day on which he had set out from Melitia, he halted at Pharsalus and bivouacked at the Apidanus River. From there, he went to Phacium and from there to Perrhaebia. At that point, his Thessalian escorts returned home, and the Perrhaebians, who were subject to the Thessalians, brought him to Dium, a town facing Thessaly at the base of Mount Olympus, in the Macedonian kingdom of Perdiccas.

79. That is how Brasidas was able to race through Thessaly before anyone could take measures to stop him and reached Perdiccas and Chalcidice. You see, Perdiccas and the people around Thrace who had revolted from Athens, terrified over Athens's military success, had invited this army over from the Peloponnese. The Chalcidians thought the Athenians would go after them first, and their neighboring cities, though not in revolt, had secretly joined in calling for the expedition. Perdiccas had called them in because though he was not openly at war with Athens, he was fearful over their long-standing differences. Mostly, however, he wanted to destroy Arrhabaeus, king of the Lyncestians.

80. The ease with which Perdiccas and the others were able to get the Peloponnesians to send an army resulted, paradoxically, from the sorry state of Spartan affairs. With the Athenians pressing the Peloponnese, and especially Laconia, hard, the Spartans were extremely eager to divert them elsewhere by sending an army to their allies in hopes of delivering a painful counterpunch—especially since the allies were prepared to feed the troops and had invited them over to assist in insurrection. They also wanted a reason to get rid of some of the helots, lest the Athenian occupation of Pylos lead them to rebel. The Spartans had always been obsessed with security in their relations with the helots. Why, once, for fear of the numbers and youthful energy of the helots, they had even done the following. They announced that there would be a contest for helots who considered themselves to have most valorously served Sparta in her wars, to see who should gain his freedom. The Spartans did this as a test, assuming that anyone who had the presumption to believe that he should be freed first would be most likely to revolt. They selected about two thousand. They were crowned with garlands and paraded around the temples, thinking that they had been awarded their freedom, and then, not much later, the Spartans disappeared them, and no one has ever found out how any of these men met his death.

On this occasion, they gladly sent seven hundred helots to serve as hoplites under Brasidas. The rest of his army were Peloponnesians who served for pay.

81. The Spartans sent Brasidas because he himself really wanted to go (although the Chalcidians were also very eager for it). He was considered to be in every way the most active man in Sparta, and after he left, he turned out to be of the greatest value to the Spartans. His moderation and fairness towards the cities in this campaign induced many of them to revolt and allowed him to take others by betrayals from within. He was thus able to lighten Athenian pressure

on the Peloponnese, and when the Spartans wanted to come to terms with Athens, as they eventually did, they were able to trade these places for others they wanted. Also, down into the last stages of the war, after the Sicilian expedition, the bravery and intelligence of Brasidas at this time, which some knew from experience and others learned by hearsay, instilled an especial enthusiasm for the Spartans in the allies of the Athenians. He was the first to go on a foreign campaign and earn a reputation for true nobility, and he left the firm belief that the other Spartans were just like him.

82. When the Athenians found out that Brasidas had reached the Thracian region, they came to the conclusion that Perdiccas was behind Brasidas's appearance and declared war on him. They also tightened security among their allies in the region.

83. Perdiccas immediately joined forces with Brasidas and his army and attacked his neighbor, Arrhabaeus, son of Bromerus and king of the Lyncestian Macedonians, a man with whom he had differences and whom he wanted to destroy. When he and Brasidas and their army reached the pass going into Lyncus, Brasidas said that he wanted to enter into negotiations with Arrhabaeus before going to war with him, to see whether he could make him an ally of Sparta. And in fact, Arrhabaeus had sent a herald to Brasidas with the message that he was prepared to submit his dispute with Perdiccas to him for mediation. Furthermore, the Chalcidian ambassadors who were accompanying the army advised Brasidas not to set Perdiccas free from all danger, so as to keep him that much more involved and hence more useful to them when they needed him. Finally, the envoys who had gone to Sparta on Perdiccas's behalf had said something to the effect that Brasidas would have the opportunity to form many alliances for Sparta in the area around Macedonia. For these reasons, then, Brasidas thought he had a right to work with Arrhabaeus in the common interest. Perdiccas said that he had not brought Brasidas in as an arbiter of local differences, but rather as an enforcer against whatever enemies he, Perdiccas, might point out. Besides, Brasidas would be wronging him if he had dealings with Arrhabaeus when he, Perdiccas, was feeding half of Brasidas's army. Despite Perdiccas's stubborn opposition, Brasidas met with Arrhabaeus and, won over by his arguments, withdrew his army before invading the country. After this, Perdiccas decided that he had been wronged and supplied a third instead of a half of Brasidas's army.

84. That same summer, right after leaving Lyncus, Brasidas, accompanied by Chalcidian troops, advanced on the Andrian colony of Acanthus a little before the grape harvest. The Acanthians fell out among themselves over whether to let Brasidas into the town. The struggle was between those who had joined the Chalcidians in calling in Brasidas and his foreign army, on one side, and the majority of the people on the other. Still, frightened because the harvest was still in the fields, the people were persuaded by Brasidas to receive him alone and then to hold their deliberations after hearing him out. He was allowed in, and came before the people. Not an ineffective speaker, for a Spartan, he spoke as follows.[8]

> 85. Men of Acanthus. The mission on which the people of Sparta have sent me and my army gives truth to the reason we proclaimed for starting the war, namely, that we were making war on Athens to free Greece. Let no one blame us if it has taken us a long time to come. We were wrong

---

8. Spartans were known for their tight, blunt, and graceless speech, hence the word "laconic" for people of few words.

in the assessment we made of the war back there, when we expected that we would quickly be able to destroy the Athenians without exposing you to any danger; but we have come now, as soon as we could, and with your help, we will try to finish them off.

That is why I am amazed to find your gates shut in my face, as though you weren't pleased that I have come. You see, we Spartans thought before we left home that we would arrive to find allies, allies of the mind and of the will, and we ran the great risk, filled with enthusiasm, of traveling through foreign soil for many days to get here. So if you have something else in mind, or if you oppose your own liberation or that of the rest of Greece, why, that would be terrible. Terrible. You see, it is not just that you would be opposing me. You would be making it difficult for anyone to join me wherever I went if you, the first people I came to, the people of a substantial city, people with a reputation for good sense, refused to accept me. And I wouldn't have any credible reason to show for it, other than that it is wrong to impose freedom, or that I have come weak and powerless to wreak vengeance on the Athenians should they attack you. And yet the Athenians, who outnumbered us, would not engage me in battle when I went to the relief of Nisaea with the very army I have with me now. So it isn't likely that they will send an army equal to what they had at Nisaea against you, especially when they have to come by sea.

86. I have passed this way not to harm, but to free the Greeks, and have sworn the government of Sparta to the most solemn oaths that the allies I recruit shall remain self-governing. Further, we will not use force or deceit just to have you fighting beside us. On the contrary, we are here to fight by your side, you who have been enslaved by the Athenians.

I do not, therefore, think it right that I, who offer the securest guarantees, should be mistrusted, nor that I should be thought a helpless ally. I think you should take heart and join me. And if anyone hangs back because he is personally afraid of someone, and thinks that I will hand the city over to this or that person, why, let him be most confident of all. I have not come to take part in a civil war, and I do not think that I would be imposing a secure freedom if, disregarding the traditions of my people, I were to enslave the many to the few or the part to the whole. That would be crueller for you than to be ruled by a stranger and would not bring us Spartans gratitude in exchange for our trouble, but curses instead of honor and reputation. In view of the indictments against the Athenians that we are attempting to prosecute by war, we would come to appear more hateful in victory than someone who never made any pretense to virtue. It is more shameful for those who are held in high regard to advance themselves by smooth deceit than by open force. In one case, you march justified by the strength that luck has given you; in the other, by the schemes of a lawless intent.

87. We take a very long view, then, about the things that matter most to us, and, in addition to our promises, you could not have a greater guarantee than the one by which deeds can be minutely compared with words to furnish the irrefutable proof that it is in our interest for us to do as we say.

I am reaching out to you, and if you say that you are powerless; if you decide that you can reject us with impunity simply because you have good will toward us; if you think freedom is dangerous, and that it may be just to impose it on those who are willing to accept it but that it must never be forced on anyone who doesn't want it—I call on the gods and local heroes to witness that having come in a good cause and failed to persuade you, I will lay waste your land and try to conquer it by force, and that I will consider myself to be doing no wrong. I will do so for two excellent and compelling reasons. First, to keep Sparta, through your "good will," from being harmed by Athens with the money that will be brought to her from you if you don't join with us, and second, to keep you from standing in the way of the liberation of the Greeks.

If it were not for the common good, Sparta would have no business freeing people who didn't want it, and it's not likely that we would do it. Again, we do not aim at empire, but rather hasten to end that of others, and we would wrong the majority if, in bringing autonomy to all, we looked the other way while you opposed it. Make the right decision, then. Lay up eternal fame as you lead in the struggle to liberate Greece. Meanwhile, your private interests will be protected from harm and you will dress your city in the most beautiful of reputations.

88. That is what Brasidas said. The Acanthians cast a secret ballot after first making many speeches on both sides of the issue. Because of the seductive way Brasidas spoke and their fears over the harvest, the majority decided to rebel against Athens. They bound Brasidas to the promises the Spartan government made before sending him out, namely that the allies he recruited would be autonomous, and decided to allow his army into the city. Not much later, the Andrian colony of Stagirus joined in the rebellion.

These, then, are the events that took place that summer.

89. The following winter had just begun. Governments in Boeotia were to be betrayed to the Athenian generals Hippocrates and Demosthenes. Demosthenes, with his ships, was to appear at Siphae, Hippocrates at Delium with his infantry. An error was made in computing the days on which the two forces were to move out. The result was that Demosthenes, with Acarnanians and many other allies from that region aboard his ships, sailed for Siphae too soon. Also, the plot was disclosed by Nicomachus, a Phocian from Phanotis, who told the Spartans, who in turn informed the Boeotians. And so Demosthenes accomplished nothing. Reinforcements arrived from all over Boeotia because Hippocrates was not yet in the field to create diversions, and Siphae and Chaeronea were secured before Demosthenes arrived. When the conspirators learned of the error, they did not create a stir in any of the cities.

90. Hippocrates, having levied the Athenians in full strength—the citizens themselves, the metics, and as many foreigners as there were—reached Delium too late, because the Boeotians had already withdrawn from Siphae. Hippocrates encamped his army and began to fortify Delium as follows. His men dug a circular ditch around the temple and its precinct and, instead of a brick wall, built up a mound with the earth from the ditch. They drove stakes in alongside the mound, and then cut down the vines around the temple and threw them into the mound, along with stones and bricks from nearby buildings that they tore down. They kept raising the height of the barricade in any way they could. They built wooden towers where they could and where the temple buildings were useless for defense—where, for example, a stoa had collapsed. They started on the third day after setting out from home, worked all that day, and continued through the fourth and into the fifth day until lunch time. Then, when most of the wall was finished, the army withdrew about a mile and a quarter from Delium and headed for home. Most of the light-armed troops kept right on going, but the hoplites put down their weapons and rested. Hippocrates stayed behind, set pickets, and worked on finishing the remaining parts of the outer defenses as needed.

91. During these days, the Boeotians were gathering at Tanagra. When they had arrived from all the cities and learned that the Athenians were headed home, ten of the boeotarchs, of whom there are eleven, would not join in recommending battle since the Athenians were no longer in Boeotia. (You see, when they put down their weapons, the Athenians were right on the Oropian border.) Pagondas, son of Aeolidas, however, was a chief magistrate from Thebes and was in command along with Arianthides, son of Lysimachides. He thought that it would be better to risk battle. Summoning his men in battalions so that they would not all leave their posts at once, he urged them to move against the Athenians and force a conflict. He spoke as follows.

92. Men of Boeotia! It should never have entered the minds of some of us chiefs that we ought not to do battle with the Athenians unless we caught up with them while they were still in Boeotia. After all, they crossed our common border and built a fortress with the intention of destroying us, and this makes them enemies wherever they are found and from wherever they set out on their errands of war. So that if any one of them thinks that he is safer for being across the border, let him think again. People who are under attack don't need to take thought about the defense of their own. Those who have their own and deliberately go about attacking others are the ones who need to do the thinking. We have traditionally defended ourselves against foreign invaders, whether at home or in the territory of our neighbors. And it is all the more necessary to defend ourselves now because the Athenians live on our borders. Neighbors who stand up to each other keep their independence; so when it comes to these particular neighbors, who not only try to enslave those who are close to them, but those who are far away, how can we avoid fighting it out to the bitter end? (We have only to take the example of how things stand with Euboea, across the strait, and with much of the rest of Greece.) And do we not realize that whereas elsewhere neighbors fight battles over boundary stones, if we are defeated, one undisputed Athenian boundary stone will be hammered in over all our land? Because they will come here and take everything we have by force. That is how much more dangerous these people are than other neighbors. Those who, as the Athenians are doing now, habitually and in the confidence of their strength invade their neighbors can more fearlessly attack when a neighbor holds his peace and only defends himself on his own soil; one who pre-emptively crosses his borders and, if the moment is right, starts the war, is less readily subdued. We've had some experience of that right here: when the Athenians took over our land during our civil wars, we defeated them at Coronea and we secured peace of mind for Boeotia up to the present day.[9] We must remember these things as we who are older strive to match our former deeds, while the young sons of the brave men of that time must try not to bring shame on their heritage of valor. With trust that the god whose temple the Athenians have fortified and occupied in contravention of all custom will be on our side, and trust in the good omens we have from the sacrifices that we have made, we must come to grips with these men and show them that whereas they may get what they want when they attack men who do not defend themselves, they will not get away without a struggle when it comes to those who nobly fight to keep free what they have and do not unjustly enslave the lands of others.[1]

9. See 1.113.
1. Thucydides tells us in 4.91 that Pagondas delivered this speech to a succession of battalions. Since it is unlikely that Pagondas delivered exactly the same speech over and over again, it is probable that this is a composite speech or the sort of speech Thucydides thought would have been or ought to have been made under the circumstances. See his discussion of his policy in presenting speeches at 1.22.

93. With this speech, Pagondas persuaded the Boeotians to attack the Athenians. It was late in the day by now, so he quickly struck camp and led his army out. When he was near the Athenian forces, he took up a position on ground where a hill between the two armies kept them from seeing each other. Then he placed his troops in formation and prepared for battle. When Hippocrates, who was near Delium, got the news that the Boeotians were on the way, he sent orders to the army telling them to get into position. Then, not much later, he arrived, after posting about three hundred cavalrymen near enough to Delium so that they could guard it if it was attacked, but also so that they could keep a lookout for just the right moment at which to join in the battle with the Boeotians. The Boeotians sent out a force to defend against these cavalry, and then, when they were ready, they appeared over the top of the hill and halted in full battle formation. There were about seven thousand hoplites, over ten thousand lightly armed troops, one thousand cavalry, and five hundred peltasts. The Thebans and their neighbors took the right wing. In the middle of the line were the Haliartians, Coronaeans, Copaeans, and others who lived on Lake Copais. The Thespians, Tanagrans, and Orchomenians held the left wing. Cavalry and light-armed troops were on both wings. The Theban phalanx was twenty-five shields deep; the other units were lined up in the order to which each was accustomed. That was the battle order and equipment of the Boeotians.

94. The whole Athenian hoplite force, equal in number to its hoplite opponents, was lined up eight deep. There was cavalry on each wing. No men especially equipped to be light-armed troops were present, nor did Athens have a designated force of light-armed citizens. The number of men who had set out on the original expedition was much greater than the enemy army, and many had gone along without heavy armor because there had been a general mobilization of whatever citizens and foreigners were available; but these men had already started for home and only a few were left. The Athenians were lined up in their order of battle and were about to attack when their general, Hippocrates, walking back and forth in front of his army, urged them on with the following words.

95. Men of Athens. This speech will be short. But that is enough for brave men, and besides, this is more of a reminder than a pep talk. None of you should think that we have no business running this risk on foreign soil, because this will be a battle for our own land on the land of these men here. If we win, the Peloponnesians, without Boeotian cavalry, will never again invade your fields. In one battle, you will annex Boeotia and liberate Athens. Advance on them in a spirit worthy of the city that each of you whose fatherland it is proudly calls the first in Greece, and in a spirit worthy of your fathers who, under Myronides, beat these men in the battle of Oenophyta and conquered all Boeotia. . . .[2]

96. That was much as Hippocrates could say. He had gotten as far as the middle of his army, but had no time for more because the Boeotians, who had just been given a brief speech by Pagondas, were banging their drums and charging down the hill. The Athenians moved up to meet them and they crashed into each other on the run. The far ends of both lines did not come to hand-to-hand combat, and for the same reason: mountain streams kept them apart. The rest stood pushing up against each other with

2. See 1.108.

their shields in a brutal battle. From the left wing to the center of the line, the Boeotians were defeated by the Athenians, who squeezed everybody here, but especially the Thespians. The Thespians who were wiped out had been defending themselves in hand-to-hand combat when their flanks gave way, and they were surrounded and butchered in a very small space. A result of the encirclement was that some of the Athenians fell out of line and killed other Athenians whom they did not know. The defeated Boeotians at this part of the line fled in the direction of the fighting; but the right wing, where the Thebans were, was beating the Athenians. At first, the Thebans pushed forward little by little, but then they started to give full chase. It also turned out that when he saw his left wing struggling Pagondas sent around two cavalry divisions from behind the cover of the mountain, and when they suddenly appeared, the victorious Athenian wing thought another army was attacking and fell into a panic. By now, with both wings collapsing from this action and the Thebans pursuing them and breaking through the ranks, the whole Athenian army turned and ran. Some headed towards Delium and the sea, some in the direction of Oropus, and some to Mount Parnes. Others scattered towards wherever they saw some hope of survival. They were pursued and killed by the Boeotians, especially by their cavalry and by the cavalry from Eastern Locris, which joined in as soon as the rout began. Night fell on the action, however, and most of the fugitives easily escaped to safety. The next day, the troops from Oropus and Delium (which, at least, they still held) left a garrison in place and made their way home by sea.

97. The Boeotians set up a victory marker, gathered their dead, and stripped the corpses of their enemies. They left a guard and withdrew to Tanagra, where they began to make plans for an assault on Delium.

A herald leaving Athens to ask for their dead met a Boeotian herald who turned him back, adding that nothing could be done until he himself returned to Boeotia. The Boeotian herald then went before the Athenians and delivered the Boeotian message that the Athenians had done wrong in transgressing against the customs of the Greeks. It had been long established for all that they should keep away from the local temples when they invaded each others' lands; but the Athenians had fortified and were living in Delium, and had done everything there that people do on profane ground, including drawing water from the wells for their own use, water that Boeotians were not to use except for handwashing before performing sacrifices. Therefore, in the name of the god and of the Boeotians themselves, invoking Apollo and the other spirits who dwelt in the temple, he publicly demanded that the Athenians leave the temple and then come back for what was theirs.

98. After the herald said this, the Athenians sent a herald of their own to Boeotia to say that they had done no injury whatever to the temple and that they would not willingly damage it in the future, because they had not entered it for the purpose of wrongdoing in the first place, but so that from it they could defend themselves against Boeotian aggression. The custom of the Greeks was this: whoever had control of a piece of land, whether large or small, owned the sacred buildings on it and was required to use them for whatever purposes they had always served to the extent possible. After all, the Boeotians, along with most other people who had expelled some other group and then occupied their land, had attacked what at first were foreign temples but which they now claimed as their own. And the same would hold true for the Athenians if they had been able to gain control of even more Boeotian territory. For now, though, the portion they occupied was theirs and they would not willingly leave it. The

water had been troubled out of a necessity that they, the Athenians, had not impiously brought about; they had been forced to use it while acting in self-defense against the Boeotians who had first invaded their land. There was every likelihood that even the god would sympathize with what men were reduced to doing by war and other hardship. After all, the altars were a sanctuary for those who had unwillingly gone astray, and "crime" was the word for evil that did not have to be done, and not for what men were emboldened to do by calamity. They, the Boeotians, were committing a much greater sacrilege in thinking it right to exchange the dead for a temple than were those who refused to take up their dead at the price of a temple. They also expressly demanded that the Boeotians not speak of "leaving Boeotian soil," because they were no longer on Boeotian soil when they had conquered it with their spears. They should make a truce by which the dead were to be "taken up according to ancestral custom."

99. The Boeotians responded that if the Athenians were in Boeotia, they should leave Boeotian soil and then come back for what was theirs; if they were on Athenian soil, they, the Athenians, knew best what to do with their dead. By this they meant that the Oropian border, where the battle had taken place and where the corpses happened to lie, was subject to Athens, and the Athenians would not take their own territory by force. Nor would the Boeotians make a treaty involving Athenian land. The proper wording for an agreement, therefore, was that the Athenians should "come back and take what they asked for after leaving Boeotian soil." The Athenian herald heard this out and left without accomplishing his mission.

100. The Boeotians sent for javelin men and slingers from the Malian Gulf. Two thousand Corinthian hoplites also came to their aid after the battle, and the Peloponnesian garrison that had abandoned Nisaea marched up, along with some Megarians. As soon as these troops arrived, they advanced on Delium and made a frontal assault on its fortifications. They tried all sorts of tactics until they brought in a siege engine, which took the wall. It was built as follows. They sawed a huge wooden ship's mast in half lengthwise and hollowed out the sections. They then snugly rejoined the halves, like a flute, and hung a cauldron from one end with chains. Next, they hammered the iron snout of a bellows into the beam's mouth and bent it down into the cauldron. Most of the beam was plated with iron. They brought this machine up from a considerable distance on wagons and moved it to the part of the wall that had been built up with the greatest amount of wood and grape vine, and then, when it was close enough, they inserted a large bellows into the end of the beam facing them and began to pump in air. The blasts streamed through the airtight tube and snout and into the cauldron full of smoldering coals, sulphur, and pitch and made such a conflagration on the wall that no one could hold his position. The defenders abandoned their posts and fled, and that is how the fortification was taken. Some of the defenders were killed and two hundred were captured. Most of the rest got down to the ships and made their way back home.

101. Delium was captured seventeen days after this battle, and not much later, when the Athenian herald (who knew nothing of what had happened) again came to ask for the bodies, the Boeotians no longer gave the same answer and returned them. A little less than five hundred Boeotians died in the battle and a little less than one thousand Athenians, including Hippocrates, the general. A large number of light-armed troops and orderlies also died.

Soon after the battle of Delium, the events surrounding the betrayal of Siphae having failed to materialize, Demosthenes, who had set out with his ships and his army of Acarnanians, Agraeans, and four hundred Athenian hop-

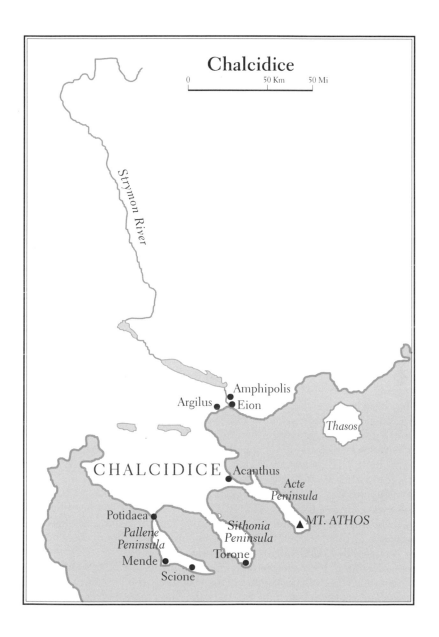

Chalcidice

0   50 Km   50 Mi

Strymon River

Amphipolis

Argilus   Eion

Thasos

CHALCIDICE   Acanthus

Acte Peninsula

Potidaea

Pallene Peninsula

Sithonia Peninsula

▲ MT. ATHOS

Mende

Torone

Scione

lites, attempted a landing in the region of Sicyon. Before all the ships could get to shore, however, the Sicyonians brought up their troops, turned back the landing force, and chased them to their ships, killing some and taking others prisoner. They set up a victory marker and returned the dead under a truce.

At the same time as the events at Delium were taking place, Sitalces, king of the Odrysians, died. He had been leading an attack on the Triballi and had been defeated in battle. His nephew, Seuthes, son of Sparadocus, became king of the Odrysians and other Thracians over whom Sitalces had ruled.

102. That same winter, Brasidas and his Thracian allies launched a campaign against the Athenian colony of Amphipolis on the Strymon River. Aristagoras the Milesian, fleeing from King Darius, had earlier tried to settle the place where the present-day city is, but he had been expelled by the Edonians.[3] Thirty-two years later, the Athenians sent out ten thousand volunteer colonists from Athens and elsewhere, but they were wiped out at Drabescus by the Thracians.[4] Twenty-nine years after that, the Athenians returned under Hagnon, son of Nicias, who had been sent out as the founder. They drove away the Edonians and settled the place, which had formerly been called Nine Roads. Their base of operations had been Eion, a coastal market town they occupied at the river's mouth, three miles from today's city, which Hagnon called "Amphipolis," or Two-sided City, because the Strymon River flows around it on two sides. He built it where it would be clearly visible from the mainland and the sea and walled it off from the upper to the lower bends in the river.

103. It was against this city, then, that Brasidas advanced after setting out from Arnae in Chalcidice. At dusk, he arrived at Aulon and Bromiscus, where Lake Bolbe flows into the sea, and then, after dinner, he marched through the night. It snowed a little in wintry weather and this made him hurry even more, in his desire to escape the notice of everyone in Amphipolis—everyone but those who were conspiring to betray the city. There were Argilians, who are colonists from Andros, inhabiting Amphipolis, as well as others. These were collaborating in the betrayal of the city, some for Perdiccas, some for the Chalcidians, but it was especially the people of Argilus who had designs on the town. They lived nearby and had always been regarded with suspicion by the Athenians. When the opportunity arose with the arrival of Brasidas on the scene, they plotted at length with their fellow citizens who lived in Amphipolis as to how the city was to be given up. That night, the Argilians rebelled against the Athenians, brought Brasidas into their city, and then positioned his army at the bridge over the river just before dawn. The town of Amphipolis is some distance from this crossing, which was not enclosed within the city wall as it is today, and there was only a light guard on duty. Partly because they had been betrayed, partly because he was falling on unsuspecting men in a storm, Brasidas easily overpowered them, crossed the bridge, and immediately captured all the country occupied by Amphipolitans living outside the city.

104. Brasidas' crossing came on the inhabitants of the city with such suddenness that what with the capture of many of those who lived outside, and the flight of others to safety behind the walls, the Amphipolitans were thrown into total confusion—especially since they did not trust each other. They say Brasidas thought that he would have taken the city if he had not allowed his army to go looting but headed straight for it. As it was, he halted his army and held still,

---

3. See Herodotus 5.124.
4. See 1.100.

since he had overrun the country and nothing he had expected from the men inside the city had taken place.

Meanwhile, there were more than enough opponents of the conspirators to keep the gates from being opened immediately, and acting in conjunction with Eucles, the general from Athens who was there to guard the place, they sent for help to the other general in command of the forces in Thrace — Thucydides, son of Olorus, who wrote this narrative, and who was in Thasos, an island colony of Paros about a half day's sail from Amphipolis. He obeyed and instantly set sail with the seven ships that were available to him, intending first and foremost to get to Amphipolis before it surrendered, or, failing that, to secure Eion.

105. While this was going on, Brasidas became concerned about the naval relief from Thasos. Also, having learned that Thucydides had the rights to the gold mines in that part of Thrace and that this made him influential with the leaders on the mainland, Brasidas was in a hurry to get possession of the city, if at all possible, lest Thucydides arrive and the majority of the Amphipolitans be unwilling to come to terms in the hope that he would bring in allies from overseas and from Thrace to keep them safe. Brasidas therefore offered them moderate terms, proclaiming that any Amphipolitan or Athenian who so desired could remain on his own property with full and equal citizenship, while any who did not so wish could leave within five days and take his possessions with him.

106. When the people heard this, they began to change their minds, especially since few had Athenian citizenship, most were of mixed nationalities, and many of those who were inside the walls were related to those who had been captured outside them. Also, they acknowledged that the proclamation fairly addressed their fears. The Athenians were happy to get out: they believed that theirs was the greater danger, and they did not expect help to arrive quickly. The rest of the people believed they would not be disenfranchised in the city and felt unexpectedly delivered from danger. As a result, once they saw that the majority opinion was beginning to turn around, and that the people were no longer paying any attention to the Athenian general who was there, the men who were working with Brasidas openly argued that the terms were right. An agreement was reached and the people allowed Brasidas and his army into the city according to the terms that he had offered. That, then, is how the people handed over the city. Thucydides and his ships sailed into Eion on the evening of the same day. Brasidas had just taken Amphipolis and was on the point of capturing Eion overnight. If the ships had not come to the rescue immediately, Brasidas would have had Eion in his hands by dawn.[5]

107. Next, Thucydides secured Eion so as to be sure of holding it in the present — should Brasidas attack — and in the future as well; and he gave refuge to whoever wanted to join him from upcountry in Amphipolis according to the terms of the agreement. For his part, Brasidas suddenly sailed down the river against Eion with a large force of merchantmen and other boats to see if he could capture the promontory that jutted out past the city wall, and thereby control the entry to the river. He also simultaneously attacked by land. But after

5. For his failure to reach Amphipolis in time, Thucydides was exiled from Athens, but he does not allude to this until 5.26. The precise charge against him is impossible to determine, and it is not known whether his fellow general Eucles was called to account as well. It was not unusual for the Athenians to impeach officials who they thought had performed badly; sometimes they were accused of treason, as may have been the case here. Thucydides' reticence in giving a coherent account — or any account — of the charges and procedures in his trial (for which he probably did not turn up) has made it very difficult to understand just what happened. For Thucydides' own views on political second-guessing of military action in the field, see 4.65.

being pushed back on both fronts, he strengthened the defenses at Amphipolis. After Pittacus, king of the Edonians, was killed by his wife, Brauro, and by the sons of Goaxis, the Edonian city of Myrcinus went over to Brasidas, and not much later, so did Galepsus and Oesyme, both colonies of Thasos. Perdiccas too appeared on the scene immediately after the capture of Amphipolis and helped arrange for these events.

108. The Athenians were greatly alarmed by the capture of Amphipolis, especially because of the city's valuable contributions of revenue and timber for ship-building, but also because the Spartans could now advance beyond the Strymon River. There had always been a route for the Spartans to Athens' allies as far as the Strymon (provided the Thessalians gave them passage), but so long as they didn't control the bridge, they could not advance any further, because a large lake was above the river while the entry to Eion was guarded by triremes. Their passage had suddenly become easy, and the Athenians were afraid that the Spartans would foment rebellion among the allies. Brasidas conducted himself with moderation in all his actions, and everywhere he spoke, he kept making the point that he had been sent out to free Greece. Athens' subject cities were all the more stirred to revolution when they learned of the capture of Amphipolis and of Brasidas' promises and his gentleness. They sent him secret envoys, asking him to come to their aid and expressing their wish to be the first to rebel. And in fact they thought it would be safe to do so, mistaken as they were about Athenian power to an extent that would become perfectly clear later on. They based their decisions more on headlong desire than on steady foresight, habituated, as all men are, to give themselves up to unconsidered hope when they want something and to reject what they don't want with rigorous analysis. Amphipolis had been captured and Athens had just been stunned in Boeotia, and Brasidas was saying—seductively but not truthfully—that the Athenians refused to engage his lone army at Nisaea; so the cities grew increasingly bold and came to believe that no one would come to punish them. Above all, in the rapture of the moment, with Spartans for the first time seemingly hot to take chances, the cities were prepared to run every sort of risk. When the Athenians learned of these developments, they dispersed what garrisons they could, in winter and on short notice, throughout the cities. Brasidas sent to Sparta asking that they send him another army; meanwhile, he prepared to build triremes on the Strymon River. The Spartans, however, did not oblige him, partly because of the envy of the leading citizens, and partly because what they really wanted was to get back the men who had been captured on the island and to end the war.

109. That same winter, the Megarians recovered their long walls, which had been held by the Athenians, and tore them to the ground; and Brasidas, after the capture of Amphipolis, took his allies and advanced on the so-called Acte, or Promontory. It extends from King Xerxes' canal and Athos, its high mountain, marks its end at the Aegean Sea.[6] It contains the cities of Sane, an Andrian colony along the canal facing the sea in the direction of Euboea; Thyssus; Cleonae; Acrothoi; Olophyxus; and Dium, all of which are inhabited by a varied mix of bilingual barbarians. Most are Pelasgian descendants of the Tyrrhenians who once lived in Lemnos and Athens, but there are also Bisaltians, Crestonians, and Edonians. There are even a few Chalcidians. They all live in small towns. Most of them went over to Brasidas, but Sane and Dium held out, so he stayed there for some time with his army and ravaged their land.

---

6. Xerxes had the canal dug in anticipation of his invasion of Greece.

110. When they still did not submit, he quickly advanced on Chalcidian Torone, which was held by the Athenians and to which he had been invited by some oligarchs who were prepared to hand over the city. He arrived while it was still dark, and by dawn he had positioned his army in front of the temple of the Dioscuri, about a third of a mile from the city. He had gone unnoticed by the rest of the city and by the Athenians who were guarding it. His collaborators knew that he would be coming, though, and a few of them had gone out in advance to watch for his approach. When he arrived, they took seven of his men, light troops armed with daggers, back into the city with them. Out of the twenty who had originally been detached for this purpose, those were the only ones who were not too terrified to go in. They were commanded by Lysistratus, an Olynthian. Unbeknownst to the sentries in the topmost guardhouse, they slipped through a hole in the part of the wall facing the sea, went up the hill on which the city is built, killed the sentries, and broke open the back gate leading out to Canastraeum.

111. Though Brasidas had advanced a little with the rest of his army, he took no action other than to send a hundred peltasts ahead, so that when some gates were opened and the agreed-on signal given, they would run in first. Time passed and the peltasts wondered what was happening. Nevertheless, they were able to advance, little by little, on the city. Inside, the Toronaeans were concerting their efforts with the men who had come in. Once the back gate had been broken open and the bar on the market gates cut through so these too could be opened, they first let in some men who had been led around to the back gate. Thus they would be able to suddenly panic the unknowing citizenry from the rear and on two sides. Then, after the pre-arranged torch signal was raised, they let the remaining peltasts in through the gates to the marketplace.

112. When Brasidas saw the signal, he ordered his army to advance and they came in at a run, shouting together and striking terror into the inhabitants of the city. Some of the men charged right through the gates; some went up planks that happened to be leaning against broken parts of the wall and that were used to drag up stones for repair work. Brasidas, along with most of his men, turned straight up to the heights of the city, wanting to make sure of taking it from top to bottom; the rest of the troops dispersed evenly throughout the town.

113. While the capture was taking place, most of the Toronaeans were in chaos: they didn't know what was happening to them. The men who had arranged for the action, and those who were pleased to see it done, immediately joined the invaders. About fifty Athenian hoplites were posted in the marketplace, where they slept, and by the time they figured out what was going on, a few had been killed in hand-to-hand fighting with the Spartans. The rest, on foot or on the two ships guarding the harbor, escaped to safety in the fort at Lecythus, which the Athenians kept as a stronghold for themselves. It was on a promontory projecting from the city into the sea and joined to the mainland by a narrow isthmus. Some Toronaeans who were friendly to the Athenians also went there for safety.

114. It was now day, and Brasidas had the city firmly in hand. He announced to the Toronaeans who had fled to safety with the Athenians that whoever wanted to could leave Lecythus and return home without fear of reprisals and with full civil rights. He also sent a herald to the Athenians ordering them to leave Lecythus under a truce, taking their possessions with them, because the place belonged to the Chalcidians. The Athenians refused to leave, but asked for a day's truce so that they could collect their dead. Brasidas gave them two

days. During this time, he strengthened the buildings nearby, and the Athenians did the same with their fort. Brasidas also called an assembly of the Toronaean people and said pretty much what he had said in Acanthus, namely that it would not be right to regard the men who had cooperated with him in the capture of the city as either cowards or traitors. After all, they had not done this to enslave the people or because they had received bribes; they had done it for the well-being and freedom of the city. Nor should those who had not taken part think that they would not be treated as equals; he had come to harm neither the city nor any particular citizen. That was why he had made that announcement to those who had fled to safety with the Athenians. It was because he did not think any the less of them for that friendship. And the Toronaeans would find on experience that they did not think less of the Spartans, he said. On the contrary, they would think more of them, because the Spartans were acting with good intentions, even though they were now feared because they were unfamiliar. He called on all of them to find ways to become steadfast allies and told them that they would only be faulted for the mistakes they made from that point on. The Spartans did not consider themselves to have been wronged in what went before; it was the Toronaeans who had been wronged by a greater power, and they were to be excused for their former hostility.

115. After reassuring them with words to that effect, Brasidas began the assault on Lecythus after the expiration of the truce. The Athenians defended themselves from a flimsy wall and from buildings that had battlements and were able to drive them back for one day. The next day, their enemies started bringing a war machine against them from which they intended to shoot fire onto the wooden bulwarks. While the army was on the move, positioning the machine near the spot they thought most assailable, the Athenians built a wooden tower on top of a building and carried up large stones and lots of jugs and wine jars full of water. Lots of men also climbed up. This overburdened structure suddenly crashed down with a tremendous noise, and although it caused more irritation than terror to the Athenians who were nearby and who could see it, those who were at a distance, and especially those who were far away, rushed to the sea and the ships, thinking that the place had been captured at that spot.

116. When Brasidas saw what had happened and learned that the Athenians were abandoning the ramparts, he immediately came up with his army and captured the fort, killing whatever men he caught. That is the manner in which the Athenians abandoned this position and made their way across to Pallene in boats and warships. Now when Brasidas was about to attack, he announced that he would give thirty mnae in silver to the first man to get over the wall; but Brasidas decided that the capture had taken place through other than human means. As it happens, there is a temple of Athena on Lecythus, so he dedicated the thirty mnae to the goddess for the temple, dismantled and leveled Lecythus, and made the whole place an inviolable sacred precinct. For the rest of the winter, he secured as much of the region as he held and planned his strategy to take what remained. And with the passing of the winter, the eighth year of the war came to an end.

117. As soon as the following summer began, the Spartans and the Athenians agreed to a one-year armistice—the Athenians, to keep Brasidas from tempting any more of their allies to revolt before they had a chance, unhindered, to take precautions, but also because they could make a more extensive agreement if that was in their interests; the Spartans, because they decided that the Athenians feared what they were in fact afraid of, and because if there was a cessation of hard times and suffering, the Athenians, who had been so sorely

tried, would be more likely to come to terms, return the prisoners to Sparta, and make a truce for a longer period of time. More than anything else, the Spartans wanted to get their men back while Brasidas' luck still held. If he advanced still further and suffered a setback, they were likely to lose the men. Meanwhile, to the Athenians it was a toss-up whether their military actions would bring victory or defeat.

This, then, is the armistice they made for themselves and their allies.

SPARTAN PROPOSAL FOR A TRUCE

118. As to the temple and the oracle of the Pythian Apollo, we have resolved that whoever so wishes may resort to them free of fear and guile according to our ancestral customs. This has been resolved by the Spartans and by those of our allies who are present; we declare that we will send a herald to the Boeotians and Phocians and, insofar as it is in our power, try to persuade them to cooperate.

As to the treasure of the god, we shall see to it that we find its robbers—we, you, and any of the other states who so wish, all justly and with due process observing our ancestral laws.

The Spartans and their allies have hereby made these resolutions concerning these matters.[7]

The following are the resolutions the Spartans and their allies will make on condition that the Athenians conclude a truce:

Each side will remain in his own territory retaining possession of what he now has. The Athenians at Coryphasium shall stay between Buphras and Tomeus.[8] The Athenians at Cythera shall have no relations with the Spartan alliance, neither us with them nor them with us.[9] The Athenians in Nisaea[1] and Minoa[2] shall not cross the road that leads from the gates of the shrine of Nisus to the temple of Poseidon and that continues from the temple of Poseidon straight to the bridge to Minoa. The Megarians and their allies shall also not cross this road. The Athenians shall hold the island that they have captured, and neither side shall have relations with the other.[3] They shall also continue to hold what they have in Troezen, according to the agreement the Troezenians made with the Athenians.[4]

As to access to the sea, the Spartans and their allies may sail along their own and allied coasts in any oared vessel, except a warship, that does not carry a cargo of more than twelve tons.

There will be a safe conduct for heralds, ambassadors, and a number of attendants as yet to be determined, to come and go by land and sea between the Peloponnese and Athens to negotiate the cessation of the war and the settlement of differences.

---

7. These guarantees were presumably given in response to Athenian demands for them as a precondition to negotiation. The Spartans and their allies controlled Delphi, and the Athenians probably wanted access to the temple before they would negotiate a truce. The people of Boeotia and Phocis, who seem not to have been present at the meeting in which the Spartans and their allies formulated the proposal, would have to be persuaded to observe the truce by allowing the Athenians and their allies to travel the Sacred Road through their territory to Delphi. It is not known what the "robbery" or other wrongdoing in connection with the temple may have been. It is possible, however, that Sparta itself took money from the Delphic treasury and that this formula for finding the culprits was agreed on to appease the Athenians. These considerations strongly suggest that it was the Spartans who initiated the peace process.
8. Coryphasium is Pylos. See 4.3 and 5.18.
9. See 4.53, 54.
1. See 4.69.
2. See 3.51.
3. It is not known what island is meant here.
4. See 4.45.

Deserters, whether slaves or free men, shall not be accepted during this time, neither by us nor by you.

You will try cases with us and we with you according to our ancestral customs and we will settle disputed points at law, not war.

These are the items that the Spartans and their allies have resolved. If some proposal seems to you more just or honorable than these, come to Sparta and explain it to us. Neither the Spartans nor their allies will reject any just proposal you advance. Let those who come have full powers, however, just as you have demanded of us.

This truce shall last for one year.

THE ATHENIAN RESPONSE

Thus have the people resolved. The Acamantis tribe held the presidency. Phaenippus was the recording secretary. Niciades was the chairman. The motion of Laches was carried (and may it bring good fortune to the Athenians) to make a truce according to the terms conceded by the Spartans and their allies and agreed by the people. The truce shall last for one year, beginning this very day, the fourteenth day of the month of Elaphebolion.[5] During this time, heralds and ambassadors shall travel between both sides conducting negotiations as to the terms for the ending of the war. Meanwhile, the generals and the prytanes shall first call an assembly to discuss the peace. . . .[6] The Athenians shall deliberate on whatever terms the Spartan embassy may bring concerning the ending of the war. The ambassadors here present before the people shall now pour wine on the ground and solemnly swear that they will abide by the truce for one year.

SPARTAN RATIFICATION OF THE TRUCE

119. The Spartans and their allies agreed to these terms with the Athenians and their allies on the twelfth day of the Spartan month of Gerastius.[7] These are the Spartans who concluded the truce and poured the wine: Taurus, son of Echetimides; Athenaeus, son of Pericleidas; Philocharidas, son of Eryxilaidas. The Corinthians were Aeneas, son of Ocytus, and Euphamidas, son of Aristonymus. The Sicyonians were Damotimus, son of Naucrates, and Onasimus, son of Megacles. The Megarians were Nicasus, son of Cecalus, and Menecrates, son of Amphidorus. The Epidaurian was Amphias, son of Eupaidas. The Athenians were the generals Nicostratus, son of Diitrephes; Nicias, son of Niceratus; and Autocles, son of Tolmaeus.

This, then, was the truce, and while it lasted, the parties negotiated with each other continuously about the broader treaty.

120. During the days in which the negotiators were traveling back and forth, Scione, a city in Pallene, revolted from Athens and went over to Brasidas. The Scionaeans say that they are descended from the Pellenians in the Peloponnese and that their ancestors were carried over to their land—where they settled—by the great storm the Achaeans underwent as they sailed from Troy.

---

5. About March 24, 423.
6. There is a break in the text here.
7. Probably the same day as in note 5.

Once the revolt began, Brasidas sailed over to Scione by night, with a friendly trireme sailing before him while he followed in a skiff. That way, he reasoned, if he encountered a vessel smaller than a trireme, the trireme would protect him, whereas another large trireme heaving in sight wouldn't bear down on the smaller craft, but on the warship, and while this was going on he could escape to safety. After he got across, he held an assembly of the Scionaeans and repeated what he had said in Acanthus and Torone,[8] adding that they deserved more praise than all the others because, although they were virtually islanders what with the Athenian hold on Potidaea blockading the isthmus of Pallene, they had, on their own initiative, progressed to freedom without waiting timidly for some outward force to impose on them what was clearly in their best interests. This was a proof that they would bravely stand firm before the greatest dangers; and if he proved able to settle things as he had a mind to, he would regard them as truly the most trustworthy of Sparta's friends and honor them with more than words.

121. All Scionaeans alike were excited and encouraged by this speech, even those who had not formerly been pleased with the developments. They eagerly made plans to carry on the war and gave Brasidas a fine reception in every way. At the public expense, they crowned his head with a golden wreath for liberating Greece, and private citizens tied the headbands of a conqueror on his head and deferred to him as to a winner in the Olympic games.

For the time being, Brasidas left a small garrison with them and crossed back over to Torone, returning not much later with a larger army. He intended to use them in an attempt on Mende and Potidaea, because he thought that the Athenians would retaliate against the Scionaeans as they would against an island, and he wanted to beat them to it. He had even had some dealings with these cities about having them betrayed to him.

122. Brasidas prepared to attack these cities, but just as he was on the point of doing so, he was visited by Aristonymus the Athenian and Athenaeus the Spartan, who were traveling around in a trireme announcing the news of the truce. They reported the agreement to Brasidas; the army crossed back over to Torone; and all the allies of Sparta in Thrace accepted the terms. Aristonymus assented to everything that had taken place, but after counting up the days and concluding that they had revolted after it had been agreed he refused to allow that the Scionaeans fell under the provisions of the truce. Brasidas argued vehemently that they had revolted sooner and would not surrender the city. When Aristonymus sent a despatch to Athens concerning these events, the Athenians were immediately prepared to launch a campaign against Scione. The Spartans sent ambassadors to Athens to declare that the Athenians would be overstepping the terms of the truce, and putting their trust in Brasidas, they laid claim to Scione and were ready to submit the decision to arbitration. The Athenians, however, were not willing to risk arbitration, but only to attack as quickly as possible, furious that people in what was by now an island should rely on an ineffectual Spartan land force and presume to revolt from them. And indeed the truth about the revolt was more like what the Athenians had claimed: the Scionaeans had rebelled two days after the truce went into effect. On a motion of Cleon, the Athenians immediately voted to drag the Scionaeans out of their city and kill them. They left everything else hanging and prepared to do just that.

---

8. See 4.85–87 and 114.

123. During this time, Mende revolted from Athens. This was a city in Pallene, a colony of Eretria. They had clearly gone over to Brasidas during the armistice, but he had accepted their overtures, indifferent to the legalities of the matter. The fact is that he had himself accused the Athenians of certain violations of the truce, which emboldened the Mendaeans all the more. They saw that he had a rough-and-ready attitude, which they also inferred from his refusal to abandon Scione. Furthermore, though they had not given up their original intention,[9] Sparta's collaborators were few; they were afraid of being exposed and had compelled the majority to act against their better judgment. When the Athenians learned of the revolt, they became that much angrier and made preparations to attack both cities. Brasidas, anticipating their naval expedition, sent the women and children of Scione and Mende off to safety in Olynthus and Chalcidice and sent the Scionaeans and Mendaeans five hundred Peloponnesian hoplites and three hundred Chalcidian peltasts, all under the command of Polydamidas. They then jointly prepared for the common defense, since the Athenians would swiftly be upon them.

124. Meanwhile, Brasidas and Perdiccas together attacked Arrhabaeus in Lyncus for the second time. Perdiccas led the forces of the part of Macedonia he controlled, along with hoplites from among the resident Greeks; Brasidas, in addition to his remaining Peloponnesians, led Chalcidians, Acanthians, and as many troops from the other tribes as each could muster. The entire Greek hoplite force of about three thousand, followed by the Macedonian and Chalcidian cavalry, a little under a thousand in all, and a large throng of barbarian soldiers, invaded Arrhabaeus' domains, and when they found that the Lyncestians had already taken up positions against them, they too deployed their forces against the enemy. The infantry were on opposite hills with a plain in between. First, the cavalry of both sides rode down into it and fought. When the Lyncestian hoplites advanced from their hill behind their cavalry, ready to fight, Brasidas and Perdiccas moved forward, engaged the Lyncestians, and routed them. Many of them were killed, and the remnant escaped to the high ground and halted. After this, Perdiccas and Brasidas erected a victory marker and held off for two or three days, waiting for the Illyrians who were supposed to be coming to Perdiccas on the promise of pay. Then Perdiccas wanted to move against Arrhabaeus' villagers and not sit around any longer, but Brasidas was not in favor of this. He preferred to pull back, because he was keeping an eye out for Mende, lest it suffer an Athenian naval attack before his return; and besides, the Illyrians had not arrived yet.

125. The two were quarreling about this when the news came that the Illyrians had betrayed Perdiccas and were with Arrhabaeus. Now both wanted to pull back for fear of the Illyrians, a nation of warriors. The quarrel had kept them from deciding exactly when they should set out, however, and night was coming on. The Macedonians and most of the barbarians instantly took fright, the way a large army tends to do, panic-stricken from out of nowhere. They decided that many more men were coming than actually were and that they were almost on top of them, so they started running and made for home. Perdiccas was at first unaware of this, but when he found out, he was forced to leave before seeing Brasidas, since both sides had camped far apart from each other. When, at dawn, Brasidas saw that the Macedonians had moved on ahead, and that Arrhabaeus and the Illyrians were about to attack, he decided to withdraw and pulled his hoplites up into a square phalanx, placing the crowd of light-

9. See 4.121.

armed troops in the middle. He ordered his youngest troops to skirmish with the enemy wherever they attacked, while he took the rearguard with three hundred picked men, intending to stand up to the front line of the enemy's advancing troops and fight them off during the retreat.

In the short time he had before the enemy got close, he rallied his soldiers as follows.

126. Men of the Peloponnese. If I didn't suspect that you were beside yourselves because you have been left alone, and because your attackers are barbarians and there are so many of them, I would not throw a lesson in along with the pep talk. As it is, though, in the face of the desertion of our allies and the numbers of our opposition, I'll try to persuade you of what is most important with a brief reminder and some advice. It is not for you to be brave in warfare because of the presence of allies on this or that occasion, but because of your innate valor; nor is it ever for you to be terrified of the numbers of others, you who do not come from the sort of city in which the many rule the few, but the few the many, owing their position to nothing but their superiority in fighting. From your previous fights with the Macedonians among these barbarians, from what I can guess, and from what I know after listening to others, it is important for you to understand that these barbarians whom you now fear out of inexperience will not be so terrible. The actual weakness of an enemy can seem to be a strength until correct knowledge about them comes to encourage the defender; but no amount of foreknowledge can make a man fight more boldly against those who are secure in their courage. These men present a terrifying prospect to the inexperienced. Just looking at the numbers of them is scary, and the loudness of their roaring is unbearable, and all that pointless brandishing of their weapons makes a great show of danger. But they won't be the same after mixing it up with men who stand up to that stuff. Since they have no formation, they won't be ashamed of being forced to abandon a post. Running away and attacking have the same appearance of valor; their manliness is not put to the test. When every man is fighting on his own, every man has a perfect excuse to save himself, and they think it's safer to run no risks by scaring you than to fight with you, hand to hand. Otherwise, they would have come to grips by now. You can plainly see that all the terrors you have attributed to them in advance are paltry in action, however impressive it may be to see and hear them. You can bear the attack if you stand up to it and then, when you have the chance, resume the retreat in good order and formation. You'll get to safety faster, and you will have learned once and for all that mobs like this will boast from a distance about their bravery against men who have withstood their first onslaught, but that when you give way to them, they eagerly show their courage when it's safe to do so—at your heels.

127. After giving this speech, Brasidas began to draw off his army. When the barbarians saw this, they bore down on the Peloponnesians with a lot of sound and fury, thinking that Brasidas was running for it and that they would catch and kill his men. But the skirmishers opposed them wherever they struck, and Brasidas and his picked troops stood up to them whenever they pressed forward, and much to the barbarians' surprise, the Greeks withstood the first charge. Thereafter, the Spartans engaged the barbarians and beat them back when they advanced and retreated when they held still. In time, most of the barbarians kept away from Brasidas and his Greeks in the open field. Next, leaving a detachment to follow and harry them, the rest of the barbarians set off on the

double after the fleeing Macedonians, killing whomever they happened to catch until, in advance of Brasidas, they took the narrow pass between two hills that leads to the territory of Arrhabaeus. They knew that Brasidas had no other line of retreat, and as he approached the most difficult stretch of the road, they began to encircle him in an attempt to cut him off.

128. When he realized this, Brasidas ordered his three hundred men to run up the hill he thought could most easily be taken. Each man was to go up as fast as he could, out of formation, and attempt to beat back the barbarians who were already on the hill before the rest of the encircling force could get there and close in on them. The three hundred ran forward and overpowered the men on the hill, after which the main body of the Greek army was more easily able to make its way up. The reason for this was that when their men turned away from the high ground, the barbarians panicked and stopped pursuing the Greeks any further. They also decided that the Greeks were on Perdiccas' borders by then and had gotten away.

After taking the high ground, Brasidas was able to continue in relative safety until, on that very day, he reached Arnissa, the first town in the domain of Perdiccas. His troops were in a rage over the desertion of the Macedonians, and whenever they came on any Macedonian oxcarts or cast-off gear on the road—as they naturally would, given the panicky nocturnal retreat—they unyoked and butchered the oxen and confiscated the gear. It was after this that Perdiccas began to regard Brasidas as an enemy. From then on, he harbored in his mind a hatred of the Peloponnesians that did not sort with his views of Athens, and abandoning his security interests, he took steps to come to terms with the Athenians and to get rid of the Peloponnesians as soon as possible.

129. When Brasidas returned to Torone from Macedonia, he found that the Athenians were already occupying Mende. He rested at Torone and held it under close guard, having decided that he was no longer able to cross over to rescue Mende. What had happened was that at around the same time as the events at Lyncus, the Athenians sailed against Mende and Scione as planned, with fifty ships (of which ten were Chian,) one thousand of their own hoplites and six hundred of their own archers, and one thousand Thracian mercenaries, along with a number of peltasts recruited from regional allies. Nicias, son of Niceratus, and Nicostratus, son of Diitrephes, were in command. They had set out in their ships from Potidaea, landed near the temple of Poseidon, and marched to Mende. The Mendaeans, three hundred Scionaean reinforcements, and the Peloponnesian allies—seven hundred hoplites in all, under the command of Polydamidas—were camped on a rugged mountain outside the city. Nicias, with one hundred and twenty light-armed Methonians, sixty picked Athenian hoplites, and all the archers, tried to get up to them via a path on the mountain, but he was wounded by the defenders and was unable to take the point. Then Nicostratus went up the mountain by another, longer, route with all of the rest of the army, but it was rough going, his men were thrown into disorder, and the whole Athenian army came within an inch of defeat. On that day, the Mendaeans and their allies would not give in; so the Athenians retreated and set up camp, while the Mendaeans returned to their city as night fell.

130. The next day, the Athenians sailed around to the east of Mende (facing Scione), captured the suburbs, and spent the whole day rampaging through the fields without anyone coming out to stop them, since it turns out that there was also some civil unrest in the city. The three hundred Scionaeans returned home at nightfall. The next day, Nicias advanced with half the army to the

Scionaean border and deforested the land, while at the same time Nicostratus with the remainder of the troops besieged Mende at its upper gates, the ones that lead out to Potidaea. It happened that the Mendaeans and their allies had stacked their weapons behind this section of the wall, so Polydamidas positioned his men for battle and urged the Mendaeans to go out the gate. The civil unrest was such that a member of the pro-democratic party answered that they wouldn't go out and that there was no need for a war. After giving this answer, he was dragged out and roughed up by Polydamidas, whereupon the people immediately took up their weapons and furiously attacked the Peloponnesians and the members of the opposition who cooperated with them. The people fell on them and routed them, partly because of the suddenness of the fight and partly because the Peloponnesians panicked when the gates were opened for the Athenians, for it was thought that the attack had been preconcerted with them. The Peloponnesians who were not immediately killed fled to the acropolis, which they had always occupied. Nicias had by now turned back toward the city, so the whole Athenian army attacked Mende (which was open to them, though not by any pre-arrangement) and proceeded to plunder it as though they had taken it by storm. It was all the generals could do to keep the whole population from being slaughtered.

After this, the generals ordered the Mendaeans to govern themselves as they always had and to bring to trial anyone they considered responsible for the rebellion. They isolated the men on the acropolis by building and garrisoning walls to the sea from both sides of the acropolis. Then, after Mende had been secured, they marched on Scione.

131. The Scionaeans and the Peloponnesians came out to oppose them and took up a position on a rugged hill in front of the city that the enemy had to take if they were to build a siege wall around Scione. The Athenians attacked the hill in full strength and pushed its defenders off in a pitched battle; they then set up camp, erected a victory marker, and prepared to build a siege wall. Not much later, while they were engaged in the work, the Peloponnesian allies who had been besieged on the acropolis at Mende reached Scione at night, after forcing their way past the guard along the seashore. Most of them got past the Athenian camp at Scione and entered the town.

132. With Scione being walled off, Perdiccas, out of hatred for Brasidas over the withdrawal from Lyncus, sent a herald to the Athenian generals and made an agreement that was immediately put into effect. At that time, Ischagoras the Spartan was about to lead his army overland to Brasidas, but Perdiccas, who had always cultivated Thessalian leaders, maneuvered his friends in Thessaly to put so many obstacles in the way of the army and its supply train that they didn't even try to get through Thessaly. He did this partly at Nicias' instigation—since they had come to terms—to give a clear signal to the Athenians that he could be trusted; and partly because he himself did not want Peloponnesians in his territory. Nevertheless, the Spartans sent Ischagoras, Ameinias, and Aristeus alone to Brasidas in order to reconnoiter the situation. Uncharacteristically, they even brought some of their young fighting men out of Sparta, so that they could install them as the magistrates of their subject cities and not have to turn affairs over to just anybody. Brasidas appointed Clearidas, son of Cleonymus, in Amphipolis, and Pasitelidas, son of Hegesander, in Torone.

133. That same summer, the Thebans tore down the wall around Thespiae, accusing the Thespians of collaborating with Athens. They had always

wanted to do this, but it became easy after what had been the flower of the Thespian army had perished in the battle with the Athenians.[1]

In the same summer, too, the temple of Hera at Argos burned to the ground. The priestess, whose name was Chrysis, had fallen asleep after placing a lighted lamp near the sacred wreaths of wool, so that they all caught fire and flamed up without her noticing it. Chrysis, terrified of the Argives, immediately fled by night for Phlius; and the Argives, following established custom, appointed another priestess whose name was Phaeinis. Chrysis had been in office during eight and one-half years, of this war when she ran away.

By the time that summer came to an end, Scione had been completely walled off. The Athenians left a guard on the wall and then withdrew with the remainder of their army.

134. The following winter, the truce between Athens and Sparta held, but Mantinea, Tegea, and their respective allies clashed in Oresthian Laodicium. The result was a disputed victory. One wing of each army turned back its opponents, so each army set up a victory marker and sent their spoils off to Delphi. Many were killed on both sides, the battle was close, and night interrupted the action. The Tegeans remained in their camp overnight and then set up their victory marker. The Mantineans withdrew to Bucolion and set up their own victory marker later.

135. When that same winter came to an end—when, in fact, it was almost spring—Brasidas made an attempt on Potidaea. He got so far as to set up ladders unobserved as night was coming on. The attack began in no-man's-land while the bell-ringer was still making his rounds—before he reached his relay-man; but they were quickly discovered before they could advance, and Brasidas withdrew his army on the double without waiting for daybreak.

And so that winter came to an end, and with it the ninth year of this war that I, Thucydides, have written down.

---

1. At Delium. See 4.96.

Book 5

In 422 Amphipolis was in the foreground once again, and Book 5 opens with the pivotal operations that claimed the lives of both Cleon and Brasidas (1–11). With Cleon and Brasidas dead, the Athenians and the Spartans decided to make peace. Thucydides gives the terms of the peace verbatim at 18–19 and goes on to tell how, as some of the Spartans' allies refused to cooperate in fulfilling conditions to which they had not agreed, the Spartans proceeded to make an alliance with Athens on their own; the terms of this alliance he also records (23). He then pauses (26) to make some general observations about the war, contending that the hostilities beginning in 431 and ending in 404 constituted a single war, and about his own work. Plainly this passage was written after the end of the war. Only in his allusion here to the time he spent out of Athens following his command at Amphipolis do we learn of the exile that was imposed upon him as a consequence of the loss of the city to Brasidas in December 424.

Sparta's failure to take its allies' concerns adequately into consideration when signing the Peace of Nicias with the Athenians provoked serious disaffection within the Peloponnesian League; in addition, the thirty years' truce between Sparta and Argos was expiring. Consequently the years following the end of the Archidamian War in 421 show a breakdown of the bipolarity that had characterized Greek international relations for some years (27–82). Sparta's former allies Corinth, Mantinea, and Elis now allied with Argos, as did Athens; Thucydides records verbatim the treaty between Athens, Argos, Mantinea, and Elis at 47. Sparta defeated the new coalition at the battle of Mantinea, however, and the Argives, replacing their democracy with an oligarchy, abandoned their alliance with Athens and allied with Sparta instead, as did Mantinea and Elis; the terms of the alliance appear at 79. It is uncertain what written records Thucydides was able to utilize in setting forth these alliances in precise wording. The book ends (84–116) pointedly with Thucydides' dramatization of the events on the island of Melos, whose inhabitants did not want to join the Athenian confederacy, and the conversations that culminated in the annihilation of the men and the enslavement of the women and children. It seems impossible to determine whether the dialogue Thucydides presents actually took place or is merely a free composition designed to focus attention on painful elements of power relations that Thucydides wished his readers to contemplate.

The Athenians were deeply divided about the best policy to follow, and these years (422–416) entailed substantial conflict among political factions; it is at 43 that Thucydides introduces the problematic Alcibiades. Thucydides' account of domestic conflict during these years needs to be supplemented from other sources, particularly Plutarch's lives of Alcibiades and Nicias, in which we read about the machinations that led to the ostracism of Hyperbolus, mentioned only casually by Thucydides at 8.73.

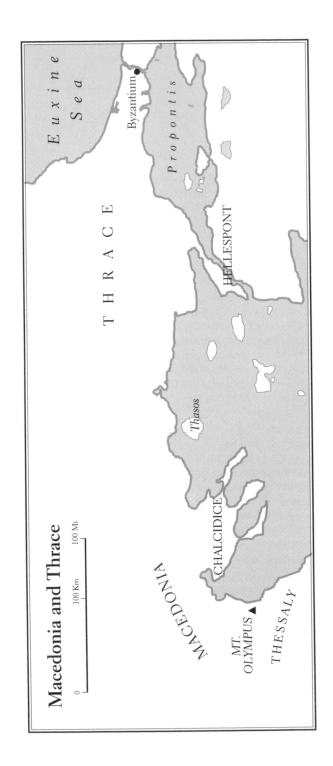

Macedonia and Thrace

Book 5

1. The following summer, the yearlong truce came to an end at about the time of the Pythian games. During the armistice, the Athenians drove the Delians out of Delos, having concluded on the basis of some ancient guilt that the Delians had not been pure enough to be consecrated to the priesthood. In the purification I referred to earlier, the Athenians thought they had made things right by removing the remains of the dead, but that purification had been deficient because of the Delians' ancient guilt.[1] Pharnaces gave the Delians Atramyttium, in Asia, and they occupied it, each man setting out on his own.

2. Cleon persuaded the Athenians to let him sail off for the Thracian region when the truce expired. He had twelve hundred hoplites, three hundred Athenian cavalrymen, an even larger allied force, and thirty ships. First, he put into Scione, which was still under siege, and reinforced his army with hoplites from the garrison there. Then he sailed down into Cophos harbor, which belongs to Torone and is not far from the city. After learning from deserters that Brasidas was not in Torone and that its inhabitants would be no match for him, Cleon sent ten ships to sail around into the harbor, and then he and his infantry left Cophos and marched on the city. First, he reached the advanced fortification that Brasidas had put up to encompass the suburbs within the town by taking down the old wall and creating one city.

3. The Spartan governor, Pasitelidas, rushed to the defense of the spot with the garrison he had and tried to fight off the attacking Athenians. But they were hard pressed, and the ships that had been sent around were simultaneously entering the harbor. Pasitelidas became alarmed that the ships would take the undefended city before he could stop them and that the fortification would also be captured, trapping him and his men. So he abandoned the fortification and ran towards the city. The Athenians got there first, however, their amphibious troops taking Torone, while the infantry followed Pasitelidas in hot pursuit, crashing into the city after him through the gap in the old wall. They killed some of the Peloponnesians and Toronaeans as soon as they got their hands on them, but they also took some alive, including the governor Pasitelidas. Brasidas rushed to the relief of Torone, but he withdrew after learning en route that it had been captured. He was about five miles short of arriving in time.

Cleon and his Athenians set up two victory markers, one at the harbor and one near the fortification. They sold the Toronaean women and children into slavery and sent the Peloponnesians and whatever Chalcidians there were back to Athens. There were seven hundred men in all. The Peloponnesian contingent was released in the peace that was made later; the rest were recovered by the Olynthians in a man-for-man exchange. At about the same time, the Boeotians captured the Athenian border fortification of Panactum after it was betrayed from within. Meanwhile, Cleon stationed a garrison at Torone and set sail around Athos with the intention of attacking Amphipolis.

4. At about the same time, on orders from the Athenians, Phaeax, son of Erasistratus, and two others set out in two ships as ambassadors to Italy and Sicily. The reason was that when the Athenians left Sicily after the agreement,[2] the Leontines naturalized a great many citizens and the people started making plans to redistribute the land. In view of what was happening, the ruling classes brought in the Syracusans and expelled the common people,

---

1. See 3.104.
2. Thucydides means the agreement that was made in 424. See 4.65.

who scattered here and there in Sicily. Then the ruling classes reached an agreement with the Syracusans whereby they stripped and abandoned Leontini and went to live in Syracuse as citizens. Disgruntled, some of them later left Syracuse and returned to Leontini. They seized a part of the city of Leontini known as Phocaeae, along with Bricinniae, a fortress in Leontine territory. Then most of the common people who had been driven out joined them. They dug in and proceeded to make war on Syracuse from the two fortified posts. The Athenians sent Phaeax after they learned of these developments, to see whether he could persuade their allies there to unite with each other and with the other cities, if possible, in order to save the people of Leontini by attacking the growing power of Syracuse. On his arrival, Phaeax won over the people of Camarina and Agrigentum, but the mood was hostile to him in Gela, so he changed his plans and did not go to the other cities, knowing that he would not be able to convince them either. Instead, he withdrew through Sicilian territory to Catana, stopping at Bricinniae along the way to give them encouragement. Then he sailed away.

5. Both on his passage to Sicily and on his return, Phaeax also negotiated with some Italian cities to bring them to terms of friendship with Athens. He also met up with the Locrian settlers who had been expelled from Messana. (After the agreement among the Sicilians, the Messanians had fallen into civil war. One faction had called on Italian Locri, which sent these Locrians out as settlers, thus putting Messana in Locrian hands for a time.) Phaeax encountered these men on their way home, but he took no hostile action against them, because the Locrians had already agreed with him to make a treaty with Athens. When the Sicilians reached their agreement, the Locrians were the only allies who did not make a treaty with Athens; and they would not have done so now had they not been hard pressed by their war with the Hipponians and Medmaeans, who were their colonists and who were on their borders. Some time later, Phaeax returned to Athens.

6. As to Cleon, he had sailed around from Torone, bound for Amphipolis. Using Eion on the Strymon River as his base of operations, he attacked the Andrian colony of Stagirus without capturing it, although he did take the Thasian colony of Galepsus by storm. He also sent envoys to Perdiccas to get him to join him with an army, according to the terms of their alliance. He sent other envoys into Thrace, to Polles, the king of the Odomantians, to get him to bring as many Thracian mercenaries as possible. Cleon himself bided his time in Eion, awaiting these men.

When Brasidas learned of these developments, he for his part took up a position opposite Cleon, in Cerdylium. This is Argilian territory on the high ground across the river, not far from Amphipolis. Brasidas could see the whole country from there, so Cleon could not escape his notice if he set out with his army. And that is what Brasidas expected Cleon to do—to go up against Amphipolis with the army he had, disdaining the small size of Brasidas' forces. Meanwhile, Brasidas got ready, calling up fifteen hundred Thracian mercenaries, along with all the Edonian peltast and cavalry forces. In addition to the forces he had in Amphipolis, Brasidas also had one thousand peltasts from Myrcinus and Chalcidice. His whole assembled hoplite force amounted to about two thousand, as well as three hundred Greek cavalry. Of these, Brasidas took fifteen hundred and stationed himself in Cerdylium. The other troops took up positions in Amphipolis under Clearidas.

7. As to Cleon, he held still for a while, but then he was forced to do what Brasidas expected he would. The reason was that his men had grown

restless sitting on their hands and had started to compare Brasidas' leadership, with his boldness and experience, to Cleon's, with his lack of skill and energy, and they remembered that they had left home and followed Cleon against their will. Cleon heard this grumbling, and not wanting his men to become demoralized from staying in the same place, he called them to arms and led them out. He had the same attitude as he had before he got lucky at Pylos and came to believe that he actually knew something. He did not so much as imagine that anyone would come out to meet him in battle. He was going out, he said, to take a look at the terrain; and he was waiting for the reinforcements not so that he could safely hold off the enemy if need be, but so that he could encircle the city and take it by storm. When he reached a steep hill in front of Amphipolis, he positioned his army there and noted the marshy area of the Strymon valley and the lay of the city in the Thracian landscape. He thought that he could withdraw whenever he wanted to, without a battle. After all, no one was visible on the city walls and no one came out the gates, which were all closed. He even thought it a mistake that he had not brought along battering rams, since there was no one to stop him from taking the place.

8. As soon as Brasidas saw the Athenians on the move, he descended from Cerdylium and entered Amphipolis. He did not formally march out and take up a position opposite the Athenians, because he was worried about his troops and thought them inferior—not in numbers—since they were just about equal, but in quality, since the ablest Athenians had gone out with the strongest Imbrians and Lemnians. Instead, he planned a surprise attack. He thought he had a better chance to prevail if the enemy didn't see him and couldn't assess his strength for what it really was than if he went out to meet them face to face with his scantily armed rabble. Therefore, selecting one hundred fifty hoplites and turning the rest over to Clearidas, he decided on a sudden attack before the Athenians withdrew, thinking that he would not be able to catch them alone like this again once their reinforcements had arrived. He then called together all his soldiers to encourage them and to explain his plan, and spoke as follows:

9. Men of the Peloponnese, it's enough for me to say that you come from a land that has always been free because of your courage, and that you, who are Dorians, are used to beating the Ionians, with whom you are about to fight. What I want to explain to you is how I intend to execute this attack, so that our small force, our refusal to risk everything, our seeming inadequacy, will not cause any of you to fear. I figure that because of their disrespect for us, our enemies haven't even dreamed that anyone will come against them in battle, and that they're slighting us by coming up to this ground now all out of formation to look around. The general who sees such tactical errors of the enemy for what they really are and attacks with the forces he has will do all right—not necessarily by standing shoulder to shoulder and out in the open, but taking the battle as it comes. The tricks by which a general deceives his enemies earn him the greatest reputation and do the most good for his friends. So while they're still confidently unprepared, and are, from what I can tell, more inclined to withdraw than stay where they are; and while their thoughts are distracted, and before they recover their presence of mind, I will take the men I have with me and do my best to get to the center of their army on the run before they have a chance to retreat. Then you, Clearidas, as soon as you see me attacking and most likely panicking them, you will open the gates—one

more thing they didn't foresee. You will then take your own men, along with the Amphipolitans and the other allies, start running, and come to grips with the enemy as quickly as possible. That's our best hope of striking terror into them. A second attack is more frightening to an enemy than the one he is already fighting. Be brave, Clearidas, as becomes a Spartan, and follow bravely, you allies, in the knowledge that fighting well is made up of three things: alacrity, fear of disgrace, and obedience to your officers. On this day, you will either be brave, gain your freedom, and call yourselves the allies of Sparta, or you will become the slaves of Athens. At best, even if you avoid death or being sold as chattels, you will suffer a harsher servitude than before and you will impede the liberation of the rest of Greece. Don't falter, knowing what this fight is about, and I will show that I am able not only to give speeches to others, but to get into the action myself.

10. After saying this, Brasidas prepared for his sortie and concentrated his other troops at the so-called Thracian gate with Clearidas so they could rush out as ordered. It was reported to Cleon (who had by now advanced far forward on his reconnaissance) that Brasidas had been seen coming down from Cerdylium into the city, which was clearly visible from outside, and that he had performed sacrifices at the temple of Athena and made preparations with Clearidas at the Thracian gate. He was also told that the whole enemy army was clearly in the city, and that the feet and hooves of many men and horses ready to rush out could be seen under the gate. When Cleon heard this, he moved up to see for himself. He did not, however, want to fight a battle before the reinforcements reached him, and he thought that he could get away before the enemy launched an attack, so he ordered that the signal to retreat be given and that they withdraw to the left, towards Eion, which was the only possible route. He thought he had plenty of time, so he turned his unshielded right flank toward the enemy and withdrew his force. At this point, with the Athenian army on the move, Brasidas saw his opportunity and told both his own men and the others, "These men won't stand up to us. It's obvious from the way their heads and spears are shaking. When men act like that, they don't usually stand up to their attackers. Somebody open the gates for me as ordered, and let's boldly run out as fast as we can." Then he sortied through the doors leading to the palisade, the ones that were at that time the first in the long wall, and after running up the straight path where you will find the victory marker now standing, which he erected in the most rugged part of the terrain, he hit the Athenians, terrified in their own disarray and stunned by his daring, and routed the center of the army. As ordered, Clearidas then ran out through the Thracian gate and charged at the army. The Athenians were thrown into confusion by the suddenness and unexpectedness of the attack from two sides, and their left wing, which had advanced toward Eion, broke up and started running. As soon as the left wing retreated, Brasidas proceeded to attack the right wing, where he was wounded and fell. The Athenians were not aware of this, however, because the men who were near him picked him up and carried him away.

The right wing was more inclined to hold its ground, but Cleon, who had never contemplated taking a stand, started running immediately and was cut off and killed by a Myrcinian peltast. Cleon's hoplites, however, massed at the top of the hill and held off two or three of Clearidas' assaults, not giving up until the Myrcinian and Chalcidian cavalry and peltasts had surrounded them, bombarded them with javelins, and put them to flight.

By now, the whole Athenian army was on the run, making its difficult way over many mountain trails, and those who weren't killed in hand-to-hand combat or by the peltasts and the Chalcidian cavalry managed to get back to Eion.

The men who picked up Brasidas and got him safely out of the battle and into the city brought him in while he still had breath in him. Not much later, he lost consciousness and died; but he knew that his men had won.

After returning with Clearidas from the chase, the rest of the army stripped the dead and set up a victory marker.

Later, all the allies in full battle gear followed the body of Brasidas and gave him a public burial in Amphipolis in front of what is now the agora. In time, the Amphipolitans built an enclosure around his grave and came to perform sacrifices to him as to a hero.[3] They instituted athletic contests and annual sacrifices in his honor and dedicated their colony to him as their founding father, after tearing down the monument to Hagnon and obliterating any trace that might survive of his having founded the city. They believed Brasidas to be their savior, and besides, in the present circumstances they cultivated the alliance with Sparta for fear of the Athenians. Because they were at war with Athens, to hold ceremonies in honor of Hagnon would not have been expedient for them or agreeable to him.

They also returned the Athenian dead. About six hundred Athenians had died, as opposed to seven of their adversaries, and they died because this was no regular engagement of troops, but a fortuitous conjunction of events in which the Athenians were panicked even before the battle began. After taking up their dead, the Athenians sailed back home, while Clearidas and his men ran things in Amphipolis.

12. At about the same time at the end of that summer, the Spartans Rhamphias, Autocharidas, and Epicydidas led a relief column of nine hundred hoplites into the region around Thrace. When they came to Heraclea in Trachis, they began to set some things to rights that they disapproved of, and while they wasted time there, the battle took place at Amphipolis.

And so the summer came to an end.

13. As soon as the following winter began, Rhamphias and his men marched as far as Pierium in Thessaly, but they turned back toward home because the Thessalians blocked their way, and because Brasidas, to whom the army was going, was dead. They decided there was no longer any point in going on, since the Athenians had withdrawn in retreat and since they lacked the resources to carry out Brasidas' strategy. Mostly, however, they pulled back because they had known from the time of their departure that the attitude of the Spartans leaned toward peace.

14. What happened immediately after the battle of Amphipolis and the withdrawal of Rhamphias from Thessaly was that both sides stopped pressing the war energetically. Instead, they inclined toward peace. The Athenians had been stung in Delium and not long after in Amphipolis, and they no longer had the same confidence in their strength that had led them to reject the treaty initially, in the belief that the luck of the moment would lead to final victory. At the same time, they feared that, encouraged by their missteps, more of their allies would revolt. They regretted that they had not come to terms when the events in Pylos had given them a favorable opportunity to do so.

For the Spartans, the war had gone differently than they had expected when they thought that they would bring low the power of Athens in a few

---

3. On hero cults, see note to 2.74.

years if they just slashed and burned their land, because a catastrophe then befell them on that island such as Sparta had never experienced before. Also, their territory was constantly being raided from Pylos and Cythera. And the helots were deserting, creating a continual anxiety that those who remained, trusting in help from those who had fled, would take the opportunity to rebel now as they had done in the past. Furthermore, their thirty years' truce with Argos was about to expire, and the Argives were not willing to renew it unless Cynuria was returned to them—the impossibility of which made it look like they would have to fight Argos and Athens both. In addition, they suspected that some of the cities in the Peloponnese would go over to the side of Argos, which in fact happened.

15. The more they thought about it, the more desirable an agreement seemed to both sides, but especially to the Spartans in their eagerness for the return of the men who had been captured on the island. Those Spartans, after all, were their best men, as well as their kin. They had begun negotiations immediately after the capture, but there was no way the Athenians, who were then doing well, would agree to a man-for-man exchange. As soon as the Athenians suffered the setback at Delium, the Spartans knew that they would be more willing to accept terms, so they negotiated the yearlong armistice that required them to meet and deliberate about the longer term.

16. Then came the Athenian defeat at Amphipolis and the deaths of Cleon and Brasidas. Both men had stood out in their opposition to peace, Brasidas because the war brought him success and esteem, and Cleon because he thought that once there was peace, his corruption would be more obvious and his false accusations less credible. But then two men who were consolidating their power in each city, Pleistoanax, son of Pausanias and king of Sparta, and Nicias son of Niceratus (the most successful Athenian general of his time) became much more ready for peace. Nicias wanted to safeguard his success while he was still highly regarded and unscathed in battle. He wanted an immediate rest from trouble for himself and his fellow citizens, and he wanted to leave behind a reputation for all time that he had lived his life without harming his city. He believed that these things would come to pass for whoever least trusted to chance and stayed safe, and he thought that peace brought safety. Pleistoanax wanted peace because he was always being attacked by his enemies over the way he had been restored to power; they created misgivings among the Spartans by saying, whenever something went wrong, that it happened because of his illegal return. They accused him and his brother Aristocles of bribing the priestess at Delphi to keep telling Spartans who went to consult the oracle that they should "bring the seed of the demi-god son of Zeus from foreign lands into their own, because if not they would plow with a silver plowshare."[4] Pleistoanax had been banished to Mount Lycaeum for having taken gifts to withdraw from Attica[5] and had lived in a house halfway inside the grounds of Zeus's temple for fear of the Spartans, but in time—after nineteen years—he persuaded the Spartans to restore him to power with the same dances and sacrifices as when they founded Sparta and instituted their first kings.

17. Pained by these accusations, Pleistoanax had become eager to come to terms. In war, it is in the nature of things for leaders to be blamed for setbacks; but he believed that in peace, with no harm coming to the city and with the return of the men, he would be beyond the reach of his enemies. They started

---

4. That is, there would be a scarcity of grain, which would be worth its weight in silver.
5. See 1.114 and 2.21.

talks that winter, and toward spring, to get the attention of the Athenians, the Spartans feinted a threat by sending a message around to all the cities in their alliance requiring them to prepare to build a fort on Athens' frontier. Then, after meetings that were accompanied by many legal claims made by one side against the other, Athens and Sparta came to an agreement whereby each side would return what it had captured in war and they would make peace. The Athenians would keep Nisaea, because when they asked for Plataea, the Thebans said that the place had neither been betrayed nor taken by force, but that it had agreed to go over to their side; the Athenians then replied that they had gained Nisaea in the same way.[6] Then the Spartans sent for their allies, who voted to end the war—all but Boeotia, Corinth, Elis and Megara, who disliked the terms. They drafted the treaty, then poured libations and swore to the Athenians, who swore to the Spartans, as follows.

18. The Athenians and the Spartans and their allies have made a treaty, sworn to by each of the cities, on the following terms.

As to our common shrines, whoever so wishes may resort to, sacrifice at, seek divinations, and officially consult oracles in them, in accordance with ancestral custom, going without fear of harm by land and sea.

The grounds and temple of Apollo at Delphi, and Delphi itself, shall be autonomous, and shall levy its own taxes and make its own laws for its people and its territory according to ancestral custom.

This treaty between Athens and the allies of Athens, and Sparta and the allies of Sparta, shall last for fifty years without prejudice or deceit, and shall be in effect on land and sea.

Neither the Spartans and their allies shall be permitted by any manner of means to bear arms with hostile intent against the Athenians and their allies, nor the Athenians and their allies against the Spartans and their allies; and if any dispute should arise among them, they shall resort to the courts and to their own oaths in such wise as they shall agree.

The Spartans and their allies shall restore Amphipolis to Athens. In such cities as the Spartans shall turn over to the Athenians, it shall be possible for people to leave for wherever they wish, taking their belongings with them. These cities shall be autonomous, but shall pay the tribute imposed in the time of Aristeides. Once this treaty is in effect, neither Athens nor its allies may bear arms against them for so long as they pay the tribute. These cities are: Argilus, Stagirus, Acanthus, Scolus, Olynthus, and Spartolus. These cities shall be allied with neither side, neither with Sparta nor with Athens. If, however, the Athenians can win any of them over and gain their assent, the Athenians may make them allies.

The Mecybernaeans, Sanaeans, and Singaeans shall live in their own cities, just like the Olynthians and Acanthians.

The Spartans and their allies shall return Panactum to Athens. For its part, Athens shall return to Sparta Coryphasium, Cythera, Methana, Pteleum, and Atalanta, as well as any Spartan men held in prison in Athens or anywhere else under Athenian control. They shall also release the Peloponnesians under siege in Scione, as well as whatever allies of Sparta are in Scione and whoever Brasidas sent into the place, along with any allies of Sparta who are in prison in Athens or anywhere else under Athenian control. The Spartans and their allies shall, by the same token, return whatever Athenians and their allies they are holding.

6. See 3.52 and 4.69.

As to Scione, Torone, Sermyle, and any other city Athens holds by conquest, the Athenians may do with them as they wish.

The Athenians shall swear oaths to the Spartans and their allies, city by city. Seventeen representatives from each city shall swear by the most revered local gods in each of the several cities. What they swear to shall be as follows: "I will abide by these articles and this truce strictly and without guile." The Spartans and their allies shall take the same oath to the Athenians. The oath shall be renewed by both sides every year, and they shall erect stelae at Olympia, Delphi, and the Isthmus, and in the city of Athens and in Sparta at the temple of Apollo at Amyclae.

If either side shall have left anything unmentioned, the Athenians and the Spartans may alter the treaty with due process and in accordance with their oaths in such wise as shall seem best to them both.

19. The treaty takes effect in Sparta under the ephor Pleistolas on the fourth day from the end of the month of Artemision, and in Athens under the archon Alcaeus on the sixth day from the end of the month of Elaphebolion. The following have taken the oath and poured libations to ratify the treaty. Of the Spartans: Pleistoanax, Agis, Pleistolas, Damagetus, Chionis, Metagenes, Acanthus, Daithus, Ischagoras, Philocharidas, Zeuxidas, Antippus, Tellis, Alcinadas, Empedias, Menas, and Laphilus. Of the Athenians: Lampon, Isthmionicus, Nicias, Laches, Euthydemus, Procles, Pythodorus, Hagnon, Myrtilus, Thrasycles, Theagenes, Aristocrates, Iolcius, Timocrates, Leon, Lamachus, Demosthenes.

20. This treaty was drafted at the end of the winter, at the coming of spring, right after the festival of the City Dionysia,[7] just a few days more than ten years from the first invasion of Attica and the beginning of this phase of the war. One should reckon the events of the past by the seasons, and not trust to checking the names of men in power off lists here and there, or to anyone's term of office. This is not an exact method because successive events may have taken place in the beginning or in the middle or at any other point in an official's term. If one reckons by summers and winters, as has been done here, with each counting for half a year, one will find that ten summers and an equal number of winters passed in the first part of the war.

21. The Spartans were chosen by lot to be the first to return what they had captured and immediately released their prisoners of war. They also sent the ambassadors Ischagoras, Menas, and Philocharidas to Thrace to order Clearidas to surrender Amphipolis to the Athenians, and to tell the other cities in the region to accept all the terms of the treaty that concerned them. These cities refused, however, saying the treaty was not to their advantage, and to oblige the Chalcidians, Clearidas refused to give up Amphipolis, asserting that he was not strong enough to enforce the surrender. Then he went straight from there to Sparta with local ambassadors to defend himself against any charge by Ischagoras' group that he had disobeyed orders. He also wanted to learn whether the treaty could be renegotiated, but when he found that it was final, he quickly returned to Thrace under orders from the Spartans preferably to surrender the territory, but if not, to pull out any Peloponnesians who were there.

22. Envoys from Sparta's allies happened to be in Sparta, and the Spartans ordered those who had not approved the treaty to do so. They refused to accept it for the same reason they had given at first, which was that the parties must agreed to fairer terms than these. Seeing that these states would not obey

---

7. The City Dionysia was a springtime festival honoring Dionysius. It was attended by visitors from all over the Greek world and featured several days of theatrical productions.

them, the Spartans dismissed them and made an alliance with Athens. They thought that the Argives, who had refused to make a new treaty with the Spartan ambassadors Ampelidas and Lichas, would be less formidable without the support of Athens, and that the rest of the Peloponnese would also be more likely to calm down. Given the chance, you see, the Argives would have shifted toward Athens. There were Athenian ambassadors in Sparta, talks took place, and the Spartans and the Athenians came to an agreement, swearing to an alliance as follows.

23. The Spartans and the Athenians shall be allies for fifty years on the following terms. If an enemy invades Spartan soil and does injury to the Spartans, the Athenians shall assist the Spartans in whatever way they can to the utmost of their power. If they come on a hit-and-run raid, that city will be an enemy to Sparta and Athens, will suffer retaliation from both, and will have to come to terms with both. All this shall be performed honestly, readily, and openly.

If any enemy invades Athenian soil and does injury to the Athenians, the Spartans shall assist the Athenians in whatever way they can to the utmost of their power. If they come on a hit-and-run raid, that city will be an enemy to Sparta and Athens, will suffer retaliation from both, and will have to come to terms with both. All this shall be performed honestly, readily, and openly.

If the slave class rises, the Athenians shall help the Spartans with all their might and to the utmost of their power.

The same men shall swear to this on both sides as swore to the other treaty. The oaths shall be renewed yearly, with the Spartans going to Athens during the City Dionysia and the Athenians going to Sparta during the Hyacinthia.[8] Both sides shall erect stelae, the Spartans at the temple of Apollo at Amyclae, and the Athenians in the city at the temple of Athena. If the Spartans and the Athenians should decide to add or remove any article of this alliance, they shall both be on their oath whatever they decide.

24. The following Spartans took the oath: Pleistoanax, Agis, Pleistolas, Damagetus, Chionis, Metagenes, Acanthus, Daithus, Ischagoras, Philocharidas, Zeuxidas, Antippus, Alcinadas, Tellis, Empedias, Menas, and Laphilus. The Athenians were Lampon, Isthmionicus, Laches, Nicias, Euthydemus, Procles, Pythodorus, Hagnon, Myrtilus, Thrasycles, Theagenes, Aristocrates, Iolcius, Timocrates, Leon, Lamachus, and Demosthenes.

This alliance was formed not long after the treaty, and with the beginning of spring of the eleventh year, the Athenians returned to the Spartans the men who had been captured on the island.

This has been the record of the first war, which lasted uninterruptedly for ten years.

25. The treaty and the alliance between Sparta and Athens were concluded at the end of the ten-year war, Pleistolas being then the ephor in Sparta and Alcaeus the archon in Athens, and there was peace among those who accepted the treaty. Corinth and some of the cities in the Peloponnese kept disrupting the arrangements, however, and yet another disturbance immediately arose among the allies in their relations with Sparta. In time, also, the Athenians became suspicious of Sparta over cases in which they did not put into effect

---

8. The Hyacinthia was a celebration of Hyacinthus, who may have been a pre-Hellenic god, but who was remembered as a hero beloved by Apollo and accidentally killed by him. The Hyacinthia lasted several days and involved sacrifices, performances, and feasting. Unfortunately, the precise date of the festival is uncertain.

the agreements they had made. They refrained from making war on each others' soil for six years and ten months; but abroad, where there was only an uneasy truce, they hurt other as much as possible. In the end, they were forced to break the truce made after the first ten years, and once again engaged in open war.

26. I, the same Thucydides of Athens, have written down these events too, in sequence, as each one occurred in summer and winter, until Sparta and her allies terminated the Athenian empire and captured the Piraeus and the Long Walls.[9] The war lasted twenty-seven years in all, for it would be a mistake not to regard this intervening agreement as part of the war. A breakdown of events in this period will show that it was a very improbable peace in which the parties neither returned nor recovered everything in their agreement. Besides this, there were violations on both sides in the war with Mantinea and Epidaurus, as well as with respect to other matters. Meanwhile, the allies in Thrace were as much at war with Athens as ever; and in Boeotia, there was a cease-fire that could be broken on just ten days' notice.

Thus counting the first ten-year war, the following uneasy truce, and the war that later grew out of it, one will, reckoning chronologically, arrive at the abovementioned twenty-seven years, plus a few days.—And for those who put their trust in oracles, only one turned out in sure accordance with the facts, because I, for one, remember very well that from the beginning of the war until its end, many alleged that it was destined to last for "three times nine years."

I have lived through the whole war and applied the full powers of my mind in the prime of my life to knowing exactly what happened. It came about, also, that I was banished from my native Athens for twenty years after my command at Amphipolis.[1] I was present at events on both sides (not least with the Peloponnesians because of my exile) so I was, without distraction, all the better able to understand them. I will, therefore, now relate the quarrels that arose after the first ten years, the collapse of the treaty, and the subsequent development of the war.

27. After the fifty-year peace was made, and then the alliance, the ambassadors from the Peloponnese who had been summoned to the meetings left Sparta. They all went home, except the Corinthians, who took a detour to Argos first to hold talks with some Argive officials.[2] They said that since Sparta had made peace and an alliance with their former worst enemies, the Athenians, not for the benefit but for the enslavement of the Peloponnese, the Argives should look to how the Peloponnese might be saved and should vote that any willing, autonomous Greek city that would equitably settle its disputes with other states could form an alliance with Argos to fight in each other's defense. They should appoint a few magistrates with full powers, so that states would not have to negotiate with the popular assembly and be embarrassed if they failed to win a majority. The Corinthians said that many would join with them out of hatred for Sparta, and after instilling this idea in the Argives, they returned home.

28. After hearing them out, the Argive officials reported their proposal to the other authorities and to the people. The Argives voted for it and elected twelve men through whom any Greek city that so desired—except Athens and Sparta—could negotiate an alliance. The men were not permitted to enter agreements with either Athens or Sparta without the consent of the people. The

9. This chapter, plainly written after 404, is sometimes called Thucydides' "second preface."
1. The campaign is described at 4.102–108, but this is Thucydides' only reference to his exile.
2. Thucydides' narrative seems somewhat confused here, because in 22 we were told that these allies were "dismissed."

Argives were all the more willing to accept this arrangement because their treaty with Sparta was about to expire and they saw a war coming. They also hoped to become the leaders of the Peloponnese. By this time, Sparta had developed a bad reputation and was despised for its misfortunes, whereas the Argives on the other hand were in an excellent position. They had not been caught up in the war in Attica and they reaped the benefits of treaties with both sides. Thus the Argives offered an alliance to whatever Greek states wanted one.

29. Mantinea and her allies, out of fear of the Spartans, were the first to join them. The reason for this was that while Sparta was at war with Athens, the Mantineans had subjected a portion of Arcadia, and they thought that Sparta would not let them keep ruling it, especially now that the Spartans had time on their hands. Thus they turned with relief to Argos as a large city perpetually at odds with Sparta, and a democracy, like themselves. The rest of the Peloponnese was abuzz over the defection of the Mantineans: they could do this too. They thought the Mantineans knew something they did not in breaking away, and they were also in a rage with Sparta, mostly because of the provision in the treaty with Athens that it would be legal to add or remove any article to which both sides agreed. This provision especially threw the Peloponnesians into an uproar and made them suspect that the Spartans, in league with the Athenians, planned to reduce them to slavery. It would have been right, they thought, for all the allies to sign on to any changes. Because of these apprehensions, most of the allies moved to make individual treaties with Argos.

30. Sparta knew that this hubbub was everywhere in the Peloponnese, and that Corinth had instigated it and was on the verge of making a treaty with Argos, so they sent envoys to Corinth hoping to forestall what was about to happen. The Spartans blamed the Corinthians for introducing the whole idea and said that they would violate their oath of allegiance if they broke away from Sparta and made an alliance with Argos. They were already in the wrong, the Spartans said, in not accepting the treaty with Athens, since all the allies were bound by whatever the majority voted unless it was objectionable to the gods or the heroes. The Corinthians, in company with other allies who had rejected the treaty and whom the Corinthians had invited beforehand, replied to the Spartans without openly stating their real grievances. These were that Sparta had not taken back Sollium or Anactorium from Athens on their behalf.[3] Instead they pretended that they did not want to betray the cities around Thrace. The Corinthians and the other allies had sworn private oaths with them when they first revolted with the Potidaeans and then other oaths later. Thus it was certainly not a violation of their oath to the alliance to refuse to enter into the treaty with Athens. They had sworn to their allies by the gods and they would be violating their oaths by betraying them. After all, the treaty did say "unless it was objectionable to the gods or the heroes," and it surely appeared that this would be a divine objection. That is what they said about their old oath of allegiance; as to the Argive alliance, they would deliberate with their friends and do what was right.

The Spartan envoys returned home, but there happened to be Argive envoys in Corinth, and they urged the Corinthians to enter the alliance without delay. The Corinthians told them to come to their next assembly.

31. Shortly thereafter, an Elean embassy arrived and made an alliance first with Corinth and then, going from there to Argos, became allies of the Argives in accordance with their instructions. Elis was engaged in a dispute

---

3. See 2.30 and 4.49.

with Sparta over Lepreum. A war had once broken out between some Arcadian tribes and the Lepreans, who called in the Eleans as allies on the understanding that the Eleans would get half the Leprean territory in return. After they had brought an end to the war, the Eleans allowed the Lepreans to work the land themselves, provided that they pay rent of a talent to the temple of Zeus at Olympia. The Lepreans paid it until the war with Athens, whereupon they stopped paying, using the war as an excuse. When the Eleans tried to make them pay, the Lepreans turned to Sparta. Sparta agreed to arbitrate the matter, but the Eleans suspected that they would not be treated fairly, suspended the proceedings, and ravaged Leprean territory. The Spartans nonetheless decided that Lepreum was independent and that Elis was in the wrong, and since the Eleans were not abiding by the arbitration, Sparta sent a hoplite garrison into Lepreum. The Eleans took the position that the Spartans had allied themselves with one of their rebel cities, and they adduced the stipulation in the agreement that a state would retain, when getting out of the Attic war, whatever it had going in. Thus since they considered themselves to have been treated unfairly, they broke away to the Argives and made the abovementioned alliance. The Corinthians quickly followed them into the Argive alliance, along with the Chalcidians in Thrace. Boeotia and Megara agreed with each other to hold back. They were being closely watched by Sparta, and they thought that since they were oligarchies, the Argive democracy would be less agreeable to them than the Spartan system of government.

32. At about the same time that summer, the Athenians, who had forced Scione to surrender, killed all its adult men, sold all its women and children into slavery, and then gave the land to the Plataeans. The also returned the Delians to Delos, motivated by the Delians' wartime sufferings and by an oracle from the god in Delphi. Also, Phocis and Western Locris went to war with each other.

Corinth and Argos, who were now allies, went into Tegea with the aim of detaching it from the Spartan alliance. Its territory was extensive, and they thought that if it came over to their side, they would control the whole Peloponnese. But when the Tegeans said that they would in no way oppose Sparta, the Corinthians, formerly so energetic, abated their zeal and became afraid that none of the other cities would come over to them. Still, they went to Boeotia and urged the city to become allied with them and Argos and to act in conjunction with them. The Corinthians urged the Boeotians to accompany them to Athens and help them negotiate a truce that could be ended on ten days' notice, like the one that came into effect between Boeotia and Athens not long after the fifty-year treaty. If the Athenians did not accept this proposal, the Boeotians should abrogate their own truce and refuse to enter into any future agreements without them. The Boeotians asked the Corinthians to refrain from saying anything more about an Argive alliance, but they did go to Athens with them, where they failed to help the Corinthians obtain the truce. The Athenians said that the Corinthians had a treaty, if, that is, they were allied with the Spartans. Then, although the Corinthians insisted that they had an agreement and reminded the Boeotians of it, the Boeotians nonetheless refused to abrogate their cease-fire. Thus Corinth had only a de facto truce with Athens.

33. That same summer, the Spartans under the leadership of their king Pleistoanax, son of Pausanias, marched out in full strength against the Parrhasians of Arcadia. They were subjects of the Mantineans, and the Spartans had been invited in by one side in a civil war. Sparta also aimed, if possible, to

raze the fortress in Cypsela. It was in Parrhasian territory, threatening Laconian Sciritis, and had been built and was now being guarded by the Mantineans. As the Spartans ravaged Parrhasian territory, the Mantineans turned over their city to the Argives and went to the defense of their ally. They were, however, unable to save the fortress at Cypsela or the cities in Parrhasia, so they withdrew. Then, after levelling the fortress and giving the Parrhasians their independence, the Spartans went back home.

34. In that same summer also, the soldiers from Thrace who had gone out with Brasidas—the ones Clearidas withdrew after the truce—returned to Sparta, and the Spartans voted that the helots who had accompanied Brasidas into battle would be free and might live wherever they liked. Then, not much later, they settled them and the freedmen in Lepreum, which lies between Sparta and Elis, and which was now at odds with Elis.[4] At the same time, the Spartans had grown afraid that their men who had been captured on the island and who had surrendered their arms might become second-class citizens as a result of their defeat. These men still had full civil rights, however, and might retaliate by engaging in radical politics. Thus although some of them were already in office, they were deprived of the right to hold office or to buy and sell property. Later, however, their civil rights were restored.

That same summer, the Chalcidians captured Thyssus, an Athenian ally at Mount Athos.

35. That summer, Athens and Sparta were in constant contact with each other, although they began to be suspicious of one another right after the treaty because of their mutual failure to return each other's territory. It had fallen to Sparta to return Amphipolis and the other places first, but they had failed to do so. They had not made their allies in Thrace accept the treaty—just as Corinth and Boeotia would not accept it—although they repeatedly said that they would join the Athenians in forcing the holdouts to submit. They also kept proposing nonbinding dates by which those who had not become parties to the treaty would become the enemies of them both. The Athenians saw that none of these things was actually happening and suspected the Spartans of not wanting to honor their commitments. Thus they did not return Pylos when the Spartans asked for it and regretted having given back the prisoners of war. They also held onto the other places, waiting until the Spartans did their part. The Spartans, however, said that they had done what they could: they had returned the Athenian prisoners they held; they had pulled the troops back from Thrace; they had done everything else that it was in their power to do. They denied that they had enough control over Amphipolis to return it. They would try to bring Boeotia and Corinth into the treaty, to recover Panactum, and to return Athenian prisoners of war from Boeotia.[5] They felt, however, that Athens should give them back Pylos, or at least withdraw their Messenian and helot troops from the place, just as Sparta had withdrawn its men from Thrace. Then the Athenians could garrison it themselves, if they wished. After frequent, lengthy talks that summer, the Spartans persuaded the Athenians to withdraw the Messenians and other helots from Pylos, along with any Spartan deserters.

---

4. Thucydides mentions this fact as if he had not already told the story of the Lepreans in 31. This and other rough spots in the narrative (note the stark exposition at the beginning of 32 and the mention of otherwise unexplained "freedmen" here in 34) suggest that Thucydides had not fully revised this part of the history.

5. See 4.100. These are presumably the same prisoners.

These men were then settled in Cranii in Cephallenia. Thus there was peace and dialogue between both sides that summer.

36. By the following winter, there were different ephors at Sparta. They were no longer the ones who had presided at the peace treaty, and some of them were even opposed to it. Ambassadors from the Spartan alliance had come to Sparta that winter, and there were also ambassadors from Athens, Boeotia, and Corinth. They delivered many speeches to each other without agreeing to anything, but after they broke up to go home, Cleobulus and Xenares, the ephors who most wanted to dissolve the treaty, held private talks with the Boeotians and the Corinthians. They urged an understanding among themselves that Boeotia try to make an alliance with Argos first and then an alliance between Argos, Boeotia, and Sparta. In this way, Boeotia would not be obligated to become a party to the peace treaty with Athens.[6] The fact is that Sparta was willing to pay the price of enmity and war with Athens if they could have friendship and alliance with Argos. Cleobulus and Xenares knew that Sparta had always been eager for the right kind of friendship with Argos, and they believed that if these alliances were accomplished, the conduct of the war outside the Peloponnese would be easier. They also asked Boeotia to give Panactum up to Sparta, so that Sparta could trade it for Pylos and thus be better able to renew the war with Athens.

37. Having received these instructions from Cleobulus, Xenares, and their other Spartan friends to be relayed to their respective governments, the Boeotians and Corinthians started for home, when they were joined by two of the highest officials of the Argive government, who had been keeping a lookout for them on the road and who entered into discussions to see whether the Boeotians would become their allies like the Corinthians, Eleans, and Mantineans. It was the Argive view that if this came about, they could, if they liked, join together to make war or peace with Sparta or anyone else. The Boeotian ambassadors were delighted with what they heard. As it happened, the Argives were asking for just what their Spartan friends had told them to do. When the Argives saw that the Boeotians were amenable to this proposal, they said that they would send ambassadors to Boeotia, and then left. When the Boeotians returned home, they reported to the boeotarchs what had happened at Sparta and at the encounter with the Argives. The boeotarchs were also delighted, and all the more eager to act since it had turned out that their friends in Sparta wanted them to do the very thing the Argives were seeking. Not much later, Argive ambassadors arrived to offer their proposals. The governors sent them back home with thanks for their offer and promised to send ambassadors to Argos to negotiate an alliance.

38. In the meanwhile, the boeotarchs, the Corinthians, the Megarians, and the ambassadors from Thrace decided to take oaths with each other to come to the defense of whoever needed it, as circumstances required, and not to go to war or reach any agreements without common consent. Thereafter, the Boeotians and Megarians (who were acting in unison) were to make a treaty with Argos. But before the oaths could be taken, the boeotarchs brought the matter before the four Boeotian councils, which have the final authority in the state. The boeotarchs recommended taking oaths with whatever cities were willing to join in their defence, but the members of the councils did not accept the proposal, fearing that they would put themselves in opposition to Sparta by taking oaths with Corinth, which had broken away from Sparta. You see, the

6. Because Sparta would have broken the treaty with Athens.

boeotarchs did not tell the councils about the events at Sparta, and how the ephors Cleobulus and Xenares as well as their friends had urged them to make alliances first with Argos and Corinth and then with Sparta itself. The boeotarchs had thought that the councils, even without being told, would vote just as they had decided to recommend.

Thus matters came to a standstill. The Corinthians and the envoys from Thrace went away empty-handed, while the boeotarchs, who had intended to try to make an alliance with Argos once this one went through, did not even mention Argos before the councils. Neither did they send ambassadors to Argos, as promised. The whole thing was delayed and neglected.

39. That same winter, the Olynthians overran and captured Mecyberna, which was being defended by Athenians.

There were constant talks between Athens and Sparta about the territory they held back from each other. Sparta hoped that if the Athenians could recover Panactum from Boeotia, they would return Pylos to them, so they sent ambassadors to Boeotia imploring them to turn Panactum and the Athenian prisoners over to them, so that Sparta could obtain Pylos in return. The Boeotians said, however, that they would not return Panactum unless the Spartans made a private alliance with them as they had done with Athens. The Spartans of course knew that this would mean violating the treaty with Athens, which stipulated that neither side would make treaties or go to war without the approval of the other, but they were desperate to take over Panactum, since they could get back Pylos in return for it. Also, those who wanted to nullify the treaty with Athens were pressing for the agreement with Boeotia. So at the end of winter, towards the beginning of spring, the Spartans made the alliance, and the Boeotians immediately began to demolish the fortifications at Panactum. With this, the eleventh year of the war came to an end.

40. At the very beginning of the following spring, the Argives, seeing that the ambassadors the Boeotians had promised had not come, that Panactum was being demolished, and that a private alliance had been made between Sparta and Boeotia, became afraid that all their allies would go over to Sparta and that they would be left alone. They believed that the Boeotians had been persuaded by the Spartans to raze Panactum and to become a party to the treaty with Athens. They also believed that the Athenians knew this, thus ruling out an alliance between themselves and Athens, when all along they had been hoping that if their treaty with Sparta was not renewed, they could exploit the differences between the two sides and at least become allies with the Athenians. The Argives were in a quandary. They were afraid that they would have to fight with Sparta, Tegea, Boeotia, and Athens combined when they had earlier not only rejected the treaty with Sparta but also been fired up about the leadership of the Peloponnese. So they sent ambassadors to Sparta as fast as they could. They chose Eustrophus and Aeson, men who were believed to be well liked by the Spartans. The Argives thought that, under the circumstances, the best thing to do was to make whatever agreement they could with Sparta and live in peace.

41. When the Argive ambassadors arrived, they held talks with the Spartans as to the terms of the treaty. First, the Argives demanded that they refer the matter of the Cynurian territory, about which they were always at odds because it is on their common border, to arbitration by some city or private person. (This territory contains the cities of Thyrea and Anthene and is occupied by Spartans). The Spartans would allow no further mention of that subject, but were prepared to agree to a treaty on the same terms as formerly. The Argive ambassadors were, however, able to get the Spartans to agree to the following: for now,

they would make a fifty years' peace, although it would be possible, provided neither the Spartans nor the Argives were afflicted by plague or war, for either side to call the other out to battle over this particular territory just as they had done once before when both sides thought they had won.[7] Pursuit by the victors across the borders of either Argos or Sparta would be forbidden. At first, the Spartans thought this proposal was childish, but then they agreed to the Argive terms and drew up a treaty. That is how eager they were for friendship with Argos. The Spartans asked, however, that before the terms be ratified, the ambassadors return to Argos and present the treaty to the people. If they were satisfied, the ambassadors should return to Sparta at the Hyacinthia to take the oaths.

42. The Argives left, but while they had been conducting these negotiations, Andromenes, Phaedimus, and Antimenidas, the Spartan envoys who had been assigned to take over Panactum and the prisoners of war from the Boeotians and restore them to the Athenians, found that the Boeotians, acting on their own, had razed Panactum to the ground. Their excuse was that long ago Athens and Boeotia had disputed the place and ended up taking oaths that neither side would occupy it, but that they could cultivate it in common. So Andromenes and his party took custody of the Athenian prisoners from the Boeotians and returned them to Athens. They explained the destruction of Panactum to the Athenians and took the position that the Spartans had restored it, too. After all, no longer would an enemy of Athens be occupying it. The Athenians were incensed at this. They said that they had been unfairly treated by Sparta with respect to the destruction of Panactum, which ought to have been handed over intact, and they were equally angry when they learned that Sparta had also made a separate treaty with Boeotia, despite earlier promises to " join the Athenians in forcing the holdouts to submit."[8] They saw other ways in which the treaty had been breached and considered themselves thoroughly deceived; and with this harsh response to the ambassadors, they dismissed them.

43. With the emergence of this dispute between Athens and Sparta, those Athenians who wanted to abrogate the treaty at once resumed their pressure. Foremost among these was Alcibiades, son of Cleinias, a man who would have been considered young in any other city, but who was highly regarded in Athens because of his distinguished ancestry. He truly believed that it would be more in Athens' interest to side with Argos, but he also opposed the treaty out of jealous ambition, since Sparta had made the treaty with Nicias and Laches, slighting him on account of his youth and failing to honor the ancient tie of proxeny between his family and their city. His grandfather had renounced this tie, but Alcibiades had thought to renew it by giving aid to the prisoners from the island. Feeling himself disrespected on all sides, he had opposed the treaty from the first. He said the Spartans were untrustworthy, and that the reason they had made a treaty with Athens was to neutralize Argos, whereupon they would again attack the now-isolated Athenians. As soon as this dispute arose, he at once privately sent to Argos, urging the Argives to come to Athens as quickly as possible with envoys from Mantinea and Elis and invite the Athenians to join their alliance. The time for this was right, he said, and he would do everything he could to help them.

44. When the Argives heard this message, they realized that Athens had not cooperated in the Spartan alliance with Boeotia but that, on the contrary,

7. See Herodotus 1.82.
8. See 5.35.

there was serious disagreement between the two. They forgot about their ambassadors, who were then away negotiating a treaty in Sparta, and turned all their attention towards Athens, which they regarded as a city friendly to them since antiquity, and which, like them, was a democracy. Athens also had a great navy, which would join them in battle should they have to go to war. They therefore immediately sent envoys to Athens to see about an alliance, and Elean and Mantinean envoys went along with them.

Spartan ambassadors also quickly arrived: Philocharidas, Leon, and Endius—men thought to be on good terms with the Athenians. The Spartans feared that out of anger, Athens might make an alliance with Argos. They also came to ask for Pylos in exchange for Panactum and to explain that they had not made the alliance with Boeotia out of any desire to harm Athens.

45. They spoke on these subjects to the council and said that they had come with full powers to resolve their differences. They made Alcibiades afraid that if they were to say the same things to the assembly of the people, they might actually win over a majority and that the treaty with Argos would be rejected. So he came up with the following trick. He personally assured them that he would see to it that Pylos was given back to them, if only they did not repeat before the people that they had come with full powers. He himself would speak on their behalf to the Athenian people as forcefully as he was now opposing them. He would also see to it that other matters were worked out. He did this because he wanted to detach them from Nicias, and so that, after denouncing their duplicity in the assembly for never being consistent in what they said, he could then make allies of Argos, Elis, and Mantinea. And that is what happened. After the Spartans went before the assembly and contradicted under questioning what they had said in the council about coming with full powers, the Athenians were fed up with them. They gave ear much more than ever before to Alcibiades, who was loudly denouncing the Spartans, and they were prepared to immediately bring forward the Argives and the others and to make an alliance with them. But there was an earthquake before anything could be finalized, and the assembly was adjourned.[9]

46. The Spartans were not the only ones who were deceived by Alcibiades when he induced them to contradict themselves about coming with full powers. Nicias had been deceived as well. But he nevertheless said at the next day's assembly that they should seek friendship with Sparta rather than Argos. He said that they should hold off on their dealings with the Argives until they could send to Sparta to find out what the Spartans really had in mind, because, he argued, avoiding war would benefit Athens and keep Sparta in an awkward position. Things were going well for Athens, and the very best thing for them was to preserve the status quo. On the other hand, Sparta had fallen on hard times, and the quickest solution for them was to take a gamble on war. Nicias persuaded them to send ambassadors to Sparta, of whom he would be one, demanding that the Spartans, if they had honorable intentions, should return an intact Panactum as well as Amphipolis and should renounce the Boeotian alliance unless Boeotia became a party to the treaty, in keeping with the stipulation that neither side could make treaties without the other's consent. The ambassadors were to say that if Athens had wanted to wrong Sparta, it would have made an alliance with Argos by now. Indeed, they should say that the Argives were in Athens for that very reason. Then, after giving them instructions regarding other

---

9. Commentators have questioned this story on the grounds that the Spartan emissaries were unlikely to have placed so much trust in Alcibiades. On the other hand, it could be that they were willing to try anything in hopes of getting Pylos back.

Athenian grievances, the assembly sent Nicias and the other ambassadors on their mission.

When they arrived, they delivered their message, concluding with the declaration that if Sparta did not give up its alliance with a Boeotia that would not join the treaty, Athens would, for its part, make an alliance with Argos and its allies. The position of Xenares and his party, as well as others of his opinion, prevailed, and the Spartans refused to give up the alliance with Boeotia. Nevertheless, they did renew the oaths of the peace treaty, at Nicias' insistence. He feared that he would return completely empty-handed and that he would be censured—as in fact he was, because he was held responsible for the treaty with Sparta. The Athenians were furious when Nicias returned and they heard that nothing had been accomplished at Sparta. They thought they had been wronged, and they made a treaty and an alliance with the Argives and their allies, who were still present and who were brought to the assembly by Alcibiades. The treaty was as follows.

47. The Athenians, the Argives, the Mantineans, and the Eleans have made a one-hundred-year treaty for themselves and whatever allies they may severally govern, which shall obtain without prejudice or deceit on land and sea. It shall be forbidden for Argos, Elis, Mantinea, and their allies by any manner of means to bear arms with hostile intent against Athens and the allies whom Athens governs, as it shall be for Athens and the allies Athens governs against Argos, Elis, Mantinea, and their allies.

Athens, Argos, Mantinea, and Elis shall be allies for one hundred years on the following terms. If a hostile force should attack Athenian soil, Argos, Mantinea, and Elis shall come to the defense of Athens, according as Athens shall require, in the most effective way they can, to the utmost of their power. If they come on a hit-and-run raid, that city shall be the enemy of Argos, Mantinea, Elis, and Athens, and shall suffer the consequences from all the aforesaid cities. It shall be forbidden for any one of these cities to end the war with the enemy city unless all the others agree. Athens shall also come to the defense of Argos, Mantinea, and Elis if hostile forces attack Argive, Mantinean, or Elean soil, as these shall require, in the most effective way it can, to the utmost of its power. If they come on a hit-and-run raid, that city shall be the enemy of Athens, Argos, Mantinea, and Elis and shall suffer the consequences from all these cities. It shall be forbidden for any one of these cities to end the war with the enemy city unless all the others agree.

It shall be forbidden to bear arms on the way to a war across each other's land or the land of the allies whom they govern, or to pass by sea, unless said crossing shall have been voted on by all the cities, viz. Athens, Argos, Mantinea, and Elis.

The city sending troops to the defense of another shall provide those men with supplies for up to thirty days from the time they enter the city that summoned them and shall also provide for them when they leave. If, however, the city that has summoned the troops wants to use them for a longer time, it shall supply food at a rate of three Aeginetan obols a day for hoplites, light-armed soldiers, and archers, and one Aeginetan drachma for a cavalryman. The city that summoned the troops shall command them when the war is on its soil. If all the cities decide to go to war together, all the cities shall share the command equally. Athens shall take this oath on its own behalf and on behalf of its allies; Argos, Mantinea, and Elis and their respective allies shall take the oath individually. The oath shall be taken over full-grown sacrificial animals, and each city shall swear by its most revered local gods.

The oath shall be as follows: " I will adhere to the alliance according to the terms we have agreed honestly and without prejudice or deceit, and I will not violate it by any manner of means whatsoever."

At Athens, the oath shall be administered by the prytaneis and taken by the council and the local magistrates. In Argos, the oath shall be administered by the Eighty and taken by the council, the Eighty, and the magistrates. In Mantinea, the oath shall be administered by the Overseers and the Warchiefs and taken by the magistrates, the council, and the other officials. In Elis, the oath shall be administered by the magistrates and the Guardians of the Law and taken by the magistrates, the chief officials, and the Six Hundred.

The Athenians shall renew the oaths by going to Elis, Mantinea, and Argos thirty days before the Olympic games, and the Argives, Eleans, and Mantineans by going to Athens ten days before the Panathenaic festival.

The articles of the treaty, the oaths, and the alliance shall be inscribed on a stone slab in the city of Athens, at the temple of Apollo at the marketplace in Argos, and at the temple of Zeus at the marketplace in Mantinea. All the cities together shall set up a bronze slab at Olympia at the next Olympic games.

If the cities shall think to add any improvements to this agreement, whatever all the cities shall decide after conferring together shall take effect.

48. In this way, the treaty and the alliance came into being; but the agreements between Sparta and Athens were not thereby renounced by either side. The Corinthians, however, who were allies of Argos, did not enter into the agreements. There had been an earlier offensive and defensive alliance formed by Elis, Argos, and Mantinea, but the Corinthians had not sworn to it. They said that they were content with their original defensive alliance, whereby they would come to each others' aid but not join in offensive operations against anyone else. Thus the Corinthians pulled back from their allies and began to turn their attention to Sparta once again.

49. The Olympic games were held that summer, the ones in which Androsthenes the Arcadian first won the prize in boxing and wrestling.[1] The Eleans prevented the Spartans from entering the temple, and thus from sacrificing and competing, because the Spartans had not paid the fine that the Eleans had won from the court under Olympic law. The Eleans said that Sparta had attacked the fortifications at Phyrcus and that they had sent a thousand hoplites into Lepreum, which belonged to Elis, during the Olympic truce. The fine was two thousand mnae—two for each hoplite, as prescribed by law. The Spartans sent envoys to contend that the verdict was unfair, since the truce had not been announced in Sparta before they sent in their hoplites. The Eleans said that the truce had already been in effect, because they always announce it among themselves first. Thus they were peacefully abiding by the truce and expecting nothing untoward while the Spartans, unbeknownst to them, were breaking the law. The Spartans replied that the Eleans would not have announced the truce at Sparta if they had thought it had been broken. No, the Eleans did it because they did not then think so; and as soon as the announcement was made, the attacks were halted. The Eleans reiterated their argument: they would not allow that they had not been wronged. If, however, Sparta would

---

1. We know that the Olympic games were held in 420. Since they were held every four years, the next time Androsthenes could have won a prize was 416. Thus 416 is the earliest possible date for this passage.

restore Lepreum to them, they would forego their share of the money and pay on Sparta's behalf the portion of the fine it owed to the god.

50. When Sparta rejected that proposal, the Eleans made another: Sparta would not have to give up Lepreum if it didn't want to. — But since the Spartans were so eager to have access to the temple, let them step up to the altar of Olympian Zeus and swear before all the Greeks that they would pay the fine after the games. Since the Spartans did not consent to this, either, they were barred from the temple and went home to perform their sacrifices. All the other Greek states participated in the Olympics except for Lepreum. Still, the Eleans feared that the Spartans would come to the temple with hoplites to perform their sacrifices, so they kept a guard of young men on alert. They were supported by Argives and Mantineans, a thousand each, as well as by some Athenian cavalrymen who had been waiting in Harpina for the games. There had been a panic during the great festal assembly that armed Spartans would come, especially since Lichas the Spartan, son of Arcesilaus, had been whipped by the referees. Lichas' team of horses had won the chariot race, but because Lichas was barred from the games as a Spartan, he had entered the team through the Boeotian stable and the Boeotian state had been announced as the winner. Nevertheless, Lichas wanted to show that the chariot was his, so he went onto the track and tied a garland on the head of the charioteer.[2] This whipping made everyone even more frightened that there would be some disturbance. The Spartans, however, decided to hold their peace and took no further action during the remainder of the games.

After the Olympic games, the Argives and their allies went to Corinth and asked them to join their alliance. Envoys from Sparta also happened to be present, and there were long talks. In the end, however, nothing was accomplished, because there was an earthquake and they broke up the meeting to go home. And so the summer came to an end.

51. The next winter there was a battle between the Heracleans of Trachis and the Aenianians, Dolopians, Malians, and some Thessalians. These tribes lived near Trachis and were hostile to it. It was in fact precisely against these people's territory that Heraclea had been fortified, and they began to oppose and harry it with all their might as soon as the fortification was built. They won this battle against the Heracleans, whose governor Xenares, son of Cnidis — a Spartan — was killed, along with many Heracleans. Then the winter came to an end, and with it ended the twelfth year of the war.

52. As soon as the following summer began, the Boeotians took charge of Heraclea, which was in a very bad way after the battle, and expelled Agesippidas the Spartan for incompetence. They took charge of the place for fear that the Athenians would seize it while the Spartans were preoccupied with their troubles in the Peloponnese. Nonetheless, the Spartans were furious with the Boeotians.

That same summer, Alcibiades, son of Cleinias, who was now an Athenian general, in company with the Argives and their allies, led a few Athenian hoplites and archers into the Peloponnese, picking up some local allies along the way, and took care of some allied business. He led his army through the Peloponnese and persuaded the people of Patrae to extend their walls to the sea. He also wanted to build a fortification at Rhium in Achaea, but the Corinthians and Sicyonians, who would have been threatened by the fort, moved men into the place and prevented it.

---

2. Referees at the Olympic and other games were equipped with rods with which they whipped athletes or other competitors who broke the rules. The passage also shows that competitors in the chariot races could enter their teams through states other than their own.

53. Also that same summer, a war broke out between Epidaurus and Argos. The excuse for it was the offering to the shrine of Apollo Pythaeus, which was mostly under the stewardship of Argos. This was an offering the Epidaurians were supposed to make as a sacrifice of atonement for the castration of bulls, but which they had not made. Alcibiades and the Argives had decided to take over Epidaurus even without a reason if they could, to keep Corinth quiet and to enable Athens to send aid to Argos the short way, from Aegina, instead of having to sail around the headland at Scyllaeum. Thus the Argives, as if on their own, prepared to invade Epidaurus to collect the offering.

54. At the same time, under King Agis, son of Archidamus, the Spartans marched out in full strength as far as Leuctra, which is on their own border in the direction of Mount Lycaeum.[3] None of the troops knew where they were going on this campaign, not even the allied cities that had sent them. They made the usual sacrifice before crossing the border, however, and the omens were not good, so they returned home. The Spartans then sent a message around to their allies to prepare for an expedition the month after next, for the next month was Carneus,[4] which was a sacred month for the Dorians. After the Spartans pulled back, the Argives marched out four days before Carneus, and calling every day the fourth day before Carneus, invaded and plundered Epidaurus.[5] Epidaurus called on its allies for help, but some used the holy month as an excuse for not coming, while others went to the Epidaurian border and halted there.

55. While the Argives were in Epidaurian territory, envoys from the various cities gathered in Mantinea at the invitation of Athens. Once the talks started, Euphamidas, a Corinthian, said that their words did not correspond to their actions, because they had sat down for a conference on peace while their allies the Epidaurians and the Argives were going up against each other with weapons in their hands. Let representatives go to the armies of both sides and disband them. Then they could come back and talk about peace. The members agreed. They left, and brought about the removal of the Argives from Epidaurian territory. They reconvened later for the same purpose as before, but were still unable to agree. Then the Argives once again invaded and plundered Epidaurian territory. At the same time, the Spartans marched out to Caryae, but the sacrifices at the border were once again inauspicious and they went back home. After ravaging about one-third of Epidaurian territory, the Argives also went home. One thousand Athenian hoplites had come to reinforce them, with Alcibiades in command, but he left when he learned that the Spartan campaign was over and that nothing further was required of them. And so passed an uneventful summer.

56. The following winter, Sparta, unbeknownst to the Athenians, slipped a garrison of three hundred men, under the command of Agesippidas, into Epidaurus by sea. The Argives went to Athens and complained that their treaty stipulated that neither side would allow enemy forces to pass through their own territory, whereas the Athenians had allowed such passage through their waters. They would consider themselves wronged, the Argives said, unless the Athenians likewise brought Messenians and helots into Pylos to raid Laconia. On the advice of Alcibiades, the Athenians subjoined to the terms of the treaty on the

3. The location of this Leuctra is not known, but it should not be confused with the Leuctra in Boeotia, where the Boeotians defeated the Spartans decisively in 371 and ended Spartan supremacy in Greece.
4. Essentially our month of August.
5. The Argives in effect stopped the clock, so as not to be accused of sacrilegiously invading a Dorian city during a holy month. This sort of trick is possible with a lunar calendar, when extra days frequently need to be inserted to make the lunar cycle come out right.

Spartan stele that Sparta had not abided by its oaths, and then they brought the helots from Cranae into Pylos so that they could plunder Laconia. They refrained from other action, however. The Argives and the Epidaurians fought throughout that winter, although there was no set battle, only ambushes and raids in which troops from both sides were killed. Towards the end of winter, just before spring, the Argives, thinking Epidaurus would be deserted because its men were out fighting, tried to scale the walls of the city with ladders and take it by storm. The attack failed, however, and they withdrew. Thus the winter came to an end, and with it ended the thirteenth year of the war.

57. In the middle of the following summer, the Spartans and their helots made war on Argos in full strength. Their Epidaurian allies were suffering, and elsewhere in the Peloponnese some cities were breaking away from them and others were growing hostile, and they realized that if they didn't take swift preventive action, things would just get worse. The Spartans were led by their king, Agis, son of Archidamus, and they were joined in the campaign by Tegea and their other Arcadian allies. Their allies inside and outside the Peloponnese gathered at the territory of Phlius. The Boeotians sent five thousand hoplites and as many light-armed troops, along with five hundred cavalry and an equal number of infantrymen to accompany the cavalry. The Corinthians sent two thousand hoplites, and their other allies what they could. The Phliasians, however, mustered in full strength, since the army had gathered in their territory.

58. The Argives had advance knowledge of the Spartan preparations, and when the Spartans marched to Phlius to join the others, the Argives also marched out. They were supported by the Mantineans and their allies, along with three thousand Elean hoplites. Moving forward, they came up opposite the Spartans at the Arcadian Divide, called Methydrium. Each side took possession of a hill. The Argives prepared to fight, since they had caught the Spartans without their allies, but Agis broke camp that night and slipped away unnoticed, making his way to Phlius and his allies. At dawn, the Argives realized what had happened and moved out, first toward Argos, and then to the road to Nemea, where they expected the Spartans and their allies to come down to the Argive plain. Agis, however, did not take the road they expected him to take. He gave the order to the Spartans, the Arcadians, and the Epidaurians to follow him down into the plain by another, more difficult, road. The Corinthians, Pellenians, and Phliasians made their way down by yet another steep road. Agis also ordered the Boeotians, Megarians, and Sicyonians to come down by the road to Nemea, where the Argives were positioned, so that if the Argives should go into the plain to attack the Spartans, the Boeotians could chase them with their cavalry. After coordinating the movements of his army and going down into the plain, Agis plundered Saminthus and other places.

59. The Argives learned of this and rushed to the defense from Nemea. It was now daylight. On the way, they had an engagement with the Phliasian and Corinthian contingent, and although they killed a few Phliasians, the Corinthians killed a slightly larger number of Argives. Then the Boeotians, Megarians, and Sicyonians advanced, as ordered, on Nemea, but they did not find the Argives there. The Argives had gone down to the plain where, seeing their territory being wasted, they positioned themselves for battle. The Spartans took up positions opposite them, and the Argives were surrounded. The Spartans and their support troops blocked their way from the plain to Argos; the Corinthians, Phliasians, and Pellenians were flanking them on the high ground; and the Boeotians, Sicyonians, and Megarians were blocking the road to Nemea. The

Argives had no cavalry, because so far the Athenians were the only allies of theirs who had not arrived.

Most of the army of the Argives and their allies did not see the danger they were in. On the contrary, they thought they would have the advantage in the battle, because they had the Spartans on their own territory, trapped between themselves and their city. Two Argive citizens, however, Thrasylus, who was one of their five generals, and Alciphron, the Spartans' proxenus, went to Agis just as the armies were about to come to grips and urged him not to fight. They told him that Argos was prepared to submit any complaints Sparta had with them to a fair and peaceful settlement, as well as to make a treaty and live in peace with them from then on.

60. These Argives spoke on their own initiative, without instructions from their assembly. Agis too accepted their proposal on his own, without consulting with his troops, and after informing only one of the officials who were on the campaign, he concluded a four month's truce in which the Argives were to make good on this verbal agreement. He then withdrew his army, without explanation to his allies. The Spartans and their allies followed him because he was their leader by law, but among themselves, they blamed Agis greatly. They believed that they had been in an excellent fighting position, that the Argives had been completely surrounded by cavalry and infantry, and that they had withdrawn without having anything to show for themselves.—And indeed, this had been the finest Greek fighting force ever assembled up to that time. It looked its best when they were still all together in Nemea, the Spartans in full strength, along with carefully chosen men from Arcadia, Boeotia, Corinth, Sicyon, Pellene, Phlius, and Megara, worthy to fight not just with the Argive alliance but with it and another army just as large. Nevertheless, full of resentment toward Agis, this army retreated, disbanded, and went home.

For their part, the Argive rank and file much more severely blamed the men who had made a truce without authority from the assembly. They too believed that they had never had a better opportunity, and that it was the Spartans who had escaped, because the battle would have been fought with many brave allies near their city. They withdrew into the Charadrus, a ditch where, before re-entering the city, the Argive army holds courts martial on cases arising in the field. There they began to stone Thrasylus. He saved himself by escaping to an altar, but his property was confiscated by the state.

61. After these events took place, the Athenians reinforcements arrived, consisting of one thousand hoplites and three hundred cavalry, led by Laches and Nicostratus. The Argives, in spite of their arrival, pulled back from breaking their truce with Sparta and ordered them to go home. The Athenians wanted to address the Argive assembly, but the Argives refused them access, until in the end the Mantineans and Eleans (who were still present) made the Argives give in. Speaking for the Athenians, Alcibiades, who was there as an ambassador, told the Argives and their allies that they had been wrong to make a truce without the approval of their other allies, and that they must now, since the Athenians had arrived just in time, resume the war. His speech persuaded the allies, and all of them except the Argives immediately marched on Orchomenus, in Arcadia. The Argives, although also persuaded, held back at first; but later they too went. They all took up positions in front of Orchomenus, besieging and attacking it. They especially wanted to take the place because Arcadian hostages were being held there for the Spartans. The Orchomenians, concerned about the weakness of their wall and the size of the army, and terrified lest they be wiped out before anyone came to help them, capitulated on

the understanding that they would join the alliance, that they would give some of their own people to the Mantineans as hostages, and that they would hand over the hostages the Spartans had placed there.

62. Now that they had Orchomenus, the allies took up the question of which town they should attack next. The Eleans wanted it to be Lepreum, the Mantineans Tegea. The Argives and the Athenians sided with Mantinea. The Eleans went home, furious that the others had voted against Lepreum. The remaining allies made preparations in Mantinea for the attack on Tegea, while some in Tegea itself were preparing to betray the city to them.

63. After making the four-month truce and withdrawing from Argos, the Spartans blamed Agis greatly for not conquering Argos when, as they thought, there had never been a better opportunity to do so—especially since it had not been easy to put together such a large allied force of crack troops. Then, when the news was brought that Orchomenus had been captured, they were all the more angry, and in a rage that was very uncharacteristic of them, they deliberated in the assembly about immediately demolishing Agis' house and fining him one hundred thousand drachmas. He begged them to do neither: he would exonerate himself with valiant deeds on the battlefield, and if not, they could then do with him as they pleased. They held off on the fine and the demolition, and for now passed an unprecedented law: ten Spartan citizens were to be appointed as Agis' advisors, without whose approval it would be illegal for him to withdraw an army from the battlefield.

64. In the meanwhile, a message came from their friends in Tegea that if they didn't come on the double, Tegea would break away from them and go over to Argos and its allies, and that in fact the Tegeans had all but revolted as it was. Thereupon with unprecedented speed, a relief column was mustered of Spartans and helots in full strength. They marched to Orestheum, in Maenalia, sending word to their Arcadian allies to assemble and follow their tracks to Tegea. When all the Spartans had gotten as far as Orestheum, they sent one-sixth of their number—consisting of their older and younger men—back to guard the home front and reached Tegea with the rest of their army. Not much later, the Arcadian allies arrived. They also sent messages to Corinth, Boeotia, Phocis, and Eastern Locris, ordering them to send reinforcements to Mantinea on the double. These allies, however, received short notice, and it wasn't easy for them to cross the enemy territory between them and Mantinea unless they waited for each other and did it together. Nevertheless, they came as fast as they could. Meanwhile, the Spartans, taking along their Arcadian allies, invaded Mantinean territory, set up camp near the temple of Heracles, and proceeded to slash and burn the land.

65. When the Argives and their allies saw them, they took up a position on easily defensible terrain that was hard to reach and then prepared for battle. The Spartans charged them immediately and advanced to within a sling shot or a javelin throw, when one of the older soldiers, seeing the rugged terrain they were approaching, called out to Agis that he was trying to cure one malady with another, by which he meant that Agis wanted to make amends for his disgraceful retreat from Argos with his now untimely zeal. Either because he heard this call or because he himself had changed his mind, Agis suddenly pulled his army back on the double before they could come to grips with the enemy. He then led his men into Tegean territory and began to divert the flow of the stream in the plain there toward Mantinea. Because this water did a great deal of damage on whichever side it flowed into, the Mantineans and Tegeans were constantly fighting over it. Agis wanted to force the men on the hill, once they found out

about the diversion of the water, to come down to prevent it, so that he could then fight them on level ground. He therefore stayed there the rest of the day diverting the course of the stream.

At first, the Argives and their allies were amazed by the sudden Spartan retreat from such close quarters and didn't know what to think, but then, after the Spartans had retreated out of sight, and they themselves had stayed put and not followed them, they once again reproached their own generals. First the generals had allowed the Spartans to escape when they had been pinned against Argos, and now that they were running away, no one was chasing them! The Spartans just marched off to safety unmolested, whereas the Argive army was being betrayed. In the heat of the moment, the generals didn't know what to do, but then they led their men down the hill and advanced into the plain, where they pitched camp with the aim of going after their enemies.

66. The next day, the Argives and their allies put themselves into the battle formation in which they would fight the enemy if they should meet him. The Spartans, meanwhile, returning from the stream to their original camp near the temple of Heracles, saw their enemy a short distance away, down from the hill and already in battle formation. The Spartans were more dismayed in this situation than they could remember ever having been. They got ready with no time to spare, hurrying themselves into formation—their king, Agis, giving the orders in accordance with Spartan law. When a Spartan king leads a campaign, he has complete control of all operations. He tells the generals what needs to be done; they tell the battalion leaders, who tell the company commanders, who tell the squadron leaders, who tell the squadrons. If any supplemental orders are necessary, they are speedily transmitted and executed in the same way. Almost every man in the Spartan army is somewhere in the chain of command, and many men are responsible for carrying out orders.

67. In this battle, the soldiers from Sciritis stationed themselves on the left wing; they are the only contingent in the Spartan army who always have this position entirely to themselves. On their right were the Thracian soldiers and Spartan freedmen who had been with Brasidas. Next were the Spartan divisions, standing side by side. Then came the Arcadians from Heraea, and next to them the Maenalians. On the right wing were the Tegeans, with a few Spartans to the extreme right, and there was cavalry on each wing. That was the Spartan battle order. As for their opponents, the Mantineans took the right wing, since the action was taking place in their territory, and to their left were their Arcadian allies. Next, there was the thousand-man special force from Argos, men to whom the city gave extensive combat training at the public expense; and then there was the rest of the Argive contingent. Next to these were the allies of Argos, the Cleonaeans and the Orneates, followed by the Athenians and their cavalry on the far left.

68. This, then, was the order and composition of both armies. The Spartan army seemed larger, although I cannot relate, because I could not ascertain, either the numbers for the separate contingents or for both sides taken together. One could not know the size of the Spartan army because of the secretiveness of their government; and one could not tell the size of the other because of people's tendency to exaggerate their strength. It is possible, however, to guess at the size of the Spartan army that was present at this battle by the following calculation: not counting the Sciritae, who are six hundred men, there were seven battalions. In each battalion, there were four companies, and in each company, there were four squadrons. Four men fought in the first rank of each squadron. The depth of the line was not always the same and depended on the wishes of

the battalion leaders, but in general the line was eight men deep. Except for the Sciritae, there were four hundred and forty-eight men in the first line.[6]

69. Just before the two armies engaged, each contingent was given the following exhortations by its commanding general. The Mantineans were told that they were fighting for their fatherland, fighting for sovereignty against subjection, fighting not to be deprived of the one and fighting never to experience the other again. The Argives were told of their ancient preeminence and recent equality in the Peloponnese. They must not allow themselves to be stripped of these forever, and they must not fail to avenge the many injustices of their neighboring enemies. The Athenians were told that it would be glorious to fight with so many brave allies and hold their own with all of them; that to defeat the Spartans in the Peloponnese meant making the Athenian empire larger and more secure, and meant that never again would anyone invade their land. The Argives and their allies were urged on in this way; but the Spartans, brave men that they were, encouraged each other man to man, as was their way in war, to remember the valor each knew so well. They understood that their safety lay more in their long training than in hasty speeches, however eloquent.

70. After this, the armies approached each other, the Argives and their allies marching with muscles taut and feelings high, the Spartans slowly and to the music of the many fifers in the ranks, who played not for religious reasons but so that the men could close on their enemy steadily and evenly and not fall out of formation, as large armies tend to do at the onset of battle.

71. While they were still moving forward, King Agis decided on a maneuver. All armies, as they come to grips, will overextend themselves to the right, and with this movement of each army to the right, they will begin to outflank the other's left. They do this out of fear, each man thrusting his naked side behind the shield of the man to his right, and thinking that this tight closeness is his best protection. The first man on the extreme right of the line is responsible for this. He leads the movement because he is eager to get his unshielded side out of the way of the enemy, and the others, who share his fear, follow him.[7] In this battle, the Mantineans had come far around the left flank of the Sciritae, and because their army was larger, the Spartans and Tegeans came still further around that of the Athenians. Now Agis feared that they would be surrounded on their left, because he saw that the Mantinean line was outflanking it too much. So he signalled to the Sciritae and to Brasidas' former troops to swing around from their line and face off against the Mantineans, and then he ordered two battalions from the right wing, under generals Hipponoidas and Aristocles, to come around and fill the breach that had been created in the line. He reasoned that he would still have more than enough troops on his own right, and that the left side would now be in a stronger position against the Mantineans.

72. The order had been given on such short notice, however—when the armies were already advancing—that Aristocles and Hipponoidas refused to shift their men. (For this act they were later exiled from Sparta on a charge of cowardice.) So the enemy attacked while the Spartans were still in disarray, because the Sciritae were no longer able to close ranks when Agis ordered them back into their regular formation after the battalions refused to move. But even

---

6. Thucydides doesn't finish the arithmetic for us, but by this calculation there were about 3,584 men in the regular battalions, making for a whole army of 4,184, counting the Sciritae.
7. Because hoplites carried their large shields on their left arms, the overlapping shields left only one man in each line unprotected: the man on the far right, whose body was covered only on the left.

though their military skills had completely failed them on this occasion, the Spartans nevertheless showed that they could prevail through sheer courage.

When the Spartan army came to hand-to-hand combat with the enemy, the Mantinean right wing routed the Sciritae and the former army of Brasidas. The Mantineans and their allies, along with the thousand special Argive troops, had poured into the unclosed breach in the line and started to slaughter the Spartans, whom they surrounded, turned back, and pushed against the Spartan supply wagons. These were guarded by the older troops, some of whom the Mantineans also killed. At this point in the line, then, the Spartans were defeated. The rest of the army, however, and especially the middle of the line, where King Agis was (surrounded by his three hundred so-called cavalry, which fought as hoplites), attacked and routed the older Argive troops and the "five companies, " as they are known, along with the Cleonaeans, Orneates, and the Athenians who were at their side. Most of them didn't even wait until it came to hand-to-hand combat, but gave up while the Spartans were still advancing. There were even some who were trampled as they tried to avoid capture.

73. When this part of the army of the Argives and their allies gave way, the whole line broke to bits. At the same time, elements of the right wing of Spartans and Tegeans were completing its encirclement of the Athenians, who were defeated here, surrounded there, and beset by danger on all sides. Indeed, if their cavalry had not been there to help them, the Athenians would have been the hardest-hit sector of the whole army.

What happened next was that Agis saw his right wing struggling with the Mantineans and the thousand Argive special forces, and he ordered the whole army to move toward the defeated right. With this, the army backed away from or swept past the Athenians, and they and the defeated Argives who were with them were able to find safety without being harassed. At this point, the Mantineans, their allies, and the Argive special forces let up the pressure on their opponents. They saw their comrades in defeat and the Spartans bearing down on them, so they fled. Most of the Mantineans were killed, but most of the Argives got away. There was not a long pursuit or a bloody retreat, however. The Spartans fight long battles and hold on to their position until they turn back the enemy, but once the enemy runs, they do not follow very long or very far.

74. That, more or less, is how the battle went. It was the greatest battle between the Greeks in a very long time, and it was fought by the most important cities. The Spartans piled up the weapons of the enemy dead, quickly set up a victory marker, and began to strip the bodies. They gathered up their own dead and brought them to Tegea, where they buried them. Then they returned the enemy dead under a flag of truce. Seven hundred Argives, Orneates, and Cleonaeans; two hundred Mantineans; and two hundred Athenians and Aeginetans, as well as both their generals, were killed. Sparta's allies did not have a hard enough time of it to make the number of their dead even worth mentioning. As to the Spartans, it was difficult to get the truth from them, but they said that about three hundred of their men had died.

75. On the eve of the battle, Pleistoanax, the other Spartan king, led out the younger and older men as reinforcements and got as far as Tegea, but he returned when he learned of the victory. The Spartans also sent messengers to turn back the allies from Corinth and outside the isthmus. Then they too went home, sent off their allies in battle, and since it was the time of their Carneian festival, they began to celebrate the holiday. With this one battle, the Spartans acquitted themselves of the charge of cowardice the other Greeks had made after the battle on Sphacteria and of the charge of indecision and sluggishness

in other matters. Now the verdict was that they had been maligned for mere bad luck, and that their character was the same as ever.

On the day before this battle, the Epidaurians also staged an invasion. Knowing that the Argive fighting men would not be there, they went into Argos in full strength and killed many of the guards who had stayed behind when the army left for battle. After the battle, three thousand Elean hoplites arrived to reinforce the Mantineans, and one thousand Athenians came to supplement the first Athenian contingent. These allies quickly marched on Epidaurus while the Spartans were still celebrating the Carneia and, dividing up the work, began to build a siege wall around it. The others gave up, but the Athenians soon finished their part of the job—a fortress on the promontory where the temple of Hera stands. All the allies contributed men for a garrison of this fortress and then returned to their respective cities. And so the summer came to an end.

76. After they had finished celebrating the Carneia, and as soon as the following winter began, the Spartans marched out of their city. When they reached Tegea, they sent peace proposals to Argos. The Spartans had for some time had friends in Argos who wanted to end the democracy, and after the battle at Mantinea, these men were finding it much easier to persuade the people to come to an agreement. Their plan was first to make a peace treaty with Sparta, then later an alliance, and thus be in a position to attack the democracy itself. Now Lichas, son of Arcesilaus, who was the Argives' proxenus in Sparta, came from the Spartans to Argos carrying two messages. He said that he was to deliver one if they wanted war, and the other if they chose peace. There were many arguments, pro and con, partly because Alcibiades was present, but the men who were working with Sparta and who could now boldly come out into the open persuaded the Argive people to accept the terms of peace. The message, which consisted of these terms, was as follows.

77. It is the decision of the Spartan assembly to make an agreement with the Argives on the following terms.

Argos shall return the children it holds hostage to the Arcadian Orchomenians, and the men it holds hostage to the Maenalians, and shall return the men kept in Mantinea to Sparta. They shall also leave Epidaurus and tear down the fortifications they built there.

If the Athenians refuse to leave Epidaurus, they shall become the enemies of Argos and Sparta and of the allies of Sparta and of the allies of Argos.

If the Spartans are holding any children hostage, they shall return them to all their cities.

As to the sacrifice of atonement for the castration of bulls, if Argos wishes, Sparta shall administer the oath of compliance to the Epidaurians. Otherwise Argos shall administer the oath.

All the cities in the Peloponnese, whether great or small, shall be self-governing in keeping with their ancestral traditions. If any state from outside the Peloponnese shall enter Peloponnesian territory with intent to do harm, Argos and Sparta shall consult each other as to how to repel the enemy, distributing the burden of defense as shall seem equitable to the Peloponnesians.

The allies of Sparta outside the Peloponnese shall be parties to this agreement on the same terms as Sparta, and the allies of Argos shall be parties to this agreement on the same terms as Argos, and all shall retain their present territories.

A copy of these terms shall be taken around to the allies and shown to them. If they should have any amendments, they shall send the document back to Sparta.

78. Once the Argives had accepted this first proposal, the Spartan army withdrew from Tegea and went home. There continued to be communication between Argos and Sparta after this, and not much later the same men in Argos were able to produce an agreement whereby the Argives would abrogate the treaty of alliance with Mantinea, Athens, and Elis and make a treaty of peace and alliance with Sparta. This agreement is as follows.

79. The Spartans and the Argives have decided on a treaty of peace and alliance to last fifty years, submitting differences to arbitration for a peaceful settlement on fair and equal terms in keeping with ancestral tradition.

The other cities in the Peloponnese shall share in the peace and the alliance as self-governing and distinct entities, retaining their own territories and submitting differences to arbitration for a peaceful settlement on fair and equal terms in keeping with ancestral tradition.

The allies of Sparta outside the Peloponnese shall be parties to this agreement on the same terms as Sparta, and the allies of Argos shall be parties to this agreement on the same terms as Argos, and shall retain their present territory.

If it should be necessary to embark on a military campaign in common, the Spartans and the Argives shall consult each other and decide how the allies shall most equitably share the burden.

If any states, either in or out of the Peloponnese, shall have a dispute, whether about their borders or anything else, they shall settle it themselves.

If any state in the alliance shall remain at variance with another, they shall submit their dispute to an impartial state for resolution.

Legal proceedings involving private citizens in foreign courts shall be conducted according to ancestral tradition.

80. Thus the treaty of peace and alliance was ratified, and Argos and Sparta resolved differences over whatever either side had taken in the war and over other matters. By this time, they were making policy together, voting to accept neither heralds nor ambassadors from Athens unless the Athenians left the Peloponnese and abandoned their fortifications there, and voting as well neither to conclude any agreements nor to declare war unless they did it jointly. They were eager to take action, and both states sent ambassadors to the cities in Thrace and to Perdiccas, whom they prevailed on to join their alliance. He did not, to be sure, immediately break off from the Athenians. He intended to do it, though, because he saw that Argos had done so, and he himself was of Argive ancestry. Argos and Sparta also renewed Sparta's old oaths with the Chalcidians and swore new ones. Argos also sent ambassadors to Athens, demanding that they abandon the fortification at Epidaurus. The Athenians, seeing that their former allies outnumbered them there,[8] sent Demosthenes to lead their men out. After he arrived, he staged an athletic competition outside the fort as an excuse for getting the other troops out of it. As soon as the allies were out, he shut the gates on them. Later, after renewing the peace treaty with Epidaurus, the Athenians unilaterally returned the fort to them.

8. See 5.75.

81. The Mantineans at first held out after the Argives left the alliance, but then, powerless without Argos, they too made an agreement with Sparta and gave up their control of the cities in Maenalia. Then the Spartans and the Argives each sent one thousand men on a joint campaign. First the Spartans, on their own, went into Sicyon and restructured the government into a smaller oligarchy than it had already been, and after that, they acted together to end the democracy in Argos and to institute an oligarchy friendly to Sparta. The winter was ending and spring was on the way when these events took place, and so the fourteenth year of the war came to an end.

82. The following summer, the Dians at Mount Athos left the Athenian alliance for the Chalcidians, and Sparta replaced the formerly unfriendly government in Achaea.

It was not long before the people of Argos pulled themselves together and got up the courage to attack the oligarchy. They waited for the beginning of the gymnastics festival at Sparta, and then, after a battle in the city, the people regained power and killed some oligarchs and exiled others. The oligarchs had kept sending for their friends in Sparta, but the Spartans delayed for quite some time, until they finally adjourned the festival and went to help. When they learned, in Tegea, that the oligarchs had been defeated, they were unwilling to advance any further, despite appeals from the exiles. Instead they returned home and resumed their festival. Later, envoys came to Sparta from both the Argive people and the exiles. The allies were also present, and after many speeches on both sides, the alliance voted that the democrats in the city were in the wrong. They decided to march into Argos, but time was wasted, and the invasion kept being postponed. During this time, the people of Argos, for fear of the Spartans, once again moved toward an alliance with Athens in the belief that this was where their greatest security lay. They also began to build long walls from the city to the sea, so that if they were cut off by land, they would be able, with the help of Athens, to obtain supplies by sea. Some other cities in the Peloponnese connived in the building of this wall, and everyone in Argos—men, women, and household slaves—was involved in its construction, aided by carpenters and stonemasons from Athens. And so the summer came to an end.

83. The following winter, on learning of the wall, the Spartans and their allies (with the exception of the Corinthians) marched into Argive territory. There were also some Argives working with them in the city. The army was led by the Spartan king Agis, son of Archidamus. Although they did not get the help they had expected from within the city, they captured the as-yet-unfinished wall and tore it down. They then took the Argive territory of Hysiae and killed all the free men they captured before pulling out and dispersing to their cities. Next, the Argives marched against the Phliasians for harboring the Argive exiles, most of whom had settled there. After plundering the place, the Argives went home.

That same winter, the Athenians blockaded Macedonia after accusing Perdiccas of joining in the alliance with Argos and Sparta. The Athenians also charged that he had been making preparations for a campaign against the Chalcidians in Thrace and Amphipolis, with Nicias to be in command, but that he betrayed the alliance by refusing to join the campaign, which then had to be given up. Perdiccas therefore became an enemy. And so this winter came to an end, and with it ended the fifteenth year of the war.

THE TALKS AT MELOS

84. The following summer, Alcibiades sailed to Argos with twenty ships, seized three hundred Argives still suspected of having Spartan sympathies, and then imprisoned them on nearby islands under Athenian control. The Athenians also sent a fleet against the island of Melos. Thirty of the ships were their own, six were from Chios, and two were from Lesbos. Their own troops numbered twelve hundred hoplites, three hundred archers, and twenty mounted archers. There were also about fifteen hundred hoplites from their allies on the islands. The Melians are colonists from Sparta and would not submit to Athenian control like the other islanders. At first, they were neutral and lived peaceably, but they became openly hostile after Athens once tried to compel their obedience by ravaging their land. The generals Cleomedes, son of Lycomedes, and Tisias, son of Tisimachus, bivouacked on Melian territory with their troops, but before doing any injury to the land, they sent ambassadors to hold talks with the Melians. The Melian leadership, however, did not bring these men before the popular assembly. Instead, they asked them to discuss their mission with the council and the privileged voters. The Athenian ambassadors spoke as follows.

85. "We know that what you are thinking in bringing us before a few voters, and not before the popular assembly, is that now the people won't be deceived after listening to a single long, seductive, and unrefuted speech from us. Well, those of you who are sitting here can make things even safer for yourselves. When we say something that seems wrong, interrupt immediately, and answer, not in a set speech, but one point at a time. — But say first whether this proposal is to your liking."

86. The Melian councillors said, "There can be no objection to the reasonableness of quiet, instructive talks among ourselves. But this military force, which is here, now, and not off in the future, looks different from instruction. We see that you have come as judges in a debate, and the likely prize will be war if we win the debate with arguments based on right and refuse to capitulate, or servitude if we concede to you."

ATHENIANS

87. Excuse us, but if you're having this meeting to make guesses about the future or to do anything but look at your situation and see how to save your city, we'll leave. But if that's the topic, we'll keep talking.

MELIANS

88. It's natural and understandable that in a situation like this, people would want to express their thoughts at length. But so be it. This meeting is about saving our city, and the format of the discussion will be as you have said.

ATHENIANS

89. Very well.

We Athenians are not going to use false pretenses and go on at length about how we have a right to rule because we destroyed the Persian empire, or about how we are seeking retribution because you did us wrong. You would not believe us anyway. And please do not suppose that you will persuade *us* when you say that you did not campaign with the Spartans although you were their colonists, or that you never did us wrong. No, each of us must exercise what power he really thinks he can, and we know and you know that in the human realm, justice is enforced only among those who can be equally constrained by it, and that those who have power use it, while the weak make compromises.

MELIANS

90. Since you have ruled out a discussion of justice and forced us to speak of expediency, it would be inexpedient, at least as we see it, for you to eradicate common decency. There has always been a fair and right way to treat people who are in danger, if only to give them some benefit for making persuasive arguments by holding off from the full exercise of power. This applies to you above all, since you would set an example for others of how to take the greatest vengeance if you fall.

ATHENIANS

91. We're not worried about the end of our empire, if it ever does end. People who rule over others, like the Spartans, are not so bad to their defeated enemies. Anyway, we're not fighting the Spartans just now. What is really horrendous is when subjects are able to attack and defeat their masters. — But you let us worry about all that. We are here to talk about benefiting our empire and saving your city, and we will tell you how we are going to do that, because we want to take control here without any trouble and we want you to be spared for both our sakes.

MELIANS

92. And just how would it be as much to our advantage to be enslaved, as for you to rule over us?

ATHENIANS

93. You would benefit by surrendering before you experience the worst of consequences, and we would benefit by not having you dead.

MELIANS

94. So you would not accept our living in peace, being friends instead of enemies, and allies of neither side?

ATHENIANS

95. Your hatred doesn't hurt us as much as your friendship. That would show us as weak to our other subjects, whereas your hatred would be a proof of our power.

MELIANS

96. Would your subjects consider you reasonable if you lumped together colonists who had no connection to you, colonists from Athens, and rebellious colonists who had been subdued?

ATHENIANS

97. They think there's justice all around. They also think the independent islands are strong, and that we are afraid to attack them. So aside from adding to our empire, your subjugation will also enhance our safety, especially since you are islanders and we are a naval power. Besides, you're weaker than the others — unless, that is, you show that you too can be independent.

MELIANS

98. Don't you think there's safety in our neutrality? You turned us away from a discussion of justice and persuaded us to attend to what was in your interest. Now it's up to us to tell you about what is to our advantage and to try to persuade you that it is also to yours. How will you avoid making enemies of states that are now neutral, but that look at what you do here and decide that you will go after them one day? How will you achieve anything but to make your present enemies seem more attractive, and to force those who had no intention of opposing you into unwilling hostility?

ATHENIANS

99. We do not think the threat to us is so much from mainlanders who, in their freedom from fear, will be continually putting off their preparations against us, as from independent islanders, like you, and from those who are al-

ready chafing under the restraints of rule. These are the ones who are most likely to commit themselves to ill-considered action and create foreseeable dangers for themselves and for us.

MELIANS

100. Well then, in the face of this desperate effort you and your slaves are making, you to keep your empire and they to get rid of it, wouldn't we, who are still free, be the lowest of cowards if we didn't try everything before submitting to slavery?

ATHENIANS

101. No, not if you think about it prudently. This isn't a contest about manly virtue between equals, or about bringing disgrace on yourself. You are deliberating about your very existence, about standing up against a power far greater than yours.

MELIANS

102. But we know that there are times when the odds in warfare don't depend on the numbers. If we give up, our situation becomes hopeless right away, but if we fight, we can still hope to stand tall.

ATHENIANS

103. In times of danger, hope is a comfort that can hurt you, but it won't destroy you if you back it up with plenty of other resources. People who gamble everything on it (hope is extravagant by nature, you see) know it for what it really is only after they have lost everything. Then, of course, when you can recognize it and take precautions, it's left you flat. You don't want to experience that. You Melians are weak, and you only have one chance. So don't be like all those people who could have saved themselves by their own efforts, but who abandoned their realistic hopes and turned in their hour of need to invisible powers—to prophecies and oracles and all the other nonsense that conspires with hope to ruin you.

MELIANS

104. As you well know, we too think it will be hard to fight both your power and the fortunes of war, especially with uneven odds. Still, we believe that our fortune comes from god, and that we will not be defeated because we take our stand as righteous men against men who are in the wrong. And what we lack in power will be made up for by the Spartan League. They will have to help us, if only because of our kinship with them and the disgrace they would feel if they didn't. So it's not totally irrational for us to feel hopeful.

ATHENIANS

105. Well, when it comes to divine good will, we don't think we'll be left out. We're not claiming anything or doing anything outside man's thinking about the gods or about the way the gods themselves behave. Given what we believe about the gods and know about men, we think that both are always forced by the law of nature to dominate everyone they can. We didn't lay down this law, it was there—and we weren't the first to make use of it. We took it as it was and acted on it, and we will bequeath it as a living thing to future generations, knowing full well that if you or anyone else had the same power as we, you would do the same thing. So we probably don't have to fear any disadvantage when it comes to the gods. And as to this opinion of yours about the Spartans, that you can trust them to help you because of their fear of disgrace—well, our blessings on your innocence, but we don't envy your foolishness. The Spartans do the right thing among themselves, according to their local customs. One could say a great deal about their treatment of others, but to put it briefly, they are more conspicuous than anyone else we know in thinking that pleasure is

good and expediency is just. Their mindset really bears no relation to your irrational belief that there is any safety for you now.

MELIANS

106. But it's exactly because of this expediency that we trust them. They won't want to betray the Melians, their colonists, and prove themselves helpful to their enemies and unreliable to their well-wishers in Greece.

ATHENIANS

107. But don't you see that expediency is safe, and that doing the right and honorable thing is dangerous? On the whole, the Spartans are the last people to take big risks.

MELIANS

108. We think they'll take on dangers for us that they wouldn't for others and regard those dangers as less risky, because we are close to the Peloponnese from an operational point of view. Also, they can trust our loyalty because we are kin and we think alike.

ATHENIANS

109. Men who ask others to come to fight on their side don't offer security in good will but in real fighting power. The Spartans take this kind of thing more into consideration than others, because they have so little faith in their own resources that they even attack their neighbors with plenty of allies. So it's not likely that they'll try to make their way over to an island when we control the sea.

MELIANS

110. Then maybe they'll send their allies. The sea of Crete is large, and it is harder for those who control the sea to catch a ship than it is for the ship to get through to safety without being noticed. And if that doesn't work, they might turn against your territory or attack the rest of your allies, the ones Brasidas didn't get to. And then the fight would shift from a place where you have no interest to your own land and that of your allies.

ATHENIANS

111. It's been tried and might even be tried for you—though surely you are aware that we Athenians have never abandoned a siege out of fear of anyone.

But it occurs to us that after saying you were going to talk about saving yourselves, you haven't in any of this lengthy discussion mentioned anything that most people would rely on for their salvation. Your strongest arguments are in the future and depend on hope. What you've actually got is too meager to give you a chance of surviving the forces lined up against you now. You've shown a very irrational attitude—unless, of course, you intend to reach some more prudent conclusion than this after you send us away and begin your deliberations. For surely you don't mean to commit yourselves to that "honor" which has been so destructive to men in clear and present dangers involving "dishonor." Many men who could still see where it was leading them have been drawn on by the allure of this so-called "honor," this word with its seductive power, and fallen with open eyes into irremediable catastrophe, vanquished in their struggle with a fine word, only to achieve a kind of dishonorable honor because they weren't just unlucky, they were fools. You can avoid this, if you think things over carefully, and decide that there is nothing so disgraceful in being defeated by the greatest city in the world, which invites you to become its ally on fair terms—paying us tribute, to be sure, but keeping your land for yourselves. You have been given the choice between war and security. Don't be stubborn and make the wrong choice. The people who are most likely to succeed stand up to their equals, have the right attitude towards their superiors, and are fair to those beneath them.

We will leave now. Think it over, and always remember that you are making a decision about your country. You only have one, and its existence depends on this one chance to make a decision, right or wrong.

112. Then the Athenians withdrew from the discussion. The Melians, left to themselves, came to the conclusion that had been implied by their responses in the talks. They answered the Athenians as follows: "Men of Athens, our decision is no different from what it was at first. We will not in this brief moment strip the city we have lived in for seven hundred years of its freedom. We will try to save it, trusting in the divine good fortune that has preserved us so far and in the help we expect from the Spartans and from others. We invite you to be our friends, to let us remain neutral, and to leave our territory after making a treaty agreeable to us both."

113. That was the Melian response. The talks were already breaking up when the Athenians said, "Well, judging from this decision, you seem to us to be the only men who can make out the future more clearly than what you can see, and who gaze upon the invisible with your mind's eye as if it were an accomplished fact. You have cast yourselves on luck, hope, and the Spartans, and the more you trust in them, the harder will be your fall."

114. Then the Athenian envoys returned to the camp. Since the Melians would not submit, the Athenian generals immediately took offensive action and, after dividing their men according to the cities they came from, began to build a wall around Melos. Later the Athenians left a garrison of their own and allied men to guard the land and sea routes and then withdrew with most of their army. The men who were left behind remained there and carried on the siege.

115. At about this same time, the Argives invaded the territory of Phlius, where they fell into an ambush set by the Phliasians and the Argive exiles, who killed about eighty of them. The Athenian raiders on Pylos took a great deal of booty from Spartan territory, but despite even this, the Spartans did not renounce the treaty and declare war. They did, however, announce that if any of their people wished to raid Athenian territory, they could do so. The Corinthians made war on the Athenians over some private quarrels, but the rest of the Peloponnesians held their peace. The Melians staged a night attack on the part of the Athenian wall opposite their market and captured it. They killed some men and withdrew into the city carrying grain and as many other useful provisions as they could, taking no further action. The Athenians kept a better watch from then on. And so the summer came to an end.

116. The following winter, the Spartans were about to march into Argive territory, but the omens from sacrifices made before crossing the border were unfavorable and they turned back. This balked expedition led the Argives to suspect some of their citizens. They arrested some, but others managed to escape. At about the same time, the Melians again captured yet another part of the Athenian wall when only a few men were on guard duty. Because of this, another contingent later came from Athens, under the command of Philocrates, son of Demeas. By now, the Melians were completely cut off, and there were traitors within the city itself. So, on their own initiative, they agreed to terms whereby the Athenians could do with them as they liked. The Athenians thereupon killed all the males of fighting age they could capture and sold the women and children into slavery. The Athenians then occupied the place themselves and later sent out five hundred colonists.

Book 6

Sicily was, literally, a land of milk and honey—or perhaps more correctly, of cheese and honey—as well as cattle, hogs, fish, horses, and, most important of all, timber and grain. Thucydides specifically identifies the decision to invade Sicily as one of the blunders of Pericles' successors that led to the loss of the war (2.65).

In recounting the events of Book 6, Thucydides compels readers to engage with several of his work's most important themes—the fallibility of human judgment, the Athenian character, and the dynamics of democracy. After explaining (6.1) that the Athenians did not realize the magnitude of the war they were undertaking against Sicily, Thucydides describes the island and its history (2–5) and discusses the Athenian decision to take military action in support of their ally Egesta (6–26), highlighting the speeches of Nicias and Alcibiades. The speeches are Thucydides' vehicle for stressing the difference in the two men's characters and personalities, differences that Thucydides suggests have wider implications for the divergent outlooks of youth and age. Chapters 27–28 deal with the nocturnal mutilation of the images of Hermes that stood outside Athenian houses, rumored parodies of the mystery religion celebrated just outside Athens at Eleusis, and the attendant accusations against Alcibiades. They are followed (30–32) by a vivid account of the sailing of the fleet—a narrative whose drama is heightened by the hindsight that Thucydides knew would enable his readers to look back upon the Athenians' high hopes with horror.

The scene then shifts to Syracuse and the speeches of the politicians Hermocrates and Athenagoras (33–40), which offer an opportunity for readers to compare Athenian and Syracusan democracy. Thucydides' account of Athenian military operations and the generals' disagreement over strategy (42–52) is broken off at 53, when the arrival of the state trireme *Salaminia* to return Alcibiades to Athens for trial inspires an important digression (53–60) on misinformation and misunderstandings about the conspiracy against the sons of Peisistratus in 514, which Thucydides views as symptomatic of the Athenian (or human) inability to gather or evaluate evidence properly. After describing Alcibiades' machinations to avoid returning home (61), Thucydides returns to the war in Sicily (62–88).

Thucydides next takes us to Sparta, where Alcibiades delivers a memorable sophistic tour de force (89–92) that seeks to justify his defection from Athens by attacking Athenian democracy. The historian also ascribes the Spartans' decision to fortify Decelea in the north of Attica to Alcibiades' counsel (93). He then returns to operations in Sicily and elsewhere (94–105), in the course of which Lamachus was killed (101).

Thucydides is not the best source for the brouhaha that erupted at Athens following the parodying of the mystery religion and the mutilation of the herms, an act of violence that people were convinced smacked of treason; a more detailed (though not necessarily accurate) account of the scandals of 415 can be found in the speech the orator Andocides delivered, *On the Mysteries*, in 399.

Book 6

1. That same winter, the Athenians decided to send another expedition to Sicily. It would be greater than the one led by Laches and Eurymedon,[1] and it would set sail with the goal of reducing the island to subjection, if possible. The majority of the Athenian people were unaware of the size of the island and of its population, both Greek and barbarian; and they were unaware, also, that they were undertaking a war only slightly less extensive than that with the Peloponnesians. After all, a merchant ship takes almost eight days to circumnavigate the island. Despite its size, however, it is separated from the mainland by only two and a half miles of water.

2. Its original settlement and the peoples who inhabited it were as follows. It is said that the earliest settlers in any part of the island were the Cyclopes and the Laestrygonians, although I can't say who they were, where they came from, or where they went. We must be content with what the poets[2] have said about them and form an opinion about them for ourselves. The Sicanians appear to have been the first inhabitants after them, although as the Sicanians themselves tell it, they were Sicily's indigenous inhabitants from the first. The truth, however, is that they were Iberians and had been forced out of the area of the Sicanus River in Iberia by the Ligurians. The island was then called Sicania after the Sicanians, having formerly been called Trinacria. The Sicanians occupy the western part of Sicily to this day.

During the capture of Troy, some Trojans fled the Achaeans in boats and reached Sicily. They settled on the borders of Sicanian territory. They were all called the Elymi, and their cities were Eryx and Egesta. Some Phocians, also coming from Troy, settled among them, after having been blown by storms first to Libya and from there to Sicily.

The Sicels, who first lived in Italy, fled to Sicily to escape the Oscans. They say, and in fact one would expect, that they crossed over on rafts after waiting for a favorable wind, although they probably also sailed over on other craft. There are Sicels in Italy to this day, and the reason the place is called Italy is that it takes its name from Italus, a Sicel king. This large army of Sicels reached Sicily, defeated the Sicanians in battle, and pushed them into the southwestern part of the island. After this crossing, nearly three hundred years before the Greeks went there, they changed the name of the island from Sicania to Sicily, and they occupied its most fertile terrain. They still live in the middle and north of the island.

At one time the Phoenicians used to live in all parts of Sicily. They took headlands jutting into the sea, as well as islets off the coast, on which they set up markets and traded with the Sicels. After large numbers of Greeks started sailing over to the island, though, the Phoenicians left most of these places and settled near the Elymi, in the confederated towns of Motya, Soloeis, and Panormus, partly because they trusted their alliance with the Elymi, and partly because it is at that point that Sicily is the least distance from Carthage. Those, then, are the barbarian peoples in Sicily, and that is how they settled it.

3. As to the Greeks, the first colonists were the Chalcidians, who had sailed from Euboea with their founder, Thucles, and settled Naxos. There they

---

1. See 3.86 and 115.
2. In the *Odyssey*, Homer includes encounters with the Cyclopes and the Laestrygonians among the adventures of Odysseus. Polyphemus, whom Odysseus blinded in his cave in Book 9, was one of the one-eyed giants known as Cyclopes; the Laestrygonians, who ate some of Odysseus' men (10.80–132), were also cannibal giants.

built the altar to Apollo the Founder, which is still standing outside of where the city now is and at which Sicilian delegates to international festivals make their sacrifices before sailing out of Sicily.

The following year, Archias, a Heraclid from Corinth[3], founded Syracuse after driving the Sicels from the island of Ortygia, which is no longer surrounded by water and where the inner city of Syracuse now stands. In later years, the city wall was extended to the settlement on the mainland, which became quite populous.

In the fifth year after the founding of Syracuse, Thucles and his Chalcidians set out from Naxos and founded Leontini after making war on the Sicels and forcing them out. After establishing Leontini, they founded Catana, although the Catanaeans themselves memorialized Evarchus as their founder.

4. At about the same time, Lamis led a group of colonists out of Megara and arrived in Sicily. He founded a place called Trotilus on the Pantacyas River. Later he went from there to the Chalcidians in Leontini in order to join their settlement, which he did for a short time, although he was later driven out and went on to found Thapsus, where he died. His followers left Thapsus to found a place called Megara Hyblaea, after the Sicel king Hyblon led them there and gave it to them. They had lived there for two hundred forty five years when they were forced out of the city and the whole region by Gelon, the tyrant at Syracuse. Before their expulsion, however, and one hundred years after they had founded Megara Hyblaea itself, they sent Pammilus out to found Selinus. A cofounder came from their mother city, Megara, to join him.

Forty-five years after the founding of Syracuse, Antiphemus led colonists from Rhodes, and Entimus from Crete, and they jointly founded Gela. The city took its name from the river Gelas, although the place where the acropolis now is, and which was fortified first, is called Lindii. The institutions there are Dorian.

Some one hundred and eight years after they built their settlement, the Geloans founded Acragas, naming the city after the Acragas River. They made Aristonous and Pystilus their founders and imposed Geloan institutions on the place.

Zancle was originally founded by raiders from the Chalcidian city of Cyme in Opicia. Later a large group of colonists came from Chalcis and the rest of Euboea and shared out parcels of land. The founders of Zancle were Perieres and Crataemenes, the former from Cyme and the latter from Chalcis. Zancle first got its name from the Sicels because the place is shaped like a sickle, and the Sicels call a sickle a "zanclon." Later the Zanclian settlers were driven out by Samians and other Ionians who landed in Sicily as they fled the Persians. Not much later, Anaxilas, the tyrant of Rhegium, forced the Samians out and himself refounded the place as a city of mixed population, changing its name to Messana after the homeland of his ancestors.

5. From Zancle, Himera was founded by Eucleides, Simus, and Sacon. Most of the colonists came from Chalcis, but they were joined by the so-called Myletidae, who were exiles defeated in a civil war in Syracuse. The language that developed was a mixture of Chalcidian and Dorian, but their institutions were predominantly Chalcidian.

Acrae and Casmenae were founded by the Syracusans, Acrae seventy years after Syracuse and Casmenae nearly twenty years after Acrae.

---

3. Like other Dorian aristocracies, that of Corinth claimed descent from Heracles.

Camarina was first founded by Syracuse, exactly one hundred and thirty five years after the founding of Syracuse itself. Its founders were Dascon and Menecolus. The Camarinaeans, however, rebelled against Syracuse, which made war on them and forced them out. Later Hippocrates, the tyrant at Gela, took the territory of Camarina as a ransom for some Syracusan prisoners of war and himself repopulated Camarina. The city's inhabitants were again driven out, this time by Gelon, and the Geloans then repopulated the city for the third time.

6. These were all the peoples, barbarian and Greek, who inhabited Sicily, and such was the size of the island on which the Athenians were determined to make war. They wanted to maintain the appearance of helping their kinsmen and their newly acquired allies, but what they really longed for was to rule over the whole island.

They were especially egged on by some ambassadors from Egesta who were in Athens and who were very eager for the Athenians to come and help them. The reason for this was that they shared a border with Selinus, with whom they had gone to war over marriage laws and disputed land. The Selinuntines had called in the Syracusans as allies, and they were squeezing Egesta by land and sea. The Egestans reminded the Athenians of the alliance they had made with Leontini during Laches' previous campaign and begged Athens to send a fleet to their defense.[4] They made a great many arguments, but the main point was that Syracuse would end up all-powerful in Sicily if it went unpunished in driving out the Leontines and in destroying the rest of Athens' allies; whereupon there would be a real danger that out of kinship, as Dorian to Dorian and as colonist to mother country, they would one day bring a large force to help the Peloponnese and would join them in destroying the power of Athens. It would therefore be prudent for Athens, along with its remaining allies, to stand up to Syracuse, especially since Egesta would provide the money they needed for the war. After hearing these arguments repeated again and again in their assemblies by the Egestans and their supporters, the Athenians voted that as a first step, they should send a delegation to Egesta to see whether there really was money in the public treasury and in the temples and to find out how things stood in the war with Selinus.

And so the Athenian delegation was sent to Sicily.

7. That same winter, the Spartans and their allies (except Corinth) advanced into Argive territory, slashed and burned some land, though not much, and then brought in wagons and carried away some grain. They also settled the Argive exiles in Orneae and detached some of their remaining army to stay with them. Then after negotiating a period during which the Orneates and the Argives would refrain from violating each other's territory, the Peloponnesian army returned home. Not much later, however, the Athenians arrived at Argos with thirty ships and six hundred hoplites, whereupon the Argives marched out in full strength with the Athenians and spent a day besieging the people in Orneae. That night, while the army bivouacked away from the town, the men in Orneae escaped. When the Argives learned of this the next day, they completely demolished Orneae. Then they returned home and so, somewhat later, did the Athenian fleet.

Next, the Athenians went by sea to the Methone, which is on the Macedonian border. They brought their own cavalry as well as the Macedonian exiles who were at Athens, and from there they conducted raids on Perdiccas' territory. The Spartans sent a message to the Chalcidians in Thrace, who had a truce with Athens that could be ended on ten days' notice, ordering them to join forces with Perdiccas, but they refused.

And so the winter came to an end, and with it ended the sixteenth year of the war that I, Thucydides, wrote down.

8. At the beginning of the following spring, the Athenian envoys, accompanied by the Egestans, returned from Sicily. The Egestans brought with them sixty talents of uncoined silver—enough to support sixty ships for a month, which is what the Egestans were going to ask for. The Athenians called an assembly and listened to a great many enticing but untrue statements from the Egestans and from their own envoys, who said that there was plenty of ready money in Egesta's treasury and temples. The assembly voted to send sixty ships to Sicily. Their commanders were to be Alcibiades, son of Cleinias; Nicias, son of Niceratus; and Lamachus, son of Xenophanes; and they were to have full authority to make decisions on the spot without checking back with the assembly. They were to support the Egestans against Selinus; to work with the Leontines in rebuilding their city, provided that the war was going well; and to do everything else in Sicily that they judged to be in Athens' best interest.

There was another assembly four days after this one, to discuss how to outfit the ships as quickly as possible and to vote whatever else the commanders might need to get under way.

Nicias, however, had been appointed to his command against his will. He believed that the city was not thinking straight. It was giving flimsy, specious reasons for its actions, but its real aim was to conquer all of Sicily—a huge enterprise. Wanting to dissuade the assembly, he came forward and gave the following advice.

9. I am aware that this assembly has gathered to discuss the preparations we must make for an expedition to Sicily, but it seems to me that we still have to look into the question of whether it is advisable to send off our ships in the first place—instead of rushing to a decision on such an important question, and trusting people of a different race in undertaking a war that is not right for us. Now, for me, war is a way to gain prominence. I also happen to have fewer fears for my own personal safety than do others, although I of course believe that a man can still be a good citizen and look out for himself and his property. Such a man, after all, is more likely than anyone else to want his city's efforts to succeed, if only for his own sake. Nevertheless, I have not in the past tried to gain your approval by speaking anything but my true thoughts, and I won't do it now. I will say what I think best for Athens. In view of the Athenian character, no argument of mine would be strong enough to persuade you to safeguard what you have and not to risk your present wealth on the uncertainties of the future.[5] I will, however, try to show you that this is the wrong time for hasty action, and that it will not be easy for you to obtain what you long for.

10. I'm telling you that you will not only be leaving many enemies behind, but that you seem determined to sail over there and bring new ones back here. Maybe you think that there is some security in the existing peace treaty, although even if you do nothing, this will be a treaty in name only, since that is what men here in Athens and among our enemies have conspired to make it. But if we suffer a setback with a large force somewhere, our enemies will be right on top of us. After

---

5. Compare this assessment of the Athenian character with the Athenians' contempt for what seems like the same trait in the Melians (5.85–113).

all, they only made the treaty in the first place because they had to—because of their own problems and because they had lost more face than we. Furthermore, we have a great many disputes over this treaty. Also, there are those who have not accepted the agreement, such as it is, and they are by no means the weakest states, either. Some of them are openly making war on us; others are just maintaining a ten-day truce because the Spartans are still keeping the peace. It is highly probable that if they catch us with our forces divided—and dividing them is what we are now in such a hurry to do—they will all eagerly attack us along with the Sicilians, whom at one time they wanted as allies above all others. These are things we must consider, and not decide to endanger our city while its fortunes are still up in the air by reaching for another empire before we have secured the one we have. The Chalcidians in Thrace, for example, have been in revolt against us for many years and need to be taken in hand, while some of our other subjects on the mainland are obeying us only reluctantly. And yet we are keen to help our allies, the Egestans here, who have been wronged, while we put off taking revenge on rebels who have been doing us wrong for a long time.

11. Furthermore, if we subdued those rebels, we could keep our hold on them; but even if we conquered Sicily, its population and its distance would make it very difficult for us to maintain our control. It is downright foolish to attack people whom you can't hold onto after you conquer them, and who leave you worse off if you fail than you were before you attacked them. It seems to me that the Sicilians, judging from their present condition, would be less dangerous to us if the Syracusans ruled over them, though this prospect is what the Egestans are trying to terrify us with. As things now stand, some Sicilians might come this way as a favor to the Spartans; but it isn't likely that a Syracusan empire would make war on our empire, because though they might join the Spartans and find a way to destroy our empire, we might just as well join the Spartans and destroy theirs in the same way. The Greeks over there will be most afraid of us if we don't go. The alternative is to make a display of our power and quickly leave, because if we should falter in any way, they would almost certainly despise us enough to join our enemies here in attacking us. We all know that the most awe-inspiring things are those that are furthest away and whose renown is least tested. And that, my fellow Athenians, is exactly what your experience with the Spartans and their allies has been. Because of your unexpected success against them—in contrast to your first fears—you now look down on them so much that you hanker after Sicily!

We must not be smug about the bad luck of our opponents; we should be confident only after we have surpassed them in planning. You must always bear in mind that because the Spartans have lost prestige, they are even now looking to trip us up any way they can and thereby set their own ugly state of affairs to rights—especially since they have worked so long and so hard to gain a reputation for valor. Thus if we are wise, we will see that our struggle is not in Sicily—for the Egestans, who are barbarians after all. It is to defend ourselves energetically against an oligarchic government that is constantly plotting against us.

12. We must also remember that we have only recently had a chance to take a brief rest from war and the great plague and to replenish our treasury and our human stock. The right thing to do is to spend this capital here, on ourselves, and not on exiles who are begging for aid, men for whom it is expedient to tell appealing lies and to offer nothing but

speeches while others run the risks. Then, if they succeed, they show a paltry gratitude, and if they fail, they take their friends down with them.

Now if a certain person, glad to be elected to a command, advises you to set sail, when he is only looking out for his own interests—especially if he is still too young for a generalship and really hopes to benefit from the perquisites of office while being admired for his fine stable of horses—don't put it in the power of such a man to endanger the city just so that he can show off. Bear in mind that such men violate the public trust and squander their private fortunes. This matter is too important for one so young to both plan and then hastily carry out.[6]

13. I am alarmed at the sight of the young supporters who have been invited to sit beside this very man here in this assembly, and I would say to any of the older men that if he happens to be sitting next to one of these youths, he should not be shamed into voting for war for fear of being thought a coward. Neither should he be madly in love with faraway things, as the young may be to their sorrow; he should realize that enterprises succeed less from enthusiasm than from forethought. He should raise his hand and vote against the greatest danger ever to face the fatherland. The boundaries between us and Sicily are the Ionian Gulf if you sail along the coast, and the Sicilian Sea if you sail through open water. The Sicilians observe them and that is fine with us. Vote to keep observing these boundaries so that Sicilians can manage their own affairs in their own country, and tell the Egestans in particular that since they started the war with the Selinuntines without consulting Athens in the first place, they should also end it by themselves. And from now on let us stop making allies in the usual way, allies whom we come to defend when they are in trouble and from whom we get nothing when we ourselves need help.

14. And you, prytanis[7], if you think it your duty to care for your city, and if you want to be regarded as a good citizen, vote to submit this question to the Athenian people again. Even if you are worried about reopening a vote, remember that with so many witnesses, you cannot be charged with setting a bad precedent. The city's mind is not right, and you must be its physician, because that is what holding office is at its best—to do as much good for your city as possible, or at least to avoid willingly doing harm.

15. After Nicias gave this speech, most of the Athenians who came forward urged making the campaign and not rescinding the vote, although there were some who spoke against. Alcibiades, son of Cleinias, was the most eager advocate of the expedition. He was determined to oppose Nicias, because he differed with Nicias' politics and because Nicias had just maligned him. Above all, he was eager to be a general and hoped to be the conqueror of Sicily and Carthage. At the same time, he hoped that his success would bring him, personally, the benefits of wealth and prestige. He was, you see, famous among the common people, and he indulged his passion for horse-racing and other extravagances far beyond his means. More than anything else, however, this relationship with the public is what later brought Athens to ruin, because most people came to fear the enormity and excess of his way of life and of the extremes to which his ambition took him in everything he did. They turned on him when they decided that what he really wanted was to become tyrant, and even though in his public capacity he was their best military strategist, they so resented his behav-

---

6. Nicias is referring here to Alcibiades, who was in his thirties in 415 and famous in Athens for his extravagance.
7. The chair of the prytaneis for that day (and hence the chair of the assembly meeting).

ior in private life that they turned over the conduct of the war to other men and quickly brought down their city.

On this occasion, then, Alcibiades came before the Athenian people and spoke to them as follows.

16. My fellow Athenians. I have more of a right to a command than anybody else. There, I had to begin like that, after the beating Nicias gave me. I also believe that I deserve a command, because all the things that make me notorious are really an honor to my ancestors and to me, as well as an advantage to the state. For example, because of my magnificent performance at the Olympic games, the other Greeks, who came expecting to find us exhausted by war, decided that our city was even greater than it is. That was because I entered seven chariots, more than any other private citizen ever, and won first, second, and fourth prizes—and I also carried myself in a style worthy of such victories. It's the way of the world to respect things like that: people think there is power behind performance. And again, when I distinguish myself here in Athens with a dramatic production or some other such thing, it's only natural for my fellow citizens to envy me; but to foreigners they are a sign of strength.[8] So this folly of mine isn't so useless after all, since at my own expense I benefit not only myself but my city. And there is nothing wrong when a man who thinks a lot of himself doesn't treat others as equals. A man who is doing badly doesn't expect anyone to share his troubles. We don't talk to anyone when he's down and out, so we have to put up with it when successful people scorn us—either that or do unto others as you would have them do unto you. I know that men of that kind, men who stand out in some way, are hated in their own lifetimes, especially among their peers, but also when they are with others. Nevertheless, men in future generations make false claims to be their descendants, and they become the pride of their countries, no longer aliens or crackpots, but favorite sons and benefactors.

I aspire to such fame, and because of it I am criticized for my private life. But look at my public acts and tell me whether I am second to anyone: I put together an alliance with the most powerful states in the Peloponnese at no risk or expense to Athens, and I made Sparta stake everything on the outcome of a day-long battle at Mantinea.[9] Yes, they emerged from that successfully, but they have not to this day recovered their courage.

17. Thus what they call my "youth" and my "insane folly" was able to find the right arguments to win over the powers of the Peloponnese, who took confidence from my spirit. So don't be afraid of that spirit now, and take advantage of what Nicias and I have to offer while I am coming into the prime of life and while Nicias is still considered lucky. Don't change your minds about sending the fleet to Sicily because it's supposed to be a great power. Their cities are populous, it is true, but they are a multicultural rabble who easily accept comings and goings in the citizen body. And since people don't feel like it's their own homeland, they don't provide themselves with weaponry or even improve their farms if they live in the

---

8. Rich citizens in Athens were required to pay for dramatic productions, the more lavish the better; the training of a chorus was one of the "liturgies" wealthy men undertook as a form of semivoluntary taxation. (Others included throwing a banquet for all the members of one's tribe or maintaining a trireme.) One advantage of performing such a service was that it provided a fund of goodwill and afforded precisely the sort of bragging rights Alcibiades claims here.

9. Alcibiades is referring to the alliance he put together with Argos, Elis, and Mantinea, although these were hardly the most powerful states in the Peloponnese. He did push the Argives into the battle of Mantinea (5.66–74), in which they and their allies were decisively beaten by Sparta.

country. They hoard whatever they make from the public treasury through pettifogging or political intrigue, knowing that if they fail they can go and live somewhere else. It isn't likely that such a disorganized group will ever be of one mind or unite for action. Elements will probably come over to us if we make offers they like—especially if there is civil unrest, as we have learned there is.

And really, they don't have as many hoplites as they like to say. It is transparently clear that the other Greek states have not had as many as they themselves listed. In fact all of Greece falsified the size of its hoplite force and has hardly been able to muster enough hoplites during this whole war.

From what I hear, the situation in Sicily will be even easier to handle than we have thought. After all, there will be a lot of barbarians who hate the Syracusans and who will join us in attacking them. And if you think about it, the situation here is no impediment either. While our forefathers were founding their empire, they had the same enemies people say we will be leaving behind now if we sail— and the Persians were their enemies besides. Their strength consisted in nothing other than the superiority of their navy. The Peloponnesians have never had so little hope of success against us as right now. Even if they were to get up their confidence, they are only strong enough to invade our land— and they could do that whether we set sail or not. No matter what, though, they would not be able to harm us with a fleet, because we would have left enough ships to match theirs.

18. So what plausible argument could we make for pulling back, or what excuse could we give to our allies there for not helping them? No, we must come to their aid because we have given them our oath, and we must not object that they have not come to help us. We didn't become their allies so that they could come to our aid here, but so that they could harry our enemies there and prevent them from coming here to attack us. That is how we and everyone else who ever ruled acquired an empire—by readily coming to the side of whoever called, whether Greek or barbarian. If we were all to sit on our hands, or make distinctions about who to help on the basis of race, we would never add anything to our empire and would actually risk losing it. You don't defend yourself against a power only when it is attacking you; you take steps to prevent it from attacking in the first place. We can't, like bean counters, decide how much empire we want. We must, seeing that we have gone this far, pre-emptively attack some and hold onto the rest, because the danger for us is that if we don't rule over others, they will rule over us.[1] Inaction doesn't mean the same thing for you as it does for others—not unless you change your ways and become like them.

In the certainty that we will increase our power here if we attack our enemies there, let's make this expedition and blow the minds of the Spartans when they see that we scorn the status quo by sailing against Sicily. The chances are that our gains there will make us the rulers of all Greece, or that we will at least damage Syracuse, which will benefit both us and our allies. Our navy will give us security whether things go well and we stay, or decide to leave. After all, we have more sea power than all the Sicilians combined. And don't let Nicias divert you with his do-nothing counsel or with his attempts to set the old against the young. Deliberate as your fathers always did, with old and young together, when they raised the city to its present greatness. In the same way, you must now attempt to raise

---

1. See Pericles' speech at 2.63 for a similar sentiment.

it even higher in the realization that old and young can do nothing without each other, just as any mixture of strong, weak, and average working together is most likely to prevail. Also the city, just like anything else, will start to fall of its own weight if it does nothing. Its skills will start to decline. But if it is constantly competing, it will acquire new skills and get into the habit of taking care of itself through deeds and not words. To sum up, I believe that an active city will be quickly ruined by a change to inactivity. The people who live in the greatest security are the ones who run their governments in keeping with their institutions and their national character, flawed though they may be.

19. That was Alcibiades' speech, and after listening to it and to the speeches of the Egestan and Leontine exiles, who came forward begging them to remember their oaths and beseeching their help, the Athenians were even more eager for the campaign than before. Nicias realized that he could no longer deter them with the same old arguments, but he thought he might still change their minds if he told them what a huge force they would need. So he came before the assembly once again and spoke as follows.

20. My fellow Athenians. I see that you are thoroughly determined to go to war, and I hope everything turns out as we would all wish. I must now tell you what I think about the task ahead. From what I, for my part, hear, we are about to set out against large, independent cities that do not yearn for a change in which they gladly throw off the hard yoke of slavery for a kinder form of government.[2] It's also unlikely that they would accept our rule in exchange for their freedom. And though Sicily is only one island, there are many Greek states on it. Except for Naxos and Catana, which I expect to be on our side because of their kinship with Leontini, there are seven other cities that have forces in every way comparable to our own. This is especially true of our main objectives, Selinus and Syracuse. They have a great many hoplites, archers, and javelin men, as well as many triremes and large populations to man them. They have great private wealth, and there is public wealth at the temples of Selinus. Also, some of the barbarians pay a tithe as tribute to Syracuse. Where they have the greatest advantage over us is in cavalry, of which they have a great many, and in the fact that they grow their own grain and so do not have to import it.[3]

21. Against a force of this size, you need more than just a fleet with a few men. A lot of infantry also needs to sail if we want to achieve our goals and not be hampered in our operations on land by all that cavalry—especially if the cities join forces out of fear of us, and leave us with no friends but the Egestans to supply us with cavalry to match that of the Syracusans. We would be disgraced if we had to leave, or if we had to send for more men later, because our initial plans were sloppy. We have to set out from here with all the men and equipment we need, in the knowledge that we are sailing far from our sources of supply, and that this is not the same thing as going to help our nearby allies against somebody or other, in which case we can easily get what we need from our friends. We are going to be very far away, in enemy country, a place from which a messenger can easily take four months getting here during the winter.

---

2. Democratic Athens could often angle for the support of the common people in campaigns against oligarchic or repressive states. Such support would not be forthcoming in Syracuse, which was also a democracy.

3. Athens, in contrast, did import its grain. Also Syracuse's self-sufficiency made it immune to a naval blockade.

22. In my opinion, we will need a great many hoplites, ours and those of our allies and subjects, and any Peloponnesians we can induce to come by persuasion or payment. We will need a great many archers and slingers with which to oppose the enemy cavalry. We will need naval superiority so that we can easily bring over supplies, and we will need merchant ships to bring food from here—wheat and toasted barley. We will need to draft and pay bakers, with a fair quota for all our mills. Thus if our ships are kept from sailing by a calm, our army will have provisions. It will be large, after all, and not every city will be able to receive it. We will have to prepare everything else as much as possible, so that we won't have to depend on others, and we must take as much money from here as we can, because you must regard the ready money that we are told the Egestans have over there as "ready" in name only.

23. We are planning to go there as a match for them, a match in everything but hoplites, which are their main strength; but even if we were to have complete military superiority, we would just barely be able to conquer them and return home safely. We must think of ourselves as going to found a city among enemies and strangers, where we must control the ground from the first day, for if we do not—and we must understand this— we will be in a wilderness of war. And that is what I am afraid of. We must plan well, and even more, we must be lucky—though luck is hard for us mortals to come by. I want to sail trusting myself as little as possible to luck; I want to sail trusting in all the security our preparations can reasonably offer. This is the best course for our city as a whole and a guarantee of safety for us, your fighting men, and if anyone thinks differently, I hereby offer to resign my command to him.[4]

24. Nicias made this speech thinking that either the Athenians would be deterred by the magnitude of the undertaking, or he would at least set out with maximum safety if he was forced to make the expedition. But the onerousness of the task did not deprive the Athenians of their enthusiasm for the voyage. On the contrary, they embraced it all the more eagerly, and the result was the opposite of what Nicias had expected: the Athenians thought that he had given them good advice. Now, surely, they would be totally safe. Thereupon everyone alike fell madly in love with the expedition: the older men because they thought that it would either conquer Sicily or return unharmed, given its great strength; the elite of military age because they longed to see far away places and broaden their minds, and because they were confident that they would come home safely; the rank and file of soldiers because they thought that they would make money right away and also acquire an empire where they could collect soldiers pay forever. Given this access of enthusiasm in the majority, anyone who disliked the plan held still for fear of being thought unpatriotic if he voted against it.

25. Finally, an Athenian citizen came before the assembly and addressed Nicias directly. The citizen told him to stop delaying and making excuses, and to come up before the whole body and say what forces the Athenian people should vote for him. Nicias reluctantly said that he would prefer to consider the matter, at leisure, with his fellow commanders, but that the way it looked to him at that moment, they had to sail with at least one hundred triremes from Athens itself, of which as many as they thought necessary would be troop transports. They would also have to send for other triremes from the allies. They would

---

4. Nicias offered to resign his command once before, in 425, when Cleon took him up on it. See 4.28.

need no less than five thousand Athenian and allied hoplites—and more, if possible. The rest of the force would be in proportion to these figures: they would need archers from Athens and Crete, and slingers too. If the generals themselves decided that anything else was needed, they would have to get it ready to go.

26. After hearing this, the Athenians immediately voted that the generals should have full powers with respect to the size of the army and the whole expedition, as they thought best for the Athenian people. After the vote, the preparations were begun by sending requisitions to the allies and drawing up lists of the eligible soldiers in Athens. The city had recently recovered from the damage inflicted by the plague and by the first period of continuous war. It had a large, new generation of fighting men, and had been able to amass wealth during the truce, so men and material were readily available. And so the Athenian people made ready for war.

27. Throughout Athens, there are those well-known, square-sectioned stone statues, carved after the custom of the country, called herms. They are very numerous, and one finds them at the doorways of temples and private houses.[5] One night, during the mobilization, the faces of most of these herms were mutilated.[6] No one knew who the perpetrators were, but the Athenians offered large rewards from the public treasury for information leading to them and voted, as well, to give immunity from prosecution to anyone, whether citizen, metic or slave, who came forward with knowledge of any other act of impiety. The Athenians regarded this as a very serious matter: it was thought to be a bad omen for the expedition, an expression of conspirators bent on revolution and the overthrow of the democracy.

28. Some metics and servants gave information, albeit not about the herms. It turned out, though, that there had previously been some mutilations of other statues by young men playing drunken pranks. There had also been irreverent parodies of the mystery religions in private homes, and Alcibiades was implicated in these. The matter was taken up by those who were especially vexed that Alcibiades prevented them from leading the people themselves. They thought that they would be on top if they could get him exiled, and so they exaggerated and decried the profanation of the mysteries and the mutilation of the herms as an assault on "the people" and maintained that none of it could have happened without Alcibiades. They also gave weight to their charges by citing incidents in which his behavior deviated from democratic norms.

29. Everything was now ready for the Sicilian campaign, but Alcibiades denied the charges then and there and said that he was prepared to stand trial before leaving to determine whether he had committed any of these acts. If convicted, he would take his punishment; if acquitted, he would get on with his command. He appealed to them not to entertain any accusations in his absence: if he had done wrong, they should kill him right away. He said that this would be wiser than sending him on such an important command with an accusation of this kind still unresolved. But his enemies feared that if he stood trial then, the army would support him and the civilians would be lenient and protect him, because he had induced the Argives and some of the Mantineans to join in the expedition. So they eagerly sought to avert a trial, planting speech-makers in the assembly to argue that the launch should not be held up and that Alcibiades should sail immediately and come back to Athens for trial within a

---

5. Herms were square pillars with a bearded head of the god Hermes on top and an erect phallus in front. They were thought to bring good luck.
6. Thucydides says that the faces of the statues were mutilated, but the phalluses were probably knocked off as well. See Aristophanes, *Lysistrata*, 1094.

prescribed period. What they wanted was to send for him and try him after his return on a more serious charge, which they were sure they could easily trump up in his absence.

The assembly voted that Alcibiades should sail.

30. It was already midsummer when the ships set sail for Sicily. Most of the allies and the ships and merchantmen carrying food, as well as all the other support craft, had already been ordered to gather at Corcyra, from which the whole fleet would cross the Ionian Gulf to Cape Iapygia; but the Athenians and some allies who were still in Athens went down to the Piraeus at dawn on the day appointed for the launch and began to man their ships.

Almost the whole population of Athens, citizen and alien alike, went down to the sea with them. The citizens came to send off their own—friends, relatives, sons—with hope and sadness, hope of conquering Sicily and sadness because they thought of how far the ships were sailing and wondered whether they would ever see their loved ones again. At that moment, just as they were about to leave each other, they were filled with dread, as they had not been when they voted for the expedition, yet they took heart from the sheer might and plenitude of what they saw.

31. The foreigners and the rest of the crowd came to see the spectacle of the city's typical mind-boggling audacity. For this first armada was the greatest, the most magnificent, and of course the most expensive ever launched by a single Greek city up to that time. The numbers of ships and hoplites were not inferior in the expedition against Epidaurus, under Pericles—the same one that went subsequently against Potidaea, under Hagnon—where there were four thousand Athenian hoplites, three hundred cavalry, and one hundred triremes, along with fifty triremes from Lesbos and Chios and a large contingent of allies.[7] Still, that force set out on a short voyage, with scant equipment and supplies, whereas this one was to go on a lengthy voyage and was much better equipped for action on land and sea, as needed. The ships had been outfitted at great cost to the state and to the trierarchs, the state paying a drachma a day out of the public treasury to each sailor, as well as supplying sixty fast unequipped triremes and forty troop transports along with first-class petty officers. Besides the basic pay from the public funds, the trierarchs supplied extra pay for the petty officers and the rowers on the top benches. They also provided the flags, insignias, and expensive fittings, each trierarch trying to make his ship excel in appearance and speed. As to the infantry, they were chosen from the best lists, and they vied with one another to deck themselves with the best arms and equipment. The result of this rivalry among the men, whatever their rank, was that it all seemed to the other Greeks more like a display of wealth and power than a preparation for war. And if one computed the expense to the city as well as to each soldier—for the city, in what it had already spent and in what it sent off with its generals—and for the men, in what each had spent on himself as well as what each trierarch had spent and would continue to spend on his ship; and if one counted, besides, each man's expenses over and above his wage on such a long campaign, and what each soldier or merchant might take along for trade, it would be found that a vast sum of money indeed was sailing away from Athens. This armada was famous as much for its awe-inspiring daring and visual splendor as for the grandeur of its scale in relation to the forces of the enemy. It was the greatest, longest voyage ever attempted from Athens, and it offered the hope of a huge addition to their empire.

7. See 2.56 and 58.

32. Once the ships were manned and everything was aboard that they planned to take with them, a trumpet sounded the signal for silence. The prayers customary before setting sail were made, not on each ship, but by a single herald speaking for all. Throughout the armada, officers and men mixed wine and water in craters and poured libations from cups of silver and gold. The prayers were joined from the shore by the crowd of citizens and anyone else who wished the men well. After the crews sang the battle hymn and the libations were completed, they put to sea. They rowed out in single file at first, and then they had a race to Aegina. The ships of their allies were gathering at Corcyra, and to Corcyra they then hastened on their way.

Reports of the expedition came to Syracuse from all sides, although nobody believed them for quite some time. Then there was an assembly in which a number of matters were discussed, including the invasion. Some believed the stories of the Athenian armada, others denied its existence, until Hermocrates, son of Hermon, who thought he had accurate intelligence about the subject, came before the assembly. His speech and recommendations were as follows.

33. You may not believe me, any more than the others, in what I am going to tell you about the coming invasion, and I know that those who are not believed, either in their own assertions or in the news they repeat, not only fail to persuade but are thought to be fools besides. But I will not hold back out of fear when our city is in danger, convinced as I am that I speak with more certain knowledge than others. However it may amaze you to hear it, the Athenians are coming to attack you with a large infantry and navy. Their pretext is their alliance with Egesta and the restoration of the Leontines, but the truth is that they want all of Sicily, and especially our city, because they think that if they conquer Syracuse, they will easily be able to take the rest of the island. They will be here soon, so you must consider how we can best defend ourselves with our existing resources. Do not look down on their forces and allow them to catch you off guard, and do not let everything slide because you don't believe they are coming. Whoever does believe this must not be frightened by the boldness and power of Athens. They can't hurt us more than we can hurt them, and their large armada may not be to their advantage. It may be much better for us, when you take the other Sicilians into consideration, because their fear may make them more willing to become our allies. I am not in the least afraid that the Athenians will gain their main objective, but it would be one of our finest achievements if we either defeated them or drove them away empty-handed—and I for one don't think this is too much to hope for. Few of the great armadas—whether Greek or barbarian—have been successful far from home. They can't outnumber the inhabitants and their neighbors, who will all unite out of fear. Also, even if they fail only for lack of supplies in a foreign land and their problems are mostly of their own making, they still confer glory on their intended victims. After the Persian armada so unexpectedly failed, the fame of these very same Athenians grew by leaps and bounds just because the Persians had attacked them, and it is not too much to hope that the same thing will happen to us.

34. So let us confidently prepare the forces we have here. Let us also send envoys to the Sicels, to secure the friendships we already have and to try to forge new friendships and alliances among them. Let us send ambassadors to the rest of Sicily to make clear that this is a threat to all of us, and let us also send ambassadors to Italy to see whether we can make them allies of ours or at least persuade them not to admit the Athenians into their harbors. I think it would also be a good idea to send an embassy to

Carthage. All this won't come as a surprise to the Carthaginians, since they have always been afraid that the Athenians will attack their city. They might decide that they too will be in danger if they turn their backs on us and so be inclined to help us somehow—whether openly or in secret doesn't matter. They are the ones who are most able to help us now, if only they want to. They have more gold and silver than anyone, and that is what sustains war and everything else. Let us also send to Sparta and Corinth, asking them to come here to help us as quickly as possible and also to get the war going over there.

Because of your typical Syracusan indolence, you are very unlikely to move quickly and seize an opportunity that won't last long—but I'll tell you about it anyway. If all Sicilians got together, or most of us anyway, and dragged every available ship into the water, taking two months' pay with us, and sailed out to meet the Athenian fleet at Tarentum and Cape Iapygia, we would show them that before they got to fight for Sicily, they would have to fight to cross the Ionian Gulf. We would stun them with this move and since Tarentum will let us use its harbor, we would make them realize that we would be operating from friendly territory as we guarded the sea lanes. They would see that there is a lot of water for them to cross with all that equipment, and that they would have a hard time staying in formation over the course of a long voyage, making them easy to attack as they approached slowly and a few at a time. If they leave their heavy transports behind and row to the attack with a mass of fast ships, we could fall on them when their oarsmen were tired. If we decide not to do that, we have the option of withdrawing to Tarentum. Since they would have come across with only enough supplies for a naval battle, they would soon run out on the barren shores of Iapygia. If they remained, they would be blockaded, and if they tried to sail down the coast, they would have to leave their support ships behind, whereupon they would become demoralized from not knowing whether the cities on the coast supported them and would receive them into their harbors. As I see it, the realization that they would be intercepted would keep them from leaving Corcyra. They would have to plan strategy and send out spies to see how many of us there were and where, and by that time, their schedule would have been pushed back to winter. Or, astounded by our unexpected move, they might disband the armada—especially since their most experienced general, as I hear tell, has taken his command unwillingly and would gladly see any sizable force of ours as an excuse to call off the expedition. You know perfectly well that reports of our size would be exaggerated, and since people form their opinions according to what they hear, those who strike first or who at least show attackers that they are going to defend themselves will be considered more frightening than before, because the attackers see that they too are in danger. And that is what would happen to the Athenians now. They are coming against us in the belief that we will not defend ourselves, and they are right to despise us, because we did not join the Spartans in trying to destroy them. But if they saw that we had some unexpected boldness in us, they would be more frightened by the surprise than by our true strength.

The best thing for you would be to take my advice and make this bold move; but if not, at least get everything ready for war as quickly as possible. Each and every one of you must understand that although we will show our contempt for the aggressor by our prowess in battle, the best thing we can do now is to act, in the knowledge that the safest preparations are made in the fear of impending danger. I know it for a fact: the enemy is not only coming but has already set sail and will soon be here.

35. That was Hermocrates' speech, and there followed a great deal of wrangling within the popular assembly. Some said that there was no way the Athenians could be coming and that there was no truth whatever in the speech. Others said that even if they did come, there was nothing they could do that couldn't be done to them, and worse. Still others were contemptuous of the whole thing and made a joke of it. Very few indeed believed what Hermocrates had said and feared for the future. Then Athenagoras came before them. He was a leader of the populace, the man most trusted by the majority in this crisis. He spoke as follows.

36. Anyone who does not devoutly wish that the Athenians had made such a crazy plan to come here and put themselves in our power is either a coward or an enemy to the state. It's not the audacity of the people who try to terrify you by spreading these rumors that amazes me, it's their stupidity in not realizing how totally transparent they are. It is they who have reason to be afraid, and they want to throw the city into a panic so that everyone's fear can mask their own. That's what these "reports" mean. They don't refer to anything that's really happening. They've been concocted by men who are always stirring up trouble. If you want to make the right decision, don't try to figure out what will probably happen by scrutinizing what these people are reporting. Look instead at the probable actions of a powerful and widely experienced people, which is how I regard the Athenians. It isn't likely, for example, that they would willingly turn their backs on the Peloponnesians when the war there isn't really over and go away to wage another equally great war—not when, as I see it, they are delighted that we, who have large and powerful cities, do not go and attack *them*.

37. Even if, as these people say, the Athenians really were coming, I believe that Sicily is better able to conduct a war than the Peloponnesians because we are better equipped in every way. Also this city of ours is much more powerful than the army they say is coming—even if it were twice as large. As I understand it, they won't be bringing horses with them, and they won't be able to get any here, except maybe a few from the Egestans. Also, considering that they are coming by sea, they won't have hoplites in numbers to equal ours. After all, it would be hard enough just to bring empty ships here on a voyage of that length. And they are going to have to bring a lot of equipment against a city the size of ours. I would go so far as to say that even if they brought over another city the size of Syracuse, planted it on our border, and made war on us, it would be hard for them to escape total destruction; so how on earth will they survive an all-out war with Sicily (because Sicily *will* unite) when they will be setting up camp from their ships and kept by our cavalry from advancing far beyond their miserable tents and short rations? In a word, I don't think they'll even be able to establish a beachhead. That's how much more powerful I think our forces are than theirs.

38. But as I say, the Athenians are aware of all this, and I am very sure that they are keeping their resources safely at home. But here, and not for the first time, men fabricate events that neither are happening nor will happen. I have always known that they want to panic the majority of you and take over the government themselves, either with speeches like these—or worse than these—or with open action. What I am afraid of is that they will keep trying and finally succeed. We are bad at taking precautions and then pouncing when we know something for sure. We have to actually be in trouble first, and that is exactly why our city is so seldom at peace and al-

ways involved in unrest and strife—as much with our enemies as with ourselves—at times to the point of having tyrannies and unconstitutional
cliques.

If you will only follow me, though, I will do everything in my power
to see that this does not happen in our time, by persuading you, the people, to punish those who are engaged in these machinations—and not
punish them only when we catch them in the act, because we're seldom
so lucky, but also for what they would do if they could. It is imperative to
defend not just against what your enemy actually does, but against his intentions as well, because not taking timely precautions means suffering
untimely grief. As to the upper classes, I would expose them, keep an eye
on them, and re-educate them. That, I think, would be the best way for me
to divert them from their wicked ways.

So come now, you men of the younger generation, tell me something
I have often wondered about. What do you *want*? Is it that you want to govern before your time? But that's against the law, and the law excludes you
not because you are competent, but because you are not. Or maybe it's that
you want to be above the law? But how can it be just for some people to be
given special treatment when we are all the same?

39. Now a person might say that democracy is stupid and unfair, and
that the rich govern best. I would say, first, that "the people" is the name
of the whole and "the elite" is the name of a part. Secondly, the rich are
the best at administering the treasury; the intelligentsia are the best at fram-
ing issues; but the people are best at hearing arguments and making decisions. In a democracy, none of these functions outweighs the other. An
oligarchy, however, spreads risk to the many and doesn't then just take
most of the benefits—it takes them all. That is what the powerful and the
young among you so eagerly desire, but that cannot be had in a great city.

But to this day, you remain the stupidest of men, the most ignorant of
all the Greeks I know, if you do not realize that you are promoting an evil
agenda. Either that, or you are the most immoral, if you do know it and
dare to keep trying.

40. Thus you can either learn or you can repent, and thereby improve the general lot of the city, in the knowledge that in this way you will
get an equal, and the best of you will get a greater, share in things. If you
decide otherwise, though, you run the risk of being stripped of what you
have. So put an end to these false reports, because you are making them
to people who know what you are up to and who are not about to entrust
you with the government. Even if the Athenians are coming, this city of
ours will do itself proud in its own defense. We have generals who will see
to that. And if none of the stories about the Athenians is true, as I believe
to be the case, this city will not have been panicked by your rumors into
choosing you as its leaders and imposing voluntary servitude on itself. It
will look into things for itself. It will judge your words as if they were deeds
and will not be deprived of its foundation of freedom because of mere reports. It will not let you do as you like, but will remain vigilant and take action to ensure its safety.

41. After Athenagoras gave this speech, one of the generals stood up and,
preventing anyone else from coming forward, spoke about the crisis as follows.

There is no point in listening approvingly as people make accusations
against each other. Instead, it would be wise for us to face this news
squarely, so that each of us individually and the city as a whole can best
prepare to fend off the attackers. Even if no action is needed, there can be

no harm in adorning the commonwealth with cavalry, armor, and all the other regalia of war. We, your generals, will undertake a diligent review of our forces. And yes, there should be fact-finding missions to other cities and anything else that seems useful. There are some matters that we have already taken care of; we will bring before you anything else that comes to our attention.

After their general spoke these words, the people of Syracuse dissolved their assembly.

42. The Athenians and all their allies were by now in Corcyra. The first thing the generals did was to review the armada once more and to decide on the order in which the ships were to anchor and the men were to camp. They divided the force into three parts and drew lots to determine each general's command. They did this to avoid sailing all together and risking shortages of water and provisions as they landed in harbors with inadequate anchorage for the whole fleet. Also the ships would keep better formations and be easier to command if they were assigned in divisions to separate generals. They then sent ahead three ships to Italy and Sicily to find out which cities there would accept them into their harbors. They had orders to come back to meet the ships so that they could know where they might land.

43. After making these preparations, the Athenians set out from Corcyra with their great fleet and began to cross the sea to Sicily. They had one hundred thirty four triremes in all, as well as two fifty-oared ships from Rhodes. One hundred of the triremes were from Attica. Sixty of these were fast fighting ships; the rest were troop transports. The rest of the fleet was supplied by Chios and the other allies. In all, there were fifty-one hundred hoplites, of whom fifteen hundred were from the troop list of Athenian citizens, and seven hundred, who served as marines, were from the lowest class of free men. The rest were allies who joined in the campaign, mostly from the subject states, but also five hundred hoplites from Argos and two hundred and fifty Mantinean and other mercenaries. There were four hundred eighty archers in all (the eighty being from Crete) and seven hundred slingers from Rhodes. There were also one hundred and twenty light-armed Megarian exiles, and there was one horse transport carrying thirty horses and their mounts.

44. That was the size of the first fighting force that sailed across to war.[8] It was accompanied by thirty grain transports, which also carried bakers, stonemasons, carpenters, and equipment needed for sieges. Another hundred ships had been pressed into service to sail with the transports, and a great many other vessels of all kinds voluntarily followed the armada to trade on their own. All of them now left Corcyra and together struck out across the Ionian Gulf. The whole fleet reached Cape Iapygia and Tarentum, from which the ships followed their own courses as they sailed along the Italian coast. There the cities refused to allow the Athenians into their markets or within their walls. They did give them anchorage and supply them with water, although Tarentum and Locri would not even do that. Finally, they reached Rhegium, at the toe of Italy. After all the ships had gathered there, the men set up camp at the temple of Artemis outside the city, because they were not allowed in. The Rhegians provided them with a market at the temple, and they rested there after pulling their ships onto the beach. They held talks with the Rhegians, urging them to help the Leontines, since they, like the Leontines, were of Chalcidian origin. The Rhegians, however, said that they would not join forces with outsiders, but would comply

---

8. Athens sent a second fleet of reinforcements to Sicily two years later.

with the collective decision of the other Italian states. The Athenians then considered how best to carry out the assault on Sicily. Meanwhile, they waited for the ships that had sailed on ahead to return from Egesta, so they could find out whether the funds the Egestan envoys had described in Athens were as they had said.[9]

45. By now, the Syracusans were getting clear intelligence from their spies and from elsewhere that the Athenian ships were at Rhegium and now, no longer doubting, they concentrated their full attention on their preparations. They sent garrisons to some Sicel cities and ambassadors to others and also despatched soldiers to man the forts in the countryside. In the city itself, they reviewed their hoplite forces, saw to it that their cavalry was in good condition, and put everything in readiness for the war that was all but upon them.

46. The advance ships from Egesta rejoined the Athenians at Rhegium with the news that the money they had been promised did not exist: it appeared that there were only thirty talents. The generals immediately became dispirited by this news, since this was their first setback—this and the refusal of the Rhegians to join them. For the attempt to win them over was the first step in the campaign, and one that had seemed very likely to succeed, since the Rhegians were kinfolk to the Leontines and had always been friendly to Athens. As to the Egestans, Nicias had always expected as much from them, but it was much harder for the other two generals to understand.[1]

The Egestans had put the following ruse into effect from the moment the Athenian ambassadors first came to Egesta to assess the extent of their wealth. They led the Athenians to the temple of Aphrodite at Eryx and showed them its heaps of votive offerings, and the silver vials, flagons, censers, and other treasures that struck their eyes concealed the underlying poverty of the state. Also, in private receptions for the crews of the triremes, they brought out goblets of gold and silver that they had collected from within Egesta itself and borrowed from neighboring towns, both Greek and Phoenician, but which they presented at these feasts as belonging to the household. They all used the same goblets, for the most part, and they showed so much of these things everywhere that they absolutely awed the Athenian crewmen, who, when they returned to Athens, spread the news about the great wealth they had seen. Those who had been deceived in turn misled others, and they were all held responsible by the troops when word got out that Egesta did not have any money. The generals now had a meeting to decide what to do under the circumstances.

47. Nicias believed that the whole force should sail for Selinus, since that was, after all, their main objective. If the Egestans then supplied enough money to pay for the whole army, they should make decisions accordingly. If not, they should demand support for the sixty ships the Egestans had originally asked for, then stay at Selinus until things were settled between the Selinuntines and the Egestans, either by force or negotiation. Next they should sail along the coast past the other cities and make a display of the power of Athens to show their support for their allies. Then, unless they could quickly help the Leontines or win over one of the cities in some unexpected way, they should return home and not endanger Athens by wasting its resources.

48. Alcibiades said that they must not leave Sicily disgraced and empty-handed, after having sailed away with a force of this size. Instead, they should

---

9. See 6.8. Thucydides seems to have forgotten to mention that these ships, which had been sent ahead to reconnoiter the situation in Italy and Sicily (6.42), were also sent to Egesta.
1. For Nicias' skepticism, see 6.22.

send envoys to all the cities except Syracuse and Selinus and try to befriend some of the Sicels and induce others to break away from Syracuse, thereby obtaining supplies and reinforcements. First, they should try to win over Messana, because that was where ships crossed and landed in Sicily and because it had the best harbor from which their forces could keep an eye on the enemy. Then, when they had won over the cities and knew what side everybody was on, they should launch an attack on Syracuse and Selinus—unless, of course, Selinus was willing to come to terms with Egesta and Syracuse allowed the resettlement of the Leontines.

49. Lamachus said that they should sail straight to Syracuse and have a battle in front of the city as quickly as possible, while the enemy was still unprepared and in the highest state of anxiety. The sudden onset of any army is absolutely terrifying, but if it wastes time coming into sight, people recover their presence of mind and are inclined to be contemptuous when they do see it. But if the Athenians struck suddenly, while the Syracusans were still dreading their arrival, they would have the best chance for victory. The Syracusans would be completely panicked by the sight of their forces (which would look their largest now), by the fear of what would happen to them, and above all by the immediate threat of a battle. Also, a lot of people who didn't believe the Athenians were coming would probably be stuck out in the countryside, so if the army held its position in front of the city, it would not want for booty from the people who would have been trying to bring their possessions inside the city walls. Furthermore, the other Sicilians would be much less inclined to ally themselves with Syracuse and would come over to Athens without waiting to see which side won. Then they should bring their ships to Megara Hyblaea, anchor them there, and make that the base of operations for their fleet. It was deserted, and it wasn't far from Syracuse by either sea or land.

50. Although that was Lamachus' plan, he nevertheless threw his support to Alcibiades. Thereupon Alcibiades sailed over to Messana in his own personal ship and tried unsuccessfully to negotiate an alliance with the Messanians. They told him, however, that although they would not allow the Athenians within the city, they would provide them with a market outside its walls. Then he sailed back to Rhegium. Then, drawing forces from all three divisions, the generals immediately manned and supplied sixty ships and sailed along the coast to Naxos, leaving the rest of the fleet at Rhegium under the command of one of them. The Naxians, for their part, did allow them into their city, after which they sailed along to Catana. When the Catanaeans did not accept them (because there were men there who supported the Syracusan side), they proceeded to the Terias River and camped on its banks for the night. The next day, fifty of the ships sailed in single file for Syracuse. Ten had been sent ahead to the great harbor to see whether any ships had been launched and to proclaim from their own vessels that the Athenians had come, as allies and kinsmen, to resettle the Leontines on their own land, and that any Leontines in Syracuse should leave and join the Athenians as friends and benefactors. After this proclamation had been made, and they had reconnoitered the city and the harbor and the terrain that would serve them best as a base of operations in the war, the Athenians sailed back to Catana.

51. There an assembly was held in which the Catanaeans voted not to allow the army into the city, but did invite the generals in to address the assembly if they wished. Alcibiades spoke, and since everyone in the city had gone to the assembly, the Athenian soldiers slipped into town unnoticed, after breaking through a badly constructed gate, and then took over the agora. When the

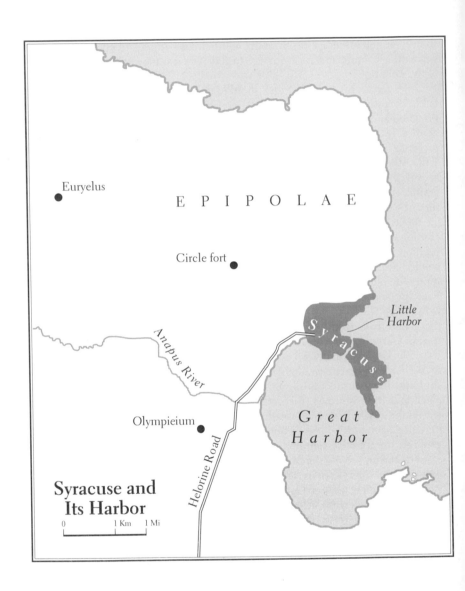

Euryelus

E P I P O L A E

Circle fort

Anapus River

Syracuse

Little
Harbor

Olympieium

Helorine Road

*Great
Harbor*

**Syracuse and
Its Harbor**

0   1 Km   1 Mi

Catanaean supporters of Syracuse saw the army inside the city walls, they immediately panicked, and a few of them even fled the city. The other citizens voted for an alliance with Athens and invited the Athenians to bring over the rest of their army from Rhegium. After this, the Athenians sailed over to Rhegium, from which they set out with their whole force for Catana, where they began to set up camp on their arrival.

52. But then a message came to them from Camarina, saying that if the army went there, the Camarinaeans would go over to them. They were also told that the Syracusans were manning a navy. The first thing they did was to sail along the coast to Syracuse with their whole fleet. Then, when they found no ships being manned, they sailed on to Camarina, where they landed on the beach and despatched a herald to the city. The Camarinaeans, however, would not allow them into the harbor. They said that their treaty bound them to accept one Athenian ship, unless they themselves asked for more.[2] Having met with no success, the fleet sailed away. They then made a landing in Syracusan territory and began to plunder the place, whereupon the Syracusan cavalry came up and killed some of the Athenian light-armed troops who were not with their regiments. After that, the fleet returned to Catana.

53. There they found the *Salaminia*, which had come from Athens to order Alcibiades to return and answer the city's charges against him, and to also bring back some soldiers who, with Alcibiades, were reported to have profaned the mysteries, and others who were said to have mutilated the herms. After the departure of the expedition, the Athenians did not let up their investigation into the actions surrounding the mysteries and the herms. They were led by their suspicions to accept every accusation without regard to the status of informers, and fully trusting the vilest of people, they seized and imprisoned some of their most prominent citizens, in the belief that it was better to conduct a thorough examination and find out what happened than to allow a reputedly honest defendant to escape without being questioned just because some riff-raff had informed on him. After all, the mass of people knew the oral tradition that the tyranny of Peisistratus and his sons had become harsh in the end, and that it had been overthrown by the Spartans and not by Harmodius and themselves. As a result, they lived in constant anxiety and regarded every event with suspicion.

54. The daring action of Aristogeiton and Harmodius was undertaken because of an incident in a love affair, and I will go into it in greater length than I have elsewhere in order to show that none of what the Athenians themselves or any of the other Greeks have to say about the Athenian tyrants or about this particular event is strictly true.[3] Contrary to popular belief, after Peisistratus died of old age while still tyrant,[4] it was his oldest son Hippias, and not Hipparchus, who took control of the government. When Harmodius was in the first bloom of youth, Aristogeiton, a middle-class citizen, became his lover and had sex with him. Then Hipparchus, son of Peisistratus, tried unsuccessfully to seduce Harmodius, and Harmodius complained about it to Aristogeiton. Aristogeiton, being in love, was tormented by this and grew afraid that, given his power, Hipparchus might take Harmodius and rape him. So he immediately formed a conspiracy—within the limits allowed by his social status—to overthrow the

---

2. The Camarinaeans are probably referring to a treaty they made with Laches in 427–25. See 3.86, although Thucydides does not there spell out the terms of the alliance, and 6.75.
3. Thucydides discussed erroneous opinions about the assassination of Hipparchus by Harmodius and Aristogeiton (514 B.C.) in 1.20.
4. In 527.

tyranny. While this was going on, Hipparchus tried again to seduce Harmodius, again without success. Hipparchus, however, did not want to resort to violence, but instead worked underhandedly to besmirch Harmodius without revealing the true reason for it. And indeed Peisistratid rule had not in general been hard on the people as a whole. On the contrary, it had been rather public-spirited. More than other tyrants, these men had been careful to conduct the public business in an intelligent and enlightened way. They only taxed crops at a rate of five percent; they improved the city with fine public works; they won their wars; and they sacrificed at the temples. And aside from making sure that one of their own would always be in office, the city observed, without interference, the laws that had previously been in force. Among those who held the annual eponymous archonship at Athens was Peisistratus, son of Hippias the tyrant. This Peisistratus was named after his grandfather, and during his administration he dedicated the altar to the Twelve Gods in the agora, as well as the altar in the sanctuary of Apollo in the Pythian precinct. Later the Athenians added to the length of the altar in the agora and so covered up the inscription on it. The inscription on the altar in the sanctuary is still faintly visible, however, and says:

THIS MEMORIAL TO HIS ARCHONSHIP PEISISTRATUS SON OF HIPPIAS
HERE DEDICATES IN THE SANCTUARY OF PYTHIAN APOLLO

55. I have more accurate knowledge than anyone of the oral tradition when I maintain that it was Hippias who held the archonship as the oldest son of Peisistratus. But one may also know it from the following. He alone of his legitimate brothers had children. The altar proves this, as does the stele standing on the acropolis of Athens as a testimony against the crimes of the tyrants. No names are inscribed on it for the children of either Thessalus or Hipparchus, whereas there are five for Hippias, whom he had with Myrrhine, daughter of Callias, son of Hyperochides. Now it is likely that the oldest son would marry first. On this same stele, too, he is listed first after his father, and not without reason, since he was the oldest son and succeeded his father as tyrant. Also, if Hipparchus had been archon when he died, I am sure that Hippias would not have been able so easily and quickly to seize power that he could have established himself as tyrant on the very same day. No, it was because of the habitual dread Hippias had instilled in the citizenry and the discipline of his hired bodyguards that he was able to prevail with an ease and assurance that a younger brother who had not been in constant and familiar touch with power would have lacked. What happened was that Hipparchus became a byword because of the unlucky way he died and was later popularly reputed to have been the tyrant.

56. Hipparchus, then, after having been rejected by Harmodius, carried out his plan to humiliate him. Harmodius had a little sister who had been invited by the Peisistratid family to carry a votive basket in one of the religious processions. But then they sent her away, saying that they had never invited her in the first place because of her lowly status. Although Harmodius was angry, Aristogeiton was even more provoked for Harmodius' sake.

They and their co-conspirators had made all the preparations for the assassination. They were only waiting for the great Panathenaic festival, which was the only day when those who were joining in the procession would not attract suspicion for assembling under arms. Harmodius and Aristogeiton were to begin the attack, whereupon the others would immediately come up to take on the bodyguards. For safety, there were not many conspirators, but they hoped that the armed citizenry, though not aware of the plot, would spontaneously join in liberating themselves from tyranny even though a very few were actually initiating the action.

57. When the day of the festival arrived, Hippias was with his bodyguard outside the city wall, in what is known as the Ceramicus[5], setting the order of the marchers in the procession. Harmodius and Aristogeiton, their daggers ready, were advancing to do their deed when they saw one of their co-conspirators chatting familiarly with Hippias, who was, by the way, easily accessible to everyone. Harmodius and Aristogeiton became frightened and thought they had been betrayed and were about to be arrested. They decided that if they could still do it before being taken, they would kill the man who had injured them and because of whom they had risked so much. So they dashed, just the two of them, through the city gates and came on Hipparchus near the part of the Ceramicus known as the temple of the Daughters of Leos. There they jumped him, instantly and without a moment's thought, and with a rage that only a jealous lover and a man stung by insult could feel, they stabbed him repeatedly and killed him. For the moment, Aristogeiton escaped the bodyguards in the confusion of the crowd. He was captured later and died a slow death; Harmodius was killed then and there.

58. Hippias did not go to the scene of the murder when the news was brought to him at the Ceramicus. Instead, he went straight to the armed members of the procession, who were outside the gate and had not yet learned what had happened. Composing his features to conceal his emotions, he pointed out an area to the marchers and ordered them to go there without their armor on. They went, thinking he was going to say something to them; but Hippias had told his guards to collect all their weapons, which enabled him to pull out men he suspected as well as anyone who was carrying a dagger, since it was customary for marchers to carry only spears and shields.

59. The plot, then, resulted from the pangs of love, and the pointless murder from the sudden panic of Harmodius and Aristogeiton. Afterward, the tyranny was harder on the Athenian people. Hippias, fearing for himself, had many of the citizens killed while at the same time looking around for some safe haven in the event of a revolution. Why, after the murder, he, an Athenian, even married his daughter, Archedice, to Aeantides—a Lampsacene and the son of Hippocles, tyrant of Lampsacus—and he did it because he had learned that the family was very influential with King Darius.[6] Archedice's tomb in Lampsacus is inscribed with this epitaph.

> THIS DUST COVERS ARCHEDICE DAUGHTER OF HIPPIAS
> THE GREATEST GREEK OF HIS TIME
> HER FATHER HER HUSBAND HER BROTHERS HER SONS WERE TYRANTS
> YET HER MIND KNEW NO IMMODESTY

Hippias remained tyrant at Athens for three more years. His rule was ended in its fourth year by the Spartans and the Alcmaeonid exiles. He was given safe conduct to Sigeum and from there he went to Aeantides in Lampsacus. From Lampsacus, he went to the court of King Darius, and twenty years later, an old man, he set out with the Persians on the campaign that took them to Marathon.

---

5. The fact that it was originally the potters' section of town gave the Ceramicus its name. It lay partly inside the city walls and partly outside. The state cemetery, where Pericles delivered his funeral oration (2.35–46), was in the Ceramicus.
6. Hippocles, it seems, in effect controlled Lampsacus for Persia.

60. The Athenian people had taken all this very much to heart. Calling to mind the traditions they knew about those events, they were suspicious and harsh toward those who were accused of having taken part in the profanation of the mysteries, and they believed that all those things had been done as part of a conspiracy to institute either an oligarchy or a tyranny.[7] They were so worked up about the affair that they threw many distinguished people in prison. There seemed to be no end to it, and the savagery of the people grew daily as more and more people were arrested. Finally, one of the prisoners[8] who was thought to be most complicitous was persuaded by a fellow inmate to testify to *something*, whether true or not: it would be plausible, one way or the other, since no one, either at the time or later, was able to say anything clear about who had done what. The inmate persuaded him that even if he hadn't actually done it, he should obtain immunity from prosecution and save himself, and at the same time put an end to the prevailing hysteria in the city. Surely his chances to save himself were better if he confessed under immunity than if he continued to deny his guilt and stood trial. Thus he informed on himself and on others in the matter of the mutilation of the herms. It had been intolerable to the public not to know who had been conspiring against them, so they were happy to get what they thought to be the truth. They immediately released the informer and any fellow prisoners he had not named and put the others who had been accused on trial. They killed those who were already in custody and passed a death sentence on those who had fled, offering a monetary reward for their deaths. This resolution of the affair left it impossible to determine whether those who suffered had been justly punished; but, under the circumstances, the city as a whole was the clear beneficiary.

61. Alcibiades' enemies continued to attack him, just as they had done before he sailed, and the Athenians were turning against him in anger. Now that they thought they knew what had happened in the case of the herms, they were more than ever convinced that the profanation of the mysteries — of which Alcibiades had been accused — had been inspired by the same logic, and that he had committed it as part of the same conspiracy against the democracy. And as luck would have it, at the very time the Athenians were in this turmoil, a small Spartan army had come as close as the Isthmus of Corinth, as part of some operations in Boeotia. The people thought the arrival of the Spartans actually had nothing to do with Boeotia, but that it resulted from an agreement the Spartans had made with Alcibiades, and that if they had not acted so quickly on their information and arrested those conspirators, the city would have been betrayed to the Spartans. In fact, there was even a night when they slept with their armor down in the city, in the temple of Theseus.

At around the same time, Alcibiades' friends in Argos were suspected of plotting to overthrow the Argive democracy. As a result, the Athenians brought back the Argive hostages they had been holding on the islands in the Aegean and turned them over to the Argive people for execution.[9] Alcibiades was now held in suspicion everywhere, and the Athenian people, wanting to bring him to trial and kill him, sent the *Salaminia* to Sicily for him and for the others who

---

7. They feared that the upper classes, in showing contempt for popular religion, would also have contempt for popular government.
8. Although Thucydides does not say so, this prisoner was the future orator and politician Andocides (c. 440–c. 390), whose speech *On the Mysteries*, delivered shortly after the end of the war, provides considerable information about the scandals of 415 (although plainly Thucydides is not convinced of Andocides' reliability).
9. See 5.84.

had been named. The ship's officers were ordered to tell him to follow them to Athens and stand trial. They were not, however, to place him under arrest, since the Athenians were concerned about upsetting their own troops and encouraging the enemy. Most of all, they were eager for the Mantinean and Argive troops to stay on, as they believed that it was Alcibiades who had persuaded them to join the expedition. Thus, in his own ship, Alcibiades and the others who had been accused left Sicily in the wake of the *Salaminia*, as though bound for Athens. But when they reached Thurii, they stopped following. Fearful that they were sailing back to a rigged trial, they left the ship and disappeared. The crew of the *Salaminia* searched for Alcibiades and his companions for a while, but they could not find them and sailed for home. Not much later, Alcibiades, now a fugitive, crossed over from Thurii to the Peloponnese by boat. The Athenians passed a sentence of death in absentia on him and the men who were with him.

62. After this, the two remaining Athenian generals in Sicily divided their force in two and drew their commands by lot. Then both divisions set sail for Selinus and Egesta together, wanting, on the one hand, to find out whether the Egestans would give them that money, and on the other, to gather intelligence about the situation in Selinus and about the extent of its differences with Egesta. They sailed along the stretch of Sicilian coast facing the Tyrrhenian Gulf, keeping the shore on their left, and stopped at Himera, the only Greek city in this part of Sicily. When the Himerans would not accept them, they continued sailing along the coast. On the way, they captured the coastal stronghold of Hyccara, which though Sicanian was hostile to Egesta. After enslaving the population, they turned the town over to the Egestans, whose cavalry had joined them. Then the troops made their way on foot through Sicel territory until they reached Catana, while their ships sailed around the coast carrying their cargo of slaves. Nicias, however, had sailed directly from Hyccara to Egesta. After settling their business and collecting the thirty talents, he returned to the fleet. They sold the slaves, from whom they made one hundred and twenty talents. Next they sailed around to the allies they had among the Sicels and asked them for troops. Then, with half the fleet, they attacked the hostile city of Hybla, in Gela, although they did not take it. And so the summer came to an end.

63. As soon as winter began, the Athenians readied their assault on Syracuse, and the Syracusans, for their part, prepared to attack the Athenians. After the Athenians had failed to attack immediately, as the Syracusans had initially feared and dreaded, the confidence of the Syracusans grew with every passing day. Next the Athenians seemed to put distance between them by sailing off to the far side of the island; and then, when the Athenians tried and failed to take Hybla by storm, the Syracusans despised them all the more and, as is the way of the masses once they gain confidence, insisted that since the Athenians would not come to them, their generals should lead them against Catana. Even the cavalrymen who were constantly being sent out from Syracuse to scout the Athenian camp taunted them, asking whether they had traveled abroad to restore the Leontines to their land or to live with the Syracusans themselves!

64. The Athenian generals, aware of this attitude, wanted to draw the entire Syracusan army as far out of the city as possible. Then they would sail along the coast by night and, unhindered, establish a beachhead on strong ground. They were well aware how much harder it would be, even with such a fleet as theirs, to make a landing against forces who were waiting for them or to try to march overland amidst an enemy who knew where they were. They had no cavalry, and the numerous Syracusan cavalry could badly hurt their infantry and

light-armed troops. Thus they wanted to take up a position where the cavalry could not seriously injure them; and some Syracusan exiles who were with them pointed out a spot near the temple of the Olympian Zeus that they eventually occupied.

The generals implemented the following plan to achieve their aim. They sent to Syracuse a man they fully trusted, but whom the Syracusan generals thought to be their friend. This man was from Catana, and he said that he had come from supporters there whose names were known to them, and whom they knew to be still in the city.[1] He told them that the Athenians slept in Catana every night away from camp and without their weapons, and that if the Syracusans were to attack the Athenian camp at dawn on a prearranged day, and in full force, he and his friends would lock the Athenians inside the city and set their ships on fire. The Syracusans could then easily attack the camp and capture the stockade. Many Catanaeans were in on this; they were ready; he had come from them.

65. In the confident mood induced by all the other events, independently of the information this man brought, the Syracusan generals had been making plans to attack Catana, so they were now much less wary of him than they should have been. They immediately set a day that they would come, and sent him back. By now, their allies from Selinus and some from elsewhere had arrived in Syracuse, and the generals put the Syracusan army on notice that it would be marching out in full strength. When everything was ready and the appointed day drew near, they set out for Catana, spending the night on the Symaethus River in Leontine territory. When the Athenians learned that they were on the march, they put their whole army and whatever Sicels and others were with them aboard their warships and other craft, and sailed away to Syracuse under cover of darkness. At dawn, the Athenians landed opposite the temple of Olympian Zeus, where they intended to set up their camp. Meanwhile, the Syracusan cavalry, which had ridden to Catana first, was finding out that the whole armada had put to sea. They wheeled around to give the news to the infantry, whereupon they all turned back to go to the defense of their city.

66. The Syracusans had a long way to go, so the Athenians were able, unhindered, to set up their camp on strong ground where they could fight whenever they chose with the least harm from the Syracusan cavalry either before or during a battle, because the cavalry would be kept off by walls, houses, trees, and a marsh on one side and cliffs on the other. They also cut down nearby trees, brought them down to the beach, and fixed them in the sand to fence in their ships. At Dascon, where the enemy had the best access to them, they quickly built a barricade with wood and whatever stones were ready to hand. They also tore down the bridge over the Anapus River. No one came out of the city to try to stop them while they were making these preparation. The first defensive force to come up was the Syracusan cavalry; later the whole infantry assembled. At first, they advanced close to the Athenian camp, but when the Athenians did not come forward to engage them, they withdrew across the road to Helorus and camped for the night.

67. The next day, the Athenians and their allies prepared for battle and took up positions as follows. The Argives and the Mantineans were on the right wing, the Athenians in the middle, and the other allies were on the left. The half of the army that was in the forward position was arrayed eight deep. The other half was also arrayed eight deep, near where they had slept, in a hollow

---

1. Catana had gone over to the Athenians and supporters of Syracuse had fled the city. See 6.51.

rectangle. Their orders were to keep a lookout and come up to support the sections of the line that were having the worst of it. The camp followers were in the center of the rectangle.

The Syracusans were in full strength, accompanied by such allied forces as had come to help them. These consisted mostly of the Selinuntines, of Geloan cavalry, two hundred in all, and of twenty cavalry and fifty archers from Camarina. The whole Syracusan hoplite force was lined up sixteen deep. No less than twelve hundred cavalry were on the right, and next to them were the javelin men. Since the Athenians intended to initiate the battle, Nicias went back and forth before each of the nationalities and spoke to all the men. What he said was as follows.

68. There is no point in making a long speech, men. We are all here to fight the same battle. It seems to me that this armada is better able to give you confidence than any fine speeches made with a weak fighting force behind you. We are Argives, Mantineans, Athenians, and the best of the islanders! How can we not have the highest hopes for victory when we have so many and such fine allies on our side? Especially when we are fighting a militia that is on the defensive, and not a picked army like ourselves. And besides, they're *Sicilians!* They can look down on us, but they can't stand up to us, because their knowledge of warfare isn't equal to their bravado. And let every one of you remember this: we are far from home, on enemy soil, and we will not conquer it unless we fight for it. What I am telling you is the opposite of what I know the enemy commanders are telling their men. They are saying, "This fight is for the fatherland!" I am telling you that you are not in your fatherland, and that it will not be easy to leave here except as conquerors, because if you try to retreat, all that cavalry will be right on top of you. Remember who you are, and attack the enemy gamely; and think of the fact that you are isolated and up against it as even more frightening than the enemy.

69. Nicias led his men forward immediately after making this speech. The Syracusans were not expecting to be fighting just then, and some of them had even gone back into the city, which was nearby, so that although they hurried back on the run, they arrived late and took up positions wherever they happened to reach the main body. They lacked neither enthusiasm nor boldness either in this particular battle or in those to come. For so long as they could count on their military skills, they were no less courageous than the Athenians, but when these failed them, they also lost their will. Now, though never expecting that the Athenians would attack first, and though forced to mount a hurried defense, they immediately took up their arms and went to meet the advancing enemy.

First the stonethrowers, slingers, and archers on both sides skirmished in front of the armies, advancing and retreating as is usual for light-armed troops. Then the soothsayers brought up the customary sacrificial animals, and the trumpeters sounded to urge the hoplites into combat, and on they marched, the Syracusans fighting for their fatherland and to save, each man, his own life now and his freedom in the future; and on the other side, the Athenians to make a foreign land their own and to spare their country a defeat; the Argives and the independent allies to share with the Athenians in the riches for which they had come and to return victorious to see their homelands once again. As for the Athenian subjects, they wished mostly for their own immediate preservation, which they had no hope for if they did not win. Also in their minds was the thought that if they helped the Athenians to make this conquest, their own yoke would be easier to bear.

70. After the men came to hand-to-hand combat, they held their ground against each other for a long time. During the battle, there happened to be some thunder and lightning and a heavy rain, and this added to the terror of the men who were least familiar with warfare and were going into combat for the first time. The more experienced men understood that this was normal weather for the time of year and were much more amazed that their opponents did not give up in defeat. It was the Argives who first pushed through the left wing of the Syracusan line, and then the Athenians broke through in the middle. Then the rest of the Syracusan line collapsed and the men started running away. The Athenians did not pursue them very far, held back by the numerous, still-unbeaten Syracusan cavalry, which fell on any Athenian hoplites they saw out of line ahead of the others. Nevertheless, the Athenians pursued the enemy as far as they safely could in formation and then turned back and set up a victory marker. The Syracusans gathered on the road to Helorus and regrouped as best they could under the circumstances. They were still able, however, to dispatch a garrison of Syracusan troops to the temple of the Olympian Zeus, fearful that the Athenians would remove the money that was deposited there. Then the rest of the men retreated into the city.

71. The Athenians did not, however, go to the temple. Instead, they gathered up their dead, burned them on a funeral pyre, and spent the night where they were. The next day, under a truce, they gave the Syracusans back their dead. (Over two hundred and sixty Syracusans and their allies had been killed, as opposed to fifty Athenians and their allies.) Then they collected the bones of their dead from the pyre, and with the weapons they had stripped from the enemy dead, they sailed back to Catana. They left because winter weather had set in, and because they decided that they could not prosecute the war at Syracuse itself until they could get horses from Athens and collect some from their Sicilian allies, so as not to be so totally outnumbered in cavalry. Money would also have to be obtained in Sicily and brought from Athens. They hoped too that after the battle, some of the cities would be more inclined to listen to them, and that these could be brought over to their side. They would also have to make other needed preparations, including stocking up on grain, in order to carry out an attack on Syracuse in the spring.

72. With these thoughts in mind, then, they sailed away to spend the winter in Naxos and Catana. The Syracusans, for their part, buried their dead and called an assembly. Hermocrates, son of Hermon, came before them. He was a man of unparalleled intelligence, more than adequate experience of war, and conspicuous bravery, and he rallied the Syracusans, refusing to let them give in to the events that had befallen them. Their resolve had not been defeated; it was their lack of training that had hurt them. And besides, they had not come up as short as you might have expected, especially since they had been fighting the most experienced soldiers in Greece—unskilled workers against craftsmen, so to speak. They had also been hurt by their large number of generals. They had fifteen of them, resulting in a multiplication of authority. The more people giving orders, the more disorder and confusion. Hermocrates said that they would have a very good chance of defeating their enemies if they had a few experienced generals training their hoplite force during the winter, giving armor to those who did not have it to maximize the number of hoplites, and requiring these men to train also. They had courage. To that would be added disciplined action. And both these things would improve together: discipline by being exercised in a situation of real danger, and courage on its own, ever more confident in sure-handed skill. Thus the generals they elected must be few, and they

must be given discretionary power and solemnly promised that they would be allowed to command to the best of their ability. In this way, secrets would be more tightly kept, and all their preparations would be made in good order and with full accountability.

73. The people of Syracuse heard Hermocrates out, voted for everything he asked for, and then elected Heracleides, son of Lysimachus; Sicanus, son of Execestes; and Hermocrates himself as their three sole commanding generals. They also sent ambassadors to Corinth and Sparta to get an allied force to come to their support, and to urge the Spartans to prosecute the war with Athens more vigorously and more openly and to do so on their behalf. In this way, the Spartans would either draw Athenians away from the Sicilian campaign or prevent them from sending more support to the army in Sicily.

74. The Athenian armada, now at Catana, soon sailed against Messana, which was to have been betrayed into their hands, but although the betrayal had been planned, it did not take place. The reason was that Alcibiades, already recalled from his command and knowing that he would go into exile, gave information to the supporters of Syracuse in Messana about what he knew to be afoot. These men, who had by now killed the conspirators, formed an armed band and compelled the city to reject the Athenians. The Athenians waited outside the city for about two weeks, but the weather was wintry, they were running out of supplies, and nothing was happening, so they sailed away to Naxos. There they fixed a perimeter around their camp, built a palisade, and prepared to spend the winter. They also sent a trireme to Athens to ask that cavalry and money be sent by spring.

75. The Syracusans spent the winter fortifying their city. To make it difficult to wall them in at close quarters in case of defeat, they included the temple of Apollo Temenites inside a wall that adjoined the city and that faced the whole length of Epipolae. They built one fort at Megara Hyblaea, another at the temple of the Olympian Zeus, and fixed stakes at landing sites all along the beach. Also, knowing that the Athenians were spending the winter at Naxos, they marched in full strength into the territory of Catana, where they slashed and burned the ground, set fire to the Athenian camp and its shacks, and then returned home. Then the Syracusans learned that Athenian ambassadors were in Camarina, to see whether they could use the alliance Camarina had made with Laches as a basis to win them over, so they sent ambassadors of their own to try to prevent it.[2] They suspected that the Camarinaeans had been less than enthusiastic in sending what troops they did to the first battle, and that, in view of the Athenian victory in that battle, they might be induced to go over to the Athenians' side on the strength of their former friendship and refuse to help in the future. The Syracusans sent a delegation headed by Hermocrates, and the Athenians sent a delegation headed by Euphemus. The Camarinaeans called an assembly, and Hermocrates, wanting to turn sentiment against the Athenians, spoke as follows.

76. Citizens of Camarina. We have not come on this mission for fear that you will be panic-stricken by the forces the Athenians have brought here, but for fear that you might be won over by the arguments they are going to make before you listened to ours. You know their pretexts for coming to Sicily, but we all have a sneaking suspicion of their true plans, and it seems to me, for one, that they don't want to resettle the Leontines so much as they want to unsettle us. It just doesn't make sense for them to

2. See 6.52.

desolate cities in their part of the world and to restore them here, or to care so much about the Leontines' kinship with the Chalcidians, when what they have done with the Chalcidians in Euboea, of whom the Leontines are colonists, is to hold them in subjection![3] And the way they hold them there is the way they now want to hold us here. They gained their pre-eminence with the consent of the Ionians and their allies of Athenian origin in order to take reprisals against the Persians, but then they subjected them, some for failure to supply troops, some for attacking each other, and some for whatever plausible accusation they could bring in each case.[4] So it turns out that Athens did not fight Persia for the liberty of Greece, and the Greeks did not do it for their own: for Athens, it was about enslaving Greece to itself rather than to Persia; for the Greeks, it was about changing to a master no less clever, just more malicious.

77. But the Athenian state is easy to blame, and we have not come to expose its injustices to those who already know them. Rather it is we Sicilians who are much more to be blamed, because we have the example of how the Greeks of the Aegean were enslaved by not defending each other. And yet now, when they give us this doubletalk about resettling Leontine kin and aiding their Egestan allies, we are disinclined to come together to show them clearly that we're not Ionians here, or islanders, or the people of the Hellespont, who are always changing masters and enslaving themselves to Persians or whoever. No, we are free men of Dorian blood, come to dwell in Sicily from the self-governing states of the Peloponnese. So then. Are we going to wait until we are conquered, one city at a time, knowing that this is the only way we can be taken, and seeing clearly that the way they are doing it is to divide some of us with specious arguments, or to promote conflict between others who hope for an alliance, or, when they have the power to do harm in a given case, to say something kind instead? Do we really think that the danger will not come to us after a distant neighbor is destroyed, and that when someone suffers before we do his hard luck is his alone?

78. So if anyone thinks that the Syracusan, and not he, is the enemy of Athens, or is outraged at the idea of endangering himself on behalf of my country, let him take this to heart: he would not be fighting for my country as much as for his own. Fighting on my soil is the same as fighting on his, and he will be that much safer if I am not destroyed first, because he will have me for an ally and not have to struggle alone. Let him also reflect that the Athenians do not just want to punish our hatred for them, they also want to use their attack on us as a way to force you into "friendship." And if anyone, out of resentment or fear (for great powers are the objects of both) wants Syracuse to be chastened and taught a lesson in humility while he survives in the hope that he will be safe, why then he is not wishing for anything within the scope of human calculation. It is not possible for a man to regulate time and tide in accordance with his wishes. And if he errs, he may well come to lament his own ills so much that he could wish to envy my good fortune once again. But that will be impossible after he abandons me and refuses to fight the danger because of what it seems to be, when he should be fighting it because of what it is. In appearance, you would be saving us; in reality, you would be saving yourselves. You Camarinaeans, who are on our border and are next in danger,

---

3. The desolated cities are undoubtedly Aegina (2.27), Potidaea (2.70), and of course Melos (5.116), although there were others. See 1.114 and 5.32. As to Chalcis, it had revolted from Athens and was subsequently reduced to subject status.
4. For the formation of the Delian League, see 1.95–97.

should have foreseen this and come to our side, instead of fighting with us reluctantly, as you do now. If the Athenians had gone against Camarina first, you would have appealed to us for help; by the same token, you should now be exhorting us never to surrender. But so far neither you nor any of the other Sicilians seems in any hurry to do this.

79. Perhaps you will adopt a legalistic standpoint towards us and the invaders out of cowardice, and say that you have an alliance with the Athenians, even though you did not make that alliance against your friends, but against the possibility that one of your enemies might attack you. You are also to help the Athenians when they are wronged by others and not, as now, when they are doing wrong to your neighbors. Why, even the Rhegians, who are Chalcidians, refuse to join in the restoration of the Chalcidian Leontines. It would be a terrible thing if the Rhegians refrained from an aggression they could justify because they surmised the reality behind the specious claims of the Athenians, while you use a plausible excuse to help your natural enemies and to destroy your kinsmen in company with their most hated foes. This is not right. Our natural claim is stronger. You must help us, and you must not fear this armada of theirs, because it isn't frightening if we all stand shoulder to shoulder, but only if we are divided, which is what these Athenians so eagerly desire. After all, even when they came up against us alone and defeated us in battle, they did not achieve their objective and quickly withdrew.

80. Thus there is no reason to lose heart if we are united, and you can join forces with us all the more confidently, since help is coming from the Peloponnesians, who are altogether better at warfare than these Athenians. And don't let the idea that you can be neutral because you are allied to both of us seem like a just policy toward us and a safe one for you, because it won't work out as justly in practice as it does in theory. If the aggressor prevails and the victim perishes because of your refusal to join the fight, then surely you, by your abstention, will have done nothing either to protect and save the victim or to restrain the aggressor from his crimes. It would be much nobler to stand by your injured kinsmen and thereby both safeguard the common good of Sicily and prevent the Athenians, who say they are your friends, from going astray.

In summary, we Syracusans say that there is no need to lecture either you or the others here on what you know as well as we. We are here to implore you, not to lecture you. But if we fail to persuade you, we also call the gods to witness that we are being victimized by people of the Ionian race—our eternal enemies—and that we, who are Dorian, are being betrayed by you, who are also Dorian. If the Athenians conquer us, they will have been victorious because of your decision, and although they will take the glory in their own name, their prize will be none other than those through whom they gained their victory. If, however, it is we who prevail, it will be you, the reason for our peril, who will endure our vengeance. So think it over, and choose between safe, instantaneous slavery, and, if you help us to survive, the rejection of a disgraceful subservience and the avoidance of our hatred, which will be long-lasting.

81. That was the speech of Hermocrates. After him, Euphemus, the Athenian ambassador, spoke as follows.

82. We came here to renew our original alliance, but since the Syracusans have attacked us, I am compelled to defend our right to our empire. Hermocrates himself gave the best testimony on our behalf when he said that the Ionians and the Dorians are eternal enemies. And so they are.

We who are Ionians were always looking for ways to avoid answering to the Peloponnesians, who are Dorian, who outnumber us, and who live nearby; and after the Persian Wars, in possession of our fleet, we rid ourselves of Spartan rule and leadership. They had no more right to give orders to us than we to them, except to the extent that they had more power at the time. We took control over, and still govern, those who had formerly been subject to the Persian King, and we do so in the belief that the forces they give us to defend ourselves make it less likely that we will be dependent on the Peloponnese. And as to the legalities of the matter, we did not unjustly trample down the Ionians and the islanders who, according to the Syracusans, are our enslaved kinsmen. After all, they joined the Persians in attacking us, their mother city. They did not have the courage to revolt and lose their homes, as we did when we abandoned our city. No, they willingly accepted slavery and were willing to impose the same on us.

83. But we rule instead. First, because we deserve to. We put the largest fleet and the most unflinching will at the service of Greece, and while we did so, our subjects put themselves at the service of the Persians and attacked us. Secondly, because we sought power to counterbalance the Peloponnesians. We won't use fine phrases and say that it is right and proper for us to rule because we alone brought the barbarian low, or that we put ourselves in danger for the freedom of our allies, when in reality we did it for everyone, including ourselves. After all, no one can be blamed for providing for his own safety. Indeed, we are here now for reasons of security, and we can see that this fact is also to your advantage, as we will show from the very slanders of the Syracusans and from your own overwrought fears.

We know that people in a state of panicky suspicion like to hear speeches that accord with their mood; but when it comes time to act, they do what is in their interest.

84. We have already said that we hold onto our empire at home out of fear. We now tell you that the same fear is why we have come to work with our friends to guarantee our security in Sicily—not by enslaving you, but by keeping you from being enslaved. Let no one suppose that your well-being is none of our business, for you must be aware that if you are secure and have the strength to stand up to Syracuse, they will be less able to send a force to the Peloponnesians with which to do us harm. You are, to this extent, very much our business. Likewise, it makes sense for us to restore the Leontines, not to be our subjects like their kinsmen in Euboea, but to be as powerful as possible, so that they can operate from their territory on the borders of Syracuse and harass them on our behalf. We are a match for our enemies at home, and one reason is the Chalcidians. The Syracusans say that it is preposterous for us to be subjecting them there and liberating them here. But it is to our advantage to keep them disarmed there, and only paying tribute, and it is to our advantage that the Leontines and our other friends here be as independent as possible.

85. Nothing expedient is pointless, either to an individual tyrant or to a city with an empire, and no one is a kinsman who cannot be trusted. One makes enemies or friends on each issue according to circumstances. What benefits us here in Sicily is not to injure our friends, but to use their strength to neutralize our enemies. You must not doubt this. After all, we govern our allies back home so as to make the best use of what they have to offer. The Chians and Methymnians are self-governing and furnish us with ships; many others need to be coerced into paying tribute; still others, though they are islanders and we could easily conquer them, are allies of

their own free will, and are valuable to us because they are conveniently located around the Peloponnese. And so now it makes sense for us to establish a position here, for our own profit and because of the fear of Syracuse of which we spoke. The fact is that the Syracusans aim to rule over you. First they want to arouse your suspicions and unite you against us; then they want to take over Sicily, either by force or by exploiting your isolation after we fail to achieve our objectives and go away. This is inevitable if you take their side. We will not have enough strength to deal with you if you unite, and they will be too strong for you after we are gone.

86. If anyone thinks otherwise, the facts refute him, because when you originally invited us here, you tried to frighten us with the argument that we would eventually be in danger if we stood by and watched you fall to Syracuse.[5] It's not fair now to distrust the same argument you used to persuade us then. Nor should we be under suspicion because, in order to match their power, we have brought a larger force than before. The Syracusans are much more deserving of your suspicion. After all, we cannot stay here without your help, and even if we were to be so base as to embark on conquest, we would not be able to hold on to our gains because of the length of the voyage here and the impossibility of policing such large cities that, though they are on an island, have the resources of cities on the mainland. The Syracusans, on the other hand, do not live in a military encampment, but in a city far larger than the force we have here now. They never miss a chance to carry out the schemes they are constantly forming against you, as their treatment of the Leontines, among other things, makes clear. And now they have the audacity to call on you, as if you were numbskulls, to oppose those who have so far held them off and kept Sicily from falling under their control! We, for our part, call you to a far more trusty security, since it is essential for us that the security arrangements between us not be violated by either side. You must realize that the Syracusans, because of their numbers, will always be prepared to take the road against you, even without allies; and you must understand that you will not often be given the opportunity to defend yourselves with the help of such a large armada as this. If, because of your suspicions, you let it go away unsuccessful or even in defeat, it will not be here to help you when the time comes that you yearn to see even a small part of it again.

87. So do not, you Camarinaeans, or any of the rest of you, be influenced by the slanders of the Syracusans. We have told you the whole truth about the things that have made you suspect us. It remains to refresh your memories with a summary that we think you will find convincing. We assert that we have an empire at home and need not answer to anybody, and that we want to liberate you here so as not to be harmed by Syracuse. We are forced to be activists because we have a lot to protect. We are here now, as we were in the past, as allies of those of you who were victims of aggression, and we did not come unbidden: you invited us. Do not sit in judgment of our actions or try to make us cease and desist with a slap on the wrist. That would be pretty hard to do! Instead, take our activism and our Athenian ways and make use of them to the extent that they are also in your interests, and be aware that our behavior has not harmed all alike; most Greeks have actually benefited from it—everyone, everywhere, even outside our sphere of influence. Those who think they are going to be attacked have the solid hope that they will obtain help from us to match their op-

---

5. Camarina was one of the allies of the Leontines who asked Athens for help in 427. See 3.86.

ponents, while those who have designs on others can expect that their enterprise will not be risk-free if we come in. The aggressor has to think twice, whether he likes it or not, and the intended victim will be kept safe without having to do very much. Do not now, therefore, reject this general security, which has been available to others who have needed it, as it is to you now. Instead, stand in a united front with us against the Syracusans, and change from always having to guard against them to posing some dangers of your own.

88. That was the speech of Euphemus. The problem of the Camarinaeans was as follows. The proximity of the Syracusans had always been a source of friction, and they were inclined toward the Athenians, except to the extent that they feared that the Athenians wanted to subject Sicily. Nevertheless, they were very afraid that the nearby Syracusans might win out without their help, which was why they had originally sent that small contingent of cavalry. They therefore decided that they would, as time went by, give real support to Syracuse, although they would keep it as modest as possible. For the time being, however, since they didn't want to appear to do less for the Athenians, who had after all come out on top in the recent battle, they would give each side the same answer. After reaching this decision, they announced that since they happened to be allied to two parties who were at war with each other, the best way to honor their oaths of alliance, under the circumstances, was to render aid to neither side. Thereupon the ambassadors of both sides left.

The Syracusans continued to prepare their territory for war. The Athenians, who were camped in Naxos, carried on negotiations with the Sicels to bring as many of them as possible over to their side. The Sicels who lived in the plains were subject to Syracuse, for the most part, and not many revolted, but the inland settlements had always been autonomous, and with few exceptions, they immediately joined the Athenians, bringing food and in some cases money down to the beach for the army. The Athenians made war on those who would not come over, and although they forced some into service, the Syracusans sent garrisons to the rescue and prevented them from doing this to others. During the winter, the Athenians changed anchorage from Naxos to Catana, rebuilt the camp that the Syracusans had burned down, and spent the rest of the winter there. They sent a trireme to Carthage on a mission of friendship, to see whether the Carthaginians would give them any help, and they also sent a ship to Tyrrhenia, where there were some cities that had volunteered to join them in the fighting. In addition, they sent messengers to the Sicels and to Egesta, ordering them to send as much cavalry as possible. They also readied iron, wooden frames for making bricks, and everything else they needed for their siege wall, with the intention of resuming the war in earnest at the beginning of the spring.

The Syracusan ambassadors who had been sent to Corinth and Sparta also stopped at towns along the Italian coast and tried to persuade these people to not just stand by and watch what the Athenians were doing, arguing that these actions were also directed at them. When they reached Corinth, they delivered speeches demanding help on the basis of their kinship.[6] The Corinthians voted to help them with all their might. They were the first to do so, and they did it on their own initiative. They also sent along ambassadors of their own to Sparta, to join the Syracusans in trying to persuade the Spartans to prosecute the war against Athens more openly in Greece and to send some sort of aid to Sicily.

---

6. Syracuse was a Corinthian colony. See 6.3.

Not only the ambassadors from Corinth were in Sparta. Alcibiades and his fellow exiles were there as well. The first thing he had done was to go straight across from Thurii to Cyllene, in Elis, aboard a merchant ship. Then he went to Sparta under a safe conduct after the Spartans themselves had sent for them: he wanted the safe conduct because he feared the Spartans on account of the business in Mantinea.[7] At the assembly in Sparta, it turned out that Alcibiades and the ambassadors from Corinth and Syracuse had all come to urge the Spartans to do the same thing. The ephors and other authorities were inclined to send ambassadors to Syracuse to try to prevent them from coming to terms with the Athenians, but they were not eager to send help. But then Alcibiades came forward and provoked the Spartans to action with the following words.

89. First, I must speak to you about the allegations made against me, so that suspicion doesn't make you unwilling to heed what I have to say about our common concerns. It is true that my ancestors gave up the hereditary office of Spartan proxenus because of accusations that had been made against them. I, however, resumed that office, and put myself at your service in many ways, especially after the disaster at Pylos.[8] I never stopped supporting you, but when you negotiated the peace with Athens, you worked through my enemies, conferring power on them and disgrace on me. Thus it served you right if you were harmed when I tilted towards Argos and Mantinea and opposed you in other ways, and now is the time for anyone who was unjustifiably angry at me over what you suffered then to face the truth and think again. Also, if anyone thought less of me because of my devotion to the common people, he has to admit that he had no right to be aggrieved on that account, either. My family has always been opposed to tyranny. "The people" is the byword for everything opposed to tyranny, and it is because of our opposition that leadership of the people has been a family tradition. Besides, the city has a democratic government, and by and large, we had to conform to the situation. Nevertheless, we did try to remain politically moderate amid the prevailing extremism. In the past, as well as now, it has been others who have taken the people down to the lowest common denominator. Why, they are the ones who exiled me! We were the leaders of *all* the people, believing that we should help preserve the government under which our city was most powerful and most independent, the government we had inherited, since those of us who had any sense knew the power of the people for what it was, and as I would come to know it more than anyone, I who have been wronged by it and who have the right to abuse it. But nothing new can be said about what everybody agrees is an absurd form of government. In any case, we decided that it would be unsafe to change it while enemies like you were perched nearby.

90. So much for the allegations against me. Now you need to know whatever confidential information I have about the matter before you. The reasons we went to Sicily were: first, to conquer it if we could; next, to conquer the Italians too; then, to attack the Carthaginian empire and Carthage itself. If we succeeded in whole or in part, the plan was to then launch an attack on the Peloponnese, bringing along all the Greek forces we would have acquired in Sicily and Italy, and hiring hordes of mercenary barbarians—Iberians and others in those parts who are generally agreed to be the most warlike savages in the world right now. We would add to our fleet of triremes many ships built with the boundless timber of

7. See 6.16.
8. See 5.43.

Italy, and we would use them to throw a naval blockade around the Peloponnese while our infantry attacked your cities by land, taking some by storm and others after building fortresses in their vicinity. We fully expected to win this war of attrition easily and to go on afterward to rule over the whole Greek world. The money and foodstuffs that our newly acquired territory in the west would supply in abundance would make all this easier to do, quite apart from the revenue provided by our empire in the Aegean.

91. So you have heard, from the man who knows them best, what our intentions were for the armada that is now on the move. If they can, the generals who remain will carry them out to the letter. Now know this: the Sicilians will not be able to win if you do not help them. They might survive, even now and despite their inexperience, if they could only join forces. But the Syracusans are alone, already defeated in a battle they fought in full strength, and blockaded by sea to boot. They will not be able to hold out against the Athenian forces that are now there. And if Syracuse is taken, Athens will have all of Sicily, and very quickly Italy too. It wouldn't be long before the danger I just foretold from that region was upon you. So let no one think that he is deliberating only about Sicily, because this situation will also affect the Peloponnese unless you do the following things. You must send an armed force to Syracuse on a ship whose rowers are also soldiers and who will be prepared to fight immediately. And, even more important than the soldiers in my opinion, you must send a Spartan officer, a man who will be able to train the Syracusan soldiers who are present and accounted for and conscript the men who have not volunteered. That way, the friends you already have will be all the more encouraged, while those who are wavering will be less afraid to come forward. Also you must openly push the war here and force the Athenians to respond, so that the Syracusans, knowing you care about them, will put up an even stiffer resistance, and so that the Athenians will be less able to send reinforcements to their men in Sicily. In addition, you must build a fort in Decelea, in Attica, which is something the Athenians have always been afraid you would do. They think that is the only calamity they have not experienced in this war, and the best way to hurt your enemy is to find out what he is most afraid of and then do it to him right away. It stands to reason that every state best knows its own peculiar weaknesses and fears them. There are many ways in which this fortification will help you and hinder them, but I will just sum up the most important. Almost everything in the vicinity will come under your control. You will capture all the property and the slaves will desert to you of their own accord. The Athenians will immediately be deprived of the revenue from the silver mines at Laurium and of whatever they get from the land—and from the law courts![9] Most importantly, less revenue will come in from their allies, who will slight them once they realize that you are prosecuting the war with vigor. I am quite sure that this is something you Spartans can do, and I am highly confident that the consequences I have predicted will come about if you take the initiative and act quickly.

92. Let none of you think less of me if, after having once seemed patriotic, I now vigorously attack my city in company with its worst enemies.

---

9. It is not clear how Athens would be deprived of money from the law courts, unless Alcibiades meant that citizens, by being forced to enter the army, would not be able to earn money by serving on juries. The Athenians were notoriously litigious, and the Spartans may have thought of them as making most of their money through jury duty. On the other hand, Alcibiades may have been making a joke by playing on a stereotype that was commonly recognized as a caricature. Aristophanes ridiculed the addiction of old men to jury duty in *The Wasps*, 422.

Nor should you discount me as a man motivated by the usual zeal of exiles. I am an exile on account of the baseness of those who drove me out, not because of the good I may do you if you accept my recommendations. The worst opponents are not those who hurt their enemies, like you, but those who force their friends to become enemies. I have no patriotic loyalty to the state in which I was a victim of injustice, only to the one in which I safely exercised my rights as a citizen. I don't regard the country I am attacking as my fatherland any longer; on the contrary, I want to restore the fatherland that is no more. The truly patriotic man is not the one who is unjustly deprived of his country and does nothing about it, but the one whose love of country makes him try anything to get it back. So I urge you Spartans to make use of me in total confidence for any task, however difficult or dangerous, bearing in mind the adage of all us exiles: If I could hurt you as an enemy, I can help you as a friend. And in the past I could only guess at the situation here, but I *know* the situation there. Remember that you are making a decision of the greatest moment. Do not pull back from campaigns in Sicily and Attica. You can save Sicily just by being on the scene with a small fraction of your men, and you can destroy the present and future power of Athens. Then you can dwell in Sparta in total security and lead all of Greece, which will follow not by force, but from good will.

93. That was the speech of Alcibiades. Even before the speech, the Spartans had been planning an attack on Athens, but it was being delayed as they watched the turn of events. Now, however, after Alcibiades' explanation of the facts, and believing that they had heard them from the man who knew them best, they were emboldened to act. They focused their attention on building a fort at Decelea, and they voted to send immediate aid to Sicily. They assigned Gylippus, son of Cleandridas, to the Syracusans as a commander and ordered him to confer with the Syracusans and the Corinthians about getting aid to Sicily as quickly and effectively as the circumstances permitted. Gylippus told the Corinthians to send two of their ships to him at Asine right away, and then to outfit as many more ships as they intended to send. These should be ready to sail with the first good weather. After making these arrangements, the Syracusans and Corinthians left Sparta.

Meanwhile, the Athenian trireme the generals had sent from Sicily for money and cavalry had arrived at Athens. The Athenians heard their message and voted to send cavalry and more pay for the army. And so the winter came to an end, and with it ended the seventeenth year of the war which I, Thucydides, wrote down.

94. As soon as spring began, the Athenians in Sicily set out from Catana and sailed along the coast to attack Megara Hyblaea, which, as I have said,[1] was evacuated by the Syracusans in the time of the tyrant, Gelon, and which they still hold. They landed and slashed and burned the fields. They also attacked a Syracusan fortification but failed to take it, so the infantry and the ships moved in tandem along the coast to the Terias River. The men went up to the plain, which they ravaged, torching the fields of grain, and happened on a small force of Syracusan soldiers, some of whom they killed. Then after erecting a victory marker, they withdrew to their ships and sailed back to Catana. After taking on provisions, the whole armada set off from there for the Sicel town of Centoripa, which surrendered and came over to their side; whereupon the Athenians left,

1. See 6.4.

burning the fields of the Inessians and the Hyblaeans on the way. When they re-
turned to Catana, they found that two hundred fifty cavalrymen had arrived from
Athens. They had tack but not horses, which were supposed to be procured in
Sicily. There were also thirty horse-archers and three hundred talents of silver.

95. That spring, the Spartans marched on Argos. They got as far as
Cleonae, but there was an earthquake, so they turned back. After this, the Argives raided the border region of Thyrea, where they seized a great deal of Spartan booty, which was sold for at least twenty-five talents. Not much later, in
summer, the people of Thespiae attacked the ruling government, but the Thebans sent reinforcements and they failed to achieve their purpose. Some of the
revolutionaries were captured and others fled to Athens.

96. That summer, the Syracusans learned that the Athenian cavalrymen
had arrived and that the Athenians were planning to attack them; but they had
been coming to realize that unless the Athenians took Epipolae, a high plateau
above Syracuse, the city could not easily be walled off, even if the Athenians
were victorious in battle. They therefore decided to secure the access roads to
Epipolae to keep the enemy from ascending to the heights unbeknownst to
them. These were the only routes by which they could get up, because the edges
of the rest of the plateau are very steep, and the ground slopes right down to the
city, from the inside of which all of Epipolae is clearly visible. The Syracusans
call it Epipolae, which means "the rise," because it rises above the rest of the
city. One day, at dawn, the whole Syracusan people went out to the meadow
along the Anapus River. Also present were the generals, including Hermocrates,
who had just been formally invested with command. A review of the troops was
conducted, and six hundred picked hoplites were at once detached, under the
command of Diomilus, an exile from Andros, to guard Epipolae and to immediately go in full force to any other point at which they were needed.

97. On the very evening of the review, however, the Athenians, unknown
to the Syracusans, left Catana with their entire force and landed near a place
called Leon, about three-quarters of a mile from Epipolae. The infantry disembarked there, and the ships put in at Thapsus, which is a peninsula off a narrow
isthmus and is not far from Syracuse either by land or sea. After building a palisade across the isthmus, the Athenian sailors rested at Thapsus, but the infantry
immediately went on the run towards Epipolae and got up there via the Euryelus before the Syracusans could get there from the review at the meadow,
where they heard the news. Diomilus and his six hundred men went up to resist the Athenians, and everyone else hurried as fast as he could to help, but they
had to cover over three miles from the meadow before they could engage with
the Athenians. Coming up in this way, all out of formation, the Syracusans were
defeated at Epipolae and fell back into their city. Diomilus and about three hundred others were killed. After the battle, the Athenians set up a victory marker
and returned the Syracusan dead under a truce. The next day, they went down
to the city itself, but when the Syracusans did not come out to fight them, they
went back up the plateau and built a fort at Labdalum at the edge of the cliffs
of Epipolae, facing Megara Hyblaea, so that they could leave their money and
equipment there whenever they went out to fight or engage in siege operations.

98. Not much later, three hundred cavalrymen and horses arrived from
Egesta, and about a hundred from the Sicels, Naxians, and various others. The
Athenians had two hundred fifty cavalrymen of their own, for whom they had
either been given mounts by the Egestans and the Catanaeans or had pur-
chased them, making for a combined cavalry of six hundred and fifty in all.
Then after leaving a garrison at Labdalum, the Athenians marched to the Fig

Tree, where they halted and quickly finished building the Circle.[2] The speed of their construction amazed the Syracusans, who sortied out of the city with the intention of fighting a battle to prevent it. The opposing armies were getting into position against each other when the Syracusan generals saw that their army was scattered and in disorder and that it could not easily be brought into formation. So they led their men back into the city—except for a portion of their cavalry, which stayed behind and prevented the Athenians from gathering stones or moving very far from the Circle. Then a contingent of hoplites and the whole force of cavalry attacked the Syracusan cavalry and put them to flight, killing some of them, and later erecting a marker to signify their victory in the cavalry battle.

99. The next day, some of the Athenians finished the wall going north from the Circle, while others brought stones and wood which they laid in a line aimed at the gully known as Trogilus, where their siege wall was to follow the shortest route from the Great Harbor to the open sea. On the advice of the generals, especially Hermocrates, the Syracusans decided not to risk any more all-out battles in full strength with the Athenians. They decided that it would be better to anticipate the Athenians by building a wall across the one they intended to build, thus putting an impediment in the way. At the same time, in case the Athenians should try to stop them, they would deploy a part of their army to counter them by occupying the approaches to their blockading wall first, planting a palisade of stakes in the ground and defending it if need be. Then the Athenians would have to break off from their work and direct their whole army against them. They therefore came out and began to build their counterwall, starting from their city at the seaward side of the Circle and continuing at a right angle to the intended Athenian siege wall. They also cut down the olive trees in the temple of Apollo Temenites and built wooden towers. The Syracusans still controlled the area around their coast. The Athenian fleet had not yet sailed around from Thapsus into the Great Harbor, and the Athenians brought their supplies over from Thapsus by land.

100. The Athenians did not move to prevent the Syracusan construction, because they feared dividing their forces and making it easier for the Syracusans to fight them, but also because they were hurrying to build their own wall. After the Syracusans decided that they had finished enough of the palisade and the counterwall, they left a division behind to guard the construction site and returned to the city. Then the Athenians destroyed the underground pipes that carried drinking water into the city.

They timed their next action for noon, when some of the Syracusan guard were in their tents or had even gone back to the city, and when the men at the palisade were getting careless. They picked three hundred men—their own hoplites, along with some carefully selected light-armed troops to whom they gave heavy weapons—and ordered them to start running as fast as possible for a surprise attack on the counterwall. Meanwhile, one of the generals took half of the army toward the city, in case they should try to intervene, and the other general led the other half to the part of the palisade that ran past the Pyramid. The force of three hundred attacked and took the palisade. Its guards abandoned it and fled behind the new wall that adjoined the city and included the temple of Apollo Temenites.[3] Their pursuers were on top of them as they went

---

2. Thucydides wrote of the Fig Tree and the Circle as if they were well known to his readers. The Fig Tree was probably just that, a fig tree so large or otherwise distinguished that it served as a landmark; and the Circle was probably the main Athenian fortification on the plateau. See also the reference to "the Pyramid" at 6.100.

3. See 6.75.

in, and got in too, but were forced back out by the Syracusans, and some Argives as well as a few Athenians were killed there. Turning back, the entire Athenian army then tore down the counterwall, pulled up the palisade, carried the stakes back to their camp, and set up a victory marker.

101. The next day, the Athenians fortified the ridge south of the Circle that, from this part of Epipolae, looks over the marshy meadow towards the Great Harbor. This point began the shortest descent for their siege wall through the level ground of the marshy meadow to the harbor. To make it impossible for the Athenians to extended their siege wall down to the sea, the Syracusans also came out while the Athenian fortification was going on and started building yet another palisade with a ditch running parallel to it, which started at the city and extended through the middle of the marshy meadow. When the Athenians had finished their work at the ridge, they made yet another attack, this time on the palisade and the ditch. They had ordered their ships to sail around from Thapsus to the Great Harbor, while the army came down before first light from Epipolae to the level ground. They went through the marshy meadow where the mud was firmest, laying down lattices and wooden planks that they walked over as they went across, and at dawn captured most of the palisade and the ditch. The rest they took later. Then a pitched battle took place, which the Athenians won, and in which the Syracusan right wing fell back on the city while the left wing retreated along the river. The three hundred picked Athenians then set off on a run for the bridge, intending to cut them off before they could cross the river. Fearing this, and encouraged by the fact that most of their cavalry was in the vicinity, the Syracusans charged the three hundred and came to grips with them. They put them to flight and then fell on the Athenian right wing. Right after they hit, the whole first division of that wing fell into a panic. When Lamachus saw what was happening, he hurried to the rescue from his own left wing, taking along a few archers and the troops from Argos. But after following some others over a ditch, he was cut off with a few of the men who had crossed with him, and he and five or six of his men were killed. Before the Athenians could get there, the Syracusans immediately grabbed the bodies and hurried across the river to safety, retreating again when the rest of the Athenian army started to advance on them.

102. Meanwhile, the Syracusans who had at first fled toward the city saw what was happening and regained their courage. They returned from the city and took up positions against the opposing Athenians. They also sent a detachment to the Circle, on Epipolae, thinking that it was undefended and that they could take it. They were able to capture and destroy the one-thousand-foot-square advance fortification, but Nicias prevented them from taking the Circle itself. He was inside, left behind because of an illness, and he ordered his aides to set fire to the scaffolding and the wood that had been left lying in front of the wall. He realized that without troops they would be unable to survive any other way. It worked. The fire stopped the forward advance of the Syracusans, and they fell back. Furthermore, the Athenians who had been pursuing the Syracusans down below had started straight back up the plateau to the relief of the Circle. Also the ships from Thapsus, as ordered, were sailing into the Great Harbor. When the Syracusans on the plateau saw this, they retreated on the double, and the whole Syracusan army then returned to the city, having decided that their available forces were not strong enough to prevent the Athenians from extending their wall to the sea.

103. After this battle, the Athenians set up a victory marker. Then they returned the Syracusan dead under a truce and carried back the bodies of

Lamachus and the men who were with him. Now that their whole armament of ships and infantry were together, they blockaded the Syracusans with a double siege wall that began at the ridge at Epipolae and ran down to the sea.

Supplies were coming to the army from all over Italy. Also a great many of the Sicels who had been awaiting developments now joined with the Athenians, and three penteconters arrived from Tyrrhenia. Everything was going just as they had hoped. What is more, since even the Peloponnesians had not sent help, the Syracusans no longer believed they could win the war and spoke only of coming to terms, both among themselves and in their dealings with Nicias, who after the death of Lamachus was in sole command. No final agreements were reached, but they were even more cut off than they had been before and were growing desperate. So there was naturally a great deal of discussion with Nicias, and even more within the city itself. In the midst of their troubles, they even became somewhat suspicious of one another, and thinking that their city had come to this pass because their generals were either treacherous or just plain unlucky, they terminated the generals' commands and elected Heracleides, Eucles, and Tellias to take their place.

104. Meanwhile Gylippus the Spartan and the Corinthian ships were already at Leucas, eager to hasten to the relief of Sicily. But Gylippus kept getting disturbing news—all false, but all to the same effect—that Syracuse was completely besieged, so he gave up hope for Sicily and decided to protect Italy instead. Taking two Spartan and two Corinthian ships, he and the Corinthian, Pythen, crossed the Ionian Gulf to Tarentum as fast as they could. The Corinthians were manning and equipping two Leucadian and three Ambraciot ships in addition to their own fleet of ten and intended to set sail later. The first thing Gylippus did at Tarentum was to send envoys to Thurii in accordance with the citizenship that had once been granted to his father. He was unable to win their support, so he set out to sail along the Italian coast; but the strong prevailing north wind in those parts caught him off the Gulf of Terinaea and carried him out to sea. After riding out an especially rough storm, he put back into Tarentum, where he dragged on shore and repaired the ships that had been most damaged by the storm.

When Nicias learned that Gylippus was sailing his way, he was dismissive of the number of his ships (as the Thurians had been). He decided that they had been outfitted more for piracy than anything else and for the time being took no precautions against them.

105. At about the same time that summer, the Spartans and their allies invaded the Argolid, slashing and burning a great deal of land, and the Athenians sent thirty ships to their aid. This act was a conspicuous breach of the treaty between Athens and Sparta. Previously, the Athenians had come over from Pylos and landed to make raids in the Peloponnese, but not in Laconia, and they had also fought alongside the Argives and the Mantineans. The Argives had frequently urged them to just land some armed men on Laconian soil and join them in ravaging a tiny little part of it before pulling out again, but they had refused. Now, however, under the command of Pythodorus, Laespodius, and Demaratus, they landed at Epidaurus Limera, Prasiae, and elsewhere, slashed and burned the ground, and gave the Spartans good grounds to claim that the Athenians had made them act in self-defense. After the Athenians left Argos in their ships, and the Spartans also withdrew, the Argives invaded the territory of Phlius, deforested some of their land and killed some of their people, and then returned home.

Book 7

The pain that Thucydides plainly wished his readers to share in contemplating the war is nowhere more evident than in Book 7, in which he recounts the collapse of the expedition against Sicily and goes to considerable effort to capture in words the miserable end of the Athenian forces there. Chapters 1–27 deal with the simultaneous operations in mainland Greece, where the Spartans fortified Decelea thirteen or fourteen miles from Athens, and in Sicily, where Gylippus arrived at Syracuse. Chapter 28 then relates the mounting expenses that led the Athenians to levy a five-percent import and export tax on their imperial subjects; and the Athenians' financial difficulties give Thucydides occasion to relate (29–30) an incident that took place when some Thracians, whom they decided they could not afford to pay, were being escorted home by Diitrephes. The Thracians' attack on the civilians of Mycalessus, in the course of which not only women and farm animals but an entire school full of young boys were slain, unquestionably made a deep impression on Thucydides, and he stresses the magnitude of the events at Mycalessus out of any proportion to their strategic significance. At 31 Thucydides resumes his account of events in Sicily, leading up to the Syracusan victory that concludes in 71. This leaves him sixteen chapters (72–87) for the wretched denouement of the unsuccessful expedition, culminating in the butchering of the Athenian army in the Assinarus River, the execution of Nicias and Demosthenes, and the fate of the Athenian prisoners of war consigned to the quarries and sold as slaves. Though he shows awareness of Nicias' limitations as a commander, Thucydides was clearly moved by the general's end.

Two points of information omitted from Thucydides' narrative are worth mentioning. Plutarch, in his life of Nicias, tells how Athenian prisoners won their way out of Sicily by reciting for their captors the verses of Euripides, who was immensely popular in Sicily; and information that has come to us from Plutarch's *Nicias* and from Xenophon's *Ways and Means* (4.14) gives an ironic twist to Thucydides' juxtaposition of the miserable life of the enslaved Athenians in the quarries with his praise of Nicias (86) as the man who least deserved his misfortune because he had "ordered his whole life in keeping with the highest standards". According to Xenophon, Nicias owned one thousand slaves from whom he received revenue by letting them out to work in the notoriously horrific silver mines of Laurium in southern Attica, having first made arrangements for compensation for that percentage of the human chattel who, inevitably, would die as a consequence of their working conditions.

Book 7

1. After repairing their ships, Gylippus and Pythen left Tarentum and sailed along the coast to Italian Locri. They now received more accurate intelligence to the effect that Syracuse was not yet completely blockaded and that it was still possible for an army to get into the city via Epipolae. They deliberated whether to go down the west coast of Sicily and take the risk of sailing into Syracuse, or to sail along the north coast to Himera first and then go overland, after gathering an army from the Himerans themselves and from anyone else they were able to win over. They decided to sail to Himera, which they could do because the four Attic ships that Nicias had sent to stand guard at Rhegium had not yet arrived. Despite his original dismissiveness, Nicias had nevertheless dispatched four Attic ships when he learned that the Peloponnesians were in Locri. So Gylippus and Pythen crossed the Straits of Messana before the ships arrived and reached Himera after calling at Rhegium and Messana. When they arrived, they beached their ships and persuaded the Himerans to follow them and fight on their side and to provide weapons to the Peloponnesian sailors who had none. They also sent envoys to the Selinuntines, asking them to meet them with an army at a place they designated. The Geloans and some of the Sicel tribes also promised to send them a small force. The Sicels were much more inclined to go over to them after the recent death of Archonidas, who had been the powerful king of some of the Sicel tribes in that region and who had been friendly with the Athenians. Also Gylippus, fresh from Sparta, projected confidence. So heading up approximately seven hundred of his own marines and armed sailors; a combined force of one thousand Himeran hoplites and light-armed troops, along with one hundred of their cavalry; some Selinuntine light-armed troops and cavalry; a few Geloans; and a total of one thousand Sicels, Gylippus marched toward Syracuse.

2. Meanwhile, the Corinthians left Leucas with the remaining ships and sailed to the relief of Syracuse as fast as they could. Gongylus, one of the Corinthian commanders, cast off last but reached Syracuse first in his unaccompanied ship, a little before Gylippus. On arrival, he found that the Syracusans were about to hold an assembly to discuss the terms of peace, but he managed to forestall that with the encouraging announcement that still more ships were on the way and that the Spartans had sent Gylippus, son of Cleandridas, to take command. Now that they knew Gylippus was near, the Syracusans recovered their courage and immediately marched out in full strength to meet him. En route, he had captured a Sicel fort at Ietae, and now, arrayed for battle, he came to Epipolae. Ascending via the Euryelus, as the Athenians had done before him, he and the Syracusans marched right up toward the Athenian fortifications. He arrived at just the moment when the Athenians had finished about a mile of the double wall down to the Great Harbor. There was a little way to go before they reached the sea, and they were working on that part. Most of the stones had been set down for the other wall toward Trogilus on the open sea, and it was finished in some places, half-finished in others. That is how close the Syracusans had come to destruction!

3. At first, the Athenians were thrown into disarray by the sudden onset of Gylippus and the Syracusans, but then they got into formation. Gylippus took up a position nearby and sent forward a herald with the message that he was prepared to make peace if they would agree to take what was theirs and leave Sicily within five days. The Athenians dismissed this offer and sent the herald back

without an answer. Then the two sides started lining up against each other for a battle. But Gylippus saw that the Syracusans were in disorder and were having trouble getting organized, so he led the army up to more open ground. Nicias, however, did not lead his men into battle and stood his ground near his wall. When Gylippus realized that the Athenians were not going to advance, he withdrew his men to the top of the spur, where the sanctuary of Apollo Temenites is located, and bivouacked there for the night. The next day, he led most of his troops to the Athenian wall and positioned them there to prevent the Athenians from going to fight elsewhere. Then he sent a detachment to the fort at Labdalum, which the Athenians could not see from where they were, and which the Syracusans took, killing all the men they captured. That day too the Syracusans captured an Athenian trireme that was keeping a watch at the Little Harbor.

4. Next the Syracusans and their allies started to build a single wall going up across Epipolae from the city at a right angle to the Athenian wall, so that the Athenians either had to stop them or give up walling off the city. After finishing the wall to the sea, the Athenians had gone up to the high ground; but there was a weak point in the wall, and Gylippus led his army out by night to attack it. The Athenians happened to be bivouacking outdoors that night and rushed to stop them when they realized what was happening. When he saw this, Gylippus quickly withdrew his men. The Athenians raised the height of the wall at this point and posted their own guards, positioning their allies along the other parts of the wall it was to be their duty to defend.

Then Nicias decided to fortify the point known as Plemmyrium. This is a promontory that runs out opposite the city and creates the narrow mouth of the Great Harbor, and it seemed to Nicias that if this could be fortified, it would be easier for him to bring in supplies, because they would have less distance to cover when performing operations against the Little Harbor (which the Syracusans controlled) and they would not, as they did now, have to sail out to the attack from the innermost part of the Great Harbor if the Syracusans made any move by sea. He was already focusing more on the naval aspect of the war, having seen that their operations on land had become less promising since the arrival of Gylippus. So he brought ships and men over to Plemmyrium and built and garrisoned three forts. There most of their equipment was deposited, and his heavy merchant vessels and his fast fighting ships made this their base. This move was a major cause of the demoralization of the crews, which now began. The water they needed was scarce at Plemmyrium, and not nearby, and they also had to forage for firewood. So whenever the sailors went out, they were harried and killed by the Syracusan cavalry, which controlled the ground. Fully one-third of the whole force of cavalry had been detailed to the village of Olympieium to prevent the men in Plemmyrium from leaving their forts on offensive operations.

Then Nicias learned that the remaining Corinthian ships were on their way, so he sent out a patrol of twenty ships with orders to lie in wait for them around Locri, Rhegium, and the crossing-point to Sicily.

5. While Gylippus was directing the construction of the wall across Epipolae—for which his men used the very stones the Athenians had earlier laid down for themselves—he was also leading the Syracusans and their allies into position in front of the Athenian fortifications. For their part, the Athenians lined up opposite them. When Gylippus decided that the time was right, he began his assault, and the two sides came to hand-to-hand combat between the Athenian siege wall and the Syracusan counterwall, at a

point where the Syracusan cavalry was useless. The Syracusans and their allies were defeated. They gathered up their dead under a truce, and the Athenians set up a victory marker. Then Gylippus called together his men and
told them that the error had not been theirs, but his. By forming them up
too close to the walls, he had deprived them of the advantage of their javelin
men and cavalry. So now he would lead them out again. He told them to
bear in mind that they would have more forces than before, and that they
should be too proud to endure the thought that they, Peloponnesians and
Dorians, could not defeat this Ionian and island trash the sea had washed
up on their shores and drive them out of the country.

6. After making this speech, he waited until the time was right and led
them against the enemy once more. Nicias and the Athenians realized that even
if the other side chose not to fight, they could not stand by and watch while the
counterwall was built right past their own. The Syracusan wall had all but
reached the end of theirs, and if it went any further, it would make no difference if they fought and won forever or never fought at all. So they went to meet
the advancing enemy. After leading his hoplites further from the walls than before, Gylippus made contact with the Athenians. He had positioned his javelin
men and his cavalry at the open ground where the work on both walls had been
left off. During the battle, the cavalry fell on the Athenian left flank, which was
in front of them, and put them to flight. As a result, the rest of the army was defeated by the Syracusans, fell to pieces, and retreated behind its fortifications.
That night, the Syracusans brought their wall past the Athenian construction.
As a result, their work was no longer hindered by the Athenians, who, even if
they won a pitched battle in the field, were stripped of all hope of blockading
the city.

7. After this, the remaining twelve Corinthian, Ambraciot, and Leucadian
ships sailed into Syracuse. Under the command of the Corinthian Erasinides,
they had evaded the Athenian patrol, and their crews now joined the Syracusans in finishing their counterwall at right angles to the Athenian wall. Meanwhile, Gylippus traveled throughout Sicily, putting together a force of ships and
infantry and bringing over those who had been either lukewarm to Syracuse or
who had avoided the war altogether. More Syracusan and Corinthian ambassadors were sent to Sparta to get a force to come over by whatever means possible—in merchant craft or any other sort of vessel—since the Athenians were
also sending for reinforcements. Syracusan confidence was now very high, and
they started manning a navy and practicing naval maneuvers in order to try their
hand at sea fighting too.

8. Nicias too sent messages. Observing these developments, and watching his enemies' strength and his own helplessness grow day by day, he had
frequently sent messengers to Athens, detailing what was happening, but
never more than now, when he was convinced that they were in desperate
straits and that they would be totally lost unless Athens either called them
back or sent another very large force immediately. Fearing, however, that the
men he sent would fail to give accurate reports, either for want of speaking
skills, or lapses of memory, or an unwillingness to displease the populace,
Nicias put his message in writing, believing that in this way none of his own
personal opinion would be lost in transmission and the Athenians would be
able to make decisions about the situation as it really was. His messengers
went off with the letter and with instructions as to what they should say,
while Nicias concerned himself with defensive measures rather than with
taking offensive action.

9. As that same summer came to an end, the Athenian general Euetion, acting with Perdiccas, led a large Thracian army against Amphipolis. He failed to take the city, but he brought triremes around to the Strymon and, using Himeraeum as his headquarters, blockaded the city from the river. And so the summer ended.

10. The next winter, the messengers from Nicias arrived in Athens. They delivered the verbal messages they had been given and answered any questions these prompted. They also delivered Nicias' letter, which the city secretary came forward and read to the Athenian people, as follows.

11. To the Athenian people. You know from many other messages what has been done so far, but now, more than ever, you must reach a decision based on accurate knowledge of the situation we are in. After we won most of our battles with the Syracusans (against whom you sent us), and finished the fortifications that we now hold, Gylippus the Spartan arrived with a force from the Peloponnese and from some of the cities in Sicily. We defeated him in our first battle, but the next day, overpowered by a large force of cavalry and javelin men, we retreated into our fortifications. Kept from finishing our siege wall by the large number of the enemy, we are now at a standstill. Nor can we deploy our whole army together, since many of our hoplites are engaged in guarding the walls. Furthermore, the Syracusans have built a single wall across the line of our siege wall, so that it is no longer possible to wall them off without attacking and taking this counterwall with a large force. It has come about that we who thought to besiege others are suffering the same fate ourselves, at least on land, since we also cannot go very far into the countryside because of the enemy's cavalry.

12. They have also sent envoys to the Peloponnese to ask for reinforcements, and Gylippus has gone off to the cities in Sicily, trying to persuade some of those who have stayed out of it to come and join them in the fighting, and to get even more infantry and naval forces, if he can, from the others. I have received intelligence that they are doing this because they intend to attack our fortifications on land and our ships at sea. And let none of you think it strange that I say "at sea." They too have information, and they have learned that whereas our fleet was at first unsurpassed in the buoyancy of its ships and in the fitness of its crews, our ships are now waterlogged from being afloat for so long, and our crews have deteriorated. We cannot beach our ships to let them drain because the equal or even greater number of enemy ships forces us to be constantly on the alert for an attack. We can see their naval maneuvers; they can attack at will. And they are not blockading anyone, so they can haul their ships up to dry.

13. Even if we had a vast superiority in ships and were not, as we are now, forced to keep them all on duty, we would barely have the enemy's advantages, because if we let up our guard in the least, we would lose our supplies, which have to pass so close to the city that they are only reaching us with difficulty as it is. This has led to a reduction in our crews, which continues as I write. Our sailors are being killed on raids and as they forage over long distances for firewood and water. Ever since we lost our superiority, our slaves have been deserting, and as to the contingents on board from our subject allies, they disperse among the cities here as soon as they can. Attracted at first by the high pay and thinking that they would be making money rather than fighting, they found to their surprise that there were actually naval and other enemy forces here to oppose them.

Some left alleging that they were not subjects but free men, and others just left. After all, Sicily is a big place. There are even some men who are so busy trading that they have bribed trierarchs to take Hyccaric slaves in their place, thereby depriving the fleet of high-quality personnel.—You know very well that a crew's period of maximum efficiency is short, and that only a few sailors get a ship under way and keep the rowers' strokes regular.

14. The most frustrating thing of all is that I, the commanding officer, cannot prevent this recalcitrance. But then, you Athenians are ungovernable by nature. I am also frustrated by not having anywhere to recruit fresh crews, whereas the enemy has many places to get them from. We must make use of what we came with and what is lost just makes that less. The allies we now have, Naxos and Catana, cannot supply us with men. If only one more thing goes the enemy's way—for example, if the places in Italy that supply us with food go over to their side after seeing what shape we are in and that you are not sending help—we will be starved out and the war will be over without another battle.

I could have put this report more agreeably than I have, but that would have made it useless, since what you need is a clear understanding of the situation here as you decide what to do. I also know the way you are. You like to hear good news, but then you cast blame later if any of it turns out differently, so I thought it would be safer to tell you the truth.

15. You can be sure that we, your commanders and your rank and file, have not failed you and have tried to achieve our initial objectives. But now that all Sicily is uniting and they are expecting another army from the Peloponnese, you must take into consideration that we are not even able to deal with the situation as it is, and decide either to recall us or to send yet another army and fleet as large as ours—and a lot of money too—as well as a replacement for me, since I am no longer able to remain with the army because of kidney disease. I believe that you will make allowances for this. After all, I did you much good service in the commands I held when I was in good health. But whatever you decide, you must do it by spring and not put it off. Our enemies will soon get their reinforcements from Sicily. The Peloponnesians will take longer, but if you do not give this matter your fullest attention, they will slip through your fingers, as they did at Leucas, and get here before you do.

16. That was the situation as described in Nicias' letter. After hearing it read, the Athenians did not relieve Nicias of command. Instead, so that he would not have to carry on sick and alone, they appointed two officers who were there with him, Menander and Euthydemus, to second him until other joint commanders could be chosen and sent. They also voted to send another fleet and an army to be selected from Athens' eligibility list and from its allies. To share command with Nicias, they elected Demosthenes, son of Alcisthenes, and Eurymedon, son of Thucles. They sent Eurymedon to Sicily right away, at around the winter solstice, with ten ships and one hundred twenty talents of silver, and with the message for the men who were there that reinforcements were coming and that they would be taken care of.

17. Demosthenes stayed behind to get the relief force ready so he could take it out by spring. He told the allies to send troops, and he raised money, outfitted ships, and mustered hoplites in Athens. The Athenians also deployed twenty ships to cruise off the Peloponnese and keep any Corinthians and Peloponnesians from crossing over to Sicily. The Corinthians were very encouraged when the ambassadors arrived with better news from Sicily, and they realized how timely their first contingent of ships had been, so they prepared to send

hoplites to Sicily in merchant ships, and the Spartans planned to send troops from the rest of the Peloponnese in the same way. The Corinthians also manned twenty-five warships to challenge the Athenian patrol at Naupactus, to force them to deal with this array of Corinthian triremes and so make them less able to keep the merchant ships from leaving.

18. In accordance with their previous decision, and at the instigation of the Syracusans and Corinthians, the Spartans also made ready for their invasion of Attica. They had learned of the relief force being prepared for Sicily and they wanted to hamper it with an invasion. Alcibiades was also tirelessly explaining why they should fortify Decelea and press the war. Most importantly, however, a certain feistiness was developing in the Spartans as they realized that Athens would be easier to topple now that it was fighting a war on two fronts—against them and the Sicilians. Also they believed that Athens had been the first to violate the treaty. In the first stage of the war, the onus had been more on them, because the Thebans had gone into Plataea in peacetime,[1] and because they themselves had refused an Athenian offer of arbitration, although it had been stipulated in the former treaty[2] that no state could resort to arms if the alleged wrongdoer was willing to submit a matter to arbitration.[3] As a result, the Spartans believed that they had deserved their misfortunes, and the disasters at Pylos and elsewhere lay heavy on their consciences. But now the Athenians had set out from Argos with their thirty ships to plunder parts of Epidaurus, Prasiae, and other places; they were raiding the Peloponnese from Pylos; and this time, whenever arguments arose over disputed points in the treaty of Nicias, it was the Spartans who offered to submit the matter to arbitration and the Athenians who refused. So the Spartans believed that the Athenians were making the same mistake they themselves had made and were now in the wrong, and the Spartans looked forward to war. During the winter, they requisitioned iron from their allies and readied the implements they would need for the fort at Decelea. They also raised a Spartan relief force to go to Sicily in merchant ships and levied men from elsewhere in the Peloponnese. And so the winter came to an end, and with it ended the eighteenth year of the war that I, Thucydides, have recorded.

19. As soon as spring began—earlier than ever before, in fact—the Spartans and their allies invaded Attica. They were led by Agis, son of Archidamus and king of Sparta. First they plundered the country around the plain, and then, dividing the work among the detachments from the several Peloponnesian cities, they started to fortify Decelea. Decelea is roughly fourteen miles from Athens and only slightly further from Boeotia. Their fort, which was clearly visible from Athens, overlooked the plain, and was built with a view to conducting hostile operations on the best land in Attica. At about the same time the Peloponnesians and their allies in Attica were building their fort, those in the Peloponnese were sending their hoplites to Sicily in merchant ships. The Spartans had selected six hundred hoplites from the best of the helots and the freedmen, with the Spartan Eccritus in command; and the Boeotians sent three hundred hoplites under the Thebans Xenon and Nicon, and Hegesander the Thespian. These were among the first to leave, and they put out to sea from Taenarus, in Laconia. Not much later, the Corinthians sent Alexarchus, one of their own officers, in command of five hundred hoplites, some of whom were Corinthian citizens and others mercenaries from Arcadia. At the same time, the

1. See 2.2 and 3.56.
2. The Thirty Years' Peace of 446/5.
3. See 1.78, 85, and 140.

Sicyonians sent two hundred hoplites under the command of Sargeus, a Sicyonian officer. While these hoplites sailed away from the Peloponnese in merchant ships, the twenty-five Corinthian ships that had been fitted out over the
winter were moored opposite the twenty Attic ships at Naupactus. That was why
they had been manned in the first place—to focus the Athenians' attention on
the triremes rather than on the merchant ships.

20. At the beginning of spring, during the fortification of Decelea, and in
the midst of all this other activity, the Athenians sent thirty ships around the
Peloponnese under the command of Charicles, son of Apollodorus. His orders
were to put into Argos and ask for hoplites for his ships under the terms of their
alliance.[4] They also sent Demosthenes to Sicily, as planned. He had sixty Athenian and five Chian ships, twelve hundred hoplites from the Athenian eligibility
list and as many from the islands as they could get, along with whatever spe-
cialized combat troops they could procure from the other subject allies. Demosthenes' orders were to join Charicles in his operations around Laconia before
going to Sicily, so he sailed ahead to Aegina and waited for straggling contingents of the armada and for Charicles to obtain the Argive hoplites.

21. Meanwhile, in Sicily at about the same time that spring, Gylippus
returned to Syracuse at the head of the biggest force he had been able to
persuade the various cities to give him. Then he called the Syracusans together and told them that they had to man as many ships as they could and
have a go at fighting a battle at sea. He had every reason to believe that it
was worth the risk and that it would have a positive effect on the war effort.
More than anyone else, Hermocrates seconded Gylippus' argument, and to
help them overcome their fear of attacking the Athenians at sea, he said that
the Athenians had not inherited their naval skill and that the sea was not
theirs in perpetuity, either. In fact, they were more landlubbers than the Syracusans and had been forced to become sailors by the Persian War. To audacious men like the Athenians, the toughest men were those who seemed
to match them in audacity. They frightened their neighbors with their boldness, brashly attacking even when they didn't have superior force, and the
Syracusans had to confront them with the same boldness. He said he was
certain that the advantage the Syracusans would gain by confounding the
Athenians with unexpectedly bold opposition at sea would be greater than
any harm Athenian skill could inflict on Syracusan inexperience. He called
on them not to flinch and to try to fight a naval battle.

Won over by Gylippus, Hermocrates, and various others, the Syracusans
decided to go for a naval battle and began to man their ships.

22. When the fleet was ready, Gylippus himself led all his infantry out
under cover of night with the objective of attacking the fortifications at Plemmyrium by land. In a concerted action, thirty-five Syracusan triremes in the
Great Harbor cast off while forty-five left the Little Harbor, where their dockyard was, and sailed around toward the Great Harbor, with orders to join forces
with their ships there and to shake up the Athenians on land and sea by going
on to attack Plemmyrium. To meet them, the Athenians quickly manned sixty
ships. They fought the thirty-five Syracusan ships in the Great Harbor with
twenty-five of them and sent the rest to oppose the ships coming around from
the dockyard. These latter immediately engaged right outside the mouth of the
Great Harbor, with neither side giving way for a long time, as the Syracusans

4. See 5.82.

kept trying to force their way in and the Athenians kept preventing them from doing so.

23. While this was going on, the Athenians at Plemmyrium had gone down to the beach, where they were distracted by the fighting. Catching them off guard, Gylippus suddenly attacked the forts at dawn, taking the largest one first, and then the two smaller ones when their guards abandoned them after seeing the largest captured so easily. The men who got down to a merchant ship and some small craft after fleeing from the first and largest fort were able to escape to the main camp, but only with great difficulty. The Syracusan ships in the Great Harbor were having a temporary advantage in the fighting, and so a single fast trireme was able to give the fleeing guards chase. But the Syracusans had already been defeated by the time the two other fortifications were captured, and so the men who ran away from those sailed through more easily. What had happened was that the Syracusan ships fighting outside the mouth of the Great Harbor had forced their way past the Athenian ships; but they became fouled up with each other as they sailed into the harbor all out of formation, thus handing the victory over to the Athenians, who put them to flight and then went after the ships who had at first been beating them inside the harbor. They sank eleven Syracusan ships and killed most of their crews, except for the men on three of the ships whom they took alive. Three Athenian ships had been lost. After dragging Syracusan wreckage onto the islet off Plemmyrium and using it for a victory marker there, the Athenians withdrew to their own camp.

24. That is how the Syracusans had done in the naval battle. On the other hand, they had the three forts at Plemmyrium, and they set up one victory marker for each of them. They destroyed one of the two forts they had captured last, and repaired and garrisoned the remaining two. Many men were killed or taken prisoner during the capture of the forts, and a great many supplies of all kinds were lost to the enemy. Since the Athenians had been using the forts for storage, there were large quantities of grain and trading goods in them. A lot of property belonging to the trierarchs was also seized: forty trireme sails and other equipment, and three triremes that had been drawn up on the beach. The fall of Plemmyrium was the first of the great blows the Athenian expeditionary force was to suffer, because supply ships could no longer enter the Great Harbor in safety. The Syracusan ships lay in wait at Plemmyrium to stop them, and from that point on, they had to fight their way in. And in general the event stunned and demoralized the army.

25. After this, the Syracusans dispatched twelve ships under the command of Agatharchus, a Syracusan officer, one of which went on to the Peloponnese with ambassadors who were to report to the Spartans about the optimism at Syracuse and urge them more strongly than ever to prosecute the war in Greece. The eleven other ships sailed for Italy, with intelligence that merchantmen loaded with cargo were en route to the Athenians. They engaged these ships, destroying most of them, and then went on to burn ship's timber that had been readied for the Athenians in the Caulonian territory. Then they went to Italian Locri, and while they were lying at anchor, one of the merchant ships from the Peloponnese sailed up carrying Thespian hoplites; whereupon they took the men aboard and sailed along the coast for home. The twenty Athenian ships were on the lookout for the ships off Megara Hyblaea and captured one of them and its crew. They were, however, unable to catch the others, which got away to Syracuse.

There was also a skirmish of light-armed troops in the Great Harbor around the stakes that the Syracusans had fixed into the beach in front of the old docks. They had put them there to prevent the Athenians from sailing in and ramming the ships anchored behind them. The Athenians now brought up a very large ship outfitted with wooden towers and bulwarks. They tied ropes to the stakes and bent them back and winched them up from the foremast. Divers also went down to saw them through. The Syracusans retaliated with slings, arrows, and spears and the men on the ship shot back, and in the end the Athenians pulled out most of the stakes. The most dangerous aspect of this palisade was the hidden stakes. These had been driven into the beach below the water level, which made it very hazardous to approach them, since a captain who did not see one could wreck his ship on it as on a sunken rock. The divers were given special pay and sawed through these as well.

It made no difference, though, because the Syracusans just drove in new stakes.

As you would expect from hostile armies at close quarters, they were constantly making moves against each other and trying all kinds of commando raids and military maneuvers.

The Syracusans also sent envoys from Corinth, Ambracia, and Sparta out to the cities in Sicily, to spread the news of the capture of Plemmyrium and to explain that the Syracusans had lost the naval battle not so much because of the strength of the enemy as because of their own disarray. They were also to report on the general optimism at Syracuse and to ask that they send ships and infantry and join them in fighting the enemy: the Athenians were expecting the arrival of another army, but the war would be over if the allies arrived first and destroyed the army that was there.

26. While the envoys were going from city to city, Demosthenes finished assembling the army he was to bring to the relief of the Athenians in Sicily and set off from Aegina for the Peloponnese, where he rendezvoused with Charicles and the thirty Athenian ships. Then they took aboard the Argive hoplites and headed for Laconia. First they plundered a part of Epidaurus Limera, and then they put into Laconia directly opposite Cythera where the temple of Apollo is. They ravaged some of the land there and fortified some country that was almost an isthmus, so that Sparta's helots could escape to the place and so that it could be used as a base for pirate raids, like Pylos. As soon as he and Charicles had secured this country, Desmothenes sailed along the coast to Corcyra to pick up some allies there and then made the voyage to Sicily as quickly as possible. Charicles remained until the place was completely fortified. Then, after leaving a garrison, he made his way back home with the thirty ships, accompanied by the Argives.

27. That same summer, there arrived in Athens thirteen hundred light-armed troops from the Dian tribe of saber-bearing Thracians. These were supposed to have sailed to Sicily with Demosthenes. They arrived too late, however, and the Athenians made plans to send them back to Thrace, from where they had come. Each of them earned a drachma a day, and it seemed extravagant to use them against Decelea. During that summer, Decelea had first been fortified by the whole Peloponnesian army. Then the cities of the Peloponnese started rotating troops through it, occupying it as the base of operations against Attica and doing Athens some of the worst damage in the war. Indeed, the destruction of property and loss of life did as much as anything else to bring down the city. The previous invasions had been brief, and the rest of the time the Peloponnesians could not stop the Athenians from cultivating their land. Now, however, Attica was continuously besieged by a garrison maintained at a constant level (although there was sometimes more than the usual number of

men), which was forced to support itself by overrunning and raiding the country. Furthermore, Agis, the king of Sparta, was there to signify that this was not just a sideshow. They did the Athenians a great deal of harm. The Athenians lost the use of their entire countryside. More than twenty thousand slaves, most of them skilled workers, deserted.[5] All the sheep and beasts of burden were slaughtered, and as for the horses, as the cavalry rode out to Decelea every day to attack the enemy or protect the land, some of them were lamed by the hard-trodden ground and the incessant labor and others were wounded in the fighting.

28. Previously, livestock had been quickly brought from Euboea to Oropus and then overland through Decelea. Now it had to be brought around Sunium by sea, at great cost. Athens had to import everything it needed, and what once had been a city was now a fort. During the day, the men took turns guarding the walls, and everyone except the cavalry guarded it by night, with some men stationed with their arms at various posts and others up on the wall itself. They suffered in winter and summer alike. What caused them more difficulty than anything was the fact that they were fighting two wars at the same time, and that they were also oppressed by a need to win so insatiable that it had to be seen to be believed. I mean, the fact that they refused to pull out of Sicily even when they were besieged by a Peloponnesian fort on their own territory; that they, for their part, were even *in* Sicily besieging Syracuse in their turn and in the same way—a city as big as Athens itself; that they had displayed such unexpected daring and power to other Greek states, who believed at the beginning of the war that if the Peloponnesians invaded their territory, the Athenians would be able to hold out for what some thought would be one, others two, and still others three years, but no one more; and that nevertheless, in the seventeenth year after the first invasion of Attica, by now exhausted by war, they had gone to Sicily and taken upon themselves a greater conflict than the one they already had with the Peloponnese!

Because of this war on two fronts and the great losses Decelea was now inflicting on them, and because of the other huge expenses they had incurred, the Athenians were going bankrupt, and it was about this time that they replaced the tribute with a five-percent tax on all the maritime business of their subjects, thinking that they would derive more income by this means. After all, their expenses were no longer the same as they had been, but were much greater in proportion as the war was greater, and their internal revenues were dwindling besides.

29. Thus at a time when there was no money, the Athenians did not want the expense of the Thracians who had come too late for Demosthenes, and they quickly sent them home. They appointed Diitrephes to escort them, and since they were sailing along the coast via the Euripus Strait, which separates Euboea from Boeotia, they ordered him to do as much harm to the enemy as possible with them. After putting them ashore in the Tanagran territory and rapidly taking some plunder, he sailed across the Euripus at nightfall from Chalcis, in Euboea, landed in the Boeotian territory, and led the Thracians against Mycalessus. They spent the night unseen near the temple of Hermes, about two miles from the town. At daybreak, they advanced on the undefended town, which is not large, attacked it, and took it. The people were caught completely by surprise. Never expecting that any one would come up so far from the sea to attack them, their wall was weak and in some places had fallen down; else-

5. Historians disagree as to how Thucydides arrived at this number, which is both large and round.

where, it was built low. In any case, their gates were open, so safe did they feel. Nevertheless, the Thracians rushed into Mycalessus, looting homes and temples and killing all the people they came across, one after another, sparing neither old nor young. They even killed women and children, even beasts of burden, every living thing they saw. For when they are on a rampage, the Thracian race is the most murderous, on a level with the worst barbarians, and on that day there was every kind of mayhem, and death took every conceivable form. They even burst into a boys' school—the biggest in the town—that the boys had just entered, and hacked them all to pieces. This disaster was sudden, horrible—none more so—and it fell upon the whole city.

30. When they learned what had happened, the Thebans rushed to the rescue. They caught up with the Thracians a little way from the town, took away their loot, put them into a panic, and chased them down to the sea at the Euripus, where the ships that had brought them were anchored. Most of the men the Thebans killed did not know how to swim and died while trying to get aboard the ships that their crews had moored out of bowshot when they saw what was happening on shore. In other respects, the Thracian retreat was not disorderly. Against the Theban cavalry, which attacked them first, they defended themselves with distinctly Thracian tactics of suddenly advancing and then retreating in a body. Very few of them died in this action, although many who had stayed behind to loot were caught and killed in the town itself. In all, two hundred fifty out of thirteen hundred Thracians were killed, and of the Thebans and others who came to the rescue, about twenty cavalry and hoplites, along with Scirphondas, a Theban boeotarch. Most of the Mycalessans were wiped out. Such was the calamity that befell Mycalessus, and given the size of the city, it was an event more deserving of lamentation than any other in the war.

31. After the building of the fort in Laconia, Demosthenes was sailing for Corcyra where he found a merchant ship moored at Pheia, in Elis, in which the Corinthian hoplites were intending to cross over to Sicily. Demosthenes destroyed the ship, but the men got away and later sailed in another ship. After this, Demosthenes reached Zacynthus and Cephallenia, where he took aboard some hoplites and sent for others from the Messenians of Naupactus. Then he crossed to the Acarnanian mainland opposite—to Alyzia and Anactorium, which were held by the Athenians. While Demosthenes was in those parts, he met Eurymedon, who was sailing back from Sicily, where he had been sent during the winter with money for the army.[6] Eurymedon gave him the news, including the news of the capture of Plemmyrium by the Syracusans, which he had learned of only after setting sail. Conon, the governor of Naupactus, also joined them and told them that the twenty-five Corinthian ships anchored opposite them were not only not ceasing hostilities, but looked like they intended to fight. He asked them to send him some ships, since his eighteen were not enough to fight their twenty-five. Demosthenes and Eurymedon put together their ten best ships and sent them to Conon's flotilla at Naupactus, and then they finished putting together the components of their armada. Eurymedon sailed to Corcyra, where he called up hoplites and ordered the Corcyraeans to man fifteen ships. (After turning aside from his voyage back to Athens from Sicily, Eurymedon had assumed joint command with Demosthenes, in accordance with his original orders.) Meanwhile, Demosthenes was recruiting a force of slingers and javelin men in the Acarnanian territory.

6. See 7.16.

32. The delegation from Syracuse that had been making the rounds of the cities in Sicily after the capture of Plemmyrium was now ready to lead back the army they had succeeded in raising. Nicias, who had advance intelligence of this, sent to the Centoripes, Alicyaeans, and other Sicel allies who controlled the passes, asking them to band together and stop the enemy from getting through. They had no other route, since the Agrigentines would not give them passage through their own territory. The enemy troops were by now on the way, but the Sicels, complying with the Athenian request, set up a triangulated ambush and, attacking suddenly, caught the army off guard and killed about eight hundred of them, along with all the ambassadors, except for the Corinthian. This man led the approximately fifteen hundred men who got away into Syracuse.

33. During these same days, the Camarinaeans also came to reinforce Syracuse, with five hundred hoplites, three hundred javelin men, and three hundred archers.[7] The Geloans also sent five ships, four hundred javelin men, and two hundred cavalry. The cities that had at first awaited developments had by now joined together in the relief of Syracuse, and so all the Greek cities in Sicily except for Agrigentum, which was neutral, were fighting with Syracuse against the Athenians.

In view of their losses in Sicel territory, the Syracusans put off any immediate attack on the Athenians. Meanwhile, their forces from Corcyra and the mainland now ready, Demosthenes and Eurymedon took the whole armada across the Ionian Gulf to Cape Iapygia. Setting out from there, they put into the Iapygian Choerades Islands and took aboard one hundred fifty Iapygian javelin men from the Messapian tribe. After renewing their old alliance with Artas, the chieftain who had supplied the javelin men, they went on to Metapontum, in Italy. Invoking the terms of their alliance, they prevailed on the Metapontines to send three hundred javelin men and two triremes with them, and after attaching these to their forces, they followed the coast to Thurii. On arrival, they found that there had just been a civil war and that the party hostile to Athens had been forced into exile. Demosthenes and Eurymedon wanted to gather the whole armada at Thurii for an inspection to see whether anything was unaccounted for. They also wanted to persuade the Thurians to cooperate as fully as possible in the campaign and, now that pro-Athenian feelings were at their highest, to win them over to a full offensive and defensive alliance. So they remained in Thurii attending to all these matters.

34. At about the same time, the Peloponnesians in the twenty-five ships that had anchored opposite the Athenians at Naupactus to protect the troop ships bound for Sicily got ready for battle. They had in fact manned even more ships, making theirs only slightly smaller than the Athenian flotilla, and they lay at anchor off Achaea, at Erineus, in Rhipic territory. They were in a crescent-shaped mooring, and infantry from Corinth and from local allies who had come to help were positioned along the promontories on both sides. The ships were in a line between the points of the crescent, which they blockaded, and the flotilla was under the command of Polyanthes, a Corinthian. From Naupactus, the Athenians sailed up to attack them with thirty three ships under the command of Diphilus. At first the Corinthians remained motionless, but then, when they decided the moment was right, they raised the signal flag and sailed out to do battle with the Athenians. For a long time, they fought to a standstill. Three Corinthian ships were destroyed, and while none of the Athenian ships

---

7. For the deliberations in Camarina, see 6.75ff.

was actually sunk, seven were rendered unseaworthy when their outriggers were rammed head on and shattered by Corinthian ships, whose anchor-blocks had been especially reinforced for this purpose. They fought dead even, although each side thought it had won. Nevertheless, the Athenians did manage to take the wrecked Corinthian ships, because the wind had driven them into open water and the Corinthians were no longer willing to press the attack. The two sides disengaged. There was no pursuit, and no men were captured: the Corinthians and Peloponnesians had fought close to the shore and easily made it to safety, while as for the Athenians, none of their ships had been sunk. Right after the Athenians returned to Naupactus, the Corinthians set up a victory marker. They claimed victory because they had put more enemy ships out of commission than they had lost, and they thought they had not been defeated for the same reason the Athenians thought they themselves had not won: the Corinthians considered it a victory not to be badly beaten, whereas the Athenians thought it a defeat not to win big. After the Peloponnesians had sailed away and their infantry had dispersed, however, the Athenians also set up a victory marker in Achaea, about two and a half miles from the Corinthian mooring at Erineus. And that was how the naval battle ended.

35. After the Thurians had finished their preparations to join the expedition with seven hundred hoplites and three hundred javelin men, Demosthenes and Eurymedon ordered their ships to sail along the coast towards Croton. Meanwhile, they would first review all the land forces at the Sybaris River and then lead them through Thurian territory. When they were at the Hylias River, the Crotonians sent word that they would not allow the army into their territory, so they followed the river down to the sea and spent the night at the mouth of the Hylias, where they rendezvoused with their ships. The next day, they boarded the ships and sailed along the coast, putting into all the towns but Locri until they reached Petra in Rhegian territory.

36. Meanwhile, the Syracusans, knowing that they were coming, wanted to have another try with their navy and with the infantry they had mustered expressly for action before Demosthenes and Eurymedon arrived. They rigged out their ships in a way the experience of the first battle had shown would give them the greatest advantage. They sawed off the prows of their ships to make them shorter and harder and attached thick anchor-blocks to them, reinforcing these with eighteen-foot struts extending nine feet down through the sides of the ship and into it. This was how the Corinthians had refitted their ships at Naupactus, when they fought the Athenians by ramming them with their prows. The Syracusans had decided that they would fare better with this construction against the Athenian ships, which were not built to withstand this new rigging. Athenian ships had light prows because the Athenians didn't ram prow to prow. They preferred to keep rowing around you and then come in to ram your side or stern. The Syracusans thought they would have the advantage in the Great Harbor, where many ships would fight in a small space. With their hard, thick prows they would ram prow to prow and smash the hollow, weak prows of the Athenians. Meanwhile, the lack of space would keep the Athenians from employing the maneuvers they relied on most, of either continuously rowing around you or sailing through your formation and quickly turning to ram you. Insofar as they were able, the Syracusans would deny them the space to sail through, while the lack of room to maneuver would prevent them from sailing around in circles. Head-on collisions, which in the first battle had been thought to result from the ineptitude of their steersmen, would now be the Syracusans' greatest weapon and would give them their greatest advantage. The Athenians would

not be able to back water because they would have nowhere to retreat but their own camp, which was just a small piece of the nearby shore. The Syracusans would control the rest of the harbor, and if the Athenians were hard pressed and all forced together into the same small space, they would run into each other and fall into disarray. (And in fact not having the whole harbor to retreat to, as the Syracusans did, is what did the Athenians the greatest damage in all the naval battles.) Not only would the Syracusans be able to retreat anywhere, but they alone would be able to turn in the open sea and row back into the harbor at will. This would keep the Athenians from sailing around the action and out of the harbor, especially since Plemmyrium was now enemy territory and the harbor mouth was small.

37. Having made these plans to suit their own abilities and strengths, and emboldened by the first sea battle, the Syracusans carried out a concerted attack with ships and infantry. Starting first, Gylippus led his foot soldiers out and marched them up to the Athenian wall at the point where it overlooked the city. Then the troops and hoplites at the temple of the Olympian Zeus, along with the Syracusan cavalry and light-armed forces, came at the wall from the other side. Immediately after that, the Syracusan and allied ships sailed out. At first, the Athenians thought the Syracusans were going to attack them with infantry alone, but when they saw the ships suddenly bearing down on them, they were thrown into a flurry, with some going atop the walls or in front of them to line up against the advancing infantry, and others going to meet the many swiftly moving cavalry and javelin men from the temple and beyond, and still others taking up positions along the shore and manning the ships, and then, when they were manned, getting off seventy-five to match the roughly eighty from Syracuse.

38. For most of the day, the ships advanced and backed water, testing each other, until they disengaged, with the infantry pulling back from the walls at the same time. Neither side gained anything worth mentioning, except for the sinking of one or two Athenian ships by the Syracusans.

The next day, the Syracusans rested, giving no sign of what they would do next. Seeing how evenly balanced the naval battle had been, and fearing that the Syracusans would attack again, Nicias ordered his trierarchs to repair any damaged ships and anchored merchantmen outside the fence that the Athenians had driven into the sea in front of their ships as a dock. He left about a hundred fifty feet between the merchantmen, so that if any of the warships was in trouble, it could easily take refuge and just as easily sail back out again. The Athenians worked at these tasks all day and finished at night.

39. The next day, with the same tactics, only earlier in the day, the Syracusans engaged the Athenians with their ships and infantry. Opposing each just as before, they once again passed the greater part of the day testing each other's strength, until a Corinthian, Ariston, son of Pyrrhichus, and the best steersman in the Syracusan navy, urged the commanders to send word to the officials in the city, ordering them to move the regular market down to the shore as quickly as possible and to make private individuals selling their own stores come to the same place. That way, the sailors could quickly disembark, eat right next to their ships, and then, after a short time, launch a surprise attack on the Athenians on the same day.

40. The commanders agreed. A messenger was sent and the market set up. Suddenly, the Syracusans backed water and rowed to the city shore, where they quickly disembarked and ate their meal. The Athenians thought they had put their ships astern and gone towards their city in defeat, so they calmly returned

to shore and, among other things, started preparing a meal in the belief that there would be no more naval battles that day. But suddenly the Syracusans manned their ships and sailed to the attack once more. In great confusion, the Athenians, most of them unfed, got aboard their ships helter-skelter and just barely made it out to meet the enemy. For a while the two sides warily held off from each other, but then the Athenians decided that they would bring about their own defeat if they exhausted themselves with delay and that they should attack immediately. So, cheering each other on, they advanced to battle.

The Syracusans met the attack, prows forward, as planned, and effectively tore through much of the outrigging of the Athenian ships with their reconfigured prows. Meanwhile, javelin men on the Syracusan decks wrought havoc among the Athenian sailors, though even more damage was done by troops in small craft continuously sailing around the Athenian ships, rowing into banks of oars and disrupting their stroke, or coming up alongside and showering the sailors with spears.

41. The Syracusans fought with all their strength and in the end, and in this way, they won. The Athenians turned and fled back to their mooring through the barrier of merchantmen. The Syracusans pursued them as far as the merchantmen, whose dolphin-shaped weights, hanging from spars extending over the entries in the dock, then prevented them from going any further.[8] Two Syracusan ships, their crews exhilarated with victory, came in close to press the attack, but both were damaged and one was captured with its crew. The Syracusans had sunk seven Athenian ships and crippled many more; they took many men prisoner; others they killed. They sailed away and set up victory markers for both naval battles. And now, with confidence in the superiority of their navy, they decided that they would also take control on land.

42. The Athenians were getting ready to resist yet another attack on two fronts when Demosthenes and Eurymedon arrived with the relief force from Athens. I calculate that they had seventy-three ships, including foreign ones, with over five thousand Athenian and allied hoplites. There were many barbarian and Greek javelin men, along with slingers, archers, and all the supplies they needed. In an instant, the Syracusans and their allies were absolutely dumbfounded at the thought that there would be no end to their danger. They saw that in spite of the fortification of Decelea, a force nearly equal to the first had arrived. Athens visibly projected power everywhere. Meanwhile, the first armada began to emerge from its afflictions into new vigor.

Demosthenes saw how things stood and realized that he must not waste time and thereby find himself in the same predicament as Nicias. (When Nicias first arrived, he struck fear into the Syracusans. But he wintered in Catana instead of immediately pressing the war and fell into contempt. Next, Gylippus caught him off guard and reached Syracuse with an army from the Peloponnese, an army the Syracusans would never have sent for had Nicias attacked right away. They had thought that they could go it alone, and would only have learned how weak they were after the city had been completely sealed off. Thus even if they *had* then sent for an army, it would not have been able to help them as much as it did.) Demosthenes took a hard look at these factors and understood that he too, at that point on the very first day, and more than at any other time, was at his most fearsome to the enemy, and decided to take the fullest advantage of the alarm caused at that moment by his army. He saw that the Syracusan counterwall—the one by which they had prevented the Athenians from

8. These weights were swung out from spars and dropped into enemy ships, smashing their hulls.

walling them off—was only a single wall. If he could take control of the way up to Epipolae and then knock out the force stationed on it, there would be no one left to oppose them and the wall could easily be captured. He eagerly turned his attention to this attack, thinking it the quickest way to bring about an end to the war. Either he would succeed and take Syracuse, or he would withdraw the armada and put an end to the drain on the army and on the whole city of Athens.

First the Athenians marched out, slashing and burning the land around the Anapus River. Just as they had at the beginning of the war, they asserted the superiority of their armada by land and sea, and the Syracusans, except for the cavalry and javelin men from the temple of the Olympian Zeus, did not come out to engage them on either front.

43. Then Demosthenes decided to make a preliminary attack on the crossing wall with battering rams, but the rams were set on fire by the enemy defenders on the walls as he brought them up, while the Athenian army was pushed back wherever else it attacked. Demosthenes decided to waste no more time. He won over Nicias and the other commanders and set about making the attack on Epipolae, as planned. He decided that it would be impossible to approach and ascend Epipolae undetected by day, so he ordered a five-day supply of food, and taking all the masons and joiners, along with archers and everything else he would need to hold his position and build a wall if he won, he, Eurymedon, and Menander advanced on Epipolae with the whole Athenian army in the dead of night. Nicias was left behind in their fortifications. When they reached Epipolae at the Euryelus River, where their first army had made the ascent, they got up without being seen by the Syracusan garrison, took the Syracusan fort at the top, and killed some of the men on guard. Most of the garrison, however, immediately fled toward their encampments, of which there were three behind advance fortifications atop Epipolae. One of these was made up of Syracusans, one of the other Sicilians, and one of the allies. The men spread word of the attack and reported it to the six hundred picked Syracusans who were the advance guard along this section of Epipolae. These men immediately rushed to the defense, and although they put up a stiff resistance, Demosthenes and the Athenians engaged them and put them to flight. Demosthenes and his men immediately moved on so as not to slow the momentum of their attack. Since the Syracusan guard did not stand and fight, some of the Athenians started to occupy the walls straight off and to tear down its battlements. The Syracusans, their allies, and Gylippus and his men went to meet the enemy from the advance fortifications. Though stunned by the unexpected daring of the Athenian night action, they attacked, but were forced, at first, to pull back. The Athenians kept advancing, falling out of formation as if they had already won. They also wanted to force their way through the whole line of the enemy that had not yet fought and to prevent them from regrouping by pressing the assault; but the Boeotians, who were the first to stand their ground, attacked, turned them back, and put them to flight.

44. Now the Athenians fell into total disarray and the confusion was so great that it was extremely difficult to find out what happened from either side. In daylight, things are clearer, but even then the combatants can't see everything and only know with difficulty what happens right nearby. How then can anyone know anything for sure in a night battle?—And this was the only night action in the whole war to be fought between large armies. The moon was bright, but as usual in the moonlight, though people could see forms coming at them, they could not know who was a friend. Large numbers of hoplites on both sides were moving around in a restricted space,

and some of the Athenians had already been defeated, while others advanced, still unbeaten, to their first contact with the enemy. Much of their army had just reached the top, but there were others still coming, and they did not know which way to go, because by now all their forward troops were in the chaos of the rapidly developing rout, and it was hard to tell the armies apart in all the shouting. It was impossible to transmit orders in the darkness, so the Syracusans and their allies, knowing they were winning, kept shouting encouragement to each other as they stood up to the brunt of the attack. The Athenians were searching each other out, and they thought everything in front of them was hostile, even if it was a retreating friend. Demands for the password were coming fast and thick because there was no other way for them to recognize each other, and in the confusion of everyone asking the password, they made it known even to the enemy. Not as many Athenians knew the Syracusan password, because the Syracusans had the upper hand and because they were in a closer formation and could more easily tell each other apart. Thus Athenians who could not answer the Syracusans were killed, whereas the Syracusans, who knew the password of the Athenians, could get away whenever they encountered superior force. What did the greatest damage were the battle hymns, because they were similar among Dorians fighting on both sides, and this completely bewildered the Athenians. Whenever Argives, Corcyraeans, and other Dorians who were with the Athenians started to sing their battle hymns, the Athenians were panicked as much as they were by the enemy himself. In the end, they started falling on one another throughout the army in mass confusion, friend against friend and countryman against countryman, not only intensifying the terror but barely escaping each other's deadly grip. The way down from Epipolae was straight and narrow, and most of those who were killed had been pursued to the cliffs where they jumped for their lives. But once men had gotten safely down from the top to level ground, most of them escaped to the camp—especially the men who had come with the first expedition and who knew their way around the terrain. Some of the later arrivals lost their way and wandered around the plain, and when day came, they were hunted down and killed by the Syracusan cavalry.

45. The next day, the Syracusans set up two victory markers, one at the top of the approach to Epipolae and one where the Boeotians first took their stand. The Athenians took up their dead under a flag of truce. They and their allies had lost a great many men, although there were far more weapons than dead, because the men who had been forced to jump from the cliffs had discarded their arms, and not all of them had died.

46. After the unexpected success of the battle, the Syracusans regained their former confidence and sent Sicanus with fifteen ships to Agrigentum, which was having a civil war, to bring the city over to their side if he could. Also, in view of the way things had turned out on Epipolae, Gylippus had hopes of taking the Athenian fortifications by storm and once again went into the rest of Sicily by land to gather yet another army.

47. Meanwhile, faced with their recent defeat and with the general impotence of the army, the Athenian generals had a meeting. They could see that their initiatives came to nothing and that the troops could no longer endure being there. They were also ridden with sickness, for two reasons. First, it was the time of year when people are most likely to get sick, and secondly, they were camped on pestilent, marshy ground. Everything just seemed hopeless to them. Demosthenes had decided that they must not remain. He had taken a chance

on his plan and now that it had failed, he would vote to waste no more time and to leave while the seas were still navigable and while they still had the upper hand at least with the ships that had come as reinforcements. He said that they would be more useful to their city against the troops who were building fortifications on their territory than they would be against the Syracusans, whom it was no longer possible to subdue. Furthermore, it didn't make sense to waste any more money continuing the siege.

48. That was the position of Demosthenes. Nicias, too, thought that they were in a very bad situation, but he would not have them make any statements disclosing their weakness or have their withdrawal betrayed to the enemy by taking an open vote in a large body, because they would have much less chance of pulling out at will if the Syracusans knew about it. For another thing, he had greater knowledge than his colleagues of the situation in Syracuse, and he still had reason to hope that it would become worse than their own if only they persevered in the siege. They could wear the Syracusans down by outspending them, especially since the ships they had now gave them much more control of the sea. Also, there was an element in Syracuse that wanted to turn the city over to the Athenians, and they kept sending Nicias messages urging him not to leave. He was bearing all this in mind and was in reality still vacillating and studying the situation. Nevertheless, he flatly refused to say publicly at that time that he would withdraw the army. He knew perfectly well, he said, that the Athenian people would not accept a pull-out unless they voted for it themselves, and the men who would pass judgment on their actions would only hear of what they had done in the criticisms of others. Their judges would not understand the situation because they had not seen it, and they would be won over by whatever slanders a glib prosecutor could produce. He said that many, if not most, of the soldiers who were now crying out against their plight would get to Athens and cry out against their generals for treacherously taking bribes to withdraw.[9] Therefore he, for one, knowing what the Athenians were like, preferred to take his chances and die in battle on his own terms rather than in disgrace after an unjust trial in Athens. And in spite of everything, he said, the situation in Syracuse was still worse than theirs. The Syracusans had spent their money supporting mercenary troops and building forts, and they had been maintaining a navy for a year now. They were already strapped and would soon be desperate. They had spent two thousand talents so far and were deeply in debt besides, and failure to pay any of their present forces would start to sap their strength, since most of their soldiers were mercenaries, not conscripts like the Athenian army. He said that they had to wear the Syracusans down with the siege and not leave in defeat on account of money, of which they had much more than the enemy.

49. Nicias stubbornly defended his position. He had accurate intelligence about the situation in the city and about their shortage of money. He knew of the large faction in Syracuse that wanted to turn the government over to the Athenians and that kept sending him messages urging him not to leave. He was also confident that they had a better chance of prevailing with their navy than they had before.

Demosthenes would under no circumstances accept the part about continuing the siege. If they had to wait in Sicily for a vote from Athens before they

---

9. In 424, the Athenian people punished Pythodorus, Sophocles, and Eurymedon for taking bribes to leave Sicily instead of remaining and taking control of the island. See 4.65.

could withdraw the armada, he said that they should move out and do it in Thapsus or Catana, from which their infantry could attack much of the countryside, living off what it could plunder from the enemy and hurting them in the process. Meanwhile, their fleet could fight in the open sea and not pent up in the harbor, which favored the enemy. Out in the open, they could make use of their experience, attacking and retreating without having to anchor and cast off behind their cramped palisades. In short, he said that there was no way he could sanction remaining where they were. They should end the siege as quickly as possible, now, without delay. Eurymedon advocated the same course, but when Nicias continued to object, there arose a mood of hesitancy and delay, reinforced by the impression that he was so obstinate because he knew something they did not.

In this way, the Athenians kept putting off a decision and stayed where they were.

50. Meanwhile, Gylippus and Sicanus arrived in Syracuse. Sicanus had failed in his campaign against Agrigentum, because the faction that was friendly to Syracuse had been expelled while he was still at Gela, but Gylippus brought another large army he had gathered in Sicily, along with the hoplites who had been sent in the merchant ships from the Peloponnese that spring and who reached Selinus via Libya. They had been driven off course into Libya, where the Cyrenaeans gave them two triremes and pilots to guide them. As they sailed along the coast, they joined forces with the Euesperitae, who were being besieged by the Libyans. They defeated the Libyans and sailed along from there to Neapolis, a Carthaginian trading post, which at two days' and one night's sail is the shortest route to Sicily. From there, they crossed the open sea and reached Selinus.

As soon as these troops arrived, the Syracusans prepared for another attack on the Athenians by land and sea, and the Athenian generals, seeing that the Syracusans had gained another army, and that their own situation was not only not getting better but was deteriorating every day in every way, and was especially aggravated by the sickness among the troops, now regretted that they had not left earlier. Now even Nicias no longer opposed the others, as he had done before, except for insisting that they should not vote openly. As secretly as possible, they gave all the men advance notice that they would be sailing out and told them to make preparations to cast off when the order was given. But when everything was in readiness, and just as they were about to sail, there was an eclipse of the moon, which happened to be full.[1] The event made most of the Athenians feel uneasy, and they urged their generals to stay; and Nicias, who was too inclined to believe in the interpretation of omens and that sort of thing, refused even to discuss a move until after they had stayed for "three times nine days," as their seers decreed. This was the reason the Athenians stayed on after all their delays!

51. The Syracusans learned of this and were all the more determined not to let up on the Athenians, since they themselves now conceded that they were no longer superior on either land or sea—otherwise they would not have planned to sail away. The Syracusans also wanted to make sure that they did not take up a position anywhere else in Sicily, which would make them harder to attack. No, they wanted to force the Athenians to fight at sea as quickly as possible, right where they were and just as they were. The Syracusans therefore manned their ships and practiced their maneuvers for as many days as they

---

1. This eclipse took place on August 27, 413.

thought necessary. When the time was right, they began by attacking the Athenian fortifications. A small force of hoplites and cavalry came out of one of the gates to engage them, but the Syracusans cut off some of the hoplites, turned them back, and chased them to the gate. The entry was narrow, and the Athenians abandoned seventy horses and lost a few hoplites.

52. That day, the Syracusan army pulled back. The next day, they sent out seventy-six ships while their infantry simultaneously advanced on the fortifications. The Athenians launched eighty-six ships to meet them. They engaged and began the fight. Eurymedon, who commanded the Athenian right wing, aimed to encircle the enemy ships opposed to him, so he extended his line by sailing close to shore. But the Syracusans and their allies broke through against the Athenian center first and cut him off in the inner bay of the harbor, where they killed him and destroyed his ships. Then they went after all the other Athenian vessels and drove them out of the water and onto the beach.

53. Gylippus, seeing that the defeated enemy ships had been borne down outside of their fences and away from the Athenian encampment, took a detachment of his army over to the breakwater in the harbor, in order to kill the men who were landing and make it easy for the Syracusans to tow away the vessels, which were now on friendly ground. When the Tyrrhenians, who were protecting the disembarking Athenians, saw Gylippus's men advancing out of formation, they rushed out to the rescue, attacked the front line, and forced them back to the marsh they call "Lake Lysimeleia." Before long, though, more Syracusan and allied troops came up, and the Athenians, terrified of losing their ships, advanced to reinforce the Tyrrhenians and made a real fight of it, which they won. They pursued and killed a few hoplites, and saved and brought back most of their ships to their camp, although the Syracusans and their allies had captured eighteen of them and put all their crews to death. Then the Syracusans tried to burn down the remaining ships by loading an old merchantman with brushwood and firebrands and launching it in flames into a wind that blew it towards the Athenians. The Athenians, fearful for their ships, escaped danger by coming up with preventive measures to put out the fire and by managing to keep the flaming merchantman from getting close.

54. After this, the Syracusans set up a victory marker for the naval battle and for the battle where they cut off the hoplites in front of the upper fortifications, where they also captured the horses. The Athenians set one up where the Tyrrhenians forced the infantry back to the marsh and one where they were victorious with the rest of the army.

55. The Syracusans had won a decisive victory, and by sea at that, for it must be remembered that they had initially panicked at the sudden arrival of Demosthenes' fleet. So now the Athenians were in utter despair, and their stunned disbelief at this incalculable defeat at sea was only exceeded by their regret over having undertaken the expedition at all. To have attacked the only cities that had a way of life similar to their own! A democratic people, like themselves! A place with ships, cavalry, and huge resources! These were people the Athenians could not take over either by exploiting the political differences between them and offering a change of government, or by the application of massive force. They had failed repeatedly and had reached a dead end before the battle, but now they had been beaten at sea, something they never thought would happen, and they were even more desperate.

56. The Syracusans immediately began to sail along the harbor's shore at will and made plans to close up its entrance so that the Athenians would never

be able to sail out unnoticed, no matter how much they wanted to. The Syracusans were no longer thinking only about their own safety—they were also thinking about denying safety to the Athenians. Under the circumstances, they thought that their position was far superior, as in fact it was, and that it would be a great achievement in the eyes of Greece for them to defeat the Athenians and their allies on both land and sea, thus immediately bringing political freedom to some Greeks and liberating others from fear. For the Athenians would no longer have enough strength to fight the war that would come to engulf them. Meanwhile they, the Syracusans, would get the glory for their downfall and would be the wonder and admiration of all mankind now and forever. The struggle would be renowned for this, but also because they would not only have prevailed over the Athenians, but over Athens' many allies as well. And they did not do it alone; they did it with the allies who had come to help them, the Corinthians and the Spartans, with whom they were taking leadership in the war, after putting their own city in peril to keep the peril from others and after rebuilding their navy.

This was the largest gathering of nations at a single city ever, although the total count of nations involved with Athens and Sparta during the war was of course higher.

57. The following is a listing of the peoples who came either to attack or to defend Sicily, and who fought at Syracuse to conquer the island or to save it, standing together neither in kinship nor to redress a grievance, but as each was brought by the accidents of compulsion or expediency.

The Athenians, who were Ionians, attacked the Dorian Syracusans of their own free will. They were accompanied by their colonists the Lemnians, Imbrians, Aeginetans (who possessed Aegina at that time) and Histiaeans, who occupied Histiaea, in Euboea. All still spoke the same language and had the same institutions as the Athenians.

The others who joined in the campaign were either subject states, independent allies, or mercenaries. Of the subject states who paid tribute, the Eretrians, Chalcidians, Styrians, and Carystians came from Euboea. The Ceans, Andrians, and Tenians came from the islands; and the Milesians, Samians, and Chians came from Ionia. The Chians, however, were independent allies and provided ships instead of paying tribute. Except for the Carystians, who are Dryopes, all of these people were Ionian and had originally come from Athens. They constituted the greater part of the force that accompanied the Athenians, and although they came as subjects, they were nonetheless Ionians against Dorians. In addition to these there were the Aeolians: Methymnians, who were required to supply ships instead of tribute; and Tenedians and Aenians, who paid tribute. The Athenians forced these Aeolians to fight against the Boeotians, who founded them and who were also Aeolians, and who fought with Syracuse. The Plataeans, who were Boeotians, did not need to be forced and were the only people you would expect to find fighting against their own race, because of their hatred of Boeotia. The Rhodians and Cytherians were both Dorian peoples. The Cytherians had been colonists from Sparta, but they bore arms with the Athenians against the Spartans under Gylippus. The Rhodians, who were Argive by race, were forced to fight against the Syracusans, who were Dorians, and against the Geloans, who were their own colonists but who were on the side of Syracuse. Of the islanders around the Peloponnese, the Cephallenians and the Zacynthians were independent, but their island position left them little choice but to follow the Athenians, who ruled the sea. The Corcyraeans were not only Dorians, but were clearly of Corinthian origin. Nevertheless, they fought against Corinth, their mother country, and the Syracusans, their kinsmen. On the face of it, they were forced to do so, but in reality they willingly followed Athens out of their hatred for Corinth. The Messenians, the current name for the people of Naupactus and Pylos, which at that time was held by Athens, were also brought by them to the war. There were also a few Megarian exiles who, as luck would have it, were fighting the Selinuntines, who were themselves Megarian.

The rest of the expedition was made up mostly of soldiers of fortune. The Argives, for example, who were Dorian, fought other Dorians with the Athenians, who were Ionian, not so much because of their alliance as because of their hatred of Sparta and the desire of each soldier for private gain. The Mantineans and other Arcadians were used to fighting as mercenaries against anyone who was pointed out to them as the enemy at any given moment. For pay, they now regarded the Arcadians who had come with the Corinthians as no less their enemy than anybody else. The Cretans and the Aetolians also fought for money, and it came about that the Cretans, who had founded Gela with the Rhodians, now came of their own free will, for pay, to fight not with their colony but against it. The Acarnanians fought in part for pay, but mostly as allies out of their friendship for Demosthenes and their good will towards Athens. All these peoples were bounded on the west by the Ionian Gulf.

In Italy, the Thurians and Metapontines were forced to fight by the conditions imposed on them by the state of their internal conflicts at the time. In Sicily, there were the Naxians and the Catanaeans. Of the barbarians, there were the Egestans, who had invited the Athenians in, and most of the Sicel tribes. Outside Sicily, there were the Tyrrhenians, who came out of enmity for Syracuse, and the Iapygians, who came for hire.

These were the peoples who fought with the Athenians.

58. On the other side, helping Syracuse, were the Camarinaeans, who bordered them, and the Geloans, who were to the west of the Camarinaeans. From the territory west of Agrigentum, which was neutral, they were helped by the Selinuntines. All of these people inhabited the part of Sicily opposite Libya. The Himerans came from the part of the island facing the Tyrrhenian Sea. They are the only Greek-speaking people in that region and the only ones from there who helped Syracuse.

Those were the Greek peoples of Sicily, all Dorian and all independent, who fought with Syracuse. The only barbarians to help were such Sicels as had not gone over to the Athenians.

Of Greeks outside Sicily, the Spartans provided one of their generals and troops consisting of freedmen and helots. The Corinthians were the only ones who sent both ships and infantry, and they were accompanied by their kinsmen, the Leucadians and the Ambraciots. There were Arcadian mercenaries sent by Corinth, Sicyonian conscripts, and from outside the Peloponnese, Boeotians. Compared with this outside help, many more troops in all categories were provided by the Sicilians themselves, who after all lived in sizable cities. They assembled large numbers of hoplites, ships, and cavalry, as well as an inexhaustible supply of common soldiers. In general, however, the Syracusans themselves gave more than all the rest, because of the size of their city and because they were in the greatest peril.

59. These, then, were the forces marshalled on both sides. At that time, they were all at Syracuse and there were no further reinforcements.

The Syracusans and their allies naturally thought it would be a great accomplishment to add the capture of the whole Athenian expeditionary force to the naval victory they had already won, and to prevent their escape by either land or sea. They began by immediately closing off the entrance to the Great Harbor, which is about a mile wide, by anchoring in it triremes, merchantmen, and small craft, all moored broadside. They also made preparations for another naval battle, should the Athenians risk it. They were definitely thinking big.

60. Seeing the harbor being sealed, and surmising the Syracusans' intentions, the Athenians realized that they had to make a plan. The generals and battalion commanders met to discuss the crisis, the worst of which was that they had run out of food and that there would be no more unless they could regain control of the sea. (You see, they had sent word to Catana before the eclipse that they were planning to leave and that the Catanaeans should send no more supplies.) They therefore decided to abandon the upper fortifications and to cut off the approach to their ships by a counterwall no bigger than would be needed to enclose their gear and their sick. This place they would garrison. Then they would get the remaining infantry aboard to man all the ships, sound and unsound alike, and fight one last battle. If they won, they would make their way to Catana; but if not, they would burn their ships and make an orderly retreat by the quickest route to friendly territory, whether Greek or barbarian. They immediately acted on their decision. They came down in stages from the fortifications on Epipolae and manned the whole fleet, forcing aboard every man of military age who could be of any use. In all, they fully manned about one hundred and ten ships, stationing on their decks large numbers of Acarnanian and other foreign archers and javelin men, and doing whatever else was necessary to carry out the desperate plan that had been forced upon them. When everything was almost ready, Nicias saw that the troops were still depressed over their completely unexpected defeat at sea, at the same time that want of food made them eager to take their chances as quickly as possible. So he called all the men together, and spoke the following words of encouragement before the battle.

61. Fighting men from Athens and from our allied states! What you have in common with the enemy is that the coming battle will be just as much about your lives and your city as about theirs. And if we beat them now with our ships, each of you will get to see his homeland once again. You must not be depressed, or suffer what happens to inexperienced men when they lose their first battles and cannot even be frightened into hoping for more than defeat. Those of you who are Athenian and have experienced many wars, and those of you who are allies and have fought with us always, remember how incalculable war is, and hope its fortunes will be on our side as we prepare to put up a fight worthy of such numbers as ours, such numbers as you yourselves can see.

62. Given the cramped space in the harbor, there will be a crush of ships. The enemy will also have troops on their decks. Those are two of the things that hurt us last time, but we have studied the situation with our pilots and have made preparations of our own to match theirs. Archers, javelin men, and a mass of troops will be aboard our ships. We would not do this if we were fighting a real sea battle in open water, because the weight of the boats would hamper our maneuvering skills, but it will be an advantage here where we are forced to fight an infantry battle from our ships. We've also learned how to rig out our ships to counter theirs, especially against their reinforced prows, which hurt us the most. We've made iron grappling hooks, and if the marines do their jobs, we'll keep their ships from backing up after they ram us. It's come to the point where we have to

fight them from our ships as if we were infantry, and our best chance is not to let them back off and not to do so ourselves—especially since the shore, except for the part our infantry holds, is enemy territory.

63. Knowing this, you must fight with all your strength and not be driven ashore. After your ships make contact, you must not disengage until you've knocked the hoplites off the enemy's decks. I'm talking to our hoplites more than to our sailors, because this is the job of the men on deck, and for the most part we can still count on beating them with our infantry. As to the oarsmen, I urge you—I beg you—not to be paralyzed by your setbacks. We have better forces on our decks now, and more ships. And bear in mind that though you are not Athenians, you have long enjoyed the pleasure of being treated as such. This is surely worth preserving. You are admired throughout Greece for speaking our language and behaving like us, and you have benefited from your share in our empire as much as we have—even more, because of the respect you have inspired in our subjects and your immunity to aggression.[2] As the only free partners in our empire, it would not be right for you to betray it now. Don't worry about the Corinthians, whom you have beaten many times, or about the Sicilians, who never saw fit to oppose our fleet when it was at its prime. Beat them back! And show them that even when we are weak and desperate, our skill is better than their lucky strength.

64. As to the Athenians among you, I want to remind you of something one more time. There remain neither ships in the docks of Athens comparable to these, nor eligible hoplites comparable to you. If we have any outcome other than victory, our enemies here will immediately sail against our city, and its existing forces will be powerless to defend it against the enemies who are there, combined with the ones who will be on the way. You men here will instantly fall into the hands of the Syracusans—and you know what you had in mind for them when you came here—while our fellow citizens in Athens will fall prey to the Spartans. If there was ever a time to stand firm, it is now, for in this one battle you are fighting for yourselves and your city, and each and every one of you must remember that on these ships you will now be the Athenian infantry and navy and what is left of Athens and of its great reputation. For the sake of our city, if any of you excels another in skill or courage, let him show it now. There is no better time to help yourself and save us all.

65. Immediately after giving this speech, Nicias gave orders to man the ships. Gylippus and the Syracusans, observing these preparations, were able to see that the Athenians were going to fight. But they also had advance intelligence of the iron grappling hooks, and they took precautions against these as against all the other Athenian measures. They spread hides over the prows and much of the upper parts of their ships, so that after a grappling hook was thrown, its prongs would have nothing to catch on to and would be more likely to slip off. When everything was ready, Gylippus and the other generals rallied their men and spoke to them as follows.

66. Men of Syracuse and allies. We think most of you know how magnificently you've done so far and how glorious the coming battle will be— otherwise you wouldn't have thrown yourselves into the struggle with so

---

2. It appears from this statement that the oarsmen and common sailors of Athens were often not Athenian, but either subjects or foreign mercenaries. See 1.121 and 1.143.

much enthusiasm. But if any of you doesn't know it as well as he should, we'll make it clear.

Having acquired the greatest empire of any Greek state, past or present, the Athenians came to this land to subjugate Sicily first and then, if they succeeded, the Peloponnese and the rest of Greece. You were the first to stand up to their navy, which swept all before it. You have defeated it in battle already, and you have every reason to expect that you will defeat it now. When men are thwarted where they assume that they excel, their self-esteem is weaker afterward than if they had never been so sure of themselves to begin with. Also, after unexpectedly falling short of their proud boasts, they collapse faster than they should, given their strength. This is probably what is happening to the Athenians now.

67. While we, on the other hand, were still inexperienced, we used the courage we were born with and boldly attacked them. We are surer now, and we have a reputation to add to our courage, because if you beat the best, you are the best. Each of you can have a double measure of hope now, and the greater the hope, the greater the zeal in any effort. As to their imitation of our fighting methods, we will be able to counter anything they do because those methods are peculiar to us. When they depart from their usual practice, and place a lot of hoplites on their decks, and have a pack of landlubbing Acarnanian javelin men and other troops aboard, they'll find that they don't know how to stand still and throw their weapons at the same time. How are they going to keep from rocking their boats and getting in each other's way as they move awkwardly around? And they won't benefit from the number of their ships, either. I say this in case any of you is afraid of fighting outnumbered. The small space will slow down any maneuvers they want to execute and will make it much easier for us to hurt them with our riggings.

But there is one thing you must know for a fact, based on what we have learned beyond a shadow of a doubt. Overwhelmed by their misfortunes and driven by desperation, they have fallen into the delusion of trusting more to luck than to their arms. They are risking everything in the only way they can to either force their way out at sea or to retreat by land if they fail, because they can't be worse off than they already are.

68. So let's go against this rabble, these hateful men whose luck has finally run out, and take them on with a vengeance! And let's remember that nothing is more lawful than to satisfy the rage in our hearts by taking a just revenge on the enemies who have attacked us, and that, as the saying goes, nothing is more sweet than to punish those we hate.[3] And this shall come to pass. For we do hate them! You all know it! We hate them more than anyone! They came here to enslave our land, and if they had succeeded, they would have visited the greatest torment on our men and the greatest insult on our women and children, and made the name of our whole city a disgrace. Bear that in mind, and let no one soften toward them or think it's best for them to just go away and not endanger us any more. Even if they win, all they can do is go away. But this will be a glorious battle indeed if we get everything we want, as we probably will, by punishing the Athenians and securing for Sicily the fruits of the freedom she has always enjoyed. There are seldom such dangers as these, where you have nothing to lose if you fail and everything to gain if you win!

---

3. The pleasure and appropriateness of harming one's perceived enemies was deeply ingrained in Greek thinking (and feeling). Plato, who was a generation younger than Thucydides, shocked his fellow Greeks by his suggestion (in *The Republic*, written perhaps in the 360s) that it was counterproductive to harm others.

69. Gylippus and the Syracusan generals finished this speech of their own to their men and then manned their ships as soon as they saw that the Athenians were doing so. Nicias, overcome by the situation, saw how great their danger was, and how near, since the ships were on the point of setting out. He thought, as generals will in great battles, that he had not done or said nearly enough, so he once again summoned each and every one of the trierarchs, calling them by their patronymics, given names, and tribes, demanding that anyone who had distinguished himself before should do his best, and telling all those who had famous ancestors not to sully the honor of their fathers. He reminded them of the unequaled freedom of their fatherland and of everyone's right to live his own life there without interference. He said other things of the kind that men say in crises, where they no longer avoid speaking in platitudes and invoke the customary all-purpose sentiments about wives, children, and ancestral gods, which they find helpful in the terror that is upon them.

After saying what he thought to be the bare minimum, even if it was still not enough, Nicias withdrew and led the infantry to the beach. He spaced them as widely as he could, so that they could help as much as possible by cheering on the men in the ships. Then Demosthenes, Menander, and Euthydemus, who were the generals aboard the Athenian ships, cast off from their camp, and with the intention of forcing their way to the open sea, headed straight for the passageway the Syracusans had left for themselves in their barrier.

70. The Syracusans and their allies had already set out with almost as many ships as in the previous battle. Part of their fleet guarded the passageway and the other part ringed the rest of the harbor, so they could come at the Athenians from all sides. Their infantry, meanwhile, was positioned to help wherever their ships fell back on shore. Sicanus and Agatharchus were in command at the wings of the Syracusan fleet, and Python was in the middle with the Corinthians. The Athenians approached the barrier, and they sailed up with such force that their momentum overpowered the ships stationed in front of it. They were trying to break up the barricade when the Syracusans and their allies bore down on them from all sides, whereupon the battle was fought more fiercely than any that had gone before, not just at the barrier, but throughout the harbor. The sailors on both sides were always ready to attack when the order was given, and the pilots vied to outdo each other at maneuver and counter-maneuver. Whenever one ship struck another, the marines also wanted to make sure that the fighting on the decks did not fall short of what their comrades were doing. Each and every man strove to distinguish himself at his post. There were about two hundred ships in all, and never did so many ships fight in so small a space. They were all driven together, with few ramming attacks because it was impossible to back up and sail through a line of ships. There were more collisions, though, as ships crashed into each other in flight or pursuit. While ships approached each other, the men on the decks would pelt their enemy with spears, arrows, and stones without number; then, when they were at close quarters, the marines would come to hand-to-hand combat as they tried to board each other's ships. Because of the small space, it often happened that a ship was itself rammed as it rammed another; two or even more ships were sometimes unavoidably fouled up around one, and the pilots were swamped with having to attack or defend not just against one danger, but against many coming from all sides; and what with the din and pandemonium of so many ships crashing into each other, it was impossible to hear the calls of the boatswains, who on both sides were shouting and urging on the men either in the performance of their duty or in the excitement of an ongoing struggle. To the Athenians they

shouted, "Break through the passageway!" and, "Take them on! Now, if ever, you're fighting to get home alive!" To the Syracusans and their allies, "How glorious to keep them from running away!" and, "You'll make your cities famous if you win!" And if the generals on either side saw a ship backing water without being forced to do so, they would call the trierarch by name. The Athenians would ask whether he was retreating because he thought enemy territory was more neighborly than the sea Athens had conquered with so much pain; and the Syracusans would say that it was obvious that the Athenians were desperate to escape by any means, so why run away from them?

71. While the battle hung in the balance, the infantry of both sides struggled on shore within the knotted confines of their own minds—the Sicilians yearning for even greater glory than they already had, and the invaders dreading that they would end up even worse off than they already were. For the Athenians, everything depended on their ships, and their anxiety over the outcome of the battle was like nothing on this earth. The conflict was chaotic and their view from the shore was necessarily incomplete. The Athenians were watching from up close, and not all of them were looking at the same thing at the same time, so that some would take heart when they saw their ships getting the best of it somewhere and call out to the gods not to deprive them of their deliverance, while others who were looking at a setback would moan and wail, more thoroughly resigning their minds to defeat after seeing the action than the men who were in it. Still others stared at a point where the battle was even, with incessantly undecided engagements. These terrified men had the hardest time of it, as their bodies swayed and swerved in accordance with their assessment of the situation, because they were always either about to escape or be destroyed. For so long as the battle was nearly even, you could hear all at once in that one and the same Athenian host every kind of cry that breaks from a large army in mortal danger—yells, wails, they're winning! they're losing! The men in the ships went through almost the same thing as the men on land, until, of course, the Syracusans and their allies, after a long, drawn-out struggle, turned back the Athenians and, clearly victorious, bore down on them and pursued them to the shore with a great deal of cheering and shouting. Then the part of the fleet that was not captured on the water was driven helter-skelter onto land, and the shipwrecked crews fled into the camp. Driven mad by defeat, with one voice now and one impulse, the whole infantry shrieked and howled, some running to help at the ships, some to guard what was left of the walls, but most of the others looking out for themselves and their safety. At that moment, the panic was greater than they had ever known. They now experienced something like what they had done to the Spartans at Pylos, where the men who had crossed over to the island were lost when the Peloponnesians lost their ships.[4] Now the Athenians, too, had no hope of saving themselves by land, unless something utterly unexpected happened.

72. Thus after a fierce battle and the loss of many ships and men on both sides, the Syracusans and their allies were victorious. They took up their wreckage and their dead, and set up a victory marker after sailing back to Syracuse. The Athenians, crushed by woe, never even considered asking to gather up their wreckage and dead, since they aimed to retreat as soon as night fell. Demosthenes did approach Nicias with a plan to man their remaining ships and try to force their way out at dawn. He argued that the seaworthy ships they had still outnumbered those of the enemy, because they had about sixty ships left, while

4. See 4.14.

the enemy had less than fifty. Nicias agreed with this view, and they were going to man the ships, but the crews, paralyzed by defeat and convinced that they could never win, refused to go aboard.

73. All the Athenians had now made up their minds to retreat by land. Hermocrates of Syracuse guessed that this was their intention and dreaded the thought of such a large army slipping away overland, occupying some part of Sicily and determined to make war on Syracuse once again. So he went to the commanding officers and told them what they themselves felt—that they must not allow the Athenians to retreat under cover of night. Instead, the Syracusans and their allies should immediately march out en masse, barricade the roads, and take and guard the chokepoints in the terrain before the Athenians got there. The commanders were no less aware of all this than he and thought it should be done, but the troops were enjoying their rest after the great sea fight, and there was also a festival (since they were sacrificing to Heracles that day), and the commanders doubted that the men would be disposed to obey. Overjoyed by their victory, many of the men were getting drunk at the festival, and the last order you could expect them to obey right now was to take up their arms and march out to battle. On this reasoning, the commanders decided that Hermocrates' plan was unworkable, and he could not persuade them to do it. So, fearful that the Athenians would get a head start and pass unhindered through the most difficult terrain by night, he took the following steps to deal with the situation on his own. As it was getting dark, he sent some of his friends to the Athenian camp with some cavalry. These men rode out to within earshot of the Athenians. Pretending to be friends (for there really were men in the city who brought intelligence to Nicias), they called for some of the troops and told them to tell Nicias not to lead the army out that night because the roads were being guarded. Instead, he should make the necessary preparations and retreat in an orderly fashion by day. After saying their piece, they left, and the men they had spoken to passed the message on to the Athenian generals, who acted on it, not knowing it to be a trick, and stayed for the night.

74. But despite their intention to leave that morning, they did not succeed in getting away promptly and decided to wait for the following day, so that the soldiers could get together the bare necessities as best they could, leaving everything else behind. They would take just what they needed to keep themselves alive and go.

Meanwhile, Gylippus and the Syracusans got out ahead of the Athenians with their infantry and blocked the roads that the Athenians were most likely to take through the countryside. They also guarded the fords in the rivers and streams and positioned troops where they thought they could best engage with and stop the Athenian army. They also sailed out by night and dragged the Athenian ships off the shore. As planned, the Athenians themselves had burned a few of them, but the Syracusans, unhurried and with no one to stop them, tied ropes to the rest where they had run aground and towed them back to Syracuse.

75. Then, two days after the naval battle, when Nicias and Demosthenes decided that their preparations were complete, the army finally started moving out. The situation was appalling in every way: they were retreating after having lost all their ships, and instead of realizing their grand expectations, they had put themselves and their very city in peril. As they abandoned the camp, there was something to inflict pain on the sight, the mind, of each and every man. For the dead were unburied, and whenever a soldier saw the body of a friend lying on the ground, he was filled with grief and terror. The sick and wounded, who were being left behind still alive, distressed the able-

bodied more than those who had perished and seemed more pitiful than the
dead. These men resorted to pleading and wailing, mortifying the others as
they insisted on being taken along, and calling out, one by one, to any friend
or relative they saw. As the buddies they had shared their tents with were
leaving, they would hang on them and follow them as far as they could, and
when the strength in their bodies failed them, many sobbed and called the
gods to witness as they were being abandoned. The whole army was so filled
with tears and desperation that they could hardly get going, even though
they were leaving enemy territory and what they had already suffered was
beyond tears as they dreaded sufferings yet unknown. And still with down-
cast eyes, they loathed themselves. They looked like nothing so much as people fleeing a starved-out city, and a large one at that, since the whole throng
of them marching away together numbered no less than forty thousand men.
All of them took whatever they could carry that would be of use, and contrary to the usual practice when they were under arms, even the hoplites
and cavalry carried their own supplies, some for want of slaves, others because they did not trust the ones they had. Some of the slaves had deserted
long before, but most were doing so now. In any case, they did not have
much to carry because there was no longer any food in the camp. The misery of their humiliation was equally distributed, and while that usually makes
suffering easier to bear, it did not help now, especially when they had ended
up so abased after beginning with such splendor and bravado. This was the
greatest defeat ever suffered by a Greek army. It was an army that had come
to enslave others, but that now retreated in dread that this would happen to
them. They had sailed out with prayers and battle hymns, and now they departed in the midst of evil portents, sailors making their way on foot, relying on their hoplites instead of on their ships. Nevertheless, all this would
have been bearable but for the immense danger still hanging over them.

76. Seeing that the army was totally demoralized and dejected, Nicias
walked up and down the ranks of his men trying to rouse and reassure them. In
his desire to help, he shouted ever more loudly as he moved among the men,
eager for the benefit of his words to reach as far as possible.

77. Soldiers of Athens! Allies! We must have hope even now. After all,
men have gotten to safety after worse than this. You must not judge yourselves inadequate because of your defeats or because of these sufferings
that are so contrary to your true worth. I'm not stronger than any of you—
after all, you see the state I'm in because of my sickness—and though I've
been more fortunate than most in my private and public life, I'm here,
hanging in the balance and sharing this danger with the humblest of men.
I have lived a religious life, and I have been just and well disposed toward
my fellow man, and because of this I have strong hopes for the future despite our predicament. So as far as our worth is concerned, these setbacks
don't scare me. And maybe our troubles will let up. The enemy has had
enough luck, because even if it was one of the gods who begrudged us this
expedition, we've been punished enough by now. Men have been the aggressors against others before this, and they have been able to endure the
punishment for their all-too-human deeds. So now we have reason to hope
that whatever god it is will be kinder to us, because right now we are more
worthy of pity from the gods than envy. And look at yourselves, and see
what fine well-armed men you are, and how many of you there are marching in tight formation! So don't be too afraid. Remember that you make
an instant city wherever you encamp, and no city in Sicily will easily stand

up to your attack or dislodge you after you take up a position. You are the ones who must make sure that our march is safe and orderly, and each of you must regard any point where you are forced to fight as your stronghold, your homeland, if you conquer it. Because our supplies are so low, we will press on day and night, and if we get to anywhere in friendly Sicel territory, you can think of yourselves as safe, because the Sicels are still afraid of the Syracusans and we can count on them. I have already sent to them with orders to meet us and to bring food.

Always remember, men, that you must be good soldiers, because there is no place nearby where you can be cowards and still find safety. If you escape your enemies now, those of you who are not Athenians will get to see the homelands you long for, and the Athenians will restore the fallen greatness of their city, because a city is its men, not empty walls and ships.

78. Nicias shouted these words of encouragement while moving through the army, and if he saw gaps in a line or men marching out of step, he brought them together and set them right. Meanwhile, Demosthenes did the same and said more or less the same things to the troops he commanded. The formation in which they marched was a hollow rectangle, with Nicias' division leading and Demosthenes' bringing up the rear. The hoplites were on the outside, surrounding the camp followers and the rest of the throng.

When they reached the crossing of the Anapus River, they found a detachment of Syracusans and their allies posted along it, but the Athenians forced them back, took control of the ford, and pressed forward. Syracusans kept harrying them, though, their cavalry galloping along their flanks and their light-armed troops hurling javelins into their midst.

That day, the Athenians advanced about five miles before bivouacking for the night on a hill. They started out early the next day, and advanced about two and a half miles before descending into a plain and camping there. The area was inhabited, and they wanted to loot some food from the houses there and to collect some water to take with them, because water was scarce in the many miles they had yet to go. While they were doing this, the Syracusans moved forward and fortified the pass that lay ahead. The place was a steep hill with a sheer ravine on both sides, and it was called the Acraean Scaur.

The next day the Athenians advanced, but they were impeded by large numbers of Syracusan and allied cavalry and javelin men harassing their flanks and throwing javelins at them. The Athenians fought for a long time before retreating to the camp in the plain. And now they could no longer procure food, since the cavalry made it impossible to leave the camp.

79. Early the next day, they broke camp and started out again. They forced their way up to the fortified hill and found the enemy infantry in front of them, drawn up many shields deep to defend the wall in the narrow pass. The Athenians advanced and repeatedly assaulted the wall, but they were bombarded by the numerous enemy force, whose missiles easily hit home from the high ground of the steep hill. Unable to force a passage, the Athenians retreated and halted. There happened to be some rain and thunder during the battle. It was getting to be autumn, and such weather is normal for that time of year, but it dispirited the Athenians even more, and they believed that even the elements were conspiring in their destruction. While the Athenians were resting, Gylippus and the Syracusan generals sent a detachment of the army to build a wall behind the Athenian rear on the road they had come by. The Athenians in turn sent back some of their own men who prevented them from doing so; but there-

after the whole Athenian army withdrew closer to the plain, where they camped for the night.

On the following day, they advanced again, and the Syracusans surrounded them and attacked them from all sides, wounding many. When the Athenians charged, they retreated; when the Athenians fell back, they attacked. They especially attacked the rear guards, on the chance that they might panic the whole army by routing the Athenians at a single point. The Athenians fought this way for a long time and then rested in the plain, after having advanced about three-quarters of a mile. The Syracusans withdrew from them to their own camp.

80. The army was now in a very bad way. They had completely run out of supplies, and many of the men had been wounded in the numerous engagements with the enemy. That night, Nicias and Demosthenes decided to light as many campfires as possible and then to lead the army away. They would take a route different from the one they had originally planned on — the one the Syracusans were now watching — and go in the opposite direction, towards the sea. The army's final destination would not be Catana, but the other part of Sicily in the direction of Camarina, Gela, and the Greek and barbarian cities in that region. So they lit the campfires and marched into the night. And then, as happens to all armies, and especially to large armies operating at night in hostile territory, running from an enemy not far distant, they became frightened, panicky, and confused. Nicias' division, which was leading the way, held formation and got far out in front; Demosthenes' division, which made up somewhat more than half of the army and which marched with less discipline, became separated. By dawn, however, they managed to reach the sea. They then turned onto what is known as the Helorine Road, intending to take it to the Cacyparis River, which they would follow up through the interior of the island, where they hoped to meet with the Sicels they had sent for. When they reached the river, they found that there too a Syracusan brigade was building a roadblock and fencing off the ford. They took this position by storm, crossed the river, and resumed their march in the direction their guides indicated, towards yet another river, the Erineus.

81. Meanwhile, when day dawned and the Syracusans and their allies realized that the Athenians had left, most of them held Gylippus responsible, accusing him of intentionally letting the Athenians get away. They quickly gave chase, and since it was not hard to find out which way they had gone, they caught up with them at around the time of the midday meal. They made contact with Demosthenes' division, which had become disoriented during the night and which was marching slowly and out of formation. The Syracusans immediately fell on them and started fighting, galloping round and round them with their cavalry — which was easy to do since they were only half the Athenian army — and herding them into one spot. Nicias' division was over six miles ahead. Nicias moved so rapidly because he thought that under the circumstances, safety lay in not standing and fighting — not if they could help it, anyway. Instead, they would retreat as fast as possible and only fight as much as they had to. Demosthenes, on the other hand, had had the harder time of it because his division was in the rear during the retreat, and the enemy always attacked his men first. Now he saw that the Syracusans were coming after them, and instead of rapidly advancing, he drew up his ranks for battle. While he was wasting his time doing this, he found himself surrounded by the enemy, and he and the Athenians who were with him were thrown into utter chaos. They were

hemmed into a place with a wall around it, thick with olive trees, and with roads on either side, and they were being bombarded from all sides. It was understandable that the Syracusans shot from long range, avoiding close combat, because risking themselves against such desperate men would have favored not them but the Athenians. Besides, everyone felt a certain reluctance to lose his life unnecessarily when victory was already assured, especially since they knew that sooner or later they were going to defeat and capture the Athenians by this method of fighting.

82. After barraging the Athenians and their allies all day from every side, the Syracusans saw that they were completely exhausted by their wounds and all their other sufferings. The first thing Gylippus, the Syracusans, and their allies then did was to frame a proclamation to the islanders, promising freedom to anyone who wished to come over to them. A few cities went over, but not many. Eventually an agreement was reached for all the men in Demosthenes' division, whereby they would surrender their weapons on condition that no one be put to death either by violence, confinement, or lack of basic sustenance. In all, six thousand men surrendered. They threw what money they had into upturned shields, filling four of them. The Syracusans immediately brought their captives back to the city.

On that same day, Nicias and his men reached the Erineus River. They crossed it and halted on high ground.

83. The Syracusans caught up with him the next day. They told him that Demosthenes and his men had surrendered, and they called on him to do the same thing. Nicias didn't believe it and sent a cavalryman under a truce to investigate. This man brought back word that they had indeed surrendered. Nicias then sent a herald with a message to Gylippus and the Syracusans that he was prepared to agree on behalf of the Athenian people to repay the Syracusans all the money they had spent in the war, provided they allow the men who were with him to leave. Until such time as the money was paid, he would give them Athenian citizens as hostages, one man per talent owed. Gylippus and the Syracusans rejected this proposal. They then went into action, completely surrounding Nicias' forces and bombarding them with spears, arrows, and stones until dusk, just as they had done to Demosthenes. And like the other division, Nicias' men were also desperately short of food and other provisions. Nevertheless, they waited for the dead of night, when they were about to continue on their way, but the Syracusans heard them taking up their weapons and raised their war cry. The Athenians saw that they had been detected, so they laid down their arms again—all but about three hundred men who forced their way past the Syracusan sentries and escaped into the night however they could.

84. When day broke, Nicias led his men out once again, and the Syracusans and their allies attacked in the same way, surrounding them and bombarding them with spears. The Athenians pushed on to the Assinarus River, all the while being devastated by the spears, arrows, and stones coming from everywhere and by the hordes of cavalry and other troops. They thought that if they could just get across the river, things would be a little easier for them. They were desperate to ease their suffering, to drink some water. When they got to the river, they broke ranks and ran into it, every man struggling to make the brutal crossing first as the enemy bore down. Driven to cross all together, they fell onto one another and trampled each other down. Some were killed immediately by their own spears; others got tangled up in their equipment and with each other and sank into the river. Syracusans positioned on the other bank, which was steep, hurled down spears at the Athenians, most of whom were jumbled together,

greedily drinking from the nearly dry riverbed. The Peloponnesians went down into the river after them and did most of the killing there; and though it quickly became fouled, the Athenians nonetheless fought among themselves to gulp the muddy water clotted with blood.

85. Finally, with dead bodies heaped atop each other in the riverbed, and the army decimated, some in the river and others—those who got across—by the cavalry, Nicias surrendered himself to Gylippus, trusting him more than the Syracusans. He told Gylippus and the Spartans to do with him what they wanted but to stop slaughtering his men. After this, Gylippus ordered his troops to take prisoners, whereupon the surviving men were brought in alive, except for the large number who had been hidden by individual Syracusan soldiers.[5] They also sent a search party out after the three hundred who had broken through the sentries by night, and captured them. All together, the number of prisoners belonging to the Syracusan state was small, but the number stolen and dispersed was great, and all Sicily was full of them. The reason for this was that they had not been captured under the terms of an agreement, like the men in Demosthenes' division. A large number, of course, were killed, for there was a great slaughter at the river, greater than any that occurred in the whole war; and quite a few were also killed in the frequent attacks on the way there. Still, many escaped and found refuge in Catana, some at the time, others when they later escaped from slavery.

86. The Syracusans and their allies formed up into one body, took their booty and as many of their prisoners as they could, and returned to the city. They brought the Athenian and allied captives out of the city and down into their stone quarries, thinking this was the safest place to hold them, and then, over the objections of Gylippus, they cut the throats of Nicias and Demosthenes. Gylippus had thought it would surpass all his other triumphs to bring the enemy generals back to Sparta. Demosthenes was their greatest foe because of Sphacteria and Pylos, and Nicias was their best friend for the same reason: he had acted on behalf of the Spartan men on the island by persuading the Athenians to make the treaty that brought about their release. As a result, the Spartans were extremely well-disposed towards him, and it was mainly for that reason that he trusted Gylippus when he gave himself up. But it is said that some of the Syracusans who had been in communication with him were afraid that he might make this contact known under torture and create problems for them in the moment of their success. Others, they say, and especially the Corinthians, persuaded their Syracusan allies to kill him for fear that he would bribe some of the authorities, since he was very rich, escape, and make trouble for them again. For this or some similar reason, this man was killed, the one Greek of my generation who least deserved such a hapless end after having ordered his whole life in keeping with the highest standards.

87. The Syracusans treated the men in the stone quarries very harshly at first. There were a great many men in a small, bare place, without a roof. In the beginning, the sun was still hot and they were oppressed by the stifling air. The cold nights that followed were just the opposite, it being autumn, and the shock to their systems made them sick. Because of the lack of space, they had to perform all their bodily functions in the same place, and the corpses of those who died from their wounds, exposure, and other causes were piled on top of each other. The stench was unbearable, and they were also afflicted by hunger and thirst, for they were given—some for up to eight months—only one cup of water

5. Who presumably wanted to hold them for ransom or sell them into slavery.

and two cups of ground wheat a day. They suffered every misery you could imagine among men in such a place. They all lived in those crowded conditions for seventy days, when all but the Athenians and any Sicilians and Italians who had fought with them were sold into slavery. It is difficult to say just how many prisoners there were in all, but there were at least seven thousand. This was the largest campaign in the war, and from what we know of the oral tradition, it seems, at least to me, to have been the largest in Greek history. It was also the most decisive for the victors and the most destructive for the vanquished. For the Athenians were totally defeated in every way and they suffered on a huge scale. All was lost—ships, men, everything. And very few of those who left ever returned to their homelands again.

These, then, were the events that took place in Sicily.

Book 8

Book 8 breaks off suddenly in 411. Though Thucydides lived to see the end of the war, he did not live to write of it. Some believe that he intended to revise the portion of Book 8 that survives and see certain features of the book—the lack of speeches, for example—as signs of its roughness; others argue that Thucydides compressed the action of these years because civil strife within Athens compelled him to add elements of domestic history to the military and diplomatic history that was his customary purview. What is certain is that Thucydides' attention to factional conflict within the city of Athens makes a striking contrast with his earlier indifference to domestic history. The subject matter of Book 8 is unique—the oligarchic interlude at Athens and the involvement of the rival Persian satraps Tissaphernes and Pharnabazus in the Greek war. Chapters 29–33 of the *Constitution of the Athenians* sometimes attributed to Aristotle also shed light on the oligarchy of 411.

Book 8 begins (1–5) with the response of the various Greek states to the dramatic developments in Sicily. Thucydides then chronicles military operations in the Aegean and the Hellespont, including the important revolt of the key Athenian ally Chios and the terms of the alliance between the Spartans and the Persians (via the satrap Tissaphernes); he gives us the terms of the original alliance at chapter 18 and then again in their revised versions at 37 and 58. Chapters 45–46 treat the negotiations between Alcibiades and Tissaphernes, leading into the segment at 47–98 in which the events of the war are laced with an analysis of the civil strife at Athens, where men seeking Persian favor overturned the democracy and agreed to recall Alcibiades as the price of Persian support; this section includes the revolt of Euboea (95) and the Athenian response to it (96). Chapters 99–109 take us back to the war in the Hellespont. The book ends with a paragraph on the rivalry of the two coastal satraps, Tissaphernes and Pharnabazus. Tissaphernes, Thucydides writes, "first went to Ephesus and sacrificed to Artemis. . . ." And so, with Tissaphernes sacrificing at Ephesus, the manuscript of Thucydides' history comes to an end.

Byzantium

Propontis

Aegospotami
HELLESPONT
Sestos
Abydos
Hellespont

Cyzicus

Lesbos
Mytilene
Arginusae Islands
AEOLIS
Phocaea
Eurymedon River

Chios
Clazomenae
I O N I A
Colophon
Notium
Ephesus
Samos
Miletus
C A R I A

**Western
Asia Minor**
0   50 Km   50 Mi

Halicarnassus

Book 8

1. For a long time after the news reached Athens, the Athenians refused to believe that the expedition had been so totally destroyed, even when the reports were unequivocal and came from soldiers who had actually escaped from the fighting. When the truth sank in, the people raged at the politicians who had promoted the armada — as if they themselves had not voted for it! They were also furious with the oracle readers, prophets, and anyone else who had given them hope in the beginning by foretelling that they would conquer Sicily. They were hard pressed on all sides in every way, and this event now gave rise to the greatest fear and bewilderment, for not only did individuals suffer private losses, but the city was now bereft of all those irreplaceable hoplites, cavalry, and young men. They saw that they no longer had enough ships in their dockyards, or crews for the ones they had, or money in their treasury, and they despaired for their safety. They thought that their Sicilian enemies would immediately attack the Piraeus with their armada — especially after having won such an overwhelming victory — and that their local enemies, who had been redoubling their preparations, would attack them in strength by land and sea, in company with Athenian allies who would revolt and join them. Even under the circumstances, however, they decided not to give up. They would build a new fleet with wood from wherever they could get it. They would raise money and make sure they could count on the governments of their allies, especially in Euboea. They would introduce austerity measures in their economy and elect a council of elders who would scrutinize all proposals before they were formally presented to the people. Like all democracies when they are frightened, they were prepared to be disciplined in dealing with the present emergency. They put these decisions into effect, and the summer came to an end.

2. The following winter, all Greece was positively elated by the Athenian catastrophe in Sicily. Neutral states thought they should no longer stay out of the war, whether they were invited in or not. They would volunteer to attack the Athenians in the knowledge that the Athenians would have done the same to them if they had won in Sicily. Besides, what was left of the war would be short, and it would be a fine thing to take part in it. Meanwhile, Sparta's allies were more eager than ever to be delivered quickly from their many hardships. Above all, Athens' subjects were ready to revolt, even if they did not have the might to do so. They let their emotions affect their judgment, and there was no question in their minds that Athens could not survive through the next summer. Sparta was encouraged by all this, especially since their Sicilian allies would probably be arriving in the beginning of the spring with a large force, now that the Athenians had forced them to acquire a navy. With every reason for confidence, the Spartans were making plans for all-out war. Their thinking was that ending the war would redound to their glory, and that they would be forevermore free of such dangers as Athens would have engulfed them with had Athens added Sicily to its arsenal. Furthermore, by toppling Athens, they themselves would be secure in the leadership of Greece.

3. Thus Agis, king of Sparta, immediately set out with an army from Decelea that winter to levy funds from their allies in order to pay for ships' crews. They went towards the Malian Gulf and seized most of the goods and chattels of their old enemies the Oetaeans, also making them pay some money. Then, against the will of the Thessalians and despite their protests, Agis forced the Achaeans of Phthiotis and the other subjects of Thessaly in the region to give

him money and hostages. These he transferred to Corinth, while he tried to bring the region into an alliance with Sparta. Then the Spartans enforced the levy on their allies for the construction of one hundred ships. They assessed themselves and the Boeotians twenty-five each; the Phocians and the Eastern Locrians fifteen; the Corinthians fifteen; the Arcadians, Pellenians, and Sicyonians ten; and the Megarians, Troezenians, Epidaurians, and Hermionians ten. Everything else was put in readiness to get on with the war by the very beginning of spring.

4. That same winter, the Athenians were also making preparations by going ahead with the plans they had made for ship-building, for which they had procured timber, and for the fortification of Sunium to ensure safe passage for their supply ships around the cape. They also abandoned the fort they had built in Laconia while sailing along the coast to Sicily,[1] along with any other installations they considered to be needlessly expensive, in accordance with their program of austerity. They were also keeping a watchful eye on their allies, to prevent them from breaking away.

5. With both sides preparing for the war as busily as they had been at its beginning, the Euboeans were the first to send envoys to Agis that winter to talk about revolting from Athens. Agis welcomed their proposals and sent to Sparta for Melanthus and Alcamenes, son of Sthenelaidas, to take charge of things in Euboea. These two arrived with about three hundred freedmen, and Agis started making arrangements for their passage to Euboea. While this was going on, some Lesbians arrived, also wanting to revolt. In conjunction with the Boeotians, they persuaded Agis to hold off on action in Euboea and to prepare the way for a rebellion in Lesbos instead. Alcamenes, who was on the point of sailing for Euboea, was put in command of the operation at Lesbos and was given ten ships by the Boeotians and ten by Agis. This was done without consulting Sparta: for as long as Agis was conducting operations around Decelea with his own army, he had full powers to send forces wherever he liked, to raise armies, and to levy funds. In fact, at that point, Sparta's allies were in general much more inclined to listen to Agis than to the officials in Sparta. After all, he had his own army and was a force to be reckoned with wherever he went.

While Agis was making these arrangements with the Lesbians, the Chians and Erythraeans were also getting ready to revolt; but instead of going to Agis, they went to Sparta. With them was an ambassador from Tissaphernes, whom King Darius, son of Artaxerxes, had put in command of his coastal provinces in Asia Minor. Tissaphernes had also been inciting the Spartans to action and had promised to maintain their troops. The King had recently pressed him for tribute he owed from the area under his administration, but which the Athenians had prevented him from collecting from the cities that were Greek. Tissaphernes thought that harming Athens would give him a better chance of collecting the tribute, of bringing Sparta into an alliance with the King, and of carrying out the King's order to either kill or capture Amorges, the illegitimate son of Pissuthnes, who was leading a rebellion in Caria.

6. The Chians and Tissaphernes were working together towards the same goal, but at about this same time a Megarian, Calligeitus, son of Laophon, and a Cyzicene, Timagoras, son of Athenagoras, also arrived in Sparta. Both were exiles from their native lands and had settled in the court of Pharnabazus, son of Pharnaces. Pharnabazus had sent them to get warships to come to the Hellespont, so that he could detach the Greek cities in his district from Athens and

---

1. See 7.26.

get their tribute, just as Tissaphernes was eager to do. The difference was that Pharnabazus wanted to be the one who made the alliance between the Spartans and the King.

Both groups—Tissaphernes' and Pharnabazus'—were working independently of each other and provoked a lively debate within the Spartan government over whether to send ships and men to Ionia and Chios first or to the Hellespont; although by far most Spartans favored Tissaphernes and the Chians, who were also helped and supported by Alcibiades. At that time, Endius was an ephor in Sparta, and Alcibiades had an especially strong family tie with him going back through his father's line. It was because of this tie that "Alcibiades," which is a Spartan name, came into his family.[2] Endius' full name, for example, was "Endius, son of Alcibiades." Despite this support for Tissaphernes and the Chians, however, the Spartans first sent Phrynis, an officer from one of the towns dependent on Sparta, to assess the situation in Chios and to see whether their navy was as large as they said and whether the city was in other respects as strong as it was made out to be. When Phrynis reported that what they had heard was true, the Spartans immediately made an alliance with Chios and Erythrae and voted to send them forty ships, in the belief that the Chians had, as they said, more than sixty ships at their disposal in the area. They originally intended to send ten of the forty ships, under the command of Melanchridas, who was their admiral-in-chief, but there was an earthquake, and instead of Melanchridas they decided to send Chalcideus.[3] They also outfitted not ten, but five, ships in Laconia. And so the winter came to an end, and with it the nineteenth year of the war that I, Thucydides, have narrated.

7. Just as the next summer began, with the Chians pressing them to send the ships and fearing that the Athenians would find out what they were doing (since all their negotiations had been conducted in secret), the Spartans sent three Spartan citizens to Corinth to tell them to drag the ships as quickly as possible across the isthmus from the Gulf of Corinth to the Saronic Gulf and send to them all to Chios—both the ones Agis had been preparing for the operation in Lesbos and the others.[4] All together, there were thirty-nine allied ships in the Gulf of Corinth.

8. Acting on behalf of Pharnabazus, Calligeitus and Timagoras did not join in the voyage to Chios. Neither did they contribute the twenty-five talents they had come with to the expedition. Instead, they planned to finance and set out with a separate fleet later. As to Agis, even he raised no objections when he saw that the Spartans were going to Chios first. The allies convened at Corinth, discussed the matter, and decided to sail to Chios first, with Chalcideus, who was in Laconia readying his five ships, in command. Then they would go to Lesbos, with Alcamenes, the man Agis had originally had in mind, in command. And finally, they would proceed to the Hellespont, for which Clearchus, son of Rhamphias, was the designated commander. At first, half the ships were to be brought over the Isthmus and then set out immediately, to distract the attention of the Athenians between the ships that had embarked and the ones that would be going across after them. They mounted this voyage openly, scorning the impotence of the Athenians, who did not appear to have much of a navy. The allies carried out their decision and immediately brought twenty-one ships across.

---

2. For more on Alcibiades' connection with Sparta, see 5.43.
3. Greeks took earthquakes as a bad omen. See 3.89 and 6.95.
4. There was a stone causeway across the Isthmus of Corinth by which ships were drawn from one side to the other, thus avoiding a time-consuming circumnavigation of the Peloponnese.

9. The allies were eager to set sail, but the Corinthians were unwilling to join in until they had finished holding the Isthmian games, which were to take place in that season.[5] On behalf of the allies, Agis was prepared to make the expedition his own private undertaking, so that the Corinthians would not have to break the truce of the Isthmia. There was a delay when the Corinthians refused to go along with this. Meanwhile, the Athenians were starting to find out about what was going on in Chios and sent Aristocrates, one of their generals, to accuse them of treason. When the Chians denied the alleged treachery, Aristocrates ordered them to send ships back to Athens with him to join the allied forces, and the Chians sent seven ships. The reason they sent the ships was that the Chian populace did not know about the plans that had been made, and the oligarchs and their co-conspirators did not want to arouse the hostility of the people until they had a firm grip on the situation. Furthermore, because the Peloponnesians were delaying, the Chians were no longer expecting them to come.

10. The Isthmian games were held while these events at Chios were taking place. The Athenians, who had been officially notified of the truce, sent representatives, and what had been going on in Chios became increasingly clear to them. When they got back to Athens, they immediately took precautions to prevent the ships at Cenchreae from embarking without their knowledge. After the games were over, the Peloponnesians set out for Chios with twenty-one ships under the command of Alcamenes. The first thing the Athenians did was to sail up to them with an equal number of ships and try to draw them out into the open sea; but the Peloponnesians declined to follow them out very far and turned back to Cenchreae, whereupon the Athenians returned to port. They did so because they did not consider the seven Chian ships in their fleet to be trustworthy. Later, however, having manned enough other ships to bring their number up to thirty-seven, they caught the Peloponnesian fleet sailing along the coast and chased it to Spiraeum, in the Corinthian territory. This is an unoccupied harbor, the last one before the Epidaurian border. The Peloponnesians lost one ship at sea, but got the others together and anchored in the harbor. The Athenians brought their ships in to attack them on the water and also landed to attack them on shore. There was great confusion and lack of military discipline, but the Athenians crippled most of the enemy ships and drove them onto the beach, and also killed Alcamenes, their commander. A few Athenians were also killed.

11. After the battle, the Athenians detached enough ships to blockade the enemy and anchored the rest at a little island not far off. There they pitched camp and then sent to Athens for reinforcements, because by the next day the Corinthians had come to the relief of the Peloponnesian ships and were followed not much later by other locals. Seeing how hard it would be to protect their fleet in this uninhabited place, the Peloponnesians did not know what to do, and even considered burning the ships, but then they decided to haul them up high and dry on the beach, stay put, and guard them with their infantry until the right opportunity came along to get away. When Agis learned of what was happening, he sent them Thermon, a Spartan officer. The first report to reach Sparta was that the ships had set out from the Isthmus, because the ephors had

---

5. Greeks held four athletic events, which also had a religious and cultural dimension, and which were sometimes occasions for political wheeling and dealing. Their duration was otherwise a time of general truce. The games at Olympia are the most famous. The others were the Isthmian games, held at the Isthmus of Corinth; the Nemean games, at Nemea; and the Pythian games, at Delphi. The Isthmian games were probably held in early July.

ordered Alcamenes to send them a cavalryman when this took place. They then immediately made plans to despatch the five ships they had, with Chalcideus in command and Alcibiades to accompany him. But just as they were about to set sail, the news came in about the ships running for cover in Spiraeum, and despondent over failing just as they were beginning the war in Ionia, they abandoned the idea of sending the ships from their own territory and even decided to recall some vessels that had already put to sea.

12. Seeing what was happening, Alcibiades once again prevailed on Endius and the other ephors not to back away from the expedition. He said that they would get there before the Chians found out about the defeat of the fleet, and that once he reached Ionia, he would easily persuade its cities to revolt from Athens, because he would be more credible than anyone else when he told them about the weakness of Athens and the enthusiasm of Sparta. Speaking privately to Endius, he said it would redound to Endius' glory to detach Ionia from Athens and to make an alliance between Sparta and the King of Persia. This achievement should not go to Agis, he said. (It so happened that Alcibiades and Agis were enemies.) Thus after winning over Endius and the other ephors, Alcibiades, accompanied by Chalcideus the Spartan, set sail with the five ships and hurried on their way.

13. At about this same time, the sixteen Peloponnesian ships that had been with Gylippus throughout the war were returning from Sicily. They were intercepted and badly mauled off Leucas by the twenty-seven Attic ships commanded by Hippocles, son of Menippus, which were on the lookout for the ships from Sicily. All but one of the ships escaped the Athenians and put in at Corinth.

14. In order to keep their coming from being reported, Chalcideus and Alcibiades seized everyone they came across on their voyage and released them in Corycus, the first place they came to on the mainland. There they held preliminary meetings with some of their co-conspirators from Chios, who told them to sail into the city without giving any advance notice. When they suddenly appeared in Chios, the populace was amazed and terrified. A meeting of the council, however, had been prearranged by the oligarchic party, in which Chalcideus and Alcibiades gave speeches announcing that a great many other ships were on the way, but saying nothing about the ships that were being blockaded at Spiraeum. Thereupon the Chians and later the Erythraeans revolted from Athens. After this, Chalcideus and Alcibiades sailed to Clazomenae with three ships and induced them to revolt also. The Clazomenians immediately crossed over to the mainland and fortified Polichna, so that if need be, they would have someplace to withdraw to from the small island on which they lived. And indeed all the rebel states were building fortifications and preparing for war.

15. The news about Chios reached Athens quickly, and they saw themselves as now surrounded by a great, clear danger, for their other allies would not stay quiescent when the largest of the subject cities had gone over to the enemy. In the prevailing fear, they immediately repealed the penalties that had been established against proposing or putting to a vote the use of the thousand talents they had been zealously holding on to throughout the war.[6] They now voted to spend this money and to man a large number of ships. They would also at once send to Chios eight of the ships that had been blockading Spiraeum. Under the command of Strombichides, son of Diotimus, these had already left

6. See 2.24.

their guard duty to go in pursuit of the ships with Chalcideus, but they had not caught up with him and had returned to Athens. These were to be reinforced a little later by twelve ships under Thrasycles, which were also to leave the blockade. They seized and brought back the seven Chian ships that were with them in the blockade at Spiraeum and set free the slaves who were aboard and threw the free men in prison. Another ten ships were quickly manned and sent off to replace all the ships that had departed the blockade of the Peloponnesian fleet, and plans were made to man yet another thirty. The Athenians were very determined and left nothing undone to regain Chios.

16. While this was going forward, Strombichides reached Samos with his eight ships. Adding one Samian ship to his force, he sailed to Teos and warned its people not to revolt. Chalcideus, however, was coming to attack Teos from Chios with twenty-three ships, aided by the Clazomenian and Erythraean infantry, which was standing by on shore. Strombichides learned of Chalcideus' attack ahead of time and set sail, but when he was on the high sea, he saw the large number of the ships coming from Chios and fled towards Samos with Chalcideus giving chase. At first, the Teians did not allow the Clazomenian and Erythraean infantry into the city, but they let them in after the Athenians ran away. The infantry did nothing, waiting for Chalcideus to come back from his pursuit. But he took his time, and the infantry began to tear down the wall that the Athenians had built on the landward side of the city of Teos. They were assisted in this operation by a few barbarians who unexpectedly arrived under the command of Stages, a subordinate of Tissaphernes.

17. After chasing Strombichides to Samos, Chalcideus and Alcibiades equipped the sailors from the Peloponnesian ships with heavy weapons and left them on Chios. Then they manned these ships and twenty others with fresh crews from Chios and sailed to Miletus with the intention of fomenting a revolt. Alcibiades, who was friendly with the leading citizens of Miletus, wanted to win the city over before the Peloponnesian ships arrived and to gain for Chios, Chalcideus, and himself—and for Endius, who sent them out, and to whom he had promised it—the prize of causing as many Ionian cities as possible to revolt by using only the forces of Chios and of Chalcideus. They were unobserved for most of their voyage, and although they barely escaped Strombichides and Thrasycles, who had just arrived with twelve ships from Athens and who joined in the chase, they sparked a revolt in Miletus. The Athenians followed close in their wake with nineteen ships, but the Milesians would not receive them, so they went to anchor on the offshore island of Lade.

Immediately after the revolt, Tissaphernes and Chalcideus negotiated the first alliance between Sparta and the King of Persia. It was as follows:

18. Sparta and its allies hereby conclude an alliance with the King and Tissaphernes on the following terms:

Such cities and domains as are held by the King and were held by the ancestors of the King, shall be the King's. Whatever money or other goods have been making their way to Athens from said cities, the King, the Spartans, and their allies shall jointly prevent Athens from receiving such money or other goods as have been going to Athens from said cities. Furthermore, the King, the Spartans, and their allies shall jointly prosecute the war against the Athenians, and it shall not be permitted to bring an end to the war against the Athenians without the consent of both sides, viz., the King on the one hand, and the Spartans and their allies on the other. In addition, if any peoples revolt from the King, they shall become the enemies of the Spartans and their allies; and if any peoples revolt from the

Spartans and their allies, they shall by the same token become the enemies of the King.

19. This was the alliance. Immediately after it was made, the Chians manned ten more ships and sailed for Anaea, wanting to get news of their men at Miletus and also to foment rebellion in the cities thereabouts, but they received a message from Chalcideus telling them to sail back, and adding that Amorges was approaching with an army by land, so they sailed to the temple of Zeus where they caught sight of sixteen ships, which Diomedon had brought out from Athens to follow Thrasycles after he left. The Chians fled as soon as they made the sighting, with one ship heading for Ephesus and the rest for Teos. The Athenians captured four of these ships empty, just after their crews got ashore; the rest escaped to the city of Teos. The Athenians then sailed away to Samos. The Chians set sail again and, assisted by the Clazomenian and Erythraean infantry, they raised revolts first in Lebedos and then in Haerae. After this, both the infantry and the navy returned home.

20. At about the same time, the twenty Peloponnesian ships that had been run into Spiraeum and blockaded there by an equal number of Athenian ships made a sudden breakout. They won the ensuing naval battle, capturing four Athenian ships, and sailed away to Cenchreae, where they once again prepared for the voyage to Chios and Ionia. Astyochus, who had recently assumed command of the whole Peloponnesian navy, arrived from Sparta to serve as their admiral.

After the infantry withdrew from Teos, Tissaphernes himself arrived with an army and tore down what was left of the wall. Then he too left. Not long after he left, Diomedon arrived with ten Athenian ships and made an agreement with the Teians whereby they would receive the Athenians also. Then he sailed along the coast to Haerae and attacked it; but he left when he was unable to take the city.

21. At about this same time, there took place in Samos the revolt of the populace against the oligarchical government. They were supported by the Athenians, who were standing by with three ships. The Samian populace put to death the most powerful oligarchs, about two hundred in all, exiled four hundred others, and distributed their land and their homes among themselves. After the revolution, the Athenians, who now considered the Samians to be trustworthy, voted to grant them self-government: henceforth the people administered the city. They denied the landed aristocracy any share in government and prohibited any intermarriage between them and the common people.

22. During that same summer, the Chians continued to raise revolts in the cities even though the Peloponnesians had not yet arrived in great strength. The Chians had lost none of their original zeal, but they also wanted as many cities as possible to share the danger with them.[7] The Spartan plan had been to go to Chios first and then to Lesbos and from there to the Hellespont, so the Chians attacked Lesbos with thirteen ships, which were placed under the command of Deiniadas, an officer from one of the towns dependent on Sparta. The ships were supported by what Peloponnesian infantry were on the scene, and by the infantry of local allies, which marched along the shore towards Clazomenae and Cyme. These men were under the command of Eualas, a Spartan officer. The ships put in at Methymna, which was induced to rebel. Leaving four ships behind, the rest of the fleet then sailed on to Mytilene and ignited a revolt there.

7. See 8.2.

23. Meanwhile, Astyochus, the Spartan admiral-in-chief, arrived at Chios after setting out from Cenchreae, as planned, with four ships. On the third day after he arrived, the Athenian fleet of twenty-five ships sailed into Lesbos under the command of Diomedon and Leon, who had left Athens after Diomedon to reinforce him with ten ships. Towards evening of the same day Astyochus cast off and sailed for Lesbos, taking along one Chian ship, to help the Chian fleet as much as he could. He reached Pyrrha and the next day went on from there to Eresus, where he learned that the Athenians had taken Mytilene by storm. The Athenians had unexpectedly sailed right into the harbor, overpowered the Chian ships, and made a landing; they then fought a battle with the rebels, won it, and seized control of the city. Astyochus learned this from the Eresians and from the men on the Chian ships that had been left at Methymna with Eubulus. These ships had fled when Mytilene was captured, and now happened to meet up with Astyochus, although there were now only three of them, since one had been captured by the Athenians. No longer bound for Mytilene, Astyochus raised a revolt in Eresus and then armed the men on board his ships and sent them on foot along the coast to Antissa and Methymna, appointing Eteonicus as their commander. Then he too went along the coast with his own ships and the three Chian ships, hoping that the sight of him would encourage the Methymnians to persevere in the revolt. But since everything on the island of Lesbos went against him, he took his troops aboard and sailed away for Chios. The allied infantry, which was to have gone to the Hellespont, also returned to their respective cities. Afterwards six of the allied Peloponnesian ships at Cenchreae went to Chios and joined Astyochus and his men. The Athenians returned things on Lesbos to the way they had been. They then sailed from there to the mainland, and after capturing Polichna, which the Clazomenaeans had been fortifying, they brought the captives back to their island city, except for those who had been responsible for the uprising. These had escaped to Daphnus. Thus Clazomenae was once again brought over to the Athenian side.

24. That same summer, the twenty Athenian ships that were anchored at Lade blockading Miletus made a landing at Panormus, in the Milesian territory. The Athenians killed Chalcideus, the Spartan commander, who had come out to engage them with a few men. They sailed over again three days later and set up a victory marker that the Milesians later tore down, since the Athenians had not really controlled the ground when they erected it. With the ships from Lesbos, Leon and Diomedon also prosecuted the war against Chios by sea from the Oenussae Islands off Chios, and from Sidussa and Pteleum, forts they held in Erythrae. The marines they commanded had been conscripted from the list of hoplite warriors. They landed in Cardamyle and Boliscus and fought and won a battle with the Chians who came out to meet them, killing many of the enemy and laying waste the country thereabouts. They defeated them again in another battle at Phanae, and in yet a third battle in Leuconium. After that, the Chians no longer went out to fight them, and the Athenians plundered well-developed land that had not been invaded since the Persian Wars. After the Spartans, the Chians are the only people I have observed who combine prosperity with prudence, and the more their city provided them with a higher standard of living, the more they secured the internal order of the state. And if anyone thinks their rebellion was a reckless move, they did not risk it until they had enlisted many brave allies to share the danger with them, in the knowledge that even Athens would admit, after the disaster in Sicily, that its affairs were in a sorry state. If they were wrong about the human imponderables of this life and believed in the swift collapse of the Athenian empire, they were joined in this mistake by

many others who held the same belief. Cut off by sea, their land ravaged, there were some who were trying to bring the city back over to the Athenians. The magistrates knew who they were, but took no action on their own; instead, they brought over from Erythrae the Spartan admiral, Astyochus, and four ships he had with him to see how they might end the conspiracy with the least violence, either by taking hostages (which is what they finally set about doing) or in some other way.

25. During the last part of that summer, one thousand Athenian hoplites put in at Samos, from which they crossed to Miletus and set up camp. They came in forty-eight ships (of which some were troop transports), under the command of Phrynichus, Onomacles, and Scironides, and they were accompanied by fifteen hundred Argive hoplites (of whom five hundred were light-armed troops who had been given heavy armor by the Athenians) and by one thousand hoplites from their allies. Marching out to do battle against the Athenians and their allies were eight hundred Milesian hoplites, along with the Peloponnesians who had come with Chalcideus and a force of foreign mercenaries with Tissaphernes, who was there in person with his cavalry. The Argives darted forward out of formation from their wing. Their advance was all the more disorderly because of their contempt for Ionians they were sure would not stand up to them; but the Milesians defeated them, killing almost three hundred of their men. The Athenians, however, began by defeating the Peloponnesians and then repelling the barbarians and their rabble. They did not engage with the Milesians, who retreated into their city after their rout of the Argives, when they saw that the rest of their forces were being defeated. The now-victorious Athenians took up a position in front of the city of Miletus. In this particular battle, it happened that Ionians defeated Dorians on both sides. That is, the Athenians defeated the Peloponnesians who opposed them, and the Milesians beat the Argives. After erecting a victory marker, the Athenians made preparations to wall off the city, which was on an isthmus. They were confident that the other cities would soon return to the fold if they could only take Miletus.

26. While they were making these preparations, the Athenians received a message in the late afternoon that the fifty-five ships from Sicily and the Peloponnese were about to arrive. Hermocrates of Syracuse had been foremost among those urging that Sicily take part in finishing off Athens,[8] and accordingly there were twenty Syracusan ships and two from Selinus. The ships that the Peloponnesians had been outfitting were now ready, and Therimenes the Spartan had been ordered to bring the combined fleets to the admiral Astyochus. First they sailed into Leros, the island off Miletus. After learning that the Athenians were attacking Miletus, they went on from there to the Iasic Gulf, wanting to find out more about the situation in the city.

Then Alcibiades arrived on horseback in Teichiussa, in the Milesian territory, which is where Therimenes and his men had bivouacked after sailing to the gulf. Alcibiades had been at Miletus and had fought side by side with the Milesians and Tissaphernes, and Therimenes and his men learned the details of the battle from him. Alcibiades urged them to go to the relief of Miletus as quickly as possible and prevent it from being walled off, unless they wanted the operation in Ionia and everywhere else to fail.

27. They decided to go to the aid of Miletus at dawn. But Phrynichus, the Athenian general, had received accurate intelligence of the fleet from Leros; and although his colleagues wanted to stay and fight it out at sea, he refused to

8. In Books 6 and 7.

do so himself or to allow them or anyone else to fight if he could help it. He
said that he would never let fear of reproach lead him to do something really
shameful, taking foolish risks now when it was possible to fight the enemy later
with a clear knowledge of just how many ships they had and how many of his
own he would be able to get ready in his own good time. It was not shameful,
he said, for Athenians to withdraw their ships in certain circumstances; but it
would be much more shameful to be defeated, no matter how it happened. And
for Athens it would not be merely a matter of shame, but of the city's falling into
the greatest danger. After its recent disasters, Athens could barely go ahead and
take the initiative even with proper preparations—and even then it had to be
absolutely necessary. How much less could it take unnecessary risks when it was
not forced to. Phrynichus urged them to put aboard their wounded, their infantry, and whatever supplies they had brought with them as quickly as possible—leaving behind any war booty they had taken, so as to make their ships
lighter—and to sail back to Samos. From there, having assembled their whole
fleet, they would launch their attacks as opportunities arose. They did as he advised. Here and later, and not just in this but in all his other decisions, Phrynichus proved himself to be a man of insight. Thus right after it got dark, and in
the manner Phrynichus had prescribed, the Athenians left Miletus without following up their victory, and the Argives, furious over this on account of their
own defeat, hurriedly sailed away from Samos for home.

   28. The Peloponnesians set out from Teichiussa at dawn and arrived to
find that the Athenians had left. They remained at Miletus for a day, but the
next day they took along the Chian ships that had previously been under Chalcideus and that had been chased into Miletus, and returned to Teichiussa to retrieve some tackle they had taken off their ships in anticipation of battle. When
they arrived, Tissaphernes came up with his infantry and persuaded them to sail
to Iasos, which was held by his enemy, Amorges. So they made a surprise attack
on Iasos, which was expecting to see only ships from Attica, and took it by storm.
The Syracusans were singled out for commendation in this action. Amorges,
Pissuthnes' illegitimate son who had rebelled against the King, was taken alive
by the Peloponnesians and handed over to Tissaphernes so that he could, at his
pleasure, deliver him to the King, as he had been commanded to do. Iasos had
been rich since antiquity and the army plundered it from top to bottom, seizing a great deal of treasure. Since most of the mercenaries with Amorges were
from the Peloponnese, the army did them no harm and took them instead into
their own ranks. They handed the town over to Tissaphernes, along with all
their captives, both slave and free, having agreed with Tissaphernes to a price
of one daric per captive.[9] The Peloponnesians then returned to Miletus and
sent Pedaritus, son of Leon, whom the Spartans had sent out to be the governor
of Chios, overland as far as Erythrae. He was escorted by Amorges' mercenaries. They also installed Philip to take charge of things right there in Miletus.
   And so the summer came to an end.

   29. The following winter, after arranging for the defense of Iasos, Tissaphernes went to Miletus, where, as had been promised in Sparta, he distributed
a month's pay to all the ships at a rate of one Attic drachma a day per man. In
the future he intended to pay a half a drachma per day until he could ask the
King for instructions. He said that if the King commanded it, he would pay the
entire drachma. Hermocrates, the Syracusan commander, objected to this.
(The reason was that Therimenes was not the admiral. He had only come along

----

9. The Persian gold coin known as the daric was worth twenty drachmas.

to hand over the fleet to the admiral, Astyochus, and he had no strong feelings about the matter of pay.) They agreed that the fleet should be divided into units of five ships in which each man would be paid more than half a drachma. Tissaphernes was therefore to pay out three talents per five ships, or thirty-three talents to fifty-five ships per month, and any squadrons over and above that number were to be paid at the same rate.

30. That same winter, another thirty-five ships, under the command of Charminus, Strombichides, and Euctemon, arrived from Athens to join the fleet in Samos. The Athenians assembled all their ships, including those from Chios, with the intention of dividing the fleet by lot and blockading the enemy fleet at Miletus with the main division, and of sending the other, along with infantry, against Chios. The lots were drawn, and it fell to Strombichides, Onomacles, and Euctemon to sail into operations against Chios with thirty warships and a battalion of the thousand hoplites who had come to Miletus—these to be conveyed in troop transports. The other generals were to remain at Samos with seventy-four ships, with which they would control the sea lanes and launch attacks against Miletus.

31. Astyochus was in Chios at that time, selecting hostages to prevent the betrayal of the island to the Athenians, but he gave that up when he learned of the arrival of the ships under Therimenes and of the improved prospects for the allies. He now cast off with ten Peloponnesian and ten Chian ships and attacked Pteleum. Failing to take it, he sailed along the coast to Clazomenae and demanded that those who were sympathetic to Athens move upcountry to Daphnus and come over to the Peloponnesian side. Astyochus was joined in this demand by Tamos, the Persian lieutenant-governor of Ionia. When the Clazomenaeans failed to comply, Astyochus attacked the town, but he could not take it even though it was unfortified. He sailed off in a high wind and made Phocaea and Cyme, although the rest of his ships put in at Marathussa, Pele, and Drymussa, all islands off the coast of Clazomenae. These ships remained at these islands for eight days on account of the wind, and their crews consumed or destroyed the stores the Clazomenaeans had hidden there; other stuff they threw on board when they sailed away to join Astyochus at Phocaea and Cyme.

32. While Astyochus was there, some Lesbian ambassadors arrived who wanted to revolt yet again. They were able to win him over, but when the Corinthians and other allies were lukewarm to the plan because of the previous failure, Astyochus put out to sea and sailed to Chios. His ships were scattered by winter storms, but they eventually reached Chios from various places. After this, Pedaritus arrived with his army, after leaving Miletus by land and crossing the strait from Erythrae to Chios. Here he assumed command of the forces, including five hundred armed troops that had been left by the five ships under Chalcideus. As the Lesbian ambassadors were still urging the revolt, Astyochus made the case to Pedaritus and the Chians that they should take the fleet to Lesbos and raise a rebellion there. They would either end up with more allies, he said, or if they failed, they would at least do damage to the Athenians. Pedaritus, however, would not hear of the plan and refused to release the Chian ships.

33. Astyochus then warned the Chians that he would never come to their aid if they needed him, and took a squadron of five Corinthian, one Hermionian, and six Megarian ships, along with the Spartan vessels he himself had brought, and sailed to Miletus to assume his command. They made Corycus, in Erythrae, where they spent the night. Meanwhile, Athenians from Samos were sailing for Chios with their army and anchored in a harbor on the other side of a hill that separated them from Astyochus; and so the two forces were

not aware of one another. That night, Astyochus received a message from Pedaritus that some Erythraean prisoners of war had returned to Erythrae, after having been released from Samos by the Athenians on condition that they betray the place. Astyochus immediately put to sea and headed back to Erythrae. That is how close he came to being caught by the Athenians! Meanwhile, Pedaritus had sailed across the channel to join Astyochus, and both interrogated the suspected traitors. When they learned that the men had only been pretending to go along in order to gain their release from Samos, they let them go and sailed away, Pedaritus to Chios and Astyochus to Miletus, as originally planned.

34. Meanwhile, as the Athenian fleet was sailing around from Corycus off Arginus, they came on three Chian warships and gave chase as soon as they saw them. A big storm blew up and the Chians just barely escaped into the harbor. Three Athenian ships that had been most hotly in pursuit were disabled and driven ashore near the city of Chios. Their crews were either captured or killed. The rest of the fleet got away to a harbor called Phoenicus under Mount Mimas. They later went on from there to Lesbos, where they put in and prepared to build their fortification.

35. That same winter, Hippocrates the Spartan set out from the Peloponnese with ten Thurian ships. Dorieus, son of Diagoras, and two other officers were in command. This squadron, along with one ship apiece from Syracuse and Sparta, put into Cnidus, which had already been incited to revolt by Tissaphernes. When the command in Miletus learned of their arrival, they ordered half of the ships to guard Cnidus and the rest to stand off Triopium and seize merchantmen that put in there from Egypt. (Now Triopium is a promontory, under the protection of Apollo, that juts out from Cnidian territory.) The Athenians received intelligence of this detachment, and sailing from Samos, they captured the six ships standing guard off Triopium, although the crews managed to escape. After this, the Athenians put into Cnidus and attacked and almost took the unwalled town. They attacked again the next day, but the Cnidians had put up better defenses under cover of night, and the crews that had escaped from the ships had come into the city from Triopium; so that this time the Athenians could not do comparable damage, and retreating from the city, they ravaged Cnidian territory before sailing back to Samos.

36. At about the time that Astyochus arrived at Miletus to assume his command, the Peloponnesian camp was still abundantly provided for. The pay was good; the large amount of booty seized at Iasos was available to the troops; the Milesians were generously contributing to the war effort. Nevertheless, the Peloponnesians decided that the first agreement Chalcideus made with Tissaphernes was flawed and not sufficiently in their interests, so while Therimenes was still on the scene, they made another agreement, as follows.

37.   THE AGREEMENT OF THE SPARTANS AND THEIR ALLIES WITH
KING DARIUS AND WITH THE SONS OF THE KING
AND WITH TISSAPHERNES

There shall be a treaty of friendship between the above on the following terms:

Neither Sparta nor its allies shall make war on or do any harm whatever to the territories or cities that belong to the King or belonged to his fathers or forefathers, nor shall Sparta or its allies exact tribute from these cities.

Neither King Darius nor any of his subjects shall make war on or do any harm whatever to Sparta or to its allies.

If Sparta or its allies shall need anything from the King, or the King from Sparta or its allies, whatever they agree to shall hold good.

They shall jointly carry on the war against Athens and its allies, and if they end the war, they shall end it jointly.

If the King summons any army to his territory, the King shall bear the expense of said army.

If any of the cities that are parties to this agreement with the King invade the territory of the King, the other cities shall do everything in their power to stop them and to defend the King; and if anyone in the King's territory or in the dominions over which he rules invade the territory of Sparta or its allies, the King shall do everything in his power to stop and defend against them.

38. After this agreement was reached, Therimenes turned the fleet over to Astyochus. Then he embarked in a small craft—and disappeared.[1]

The Athenians had by now crossed from Lesbos to Chios with their army. With control of land and sea, they started to build their fortification at Delphinium, a place that had harbors, strong natural defenses by land and proximity to the city of Chios. The Chians had been badly beaten in many of their previous battles and their internal politics were turbulent besides. Pedaritus had executed the followers of Tydeus, the son of Ion, on a charge of collaborating with the Athenians, and the city had been forced into an oligarchical form of government. The prevailing mood was one of quiescence and mutual distrust. As a result, neither the Chians nor the mercenaries with Pedaritus considered themselves a match for the Athenians on the battlefield. They therefore sent to Miletus asking Astyochus to come and help them. When Astyochus turned a deaf ear to them, Pedaritus sent a despatch to Sparta accusing him of misconduct.

This was the situation the Athenians found at Chios. Meanwhile, their fleet at Samos made forays against the fleet at Miletus; but since the enemy did not come out to fight them, they returned to Samos and stayed there.

39. That same winter, the twenty-seven ships that Calligeitus the Megarian and Timagoras the Cyzicene had commissioned on behalf of Pharnabazus, and which the Spartans had outfitted, put to sea from the Peloponnese at around the time of the solstice under the command of a Spartan officer, Antisthenes, and headed for Ionia. The Spartans had put aboard Lichas, son of Arcesilaus, and ten other Spartan officers, as a panel of advisors for Astyochus. Their instructions: to take charge of things when they reached Miletus and make the best arrangements they could; to despatch the twenty-seven ships—or more, or fewer, as they thought best—to Pharnabazus at the Hellespont under the command of Clearchus, son of Rhamphias, who had gone along with them; and, because Pedaritus' despatches had aroused suspicion against him, to relieve Astyochus of command, if the eleven commissioners saw fit, and to put Antisthenes in his place. From Malea, the ships sailed across the open sea until they made landfall at Melos. Here they chanced on ten Athenian ships, of which they captured three without their crews and set them on fire. After this, they feared that the Athenian ships that had escaped from Melos would give the news of their coming to the fleet at Samos—as in fact, they did. So as a precaution, they extended the length of their route and sailed to Asia via Crete, putting into

---

1. This is the last we hear of Therimenes the Spartan. He should not be confused with Theramenes the Athenian, son of Hagnon, who is introduced below at 8.68.

port at Caunus. Now that they had reached safety, they sent a message from Caunus to the fleet at Miletus, requesting an escort to take them up the coast.

40. At about the same time, and despite Astyochus' unwillingness to act, the Chians and Pedaritus sent messengers to him demanding that he come to the aid of their besieged city with his whole fleet and not stand by while the largest of Sparta's allies in Ionia was being cut off by sea and plundered by land. To make matters worse, there were a great many slaves on Chios, more than in any one state besides Sparta. Because of their number, these slaves were very harshly punished for any misconduct.[2] When the Athenian army seemed to be securely entrenched behind their wall, most of the slaves immediately deserted to them, and these slaves did the greatest damage because they knew the country. Thus the Chians said that it was imperative for Astyochus to come to their aid while there was still hope of doing something to stop the Athenians. They were fortifying Delphinium, but they were still not finished, and they were still building an extra wall to defend their ships and men. Astyochus had warned the Chians in the past that he would never help them, and he had meant it, but he saw how committed the allies were and immediately took steps to come to the relief of Chios.

41. While this was going forward, Astyochus received a message from Caunus that the twenty-seven ships and the Spartan board of advisors had arrived, and he decided that this must be given priority over everything else. In order to gain greater control over the sea, he had to escort such a large force as this up the coast and add it to his fleet, and he also needed to provide safe passage to the Spartans who had come to review him. So he immediately gave up his plan of going to Chios and set sail for Caunus.

While sailing down the coast, he made a landing at Meropis, on the island of Cos. The unwalled city had just been demolished by the worst earthquake in human memory. Its inhabitants had fled to the mountains, so Astyochus and his men looted the ruins and rampaged through the country, taking away everything but the free citizens, whom they let go. They then left Cos and reached Cnidus by night. Urged on by the Cnidians, Astyochus felt compelled not to disembark his men, but to keep right on sailing against twenty Athenian ships with which Charminus, one of the commanders from Samos, was keeping a lookout for the twenty-seven ships coming from the Peloponnese — the same ships Astyochus was sailing down the coast to meet. The command at Samos had received news of their coming from Melos, and Charminus was keeping a watch off Syme, Chalce, Rhodes, and Lycia. He already had intelligence that they were at Caunus.

42. Astyochus sailed on, just as he was, in the direction of Syme, in hopes of catching the Athenians on the open sea before his coming was known. It was raining and the sky was heavily overcast, and the ships were thrown into confusion as they strayed off course in the darkness. By dawn, the fleet was scattered, with most still floundering at various points around the island, but their left wing was visible to the Athenians, and Charminus cast off on the double with fewer than his twenty ships, thinking these were the ships from Caunus they were looking for. They made contact with the enemy and immediately sank three of his ships and disabled others. They were winning the battle until the greater part of the enemy fleet seemed to come out of nowhere, and they found themselves completely surrounded. They now ran for it and lost six ships, al-

---

2. Probably Thucydides means that there were *proportionally* more slaves in Chios than in any other Greek state. Surely in absolute numbers there were more slaves in Athens than in Chios.

though the rest got away to the island of Teutlussa, from which they went on to Halicarnassus. After the battle, the Peloponnesians put into Cnidus where they joined forces with the twenty-seven ships from Caunus. Then they all sailed out to Syme, set up a victory marker, and returned to anchor at Cnidus.

43. After the Athenians at Samos learned the details of the battle, they sailed to Syme with their whole fleet. They did not, however, move on the fleet at Cnidus, which did not, for its part, move on them. Instead, the Athenians picked up the tackle Charminus' ships had left on Syme and attacked Loryma, on the mainland. Then they sailed back to Samos.

The combined Peloponnesian contingents were now at Cnidus, making necessary repairs. Meanwhile, the eleven-man Spartan board of advisors conferred with Tissaphernes, who had come to Cnidus, about any existing arrangements they did not like, and about how to carry on the war in the future in accordance with the best interests of both sides. Lichas was especially critical of what had been done and said that neither of the two agreements framed by Chalcideus and Therimenes was well advised. It was outrageous for the King to claim that he still ruled over the same territories as his forefathers. That would mean returning to slavery all the islands, as well as Thessaly, Eastern Locris, and everything as far as Boeotia, and instead of freeing Greece, the Spartans would be putting a Persian yoke around its neck. He called for another, fairer treaty, because the authorities at Sparta were not going to observe either of these and would not accept any payment on such terms.

Tissaphernes was incensed and left them in a rage without reaching any agreement.

44. Meanwhile, the Peloponnesians had been getting messages from the most powerful men in Rhodes asking them to intervene, and they made up their minds to sail there. They hoped to bring over to their side an island that had sizable forces of sailors and infantrymen. They also thought that this would make them able to depend on their own alliance to maintain their fleet, without having to ask Tissaphernes for money. So they immediately set sail that same winter from Cnidus with ninety-four ships and fell first on the Rhodian town of Camirus. Not knowing about the conspiracy, the terrified populace fled, especially since the town was unwalled; but the Spartans called an assembly of the people of Camirus, and of the two other Rhodian cities of Lindos and Ialysus, and persuaded the Rhodians to revolt from Athens. And indeed Rhodes did go over to the Peloponnesians. The Athenians had received intelligence at about this time of what the Peloponnesians were doing and set sail from Samos with the fleet, in hopes of getting to Rhodes first. They could be seen coming out of the open sea, but they were just a little too late. So they sailed away to Chalce for the time being, and from there to Samos. They later made war on Rhodes, launching attacks from Chalce and Cos; but the Peloponnesians, who had collected thirty-two talents from the Rhodians, drew their fleet up onto the beach and took no action for eighty days.

45. While this was going on, and even earlier, before the Peloponnesians set out for Rhodes, the following events were unfolding. After the battle of Miletus and the death of Chalcideus, the Peloponnesians became suspicious of Alcibiades, and at their instigation a despatch was sent from Sparta to Astyochus ordering his death. (Even Agis hated him, after all, and in any case he seemed to be generally untrustworthy.) Terrified, the first thing he did was to escape to the court of Tissaphernes. Next he did everything he could to undermine Peloponnesian interests. He became Tissaphernes' advisor on all matters Greek and brought about the abovementioned reduction of the Peloponnesian salary from

one Attic drachma to a half drachma, advising Tissaphernes not to pay even that regularly. He told Tissaphernes to explain to the Peloponnesians that the Athenians, who had longer experience in managing a navy than they, only paid half a drachma to their sailors. They did this not so much from poverty as to keep the crews from being spoiled by high pay, in some cases neglecting physical fitness by spending their money on things that were bad for their health, and in others by staying ashore without leave—which they would not do if it meant forfeiting their back pay. Alcibiades persuaded Tissaphernes to induce both the trierarchs and the generals of the allied cities to go along with this reduction by giving them bribes. This worked with all but the Syracusans, whose general, Hermocrates, alone opposed Alcibiades in the name of the alliance.

Alcibiades dismissed allies who came to ask for money by telling them in Tissaphernes' name how shameless the Chians were. They were the richest of the Greeks, and although they were being saved by outside help, they still had the nerve to demand that others pay not only with their lives, but also with their treasure for Chian freedom. To the other cities, he said that they had paid a tribute to Athens before revolting, and it would be totally unjustifiable if they were now unwilling to contribute as much and even more to their own cause. He added that Tissaphernes was financing the war with his own money just then, so he naturally had a tight budget; but if money ever came from the King, Tissaphernes would restore full pay and would do everything he reasonably could to help the cities.

46. Alcibiades also advised Tissaphernes not to be in too much of a hurry to end the war and to neither bring in the Phoenician ships he was getting ready nor pay for more contingents of Greek seamen, thereby giving power over land and sea to the same state. Instead, he should maintain a balance of power between Athens and Sparta so that the King would always be able to play one side against the other whenever it gave him trouble. If control of land and sea were to fall into the hands of a single state, the King would have no one to help him wrest it away, unless he himself at some point led a campaign and fought it out at great cost and risk. What would be cheaper—at a fraction of the cost and at the same time safer for the King personally—would be to let the Greeks grind themselves down fighting each other. Alcibiades did say, however, that it would be more expedient for the King to share his empire with the Athenians, because they would be less likely to have designs on his mainland territory. Also, Athenian policy and practices in carrying on the war were in the King's interest, because Athens and the King could join each other in subjugating their enemies. The Athenian share would be the islands in the Aegean, and the King's would be the Greeks who inhabited his domains. The Spartans, on the other hand, came as liberators, and it was likely that after freeing the Greeks from Greeks, they would also want to free them from barbarians—unless, of course, the Persians got them out of the way. Alcibiades' advice, therefore, was to first wear both sides down, and then, after the King had gotten as much as he could out of the Athenians, to immediately rid his country of the Peloponnesians. Tissaphernes inclined to these views for the most part, at least as far as one could tell from his actions. Because of this counsel, for example, he took Alcibiades into his confidence as a trusted adviser on these matters. He was also stingy with pay for the Peloponnesians and would not allow them to fight the Athenians at sea, insisting that they would fight with superior numbers when the Phoenician ships arrived. Thus he undermined the Peloponnesian position, blunting the fighting edge of a fleet that had become so strong, and in other ways made it too obvious to escape notice that he was not a willing ally.

47. Alcibiades, having gone over to Tissaphernes and the King, gave this advice both because he thought it best and because he was working hard to return to his homeland. He knew that if he kept Athens from being destroyed, he might one day persuade the Athenians to let him come back from exile, and he believed that he would be most persuasive if everyone saw that Tissaphernes was his friend. He proved to be right. He had already sent word to the most influential men among the troops at Samos, asking them to work on his behalf among the nobility and to say that he wanted to return as their fellow citizen to establish an oligarchy instead of the democracy of the lowest common denominator that had expelled him. He also offered Tissaphernes as a friend; but although the forces at Samos saw Alcibiades wielding such great influence with Tissaphernes, it was largely for reasons of their own that the trierarchs and the most powerful Athenians at Samos took steps to dissolve the democratic government.

48. This movement began in the fleet and later spread from there to the city of Athens. A few men crossed over from Samos and went to confer with Alcibiades. He dangled the prospect of friendship, first with Tissaphernes and then with the King, provided they abandoned democratic government, since that was the best way to gain the King's trust. (In general, the most powerful citizens—those who bore the greatest burden of the war—had high hopes of getting control of the government and of prevailing over the Spartans.) When those who met with Alcibiades returned to Samos, they brought the most important men into the inner circle and publicly announced to the rank and file that the King would be their ally and give them pay, provided Alcibiades was restored and they gave up their democracy. Even though they at first grumbled over what had been done, the rank and file sat still for it because of their naive hope of money from the King. After making their plans known to the whole camp, the leaders who were organizing the oligarchy once again scrutinized the offers Alcibiades had made, both among themselves and with the majority of their faction. Most thought that they were trustworthy and that he could deliver on them, but Phrynichus, who was still general, did not like them at all. It seemed to him— and this was in fact the case—that Alcibiades was not interested in oligarchy any more than in democracy, and that all he wanted was to change the existing government in the city so that he could be called in by his own friends and restored to citizenship. This was something they must bear in mind to avoid quarreling among themselves, Phrynichus said. The most expedient course for the King was not to make trouble for himself by taking sides with the Athenians, whom he distrusted— not when it was in his power to befriend the Peloponnesians, who had never done him any harm, and who had as much of a presence at sea as the Athenians and held large cities in the King's domains besides. As to the allied states, who had been promised oligarchical government because Athens too was going to abandon democracy, Phrynichus said that he was sure that an Athenian revolution would not bring the rebellious cities to make terms with an Athenian oligarchy and that the cities still in the empire would not be more loyal to Athens on that account. Those cities did not want to be subjects, whether under a democracy or an oligarchy; either was fine, provided they were free. And as for the so-called "best and brightest," the subjects did not believe *they* would deliver more concrete advantages than the democracy, since, from the subjects' point of view, it was they who introduced criminal measures to the people, egged them on to commit them, and then enriched themselves. Once in power, they would kill subjects brutally and without trial. As far as the subjects were concerned, then, the Athenian people were

a refuge and a check on this class. The subject cities were well acquainted with their behavior, said Phrynichus, and he had certain knowledge that such was their thinking. That was why he, for his part, liked neither Alcibiades' proposals nor what was then being done on his behalf.

49. The members of the faction decided to stick to their original plan and to leave things as they were. They then got ready to send Peisander and other envoys to Athens to prepare the way for the return of Alcibiades, the abolition of the democracy, and the friendship between Athens and Tissaphernes.

50. Phrynichus knew that there would be a debate at Athens about the return of Alcibiades and that the Athenians would finally go along with it. Because he had spoken out against this, Phrynichus also feared that if Alcibiades did return, he would try to harm him for having stood in his way. So he took the following steps against this eventuality. He sent a secret message, in writing, to the Spartan admiral Astyochus, who was still off Miletus, telling him that Alcibiades was wrecking Sparta's plans by creating a friendship between Tissaphernes and Athens. Phrynichus clearly detailed everything that had happened and asked Astyochus to excuse him for devising a way to hurt an enemy, even if it meant damaging the interests of his city. Astyochus, however, did not even consider punishing Alcibiades, especially since Alcibiades was no longer in his power. On the contrary, Astyochus went up to Magnesia and, turning informer, told both Alcibiades and Tissaphernes about the letter from Samos. It is said that in return for a payoff, he also offered himself to Tissaphernes as a source of information about this matter and everything else, and that this was why he did not take a hard-line stance on the reduced pay.[3] Alcibiades immediately sent a despatch to the authorities in Samos, denouncing what Phrynichus had done and demanding that he be put to death. In great consternation as well as in the greatest danger because of this indictment, Phrynichus sent another letter to Astyochus, complaining that the secrecy of the first letter had been breached and saying that he was now prepared to hand over the whole Athenian army at Samos for destruction. Samos was unfortified, and he gave details in writing about how he would go about betraying it. He said that no one could blame him, now that his greatest enemies had put his life in danger, for doing this or anything else rather than be destroyed by them.

51. Astyochus gave this information to Alcibiades also. But by now Phrynichus knew that Astyochus was betraying him, and that a letter was about to arrive from Alcibiades about his offer. Just in time, he turned informer and told the army that the enemy was going to attack because Samos was unfortified and not all the Athenian ships were moored in the harbor. He said that he knew this for sure, and that it was imperative to fortify Samos immediately and to take every precaution. As a general, he could take these actions on his own authority. So because of Phrynichus, the army set about building fortifications; they had been planned in any case, but the result was that Samos was fortified that much sooner. Not much later, the letter arrived from Alcibiades, saying that Phrynichus had betrayed the army and that the enemy was about to attack. The Athenians, however, did not trust Alcibiades. They thought that he had foreseen the enemy's plans and had tried to pin complicity onto Phrynichus out of hatred for him. Thus Alcibiades did Phrynichus no harm and even corroborated him by giving the same information.

52. After these events took place, Alcibiades went to work on Tissaphernes, trying to persuade him to be on friendly terms with the Athenians. Tis-

saphernes feared the Peloponnesians because they had more ships on the scene than the Athenians, but he still wanted to be won over, if at all possible, especially since he was still angry with the Peloponnesians because of the quarrel at Cnidus over the treaty with Therimenes.[4] (This quarrel had already taken place—the Peloponnesians were now at Rhodes.) At that time, what Alcibiades had previously said about the Spartans liberating all the cities was borne out by Lichas, who repeatedly said that Sparta could not uphold an agreement whereby the King controlled the cities that either he himself or his ancestors had formerly ruled. And Alcibiades, who was playing for high stakes, was in constant attendance on Tissaphernes, eagerly pressing his case.

53. Meanwhile, the Athenian envoys who had been despatched with Peisander from Samos reached Athens and addressed the assembly. They emphasized their main points, in particular that if they restored Alcibiades and changed to a "different form of democracy," they could form an alliance with the King of Persia and defeat the Peloponnesians. Many people objected to the proposal about changing the form of the democracy, while at the same time Alcibiades' enemies shouted that it would be outrageous if he returned after having broken the law. The Eumolpidae and the Ceryces invoked the mysteries—which had been the reason for his exile—and adjured the gods to prevent his return.[5] At that point Peisander came forward. In the face of the indignant outcry, he called his opponents before him one by one and, reminding them that the Peloponnesians had as many ships ready for action as they, that the Peloponnesians had more allies, and that Tissaphernes and the King were supplying the Peloponnesians with money while Athens was bankrupt, he asked them one by one whether they had the slightest hope that their city could be saved unless they could persuade the King of Persia to come over to their side.

Each of them answered "No."

Then Peisander flatly said, "No, and we will not survive unless we have more discipline in our government and put it into the hands of fewer people, so that the King will trust us. Right now, we should be talking not about our form of government, but about our very survival! After all, if there's anything about the new government we don't like, we will always be able to return to democracy later. So let's bring back Alcibiades, the only man alive who can save us!"

54. On first hearing the proposal for an oligarchy, then, the people reacted angrily, but when Peisander clearly demonstrated that there was no other way to save themselves, they became frightened and gave in—although at the same time they were consoled by the hope that they would be able to change back to a democracy. They voted to send Peisander and ten others off by ship to do whatever they thought best as far as Tissaphernes and Alcibiades were concerned. Also, based on accusations by Peisander, the people relieved Phrynichus and his colleague Scironides of command and sent Diomedon and Leon to take charge of the fleet. Peisander slandered Phrynichus—for betraying Iasos and Amorges—because he knew that Phrynichus was hostile to the negotiations with Alcibiades. Political clubs already existed in Athens to further their members' interests in trials and elections,[6] and Peisander went to all of these and called on them to band together and take common action to overthrow the

---

4. See 8.43. This passage is unclear and has been variously emended. It has also been taken, along with other passages in Book 8, as an indication that much of the book is an unrevised first draft.
5. The Eumolpidae and Ceryces were the two families that provided the priests who officiated over the Eleusinian mysteries.
6. Political clubs at Athens were generally composed of affluent young men who sometimes had oligarchic leanings. Democrats regarded these clubs with suspicion.

democracy. When he had finished preparations to ensure that there would be absolutely no delay in taking advantage of the situation in the city, Peisander and his ten companions cast off on their voyage to Tissaphernes.

55. By this time that winter, Leon and Diomedon had taken command of the Athenian fleet and made a naval attack on Rhodes. They found that the Peloponnesian ships had been hauled ashore, but they made a landing and defeated some Rhodian defenders who came out to fight them. They then withdrew to Chalce and carried on the war from there rather than from Cos, because at Chalce they could more easily observe any movements of the Peloponnesian fleet.

At about this time also, Xenophantidas, a Spartan, arrived in Rhodes with the message from Pedaritus, at Chios, that the Athenians had just finished their fortification of Delphinium,[7] and that if the Peloponnesians did not come to the rescue with their whole fleet, the cause at Chios would be lost. So the Peloponnesians began to plan their rescue mission. Meanwhile, however, Pedaritus led out his mercenaries, along with the Chian army, in full strength and stormed the wall surrounding the Athenian ships. They took a part of it and captured some ships that had been drawn up on shore, but then the Athenians struck back, and after first driving off the Chians, they defeated the rest of Pedaritus' forces, killing Pedaritus himself, along with many Chians, and capturing a great many weapons.

56. After this, the Chians were even more cut off by land and sea than before, and there was terrible starvation in the place.

Meanwhile, Peisander and the Athenian ambassadors who were with him reached Tissaphernes and held talks with him about an agreement. Now Alcibiades was not fully confident of his ability to deliver Tissaphernes, who feared the Peloponnesians more than the Athenians, and who, as Alcibiades himself had advised, still wanted to wear down both sides; so he adopted a stratagem whereby Tissaphernes would make the greatest possible demands on the Athenians so that the talks would fail. In my view, Tissaphernes had the same idea—he because he was motivated by fear, and Alcibiades because he saw that Tissaphernes was not about to reach an agreement, and because he did not want the Athenians to think he could not win him over. Instead, he wanted it to look as if Tissaphernes had indeed been persuaded to go over to them and had really been eager to come to terms, except that the Athenians had not given him enough. Speaking on behalf of Tissaphernes, who was present, Alcibiades piled demand on demand to put the Athenians in the wrong no matter what, even though they were for a long time willing to go along with whatever he asked for. They acquiesced, for example, when he demanded that they give up all of Ionia, and again when he asked for its offshore islands and other territory. Finally, in their third meeting, terrified that he would be exposed as having no power at all, Alcibiades demanded that they permit the King to build a fleet and to cruise off Attica wherever and with as many vessels as he pleased. That was the last straw. The Athenians decided that further talks were useless and that Alcibiades had made fools of them. Furious, they left and went back to Samos.

57. Immediately afterwards that same winter, Tissaphernes went to Caunus, wanting to bring the Peloponnesians back to Miletus and to conclude yet another treaty with them on whatever terms he could get. He was willing to pay them, so as not to make them outright enemies, but also because he feared that if the Peloponnesians could not support their many ships, the Athenians

7. See 8.38.

might force them into a battle and defeat them, or that their crews might desert, whereupon the Athenians would end up getting what they wanted without him. He was especially afraid that in their search for food, the Peloponnesians might raid the mainland. After weighing all these considerations and their consequences and wishing, as he did, to maintain a balance of power between Athens and Sparta, Tissaphernes sent for the Peloponnesians, paid them, and concluded a third treaty, as follows.

58. On the plain of the Meander River, in the thirteenth year of the reign of Darius, and when Alexippidas was ephor in Sparta, a treaty was made between the Spartans and their allies on one side and Tissaphernes, Hieramenes, and the sons of Pharnaces on the other, concerning the affairs of the King and of the Spartans and their allies.

The territory of the King that is in Asia shall remain the King's, and the King shall do as he pleases with his own territory.

The Spartans and their allies shall not enter the King's territory with hostile intent, nor shall the King enter the territory of Sparta or its allies with hostile intent. If any Spartans or Spartan allies enter the territory of the King with hostile intent, the Spartans and their allies shall put a stop to it; and if anyone from the territory of the King enters the territory of Sparta or its allies with hostile intent, the King shall put a stop to it.

Tissaphernes shall support the existing ships according to the terms that have been agreed until such time as the King's ships arrive. When the King's ships arrive, the Spartans and their allies shall, if they wish, themselves bear the expense of their own ships. If the Spartans and their allies prefer that Tissaphernes pay for their ships, he shall do so, but the Spartans and their allies shall, at the end of the war, repay to Tissaphernes whatever money they have taken. When the King's ships arrive, the ships of the Spartans and their allies and the ships of the King shall carry on the war in accordance with the decisions of Tissaphernes and of the Spartans and their allies. If, however, they wish to make peace with the Athenians, peace shall only be made if all parties consent.

59. This was the treaty, and after it was concluded, Tissaphernes made preparations to bring over the Phoenician ships, as he had promised, and to honor all his other commitments—in any case, he made a great show of doing so.

60. Just as that winter was coming to an end, Oropus, which the Athenians were garrisoning, was betrayed to the Boeotians from within. They captured it with the help of some men from Eretria and from Oropus itself, all of whom were plotting to foment revolt in Euboea. The reason they needed Oropus was that it was opposite Eretria, and revolt was impossible in Eretria while the Athenians held Oropus, because they could do great damage in Eretria and the rest of Euboea. But now that they had Oropus, the Eretrians went to Rhodes and called on the Peloponnesians to help them. The Peloponnesians, however, were more eager to go to the relief of Chios, which was desperate, and they sailed there from Rhodes with their whole fleet. Near Triopium they spotted the Athenian fleet on the open sea sailing away from Chalce, but they did not attack each other. The Athenians went on to Samos and the Peloponnesians to Miletus, having seen that it was no longer possible to relieve Chios without first fighting it out at sea. And then that winter finally came to an end, and with it ended the twentieth year of the war whose history I, Thucydides, have written.

61. Early in the following spring, Dercyllidas, a Spartan officer, was sent overland along the coast to the Hellespont with a small force, in order to foment

revolt at the Milesian colony of Abydos. Meanwhile, because Astyochus could not find a way to help them, the Chians were compelled by the hardship of the blockade to fight a battle with the Athenians at sea. Astyochus was still at Rhodes, but Leon, a Spartan officer, had come to Chios from Miletus. He had sailed out with Antisthenes from the Peloponnese as a squadron commander and had been sent over to take charge after the death of Pedaritus. He had brought twelve ships, which had been on guard at Miletus—five from Thurii, four from Syracuse, one from Anaea, one from Miletus, and one belonging to himself. The Chian army came out in full force and seized a strong position. Simultaneously, they put to sea with thirty-six ships and fought with the thirty-two Athenian ships. The battle was intense, but the Chians gave somewhat better than they got, and at dusk they and their allies fell back on their city.

62. By now Dercyllidas had reached the Hellespont from Miletus, and immediately after the battle at Chios, Abydos went over to him and to Pharnabazus, with Lampsacus following two days later. Strombichides received intelligence of these events and rushed there from Chios to put down the revolt with twenty-four Athenian ships, some of which were troop ships carrying hoplites. The Lampsacenes came out to do battle with him, but he defeated them and captured the unwalled town without meeting further resistance. He took goods, chattels, and slaves as booty, but allowed the freeborn citizens to return to their homes, and then went on to Abydos. But the people of Abydos did not surrender, and he was unable to take the town after repeated assaults, so he sailed across the Hellespont to Sestos, a town in the Chersonese opposite Abydos that the Persians once held. There Strombichides built a fort from which to keep watch over the whole Hellespont.

63. Meanwhile, the Chians had gained more command of their sea lanes, and Astyochus and his men at Miletus were encouraged to learn of the naval battle at Chios and of Strombichides' departure from Abydos with his ships. Astyochus then sailed along the coast to Chios with two ships. He left there with Leon's squadron, rendezvoused with his main fleet, and showed his sails off Samos; but he went back to Miletus when mutual suspicion among the Athenians kept them from coming out to fight him. For at about this time, and even sooner, the democratic government in Athens had been overthrown, and after the delegation with Peisander had returned to Samos from Tissaphernes, they took an even tighter grip on the army and urged the most powerful Samians to join in setting up an oligarchy, even though the same men had just led an insurrection against one.[8] The Athenian leadership on Samos had decided among themselves to give up on Alcibiades, since he had failed to help them—and besides, he was not the right man for an oligarchy. They themselves, the ones who were taking the risks, would determine how to keep their plans from unraveling. They would also carry on the war and willingly contribute money and anything else that was needed out of their own resources, since the burdens they bore would be for themselves and not for others.

64. Immediately after formulating this policy, they sent Peisander and half of his delegation to promote it back in Athens, with orders to try to set up oligarchies in any of the subject cities where they stopped along the way. The other half of the delegation was sent in other directions to the other subject cities. Diitrephes, who was near Chios, was sent off to assume command of the forces in the Thracian region, to which he had been appointed. On arrival in Thasos, he dissolved the democracy, but about two months after he left, the Thasians began

8. See 8.21.

to fortify their city: they no longer wanted to be governed by aristocrats tied to Athens, when they were expecting to be liberated by the Spartans from one day to the next. In fact, Thasian exiles who had been expelled by the Athenians were now with the Peloponnesians, and acting with friends in the city, they were working hard to bring over a squadron of ships and openly break away from Athens. And indeed things were working out as they wished: the form of government had been set right without danger to themselves, and the democracy that would have opposed them had been dissolved. Thus as far as Thasos was concerned, things turned out the opposite of what the Athenian oligarchs wanted, and in my opinion this was the case in many of the other subject cities as well. For now that the cities could institute more disciplined governments without fear of reprisals, they gravitated toward outright independence and spurned Athenian "good government," which was rotten to the core.

65. Peisander and his colleagues continued on their voyage, and as ordered, they dissolved the democracies in the cities they put into. Hoplites from some of the places helped them and went on with them to Athens. They arrived to find that most of their program had already been carried out by the political clubs.[9] Some of the younger members, for example, had banded together and murdered Androcles, one of the most prominent democrats and one of the leaders in banishing Alcibiades. The killers were never caught. They murdered him for two reasons: because he was a populist; but even more because they thought it would please Alcibiades, whom they expected to return and make an alliance with Tissaphernes. They had also killed some other troublesome people, also without being caught. The political clubs had also publicly articulated as their platform that no one but men in military service would receive public pay; that no more than five thousand men would have a say in government; and that these would be the men whose lives and property were most beneficial to the state.

66. This platform was meant to appease the populace, since only the revolutionaries would be running the city. The assembly and the council, which were chosen by lot, still convened; but they only deliberated on proposals that had been approved by the inner circle. Furthermore, the speakers all came from this group, which first vetted everything they said. None of the others spoke in opposition, because they saw how extensive the conspiracy was. If any one did speak out, he quickly and conveniently turned up dead. There was no investigation; no suspects were brought to justice. The people just kept quiet, and the terror was such that even those who kept their mouths shut thought they were lucky if nothing bad happened to them. Their minds were overcome with fear, because they imagined that the number of conspirators was far greater than it really was, and no one could find out the truth, because the size of the city made it impossible for people to know each other. For the same reason, it was impossible for someone who was persecuted to vent his anger to someone else and plot revenge. He could not talk to strangers, but he also could not trust his friends. People in the former democratic government approached each other very warily: anyone could be in on the conspiracy. Even people of whom you would never have dreamed it possible had joined the oligarchs. In fact, by planting suspicion among the former democrats, these people created the greatest distrust toward everyone else and did the oligarchs the great service of making them more secure.

9. See 8.54.

67. It was at this point that Peisander and his colleagues arrived in Athens, and they immediately took over from there. First, they convened the assembly and moved that ten citizens be elected as independent commissioners. These commissioners would, on a given day, present to the assembly their proposals as to how the city should best be governed. On the appointed day, they cooped the assembly up in the temple of Poseidon at Colonus, which is about a mile and a quarter outside the walls of the city, and the commission made one and only one proposal, which was that any Athenian could deliver any opinion he wished. Anyone who indicted the speaker for having made an illegal proposal or tried to harm him in any other way would be subject to heavy fines. And then it all came out. It was moved that from then on, no one would hold office or receive pay for public service under the old constitution, and that five men would be chosen to preside over the selection of one hundred men, who would in turn appoint three men apiece. This would make four hundred men who would enter the council chamber with full power to govern as they thought best and to convene the Five Thousand when they saw fit.

68. The speaker who made this motion was Peisander, and to all appearances he was the most zealous of those who were dismantling the democracy. But the man who conceived the whole movement, who was most involved in its organization and who brought it to fruition, was Antiphon. Of all the Athenian men of his generation, he was second to none in the force of his character, in the strength of his intellect, and in his powers of expression. He did not willingly come forward to speak in the assembly, however, or indeed in any public forum, because his reputation for craftiness made the people wary of him. But more than anyone else, he was able to help parties who consulted him concerning trials and other legal procedures. Later the democracy underwent yet another change.[1] There were trials, and the members of the government of the Four Hundred were prosecuted by the new assembly. At that time, Antiphon, charged with having helped to set up the oligarchy, put up the best defense ever made by a man on trial for his life.[2]

It was Phrynichus, however, who proved to be the most fervent supporter of the oligarchy, in part because he feared Alcibiades and knew that Alcibiades was aware of his negotiations with Astyochus while he was at Samos. An oligarchy, he thought, was least likely to allow Alcibiades to return. Once he had committed himself to the oligarchy, Phrynichus was the man most to be trusted in dangerous situations.

Another of the leaders in overthrowing the democracy, and a man of considerable judgement and oratorical ability, was Theramenes, son of Hagnon.[3]

It is no surprise, then, that an effort carried out by so many able men succeeded, difficult though it was. It was hard, almost a century after the tyrants were overthrown, for the Athenian people to relinquish their freedom, especially when they had not only been an independent people, but had, for over fifty years, grown used to ruling over others.

69. The assembly passed these measures without a word of dissent and then dissolved. Sometime later, they brought the Four Hundred into the council chamber, and they did it in the following way. Because the enemy was at Decelea, all Athenians were at all times either guarding the walls or on alert, going about their business but ready to take up arms at stations throughout the city.

1. To the government of the Five Thousand.
2. The speech (except for a fragment) does not survive. Neither did Antiphon; he lost his case and was executed in 411.
3. Not to be confused with Therimenes the Spartan, who is last seen sailing off in a boat at 8.38.

On the appointed day, the revolutionaries allowed those who were not in on the conspiracy to leave their stations, as usual, but quietly told their co-conspirators to stay not with, but close enough, to their weapons to be able to arm themselves and intervene in case anyone tried to block the entrance of the Four Hundred. Also present were Andrians, Tenians, three hundred Carystians, and some colonists whom the Athenians had sent to settle in Aegina.[4] They had come, with their own arms, for the same purpose as the conspirators and had been given the same instructions. With these troops in place, the Four Hundred arrived, each one carrying a concealed dagger. Accompanied by one hundred twenty young thugs whom they used whenever they needed to resort to violence, they suddenly broke into the council chamber and ordered the five hundred councillors, who were chosen by lot, to take their pay and get out. The Four Hundred were carrying all the pay that was owed to the councillors for the remainder of their terms, and they paid it to them as they left.

70. In this way, the council skulked away without a word, and all the other citizens kept quiet and offered no resistance. The Four Hundred then took their seats in the council chamber. On that occasion, they only drew lots among themselves to select their presiding officers and gave the prayers and sacrifices to the gods customary on taking office; but over time they radically altered the democracy's internal administration. They did not allow exiles to return, because Alcibiades was one of them, but in every other respect they governed the city with an iron hand. Some were killed—not many—whom they decided it would be easier to just quietly get rid of; some were thrown in jail; yet others were banished. They also sent heralds to Agis, king of Sparta, who was at Decelea, saying that they wanted to make peace and that they supposed he would be readier to reach an agreement with them than with the fickle mob.

71. Agis could not believe that the city would so quickly give up its ancient freedoms and thought that the people would not be so quiet if they saw a large army at their gates. In fact, he was quite sure that Athens was in a state of civil war. In any case, he responded unfavorably to the envoys who came from the Four Hundred, and shortly after his talks with them broke off, he sent to the Peloponnese for a large army to come and join him. Then, with his own garrison at Decelea and the newly arrived forces, Agis marched to the very walls of Athens itself. He was hoping that the Athenians would panic and capitulate unconditionally or that, beset by internal and external danger, the city could be taken by storm. He was sure, no matter what, to capture the Long Walls, which would have been abandoned in the civil strife.

But as Agis approached, there was no disarray whatever among the Athenians behind the walls as they sent out cavalry and a force of hoplites, light-armed troops, and archers, which killed some of the Peloponnesians who had come too close and then seized some weapons and corpses. Agis pulled his army back, finally realizing what the situation in the city was. He and his garrison resumed their positions at Decelea, but he ordered the reinforcements home after they had been in Attica for only a few days. After this, the Four Hundred continued to send envoys to Agis. This time, he was more willing to listen to them; and at his suggestion, the Four Hundred, who were eager for an agreement, sent ambassadors to Sparta to talk peace.

72. They also sent ten men to Samos to reassure the army there and to explain that the oligarchy had not been set up to harm Athens or its citizens, but to save the state. It was not merely four hundred, they were to say, who brought

---

4. These may be the hoplites mentioned at the beginning of 8.65.

it about, but five thousand—although Athenians, because of military campaigns and official business abroad, had never been able to bring five thousand men together to deliberate any subject, no matter how weighty. They briefed them on the right thing to say about other matters and sent them off. They did this immediately after coming to power, fearful (with good reason, as it turned out) that the sailors would mutiny under an oligarchic government, and that trouble that began at Samos would end with their own overthrow in Athens.

73. In Samos, resistance to the oligarchy had in fact already begun, and it happened to coincide with the very period in which the Four Hundred was taking power. The Samians who had revolted against the oligarchs and instituted a democracy had changed sides again.[5] Then, at the instigation of Peisander (just back from Tissaphernes)[6] and his Athenian co-conspirators on the island, they formed a conspiracy of their own, consisting of three hundred men, and prepared to attack their fellow democratic revolutionaries on the ground that they were democrats! They also murdered Hyperbolus, one of the Athenians at Samos and a thoroughly disreputable man. He had been ostracized from Athens, not because of his power or because anyone feared his position in society, but because he was a lout and a total disgrace to the city.[7] They were joined in the assassination by one of the generals, Charminus, and by some of the Athenians who had egged them on, thus showing these men that they could be trusted. They committed other, similar acts with them and were straining to attack the democratic party. But the democrats learned of their plans and disclosed them to Leon and Diomedon, two generals who were respected by the people and who only unwillingly went along with the oligarchy. They also told Thrasybulus, a trierarch, and Thrasyllus, a hoplite, and others who had always opposed the Athenian conspirators. They begged these men not to stand by while they were killed and Samos was detached from the Athenian empire, since it was because of Samos alone that the Athenians had had their empire for so long. After hearing them out, these Athenians implored the rank-and-file soldiers, one by one, not to give in—above all the crew that sailed aboard the *Paralus*, freeborn Athenian citizens every one, who were ever on the alert against oligarchy, even where it did not exist. Whenever Leon and Diomedon sailed somewhere else, they left behind some ships to guard the Samian democrats. Thus when the three hundred conspirators attacked them, all these crews came to the rescue, but especially the crew of the *Paralus*, and the Samian democracy was saved. Some thirty of the three hundred were executed, and the three main ringleaders were sentenced to exile. The rest were given amnesty and thereafter exercised their civil rights in a democratic state.

74. The Samians and the army, not yet aware that the Four Hundred had taken power, immediately sent Chaereas, son of Archestratus, an Athenian citizen who actively supported the return to democracy, aboard the *Paralus* to Athens to report the news. As soon as the ship landed, the Four Hundred threw two or three of its crew into prison and pulled the rest of the crew off *Paralus* duty and transferred them to a troop ship assigned to keep guard off Euboea. When Chaereas understood the situation, he quickly took steps to elude cap-

5. See 8.21.
6. See 8.63.
7. Although Thucydides claimed (2.65) that divisive competition among various politicians after Pericles' death played a large role in the Athenians' loss of the war, he in fact tells us very little about any of these leaders except Cleon, Alcibiades, and Nicias. Hyperbolus seems to have become important after Cleon's death. The date of Hyperbolus' ostracism is uncertain, perhaps 417; Plutarch discusses it in two of his biographies (*Nicias*, 11 and *Alcibiades*, 13). Thucydides' contemptuous dismissal of him here echoes his attitude toward Cleon.

ture and returned to Samos, where he greatly exaggerated what was happening in Athens, saying that everyone was being punished with whipping, that it was impossible to speak out against the leaders of the government, that the wives and children of the men at Samos were being abused, and that the relatives of all those stationed at Samos who were not of the same mind as the Four Hundred would be arrested, jailed, and, if the army did not then submit, put to death. Chaereas also told a great many other lies besides these.[8]

75. When the troops heard this, they descended on the ringleaders of the oligarchy, along with anyone else who had a hand in it, and wanted, at first, to stone them to death. They stopped, however, restrained by moderates who explained that they were risking disaster with their Peloponnesian enemies anchored nearby, prows pointing their way. After this, Thrasybulus, son of Lycus, and Thrasyllus, who had taken the lead in the reversion to democracy on Samos, wanted to make it clear that the change was irrevocable and administered the most solemn oath to all the troops, especially those who had gone along with the oligarchy. Henceforth they would practice democratic government; they would have a unity of purpose; they would vigorously prosecute the war against the Peloponnesians; they would regard the Four Hundred as their enemies and refuse to treat with their envoys. All men of military age on Samos took the same oath together, and the Athenian soldiers threw in their lot with the Samians, to share the same dangers and suffer the same fate, in the belief that there was no safety either for the Samians or for themselves, and that, whether it was the Four Hundred or their enemies at Miletus who prevailed, they would be destroyed.

76. During this time, then, a great struggle was taking place between the army, which wanted to reimpose a democracy on Athens, and the Four Hundred, which wanted to force an oligarchy on the army. The soldiers called an assembly in which they ousted their former generals and any of the trierarchs whom they distrusted, including, of course, Thrasybulus and Thrasyllus, and elected others in their places. The men rose to give each other encouragement and to say that they must not become demoralized because their city had abandoned them, since it was the few who had revolted from them, the many, and they were far better able to take care of themselves. They had the whole fleet, for example, and could compel the subject states to pay them tribute, just as if they sailed from Athens. After all, Samos, the city that belonged to them now, was no weakling, and during its war with Athens, it had almost managed to wrest from the Athenians their control of the sea.[9] And as to the enemy, they would have to be on guard against their coming from Miletus, just as they had been before. With the fleet also, they would be better able to obtain supplies than the Athenians. In the past, the Athenians had been able to control the sea lanes into the Piraeus because they, the navy, had been an advance guard based on Samos. Now, if the oligarchs did not give them back their democratic government, and it came right down to it, they were in a better position to keep the Athenians off the sea than the other way around. Anyway, the help the city gave them to defeat the enemy was worthless, so it was no great loss. The oligarchs no longer had any money to send, since the soldiers were fending for themselves, and they did not even give the kind of useful direction with which cities retain control of their armies. Besides, the oligarchy had gone very

---

8. Thucydides seems to be labeling as lies some of the things he himself attributed to the oligarchy in earlier chapters. See 8.65 and 66.
9. Thucydides underlines here the seriousness of the Samian rebellion of 440; see 1.115–117.

far astray in undoing their ancestral laws; it was the army that was trying to preserve them and to make the oligarchy adhere to them. So any soldier who gave the army useful advice was just as good as an oligarch. Furthermore, if the army gave Alcibiades safe return, he would be very happy to secure for them the alliance with the King. But most importantly, if all else failed, with a fleet this size they could retreat to many a safe haven where they would find both cities and land.

77. These are the kinds of things they said to raise each other's morale during their assembly; meanwhile, they prepared for war as energetically as ever. The envoys sent to Samos by the Four Hundred learned of these events when they reached Delos and stayed put there.

78. At about this time, there was also grumbling among the crews of the Peloponnesian fleet at Miletus, who complained to one another that their position was being undermined by Astyochus and Tissaphernes. Astyochus would not fight the Athenian fleet earlier, when it was small, and when their own morale was high, and he would not fight now that the Athenians were said to have fallen out among themselves and their fleet was divided. This waiting for Tissaphernes' Phoenician ships, which he only talked about but never sent, was wearing them down. Tissaphernes was never going to give them those ships, and he impaired the fleet by not paying them in full and on time. No, they said—and it was the Syracusans who urged it most—they must fight it out at sea now and not wait any longer.

79. Astyochus and the allies got wind of this discontent and, after a meeting, made up their minds to fight it out at sea. Then, when they received intelligence of the disturbances on Samos, they put out to sea with all their ships (amounting to one hundred twelve) and headed for Mycale, after ordering the Milesians to march there along the coast. At the time, the Athenians with the eighty-two ships from Samos were moored in the vicinity of Mycale, at Glauce, a place on the mainland that is a short distance from Samos on the way to Mycale; and when they saw the Peloponnesian fleet bearing down on them, they decided that they did not have enough ships to risk everything on a battle and withdrew to Samos. Also the Athenians had advance knowledge that the Peloponnesians had been planning to leave Miletus and offer battle, and they were waiting for Strombichides, to whom they had sent a messenger, to arrive from the Hellespont to reinforce them with the Chian ships he had taken to Abydos.[1] For these reasons, then, the Athenians withdrew to Samos and the Peloponnesians put into Mycale, where they and the Milesian infantry, as well as infantry from nearby cities, set up camp. The next day, just as they were about to attack Samos, they got word of the arrival of Strombichides from the Hellespont and immediately sailed back to Miletus. And now the reinforced Athenians set out for Miletus with one hundred and eight ships wanting to fight to the finish, but they sailed back to Samos when the Peloponnesians did not come out to engage them.

80. The Peloponnesians did not go out to meet the Athenians because they decided that they were no match for the combined Athenian fleet. They were also casting about that same summer for places from which to get the money to support their large navy, especially since Tissaphernes paid them so poorly. So they hurriedly sent Clearchus, son of Rhamphias, to Pharnabazus with forty ships, this being the order Clearchus had originally been given in the Peloponnese. After all, Pharnabazus had been inviting them to come and was

1. See 8.62.

prepared to support them. Also Byzantium had sent heralds to them, saying they wanted to revolt. The Peloponnesian ships that set out on this voyage sailed into the open sea to keep from being seen by the Athenians, but they were caught in a storm, and although most of the ships under Clearchus made Delos, they later returned to Miletus. (Clearchus later got to the Hellespont by land and assumed command there). The ten ships that were with Helixus, the Megarian general, reached the Hellespont safely and fomented a revolt in Byzantium. The Athenian fleet on Samos later received intelligence of this and sent a squadron of reinforcements to patrol the Hellespont. There was even a brief naval battle off Byzantium, with eight ships on each side.

81. After the restoration of the democracy, the leaders on Samos—and especially Thrasybulus—clung to their original intention of restoring Alcibiades. Finally, there was an assembly in which Thrasybulus won over the majority of the troops, who voted to pardon Alcibiades and bring him back from exile. Then, in the belief that the Athenians' only hope was to get Tissaphernes to change sides, Thrasybulus went to Tissaphernes by ship and brought Alcibiades back with him to Samos. During an assembly, Alcibiades loudly bemoaned his personal suffering during his exile and blamed this suffering for what he had done. He also had much to say about public matters and raised in his hearers high hopes for the future. In an access of hyperbole, he greatly exaggerated his influence with Tissaphernes, and he did so for a number of reasons. He wanted the oligarchs back home to fear him and to be more inclined to break up the political clubs. He also wanted to increase his worth to the men on Samos and to raise their morale. And finally he wanted to deflate Peloponnesian expectations and to create as much dissension between them and Tissaphernes as possible.

Then, boastfully, Alcibiades gave them this great assurance: Tissaphernes had promised him that if he could trust the Athenians, they would want for nothing—not for as long as there was anything left in his own personal estate, no, not even if it came to selling his very own bed. Tissaphernes promised also that he would send the Phoenician ships at Aspendus to the Athenians and not to the Peloponnesians. But the only way that he could regard the Athenians as trustworthy would be if a safely restored Alcibiades vouched for them.

82. After hearing this and much more besides, they immediately made Alcibiades a general, along with the ones they had already elected, and put him in charge of all their affairs. Not for anything would the men give up their newly aroused hope of saving themselves and punishing the Four Hundred, and infatuated by Alcibiades' words, they were quite prepared to ignore the enemy at Miletus and to set sail at once for the Piraeus. Although there was a lot of support for it, Alcibiades flatly vetoed the idea of leaving their nearby enemies behind and sailing for the Piraeus. Now that he had been elected general, he said, he must first sail to Tissaphernes and make plans for carrying on the war. Alcibiades left immediately after the assembly, to make it seem that everything was being done in concert with Tissaphernes. He also wanted to magnify his importance to Tissaphernes, and to show that he had already been elected general, and that it was in his power to help or hurt him. Thus Alcibiades impressed the Athenians with Tissaphernes and Tissaphernes with the Athenians.

83. The Peloponnesians at Miletus were already suspicious of Tissaphernes, but when they learned of the return of Alcibiades, they became much more estranged. Their ill will began when Alcibiades took refuge with him, and it grew to hatred when his payments waned after they refused to come out to

fight the Athenian fleet that had sailed on Miletus. As before, the soldiers came together in groups and did their addition—and not just the rank and file, but some officers also. They concluded that they had never been fully paid, that their wages had been paltry and, to make matters worse, sporadic, and they decided that they would jump ship if they did not either fight one decisive battle at sea or go someplace where there was food. They blamed everything on Astyochus, who, they said, truckled to Tissaphernes for his own gain.

84. While the men were mulling these things over, the following disturbance involving Astyochus took place. Because most of the Syracusan and Thurian sailors were free men, they were that much more audacious in crowding around him and demanding their money. Astyochus, however, took a hard line in his responses and resorted to threats, and when Dorieus, the commander of the Thurian ships, spoke on behalf of his men, Astyochus even raised his staff against him. When the rank and file saw this (they were sailors, after all), they rioted and rushed Astyochus with the intention of stoning him to death. When he saw them coming, he ran away and took refuge at an altar. He was unhurt, and the mob broke up.

The Milesians, also, made a sneak attack on a fort that Tissaphernes had built at Miletus. They captured it and threw out its garrison. The other allies gave their approval to this action, especially the Syracusans. Lichas, however, did not approve, and said that the Milesians and others within the King's territory were bound, though within limits, to submit to Tissaphernes' demands and to stay on his good side, at least until they had won the war. The Milesians were furious with him for this and similar actions, and when he later fell sick and died, they would not allow him to be buried on the ground the Spartans at Miletus had chosen.

85. While the sailors were in conflict with Astyochus and Tissaphernes, Mindarus, who had come out from Sparta to succeed Astyochus in the regular rotation, assumed command of the fleet. Astyochus sailed home, and Tissaphernes sent with him an envoy named Gaulites, a bilingual Carian who was a member of his entourage. Tissaphernes knew that the Milesians were on the way to Sparta expressly to denounce him, and he sent Gaulites to protest the action of Miletus against the fort and to speak on his behalf. The Milesians were accompanied by Hermocrates, who wanted to expose Tissaphernes as a man who, abetted by Alcibiades, was undermining the Peloponnesian cause and playing one side against the other. (Hermocrates had always been at odds with Tissaphernes over the question of payments, and when, finally, Hermocrates was banished by the Syracusans, and Potamis, Myscon, and Demarchus went to Miletus to command the Syracusan fleet, Tissaphernes took advantage of Hermocrates' exiled state to attack him as a man who had become an enemy only because his request for a personal loan had not been granted.) And so Astyochus, Hermocrates, and the Milesians set sail to Sparta from Miletus.

86. By now, Alcibiades had made the crossing back to Samos from Tissaphernes, and while he was there, the envoys from the Four Hundred arrived from Delos. They had been sent to explain the situation and to reassure the men at Samos. An assembly was held, and they tried to speak, but the soldiers at first refused to listen to them and cried out instead for the death of those who had overthrown the democracy. Later, however, they held their peace—but just barely—and heard the speakers out. The envoys announced that the change in government had not been made to destroy the state, but to save it, and that it had not been made to betray Athens to the enemy.

(The Spartans had already attacked while the oligarchs were in power, after all, and the city could have been betrayed then.) They said too that everyone would take his turn as a member of the Five Thousand.[2] Also their families were not being abused, as Chaereas had slanderously reported. On the contrary, they had suffered no harm whatsoever, and all were still living in their rightful homes. They said a great deal more, but the sailors paid less and less mind. Instead, they began to vent their anger again, with different people making various proposals, the most frequently heard being to set sail for the Piraeus. And now Alcibiades performed his first service to Athens—as great as any—because when the Athenians at Samos were straining to sail against their fellow citizens in Athens, which would clearly have led to the enemy's immediate seizure of Ionia and the Hellespont, Alcibiades prevented them from doing so. At that moment, there was no other man who could have restrained that crowd. Alcibiades put a stop to the voyage and with sharp rebukes kept the mob from taking out its anger on the envoys physically. It was he who gave them a formal answer and sent them away. He told them that he had no objection to the government of the Five Thousand, but he demanded that they dismiss the Four Hundred and restore the old Council of Five Hundred. He highly congratulated them, however, if their budget cuts resulted in more supplies for the fighting men in the field. His final injunction to them was to stand firm and never surrender to the enemy. If only Athens came through safely, there was every hope that they could all make their peace with one another; but once either side lost, either in Samos or in Athens, there would be no one left with whom to be reconciled.

Also present were some ambassadors from Argos, offering aid to the "Athenian Democracy at Samos." Alcibiades thanked them, and after asking them to be ready to come when called for, he sent them away. Escorting the Argives were the former crew of the *Paralus*—the men whom the Four Hundred had ordered to patrol Euboean waters in a troop ship. After that duty, the Four Hundred then detailed them to take Laespodius, Aristophon, and Melesias, the Athenian ambassadors who were conducting peace talks, and transport them to Sparta. But as they were sailing off Argos, the crew seized the ambassadors and handed them over to the Argives as having been instrumental in overthrowing the democracy. The crew did not then return to Athens, but brought the Argive ambassadors to Samos in their trireme.

87. In that same summer, just when the Peloponnesians were most disgusted with Tissaphernes for all sorts of reasons and especially because of Alcibiades' return to Samos from exile (which they took as proof that Tissaphernes was openly siding with the Athenians), Tissaphernes strove to give the appearance of clearing himself of their charges. He therefore made preparations to go to the Phoenician fleet at Aspendus, and he asked Lichas to go with him. He attached his subordinate, Tamos, to the Peloponnesian force with instructions to pay them while he was gone. There are conflicting reports of this event, and it is difficult to know what Tissaphernes had in mind in going to Aspendus and why, after going, he did not bring back the Phoenician ships. There is no doubt that one hundred forty-seven Phoenician ships came as far as Aspendus, but there have been numerous guesses about why they did not go on to Miletus. Some say that Tissaphernes went to Aspendus in keeping with his plan to de-

2. This is the most likely translation of the Greek text here, but if the envoys really said it, then they must have considered their audience very gullible, since it is a patent lie. Many scholars interpret the Greek as meaning that each member of the Five Thousand would take his turn at governing, which, though also a lie, would have been somewhat more credible.

moralize the Peloponnesians—and in fact, now that Tamos was managing things, the pay got worse, not better. Others say that he never had any intention of using the Phoenicians, that he had led them on to get money out of them in exchange for releasing them from service. And still others say that it was because of the outcry in Sparta: he went to be able to say that he had not treated them unfairly, but had demonstrably gone to ships that were truly manned and ready for action. To me, the most trenchant explanation for not bringing over the ships is that he wanted to wear down and check the Greek powers. Attrition would result from remaining at Aspendus and wasting time there; stalemate from refusing to incline to either side and make it stronger. It is clear to me that if he had wanted to, he could have acted decisively to end the war, because by bringing over the Phoenician ships, he would in all probability have handed victory to the Peloponnesians, who were at that time anchored opposite the Athenians and were at least a match for them. The excuse Tissaphernes gave for not bringing in the ships gives him away. He said that fewer ships had gathered than the King had commanded. It seems to me, though, that the King would have been more grateful to him if he had used fewer ships, because he would have saved the King a lot of money and would have achieved the same result with less.

Whatever he may have had in mind, though, Tissaphernes went to Aspendus and held talks with the Phoenicians. And at his request, the Peloponnesians sent a Spartan citizen, Philip, with two triremes to lead back the Phoenician ships.

88. When Alcibiades learned that Tissaphernes was going to the fleet at Aspendus, he took thirteen ships and sailed there himself after guaranteeing the men at Samos a great boon: he would either bring the Phoenician ships to them or else see to it that they did not go to the Peloponnesians. He had probably known for a long time that Tissaphernes had no intention of bringing the ships back to the Peloponnesians, and he no doubt also wanted to use Tissaphernes' seeming friendship with himself and with the Athenians to widen the gap between Tissaphernes and the Peloponnesians, and then to use that estrangement to force Tissaphernes over to the Athenian side. So he put out to sea and sailed south, in the direction of Phaselis and Caunus, and then turned east, directly into the King's domain.

89. When the envoys from the Four Hundred who had gone to Samos returned to Athens, they reported Alcibiades' message about standing firm and never surrendering to the enemy, and about his high hopes that the army and the oligarchy would be reconciled and go on to defeat the Peloponnesians. The fact is that most of rank and file in the oligarchy were unhappy with it from the first and would willingly have quit the government if they could safely have done so. This message raised their spirits considerably. They now began to meet and to criticize the conduct of affairs, and had as their leaders men who were at the heart of the oligarchy and who held government office, men like Theramenes, son of Hagnon, and Aristocrates, son of Scelias, among others— all leading decision-makers. These men said that they feared the forces at Samos, and especially Alcibiades, but that they also feared that the ambassadors who were being sent to Sparta might compromise the city against the will of the main body of those who had supported the revolution. They said that what they wanted was to be rid of the extreme oligarchy and instead to set up the Five Thousand, which was now just a fiction, as well as to institute a more equal constitution. But this was not the constitution they really had in mind. Most of the oligarchs had fallen into the fierce internal rivalry that tends to be the downfall

of oligarchies that originate in democracies. From the very first day they take power, each and every one of them considers himself not only not the equal of the others, but by far the foremost among them. (It is easy, on the other hand, to endure defeat in democratic elections, because the losers can think they have been defeated by nobodies.) Two things drove these men: the power of Alcibiades on Samos, and their sense that the oligarchy would not last; and so each one of them was in a race to become the hero of the people.

90. The leaders of the Four Hundred most opposed to this movement were Phrynichus, who had come out against Alcibiades while in command at Samos; Aristarchus, a man who had long and vehemently opposed the democracy; Peisander; Antiphon; and the other most influential oligarchs. These were the men who, as soon as they were in power, and then again when the forces on Samos had rebelled and stood up for democracy, had sent ambassadors from among their ranks to Sparta to press for an agreement, and who were building a wall in the area known as Eetionia. These men became more determined than ever once their envoys returned from Samos, and they saw that the general public, as well as some of the people in their own party whom they had formerly considered to be reliable, were changing their minds. Apprehensive about the situations in both Athens and Samos, they quickly sent Antiphon, Phrynichus, and ten others to Sparta to make peace on any acceptable terms they could. Meanwhile, they hurried up the construction of the wall at Eetionia. According to Theramenes and the men in his circle, the real reason for this wall was not to keep the fleet at Samos out of the Piraeus, in the event that they sailed against the city, but rather to give the enemy access to the Piraeus with ships and infantry whenever they chose. Now Eetionia is the breakwater of the Piraeus. Ships sail straight past it into the harbor, and the wall was being built to join with the already-existing wall on the landward side, so that a few men posted on it could control the entrance to the harbor. On one side of the narrow mouth of the harbor, there was an old tower facing the mainland at the point where the existing wall ended. There was another tower, which was now inside the wall that was being built facing the sea. A wall was built across the hypotenuse of these two walls, thus enclosing a storehouse—the largest in the Piraeus and the closest to the wall facing the sea. The oligarchs kept direct control over it, depositing the city's existing grain reserves there and requiring that all cargos of imported grain be discharged there before their owners could take them out for sale.

91. Theramenes had for some time been spreading rumors about the reason for the wall, and when the ambassadors returned from Sparta without having agreed on anything that would satisfy all the Four Hundred, Theramenes declared that the wall put the city at risk of destruction. He said so because of a fleet of forty-two ships that the Euboeans had requested from the Peloponnese, of which some were Locrian and Tarantine ships from Italy and some others were from Sicily. At this time, these ships were anchored at the Laconian naval base at Las, under the command of a Spartan, Agesandridas, son of Agesander, and they were getting ready to make the voyage to Euboea. Theramenes insisted that these ships were not sailing to Euboea, but to the men who were fortifying Eetionia, and that unless protective measures were taken immediately, the city would be caught napping and destroyed. This accusation was not a mere slander—there was some truth in it, because above all, what the Four Hundred wanted was to keep an oligarchic government and to retain Athens' hegemony over its allies. Failing that, they wanted to hold onto the fleet and the walls and to remain an independent city. Deprived even of that, rather than be the first to

be killed by a restored democracy, they would bring the enemy into the city, surrender the ships and the walls, make peace, and keep whatever power they could—all provided they could save their own lives. This was why they were in such a hurry to finish building a wall that had gates and other means of bringing in the enemy.

92. At first, the rumors were secretly whispered among a small group. But then Phrynichus, who had just returned from the embassy to Sparta, was treacherously stabbed by a militiaman in the crowded agora not long after he had left the council chamber. He died on the spot. The assassin escaped, but his Argive accomplice was captured and questioned under torture by the Four Hundred. He did not disclose the name of the man who had ordered the murder, or say anything except that he knew that numerous men used to meet in the house of the chief of the militia and in other houses as well. The Four Hundred took no further action in the matter, but now an emboldened Theramenes got to work, along with Aristocrates and some like-minded members (and nonmembers) of the Four Hundred. Meanwhile, the ships at Las had sailed around the coast, anchored at Epidaurus, and raided Aegina. Theramenes said that it was unlikely that they were on their way to Euboea if they darted into the Saronic Gulf, attacked Aegina, and then returned to their moorings at Epidaurus. They would only do this if they were responding to an invitation to appear at the rendezvous he had always indicated. The time had come to act. After many seditious speeches and furtive glances, Theramenes and his followers finally took decisive action. The hoplites who were building the Eetionia wall in the Piraeus, one of whom was Aristocrates, in command of the contingent of troops from his own tribe, seized Alexicles, a general who was one of the oligarchs and who had close ties to the political clubs, and then led him to a house and held him there. Others joined them, including Hermon, the commander of the militia at Munychia; but the most important thing was that the hoplite rank and file had revolted. When the news reached the Four Hundred, who were seated in the council chamber, all but those who were involved in what had happened hurled threats at Theramenes and the men who were with him, and started for the local armories to take up their weapons. But Theramenes spoke in his own defence and said that he was prepared to join the rescue party for Alexicles. Taking along a general who shared his views, he went to the Piraeus guarded by Aristarchus and some young cavalrymen. There was general chaos and confusion. People in the city thought that the Piraeus had been captured and that Alexicles had been killed, while the hoplites in the Piraeus thought that troops in the city were about to descend on them. Some of the older men were able to keep people from running through the city to get their weapons. Thucydides of Pharsalus, who was the Athenian proxenus there, was on the scene and repeatedly barred people's way, shouting that they should not rend their fatherland with civil strife when the enemy was lurking nearby. With great difficulty, the people calmed down and refrained from killing each other. When Theramenes, who was himself a general, reached the Piraeus, he was incensed with the hoplites—or so it seemed from all his shouting, anyway. Aristarchus and those who were opposed to the hoplites were truly furious. Most of the hoplites were unswayed, however, and were ready for a set-to. They asked Theramenes whether he thought there was a good reason for the wall to be built or whether it would be better to tear it down. He said that if they thought it should go down, he thought so too, whereupon the hoplites and many of the men in the Piraeus immediately climbed up on the wall and began to demolish it. Among the mass of people, the slogan was, "If you want a government not

of the Four Hundred, but of the Five Thousand, get to work!" They used the name "Five Thousand" to cover up their real intentions, to avoid coming right out and saying, "If you want a government of the people." People feared that the Five Thousand might actually have been designated and that it could be a blunder to say something to a stranger about the government of the people. It was for this reason that the Four Hundred did not want the Five Thousand to exist or to have people know that it did not exist. Sharing power with so many was tantamount to democracy, they thought, while ignorance brought the benefit of making people wary of each other.

93. The next day, despite their agitation, the Four Hundred met in the council chamber. Meanwhile, the hoplites in the Piraeus released Alexicles, whom they had been holding, finished demolishing the wall, and then went to the theater of Dionysus near Munychia, where they laid down their weapons and held an assembly. They decided to march on the city, which they did immediately, halting at the temple of the Dioscuri. Some carefully chosen members of the Four Hundred then came out to confer with them. The envoys singled out the individuals who looked most like leaders and tried to persuade them to simmer down and restrain the others. They said that the names of the Five Thousand would be announced, and that the Five Thousand would then decide who would take turns from among themselves to make up the Four Hundred. Meanwhile, the hoplites should in no way disrupt the city or push it into the hands of the enemy. After a great deal of give and take, the whole body of hoplites calmed down and began to fear for the very existence of Athens. They agreed with the envoys on a date for a general assembly at the theater of Dionysus to discuss solidarity.

94. When the day of the assembly arrived, and people were getting seated, there was a report that Agesandridas and his forty-two ships had left Megara and were sailing along the coast of Salamis. Everyone thought this was the same event that Theramenes and his friends had been warning about. These ships were sailing to the wall, and it was a good thing that it was down. It may have been by arrangement that Agesandridas lingered around Epidaurus and was now off Salamis, but he probably waited in the area because he hoped that, given the divisions in Athens, he might be able to take advantage of the situation. As soon as the news reached them, every Athenian citizen immediately ran to the Piraeus as fast as he could. This was the enemy. He was nearby, off their harbor, and the war with him was far more important than their private quarrels with one another. Some boarded whatever ships were on the water, while others dragged ships down off the shore. Still others manned the walls and ran to defend the mouth of the harbor.

95. The Peloponnesian ships, however, continued on along the coast and rounded Cape Sunium. They anchored between Thoricus and Prasiae and later reached Oropus. Now that Attica was closed off, Euboea was everything to the Athenians. It was critical, and they had to go to its relief instantly, but because of their civil war, they were forced to quickly put together crews that were unused to rowing with each other. They sent Thymochares to Eretria in command of a squadron that, when it arrived and joined the ships already at Euboea, made up a fleet of thirty-six ships. They were forced to fight immediately: right after breakfast, Agesandridas cast off from Oropus, which is about seven miles by sea from the city of Eretria. As Agesandridas approached, the Athenian commanders, thinking that their crews were near the ships, moved to get the men aboard. But they were not getting their breakfast at the market, because the Eretrians, in order to make it more time-consuming to man the ships, had

arranged to have food sold not at the market, but in houses at the far end of town. The enemy now had the jump on the Athenians and were bearing down fast, absolutely forcing them to put to sea with whatever men they could get aboard. The Eretrians had also raised a signal telling the fleet at Oropus when it should put to sea. Unprepared for battle, the Athenians cast off and fought near the harbor of Eretria. Despite their disarray, they managed to hold off the enemy for a short time, but eventually they were put to flight and chased onto the shore. The men who had the worst of it were those who were murdered by the Eretrians after fleeing to the city in the belief that it was friendly. Others survived after fleeing to the fort that the Athenians held in the territory of Eretria, and some of the ships were able to get to Chalcis. The Peloponnesians captured twenty-two Athenian ships, putting some men to death and taking the rest prisoner, and then they set up a victory marker. Not much later, they brought all of Euboea into revolt, except for Oreus, which was occupied by native Athenians, and then proceeded to take the necessary measures for the defense of the island.

96.   When the news of the events in Euboea reached Athens, it caused the greatest panic in the history of the city. Nothing had ever terrified them so much, not even the disaster in Sicily, which had seemed so overwhelming at the time. And was there not cause for despair? The army in Samos had mutinied. They had neither ships nor crews to man them. They themselves were torn by civil strife and fighting could break out among them at any time. And added to that now came this new catastrophe, in which they had lost their ships, and worst of all, Euboea, from which they received more goods than from Attica itself. The most crushing thought was how close the danger would be if the emboldened enemy, flushed with victory, were to immediately sail on a defenseless Piraeus with their fleet—and in fact, the Athenians thought they would arrive at any moment. And had the Peloponnesians only been more daring, they could easily have done just that. Then if they had conducted a naval blockade, they could have even further divided the people; or if they had settled down into a regular siege, they would have forced the men at Samos to come to the rescue of their families and of their very society, despite their hatred for the oligarchy. In the latter case, the Peloponnesians would have gained the Hellespont, Ionia, the islands in the Aegean, and everything up to and including Euboea—in other words, the whole Athenian empire. But now, as on many other occasions, the Athenians were lucky to have the Spartans as their enemies, for their temperaments were totally different: the Athenians being quick, the Spartans slow to act; the Athenians being enterprising, the Spartans cautious. And the Spartan character especially benefited a maritime empire like Athens'. The Syracusans prove the point: they were most like the Athenians, and they put up the best fight against them.

97.   But even in the face of this news, the Athenians managed to man twenty ships. Then they hastily convened the first of many assemblies at the place called the Pnyx, where they used to gather before the change of government.[3] At this meeting, they deposed the Four Hundred and voted to turn over the government to the Five Thousand, who were to comprise all citizens who could afford the weapons of a hoplite. No one was to receive pay for any government service, on penalty of the most profound imprecations. The meetings that followed fast and thick voted to create a constitution that would include, among other things, a commission of "lawgivers" who would review all legislation. Indeed, for the first time (in my life at least) the Athenian government

---

3. The hill known as the Pnyx was the customary location for the Athenian assembly.

seems to have run smoothly, and the reason was that there was a good balance of democratic and oligarchic elements. It was this efficient government that began to bring the city up out of its sorry state.

The assemblies also voted to rescind the exile of Alcibiades and others with him, and sent messengers to him and to the fleet at Samos urging them to accept the new government.

98. Right after the change of government, the followers of Peisander and Alexicles, as well as the most committed of the oligarchs, slipped away to Decelea. Aristarchus, who was also a general, was the only one who did not join them. Instead, he took a detachment of the most brutal barbarian archers and marched to Oenoe, an Athenian fortification on the Boeotian border. Acting independently of their allies, the Corinthians had been besieging the place since some of their men, going home from Decelea, were wiped out by the Athenians there. The Corinthians had also called in help from the Boeotians. After consultations with the Corinthians, Aristarchus tricked the Athenians in Oenoe by telling them that their compatriots in the city had made a peace treaty with the Spartans, one of the terms of which was that the garrison must be turned over to the Boeotians. They believed him—he was an Athenian citizen and a general, after all—and besides, they had no idea of what had been going on because they had been besieged, so they left the garrison under a flag of truce.

Thus Oenoe was taken over and occupied by the Boeotians, and oligarchy and civil strife in Athens came to an end.

99. It was about the same time that summer, and the Peloponnesians in Miletus had still not been paid by the subordinates Tissaphernes had left in charge when he went to Aspendus. Furthermore, neither the Phoenician ships nor Tissaphernes had come. Philip (who had been sent along with Tissaphernes) and Hippocrates, a Spartan who was in Phaselis, had both written a letter to the admiral Mindarus, telling him that the Phoenician ships were never going to arrive and that Tissaphernes was being totally dishonest with him. Meanwhile, Pharnabazus had been inviting the Peloponnesians to come to him with their fleet. Hoping to increase his power, he was eager to bring into revolt the cities in his domain that were still under Athenian control, just as Tissaphernes had done. Accordingly, Mindarus abruptly gave the order, and his seventy-three ships pulled out of Miletus in tight formation and set sail for the Hellespont, where seventeen of his ships had gone earlier that summer and raided a part of the Chersonese. He left so suddenly because he wanted to escape notice by the Athenian fleet in Samos. The fleet was caught in a storm, however, and was forced to put in at Icarus, where they were becalmed for five or six days before going on to Chios.

100. At Samos, when Thrasyllus learned that Mindarus had left Miletus, he immediately put to sea with fifty-five ships, anxious to prevent the Peloponnesians from getting into the Hellespont before him. Receiving intelligence that they were at Chios and calculating that they would stay there, he posted lookouts on Lesbos and on the mainland opposite Chios, so that they could not move without his knowing it. He himself sailed along the coast of the island to Methymna and ordered his men to take on barley meal and other supplies so that they could, if they had a long wait, use Lesbos as a base from which to make attacks on Chios. He also wanted to sail to Eresus, which had revolted from Lesbos, and destroy it if possible. (What had happened was that powerful Methymnian exiles had taken about fifty friendly volunteer hoplites over from Cyme, along with mercenaries from the mainland, to make a total of about three hundred. Anaxander, a Theban, was put in command because Lesbians

are of Theban descent. This force first attacked Methymna, but their assault was beaten back by the Athenian garrison at Mytilene, which had reached Methymna first. They were again defeated in a battle outside the city, but made their way over the mountains to Eresus, which they brought into revolt.) Thrasyllus therefore sailed to Eresus, intending to attack it with all his ships. When he arrived, he found that Thrasybulus had already gone there with five ships from Samos as soon as he got word that the exiles had gone across. Thrasybulus had arrived too late to do anything and was moored off the city. They had been joined by a couple of ships going home from the Hellespont and by five ships from Methymna. In all, there were now sixty-seven ships on the scene. Thrasyllus created a landing force out of the crews and prepared with offensive weapons and any other means to take Eresus by storm, if he could.

101. Meanwhile Mindarus and the Peloponnesian fleet had spent two days taking on supplies and collecting from the Chians three Chian coins called "fortieths" for each crew member. On the third day, they hurriedly left Chios. They did not put out into the open sea for fear of coming across the fleet at Eresus. Instead, they made for the mainland, keeping Lesbos on their port side. They put into the harbor of the Phocaean island of Carteria, where they had breakfast. Then they sailed along the coast of Cyme and had dinner at Arginusae on the mainland opposite Mytilene. They continued along the coast from there in the dead of night until they reached Harmatus, which is on the mainland right across from Methymna. There they had a quick breakfast and then continued sailing along the coast past Lectum, Larissa, Hamaxitus, and the other places in that area until they came to Rhoeteum, which is in the Hellespont, shortly before midnight, although some of the ships put into Sigeum and other places in the region.

102. The Athenians at Sestos had eighteen ships. Their lookouts had been signalling to them with beacons, but they also knew, from the sudden appearance of campfires on the enemy shore, that the Peloponnesians were about to sail into the Hellespont. That very night and just as they were, they quickly cast off, stealthily hugging the Chersonese shore as far as Elaeus, aiming to sail past the enemy ships into the open sea. The squadron of sixteen ships standing guard at Abydos had been told that a friendly Peloponnesian fleet was coming and had been warned to keep a sharp lookout lest the Athenians try to get away, but the Athenians got past them nonetheless. At dawn, though, Mindarus' ships caught sight of the Athenians and instantly gave chase, but were unable to catch up with all of them. Most of them managed to escape to Imbros and Lemnos, but four ships that lagged behind were overtaken off Elaeus. One of them ran aground on the shore below the temple of Protesilaus and was captured with its crew. Two others were captured without their men, and one abandoned ship was burnt at Imbros. After this, the Peloponnesians were joined by the squadron from Abydos, making eighty-six ships in all, and they spent the rest of the day standing off Elaeus. The city did not capitulate, however, and they sailed back to Abydos.

103. Failed by their lookouts and never thinking that the enemy could sail past them along the coast without their knowing it, the Athenians pressed on with the siege of Eresus. When they did find out what had happened, however, they immediately left Eresus and sailed to the Hellespont as fast as they could. They came across and captured two Peloponnesian ships that had overconfidently sailed too far out into the open sea during the pursuit of the Athenian ships from Abydos. The next day, they reached Elaeus, where they anchored

and brought over the ships that had escaped to Imbros. They then spent five days getting ready to fight.

104. At the end of that time, the two sides fought a naval battle that was conducted as follows. The Athenians sailed to Sestos close to the shore in single file, and when the Peloponnesians saw them, they set out from Abydos to meet them. The two sides realized that a battle was coming, and the Athenians, with seventy-six ships, extended their line along the Chersonese from Idacus to Arrhiana; the Peloponnesians, with eighty-six ships, extended theirs from Abydos to Dardanus. The Syracusans held the right wing of the Peloponnesian fleet, while the left wing, which had the best ships, was personally commanded by Mindarus. Thrasyllus commanded the left wing for the Athenians, and Thrasybulus the right. The other generals were at various posts. The Peloponnesians were eager to be the first to engage because their strategy was to outflank the Athenian right flank with their left, if possible, thus closing off their escape route, and to push their center back onto the not very distant shore. The Athenians perceived this, sailed out to where the enemy aimed to outflank them, and beat them to the point. Meanwhile, the Athenian left wing had already rounded the Cynossema promontory, which left their center weak and overextended, especially since they had fewer ships and the sharply angled promontory kept ships on one side of it from seeing what was happening on the other.

105. The Peloponnesians accordingly headed for the Athenian center, forcing their ships up onto dry land and disembarking to fight on shore. They were far and away the victors in this action, and the Athenian center could be helped neither by ships from Thrasybulus' right wing, which was beset by large numbers of enemy vessels, nor by Thrasyllus on the left, both because his view was blocked by the promontory and because Syracusan and other ships equal in number to his own prevented him from doing so. Eventually, however, as the victorious Peloponnesians were recklessly dispersing to chase individual ships, a part of their line became disorganized, and Thrasybulus saw this. He stopped stretching his line past the Peloponnesian left wing that opposed him and immediately turned, and then engaged with and routed the enemy. He then went after the victorious but scattered Peloponnesian center and hit them so hard that most of them panicked and offered no resistance. Meanwhile, the Syracusans had been losing ground to Thrasyllus and were more inclined to run away once they saw what had happened to the others.

106. There was a general rout, and most of the Peloponnesians fled first to the Midius River and then to Abydos. The Athenians captured few ships, because the Hellespont is narrow and the enemy did not have far to go to escape, but this victory at sea nevertheless came to them at just the right time. They had been afraid of the Peloponnesian navy for quite some time, because of a number of minor defeats and because of the catastrophe at Sicily, but after this victory, they stopped deprecating themselves or thinking of the enemy as being any good at sea. They were, however, able to capture eight ships from Chios, five from Corinth, two apiece from Ambracia and Boeotia, and one each from Leucas, Sparta, Syracuse, and Pellene. They themselves lost fifteen ships. They set up a victory marker on the promontory of Cynossema and then collected wreckage. They returned enemy dead under a flag of truce and then sent a trireme to Athens with news of the victory. When the ship arrived and the Athenians heard of their unexpected good fortune, coming as it did on top of the recent disaster in Euboea and of their political troubles, their spirits revived and they thought they still had a chance, that if they got a firm grip on themselves, they could win through to victory in the end.

107. Four days after the battle, having quickly repaired their ships, the Athenians at Sestos sailed for Cyzicus, which had revolted. On the way, however, they sighted the eight ships from Byzantium anchored off Harpagium and Priapus, so they attacked and captured them after defeating their crews, who were on shore. They then went on to recapture Cyzicus, which is unwalled, and collected the tribute that was in arrears. Meanwhile, the Peloponnesians had sailed from Abydos to Elaeus and recovered as many of their captured ships as were still sound—the Elaeusians had burned the rest. They also sent Hippocrates and Epicles to Euboea to bring back the ships that were there.

108. At about the same time, Alcibiades sailed back to Samos from Caunus and Phaselis with his thirteen ships, and reported that he had succeeded in preventing the Phoenician ships from going to the Peloponnesians and that he had made Tissaphernes a better friend to the Athenians than ever. He then manned nine ships, which he added to his thirteen, and exacted a large sum of money from the Halicarnassians. He also fortified Cos and installed a governor there, and then, since it was getting to be late in the autumn, he sailed back to Samos.

As for Tissaphernes, when he learned that the Peloponnesian fleet had left Miletus for the Hellespont, he broke camp at Aspendus and rushed back to Ionia.

After the Peloponnesians arrived at the Hellespont, the Antandrians, who are Aeolians, obtained from them at Abydos a force of hoplites whom they led over Mount Ida and brought into their city. They were being oppressed by Arsaces, a Persian subordinate of Tissaphernes. The people of Delos had settled in Atramyttium when the Athenians purified the island and expelled its population, and Arsaces, feigning some mysterious feud, recruited from them a land force made up of their best fighting men. He led them out, as friends and allies, and then, waiting until they were having their first meal, he surrounded them with his own troops and killed them with arrows, stones, and spears. This act made the Antandrians afraid that Arsaces might commit a similar atrocity against them. Besides that, he had been taxing them beyond endurance. So they used these hoplites to help them drive his garrison out of the town's acropolis.

109. When Tissaphernes found out that the Peloponnesians were responsible for this too, and not just for the expulsion of his garrisons in Miletus and Cnidus (for they too had been driven out), he realized that they had become his enemies and he feared that they would hurt him in other ways. It also vexed him that by joining forces with the Peloponnesians, Pharnabazus would spend less time and money than he, and probably get better results in the war with the Athenians. So he decided to visit the Peloponnesians at the Hellespont, in order to lodge a complaint about their hostility toward him and about what had happened at Antandros. He would also give the most plausible explanation he could about the Phoenician ships and their other grievances. He first went to Ephesus and sacrificed to Artemis. . . .

BACKGROUNDS
AND
CONTEXTS

XENOPHON

The frustrating close of Thucydides' narrative while he was recounting the events of 411 throws those who would learn how things turned out back on writers of lesser talent—men who cannot match Thucydides either in intellectual curiosity or in analytical skill. The account of the last years of the war that comes closest to being contemporary comes from another Athenian, Xenophon, who grew to adulthood during the course of the war.

Where Thucydides seems to have written one monumental work, Xenophon wrote many. Though we are not sure when Xenophon was born (probably around 430–425 or died (probably sometime in the 350s), we know much more about his life than we do about that of Thucydides, Xenophon's family was wealthy. His age suggests he must have fought in the Peloponnesian War and attended at least some of the assembly meetings held during its later years. Like Thucydides, he spent a good deal of time away from Athens. A military man, he became involved in an exciting expedition in 401 designed to make a king of Prince Cyrus of Persia, who had resolved to replace his brother Artaxerxes on the throne. When Cyrus was killed in battle, the Greek soldiers in his employ faced a stiff challenge in making their way back to Greece alive. Xenophon not only helped lead the Greeks to safety but wrote an engaging narrative of the adventure, the *Anabasis* or *The March Up-Country*, composed in language so readable that generations of Greek students have cut their teeth on it before proceeding to more challenging texts like Thucydides' history.

Several years after his return from Persia, Xenophon struck up a warm friendship with King Agesilaus of Sparta, and he lived for over twenty years on an estate near Olympia with which Agesilaus had rewarded him for loyal service in the Spartan army. Although the exile from Athens that his pro-Spartan sympathies had earned him was eventually revoked, he nonetheless declined to return to Athens, with whose democracy he had little sympathy, and remained in the Peloponnese, eventually dying in Corinth. It is difficult to attach dates to his writings, which included a work on *The Education of Cyrus*—a cross between a pedagogical treatise and a historical novel—an encomiastic life of Agesilaus, an essay on horsemanship, and a treatise on the Spartan constitution that is of particular value because of the Spartans' reticence about describing their own civilization in writing.

Xenophon also wrote the *Hellenica (Greek Affairs)*. It seems to have been written in stages, with a clear break after the end of the war (2.3). Xenophon seems to have started writing some time after Thucydides' death, which means he knew as he was writing that Sparta would win the war, but the precise date of composition is unknown. He tried to follow Thucydides' practice of dividing up his narrative by summers and winters, but in most respects he differs markedly from his great predecessor, lacking Thucydides' passion for investigation and analysis. Thucydides' history is about power and persuasion, about calculation and human error; Xenophon's (insofar as it is about anything in particular) is about virtue and vice. But there are excellent bits—the message sent home to Sparta after the death of Mindarus (1.1), Alcibiades' return to Athens (1.4), the uproar in Athens after the massive loss of life following the naval victory off the Arginusae Islands (1.7), and most of all the climactic moment when the Athenians get word of the defeat at Aegospotami that meant the end of the war (2.2). In his use of storytelling, Xenophon in some ways resembles Herodotus.

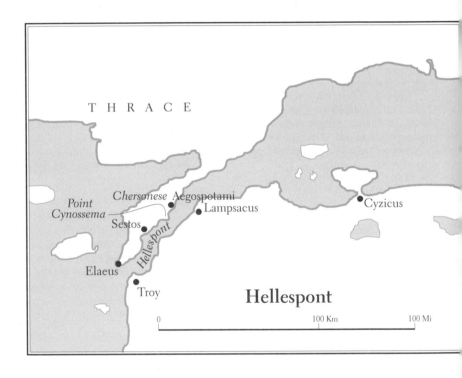

Hellespont

THRACE

Point Cynossema
Chersonese   Aegospotami
Sestos   Lampsacus
                              Cyzicus
Hellespont
Elaeus
Troy

0   100 Km   100 Mi

Hellenica[†]

Book 1

1. Not many days after this,[1] Thymochares arrived from Athens with a few ships, and the Athenians and Spartans immediately fought another battle at sea. Under the command of Agesandridas, the Spartans won.

At the beginning of winter, not long after this battle, Dorieus, son of Diagoras, sailed into the Hellespont from Rhodes with fourteen ships. He arrived at dawn, and the Athenian lookout signalled the generals as soon as he caught sight of him. They put to sea against him with twenty ships. Dorieus ran away from them, heading for shore, and positioned his triremes on the beach near Rhoeteum as soon as he opened up some distance between himself and the Athenians. When the Athenians drew near, the two sides fought from their ships and on land until, failing to gain any advantage the Athenians sailed away to the rest of their fleet at Madytus.

Mindarus was at Ilium sacrificing to Athena when he noticed the battle. He ran down to the shore, launched his triremes, and sailed off to convoy Dorieus' ships. The Athenians put out against them and they fought off the beach near Abydos until dusk. Victory hung in the balance until Alcibiades sailed into the Hellespont with eighteen ships. At that point, the Peloponnesians fled towards Abydos, and Pharnabazus rose up to help them. He rode his horse into the water as far as he could and fought there, shouting encouragement to his cavalry and infantry. Meanwhile, the Peloponnesians made a barricade of their ships, took up positions on the beach, and prepared to fight. The Athenians, however, sailed away to Sestos, taking with them thirty abandoned enemy ships, and recovering ships that they themselves had lost.[2] From Sestos, all but forty of the ships sailed off to different places outside the Hellespont to collect tribute, and Thrasyllus, who was one of the generals, set sail for Athens to give them the news and to ask for ships and men.

After this, Tissaphernes came to the Hellespont. When Alcibiades, bearing gifts, visited him in a single trireme, Tissaphernes had him arrested and imprisoned in Sardis, saying, "The King ordered you to fight *against* the Athenians." Thirty days later, Alcibiades and Mantitheus (who had been captured in Caria) managed to get hold of some horses and escaped to Clazomenae.

Meanwhile, the Athenians at Sestos fled to Caria by night, after receiving intelligence that Mindarus was planning to sail against them with sixty ships. From Clazomenae, Alcibiades also went to Cardia with five triremes and a skiff, but when he received intelligence that the Peloponnesians had put to sea from Abydos and were bound for Cyzicus, he ordered his ships to sail around to Sestos and went there himself on foot. When he arrived, he was about to set out to offer a naval battle when Theramenes sailed into the Hellespont from Macedonia with twenty ships and Thrasybulus sailed in from Thasos with twenty more. Both had been off collecting money. He ordered them to follow him after they had furled their large sea sails, and then he sailed to Parium. There were eighty-six ships in all after they rendezvoused at Parium. The next night they put to sea, reaching Proconnesus the following day at breakfast-time. There they

---

† Translated by Walter Blanco for this edition. All dates are B.C. unless otherwise noted.

1. Xenophon envisions his narrative taking up precisely where Thucydides had left off. In fact, some time has passed.
2. A different account of the battle of Abydos appears in the *World History* of Diodorus of Sicily, 13.45–46.

learned that Mindarus was at Cyzicus with his fleet and that Pharnabazus was there with his infantry. They remained at Proconnesus for the rest of that day, and on the next day Alcibiades called an assembly of the troops and informed them that they were going to have to fight at sea and on land, and also engage in siege warfare. "You see, we have no money," he said, "but our enemies have an unlimited supply, thanks to the King." (As soon has they had anchored on the previous day, he rounded up all the vessels in the harbor—including the small craft—so that no one could get out and report the size of his fleet to the enemy. He also announced that the punishment of anyone caught sailing over to the other side would be death.)

After the assembly, he got ready to fight at sea and then set sail for Cyzicus in a heavy rain. As he approached Cyzicus, the sky cleared and the sun came out from behind the clouds, and he saw Mindarus' sixty ships engaging in maneuvers far from the harbor—cut off from it in fact by his ships. When the Peloponnesians saw that the Athenians were in front of the harbor with many more ships than they had had before, they fled towards the shore and, anchoring their ships together, they fought the enemy as they bore down into them. Alcibiades, for his part, made a flanking movement and landed on the beach. When Mindarus saw this, he too went ashore, where he fought and was killed, although his men managed to escape. When the Athenians left the scene of the battle for Proconnesus, they took with them all the ships except those from Syracuse, which the Syracusans themselves had burned.

The next day, the Athenians sailed from Proconnesus to Cyzicus. The Peloponnesians and Pharnabazus had abandoned the place, so the townspeople allowed the Athenians in. Alcibiades stayed there for twenty days. He confiscated a lot of their money, but did not harm the city otherwise, and then sailed back to Proconnesus. From there, he sailed on to Perinthus and Selymbria. The Perinthians allowed his army to come into the city, and although the Selymbrians did not allow them in, they did give him money. From there, the Athenian army went on to Chrysopolis, in the Chalcedonian territory, and fortified it. They also set up a customs house and began to collect a duty of ten percent on the cargo of ships coming out of the Pontus. They left a garrison of thirty ships and two generals—Theramenes and Eumachus—to command the compound, regulate outgoing ship traffic, and do whatever else they could to harm the enemy. Then the other generals returned to the Hellespont.

A message from Hippocrates, second in command to admiral Mindarus, was intercepted on the way to Sparta and brought to Athens. It read as follows: "Ships lost. Mindarus dead. Troops starving. Don't know what to do."[3] Meanwhile, however, Pharnabazus had been urging the whole Peloponnesian fleet and their allies not to despair over mere ship's timber. There was plenty of that in the King's domains, he said. The important thing was that they were alive. He gave every man a cloak and two months' pay and provisions. He then armed the sailors and detailed them to guard the coastline of his territory. He also convened a council of generals and trireme captains from the cities and told each one to build in Antandros as many triremes as he had lost. He gave them money and authorized them to get their timber from Mount Ida. While the ships were being built, the Syracusans finished a part of the wall for the Antandrians and pleased everyone by the way they guarded it. Because of this, the Syracusans are

---

3. Diodorus (13.52–53) says the Spartans sued for peace after this battle. The popular leader Cleophon, he claims, dissuaded the Athenians from accepting their offer. (For the death of Cleophon, see Xenophon 1.7.) Diodorus' account of the battle at Cyzicus (13.49–51) differs from Xenophon's.

regarded as benefactors in Antandros and have rights of citizenship. As to Pharnabazus, he went to the aid of Chalcedon immediately after making these arrangements.

At this time, a message arrived from home telling the Syracusan generals that they had been banished by the people. They therefore called an assembly of the men under their command and, with Hermocrates speaking on their behalf, they loudly bemoaned their fate on the grounds that they had been banished unjustly and illegally. They exhorted their men to be as energetic in the future as they had been in the past, and to follow bravely every order they were given, remembering all the battles they had won at sea and all the ships they had captured on their own, as well as all the battles in which they, at least, had been unbeaten when they fought with the allies under their generals' command, holding the most perilous positions in battle because of the excellence of their generals and their own energy, whether on land or sea. They ordered them to elect generals who would serve until the men who had been designated by Syracuse came to take command. With a shout, the men, especially the trierarchs, marines and helmsmen, cried out that they should remain in command. The generals were unwilling to be at odds with their own city—but if anyone had any accusation to make against them, they should be given a chance to defend themselves. No one made any accusations, however, and they remained in command at the soldiers' request until the arrival of Demarchus, son of Epicydes; Myscon, son of Menecrates; and Potamis, son of Gnosis, who were the generals who would replace them. After most of the trireme captains vowed to restore the generals when they returned to Syracuse, the army thanked them all for their service and sent them away to the places of exile they had chosen. The individuals who had most closely associated with Hermocrates missed his concern, his energy, and his accessibility. Every morning and evening he would bring together in his tent the ablest men he knew, including trireme captains, helmsmen, and marines, and confer with them about what he was planning to say or do. He also taught them to make speeches, assigning them some speeches to be given on the spur of the moment and others with preparation. Because of these lessons, Hermocrates was very highly regarded in the council, where he was thought to be the most powerful speaker and advisor. He went to Pharnabazus, and because he had denounced Tissaphernes in Sparta (where he was seconded by Astyochus) and had been thought there to describe the situation in Ionia as it really was, Pharnabazus gave him money without his having to ask for it.[4] He now spent his time putting together a force of triremes and mercenaries in preparation for his return to Syracuse from exile. Meanwhile, the replacements from Syracuse arrived in Miletus and assumed command of the fleet and the army.

At about this time, there was a civil war in Thasos, and the supporters of Sparta were banished, along with the Spartan governor, Eteonicus. Pasippidas, a Spartan, was accused of fomenting this civil war in conjunction with Tissaphernes and was banished from Sparta. Meanwhile, Cratesippidas was dispatched to Chios to take over the fleet that Passipidas had collected from the allies.

During this same period, while Thrasyllus was in Athens, Agis sortied out of Decelea and came up to the very walls of Athens. Thrasyllus led out the Athenian citizens and everyone else who was in the city and took up a position next to the Lyceum, prepared to fight if the enemy advanced. When Agis saw

---

4. Cf. Thucydides 8.85, where Tissaphernes spreads rumors about denying Hermocrates a loan.

this, he quickly pulled back, and a few of his rearguard were killed by the Athenian light-armed troops. As a result, the Athenians were all the more eager to give Thrasyllus what he had come for, and voted to let him select 1,000 hoplites from the hoplite list, as well as 100 cavalry and fifty triremes.

Agis saw that a large number of grain ships were putting into the port of the Piraeus and told Sparta that it was pointless for his men to spend all this time cutting the Athenians off from their land unless Sparta also controlled the source from which the grain was being imported by sea. The best thing for them to do would be to send Clearchus, son of Rhamphias, who represented Byzantine interests in Sparta, to Byzantium and Chalcedon.[5] Sparta decided to do just that, and fifteen ships—troop transports rather than warships—were manned by Megarians and Sparta's other allies and sent off. Three of Clearchus' ships were destroyed in the Hellespont by nine ships from Attica, which were always on guard there to protect Athenian merchantmen, but the rest got away to Sestos, and from there they continued on safely to Byzantium.

And so the year came to an end, a year in which the Carthaginians, led by Hannibal, campaigned in Sicily with an army of one hundred thousand men and in three months captured the two Greek cities of Selinus and Himera.

2. The next year was the year of the ninety-third celebration of the Olympic games, in which Evagoras of Elis won the newly added event of the two-horse chariot race and Eubotas of Cyrene won the two-hundred-meter track event. It was also the year in which Euarchippus was ephor in Sparta and Euctemon was archon in Athens. In that year, the Athenians fortified Thoricus, and, after making shields for five thousand of his sailors so that they could also serve as peltasts, Thrasyllus set sail for Samos at the beginning of spring with the ships that had been voted for him. He stayed in Samos for three days and then sailed to Pygela, where he plundered the countryside and attacked the city wall. Some troops came up from Miletus to help the Pygelans and went in pursuit of the Athenian light-armed troops, who were separated from the main body. But the peltasts and two companies of hoplites came up to support their light-armed troops and wiped out all but a few of the reinforcements from Miletus, capturing two hundred shields and setting up a victory marker. The next day they sailed to Notium and went overland from there to Colophon, after making the necessary preparations. The Colophonians came over to their side. The next night they invaded Lydia, where the grain was beginning to ripen, and torched many villages, seizing money, slaves, and a great deal of other booty. It happened, however, that Stages the Persian was in the vicinity, and when Athenian troops dispersed from their camp in search of private booty, he took one of them alive and killed seven, despite the fact that the Athenian cavalry tried to rescue them. After this, Thrasyllus led the army back to the coast, intending to sail to Ephesus. But when Tissaphernes received intelligence of Thrasyllus' expedition, he mustered a large army and a force of cavalry and sent them off with orders to rendezvous at the temple of Artemis, in Ephesus. On the seventeenth day after the invasion, Thrasyllus sailed into Ephesus, where he landed his hoplites at the base of Mount Coressus and his cavalry, peltasts, marines, and all other troops in front of the marsh at the opposite side of the city. At dawn, he advanced on these two fronts. Out from the city to meet him came the Ephesians; their allies, led by Tissaphernes; the Syracusans from the original twenty ships and from five others that had just arrived under the command of Eucles, son of Hippon, and Heracleides, son of Aristogenes; and the crews of two Seli-

---

5. This conflicts with Thucydides' statement (8.80) that Clearchus was sent out in 411.

nuntine ships. This whole force fought first against the hoplites at Mount Coressus, routing them, killing about a hundred of them and then chasing the rest down to the beach. Then they turned toward the marsh. The Athenians were also turned back there, with a loss of about three hundred men. The Ephesians set up a victory marker there and another at the base of Mount Coressus. The Ephesians also gave rewards to the Syracusans and Selinuntines who had been most distinguished for bravery, giving them both to whole companies and to many individuals; and they also granted everyone the right to live in Ephesus tax-free whenever he so desired. And when Selinus was later destroyed, they conferred citizenship on its inhabitants.

Under a truce, the Athenians gathered up their dead and sailed back to Notium. They buried the dead there and then sailed away to Lesbos and the Hellespont. While they were moored at Methymna, in Lesbos, they saw the twenty-five Syracusan ships sailing along the coast from Ephesus. They immediately put out to sea against them and captured four of them with their crews. The rest they chased back to Ephesus. Thrasyllus sent the captives back to Athens as prisoners of war—all but Alcibiades, an Athenian who was the cousin and fellow exile of Alcibiades, son of Cleinias. Thrasyllus ordered this Alcibiades to be stoned to death. From Methymna, Thrasyllus took his fleet to the rest of the army at Sestos, and from Sestos, the whole army crossed over to Lampsacus.

The winter then set in, during which the Syracusan prisoners of war, who were confined in a quarry in the Piraeus, dug a tunnel through the rock and then escaped by night, most to Decelea but some to Megara. At Lampsacus, meanwhile, Alcibiades tried to integrate both armies, but the original troops did not want to combine with Thrasyllus' men on the grounds that they had never been defeated, while Thrasyllus' men had just come off a defeat. Nevertheless, all the men spent the winter at Lampsacus and passed their time fortifying the place. They also made an attack on Abydos, where they defeated and routed Pharnabazus, who had come to its relief with a large force of cavalry. Alcibiades pursued him with his cavalry and with one hundred and twenty hoplites under the command of Menander, until their pursuit was broken off by darkness. Because of this battle, the army came together and the original soldiers accepted the men under Thrasyllus. They made a few other forays that winter into the hinterland, plundering the King's territory.

During this time, the Spartans allowed the rebellious helots who had fled from Malea to Coryphasium[6] to leave Coryphasium under a safe-conduct. At about the same time, the Achaeans betrayed the colonists in Heraclea Trachinia when they were both lined up for battle against their enemies, the Oetaeans, resulting in the death of around seven hundred of the colonists, along with their Spartan governor, Labotas.

And so the year came to an end, a year in which the Medes who had revolted from Darius, King of Persia, made their peace with him again.

3. The following year, the temple of Athena in Phocaea caught fire after being struck by lightning during a hurricane. At the end of winter and the beginning of spring, when Pantacles was ephor in Sparta and Antigenes was archon in Athens, and the war had been going on for twenty-two years, the Athenians sailed to Proconnesus with their whole force. They marched out from there against Chalcedon and Byzantium and took up a position in front of Chalcedon. When the Chalcedonians found out that the Athenians were on

6. Pylos.

the way, they deposited everything the Athenians might plunder with their neighbors, the Bithynian Thracians. Alcibiades, however, took a small contingent of hoplites and cavalry, ordered the fleet to sail along the coast, and went to the Bithynians demanding the Chalcedonian property. They gave it to him after he said that if they did not, he would make war on them. After concluding a treaty with the Bithynians, Alcibiades returned to camp with his plunder and began the siege of Chalcedon with his whole army by building a wooden wall from one shore to the other, which also blocked off as much of the river as possible. Now Hippocrates, the Spartan governor, led his army out of the city and into battle. The Athenians lined up against him, while Pharnabazus was coming up outside the siege wall to help Hippocrates with a large reinforcement of infantry and cavalry. Hippocrates and Thrasyllus fought with their hoplites for a long time, until Alcibiades came to the aid of Thrasyllus with some hoplites and cavalry, whereupon Hippocrates was killed and his men fled into the city. While this was going on, Pharnabazus was unable to join Hippocrates because of the narrow passage between the siege wall and the river, so he returned to this camp at the temple of Heracles in the Chalcedonian territory.

After this battle, Alcibiades went to the Hellespont and the Chersonese to exact money from them, while the other generals reached an agreement with Pharnabazus over Chalcedon whereby the Athenians would lift the siege if Pharnabazus gave them twenty talents and brought Athenian ambassadors to the King. They also exchanged oaths that the Chalcedonians would pay the tribute they owed and then go on paying the usual amount, while the Athenians would not make war on Chalcedon, at least until the ambassadors returned from their visit to the King. Alcibiades, however, was not present for these oaths because he was campaigning near Selymbria. Then, after capturing that city, he went to Byzantium, bringing with him all the forces from the Chersonese as well as soldiers and more than three hundred cavalry from Thrace.

Pharnabazus believed that Alcibiades should also take the oath, so he waited in Chalcedon until Alcibiades came from Byzantium. When he did arrive, he refused to take an oath to Pharnabazus unless Pharnabazus also took one to him. Finally, Alcibiades took an oath at Chrysopolis to Mitrobates and Arnapes, the representatives of Pharnabazus, while Pharnabazus took an oath to Euryptolemus and Diotimus, the representatives of Alcibiades. Both men took the general oath and also gave personal assurances to each other. Pharnabazus left immediately after this, instructing the ambassadors who were going to the King to meet him in Cyzicus. The ambassadors who were sent by the Athenians were Dorotheus, Philocydes, Theogenes, Euryptolemus, and Mantitheus. They were accompanied by Cleostratus and Pyrrholochus, both from Argos. Pasippidas and other Spartans also went, and with them Hermocrates—who was by now in exile from Syracuse—accompanied by his brother, Proxenus.

While Pharnabazus was leading the ambassadors to the King, the Athenians had built a wall around Byzantium and were besieging the city, assaulting its walls frontally and with spears, slings, and arrows. Clearchus, the Spartan governor, was in Byzantium, and with him were some inhabitants of the towns around Sparta; a few Spartan freedmen; some Megarian troops under the command of a Megarian, Helixus; and a force of Boeotians under Coeratadas. The Athenians, however, were unable to achieve anything by force, so they prevailed on some of the Byzantines to betray the city. Clearchus, the governor, never thinking that anyone would do such a thing, set up the best defenses he could, turned the city over to Coeratadas and Helixus, and then crossed over to Pharnabazus to collect pay for his troops and to put together a fleet. He would do this with ships Pasippidas had left on guard duty in various parts of the Hellespont, and with the ships that Mindarus' subordinate Agesandridas had for operations in Thrace. He would also have ships built in Antandros. When they were all together, he would use them to raid the allies of Athens, thereby drawing its army away from Byzantium. After Clearchus sailed away, though, the men who had been planning to betray the city carried out their plan, and by night opened the gates to what is known as the Thracian Road and let in Alcibiades and his army. (Now the men who committed this act were Cydon, Ariston, Anaxicrates, Lycurgus, and Anaxilaus. Because of this betrayal, Anaxilaus was later put on trial for his life in Sparta, but he got off by saying that instead of betraying the city, he had saved it. He was a Byzantine, he said, and not a Spartan, and he had been watching women and children dying of starvation while Clearchus was giving what food there was in the city to the Spartan soldiers. That, he said, was why he let the enemy in—not for money or for hatred of the Spartans.)

Helixus and Coeratadas, knowing nothing of what was happening, rushed into the agora with all their troops, but surrendered when they saw that the enemy completely controlled the city. Helixus and Coeratadas were sent to Athens, but as they were disembarking, Coeratadas lost himself in the crowd at the Piraeus and escaped to Decelea.

4. Pharnabazus and his party of ambassadors were in Gordium, in Phrygia, for the winter when they heard the news of the events in Byzantium. At the beginning of spring, while they were back on the road to visit the King, they were met by the returning Spartan ambassadors, Boeotius and his delegation, as well as others, who told them that Sparta had gotten everything it wanted from the King. Cyrus[7] was also with Boeotius, and he was going to rule over everything on the coast and to join the Spartans in fighting the war. Cyrus was carrying a letter, with the King's seal on it, addressed to all the people living on the coast, which included the following statement: "I am sending Cyrus down to the coast to be the karanos over all those whose capital city is Castolus." (Now, a karanos is a "lord" in Persian.) When the Athenian ambassadors heard this, and when they saw Cyrus, they wanted either to continue upcountry to the King or to go straight home. Cyrus, however, told Pharnabazus to hand the ambassadors over to him; but if he did not, he should not yet send them back to Athens, since Cyrus did not want the Athenians to know what had happened. To avoid running foul of Cyrus, Pharnabazus detained the ambassadors, sometimes telling them that he was going to take them up to the King and at other times telling them that he was going to send them home. After three years, however, he asked Cyrus to let them go, on the grounds that he had sworn to bring them back to the coast, since he was not taking them to the King. So Cyrus and Pharnabazus sent the ambassadors away, with instructions to Ariobarzanes to escort them. He brought them as far as Cius in Mysia, and they sailed from there for the Athenian army.

Alcibiades, who was determined to sail away for home with his army, headed straight for Samos. From there, he took twenty of the ships and sailed to the Ceramic Gulf, in Caria, and then, after collecting a hundred talents there, he went back to Samos. Meanwhile, Thrasybulus went to attack Thrace with thirty ships. When he got there, he subdued the areas that had gone over to the Spartans, including Thasos, which was in a bad way because of war, civil strife, and starvation. Thrasyllus, for his part, sailed back to Athens with the rest

---

7. Cyrus was the son of Darius II.

of the army; but before he arrived, the Athenian people elected three generals: Alcibiades, who was still in exile; Thrasybulus, who was not in the city; and, from the eligible candidates at home, Conon. Alcibiades left Samos with his money and sailed to Paros with twenty ships. From there, he headed straight for Gytheium on a spying mission, to see the thirty ships he had learned the Spartans were preparing there. He also wanted to get a sense of how the Athenians viewed his return. When he saw that they were well disposed toward him—that they had elected him general, and that his friends were privately urging him to come back—he sailed into the Piraeus on the day the city was observing the Plynteria[8] and the seated statue of Athena was covered up. Some saw this as a bad omen and thought it would be prejudicial to Alcibiades and to the city. You see, no Athenian would on this day dare to undertake any weighty business.

As Alcibiades was sailing in, the populace from the Piraeus and the city crowded near his ship, awed by the great Alcibiades and eager to see him. Some said that he was the greatest of all the citizens, and that he was the only one who had been unjustly exiled. They said that he had been conspired against by people less powerful than he, people who talked out of both sides of their mouths and who were only in politics for their own gain. Alcibiades, on the other hand, was always promoting the common good, both with his own resources and with the power of the state. At the time he fell under suspicion, when he was accused of profaning the mysteries, he had wanted to be tried immediately, but his enemies put off a fair trial, and then, when he was away, they made him a man without a country. Then, in bondage to helplessness, he was forced into the service of the people he hated most, each and every day running the risk of death. And when he saw the citizens who were closest to him, and his own family, and indeed the whole city, going astray, his exile prevented him from helping them. A man like Alcibiades, people said, did not want revolutions or changes in government, because democracy made it possible for him to be distinguished above his own age group and to be no less eminent even than his elders. His enemies, meanwhile, were as undistinguished as they had always been, and then, when they were in power, they killed the ablest men, and the citizenry had to be content with them because they could not press other, better men into service—these were all that were left.

There were others, though, who said that Alcibiades was solely responsible for the evils of the past, and that it would probably be he alone who led them into the perils that threatened the city in the future.

Meanwhile, Alcibiades was anchored near shore but took his time disembarking, for fear of his enemies. Standing on deck, he looked around to see if any of his friends were in the crowd. After catching sight of his cousin, Euryptolemus, son of Peisianax, and other relatives, together with friends, he disembarked and went up to the city with an entourage that was ready to repel any attack anyone might make on him. He defended himself before the council and the assembly against the charge of profanation, saying that he had been the victim of injustice, and a great deal more along the same lines. No one spoke out against him, because the assembly would not have permitted it, and he was proclaimed the supreme commander with broad powers, as the one man who could restore the former power of the city. The first thing he did was to lead out the whole army and carry Athens' mystical implements and ornaments overland to Eleusis, a procession that had

---

8. The Plynteria was celebrated early in the summer and was the day on which the cloth garment on the statue of Athena Polias, as well as the statue itself, was washed. The Athenians regarded the day as unclean and unlucky.

been going by sea because of the war. After this, he selected a force of fifteen hundred hoplites, one hundred fifty cavalry, and one hundred ships. Then, four months after he had sailed back home, he set out for Andros, which had broken away from Athens. Aristocrates and Adeimantus, son of Leucolophides, were sent out with him to command infantry.

Alcibiades landed the army at Gaurium, on the island of Andros, and when the Andrians and the Spartans who were there came out to resist them, the Athenians put them to flight, penned them up in their city, and killed a few of them. Alcibiades set up a victory marker, and after remaining for a few days, he sailed to Samos, which he used as a base to carry on the war.

5. Not long before these events took place, the Spartans had sent out Lysander as admiral because Cratesippidas' commission had expired. Lysander arrived in Rhodes, took some ships from there to Cos and Miletus, and then sailed on to Ephesus, where he waited with seventy ships until Cyrus reached Sardis. When Cyrus got there, he went up to see him with the ambassadors from Sparta. They flatly denounced Tissaphernes for what he had done and implored Cyrus to be as energetic as possible in the conduct of the war. Cyrus said that his father's instructions were in accord with their wishes, and that he himself had no other intention than to do everything he could. He said that he had come with five hundred talents, and when that ran out, he would spend the money his father had given him for his own use. And if even that was not enough, he would melt down the very throne he was sitting on, which was made of silver and gold. Lysander and the ambassadors applauded this attitude and called on Cyrus to pay each Peloponnesian sailor one Attic drachma a day, explaining that if this was their pay, the Athenian sailors themselves would go over to them for it and he would actually end up spending less money! Cyrus answered that this was cleverly said, but that it was not in his power to do otherwise than his father had instructed. Besides, their agreement was that the King would pay three thousand drachmas a month for every ship, regardless of the number of ships the Spartans wanted to support. Lysander held his tongue for the time being, but after dinner, when Cyrus proposed a toast to him and asked what he could do that would please him most, he answered, "Add an obol to the pay of each sailor." After this, the pay was four obols a day, when it had previously been three. Cyrus then not only paid the Spartans the money they were owed, but gave them a month's pay in advance, so that the army would work with even more of a will.

This was discouraging news for the Athenians, and they sent ambassadors to Cyrus via Tissaphernes. Cyrus refused to receive them, however, despite being asked to do so by Tissaphernes, who also told him what he had done in accordance with Alcibiades' advice to find ways to keep any Greek state from becoming too strong, and to keep them all weak through constant quarreling among themselves.

As to Lysander, after he had organized his fleet, he drew the ninety ships at Ephesus up on the beach and waited until they were repaired and dried out. Meanwhile, Alcibiades sailed over to Thrasybulus after hearing that he had gone out of the Hellespont to besiege Phocaea. He left his own helmsman, Antiochus, behind in command of the fleet, with orders not to attack Lysander's ships; but Antiochus took his own ship and one other and sailed out of Notium, into the harbor of Ephesus, and right along the very prows of Lysander's fleet. At first, Lysander launched a few ships and went after him, but when the Athenians sailed out to help Antiochus with more ships, Lysander launched his whole fleet and went to the attack. At that point, the rest of the Athenians launched their remaining triremes and put out to sea as soon as each one got clear of the beach. From then on, they fought it out at sea, the Peloponnesians in formation, the Athenians scattered about, until the Athenians fled with the loss of fifteen triremes. Most of the crewmen managed to get away, but some were captured. Lysander took possession of the enemy ships, and after setting up a victory marker at Notium, he sailed across to Ephesus. The Athenians, for their part, went to Samos. After this, Alcibiades went to Samos and put to sea with the whole fleet, bound for the harbor of Ephesus, where he positioned his ships in front of the harbor mouth to see if the enemy wanted a fight. But he sailed back to Samos when Lysander, whose fleet was much smaller, did not come out. A little later, the Spartans captured Delphinium and Teos.

When the Athenians back home received the news of the naval battle, they were furious with Alcibiades. They thought that the ships had been lost because of dereliction of duty and indiscipline, and they elected ten new generals: Conon, Diomedon, Leon, Pericles,[9] Erasinides, Aristocrates, Archestratus, Protomachus, Thrasyllus, and Aristogenes. As a result, Alcibiades, who was also in bad odor with the army, took a trireme and sailed away to his own private fort in the Chersonese. After this, with the twenty ships the Athenians had voted for him, Conon set out from Andros for Samos to take command of the fleet. They sent out Phanosthenes, with four ships, to take Conon's place. On the way, Phanosthenes came upon two Thurian triremes, which he captured, along with their crews. The Athenians put all the prisoners in chains, but they took pity on their commander, Dorieus, and released him without even imposing a fine. This man was a Rhodian who now had Thurian citizenship and whom the Athenians had in the past exiled from Athens and Rhodes, passing a sentence of death on him and his relatives. When Conon reached the fleet at Samos he found the men extremely demoralized, but he fully manned seventy triremes (instead of the former number of more than a hundred), and then put to sea, taking along the other generals, and made landings and raids in various parts of enemy territory.

And so the year came to an end, the twenty-fourth year of the war—a year in which the Carthaginians campaigned in Sicily with one hundred twenty triremes and an infantry of one hundred twenty thousand men and (despite having been defeated in battle) starved Acragas into submission after besieging it for seven months.

6. The following year, in which there was an eclipse of the moon one evening, and the ancient temple of Athena in Athens burned down, and when Pityas was ephor in Sparta and Callias was archon in Athens, the Spartans sent Callicratidas to take command of the fleet, the commission of Lysander having expired. When Lysander turned over the ships, he told Callicratidas that he was giving them to him as master of the sea and victor in battle. Callicratidas then asked him to sail off Ephesus and along the coast, keeping Samos, where the Athenian ships were based, on his port side, and to transfer command of the fleet to him in Miletus. *Then*, said Callicratidas, he would acknowledge that Lysander was master of the sea. Lysander, however, said that he would never interfere in another man's command, so Callicratidas took over Lysander's ships and then manned and equipped fifty more ships taken from Chios, Rhodes, and other allied states. When all these ships, now numbering one hundred forty, were together, Callicratidas prepared to go out and confront the enemy. But then he learned that a clique of Lysander's friends was undermining his efforts.

9. Son of the famous Pericles.

They were not only performing their duties slackly, but they were also spreading the rumor in the cities that the Spartans were making a big mistake in this constant rotation of command. These men were frequently unfit for service, they said, with only the most rudimentary understanding of how to run a navy, and no knowledge whatever of the best way to manage men. If the Spartans kept sending out these landlubbers who were unknown to the people in the region, they were running a serious risk of defeat by doing so. Because of all this, Callicratidas called together the Spartans who were on the scene and spoke to them as follows.

> I would be happy to stay home, and if it were up to me, I would not stand in the way if either Lysander or any other man insisted that he had more experience in naval affairs than I. But the state sent me out to take command of the fleet, and I cannot do otherwise than to obey my orders to the best of my ability. You know as well as I do what I am competing for and what our city is being blamed for, so advise me of what you think best. Should I stay, or should I sail away for home and tell them what the situation here is?

No one dared to say anything other than that he should obey the orders he had been given in Sparta, and do what he had come to do.

Next he went to Cyrus to ask for pay for his men, but Cyrus told him to wait for two days. Callicratidas was offended by the delay and furious over being kept waiting at Cyrus' doorstep. He said that it was pathetic for Greeks to be sucking up to barbarians for money. He also said that if he managed to get safely back home, he would do everything in his power to make peace between Athens and Sparta; and with that, he sailed away to Miletus, where he sent triremes to Sparta to obtain money and then called an assembly of the Milesians, at which he spoke as follows.

> Citizens of Miletus. I have no choice but to obey the authorities in Sparta. I must, however, insist that you be more energetic in fighting this war because you live among barbarians and have already suffered great harm from them. You must take the lead and show the other allies how we can hit the enemy quickly and hit them hard until the men I sent to Sparta bring back money—since Lysander gave the money that was here to Cyrus before he left, as if it were a surplus. Meanwhile, Cyrus constantly put off talking to me when I went to visit him, and I could not bring myself to wait around at his doorstep. I promise you, though, that I will repay you handsomely for whatever good results we achieve while we are waiting for the money. With the help of the gods, then, let us show the barbarians that we do not have to worship them in order to take vengeance on our enemies.

After he said this, a great many men stood up in alarm—especially those who had been accused of opposing him—and proposed a levy of money. They even declared that they would contribute their own private funds. Callicratidas took this money, and from Chios paid out five drachmas apiece for his sailors. Then he sailed against the hostile city of Methymna, in Lesbos. The city was defended by Athenians and governed by people who were collaborating with Athens, so it refused to surrender; but Callicratidas attacked it and captured it by storm. The troops looted all the property in Methymna, and Callicratidas herded all the prisoners into the market place. The allies called on him to sell the Methymnians as well as the Athenians into slavery, but Callicratidas said that if he could help it, no Greek would be sold into slavery while he was in command. And the next day, he released the free Methymnians, selling only the Athenian garrison and all the captives who were already slaves. Then he sent word to Conon that he would put a stop to his use of the sea as his own personal whore. He caught sight of Conon putting out to sea at daybreak and went after him, with the intention of cutting off the route to Samos so that he could not escape there. Conon had selected the best oarsmen from all the crews, so his ships made good headway as he fled; but as he and two of the ten generals, Leon and Erasinides, tried to escape into Mytilene, on Lesbos, Callicratidas sailed into the harbor at the same time with his one hundred seventy ships. The enemy ships got ahead of Conon, and his progress was stopped, so he was forced to fight in front of the harbor, where he lost thirty ships. His crews managed to escape to shore, however, and he hauled his forty remaining ships onto the beach, under the walls of the city. Then Callicratidas anchored in the harbor, controlling the way out and blockading him on the beach. Meanwhile, he ordered the Methymnians to come overland in full strength and brought his army over from Chios. He was also getting money from Cyrus.

Conon was now blockaded by land and sea and was unable to obtain food from anywhere. There were many people in the city, and the Athenians could not come to the rescue because they did not know what was happening. So, before daybreak, he would man and launch two of his fastest ships. He had picked the best oarsmen from all his crews and stretched leather screens along the bulwarks to conceal the marines he had transferred to the holds. The ships would maneuver in the harbor all day, but would only disembark at night, when it was dark, so that the enemy would not see what they were doing. On the fifth day, Conon put a moderate supply of food aboard the ships, but this time he launched them at noon, when the crews of the blockading ships were not paying attention. Some of the men were on shore, eating their midday meal, and some of the men were even taking naps, so Conon's two fast ships were able to sail out of the harbor—one making for the Hellespont, the other for the open sea. The blockaders woke up in a hurry, cut away their anchors, and put to sea in great confusion as best they could. The crews on shore boarded their ships and took off after the Athenian vessel that had headed out into the open sea. They caught up with it at sunset, overcame its resistance, and towed it back to their camp, crew and all. The ship that had made for the Hellespont escaped and was able to get to Athens with news of the blockade. Meanwhile, Diomedon came over to help the blockaded Conon and anchored his twelve ships in the Strait of Mytilene. Callicratidas attacked him unexpectedly, however, and captured ten ships, although Diomedon managed to escape with his own and one other ship.

When the Athenians heard the news of what had happened and of the blockade, they voted to go to the rescue with one hundred ten ships and to embark every available man of military age, whether slave or free. They manned the one hundred ten ships in thirty days and put to sea. Even the elite cavalrymen went aboard and served as seamen. They put into Samos, where they got ten ships. They put together thirty more from their other allies, forcing everybody to serve. They also brought along any Athenian ships that happened to be at sea. In all, they had a fleet of more than one hundred fifty ships. When Callicratidas heard that this relief expedition was at Samos, he left fifty ships to continue the blockade under the command of Eteonicus. He himself set out with the remaining one hundred twenty ships, stopping to eat dinner at Cape Malea, on Lesbos. It so happened that on the same day, the Athenians were having dinner at the Arginusae Islands, which lie opposite Mytilene. Callicratidas saw fires in the night, and when he received reports that it was the Athenians, he made up his mind to sail out at midnight and take them by surprise. But a heavy thunderstorm came on and prevented the launch. When it stopped, at daybreak, Callicratidas set sail for the Arginusae Islands.

The Athenians put out to sea to oppose him, leading with their left wing. Their formation was as follows. Aristocrates took the lead, commanding the left wing with fifteen ships. After him came Diomedon with fifteen more. Pericles was stationed behind Aristocrates, and Erasinides behind Diomedon, and the Samians were positioned next to Diomedon with ten ships in single file. The name of the Samian commander was Hippeus. Ten ships, belonging to the officers who commanded the squadrons furnished by each of the ten Athenian tribes, were positioned next to the Samian ships, also in single file. The three subordinate officers' ships were alongside escorted by some ships from the allies. Protomachus commanded the right wing with fifteen ships, and alongside him was Thrasyllus, with another fifteen. Lysias was stationed behind Protomachus, in command of the same number of ships, and behind Thrasyllus was Aristogenes. That was their formation. Their sailors were not as good as the enemy's and they adopted the formation to prevent him from sailing through their line. The Spartan sailors were better, and all their ships were arrayed single file in order to sail through and around the enemy line and ram its ships. Callicratidas was in command of the right wing. His pilot, a man from Megara named Hermon, told him that he should retreat because the Athenians had far more triremes than he. But Callicratidas said that Sparta would be none the worse for his death, whereas he would be disgraced if he fled.

After this the battle began. They fought for a long time, at first in tight formation, but later in scattered engagements. But then Callicratidas fell overboard and disappeared into the sea as his ship was ramming an enemy vessel, and Protomachus and his ships on the Athenian right wing defeated the Spartan left wing, whereupon most of the Peloponnesians fled toward Chios, though some went to Phocaea. Meanwhile, the Athenians sailed back to the Arginusae Islands. The Athenians lost twenty-five ships with all their crews, except for a few men who were borne back toward shore. Of the Peloponnesian ships, the Spartans lost nine of their ten vessels, while the other allies lost more than sixty. The Athenian generals then decided that the trireme captains Theramenes and Thrasybulus, accompanied by some of the squadron commanders, should sail to the aid of their disabled craft and shipwrecked crews with forty-seven ships, while the rest of the fleet sailed off to attack the ships with which Eteonicus was blockading Mytilene. A large storm of wind and rain prevented them from carrying out this plan, however, so they set up a victory marker and camped where they were.

Meanwhile, a Peloponnesian tender brought Eteonicus a full report on the battle, but he sent the boat back out to sea, ordering the crew to sail away in silence without a word to anyone. They were then to sail immediately back to his camp wearing wreaths and shouting that Callicratidas had won a great victory at sea and that the whole Athenian fleet had been destroyed. The men did so, and as they were putting into shore, Eteonicus starting offering sacrifices to the gods over the good news. He ordered his troops to have dinner and then, since the wind was favorable, he told the traders to quietly load their merchandise onto their boats and sail to Chios. He also ordered his triremes to sail there as quickly as possible. Then he set fire to the camp and withdrew with his infantry to Methymna. The enemy had run away and the weather was good, so Conon launched his ships. The Athenians had by now set out from the Arginusae Islands, and Conon told them what Eteonicus had done after meeting them at sea. The Athenians sailed into Mytilene and from there to Chios. But they were unable to accomplish anything there, so they sailed back towards Samos.[1]

Meanwhile back in Athens, the people relieved of command all the generals in this theater except Conon, and chose Adeimantus and Philocles to command with him. Two of the generals who had commanded at the battle of Arginusae—Protomachus and Aristogenes—did not return to Athens. The other six—Pericles, Diomedon, Lysias, Aristocrates, Thrasyllus, and Erasinides—did go home. There Archedemus, who was the leader of the popular party and also in charge of the relief fund for needy citizens, brought an accusation against Erasinides in court and demanded that he be fined. He accused Erasinides of keeping money from the Hellespont that belonged to the people and made allegations concerning the performance of his duties as general. The court's verdict was that Erasinides should be imprisoned. After this, the generals gave detailed testimony to the council concerning the naval battle and the violence of the storm. Then Timocrates moved that these generals, too, should be imprisoned and bound over to the assembly for trial, and the council so ordered. Next there was a meeting of the assembly in which a number of people, but especially Theramenes, spoke against the generals and said that they should show cause why they should not be held accountable for failing to pick up their shipwrecked men. To show that the generals alone were responsible, he produced a letter that the generals had sent to the council and to the assembly blaming their failure solely on the storm. After this, each of the generals made a brief statement on his own behalf, because they were denied the opportunity to mount the defense the law allows. They explained their actions, saying that they had given the order to attack the enemy, and that they had assigned the rescue of the shipwrecked men to capable officers who had themselves already been generals—Theramenes, Thrasybulus, and others like them. If the assembly insisted on blaming anyone in the matter of the rescue, it could only be the men who had been ordered to carry it out. "And just because Theramenes and the others are bringing these accusations against us," they said, "we will not perjure ourselves by saying that it is they who are to blame, when in fact it was the violence of the storm that prevented the rescue effort." They offered to produce pilots and many other men who sailed with them on that day to bear witness to what they said. These statements were winning over the assembly, and many private citizens rose, wanting to put up bail for them. Because it was getting late and a show of hands could not be seen, however, the assembly decided that the matter should be postponed to another meeting of the assembly and that the council should refer a resolution to the assembly concerning the way in which the generals should be tried.

After this came the Apaturia, a festival in which fathers and other relatives gather to celebrate with one another. During the festival, Theramenes and his supporters arranged to dress a large number of people in black, to have their heads shaven, and to bring them into the assembly pretending to be relatives of the shipwrecked men who were lost at sea. They also bribed Callixeinus to bring an indictment against the generals in the council. Then they called a meeting of the assembly, to which the council presented its resolution, based on the motion of Callixeinus, as follows: "Now that the accusers have made their charges against the generals, and the generals have spoken in their own defense, be it resolved that all the people now vote by tribes. Let two urns be given to each

---

1. For a different account of the battle of Arginusae, see Diodorus 13.97–100.

tribe, and let a herald announce to each tribe that those who believe the generals were guilty of failing to pick up the sailors who were victorious in the naval battle should cast his votes in the first urn, while those who believe they were not guilty should cast their votes in the second. If they should be found guilty, they should be sentenced to death and turned over to the Eleven.[2] Their property should also be confiscated, and one tenth of it given to Athena."

Then a man came before the assembly to say that he had been saved by floating on a grain-barrel, and that those who were dying had told him, if he got to safety, to report to the Athenian people that the generals did not pick up the men who had been bravest in the service of the fatherland.[3] At this point Euryptolemus, son of Peisianax, and various others demanded that Callixeinus be put on trial, alleging that he had drawn up an illegal motion. Some of the people approved of this, but the majority shouted them down, saying that it would be an outrage if anyone prevented the people from doing whatever they pleased. At this point Lyciscus moved that Euryptolemus and the others should be judged by the very same vote as the generals unless they withdrew their charges. There was another uproar in the crowd, and Euryptolemus was forced to withdraw the charges. When some of the prytaneis refused to put an illegal resolution to the vote, Callixeinus mounted the speaker's platform and demanded the same action against them as against Euryptolemus, and the people shouted out that those who refused to put the resolution to the vote should be put on trial. The terrified prytaneis now unanimously agreed to put the question—everyone but Socrates,[4] son of Sophroniscus, who refused to do anything that was not in accordance with the law. After this, Euryptolemus got up on the speaker's platform and spoke as follows in defense of the generals.

> Men of Athens. I stand here before you partly to make an accusation against my relative and good friend, Pericles, and my friend Diomedon, partly to speak on their behalf, and partly to give my advice about what seems to me best for our city as a whole. My accusation is that they changed the minds of the other generals in command, who wanted to send a letter to the council and to you saying that they had assigned forty-seven triremes to Theramenes and Thrasybulus with orders to pick up the shipwrecked men, and that Theramenes and Thrasybulus failed to do so. But should Pericles and Diomedon now share the blame with Theramenes and Thrasybulus when it was these two alone who committed the crime? Is the payment for their concern for the lives of others after the battle to be that their own lives are in danger now, because of the plots of these two men and a few others? No, not if you listen to me and obey the laws of the gods and of men, for this will best help you to learn the truth and keep you from finding out later, to your own regret, that it was you who committed the greatest crime against the gods and against yourselves. As to the advice I have for you, it will prevent you from being deceived by me or by anyone else; and it will let you, with full knowledge of the truth, punish the wrongdoers—whether all together or one at a time—with whatever punishment you wish. My advice is to put your trust more in yourselves than in others and to grant these men one day, if not more, in which to speak in their own defense. You, the citizens of Athens all know that the decree

---

2. The board of executioners.
3. There is some question whether the rescue operation was designed to retrieve bodies for burial or also to save lives. Compare the account of this important trial in Diodorus 13.101–103.
4. The philosopher.

proposed by Cannonus is very harsh,[5] because it provides that anyone
who has wronged the Athenian people shall come before the people in
chains to defend himself, and that if he be found guilty, he shall be
put to death by being thrown into the pit, and his property shall be confiscated with one tenth going to Athena. I call on you to judge these
generals under this decree, and by Zeus, let my relative Pericles be the
first to stand trial, if that is what you think best. For it would be shameful in me to put him above the well-being of Athens. If you choose not
to do this, judge them under the law that applies to temple-robbers and
traitors, which decrees that anyone who betrays Athens or steals temple
property shall be tried in court, and that if he is found guilty, he shall
be denied burial in Attica and his property shall be confiscated by the
state. Let these men be tried under whichever of these decrees you
choose, O men of Athens, and let them be tried one at a time on a day
that shall be divided into three parts—one in which the accusers make
their case; another in which the accused makes his defense; and a third
for deliberating and voting.

  If these steps are followed, the guilty will suffer the harshest punishment, and the innocent will be set free by you, the citizens of Athens, and
will not be put to death unjustly. With piety towards the gods and fidelity
to your oaths, judge these men in accordance with the law, and do not become the allies of Sparta by illegally executing without a trial men who defeated and captured seventy Spartan ships. And what are you so afraid of,
that you are in such a hurry? Do you fear that you will be unable to release
or put to death anyone you please, provided you do it under cover of law?
Or are you afraid that you will be unable to do it illegally, like Callixeinus,
who persuaded the council to bring a resolution before the people asking
them to judge all these men by a single vote? But you just might be putting
an innocent man to death—and remember how painful and frustrating it
always is to later regret what one has done, especially when one had made
a mistake about a human life. Why, you once granted to Aristarchus, the
man who overthrew our democracy, and who betrayed Oenoe to our Theban enemies, a day in which to defend himself any way he wanted,[6] and
you observed the due process of the law in all other ways. It would be outrageous if you deprived of the same rights the generals who followed your
instructions to the letter and who defeated your enemies in battle. Do not
do this, men of Athens. Uphold your very own laws, which have made you
the greatest people on earth, and do not try to take any action without
them.

  But let us return to the situation in which the generals are considered
to have made their mistakes. When they sailed to shore after winning the
battle, Diomedon urged that they should all put to sea in single file to pick
up wreckage and shipwrecked crews, while Erasinides insisted that they
sail against the enemy at Mytilene as quickly as possible. Thrasyllus said
that they could do both if they left some ships where they were and sailed
against the enemy with the rest. Each of the eight generals was to leave
three ships from his own division. Ten were to be taken from the squadron
leaders, ten from the Samian contingent, and three from the navarchs'
ships. There would be forty-seven ships, four for each of the twelve lost vessels. Among the squadron leaders who were left behind were Thrasybulus

---

5. Although Euryptolemus does not say so, apparently the decree of Cannonus (about which little is known)
   also provided a separate trial for each defendant; otherwise it would not be particularly relevant here.
6. See Thucydides 8.98.

and Theramenes, and it was Theramenes who made accusations against the generals in the previous meeting of the assembly.

They intended to sail against the enemy with their remaining ships. Was there anything incompetent or inadequate about these plans? It is right for those who were assigned to attack the enemy, but failed to do so effectively, to answer for their actions. Likewise, those who failed to carry out their generals' orders to pick up the men should answer for theirs. What is to be said in defense of both sides, however, is that the storm completely prevented them from carrying out any of the generals' plans. These are facts witnessed by those who were saved by a fluke, among whom is one of your generals, who managed to save himself on a crippled ship. And yet you are now being called upon to judge this man, a man who himself needed to be rescued at the time, by the same vote as those who were allegedly derelict in their duty! Do not, citizens of Athens, in this moment of victory and good fortune, behave like unlucky men who have suffered defeat, and don't make an ill-advised decision about what is really an act of god by pronouncing a verdict of treason instead of helplessness on men who were rendered incapable of carrying out their duties by a storm. On the contrary, it would be much more just to honor these victorious men with wreaths than to listen to these malicious men and sentence them to death.

After making this speech, Euryptolemus moved that the men be tried, one at a time, under the decree of Cannonus. The resolution of the council had been to judge them all by the same vote. There was a show of hands to decide between these two proposals, and they at first voted for that of Euryptolemus. But then Menecles, on his oath, raised a point of order; whereupon the vote was taken again and it went to the resolution of the council. After this, they condemned the eight generals who had commanded in the naval battle and put to death the six who were in Athens.

Not much later, the Athenians had regrets about what they had done, and they voted that charges should be brought in the assembly against anyone who had deceived the people (one of whom was to be Callixeinus) and that they produce men who would vouch for them until they stood trial. Four others were indicted and were taken into custody by those who promised to vouch for them. Later fighting broke out between two political groups, in which Cleophon was killed.[7] The perpetrators escaped before they could be brought to trial. Callixeinus did return, when the Piraeus party returned to Athens, but he was shunned by everyone and he died of starvation.[8]

7. See Lysias 13.12.
8. While the pro-Spartan puppet government known as the Thirty Tyrants ruled Athens, democratic dissidents gathered in Piraeus. In 403 they returned to Athens and the democracy was restored.

Book 2

While the summer lasted, the troops who were with Eteonicus on Chios lived on the harvests of the season and earned money by working throughout the island. By winter, however, they had no food, and they were also improperly clothed and barefoot, so some of them got together and began to organize an attack on the city of Chios. The men decided that whoever wanted in on the plot should carry a reed, so that they would be able to see how many they were. When Eteonicus found out about the plan, he did not know what to do about it, because of the large number of men who were carrying reeds. To attack them openly seemed risky, because they might make a dash for their weapons, take control of the city, turn mutinous, and, if they were ultimately victorious, wreck the whole enterprise. At the same time, it seemed equally dangerous to kill so many allied troops, because it might create a prejudice against Sparta among the other Greeks too and alienate the soldiers from the enterprise. What Eteonicus did was to take with him fifteen men armed with daggers and make his way through the city. Then, coming upon a man suffering from ophthalmia leaving a doctor's house and carrying a reed, they killed him. A commotion ensued, and when people asked why the man had been killed, Eteonicus ordered his men to spread the word that it was because he was carrying the reed. As this message circulated, every man who heard it and who was carrying a reed threw it away for fear that he might be seen with it. After this, Eteonicus called the Chians together and asked them to give him some money so that the soldiers could be paid and not do anything rash. The Chians gave him the money, whereupon he gave the order to board ship. Then he went past each ship in turn, dispensing encouragement and advice as though he knew nothing of what had been going on, and giving each man a month's pay.

To deal with the situation, the Chians and the other allies met at Ephesus and decided to send ambassadors to Sparta to tell them what was happening and to ask that Lysander come out to command the fleet. He was well regarded by the allies because of his former command, when he won the naval battle at Notium. The ambassadors were sent, accompanied by ambassadors from Cyrus with the same message. The Spartans did give them Lysander, but only as vice-admiral. The admiral was Aracus, because it was against Spartan law for the same man to serve as admiral twice. The ships, however, were put under Lysander's command.

[By now, twenty-five years had gone by in the war, and it was in this year that Cyrus killed Autoboesaces and Mitraeus, the sons of Darius' sister, who was the daughter of his father, Xerxes. He did so because they did not, when they met him, extend their hands beyond the kore, something Persians only do for the King. (The kore is a long sleeve reaching over the hand, and is longer than the loose arm-sleeve, and someone who has his hand inside the kore cannot do anything with it). Because of these killings, Hieramenes and his wife told Darius that it would be terrible if he ignored such an atrocity, and Darius, pretending to be ill, sent messengers telling Cyrus to come to him.][1]

In the following year, when Archytas was ephor in Sparta and Alexias was archon in Athens, Lysander arrived in Ephesus and summoned Eteonicus from Chios with his fleet. He also brought together and repaired all other available ships, while at the same time he had ships built at Antandros. Then he went to Cyrus and asked for money. Showing him how much the admirals had received, Cyrus told him that the money allowed by the King had been spent, and much more besides, but he gave him the money nevertheless. After getting the silver,

1. This passage is probably spurious.

Lysander appointed a captain to each trireme and paid the sailors the money they were due. Meanwhile, the Athenian commanders were getting ready their fleet in Samos.

A messenger now came to Cyrus from his father, telling him that his father was sick and calling him to his side at Thamneria, in Media, near the rebellious Cadusians, against whom he was campaigning. So Cyrus sent for Lysander and forbade him to have a battle at sea with the Athenians until he had many more ships than they. He said that there was a great deal of money available, both his father's and his own, and that they could use it to man a large fleet. He then transferred to Lysander all the revenue that came in from the cities he governed, which belonged to him personally, and he also gave him the balance he owed him. He then reminded him of his friendship for the Spartan people and for him personally and set out for the trip upcountry to his father.

After Cyrus had given Lysander all his money and left to answer the summons to see his sick father, Lysander paid his troops and set sail for the Ceramic Gulf, in Caria. There he attacked a city allied to Athens called Cedreiae, taking it by storm on the second day and selling into slavery its inhabitants, who were of mixed Greek and barbarian stock. From there he sailed away to Rhodes. Meanwhile, the Athenians were using Samos as a base to raid the territory of the King, attacking Chios and Ephesus as well. They too were preparing for a naval battle, and chose Menander, Tydeus, and Cephisodotus to join the commanders they already had. Lysander left Rhodes and sailed along the Ionian coast to the Hellespont to attack merchant ships sailing through, as well as towns that had revolted from Sparta. The Athenians were also headed for the Hellespont, but they were sailing across the open sea because Asia was hostile territory. Lysander sailed along the coast from Abydos to Lampsacus, which was allied to Athens. Meanwhile, forces from Abydos and other towns under the command of Thorax, a Spartan officer, kept pace with him on shore. They attacked Lampsacus and took it by storm. It was a rich city, abounding in wine, grain, and other supplies, and the troops proceeded to plunder it, although Lysander released all the free inhabitants. The Athenians were right behind Lysander and anchored in Elaeus, in the Chersonese, with one hundred eighty ships. While they were taking their midday meal there, they got word of what had happened in Lampsacus, and they immediately put to sea and went to Sestos. There they took on supplies, and then sailed to Aegospotami, which is about two miles across the Hellespont from Lampsacus. They had dinner at Aegospotami. The following night, just before dawn, Lysander told his men to have breakfast and get aboard ship. He made everything ready for a battle and had the leather screens stretched along the bulwarks, but he ordered that no ship should leave its place in line or put out to sea. At dawn, the Athenians lined their ships up for battle at the mouth of the harbor. But when it started to get late, and Lysander still had not come out to engage them, they sailed back to Aegospotami. Then Lysander ordered his fastest ships to follow the Athenian fleet, to observe what they did when they disembarked, and to sail back and report to him. He did not allow his men off their ships until these fast ships had returned, and he repeated this action for four days, during which the Athenians continued to sail out to the mouth of the harbor and get into battle formation. Meanwhile, Alcibiades had noted from his fortress that the Athenians were anchored on an open shore and were not near a city. They were getting their supplies from Sestos, which was about two miles from their fleet,[2] while the enemy

---

2. Xenophon was wrong about the distance, which is actually about fifteen miles.

was in harbor near a city from which it got everything it needed. He told them that they had a bad anchorage and that they should move it to Sestos, from which, he said, "you can fight whenever you please." But the generals, and especially Tydeus and Menander, told him to go away: they were the generals now, not him. And so Alcibiades left.

On the fifth day that the Athenians sailed out, Lysander met with the crews who regularly followed them back. He told them that when they saw the Athenians get off their ships and disperse around the Chersonese—something they did more and more every day, partly because they had to buy food far away, and partly because they disrespected Lysander for not coming out to oppose them— they should sail back towards him and raise a shield halfway across the strait. The men followed his orders to the letter, whereupon Lysander gave the order to cast off as quickly as possible—and this time Thorax was on the ships with his infantry. When Conon saw the enemy bearing down on them, he raised the signal that everyone should come to the defense of the ships with all their might. But the men were scattered here and there. Some of the ships had only two banks of oarsmen, some one, and some had no crews at all. Conon's ship and seven others in his squadron were fully manned and they managed to put to sea together, accompanied by the *Paralus*. But Lysander was able to capture all the other ships on the beach and to round up most of the men on shore, although some escaped to small fortresses nearby.

When Conon, fleeing with his nine ships, realized that they had been utterly defeated, he put in at Abarnis, which was the promontory of Lampsacus, and seized the large sails of Lysander's fleet. Then he sailed with eight ships to Evagoras, the ruler of Cyprus, while the *Paralus* went to Athens with news of what had happened. Lysander took ships, prisoners, and everything else they had captured back to Lampsacus—including Philocles and Adeimantus and a number of other generals. On the day he won his victory, Lysander also sent the Milesian pirate Theopompus to Sparta with the news of what had happened, which he delivered on the third day. Next Lysander brought together the allies and told them to decide what to do with the prisoners. There followed a great many accusations against the Athenians concerning atrocities they had already committed, such as capturing a Corinthian and an Andrian trireme and throwing all their crews overboard, as well as actions they had voted to take if they won the battle, such as cutting off the right hand of any man they took alive. Philocles was identified as the Athenian general who had thrown the crews overboard. Many other charges were made, and the allies decided to kill all the Athenian prisoners except Adeimantus, who was the only one to oppose the vote in the assembly to cut off hands, but who had been accused by some of betraying the fleet. As to Philocles, Lysander began by asking him what punishment he deserved for being first to commit atrocities against Greeks, and then he cut his throat.

After settling matters at Lampsacus, Lysander sailed to Byzantium and Chalcedon. These towns accepted him, sending the Athenian garrisons away under a flag of truce. The men who had betrayed Byzantium to Alcibiades now fled to the Pontus, and later to Athens, where they became Athenian citizens. Lysander sent all Athenians, whether garrisoning troops or others, back to Athens. He gave them a safe conduct there, though nowhere else, and he did so because he knew that the more people were crowded into the city and the Piraeus, the faster they would run out of food. Then he left Sthenelaus, a Spartan, as governor of Byzantium and Chalcedon, and himself sailed back to Lampsacus to repair his ships.

It was night when the *Paralus* arrived in Athens with news of the disaster. The lamentation could be heard from the Piraeus and through the Long Walls to the city as word passed from man to man. That night no one slept. They grieved much less for the dead than for themselves, thinking of what they had done to the Melians, who were colonists from Sparta and whom they starved out in a siege, and to the people of Histiaea, of Scione, of Torone, of Aegina, and so many other Greeks.[3] The next day they held an assembly in which they voted to dam up all the harbors except one, to repair and man the walls, and generally to prepare the city for a siege.

While the Athenians were busy with these preparations, Lysander sailed from the Hellespont to Lesbos with two hundred ships and arranged things to his liking in Mytilene and the other cities on the island. He also sent ten triremes to Thrace, commanded by Eteonicus, who brought governments there over to the Spartan side. Immediately after the battle, all the rest of Greece broke away from Athens except for the Samians, whose people cut the throats of the rich and took control of the city. Next, Lysander sent word to Agis, at Decelea, and to Sparta that he was coming with two hundred ships. At this point, the Spartans marched out in full strength, as did the rest of the Peloponnese, except for Argos, on orders from Pausanias, the other Spartan king. When all the forces were together, Pausanias led them to Athens and set up camp in the Academy. Lysander, meanwhile went to Aegina and restored the city to the Aeginetans after gathering together as many of them as he could, and he did the same for the Melians and for all the other people whose cities had been taken from them. Next, after plundering Salamis, he anchored off the Piraeus with one hundred fifty ships and prevented supply ships from getting in.

Blockaded by land and sea, and without ships, allies, or food, the Athenians were at their wits' end. They thought they had no choice but to undergo what they themselves had done to others, not in retaliation but out of sheer hubris, when they destroyed small states for no other reason than that they were allied with the enemy. These feelings led them to grant civil rights to those who had none and to persevere without discussing peace, even though many in the city were dying of starvation. When the food supply had been utterly exhausted, however, they sent envoys to Agis offering to become the allies of Sparta, provided they could make a treaty whereby they kept their walls and the Piraeus. Agis said that he did not have the authority to make terms and told them to go to Sparta; and when the envoys reported this message to the Athenian people, they sent them there. But when they were in Sellasia, near Laconia, and the ephors learned what they had to say—which was the same thing they had said to Agis—the ephors told them to turn right around and go home, and if they really wanted peace, to come back with better offers than these. When the envoys returned home and reported this message in the city, the people fell into utter despair. They believed that they were going to be sold into slavery, and that many would die of starvation while new envoys were performing their mission. Nevertheless, no one was willing to advise tearing down the walls, because when Archestratus said in the council that the best thing to do would be to make peace on the terms the Spartans offered, which were that a mile and a quarter of each of the two Long Walls should be demolished, he was thrown into prison and a resolution was passed prohibiting such proposals.[4]

---

3. Thucydides 5.116; 1.114; 5.3; 5.32; 2.27.
4. Xenophon declines to name Cleophon here, but Aeschines (2.76) and Lysias (13.8) identify him as the moving force behind the Athenians' intransigence.

This was the situation when Theramenes said in the assembly that if they sent him to Lysander, he would come back knowing whether the Spartans insisted on the destruction of the walls because they wanted to enslave the city or because they saw it as a sign of good faith. After he was sent, however, he spent more than three months with Lysander, waiting for the time when the Athenians would be brought by the total exhaustion of all their supplies to agree to whatever the Spartans said. When he returned in the fourth month, he told the assembly that Lysander had detained him all that time and had then told him to go to Sparta because the ephors, and not he, had the authority to answer his questions. After this, Theramenes was elected ambassador to Sparta, with full powers, in a delegation of ten other men. Meanwhile, Lysander sent some Spartans and Aristoteles, an Athenian exile, to the ephors to say that Lysander had told Theramenes that they alone had the power to make peace and war. When Theramenes and the other ambassadors were asked in Sellasia what they had come to say, they answered that they had full power to negotiate a peace, whereupon the ephors gave orders that they should be summoned to Sparta. When they arrived, the ephors called an assembly, in which many Greek states, but especially Corinth and Thebes, argued that they should not make peace with Athens but annihilate it. The Spartans, however, refused to enslave a Greek city that had done Greece the greatest service in times of the greatest danger. Instead, they offered peace on terms whereby the Athenians razed the Long Walls and the Piraeus to the ground; surrendered the fleet, except for twelve ships; restored the exiles; made an offensive and defensive alliance with Sparta; and submitted to Spartan leadership everywhere, whether on land or sea.

Theramenes and his delegation brought this message back to Athens, and as they entered the city, they were surrounded by a great throng of people terrified that they had returned empty-handed, because so many people were dying of starvation that there was no more time for delay. The next day, the ambassadors reported the terms on which the Spartans would make peace. Speaking for the delegation, Theramenes said that they should comply with the Spartan demand and tear down the walls. A few people disagreed, but the overwhelming majority agreed, and they decided to accept the terms of peace. After this, Lysander put into the Piraeus, and the exiles returned; and with wild excitement the Peloponnesians began to tear down the walls of Athens to the music of flute-girls, in the belief that this day was the beginning of freedom for Greece.

And so the year came to an end, in the middle of which Dionysius of Syracuse, son of Hermocrates, became tyrant after the Syracusans had defeated the Carthaginians, who nevertheless starved out and captured Acragas after the Sicilians abandoned the city.

The following year was a year in which the Olympic Games were held. Crocinas the Thessalian won the two-hundred-meters race, Endius being the ephor in Sparta, and Pythodorus the archon in Athens. But because he was elected during the oligarchy, the Athenians do not designate the year by Pythodorus' name, and call it "the year without an archon" or "the anarchy" instead. The oligarchy came about in the following way. The people voted to choose thirty men who would frame a written constitution, based on the ancestral laws, by which they would be governed. The men they chose were Polychares, Critias, Melobius, Hippolochus, Eucleides, Hieron, Mnesilochus, Chremon, Theramenes, Aresias, Diocles, Phaedrias, Chaereleos, Anaetius, Peison, Sophocles, Eratosthenes, Charicles, Onomacles, Theognis, Aeschines, Theogenes, Cleomedes, Erasistratus, Pheidon, Dracontides, Eumathes, Aristoteles, Hippomachus, and Mnesitheides. After these men were selected, Lysander sailed to Samos, and Agis withdrew his infantry from Decelea and sent the men back to their various cities.

At about this time, and near the time of the eclipse of the sun, Lycophron of Pherae, ambitious to rule over all of Thessaly, defeated in battle his Thessalian opponents—the Larissans and others—killing a great many of them.

At the same time, Dionysius, the tyrant in Syracuse, was defeated in battle by the Carthaginians and lost Gela and Camarina. Soon afterwards the Leontines, who had been living among the Syracusans, broke away from them and from Dionysius and went back to their own city. Immediately afterwards, Dionysius sent the Syracusan cavalry to Catana.[5]

Meanwhile, Lysander was completely blockading the Samians because they had at first refused to come to terms. But just as he was on the point of making a direct assault, they agreed to capitulate on condition that every freeborn citizen could leave with one cloak—everything else would be given up. And on these terms, they left Samos. Lysander turned the city and everything in it over to its former citizens and appointed ten archons to govern it. Then he sent the allied ships in his fleet back to their cities and sailed back to Sparta with the Spartan contingent, taking with him the prows of the ships he had captured and all but twelve of the triremes from the Piraeus. He also had the crowns that the cities had given him as private gifts and four hundred seventy talents in cash, which was what was left over from the tribute money Cyrus had given to him to finance the war. He gave this and all the other booty he had acquired in the war to Sparta. And so the summer came to an end, and with it ended the twenty-eight years and six months of the Peloponnesian War.

[The remainder of Book 2 of the *Hellenica* is devoted to the aftermath of the war and the imposition of the Spartan-backed oligarchy of the Thirty Tyrants in Athens, and it includes the confrontation between the oligarch Critias (a relative of Plato's) and the moderate Theramenes. Xenophon uses invented dialogue to tell a memorable tale that culminates in Theramenes' execution, and Book 2 ends with the agreement between the oligarchs and the democrats that ended this dismal experiment—the first recorded amnesty in history. Books 3 through 7 then carry the history of Greece down to 362.]

HERODOTUS

Thucydides' great predecessor was born during the wars between Greece and Persia that lasted, with interruption, from 490 to 479. Inspired by the magnitude of the conflict and seeing its roots deep in the past, Herodotus took the occasion of writing about the war to synthesize an enormous amount of research and reflection on the Greeks and the many peoples that went to make up the Persian empire—including, for example, the Egyptians, about whom he wrote at length.

Herodotus began his history of the Persian Wars by tracing the conflict of East and West to a series of kidnappings. These included the abduction of Helen from Sparta that began the Trojan War. The principal source for Helen's role in the war in Herodotus' day was, and still is, Homer's *Iliad*. Herodotus also had access, however, to another poem now lost, the *Cypria*. His treatment of Helen reveals not only his gift for storytelling but also his methods of analyzing evidence.

5. These two paragraphs are probably spurious.

The Histories[†]

[Reconstructing the Past: Helen and the Trojan War]

BOOK 2, CHAPTERS 111–20

They said that a man from Memphis whose name, in Greek, was Proteus inherited the Egyptian throne from Pheros. His sacred precinct is in Memphis. It is richly ornamented and very beautiful and lies to the south of the temple of Hephaestus. Phoenicians from Tyre live around this precinct, and the whole region is called the Tyrian Quarter. There is a temple of the so-called Foreign Aphrodite in the precinct of Proteus. I suspect that this temple belongs to Helen, the daughter of Tyndareus, in part because of a story I heard that Helen had stayed with Proteus, but mostly because the temple is named for the Foreign Aphrodite. You see, no other temple to Aphrodite is called foreign.

The priests told me when I inquired that these were the circumstances surrounding Helen. After Alexander[1] had abducted Helen from Sparta, he sailed away toward his own country, but when he was in the Aegean the winds blew him off course and forced him into the Egyptian Sea. From there (for the winds did not abate) he came to Egypt, that is, into what is now called the Canobic mouth of the Nile and its salting factories. On the shore there was, and still is, a temple to Heracles, and if the servant of any man whatever flees there he may not be seized, provided he is branded with the sacred branding iron and dedicates himself to the god. This custom has been practiced in the same way from the very beginning to my own time. Now, some of Alexander's servants found out about the custom in this temple and deserted him. They sat as suppliants before the god and intended to harm Alexander by denouncing him and revealing the whole story about Helen and the injustice he had done Menelaus.[2] They made these accusations before the priests and before Thonis, the officer in charge of this mouth of the Nile.

Thonis heard them out and immediately sent a message to Proteus in Memphis, saying, "A stranger from the tribe of Teucer has arrived after having been driven to your land by the winds. He has committed an impious deed in Greece, for he has seduced the wife of his own host and carried her and a great deal of wealth away from him. Should we allow him to sail away unharmed, or should we confiscate his cargo?" Proteus responded by saying, "Whoever this man who has committed such impious deeds against his own host may be, arrest him and bring him to me so that I may hear what he has to say."

When Thonis heard this, he arrested Alexander, impounded his ships, and then led him, Helen, and the property to Memphis. He also brought the supplicants. After they all arrived, Proteus asked Alexander who he was and where he had sailed from. Alexander recited his lineage, gave the name of his native land, and disclosed where he had begun his voyage. Then Proteus asked him where he had gotten Helen, and when Alexander was evasive in his story and did not tell the truth, he was given away by the suppliants, who told the whole story of the crime. Finally, Proteus passed this sentence on them: "If I did not make it a rule never to kill a stranger, especially one who has come to my land after being blown off course by the wind, I would punish you for what you have

---

† Herodutus, The Histories, translated by Walter Blanco, edited by Walter Blanco and Jennifer Tolbert Roberts, pp. 103–07 and pp. 117–20. Copyright © 1992 by W. W. Norton and Company, Inc.
1. An alternative name for King Priam's son Paris, the Trojan prince.
2. Helen's original husband, the king of Sparta.

done to this Greek, you, you vilest of men, who have repaid the hospitality you received with a most unholy deed. You lay with the wife of your own host, but that wasn't even enough for you, because you have carried her away with you on the wings of seduction. And not even that was enough, for you come here after looting your host's house! Now then, though it is my policy not to kill strangers, I will not allow you to take away this woman and these goods. Instead, I will hold them in safekeeping for the Greek stranger until he himself comes and takes them away. As for you and your fellow sailors, I command you to change your moorings within three days to some land other than mine. If you do not, I will treat you as enemies."

The priests said that this is how Helen came to Proteus, and it seems to me that Homer knew this story, but that it wasn't as suitable to his epic as the one he used. So he set the story aside, but made it clear that he knew it anyway. It is clear that in the *Iliad* he let slip his knowledge of the wanderings of Alexander (and this is the only place where he trips himself up), where he says that Alexander carried away Helen and wandered to many places, including Phoenician Sidon. He refers to this in the Exploits of Diomedes where he says,

> There were the robes, richly wrought, the work of Sidonian
> Women, robes Alexander, in form like a god, himself fetched
> From Sidon while sailing the wide sea
> When he led away well-born Helen.[3]

And in fact he mentions it also in these lines in the *Odyssey*:

> The daughter of Zeus had such excellent subtle drugs,
> The gift of Polydamna the Egyptian, the wife of Thon.
> For there the grain-giving fields yield many drugs,
> Many prepared for good, and many for evil.[4]

And again, Menelaus speaks this other line to Telemachus:

> The gods held me in Egypt, though I yearned to be home
> Because I had not given them perfect hecatombs in sacrifice.[5]

In these lines, Homer makes it clear that he knew of Alexander's straying into Egypt, for Syria borders on Egypt, and the Phoenicians—to whom Sidon belongs—live in Syria. The lines in these passages are the greatest proof that the Cyprian epic is not by Homer but by someone else, for in the *Cypria* it is said that Alexander took advantage of a fair wind and a smooth sea to arrive at Ilium with Helen on the third day after leaving Sparta, while in the *Iliad* it says that he wandered around with her.

But let us bid adieu to Homer and the Cyprian epic.

When I asked the priests whether the story the Greeks tell about what happened at Ilium is a mere fiction or not, they told me what they said they knew from asking Menelaus himself. After the abduction of Helen, a large Greek army went to Troy on behalf of Menelaus. The Greeks disembarked, set up camp, and sent messengers to Ilium,[6] among them Menelaus himself. When

---

3. *Iliad*, 6.289–92.
4. *Odyssey*, 4.227–30.
5. *Odyssey*, 4.351–52. A hecatomb was a sacrifice of a hundred cattle.
6. Troy.

they had entered the walls of the city, they demanded the return of Helen and of the property which Alexander had stolen. They also demanded damages for the harm that had been done. The Trojans said the same thing then as later, sometimes on their oath and sometimes not: they had neither Helen nor the money in question. It was all in Egypt, they said, and it wasn't right for them to be responsible for damages on what Proteus the Egyptian was holding. The Greeks, thinking they were being trifled with, besieged the city until they captured it. When there was still no Helen after they had stormed the walls of Troy, and they heard the same story as they had at first, the Greeks believed the original story and sent Menelaus to Proteus.

Menelaus arrived in Egypt and sailed upriver to Memphis. After truthfully describing the situation, he was richly entertained and received Helen—and all of his property—back unharmed. After all this, however, Menelaus did the Egyptians a wrong. You see, although he was eager to sail, he was detained by contrary winds. When this situation lasted for a long time, he came up with an unholy solution. He kidnapped two infants belonging to native men and sacrificed them as propitiatory offerings. He was hated and pursued when his deed became known, and he fled with his ships straight for Libya. The Egyptians could not say where he went next. They told me that they knew about some of this story through inquiry, whereas they could only speak with certainty about what had happened in their own country.

This is what the Egyptian priests said. I myself agree with their version of the Helen story for the following reason. If Helen had been in Ilium, she would have been returned to the Greeks whether Alexander liked it or not, for neither Priam[7] nor his relatives were so addlebrained that they would risk their city and their own lives and the lives of their children just so that Alexander could live with Helen. If they had any such idea in mind at first, after seeing that so many Trojans died whenever they had a melee with the Greeks, and that there was not an occasion when two, three, or even more of Priam's own sons did not die in battle (if we may believe the epic poets)—why, all these things being so, I expect that even if Priam himself had been living with Helen he would have given her back to the Achaeans if there was any chance of getting out of the trouble they were in. Nor did the throne even devolve on Alexander, which would have left the affairs of state up to him, in view of Priam's age. Instead, Hector, who was older and much more of a man than Alexander was, would inherit the throne on the death of Priam; and it was not fitting for Hector to give in to his outlaw brother, especially when Alexander was the cause of so much misery to Hector personally and to all the rest of the Trojans combined. But the fact is that the Trojans did not have Helen to give back, and that the Greeks did not believe them when they told the truth. Because—and I'm now declaring my own theory—the gods arranged things so that the Trojans, through their total annihilation, would make it perfectly clear to all mankind that great wrongs bring great retributions from the gods. This is said in keeping with my own beliefs.

[The Debate on Government]

BOOK 3, CHAPTERS 80–88

[The debate Herodotus sets in Persia late in the sixth century B.C. is the earliest substantive discussion of political theory that survives from antiquity. Whether this con-

---

7. The king of Troy.

versation actually took place has been hotly debated, but its appearance in Herodotus' work makes plain at the very least the currency of these concerns in his time. Herodotus places the conversation in the year 522: three men involved in killing the previous ruler of Persia contemplate the best form of government to establish now that they have a free hand.]

Speeches were made which some Greeks find impossible to believe—but they were made, all right. Otanes demanded that the government be left up to the Persian people, and said:

"I don't think that we should have a monarchy any longer. It is neither agreeable nor advantageous. You have seen what pitch the arrogance of Cambyses soared to, and you have also had your share of the arrogance of the Magi.[1] How could monarchy be a well-ordered thing when the monarch is able to do whatever he wants without accountability to anyone? Even the noblest of men would change his way of thinking if he had that kind of power. Arrogance would develop from his good qualities themselves, while envy has been natural to mankind from the very beginning; and when the monarch has these two things he has all he needs to do evil, for, glutted with arrogance and envy, he will commit the most monstrous atrocities. Now, the tyrant ought not to feel any envy, since he has all the good things he wants, but he is really just the opposite in the way he treats his subjects. He envies the best of them simply for being alive, while he delights in his most contemptible subjects and loves, above all, to listen to slanderous gossip. And the most incongruous thing of all: if you admire him appropriately, he is angry because you are not totally subservient to him; but if you are totally subservient, he is angry at you for being a flatterer. But I have yet to mention the worst things: he will disrupt the settled customs of our ancestors, rape our women, and murder indiscriminately.

"Majority rule, on the other hand, is called by the fairest of terms: Equality before the Law. Furthermore, it requires something the tyrant never allows: people hold office by lot, they are accountable for the actions of their administrations, and their deliberations are held in public. I propose, therefore, that we abolish the monarchy and increase the power of the people, for in the many is all our strength."

Otanes, then, advanced this position, but Megabyzus exhorted them to adopt an oligarchy. He said:

"I agree with Otanes when he says that we must abolish the monarchy, but he misses the mark when he urges us to hand power over to the people, because there is nothing stupider or more arrogant than an idle mob. It would be absolutely unbearable to flee the arrogance of a tyrant and to fall prey to the arrogance of the unbridled masses. At least the tyrant knows what he is doing; the common people don't know anything. How could they know when they are uneducated and have never learned anything on their own and when, like a raging river, they mindlessly rush in and sweep away the business of government? Let those who bear ill will toward the Persians be governed by the people; let us select a group of the best men and give power to them, for we ourselves will be in that group, and it is natural for the best men to produce the best counsels."

This, then, was the opinion Megabyzus advanced. Darius expressed yet a third opinion, and said:

"I think Megabyzus is right in what he said about the majority but wrong in what he said about an oligarchy. For of the three forms of government set

---

1. The previous rulers of Persia. The autocracy and eventual madness of Cambyses figure prominently in Herodotus' narrative.

forth in debate as the best—democracy, oligarchy, and monarchy—I say that monarchy is far and away superior. After all, no one could be better than the one best man, and in the implementation of his own best counsel the monarch can faultlessly govern his people and keep his own secrets while carrying out his plans against his enemies. Powerful private hatreds always arise in an oligarchy when a large group of men vies for preeminence before the public. When each man wants to be the leader and wants his opinions to prevail, all come to hate each other immensely, and from this comes civil strife, and from civil strife comes bloodshed, and after the bloodshed you end with a monarchy—and in this way it becomes clear how much better the monarch is.

"It is impossible for a democracy to avoid corruption, but when corruption arises in government, it engenders strong friendships instead of hatreds because those who huddle to corrupt the government have to act together. This goes on until a man of the people comes forward and puts a stop to it. As a result, he becomes the admiration of the people, and after being an object of admiration he shows himself, of course, to be a monarch. In this way he, too, makes it clear that monarchy is the best form of government. In short: Where did our freedom come from? Who gave it to us? Was it from the people or from an oligarchy or from a monarchy? I believe that since we were liberated by one man, we should preserve the monarchy and that we should, in addition, retain the ancestral customs which have served us so well. This is our best course."

These three proposals were advanced, and four of the seven[2] chose that of Darius. When Otanes was defeated after urging the view that the Persians should adopt a government of equality before the law, he openly made this announcement to the group:

"It is as plain as can be, my fellow revolutionaries, that one of us is going to be king, whether we choose him by lot, leave it up to the Persian people to elect him, or find some other way. I will not compete with you for it, though. I will neither rule nor be ruled. But I give up all claim to the throne on one condition, the condition that I will never be subject to any of you, neither I myself, nor any of my offspring forever." The seven went along with what he had proposed, and he did not, indeed, compete with them but maintained a strict neutrality. To this day, only the house of Otanes continues to be free in Persia and, without breaking any of the laws of Persia, only obeys the king to the extent that it chooses.

The rest of the seven deliberated about the fairest way to institute a monarchy. But first they decided that if one of them became king, Otanes and his offspring would forever annually be given the choicest Median wardrobe and all the other most cherished gifts of Persia. They decided that he should be given these things because he was the first to plan the coup and to bring the seven together. These privileges were set aside for Otanes, but the following rules were to apply to them all. Any one of the seven could enter the royal palace without announcing it in advance, unless the king was in bed with one of his wives. Also, the king would not be permitted to marry anyone outside the families of his co-revolutionaries. As to the question of who should get the throne, this is what they decided: they would all mount their horses and ride out to the city limits, and that man would have the throne whose horse was the first to neigh after sunrise.

Now, Darius had a shrewd groom whose name was Oebares, and after the meeting broke up, this is what Darius said to the man: "Oebares, this is

---

2. The total number of those involved in the coup.

what we've decided to do about who gets the throne. The first one of us whose horse neighs when we're riding at sunrise is going to be king. So if you have the skill to do it, work out a way for us, and not somebody else, to win this prize."

Oebares answered, "Well, Master, if that is what being king or not being king depends on, take heart and don't worry, because no one will be king but you. I have just the medicine we need."

And Darius said, "If you know some trick, waste no time and play it now, because we're going to have our contest tomorrow."

After Oebares heard this, he did the following: he took the mare Darius' horse loved best and led her out to the city limits. He tethered her there, and then brought out Darius' horse and led him around and around the mare, getting closer every time, until finally the groom allowed him to cover her.

With the first rays of dawn, the six arrived on their horses, as agreed. They rode out to the city limits, toward the very place where the mare had been tethered the night before. Suddenly, Darius' stallion galloped ahead and began to neigh, and at the same moment as the horse did so, there was thunder and lightning in a perfectly clear sky. This unexpected event confirmed Darius as if by some covenant, and the others sprang down from their horses and prostrated themselves before him.

That is what some say about the trick Oebares played, but others say—and both stories are told by the Persians—that he rubbed the mare's vagina with his hand, which he then kept hidden in his pants. As the horses were about to be released at sunrise, this Oebares pulled his hand out of his pants and brought it up to the nostrils of the horse, who began to snort and neigh as soon as he recognized the smell.

Thus was Darius, the son of Hystaspes, chosen king.

PLATO

Like Thucydides, the philosopher Plato (c. 429–347 B.C.) lived through the Peloponnesian War and watched the internecine warfare of the Greek city-states with concern. Plato shared Thucydides' fascination with the human drive to power. For Plato, the goal of life was the development of moral virtue, a process that went hand in hand with increasing understanding of justice. Similarly, a person's greatest misfortune was to do injustice. These views, as Plato well knew, clashed with the popular way of conceiving the highest goal as the acquisition of power and the capacity to inflict harm on others. Plato was deeply affected by the execution of Socrates in 399 B.C., and shortly after Socrates' death he set about writing dialogues in which Socrates led young men in a search for understanding. In *Gorgias*, Socrates encounters the Sicilian rhetorician Gorgias and some of his friends and engages with them in a discussion of rhetoric and virtue. The most memorable character in the dialogue is Callicles, who may or may not have been a real person in Athens. Callicles argues that it is right for a man of conspicuous excellence to take as much as possible for himself and claims that this is in accord with *physis*, nature. *Nomos*, on the other hand—convention—is at odds with nature and seeks to suppress natural talent. The issues raised in the passage cited here are evocative of some that appear in the speeches in Thucydides' *History*.

Gorgias[†]

479d–484c

SOCRATES   So it turns out then that the greatest evil is injustice and doing wrong?

POLUS   So it seems.

SOCRATES   Furthermore, the way to be rid of this evil is to make amends?

POLUS   Looks like it.

SOCRATES   And not making amends means that the evil persists?

POLUS   Right.

SOCRATES   Actually, doing wrong is only the second-greatest evil. The first and greatest of all is for the wrongdoer not to make amends.

POLUS   So it would appear.

SOCRATES   And wasn't this what our dispute was about—you praising Archelaus[1] for doing great wrongs and never making amends, and I maintaining the opposite, and saying that if Archelaus or any other man did wrong and did not make amends, he deserved to be more miserable than all others? And didn't I also say that the wrongdoer is always more miserable than the victim of injustice, just as the man who does not make amends is more miserable than the one who does? Isn't that what I said?

POLUS   Yes indeed.

SOCRATES   And it's been shown that what I said was true?

POLUS   It seems so.

SOCRATES   Well then. If this is true, Polus, then what good is rhetoric? Based on what we've agreed, a man has to make sure to keep from wrongdoing, because he knows that he'll have plenty of trouble if he doesn't. Right?

POLUS   Absolutely.

SOCRATES   In fact, if he or anyone he is responsible for does wrong, he must immediately and of his own accord go anywhere and everywhere to take his punishment, hurrying to the judge as to a doctor to keep the disease of injustice from taking root and festering incurably in his soul. Wouldn't you say so, Polus—if, that is, we stick to our original understanding? Isn't this the only way these conclusions can jibe with what we said before?

POLUS   What else *can* we say, Socrates?

SOCRATES   Then rhetoric is absolutely useless to us to explain away our own wrongdoing, or that of our parents, friends, children, or country. It is only useful for the opposite purpose—to prosecute, especially ourselves, and then our relatives and any other loved ones who happen to be doing wrong at any given time. It must be used not to conceal injustice, but to bring it to light, so that we may make amends and become healthy, and it must force us and others to be brave and to take our punishment like men, just as we do when a doctor makes an incision or cauterizes a wound. We must not pay any attention to the punishment. If we deserve a whipping for our injustice, we must be whipped; if imprisonment, we must go to jail; if a fine, we must pay it; if exile, we must go; and if the punishment is death, then death it shall be. We must be the first to prosecute ourselves and our relatives, and that is the purpose of rhetoric—to bring our own injustice to light and to free ourselves from doing wrong, which is the worst thing that can happen to us.

---

† Translated by Walter Blanco for this edition.
1. Ruler of Macedon, assassinated in 399 B.C.

Is that how we would put it, or not, Polus?

POLUS It seems bizarre to me, Socrates, but it does follow from what you have already said.

SOCRATES So we must either refute that argument or accept this one?

POLUS That's right.

SOCRATES Now let's look at the other side of the coin. Assuming we are obligated to harm someone, whether an enemy or whoever, provided only that it's not us that this enemy has wronged—which is the tricky part—when our enemy does wrong to someone else, we must use every means at our disposal, whether word or deed, to keep him from making amends or from going before a judge. If he does go to court, we must work it out so that he is acquitted and doesn't have to face justice. If he has stolen a large sum of money, he must not give it back, but must hold on to it, unjustly and impiously frittering it away on himself and his family. If he has committed a wrong that deserves to be punished by death, we must see to it that he does not die, preferably not ever, so that he can be miserable and immortal. Failing that, he must live in this condition for as long as possible. It is for such a purpose, Polus, that rhetoric seems useful to me, since I think it has only minor utility for those who are not about to engage in wrongdoing. If, that is, it has any use at all, which did not seem to be the case judging from what we said before.

CALLICLES Tell me, Chaerephon, is Socrates joking or is he serious about this?

CHAEREPHON He seems very serious to me, Callicles, but why don't you ask him?

CALLICLES I'd love to, by god. Tell me, Socrates, are we to assume that you are serious or that you are joking? If you are serious, and what you are saying is the truth, human life is turned completely upside down and we are probably doing everything the opposite of the way we should.

SOCRATES You know, Callicles, if people didn't have feelings in common, some sharing one feeling and some another, but some of us instead had feelings different from everyone else's, it would be very difficult to make our experience known to others. I say this because I know that you and I happen to be having the same experience right now. We are two men who are both in love with two things—I with philosophy and with Alcibiades, the son of Cleinias, and you with the Athenian demos[2] and with Demos, son of Pyrilampes. Now although you are a formidable man, every time I have observed you, you have been unable to stand up to your darlings no matter what they say, but instead go twisting and turning every which way. If you are speaking in the assembly and the Athenian people deny the truth of what you say, you turn around and say what they want. You also go through the same thing with your handsome young son of Pyrilampes. You are unable to resist either the wills or the arguments of your two sweethearts, so that if one were to express amazement at the strange things you keep saying on their account, you might, if you were inclined to tell the truth, answer that if nobody stopped your darlings from making these arguments, you wouldn't ever stop making them either! You must realize that you are going to hear other things of the same kind from me, and you must not be amazed that I say them. Instead you will have to stop *my* sweetheart, philosophy, from saying them. Because, my dear friend, philosophy always says what you are hearing from me now, and is much less fickle with me than my other lover. The son of Cleinias says different things at different times, but philoso-

---

2. I.e., the Athenian people.

phy always says the same things, things you now marvel at although you actually heard them spoken. You must either refute philosophy by disproving that doing wrong and doing wrong without making amends are the worst of all evils, as I have just argued. Or, if you let this go unrefuted, by the dog-headed god of Egypt, you, Callicles, will not agree with yourself, and you will differ with yourself for the rest of your life. And as for me, my dear fellow, I think it would be better for me to unstring the lyre and make it jangle, or to disrupt the choreography of the dance, or to be in disagreement with the majority of my fellow men and be constantly at odds with them than to contradict or be out of tune with myself, though I am only one man.

CALLICLES   It seems to me, Socrates, that you run off at the mouth like a boy, like a regular rabble-rouser, and now you are going on about this because you have done the same thing to Polus that Polus said you did to Gorgias.[3] He said that you asked Gorgias whether he would teach someone who came to him asking for lessons in rhetoric if that person was totally ignorant of right and wrong. Gorgias was shamed into saying that he would teach him, since that was the way of the world, and because people would complain if he refused. Because of this concession, you forced him into contradicting himself, which is what you love to do. At the time, Polus ridiculed you—rightly, I thought—but now he's in the same predicament. That's the point where my respect for Polus breaks down, where he agreed with you that it is worse to do wrong than to suffer it. This concession let you bind and gag him with your arguments, because he was ashamed to say what he thought. The fact is, Socrates, that you steer discussion into this kind of vulgar, populist rant. You say that you are seeking after truth, but there is nothing by nature admirable in your ideas. They are only admirable according to convention; and nature and convention[4] are for the most part opposed to each other, and when one shrinks from boldly saying what he thinks, he is forced to contradict himself. In fact, this is the trick you have devised for cheating in argument: if someone speaks of conventional ideas, you sneak in ideas about nature; and if he speaks of nature, you sneak in convention, as in doing wrong and being wronged, to take the nearest example. When Polus said that doing wrong was dishonorable, he was speaking of social convention, but you followed up the argument on the basis of nature. But in nature, it is definitely more dishonorable and base to be the victim of wrongdoing. It is only by convention that doing wrong is dishonorable. Furthermore, a real man doesn't put up with being wronged—only a slave for whom it is better to die than to live, and who is unable to avenge himself and those he is responsible for when he is wronged and trampled in the mud, would do so. I believe that those who make the laws are the weak and the many. They make these laws and dispense praise and blame for themselves and for their own advantage. They also try to frighten more powerful men and to keep them from exercising their power to get more for themselves by saying that it is shameful and unjust to have any advantages, and that becomes the definition of injustice: to want to have more than others. I think the reason is that they are inferior, and they love it when everybody is made equal.

As a result, wanting to have more than the many is called unjust and "shameful" as a matter of convention. But I believe that nature shows that it is, quite to the contrary, just for the better man to have more than the in-

---

3. Earlier in the dialogue, at *Gorgias* 473d3.
4. The Greek words are *physis* (nature) and *nomos* (convention). The relationship between them (often but not always construed as an opposition) was a frequent topic of debate in ancient Greece.

ferior one, and for the stronger to have more than the weak. It is obvious in many ways that this is the case—it is true of other animals, and in the human realm, it is true of the relations between states and races, where right has always been deemed to be the strong ruling over the weak and having more than they. Otherwise, where was the justice of Xerxes attacking Greece, or his father attacking Scythia? And you could cite tens of thousands of similar examples. I believe that these men performed those acts in keeping with the true nature of justice—in keeping with the Law of Nature, by god!—although perhaps not in keeping with the laws that we have laid down. For we mold the best and strongest among ourselves by taking them young, like lions, lulling them with songs, casting a spell over them and turning them into slaves by telling them that equality is natural and that this is beautiful and just. I think that if ever a man was born with a nature strong enough to shake all this to its foundations, to smash it to pieces and rise up free of it, he would trample down our scribblings and tricks, spells and laws, and make it clear that the slave is now our master, and from that point on natural justice would blaze forth. I think Pindar refers to what I am talking about when he says in one of his odes that

> Custom is king of mortals and immortals alike.

"And custom", he goes on

> With sovereign hand makes just the greatest violence.
> I cite the labors of Hercules, when unbought—

I don't know the ode by heart, but it goes something like that, and it says that Hercules took Geryon's cattle, which he had neither paid for nor been given, because this was natural justice, and because the cattle and all the other chattels of the weak and lowly belong to the noble and the strong.

488b–492c

SOCRATES Let's take it from the beginning. What is this natural justice, according to you and Pindar? Is it the stronger taking from the weaker by force, and the superior ruling over the inferior, and the better having more than the worse? Did you say that justice was anything else, or do I remember right?

CALLICLES That's what I said then, and that's what I say now.

SOCRATES So when you refer to the superior, you mean "the stronger"? Because I didn't quite get what you meant. Is it that by "the stronger", you mean "the more powerful"—which is what I think you meant then—and that the weaker must obey the stronger, as for example when large states attack small ones in accordance with "natural justice," because they are stronger and more powerful? Are "stronger," "more powerful," and "superior" all the same, or is it possible to be "superior" on the one hand, but "weak" and "feeble" on the other, or "strong" and yet "lowly"? Or do we define "the superior" and "the stronger" in the same way? Spell this out clearly for me, please. Are "the stronger," "the superior," and "the more powerful" the same or different?

CALLICLES I tell you clearly that they are the same.

SOCRATES Therefore the many are stronger than the one by nature? The many, I mean, who make laws to govern the one, as you just said.

CALLICLES Certainly.

SOCRATES The laws of the many, then, are those of the stronger?

CALLICLES   Of course.

SOCRATES   And therefore of the superior? Because according to you the stronger are superior.

CALLICLES   Yes.

SOCRATES   Therefore the laws of the many are naturally good, since the many are stronger?

CALLICLES   Yes indeed.

SOCRATES   But the many believe, as you also just said, that equality is just and that it is more shameful to do wrong than to be wronged. Isn't that right? Don't let yourself be shamed into falling into the same trap as Polus and Gorgias. Tell me, do the many believe, or do they not believe, that it is not having more but equality that is just, and that it is more shameful to do wrong than to be wronged? Come, don't hold back. Give me an answer, Callicles, if you agree with me, so that I can be reassured at last—by you, a man who is fully able to make the decision and who sees things my way.

CALLICLES   Well, the populace does think those things.

SOCRATES   So it is not merely by social convention that it is more shameful to do wrong than to be wronged, or that equality is just. These things are also true by nature. And it looks like you weren't telling the truth in your former statements, and that you wrongly attacked me when you said that custom and nature were opposed to each other, and that I knowingly cheated at argument by bringing in custom when someone was speaking of nature and vice versa.

CALLICLES   This man simply will not stop talking nonsense! Tell me, Socrates, aren't you ashamed to be mincing words like this at your age and to be making such a big deal out of another man's slips of the tongue? Do you think I meant anything other than that the superior is the stronger? Didn't I tell you before that I maintain that the superior and the stronger are the same? Or do you think I meant that when the scum of the earth—slaves and nobodies who are good for nothing but manual labor—that when these people say something, that thing should be law?

SOCRATES   Callicles, you are a marvel of intelligence! So that's what you mean?

CALLICLES   Absolutely.

SOCRATES   What a strange fellow you are. But I suspected that you meant something like that by "stronger," and I only asked you because I was dying to know your real meaning clearly. You don't then regard two as superior to one, or your slaves as superior to you because they are stronger than you. But begin again from the beginning and tell me this. Who are the superior people, since they are not the stronger ones? And by the way, please conduct my education more gently, or I'll quit your school.

CALLICLES   You're only pretending to be ignorant, Socrates.

SOCRATES   No, by the same divinity you invoked when you feigned ignorance towards me! But come, tell me, who do you mean by "the superior people"?

CALLICLES   I mean the better people.

SOCRATES   But don't you see that you yourself are mincing words, and that you're not really explaining anything? Will you please tell me whether by the superior and the stronger you mean the more intelligent or some other kind of person?

CALLICLES   Yes, by god, I certainly do mean them.

SOCRATES   It will frequently happen then, according to your argument, that one intelligent man is stronger than ten thousand unintelligent ones, and that he ought to rule and they to be ruled, and that the ruler ought to have more than the ruled. That, anyway, is what I think you intend to say—and I am not mincing words here—if one man is stronger than ten thousand.

CALLICLES   But that's just what I mean! That's exactly what I think natural justice is—for the superior and more intelligent man to rule and to have more than the inferior ones!

SOCRATES   But wait a minute. What are you saying now? Let's assume that we are together all in one place—as we are now—and that there is a large quantity of food and drink in the public storehouse. Let's say that we are people of all kinds, some strong, some weak, but that one of us is more intelligent on the subject of food and drink—a doctor, let's say. As you might suppose, he is stronger than some, weaker than others, and different in other ways. Would you say that since he is more intelligent than we, he is superior and stronger with respect to food and drink?

CALLICLES   Of course.

SOCRATES   Then he should have more of these foodstuffs than we, because he is superior, and he should distribute the food by virtue of his authority? If he doesn't want to damage his health, though, he shouldn't have more than his share to use for himself. He should have more than some, and less than others; and if, by chance he is the frailest of all, then the least amount of all would go to the superior person. Isn't that, my dear Callicles, the way it would be?

CALLICLES   You're the one who's talking about food and drink and doctors and nonsense, not me.

SOCRATES   Didn't you say that the more intelligent person was superior? Yes or no?

CALLICLES   I did.

SOCRATES   And that the superior person should have more?

CALLICLES   Yes, but I wasn't talking about food and drink!

SOCRATES   I get it. But—well, what about clothes, then? Should the best weaver have the biggest cloak and go around wearing the largest and finest wardrobe?

CALLICLES   What do clothes have to do with it!

SOCRATES   And when it comes to shoes, it's obvious that the most intelligent and therefore superior person in this regard ought to have more. No doubt the shoemaker should have the most sandals and should walk around wearing the biggest ones.

CALLICLES   What do sandals have to do with it! You keep talking nonsense.

SOCRATES   But if that's not the kind of thing you're talking about, maybe it's this: maybe an intelligent, good, and worthy farmer ought to have more seed than others so that he can use the most seed on his land.

CALLICLES   As usual, you say the same things, Socrates.

SOCRATES   Not only that, but I say them about the same subjects!

CALLICLES   Yes, by god, you simply will not stop talking about shoemakers, fullers, cooks, and doctors! As if those were the people we are talking about!

SOCRATES   Well then, would you please say who we *are* talking about, and just what things the stronger and more intelligent ought to have more of? Or is it that you will neither endure my suggestions nor tell me yourself?

CALLICLES   I have been telling you for some time now. In the first place, I mean by the strongest not those who are shoemakers and cooks, but men who are intelligent about the state and about the best way of running it. In addition to being intelligent, these people are manly, fully capable of realizing their plans, and they do not flag because of spiritual softness.

SOCRATES   Don't you see, Callicles, that I can accuse you of something different from what you fault in me? You blame me for always saying the same thing, but I have the opposite criticism, because you never say the same thing about the same subjects. Once, you defined the superior, and the stronger, as the more powerful; then it was the more intelligent; and now you come up with a new idea. According to you, the superior and the stronger are also the more manly. Tell me once and for all, my dear fellow, who you mean by the stronger and the superior, and just what they are stronger and superior at?

CALLICLES   I just said that they are manly and intelligent about the state. These are the men who should be running the government, and justice means for them—the rulers—to have more than the ruled.

SOCRATES   And what of themselves, my friend?

CALLICLES   What?

SOCRATES   Do they govern themselves or are they governed?

CALLICLES   What in Hades are you talking about?

SOCRATES   I maintain that every man must govern himself. Or is that not necessary, but only to rule over others?

CALLICLES   What do you mean by "governing yourself"?

SOCRATES   Nothing fancy, just what everybody means—being prudent, having self-control, governing your pleasures and desires.

CALLICLES   What a simpleton you are! By prudent, you mean foolish.

SOCRATES   How so? Anyone can see that is not what I mean.

CALLICLES   It certainly *is* what you are saying, Socrates. How could a man be happy and subject himself to anything? I'm going to speak freely now and tell you what natural justice and goodness are. The man who is living rightly must allow his desires to expand as much as possible and not suppress them. However grand they are, he will be capable of gratifying them by virtue of his manliness and his intelligence, and he will be able to satisfy any desire he may have. I think, though, that this is not possible for the majority of people, and that is why they censure such men. It is because of their own shame and in order to conceal their own impotence. They say that imprudence is shameful, and, as I said earlier in our discussion, they make slaves out of men who are naturally superior. Powerless to take their pleasures to the full, they praise prudence and justice—and all because they aren't men enough. For those who begin as the sons of kings, or who are by nature able to grasp power, whether as a tyrant or as a member of a ruling clique—what could be more shameful or more cowardly, really, for such men than prudence and justice? These are men who can enjoy the good things in life with nothing to stand in their way. Should they impose on themselves the common man's despotism of prudery, blather, and law? And how could they not be ground down by this "virtue," this justice and prudence, unable to reward their friends more than their enemies, and this when they are the masters in their own cities? You say that you are seeking after the truth, Socrates, so this is it. When you are in charge, luxury, licentiousness, and freedom constitute virtue and happiness. Everything else is pretty talk, and the worthless nonsense of man's artificial conventions.

NICCOLÒ MACHIAVELLI

The Florentine intellectual and bureaucrat Niccolò Machiavelli (1469–1527) is best known as the author of the daring handbook for aspiring rulers called *The Prince*, written in exile after his bad relations with the Medici family ended his political career. Machiavelli shared Thucydides' interest in the workings of power, and the absence of sentimentality and didactic moralizing from their writings has often led the two men to be studied together. Some articles connecting Machiavelli's thought with that of Thucydides appear in the bibliography on pp. 539–43.

The Prince[†]

XVIII

The Way Princes Should Keep Their Word

How praiseworthy it is for a prince to keep his word and live with integrity rather than by craftiness, everyone understands; yet we see from recent experience that those princes have accomplished most who paid little heed to keeping their promises, but who knew how to manipulate the minds of men craftily. In the end, they won out over those who tried to act honestly.

You should consider then, that there are two ways of fighting, one with laws and the other with force. The first is properly a human method, the second belongs to beasts. But as the first method does not always suffice, you sometimes have to turn to the second. Thus a prince must know how to make good use of both the beast and man. Ancient writers made subtle note of this fact when they wrote that Achilles and many other princes of antiquity were sent to be reared by Chiron the centaur, who trained them in his discipline. Having a teacher who is half man and half beast can only mean that a prince must know how to use both these two natures, and that one without the other has no lasting effect.

Since a prince must know how to use the character of beasts, he should pick for imitation the fox and the lion. As the lion cannot protect himself from traps, and the fox cannot defend himself from wolves, you have to be a fox in order to be wary of traps, and a lion to overawe the wolves. Those who try to live by the lion alone are badly mistaken. Thus a prudent prince cannot and should not keep his word when to do so would go against his interest, or when the reasons that made him pledge it no longer apply. Doubtless if all men were good, this rule would be bad; but since they are a sad lot, and keep no faith with you, you in your turn are under no obligation to keep it with them.

Besides, a prince will never lack for legitimate excuses to explain away his breaches of faith. Modern history will furnish innumerable examples of this behavior, showing how many treaties and promises have been made null and void by the faithlessness of princes, and how the man succeeded best who knew best how to play the fox. But it is necessary in playing this part that you conceal it carefully; you must be a great liar and hypocrite. Men are so simple of mind, and so much dominated by their immediate needs, that a deceitful man will always find plenty who are ready to be deceived. One of many recent examples calls for mention. Alexander VI[1] never did anything else, never had another

---

† Niccolò Machiavelli, *The Prince*, trans. Robert M. Adams, pp. 47–49 and 67–69. Copyright 1992, 1977, by W. W. Norton and Company, Inc.

1. Alexander VI, who served as pope from 1492 to 1503, belonged to the notorious Borgia family; the suspected murderers Cesare and Lucrezia Borgia were among his four illegitimate children. Like other Renaissance popes, he was heavily involved in politics and international relations [*Editor*].

thought, except to deceive men, and he always found fresh material to work on. Never was there a man more convincing in his assertions, who sealed his promises with more solemn oaths, and who observed them less. Yet his deceptions were always successful, because he knew exactly how to manage this sort of business.

In actual fact, a prince may not have all the admirable qualities listed above, but it is very necessary that he should seem to have them. Indeed, I will venture to say that when you have them and exercise them all the time, they are harmful to you; when you just seem to have them, they are useful. It is good to appear merciful, truthful, humane, sincere, and religious; it is good to be so in reality. But you must keep your mind so disposed that, in case of need, you can turn to the exact contrary. This has to be understood: a prince, and especially a new prince, cannot possibly exercise all those virtues for which men are called "good." To preserve the state, he often has to do things against his word, against charity, against humanity, against religion. Thus he has to have a mind ready to shift as the winds of fortune and the varying circumstances of life may dictate. And as I said above, he should not depart from the good if he can hold to it, but he should be ready to enter on evil if he has to.

Hence a prince should take great care never to drop a word that does not seem imbued with the five good qualities noted above; to anyone who sees or hears him, he should appear all compassion, all honor, all humanity, all integrity, all religion. Nothing is more necessary than to seem to have this last virtue. Men in general judge more by the sense of sight than by the sense of touch, because everyone can see but only a few can test by feeling. Everyone sees what you seem to be, few know what you really are; and those few do not dare take a stand against the general opinion, supported by the majesty of the government. In the actions of all men, and especially of princes who are not subject to a court of appeal, we must always look to the end. Let a prince, therefore, win victories and uphold his state; his methods will always be considered worthy, and everyone will praise them, because the masses are always impressed by the superficial appearance of things, and by the outcome of an enterprise. And the world consists of nothing but the masses; the few have no influence when the many feel secure. A certain prince of our own time, whom it is just as well not to name, preaches nothing but peace and mutual trust, yet he is the determined enemy of both; and if on several different occasions he had observed either, he would have lost both his reputation and his throne.

* * *

XXV

The Influence of Luck on Human Affairs and the Ways to Counter It

I realize that many people have thought, and still do think, that events are so governed in this world that the wisdom of men cannot possibly avail against them, indeed is altogether useless. On this basis, you might say that there is no point in sweating over anything, we should simply leave all matters to fate. This opinion has been popular in our own times because of the tremendous change in public affairs during our lifetime, that actually is still going on today, beyond what anyone could have imagined. Indeed, sometimes when I think of it, I incline toward this opinion myself. Still, rather than give up on our free will altogether, I think it may be true that Fortune governs half of our actions, but that even so she leaves the other half more or less in our power to control. I would compare her to one of those torrential streams which, when they overflow, flood the plains, rip up trees and tear down buildings, wash the land away here and deposit it there; everyone flees before them, everyone yields to their onslaught, unable to stand up to them in any way. This is how they are; yet this does not mean that men cannot take countermeasures while the weather is still fine, shoring up dikes and dams, so that when the waters rise again, they are either carried off in a channel or confined where they do no harm. So with Fortune, who exerts all her power where there is no strength [*virtù*] prepared to oppose her, and turns to smashing things up wherever there are no dikes and restraining dams. And if you look at Italy, which is the seat of all these tremendous changes, where they all began, you will see that she is an open country without any dikes or ditches. If she were protected by forces of proper valor [*virtù*], as are Germany, Spain, and France,[2] either this flood would never have wrought such destruction as it has, or it might not even have occurred at all. And let this much suffice on the general topic of opposing Fortune.

But coming now to the particulars, let me observe that we see a prince flourishing today and ruined tomorrow, and yet no change has taken place in his nature or any of his qualities. I think this happens, primarily, for the reasons discussed at length above, that is, that a prince who depends entirely on Fortune comes to grief immediately she changes. I believe further that a prince will be fortunate who adjusts his behavior to the temper of the times, and on the other hand will be unfortunate when his behavior is not well attuned to the times. Anyone can see that men take different paths in their search for the common goals of glory and riches; one goes cautiously, another boldly; one by violence, another by stealth; one by patience, another in the contrary way; yet any one of these different methods may be successful. Of two cautious men, one will succeed in his design, the other not; so too, a rash man and a cautious man may both succeed, though their approaches are so different. And this stems from nothing but the temper of the times, which does or does not accord with their method of operating. Hence two men proceeding in different ways may, as I have said, produce the same effect; while two men proceeding in the same way will vary in their effectiveness, one failing, one succeeding. This too explains the variation in what is good; for if a prince conducts himself with patience and caution, and the times and circumstances are favorable to those qualities, he will flourish; but if times and circumstances change, he will come to ruin unless he changes his method of proceeding. No man, however prudent, can adjust to such radical changes, not only because we cannot go against the inclination of nature, but also because when one has always prospered by following a particular course, he cannot be persuaded to leave it. Thus the cautious man, when it is time to act boldly, does not know how, and comes to grief; if he could only change his nature with times and circumstances, his fortune would not change.

* * *

I conclude, then, that so long as Fortune varies and men stand still, they will prosper while they suit the times, and fail when they do not. But I do feel

2. Italy in Machiavelli's day was composed of numerous independent states that fought with each other (rather like the city-states of ancient Greece), making the peninsula easy prey for growing nations like France, Spain, and Austria. *The Prince* was in part an appeal for Italian unity against "inundation" by these other countries [*Editor*].

this: that it is better to be rash than timid, for Fortune is a woman, and the man who wants to hold her down must beat and bully her. We see that she yields more often to men of this stripe than to those who come coldly toward her. Like a woman, too, she is always a friend of the young, because they are less timid, more brutal, and take charge of her more recklessly.

The Discourses[†]

In his *Discourses*, Machiavelli treated a wide variety of issues in political life, using the history of Rome composed by Livy around the birth of Christ as a frame of reference. Machiavelli's belief in the constancy of human nature made Livy's work appear useful to him as a vehicle for analyzing the problems of his own day and indeed of all societies. The non-Roman worlds he discusses included classical Athens, in connection with which Thucydides' writing prompted him to adduce the events of the Peloponnesian War and particularly the invasion of Sicily as evidence of the problematic nature of popular government, something the instability of Renaissance Italy led many thinkers to denigrate.

[Book 1,] Chapter 39. Among Different Peoples the Same Events Often Occur

[Human nature always the same]

He who considers present affairs and ancient ones readily understands that all cities and all peoples have the same desires and the same traits and that they always have had them. He who diligently examined past events easily foresees future ones in every country and can apply to them the remedies used by the ancients or, not finding any that have been used, can devise new ones because of the similarity of the events. But because these considerations are neglected or are not understood by those who read or, if they are understood, are not known to rulers, the same dissensions appear in every age.

[Book 1,] Chapter 53. The Populace Deceived by a False Appearance of Good Things, Many Times Decrees its Own Ruin, and Great Hopes and Mighty Promises Easily Move It

* * *[T]he people, deceived by a false image of good, many times desire their own ruin. And if somebody in whom they have faith does not convince them that what they want is bad and explain what is good, countless dangers and losses come upon the republic. And when chance causes the people to have faith in no one, as sometimes happens, since they have been deceived in the past both by things and by men, of necessity the republic is ruined.

* * *

Therefore, considering when it is easy and when it is hard to get a people to accept something, one can make this distinction: either what you are trying to persuade them of shows on its surface gain or loss; or the decision to be made

---

† From *Machiavelli: The Chief Works and Others*, trans. Allan Gilbert, vol. 1 (Durham: Duke University Press) 278; 303–5; 468–69. Copyright © 1989 by Allan Gilbert. Reprinted by permission of Duke University Press.

seems courageous or cowardly. When in a plan put before the people gain is apparent, even though loss be hidden beneath, and when it seems courageous, even though the ruin of the republic be hidden beneath, always the multitude is easily persuaded to approve. Likewise the multitude is always with difficulty persuaded to accept proposals in which either cowardice or loss appears, even if beneath them be hidden safety and gain.

* * *

In Greece, in the city of Athens, never could Nicias, a very influential and prudent man, persuade the people that it was unwise to attack Sicily; yet when that decision was made against the opinions of the wise, the total ruin of Athens resulted.

[Book 3,]Chapter 16. In Difficult Times True Ability is Sought for; In Easy Times Able Men Do Not Hold Office, But Those Who Through Riches or Family are Most Popular.

[Nicias as an example]

It always has been and always will be true that in republics great and exceptional men are neglected in times of peace; at such times envy of the reputation their ability gives them raises in many citizens a desire to be not merely their equals but their superiors. On this there is a good passage in Thucydides the Greek historian, showing that when the Athenian republic had the advantage in the Peloponnesian War and had bridled the pride of Sparta and almost subjugated all the rest of Greece, she became so proud that she planned to conquer Sicily. This undertaking was debated in Athens. Alcibiades and some other citizens advised the attempt, in their concern not with the public good but with their own reputation, since they planned to be in charge of such an expedition. But Nicias, the man of highest reputation in Athens, spoke against it. In addressing the people, the chief argument he brought forward to give them faith in him was this: when he advised that war should not be made, he advised something not to his own advantage, because he knew that, when Athens was at peace, countless citizens were eager to be advanced ahead of him, but if they made war, he knew that no citizen would be superior or equal to him.

[In quiet times republics neglect capable men]

We see, then, that republics show this defect: they pay slight attention to capable men in quiet times. This condition makes such men feel injured in two ways: first, they fail to attain their proper rank; second, they are obliged to have as associates and superiors men who are unworthy and of less ability than themselves. This abuse in republics has produced much turmoil, because those citizens who see themselves undeservedly rejected, and know that they can be neglected only in times that are easy and not perilous, make an effort to disturb them by stirring up new wars to the damage of the republic. When I consider possible remedies, I find two: the first is to keep the citizens poor, so that, when without goodness and wisdom, they cannot corrupt themselves or others with riches; the second is to arrange that such republics will continually make war, and therefore always will need citizens of high repute, like the Romans in their early days.

THOMAS HOBBES

The name of Thomas Hobbes (1588–1679) is frequently linked with that of Thucydides, whose history he translated. Both writers engage vital questions regarding the roles of reason and the passions in shaping human actions. Some scholars have found their depictions of the human condition distinctly similar, while others identify vital differences. What is certain is that Hobbes himself was drawn to Thucydides and found his own view of the world reflected in Thucydides' history of the Peloponnesian War. He took care in his introductory remarks "To the Readers" to underscore the virtues of Thucydides' text.

To the Readers[†]

   Though this translation have already past the censure of some, whose judgments I very much esteem: yet because there is something, I know not what, in the censure of a multitude, more terrible than any single judgment, how severe or exact soever, I have thought it discretion in all men, that have to do with so many, and to me, in my want of perfection, necessary, to bespeak your candour. Which that I may upon the better reason hope for, I am willing to acquaint you briefly, upon what grounds I undertook this work at first; and have since, by publishing it, put myself upon the hazard of your censure, with so small hope of glory as from a thing of this nature can be expected. For I know, that mere translations have in them this property: that they may much disgrace, if not well done; but if well, not much commend the doer.
   It hath been noted by divers, that Homer in poesy, Aristotle in philosophy, Demosthenes in eloquence, and others of the ancients in other knowledge, do still maintain their primacy: none of them exceeded, some not approached, by any in these later ages. And in the number of these is justly ranked also our Thucydides; a workman no less perfect in his work, than any of the former; and in whom (I believe with many others) the faculty of writing history is at the highest. For the principal and proper work of history being to instruct and enable men, by the knowledge of actions past, to bear themselves prudently in the present and providently towards the future: there is not extant any other (merely human) that doth more naturally and fully perform it, than this of my author. It is true, that there be many excellent and profitable histories written since: and in some of them there be inserted very wise discourses, both of manners and policy. But being discourses inserted, and not of the contexture of the narration, they indeed commend the knowledge of the writer, but not the history itself: the nature whereof is merely narrative. In others, there be subtle conjectures at the secret aims and inward cogitations of such as fall under their pen; which is also none of the least virtues in a history, where conjecture is thoroughly grounded, not forced to serve the purpose of the writer in adorning his style, or manifesting his subtlety in conjecturing. But these conjectures cannot often be certain, unless withal so evident, that the narration itself may be sufficient to suggest the same also to the reader. But Thucydides is one, who, though he never digress to read a lecture, moral or political, upon his own text, nor

---

†   Richard Schlatter, *Hobbes' Thucydides* (New Brunswick: Rutgers University Press, 1975) 6–7. Reprinted by permission of Rutgers University Press.

enter into men's hearts further than the acts themselves evidently guide him: is yet accounted the most politic historiographer that ever writ. The reason whereof I take to be this. He filleth his narrations with that choice of matter, and ordereth them with that judgment, and with such perspicuity and efficacy expresseth himself, that, as Plutarch saith, he maketh his auditor a spectator. For he setteth his reader in the assemblies of the people and in the senate, at their debating; in the streets, at their seditions; and in the field, at their battles. So that look how much a man of understanding might have added to his experience, if he had then lived a beholder of their proceedings, and familiar with the men and business of the time: so much almost may he profit now, by attentive reading of the same here written. He may from the narrations draw out lessons to himself, and of himself be able to trace the drifts and counsels of the actors to their seat.

[Hobbes's *Leviathan* has often been considered the greatest masterpiece of political philosophy in the English language. The selection that appears below contains Hobbes's famous characterization of life as "solitary, poor, nasty, brutish, and short."]

Leviathan[†]

Chap. XIII.

Of the NATURALL CONDITION *of Mankind, as concerning their Felicity, and Misery.*

Nature hath made men so equall, in the faculties of body, and mind; as that though there bee found one man sometimes manifestly stronger in body, or of quicker mind then another; yet when all is reckoned together, the difference between man, and man, is not so considerable, as that one man can thereupon claim to himselfe any benefit, to which another may not pretend, as well as he. For as to the strength of body, the weakest has strength enough to kill the strongest, either by secret machination, or by confederacy with others, that are in the same danger with himselfe.

And as to the faculties of the mind, (setting aside the arts grounded upon words, and especially that skill of proceeding upon generall, and infallible rules, called Science; which very few have, and but in few things; as being not a native faculty, born with us; nor attained, (as Prudence,) while we look after somewhat els,) I find yet a greater equality amongst men, than that of strength. For Prudence, is but Experience; which equall time, equally bestowes on all men, in those things they equally apply themselves unto. That which may perhaps make such equality incredible, is but a vain conceipt of ones owne wisdome, which almost all men think they have in a greater degree, than the Vulgar; that is, than all men but themselves, and a few others, whom by Fame, or for concurring with themselves, they approve. For such is the nature of men, that howsoever they may acknowledge many others to be more witty, or more eloquent, or more learned; Yet they will hardly believe there be many so wise as themselves: For they see their own wit at hand, and other mens at a distance. But this

† From Thomas Hobbes, *Leviathan*, Chapter XIII, eds. Richard E. Flathmann and David Johnston (New York: W. W. Norton & Company, 1997).

proveth rather that men are in that point equall, than unequall. For there is not ordinarily a greater signe of the equall distribution of any thing, than that every man is contented with his share.

From this equality of ability, ariseth equality of hope in the attaining of our Ends. And therefore if any two men desire the same thing, which neverthelesse they cannot both enjoy, they become enemies; and in the way to their End, (which is principally their owne conservation, and sometimes their delectation only,) endeavour to destroy, or subdue one an other. And from hence it comes to passe, that where an Invader hath no more to feare, than an other mans single power; if one plant, sow, build, or possesse a convenient Seat, others may probably be expected to come prepared with forces united, to dispossesse, and deprive him, not only of the fruit of his labour, but also of his life, or liberty. And the Invader again is in the like danger of another.

And from this diffidence of one another, there is no way for any man to secure himselfe, so reasonable, as Anticipation; that is, by force, or wiles, to master the persons of all men he can, so long, till he see no other power great enough to endanger him: And this is no more than his own conservation requireth, and is generally allowed. Also because there be some, that taking pleasure in contemplating their own power in the acts of conquest, which they pursue farther than their security requires; if others, that otherwise would be glad to be at ease within modest bounds, should not by invasion increase their power, they would not be able, long time, by standing only on their defence, to subsist. And by consequence, such augmentation of dominion over men, being necessary to a mans conservation, it ought to be allowed him.

Againe, men have no pleasure, (but on the contrary a great deale of griefe) in keeping company, where there is no power able to over-awe them all. For every man looketh that his companion should value him, at the same rate he sets upon himselfe: And upon all signes of contempt, or undervaluing, naturally endeavours, as far as he dares (which amongst them that have no common power to keep them in quiet, is far enough to make them destroy each other,) to extort a greater value from his contemners, by dommage; and from others, by the example.

So that in the nature of man, we find three principall causes of quarrell. First, Competition; Secondly, Diffidence; Thirdly, Glory.

The first, maketh men invade for Gain; the second, for Safety; and the third, for Reputation. The first use Violence, to make themselves Masters of other mens persons, wives, children, and cattell; the second, to defend them; the third, for trifles, as a word, a smile, a different opinion, and any other signe of undervalue, either direct in their Persons, or by reflexion in their Kindred, their Friends, their Nation, their Profession, or their Name.

Hereby it is manifest, that during the time men live without a common Power to keep them all in awe, they are in that condition which is called Warre; and such a warre, as is of every man, against every man. For WARRE, consisteth not in Battell onely, or the act of fighting; but in a tract of time, wherein the Will to contend by Battell is sufficiently known: and therefore the notion of *Time*, is to be considered in the nature of Warre; as it is in the nature of Weather. For as the nature of Foule weather, lyeth not in a showre or two of rain; but in an inclination thereto of many dayes together: So the nature of War, consisteth not in actuall fighting; but in the known disposition thereto, during all the time there is no assurance to the contrary. All other time is PEACE.

Whatsoever therefore is consequent to a time of Warre, where every man is Enemy to every man; the same is consequent to the time, wherein men live without other security, than what their own strength, and their own invention shall furnish them withall. In such condition, there is no place for Industry; because the fruit thereof is uncertain: and consequently no Culture of the Earth; no Navigation, nor use of the commodities that may be imported by Sea; no commodious Building; no Instruments of moving, and removing such things as require much force; no Knowledge of the face of the Earth; no account of Time; no Arts; no Letters; no Society; and which is worst of all, continuall feare, and danger of violent death; And the life of man, solitary, poore, nasty, brutish, and short.

It may seem strange to some man, that has not well weighed these things; that Nature should thus dissociate, and render men apt to invade, and destroy one another: and he may therefore, not trusting to this Inference, made from the Passions, desire perhaps to have the same confirmed by Experience. Let him therefore consider with himselfe, when taking a journey, he armes himselfe, and seeks to go well accompanied; when going to sleep, he locks his dores; when even in his house he locks his chests; and this when he knowes there bee Lawes, and publike Officers, armed, to revenge all injuries shall bee done him; what opinion he has of his fellow subjects, when he rides armed; of his fellow Citizens, when he locks his dores; and of his children, and servants, when he locks his chests. Does he not there as much accuse mankind by his actions, as I do by my words? But neither of us accuse mans nature in it. The Desires, and other Passions of man, are in themselves no Sin. No more are the Actions, that proceed from those Passions, till they know a Law that forbids them: which till Lawes be made they cannot know: nor can any Law be made, till they have agreed upon the Person that shall make it.

It may peradventure be thought, there was never such a time, nor condition of warre as this; and I believe it was never generally so, over all the world: but there are many places, where they live so now. For the savage people in many places of *America*, except the government of small Families, the concord whereof dependeth on naturall lust, have no government at all; and live at this day in that brutish manner, as I said before. Howsoever, it may be perceived what manner of life there would be, where there were no common Power to feare; by the manner of life, which men that have formerly lived under a peacefull government, use to degenerate into, in a civill Warre.

But though there had never been any time, wherein particular men were in a condition of warre one against another; yet in all times, Kings, and Persons of Soveraigne authority, because of their Independency, are in continuall jealousies, and in the state and posture of Gladiators; having their weapons pointing, and their eyes fixed on one another; that is, their Forts, Garrisons, and Guns upon the Frontiers of their Kingdomes; and continuall Spyes upon their neighbours; which is a posture of War. But because they uphold thereby, the Industry of their Subjects; there does not follow from it, that misery, which accompanies the Liberty of particular men.

To this warre of every man against every man, this also is consequent; that nothing can be Unjust. The notions of Right and Wrong, Justice and Injustice have there no place. Where there is no common Power, there is no Law: where no Law, no Injustice. Force, and Fraud, are in warre the two Cardinall vertues. Justice, and Injustice are none of the Faculties neither of the Body, nor Mind. If they were, they might be in a man that were alone in the world, as well as his Senses, and Passions. They are Qualities, that relate to men in Society, not in

Solitude. It is consequent also to the same condition, that there be no Propriety, no Dominion, no *Mine* and *Thine* distinct; but onely that to be every mans, that he can get; and for so long, as he can keep it. And thus much for the ill condition, which man by meer Nature is actually placed in; though with a possibility to come out of it, consisting partly in the Passions, partly in his Reason.

The Passions that encline men to Peace, are Feare of Death; Desire of such things as are necessary to commodious living; and a Hope by their Industry to obtain them. And Reason suggesteth convenient Articles of Peace, upon which men may be drawn to agreement. These Articles, are they, which otherwise are called the Lawes of Nature.

WALTER KARP

The wars of the twentieth century have frequently brought Thucydides to the minds of those intrigued by the persistence of conflict within the human community. World War I, World War II, the Korean War, the cold war, the Vietnam War and even the brief Gulf War of 1991 led journalists and politicians to invoke the poignance of Thucydides' perspective. In 1981 Walter Karp explored the relevance of Thucydides' perspective across the decades of his own adult life.

The Two Thousand Years' War†

Around the time Republicans were vowing to "roll back Communism," a wise old college professor of mine suggested that his Humanities 1 class might get more out of Thucydides if it compared the Peloponnesian War to the ongoing struggle between America and Russia, then only recently named the Cold War. This, he assured us (quite needlessly), would not do violence to the great Athenian historian, since Thucydides himself believed that "human nature being what it is, events now past will recur in similar or analogous forms." Of the profundity of that remark Humanities 1 had not the slightest inkling. Nonetheless, analogies fell at our feet like ripe apples.

The combatants we identified readily. Authoritarian Sparta, ruling over a mass of terrified helots, was plainly the Soviet Union. Democratic Athens was America, of course. There were even neat correspondences between the two sets of foes. Sparta, as Thucydides tells us, was an insulated, agricultural, and sluggish state, rather like Russia. Athens, like America, was commercial, fast-moving, and far-ranging. "They are never at home," complained a Corinthian envoy to the Spartans, "and you are never away from it." In Athens and America, commerce and democracy seemed, 2,300 years apart, to have nurtured the very same kind of citizen. "I doubt if the world can produce a man," said great Pericles, "who, where he has only himself to depend upon, is equal to so many emergencies and graced by so happy a versatility as the Athenian." What the Athenians possessed, concluded Humanities 1, was Yankee ingenuity.

More striking than the analogies between past and present combatants were the resemblances between the two conflicts. In neither struggle do the enemies fight alone. Like America and the Soviet Union, Athens and Sparta are leaders of great confederations of inferior and subordinate allies. Similarly, they represent hostile political principles, Athens championing democracy, Sparta a traditional oligarchy. In the Peloponnesian War, as in the Cold War, the enemies are "ideological" foes. And neither is physically capable of winning. Sparta, with its invincible infantry, is so superior by land that Athens avoids pitched battles at all costs. Athens is so superior by sea that Spartan ships flee her peerless navy on sight. As a result, the Peloponnesian War, like the Cold War, is fought indirectly, peripherally, and spasmodically.

That was about as far as Humanities 1 got in its hunt for analogies between the ancient struggle for supremacy in Hellas and the ongoing struggle for supremacy in the modern world. Youth and ignorance doubtless limited our inquiry, but a greater handicap was the fact that the Peloponnesian War lasted twenty-seven years while the Cold War had not yet survived six.

That was nearly three decades ago, decades in which the struggle for supremacy between America and Russia did not cease for a single day. When I decided to reread Thucydides, the struggle was about to enter a new and more vigorous phase, under a newly elected president and a political faction that Thucydides would have unhesitatingly described as the war party. Two things struck me as I read: that the Cold War, now so long protracted, had come to resemble the Peloponnesian War more than ever and that in this resemblance lay a wholly unexpected vindication of political history, created by Thucydides.

* * *

The grounds for vindication are clear enough. Ancient Hellas and the modern world have nothing in common technologically, economically, or socially, none of those "factors" so dear to the hearts of the modern historian. If the ancient war and the modern war bear strong and essential resemblances, only political causes could have produced them; precisely those political causes that Thucydides' titanic genius found operating in the Peloponnesian War.

"Of the gods we believe, and of men we know," an Athenian envoy tells an ally of Sparta's, "that by a necessary law of their nature they rule wherever they can." Our nature as *political* beings is what Thucydides describes. Nothing compels men to enter the bright, dangerous arena of political action, but what lures them there—love of fame, power, glory, fortune, distinction—makes it fairly certain, a "law," that they will strive to rule over others. According to Pericles, Athenians, out of a love of splendid deeds and for the glory of their city, "forced every sea and land to be the highway of [their] daring." In doing so they also forged a far-flung empire, which they had to struggle continuously to maintain; for if men strive for dominion, others strive to resist it. "You risk so much to retain your empire," the Athenian envoy is told, "and your subjects so much to get rid of it."

In the striving to gain dominion and in the inevitable struggle to maintain it, men produce one thing with certainty—they "make" history. Such was Thucydides' great discovery. History is the story woven by men's deeds, and the political nature of man provides a completely intelligible account of the story. That is why the great Athenian dared to predict that the tragic events of the Peloponnesian War would one day recur in similar forms.

Consider the origins of the Peloponnesian War. Thucydides describes the petty squabbles that poison relations between certain allies of mighty Sparta and those of upstart Athens. The squabbles set in motion the great train of events, but, like Soviet–American squabbles over the Yalta accords[1], they are not, says Thucy-dides, the "real cause" of the war. "The growth of the power of Athens and the alarm which this inspired in Lacedaemon [Sparta] made war inevitable."

In 432 B.C. the Hellenic world reached a political condition that the mod-ern world was to duplicate in 1945 A.D.—and with much the same result. Two superpowers, Athens and Sparta, have so completely absorbed all the available power in Hellas that any further gain by one appears a menacing loss to the other. Under such conditions no real peace is possible. Of course if men and states accepted the diminution of their power there would have been no Pelo-ponnesian War (and precious little human history), but that is just what men and states do not accept.

War with Sparta is unavoidable, Pericles tells the Athenian assembly (it is pondering whether to accede to a Spartan fiat), because "we must attempt to hand down our power to our posterity unimpaired." Moral scruple has nothing to do with it. The Athenian empire "is, to speak somewhat plainly, a tyranny," says Pericles, referring to Athens' crushing subjugation of her nominal allies. "To take it [the empire] perhaps was wrong, but to let it go is unsafe." With re-spect to its unwilling allies. Athens resembles the Soviet Union and, like it, must expend a great deal of her strength keeping her "allies" down.

Because such tyranny is inherently unstable, Pericles urges his country-men to fight a strategically defensive war and seek no "fresh conquests" in the course of it. The result of the Periclean policy reveals the extraordinary, history-making dynamism released by merely trying to hang on to one's own. Framed by a statesman of the highest genius, the policy scores a brilliant success and then leads Athens to its ultimate ruin.

To the astonishment of the Hellenic world, the newfangled Athenian navy, as Pericles foresaw, proves tactically superior to Sparta's great infantry, which the Athenians, safely walled up in their city, can avoid with impunity. Facing a foe so swift, so daring, so immune to injury, Sparta, after seven years of war, be-comes deeply unnerved. "Being new to the experience of adversity," observes Thucydides, "they had lost all confidence in themselves."

Buoyed up by their unexpected triumphs over the traditional leader of Hel-las, however, the Athenians fall prey to the fateful temptation inherent in all po-litical action—rashness. Success "made them confuse their strength with their hopes," says Thucydides, providing, at least, a definition of political rashness that cannot be improved upon. After a Spartan garrison surrenders without a fight, something unprecedented in Spartan history, the Athenians are ripe for any daring folly; just as President Truman, blinded by General MacArthur's sweeping victory at Inchon[2], rashly attempted to conquer North Korea; and just as President Kennedy, puffed up by his Cuban missile triumph[3], was ripe for the Vietnam war—a confusion of strength and hope that drained the country of both.

The Peloponnesian War, like the Cold War, brings civil war and revolu-tion in its wake. The political causes are the same in both cases. When states are at peace, hostile factions and classes within countries are willing to rub along together. But when the great powers are desperately competing for allies,

1. Most terms of the agreement reached at Yalta in February 1945 by Winston Churchill, Franklin Roo-sevelt, and Joseph Stalin remained secret until the end of World War II. When that war ended and the cold war began, the Yalta agreements came under heavy criticism and disagreements arose concerning their implications [*Editor*].
2. In 1950, during the Korean War [*Editor*].
3. In 1962 [*Editor*].

domestic rivals are no longer willing to preserve internal peace. Popular leaders can call on the opposing power to put their domestic enemies to the sword; oligarchic factions, to set their own cities aflame.

Love of dominion, the desire for "the first place in the city" (never far from the surface in peacetime), convulses all Hellas in wartime. Men betray their own cities without scruple and cheer foreigners for killing their own countrymen. Political exiles, aided by foreign powers, wage ceaseless war against their own cities. The Peloponnesian War, which spawns a half dozen analogues of the Bay of Pigs[4] and of Moscow-trained revolutionary brigades, blights the integrity of the city-state, just as the Cold War now erodes the integrity of the nation-state.

Athens is by no means immune to the war's corrupting effects on domestic politics. At one point Athenians undergo a spasm of political paranoia that duplicates with remarkable fidelity the American McCarthy era[5]. The causes here, too, are the same, as the sequence of events clearly shows. Shortly after the Spartan garrison's stunning surrender, Sparta humbly sues for peace, and the Athenians, a little out of breath themselves, reluctantly and ruefully accept. Thucydides regards the peace, which lasts six years, as a mere incident in a continuous war. It was, says Thucydides, "an unstable armistice [that] did not prevent either party doing the other the most effectual injury."

The chief reason for the instability is the emergence in Athens of a self-serving war party. Ten years have passed since the outbreak of war. Great Pericles is dead; new men have arisen with ambitious of their own, Pericles' own ward Alcibiades among them. The Periclean policy of deadlock, based on the determination to preserve past glories, does not content them. They want to win fresh glory for themselves, and with it, says Thucydides, "the undisturbed direction of the people." Their real complaint about the peace with Sparta is that it is an unambitious use of Athenian power (which is exactly what the American foes of détente believe).

Confusing strength with hope, the leaders of the war party think Athens can do far more than merely hold Sparta at bay; it can destroy Spartan pretensions forever. Like the Republicans of 1951–52, the war party will accept, in effect, "no substitute for victory." Like millions of Americans in 1951–52, the Athenian people, "persuaded that nothing could withstand them," find deadlock exasperating. Why must irresistible Athens suffer the endless tensions of the unstable armistice? Is it possible that there are oligarchy-loving pro-Spartans in their midst?

A shocking act of impiety, analogous to the Alger Hiss trial[6], turns baseless suspicion into angry conviction: "oligarchical and monarchical" Athenians are conspiring to subvert the democratic constitution. The enraged citizenry demands arrests; blatant perjurers supply the evidence; nonconformists, including Alcibiades, fall prey to the mania. At the war's outset Pericles had proudly noted the extraordinary personal freedom enjoyed by Athenians, who "do not feel called upon to be angry with our neighbor for

---

4. The unsuccessful Bay of Pigs invasion (1961) revealed the willingness of the United States to back insurgents involved in civil wars. The Cuban exiles who failed in their attempt to overthrow the communist regime of Fidel Castro had been trained by the American Central Intelligence Agency [Editor].
5. During the early 1950s, U.S. Senator Joseph McCarthy of Wisconsin (1908–57) exercised a reign of terror in the Senate, accusing numerous private citizens and public officials of communist sympathies. By the time his influence began to wane in 1954, many lives and careers had been ruined [Editor].
6. Substantial public controversy surrounded the case of Alger Hiss (1904–96), who was suspected of espionage during the cold war and sentenced to a five-year prison term in 1950 for perjury. Many people have believed that the Federal Bureau of Investigation tampered with the evidence in order to secure his conviction [Editor].

doing what he likes." Now those who live differently from their neighbors fall under suspicion of treason. A war begun to safeguard the power of a democracy profoundly corrupts democracy.

Firmly in control of a rapidly degenerating polity, the war party launches its grandiose plan to tilt the balance of power once and for all against the Spartans. Beyond the little world of Hellas, across the Ionian Sea, lie the broad island of Sicily and a dozen Greek colonial city-states. The Athenians, as Thucydides icily remarks, do not even know Sicily's size; they are ignorantly contemptuous of the island's colonial "rabble." Nonetheless, the self-vaunting, overconfident Athenians intend to conquer it and use that huge accession of imperial power to throw down Sparta itself. When an opponent of the enterprise warns Athenians of the enormous costs and hazards of a war so far from home, enthusiasm for the expedition grows even warmer.

In the seventeenth year of the Peloponnesian War, "by far the most costly and splendid Hellenic force that had ever been sent out by a single city" sets sail for faraway Sicily. Vietnam is but a pale analogy to what fortune inflicts on the great armada. Thucydides' account of its hideous, heartbreaking fate—how its leaders blundered, how its strength drained away, how its dauntless Athenian oarsmen, the backbone of the democracy, lost their nerve and their courage— is one of the great feats of historical writing. On the hostile shores of a distant island, before the walls of an underestimated enemy, the power of Athens crumbles away forever.

Since the Cold War continues with no end in sight, its story remains incomplete. Still, it seems fairly certain even now that the same principle that makes the Peloponnesian War intelligible, 2,300 years after its end, will make the Cold War intelligible to posterity: "Of the gods we believe, and of men we know, that by a necessary law of their nature they rule wherever they can."

INTERPRETATIONS

THEODOR GOMPERZ

Thucydides found a receptive audience in nineteenth-century positivists who denigrated speculation and subjectivity and valued above all else what they viewed as the objective gathering and analysis of data. The German classicist Theodor Gomperz (1832–1912) wrote admiringly of Thucydides in his monumental *Greek Thinkers*, composed over a period of more than ten years. The Thucydides of Gomperz is a rationalist whose secular world view contrasted sharply with that of his fellow Athenians.

[Secular Thucydides][†]

There is hardly any pair of contemporaries who offer a more glaring contrast than Herodotus and Thucydides. Barely a score of years divided their works from one another, but a gulf of centuries seems to yawn between their temper and inspiration. Herodotus creates throughout an entirely old-fashioned impression; Thucydides is a modern of the moderns. He made a clean sweep of the poetical and religious bias, the legendary and novelistic sympathies, and the primitive beliefs, rarely mitigated by the light of criticism, which marked the elder historian. The gaze of Thucydides was primarily fixed on the political factors, on the actual relations of forces, on the natural foundation, so to speak, of historical phenomena. He looked for their springs, not in the dispensations of supernatural beings, nor yet, except in a moderate degree, in the caprices and passions of individual men. Behind those he always sought for the universal forces that animated them, for the conditions of the peoples, and the interests of the states. Thus he prefaced his discussion of all the points of difference which led to the Peloponnesian war by the pregnant observation —

> "The real though unavowed cause (of the war) I believe to have been the growth of the Athenian power, which terrified the Lacedæmonians and forced them into war."[1]

His biographer states that he was a pupil of Anaxagoras, the mechanical physicist, and the report, whether true or not, is fully in harmony with his view of the world as well as with his treatment of history. It was his constant endeavour to describe the course of human affairs as though it were a process of nature informed by the light of inexorable causality. His pursuit of strict objectivity was so keen that long passages of his work may be read without obtaining a hint to which side his favour inclined, and to which side his disfavour. Yet his power of dispassionate narration is no proof of the absence of passion. No one can doubt this who knows that complete devotion to human affairs, and their faithful reproduction, can only successfully be founded on an intense and absorbing personal interest. Moreover, it is not in isolated instances alone that the objective tranquillity which Thucydides so carefully preserved was interrupted by a sudden outcry of emotion; his description of the fatal Sicilian expedition affects us with the pathos of tragedy.

Herodotus wrote history "in order," in his own words, "that the actions of men may not be effaced by time, nor the great and wondrous deeds . . . deprived

---

† Theodore Gomperz, *Greek Thinkers: A History of Ancient Philosophy* (John Murray, 1920) 503–12. Greek words or phrases have been deleted when preceded or succeeded by an English translation.
1. Thuc., i.23: trans. Jowett.

of renown."[2] Nor is there any doubt that Thucydides, in his inmost soul, was moved by similar impulses. But in the foreground of his narrative, as though in self-justification, he wrote—

"But if he who desires to have before his eyes a true picture of the events which have happened, and of the like events which may be expected to happen hereafter in the order of human things, shall pronounce what I have written to be useful, then I shall be satisfied."[3]

In this sense, and because he was conscious that the rejection of all legendary issues had made his work less "fascinating," he spoke of it with strong but just self-respect as "an everlasting possession, not a prize composition which is heard and forgotten."[4] The strict sobriety in the demarcation of his purpose was reproduced by Thucydides when he came to choose the means to his end. Surprise has recently been expressed that he preferred to deal with a short span of contemporary history rather than to fill his canvas with pictures of universal historical interest. But the historian has returned his own reply to such expressions of surprise. Again and again he bitterly complained of the difficulty of attaining complete accuracy about the events even of his own day:—

"Of the events of the war I have not ventured to speak from any chance information, nor according to any notion of my own. I have described nothing," he continued, "but what I either saw myself, or learned from others of whom I made the most careful and particular inquiry. The task was a laborious one, because eye-witnesses of the same occurrences gave different accounts of them, as they remembered or were interested in the actions of one side or the other."[5]

Bitter indeed is the complaint: "So little trouble do men take in the search after truth; so readily do they accept whatever comes first to hand." ***With that delight in criticism which the Greeks seemed to imbibe with their mothers' milk, and the influence of which Herodotus himself, good-humoured though he was, did not escape in respect to his predecessor Hecatæus,[6] Thucydides likewise was infected. He sought out errors which Herodotus had committed with special reference to Spartan institutions, and accompanied them with the remark that "there are many other matters, not obscured by time, but contemporary, about which the other Hellenes are equally mistaken."[7]

Nevertheless, Thucydides could not or would not altogether avoid the claims of the history of dim antiquity. On such occasions, his method was marked by certain peculiarities, which require to be characterized. Two essential points may be mentioned. Thucydides was the first historian to employ the method of inverse deduction. When trustworthy authority failed him, he would argue back from the conditions and institutions—even the names—of the present to those of times past. Thus, in seeking to establish the fact that the room occupied by the Acropolis at Athens had once contained the whole city, he reminded his readers of the vernacular usage by which the word "city," or Polis, signified Acropolis, or "the city on a height." And a similar purpose inspired the second fact quoted by him in this connection, namely, that the most important shrines of the gods were partly included in that district and partly found in its

2. Herod., i.1: trans. Cary.
3. Thuc.. i.22: trans. Jowett.
4. Thuc., i.22: trans. Jowett.
5. Thuc., i.22: trans. Jowett.
6. Ethnographer, geographer, and historian (c. 500 B.C.) whose writings survive only in fragments. Hecataeus apparently made use of myth in his attempts to reconstruct history [Editor].
7. Thuc., i.20: trans. Jowett.

immediate neighbourhood, and that certain religious rites were associated with a spring situated in that spot. The same method may be observed in Aristotle's constitutional treatise, which has been discovered in quite recent times.[8] The second point to be noted is the use made by Thucydides—and by him first of all—of the present conditions of less highly developed peoples to illustrate the earlier stages of civilization of more advanced communities. The historians of morality, religion, and law in our own day employ them to the full extent of their capacity, and have brought the study of ethnology into close connection with that of prehistoric man. In Central Brazil, for instance, there is still an actual "Stone Age," and the pile-work in the New Guinea of to-day recalls the similar buildings in prehistoric Europe. At this point we may give an instance of the comparative method of Thucydides. Nestor in the *Odyssey*, in questioning Telemachus, on his arrival at Pylos, about the objects of his voyage, mentions piracy in the same breath as the business of commerce, and with no trace of moral disapproval. The courtly *savants* of Alexandria and the dry-as-dust scholars of the nineteenth century have vied with one another in their painful astonishment at the state of Nestor's conscience, and in their attempts to explain it away. The first had lost their sympathy with the naïve primitiveness of the ancients, and the second has not yet regained it. In this respect Thucydides stood on a pinnacle above them both. He had no intention or desire to force the Homeric verses into a Procrustean bed of meaning. He was rather at pains to shed a brilliant light on the rude minds of Homeric heroes by comparing them with the modes of life and sentiment among backward Greek tribes of his own day. For here, as in other passages, he was true to his principle of vivifying and enriching his picture of antiquity by appropriate parallels.

No doubt can subsist as to the legitimacy of this use of the evidence of Homer. If popular poems can tell us nothing else with certainty, at least they afford trustworthy evidence of the sentiment of those for whom they were intended. But Thucydides went further. He summoned the Homeric poems to the bar of history in his attempt to reconstruct the early annals of Greece. And if we measure that attempt by modern canons of criticism, we are constrained to arraign Thucydides, with Herodotus, on the charge of adopting the semi-historical method. But at least he erred in good company. To the names of Hecatæus and Herodotus must be added that of Aristotle and those of almost all the thinkers and authors of antiquity. We may accordingly try to fix more precisely the point of view from which Thucydides surveyed his theme. He believed on the whole in the historical reality cf the human personages and of their deeds mentioned in the epic poems; and to a certain extent in legend generally. Hellen, the ancestor of the Hellenic race, was as good an historical personage for Thucydides as Ion, the ancestor of the Ionians, was for Aristotle. So far, then, the issues are quite clear. We are justified of our scepticim, and even the most critical of the Greeks were the victims of their own credulity. But when we come to the race of the Atridæ[9], to Agamemnon, and to the Trojan War, we cannot speak with equal certainty. Scholarship at least has not yet said its last word on these matters. It is the habit of heroic legends in the great majority of instances to go to reality for their central figures and their chief events, however freely they may subsequently deal with them. The mediæval epicists in France, for example, turned the ages upside down and made Charlemagne participate in the Crusades. But despite this violence to chronology, they cannot be said to

---

8. The treatise known as *The Constitution of the Athenians* was discovered in 1880 and published in 1891. Its attribution to Aristotle is uncertain; if he did not write it, then one of his pupils did [*Editor*].
9. The Atridae (sons of Atreus) were Agamemnon and Menelaus [*Editor*].

have invented either Charlemagne or the Crusades, nor yet to have borrowed
them from the storehouse of mythology. And when we revert to the method of
Thucydides, we find that his faithfulness to tradition was limited to the principal features displayed by the narratives of the poets. Again and again he expressed in emphatic language his distrust of the details of their stories, and he
never lent the least favour to the method of historical patchwork so much
beloved by his predecessor. It was not his purpose to transform, nor to harmo-
nize, but rather to supplement the materials with which he dealt. He was clearly
convinced that he had no means at his disposal which would enable him to extract anything like a trustworthy picture of the distant past from the embellish-
ments, exaggerations, and disfigurements of the poets. Accordingly he struck
out a wholly new path of investigation, and pursued it in a manner which tes-
tifies at once to the depth of his insight and the breadth of his mental horizon.
The great instrument which the historian employed, without fear, but without
temerity, was the deductive method, in the sole form in which it is adapted to
unravel the problems of history, namely, as inverse deduction. This, then, was
the equipment of Thucydides. He was, further, gifted with a faculty of vision,
to which nothing was too great or too small, and he was free from every bias and
limitation of national conceit or flattering predilection. Dowered with these advantages, and employing the handful of data which he considered trustworthy,
he succeeded in producing a sketch of the earliest stages of Greek evolution,
which in its outline is certainly correct. We may briefly summarize its chief features. It showed that the Greeks were late in evolving the consciousness of national unity; that in an earlier phase of their civilization they were hardly
distinguishable from the Barbarians or non-Greeks; that pillage and piracy by
land and by sea afforded them a chief means of subsistence; and that their advance was retarded for a long time by the difficulties of intercourse and by the
sparseness and poverty of the population. Moreover, the evidence was adduced,
and skillfully employed, of the changes effected in course of time in the situation of cities, of the gradual progress in the art of shipbuilding, of the fashion in
clothing and headgear, and of the alterations in the garb of the competitors at
the Olympic games. Nor did Thucydides omit to mention the sterility of the soil
of Attica, the security thus guaranteed from foreign attack, and the stability
which was thus afforded—a stability favourable in turn to the immigration of
foreign families, with its natural consequence in the more rapid increase of population, and the eventual colonization of Ionia. Similarly, he noted the diminished sedentary habit and the increased love of wandering among Greek tribes,
due to the lack of regular agriculture; he was aware of the change of proprietors
which fell most frequently on the most fertile regions; and he remarked how the
increase of wealth assisted the transformation of the patriarchal monarchy into
the so-called tyranny. With the foregoing examples we may fitly illustrate the
deductive method as employed by Thucydides, and the conclusions to which
it led him.

    The attitude of our historian towards the poets in their accounts of human
events and natural contingencies may be described as one of cool scepticism.
In respect to their tales of gods and miracles, however, his distrust rose to absolute repudiation. Moreover, it is apparent that he belonged to a circle of
thoughtful minds within which this disbelief passed as something self-evident
and not requiring any special mention or justification. There is no trace, for example, of the boisterous tone in which Herodotus contested the truth of some
of the tales which he considered incredible. Thucydides obviously never conceived the possibility that he could be suspected of giving credence to an in-

terruption of the course of nature. Accordingly he treated the oracles and sooth-sayers with chilling contempt, sometimes diversified by biting satire. Moreover, he was thoroughly aware of the weaknesses of the mind which foster such su-perstitions, and he characterized them in places with a brilliant word. Thus when the outbreak of the plague at Athens increased the sufferings of war, some people remembered an alleged ancient oracle which ran: "A Dorian war will come, and a plague with it." This saying led, according to the historian's ac-count, to a conflict of opinions, some people maintaining that the verse referred to *limos* ("a famine") and not to *loimos* ("a plague"):—

> "Nevertheless, as might have been expected, for men's memories reflected their sufferings, the argument in favour of *loimos* prevailed at the time. But if ever in future years another Dorian war arises which happens to be ac-companied by a famine, they will probably repeat the verse in the other form."[1]

Nor was the destructive satire of Thucydides confined to a piece of anony-mous vaticination. He expressed himself with equal emphasis about an oracle of the Pythian god. When the people streamed into Athens from the country-side devastated by the Peloponnesians, the so-called Pelasgic or Pelargic field to the north-west of the Acropolis was also invaded by the fugitives, despite an an-cient oracle prohibiting such occupation. Necessity took no account of the di-vine prohibition, but its violation was presently burdened with a part of the guilt for the heavy calamities with which Athens was afflicted:—

> "And to my mind the oracle came true in a sense exactly contrary to the popular expectation; for the unlawful occupation to which men were dri-ven was not the cause of the calamities which befel the city, but the war was the cause of the occupation; and the oracle without mentioning the war foresaw that the place would be inhabited some day for no good."[2]

And Thucydides denounced not merely as baseless, but as positively hurt-ful, the superstitious

> "error of which so many are guilty, who, although they might still be saved if they would take the natural means, when visible grounds of confidence forsake them, have recourse to the invisible, to prophecies and oracles and the like, which ruin men by the hopes which they inspire in them."[3]

Bearing these and kindred utterances in mind, we may fairly assume that the historian's mention of the sole piece of prophecy which he knew has been fulfilled—that, namely, which stated that the Peloponnesian war "would last thrice nine years"—was merely intended to point to a noteworthy coincidence. Much the same explanation applies to the catalogue of natural occurrences partly ominous and threatening in character, and partly destructive, which ac-companied the course of the great war and enhanced its terrors. At that point of his exordium Thucydides stood on the threshold of the mighty drama on which the curtain was to be raised. He was ready to turn the limelight on the majesty and greatness of the period to which he had consecrated his pen, and it would have been wholly inappropriate in that place to introduce a recommendation to caution. At another time he did not withhold it. When he was telling his read-ers of the prophecies of the soothsayers and of the earthquake at Delos, which, as was "generally believed," presaged the outbreak of war, Thucydides did not

1. Thuc., ii.54: trans. Jowett.
2. Thuc., ii.17: trans. Jowett.
3. Thuc., v.103: trans. Jowett.

omit to utter the pregnant hint, "and everything of the sort which occurred was curiously noted."[4]

It is perfectly obvious by this time that the great Athenian had been thoroughly alienated from the faith of his countrymen. The word "mythical" on his lips carried the same derogatory sense as on the lips of Epicurus.[5] It would be interesting to know, however, not what he denied, but what he affirmed; above all, what attitude he took towards the great problems of universal origin and government. There is no word in his works from which his views on those subjects may be gathered. We have already sufficiently shown that he did not subscribe to the belief in supernatural interventions. He was fond of tracing back to their natural causes phenomena which had been regarded as miraculous or at least as significant. In this manner he disposed of eclipses, thunderstorms, floods, and the vortex of Charybdis; and apart altogether from his campaign against superstition, he was admirably fitted by taste and endowment for the observation and interpretation of nature. In this connection we need but recall his extremely careful discussion of the geographical conditions which brought the group of islands situated near the mouth of the Achelous ever nearer and nearer to the mainland, or, again, his masterly description of the plague at Athens which has been the admiration of experts in every age. In so far, then, we may assume that the sympathies of Thucydides tended to the physicists and the "meteorologists," and we must regard it as an especial boon that he preferred, notwithstanding, historiography to physics. But we can scarcely assume that he was satisfied for any length of time with either of the attempts then hanging in the balance to solve the great riddle of the universe, whether with that of Leucippus or with that of Anaxagoras.[6] His repugnance to both would probably have been due not so much to their divergence from the tenets of popular religion as to their intrinsic boldness and undemonstrableness. Thucydides himself complained that it was impossible to obtain information on the course of a battle from the depositions of soldiers on both sides who had participated in it. Every one, he remarked, could only accurately relate the events in his immediate neighbourhood. And, guided by this attitude, we may fairly assume that he would have withheld his assent from the philosophers who presumed to report on the origin of the universe with the circumstantial precision of an eyewitness. Doubtless Thucydides gave his deep attention to the greatest questions which can occupy the human mind, but we can best characterize the results of his long and earnest thought as a halting suspension of judgment.

FRANCIS M. CORNFORD

By 1900 classical scholarship was well established in both Germany and England, and one of its central tenets was that Thucydides was the first modern, scientific, objective historian. Thucydides, in short, was the first historian to whom college professors were completely comfortable according the name—the first one they embraced as one of their own. (Inevitably, the consequences for Herodotus' reputation were unhappy, though it has recently experienced some-

4. Thuc., ii.8: trans. Jowett.
5. Epicurus (341–270 B.C.) grounded his philosophy in the material world view set forth by the Greek physicists of Thucydides' day [Editor].
6. Leucippus was reputed to be the founder of the atomic theory that all matter was composed of tiny particles that were indivisible (a-tomoi, or "uncuttable"). In the atomist view, these particles acted entirely according to the principles of nature; the philosopher Anaxagoras differed from the atomists in viewing matter as shaped and guided by a force he called nous [mind] [Editor].

thing of a renaissance.) One voice, however, cried out against the common view of Thucydides as a committed rationalist who kept myths and oracles, gods and poets at a far remove. In his book *Thucydides Mythistoricus*, published in 1907, Francis Cornford (1874–1943) made a powerful case for a much more complex Thucydides, one for whom the nonrational forces so important to other Greeks played a key role.

[Thucydides and the Irrational][†]

1. Thucydides' Conception of History

If we would understand Thucydides, we must not regard a human action as partly caused by innumerable influences of environment, and by events that happened before the agent was born, right back into an immeasurable past; nor must we think of it as a single point in the total state of the world at a given moment, which state can be completely accounted for only by the total state at the previous moment, and so on. We must think of it as springing then and there out of the man's passions and character, and rid our minds, moreover, of the notion of *law* as applying to human actions and events. The fundamental conception which all our thought about the world implies must be banished—the conception, namely, that the whole course of events of every kind, human or non-human, is one enormous concatenation of causes and effects stretching forward and back into infinite time, and spreading outwards over immeasurable space, a concatenation in which every link is necessarily connected with all the rest, however remote. The world upon which the Greek looked out presented no such spectacle as this. Human affairs—the subject-matter of history—were not to him a single strand in the illimitable web of natural evolution; their course was shaped solely by one or both of two factors: immediate human motives, and the will of gods and spirits, of Fortune, or of Fate. The rationalist who rejected the second class was left with the first alone—the original and uncaused acts of human wills. That is why Polybius[1] expressly limits the term 'cause' (*aitia*) in relation to history to one class of things—motives. Thucydides takes the limitation for granted.

On this all-important point we part company with many recognized authorities. We will quote a typical statement from Professor Gomperz' brilliant review of Greek thought:—

'There is hardly any pair of contemporaries who offer a more glaring contrast than Herodotus and Thucydides. Barely a score of years divided their works from one another, but a gulf of centuries seems to yawn between their temper and inspiration. Herodotus creates throughout an entirely old-fashioned impression; Thucydides is a modern of the moderns. He made a clean sweep of the political and religious bias, the legendary and novelistic sympathies, and the primitive beliefs, rarely mitigated by the light of criticism, which marked the elder historian. The gaze of Thucydides is primarily fixed on the political factors, on the actual relations of forces, on the natural foun-

---

† From Francis M. Cornford, *Thucydides Mythistoricus* (London: Edward Arnold, 1907). Reprinted by permission of James Cornford and William John Bellamy.

1. The Greek historian Polybius (c. 204–c. 122) was taken hostage by the Romans when they conquered Greece and thus was well acquainted with both Greek and Roman civilization. He was a thoughtful historian who wrote an account of the period from 220 to 146 [*Editor*].

dation, so to speak, of historical phenomena. He looks for their springs, not in the dispensations of supernatural beings, nor yet, except in a moderate degree, in the caprices and passions of individual men. Behind those he always sought for the universal forces that animated them, for the conditions of the peoples, and the interests of the states. . . . It was his constant endeavor to describe the course of human affairs as though it were a process of nature informed by the light of inexorable causality.'[2]

This passage is perhaps unguarded in expression, and it seems somewhat ungracious to fasten upon details; we take it only as a typical instance of what seems to us a fallacy very prevalent in modern histories of ancient thought. What lies behind the positive statements in Professor Gomperz' paragraph is the very different and merely negative proposition that Thucydides records nothing which is not consistent with a scientific conception of the world—that he tacitly rejects supernatural causes. Let us admit, for the present, that this is true. The fallacy consists in passing from this negative statement to the assertion, implied throughout the paragraph, that the void left by the rejection of supernaturalism was filled by modern science.

The chief point in which we differ from Professor Gomperz arises over his last statement, that Thucydides endeavoured to describe the course of human affairs as though it were a process of nature informed by inexorable causality. This is precisely what we have seen reason to deny. Human affairs have, for Thucydides, not even an analogy with processes of nature; much less are they identified with one of the processes of nature; much less, again, is their course informed by inexorable causality. Man, isolated from, and opposed to, Nature, moves along a narrow path, unrelated to what lies beyond, and lighted only by a few dim rays of human 'foresight' (*gnōmē*) or by the false, wandering fires of Hope. He bears within him, self-contained, his destiny in his own character; and this, with the purposes which arise out of it, shapes his course. That is all, in Thucydides view, that we can say; except that, now and again, out of the surrounding darkness come the blinding strokes of Fortune, unaccountable and unforeseen. We shall try to prove later, in detail, that Thucydides' history can only be understood when we start from some such conception as this. If we presuppose the very modern view—it is not yet a century old—that human affairs are a process of nature indissolubly woven into one world-process by causal law, we shall be misled at every turn.

And, besides rejecting this general conception, we must beware of saying that Thucydides looked for such entities as 'political factors', 'relations of forces', 'the natural foundation of historical phenomena,' 'universal forces which animate men.' We are not merely objecting to forms of words; we are protesting against the attribution to Thucydides of the whole class of categories and conceptions and modes of thought of which these and similar phrases are the expression. It is precisely in respect of these conceptions that modern history differs from ancient. They have been imported, but yesterday, from Darwinian biology and from branches of mathematical and physical science which in fifth-century Athens were undiscovered, and which, if they had been discovered, no one would have dreamed of bringing into connexion with human history. Perhaps the importation has not been all to the good. A combination of political forces is a bloodless and inhuman entity, and in the manipulation of these mechanical categories we seem to lose touch of the realities they conceal—the pulse and play of warm, live passions, the beating hearts of men who

---

2. Gomperz, *Greek Thinkers* (E.T.), i. 503 [cited in this volume, pp. 407–12]. We are sorry to quote this interesting work only to express disagreement.

suffer and aspire. We are sometimes put off with phrases instead of explanations; and the language of cogs and pulleys fails, sometimes, to illuminate the workings of the spirit.

Further, not only has History proper been invaded by these abstract sciences, but also—and partly as a consequence—a number of ancillary sciences, fast growing up round the old method of narrating human actions, are parcelling out the field occupied by the ancient descriptive science of Politics. Collectively, they may be called Sociology. The best established of them is Economics, which studies the phenomenon known to the Greeks by the moral term, *pleonexia*, 'covetousness,' that vice of human character which makes a man want to 'have more' than his neighbour. It was in ancient days the topic for a chapter in Ethics or for a character sketch, like those of Theophrastus, of 'the covetous man'. Now it is studied in almost complete abstraction from anything psychological. The fluctuations of the money market are traced in columns of figures and in curves on a diagram.

The laws which Economics attempts to establish, the categories of its ideal constructions, the abstract methods of this science and of others like it, find their way into History. The modern historian deals in vague entities, in groups and tendencies and the balance of forces. Further, he is always aware of a vast accumulation of ordered knowledge in the background. The comparative method and the survey of evidence drawn from remote lands and from unnumbered centuries have taught him to take nothing for granted, and to seek for connexions between phenomena which his ancestors never dreamed of correlating.

The course of human events, then, is to be thought of as shaped by the wills and passions of individual men or of cities, not as a part of what lies around it and beyond. And what does lie beyond? For Thucydides, the answer is: the Unknown. This was the only answer possible to a man of his temperament, a man whose spirit needed, above all, what was clear and definite. Like a few other enlightened men of his time, he had rejected every systematic explanation of the world that he could think of. Supernatural causes—the will of personal gods and spirits—these men denied. Thucydides ought not, perhaps, to be described as a sceptic; the word has come to suggest a certain hardness of intellect and a degree of positive antagonism which are not, we think, characteristics of his mind. It is better to call him an agnostic, not of the dogmatic sort who know so much about the unknown that they confidently assert it to be unknowable; but of the sober, unprejudiced kind, whose single desire is to reach, and to observe religiously, the limit of what is known. Vulgar superstition is nothing to him, except at the few points where it stands in the path of knowledge; there he can treat it with cool irony. He could respect the piety of Nikias and love the man, while gravely condemning his credulity in one fatal matter where it blinded him to a definitely ascertained fact. He will note with grave severity how, in time of stress, men who profess religion fall short of their ideals; but for his own part he seems to stand aside, rejecting, we may imagine, with more scorn than ignorant faith would deserve the philosophizing compromises and senile allegorizings of an age too sceptical, and not quite sceptical enough, to be at ease with itself. In his attitude towards religion (which must not be confounded with the quackeries of strolling oracle-vendors) there is never a trace of lightness or irreverence.

The men of the enlightenment were agreed in rejecting religion; but Thucydides had gone yet further in agnosticism than most of them, and rejected also the 'philosophical' schemes of the universe. With his strong and

steady desire for literal, certain truth, knowing by experience how hard it is to
get a consistent account of things actually seen and done from the men who
saw and did them, he had not much respect for philosophies which, when science was still a blind and babbling infant, professed to reveal how the universe
came into being.

Well-meaning efforts have been made to furnish him with a belief in some
providential government of the world. But there is not a shadow of proof that
he recognized the 'Mind' of Anaxagoras any more than the Zeus of Aeschylus.[3]
Indeed, his avoidance of the word *nous* (to which he prefers *gnōmē*) may indicate a definite wish to renounce the philosophic theory associated in his day
with the term. From Anaxagoras and other 'philosophers' he accepted a few results of scientific observation—about eclipses, earthquakes and the like—all
that had yet been won from the vast field of the unknown by the first inroads of
knowledge. That is the extent of his debt to 'philosophy', in the way of positive
results; all it had done for him otherwise was of a negative sort. Since Parmenides[4] had declared the sensible world to be an illusion, agnosticism in one
form or another had taken possession of many thoughtful minds. It is only in
this way that Thucydides owed to philosophy his marvellous sense of the limits
of certain knowledge.

If we would put ourselves at the point where Thucydides stood when
he began his task, we must perform an almost impossible feat. To rid our
minds of religious and metaphysical beliefs which are not identical with our
own is comparatively easy. What is exceedingly difficult but equally necessary, is to throw off the inheritance to which we are born, of concepts distinguished and defined by a vast and subtle terminology, logical, metaphysical,
scientific, created by Aristotle, refined by the schoolmen, and enlarged by
centuries of discovery. Thucydides lived at the one moment in recorded history which has seen a brilliantly intellectual society, nearly emancipated from
a dying religion, and at the same time unaided by science, as yet hardly
born. Nowhere but in a few men of that generation shall we find so much
independence of thought combined with such destitute poverty in the ap-
paratus and machinery of thinking.[5] The want of scientific categories, and
above all of the cardinal conception of law as applying to human actions,
make a gulf between Thucydides and ourselves immensely greater than any
which his want of superstitious beliefs makes between him and Herodotus.
We must rid our minds of scientific terminology, as well as of religion and
philosophy, if we are to appreciate the unique detachment of Thucydides'

3. The Athenian tragic playwright Aeschylus, who died around the time of Thucydides' birth, put forward
   in his plays a fairly traditional view of the Greek gods. The Ionian philosopher Anaxagoras, who lived in
   Athens when Thucydides was young, saw *nous* (mind) as the guiding principle that organized the infi-
   nitely divisible particles that made up the material world. Anaxagoras also claimed that the sun was not
   a divinity but rather a white-hot stone a little larger than the Peloponnese. He was accused of impiety a
   few years before the outbreak of the Peloponnesian War and forced to flee Athens [*Editor*].
4. The philosopher Parmenides of Elea visited Athens around 450. He was famous for denying the validity
   of sense perception and the possibility of motion [*Editor*].
5. It is not easy for us to realize how impossible it was to think clearly in a language which did not supply,
   as modern languages do, a refined and distinct terminology. When Thucydides' contemporary, Democritus, wrote: 'By convention sweet, by convention sour; in truth atoms and void,' he *meant*, we say,
   something of this sort: that the primary qualities of matter are objectively real, while the secondary are
   only subjective. But to offer this proposition, or anything like it, as a paraphrase of the Greek is utterly
   uncritical. It is to disguise the fact that the Greek [expression "by *nomos*"] rendered 'subjective', is de-
   plorably ambiguous, and means 'legal', 'conventional', 'artificial', 'unnatural', 'arbitrary', and a number
   of other things. Enough remains of the controversies of the time to show that this ambiguity lay, not in
   language only, but in thought. These ideas, all covered by one word in the only tongue known to the
   Greeks, were simply not distinguished, and to import a distinction by assigning one meaning to the word
   to the exclusion of the rest is to commit the fallacy into which Professor Gomperz seems to us to have
   fallen.

mind, moving in the rarest of atmospheres between the old age and the new. Descartes,[6] for all his efforts, was immeasurably less free from metaphysical preoccupation; Socrates appears, in comparison, superstitious.

2. The Luck of Pylos

[Cornford now explores the paradigm for construing the world that is revealed in Thucydides' account of a single event: the occupation of Pylos in Book 4.]

We have here * * * a narrative which is unlike any earlier part of Thucydides' story. Hitherto he has told a plain tale, lucid, intelligible, natural. Now we find an episode in which facts of cardinal importance for the understanding of the events are left unmentioned, and indispensable links are wanting. If the missing facts and connexions were within the author's knowledge, why are they omitted? If they were not, we might at least expect that he would avow his ignorance and draw some attention to the blanks, instead of passing over them as if he were unconscious of their existence.

The question then is this: Why has Thucydides represented the occupation of Pylos as the merest stroke of good luck, undertaken with the least possible amount of deliberate calculation, and furthered at every turn of events by some unforeseen accident?

The simplest of all answers would be that as a matter of fact so it was. Accidents do happen; and there certainty was a considerable element of luck. No one can foresee the occurrence of a storm. The festival at Sparta was a coincidence—though we note by the way that it was not a festival sufficiently important to prevent the army of invasion from being absent in Attica. The Messenian privateer might conceivably have come by accident—though the supply of spare arms on so small a vessel is certainly odd. And so on. But all this does not explain the blanks and incoherencies we have noticed; and it is fair to add that every additional accident increases the strain on our belief. As soon as we reject this first answer, we have admitted that Thucydides—for whatever reason—is not telling the story just as it happened and just as we should tell it. There is some unexplained factor at work, something of which we have not yet taken account.

The solutions that have been offered, when the problem before us has been faced at all, fall under two heads. We are told either that Thucydides is 'moralizing' on the uncertainty of war, or that he is actuated by some personal feeling of 'malignity' and indulging it in detraction. The first of these hypotheses is, in our opinion, a grave charge against him as a man of sense; the second is a still graver charge against his moral character.

It is true that the uncertainty of war is one of the most frequent topics in the speeches; and small wonder that it is so. Thucydides' generation lived through a life-and-death struggle waged almost continuously for twenty-seven years. A nation at war is always, more or less, in a fever; when the nation is intelligent and excitable by temperament, and the war is close at home, the fever will run high. For these twenty-seven years no Athenian mind was ever quite at rest. Not a record or document of this period but we find in it the mark of this unhealthiness, of nerves on the strain with watching, of the pulse which beats just too fast. Every capricious turn of good or ill luck in the struggle sent a thrill through their hearts. But, can we think that Thucydides would deliberately dis-

6. The French philosopher and scientist René Descartes lived from 1596 to 1650 [Editor].

tort the facts of the occupation of Pylos, solely in order to illustrate the truth that accidents will happen? The question hardly needs an answer. No man of common intelligence could say to himself, 'In order to show how uncertain are the chances of war, I will describe a series of events *not just they happened, but with the causal links, which would show that the events were not fortuitous, disguised and almost suppressed.*' There were plenty of real instances of good and ill luck. What need of this perverse invention of a spurious one?

Plainly, then, this is not a case of 'moralizing'; there is some other reason; and so we fall back on the hypothesis of 'malignity'. The malignity could only be directed either against Cleon, whose exploit at Sphacteria followed on the occupation of Pylos, or against Athens. There is, on this supposition, some personal grudge, against the hated political opponent, or against the city which banished Thucydides.

With regard to Cleon, this hypothesis will not fit the facts. The occupation of Pylos was the exploit not of Cleon, but of Demosthenes. For Demosthenes, the only soldier of genius whom the Athenians could match with Brasidas, Thucydides consistently shows a marked admiration. The capture of Pylos was his master-stroke, and there was no motive for belittling the achievement. Cleon does not appear till later, when he goes to the scene of action and co-operates in the capture of Sphacteria. Malignity against him might be fully satisfied either by representing that subsequent operation as favoured by fortune or by attributing all the skill involved in its success to his colleague, Demosthenes. Thucydides actually does both these things—whether from malignity or because he thought it was true, is no matter for our present problem. But a personal grudge against Cleon could not be satisfied, or be in question at all, in the earlier narrative of the seizure of Pylos.

Was it, then, a grudge against Athens that moved him? Did he hate the city which condemned him to banishment for his failure at Amphipolis, and desire to represent—or rather to misrepresent—her most successful feat in the war as a mere stroke of luck? This, we believe, is an hypothesis which is now, reluctantly and with many attempts at palliation, allowed to pass current. It cannot be so easily and certainly dismissed as the other suggestions. It is a possible motive—possible, at least to some men—and it would account for those facts we have hitherto considered. We cannot at this point finally disprove it; the facts which it will not account for have yet to be discussed. But we do not believe that any one who knows Thucydides is really satisfied with imputing to him a motive which, candidly described, is dishonourable, ignoble, mean. The imputation does not fit in with our general impression from the rest of the History. If there is any one who is satisfied with it, we will ask him to read once more the story of the retreat from Syracuse. Were those pages written by a man who hated Athens and triumphed in her fall?

We cannot think of any other motive which could have induced Thucydides deliberately to represent as fortuitous a series of events which we, after some reflection, can see to have been in great measure designed. We next observe that the supposition of 'malignity' is itself based on the tacit assumption that Thucydides is writing from the same standpoint, and handling his story on the same methods, as a modern historian. If a modern had written the narrative of Pylos, we could say with the highest degree of moral certainty, that the distortion was deliberate and the motive must be at least dishonest, if not ignobly personal. Hence we assume, unconsciously, that Thucydides' motive must have been of this sort. In our eagerness to hail him as 'a modern of the moderns', we thought we were paying him a compliment; but now the epithet turns out to carry with it a most damaging accusation. If we decline to regard Thucydides as a modern, and recur to our thesis that, being an ancient, he must have looked at the course of human history with very different eyes from ours, it seems that an alternative explanation may yet remain.

The suggestion which we would put forward is that Thucydides thought he really saw an *agency*, called 'Fortune', at work in these events. When we say 'chance favoured the designs of Demosthenes',[1] of course we mean, not that any of the accidents had no natural cause, but only that they were such as could not have been foreseen. But have we any ground for saying that this, and nothing more, was what Thucydides would have meant?[2]

We will, for the moment, leave the notion of Fortune without precise definition. It is enough to take a belief in Fortune as meaning a belief in any non-natural agency, which breaks in, as it were, from outside and diverts the current of events, without itself being a part of the series or an effect determined by an antecedent member of it. Now, we have already pointed out that human actions are not to be fitted into such a series. Their only causes—if we are to speak of causes at all—are motives, each of which is itself uncaused by anything preceding it in time; all human motives are absolute 'beginnings of motion'. A view of the universe in which this irruption of free human agency is tacitly assumed is at any rate illogical if it denies the *possibility* of similar irruptions into the course of Nature by non-human agencies.

But we can go further than this. We observed that Thucydides had no word at all for 'cause' in our sense. From the fact, among others, that instead of discussing the causes of the war, he thought he had completely accounted for its origin when he had described the grievances (*aitiai*) of the combatants, it appeared that it was not only the word that was missing, but the concept. Having no clear conception of cause and effect, he cannot have had any clear conception of a universal and exclusive reign of causal law in Nature. In criticizing Professor Gomperz we denied that Thucydides conceived the course of human affairs as 'a process of Nature informed by inexorable causality', or as having anything in common with such a process. We may now further deny that he could have thought of the *processes of Nature themselves* as informed by causality, in our modern sense—the sense, namely, that every event has a place in one total series of all events, and is completely determined by previous events, and so on backwards into infinity; and that this is true of the future as well as of the past. By an *aitia*, in nature as in man, Thucydides does not mean a member of such a series, but a *free* agency, a '*beginning* of motion', an incursion of fresh original power. If this is so, there was nothing whatever in his view of the universe to exclude the *possibility* of extraordinary intervention on the part of some undefined non-human powers. We shall presently see that his language elsewhere implies that such a possibility was admitted by him.

That Thucydides had, on the contrary, a quite definite notion of causal law is commonly taken for granted, or actually asserted. M. Croiset, for instance, after contrasting Thucydides with his predecessors, continues: 'Hence his conception of history. If the facts are tied together by permanent and necessary laws, the knowledge of causes and effects in the past may make it possible to predict

1. [J.B.] Bury, *Hist. of Greece* (1900), p. 429.
2. That Thucydides would have meant just what we mean is commonly *assumed*, as for instance by Mr. Forbes, Introduction to Book I (p. xxxii): 'Chance (that is, the operation of unknown causes) is strong, the future is hard to foresee, hope is dangerous; we must look facts in the face, whether we like them or not, and "think it out"'.

the return of the same effects, produced by the same causes, in accord with the pattern of human affairs.'[3] This passage suggests that Thucydides based his conception of history on a belief in permanent and necessary laws, connecting events *in such a way that from a sufficient knowledge of the present state of the world the future could be predicted with certainty.* If this is true, it of course excludes the operation of Fortune.[4] Let us, however, examine the passages to which M. Croiset refers in his note, as the foundation of the above statement.

The first is as follows: 'For recitation to an audience, perhaps the absence of the "mythical" will make these facts rather unattractive; but it will be enough if they are judged useful by those who shall wish to know the plain truth of what has happened *and of the events which, according to the course of human things, are likely to happen again, of the same, or much the same, sort as these'.*[5] What Thucydides here has in his mind, we know from the other passage to which M. Croiset refers. Thucydides is there explaining why he gives an account of the outbreak of plague at Athens. 'Others may say, each according to his judgement, whether he be physician or layman, from what it probably arose, and assert that whatever he considers were the agencies of so great a change, *were sufficient to acquire power to (produce) the transformation.*[6] But I shall say what it was like when it happened; and I shall set forth *the things from which, if it should ever come on again, one who considers them might best be able, knowing them beforehand, to recognize it without fail.* I fell ill myself, and I saw with my own eyes others suffering.'

Thucydides will record the *symptoms* of the plague, from personal observation, so that posterity may recognize the disorder if it should break out again. This is all he thinks useful. He hints that the guesses of physicians are not worth much more than those of laymen, about the 'agencies responsible' which they consider were *'sufficient to acquire power* to (produce) such a transformation'. Had the man who wrote that phrase anything in his mind remotely resembling the modern notion of cause and causal law? The phrase is the very contradiction of it. The notion it conveys is that of an unknown, probably an unknowable, something, responsible for the plague, and from time to time *acquiring* enough power to produce an outbreak. Thucydides rejects all attempts to scrutinize the nature of this something, and does not even directly commit himself to a belief in its existence. He will confine himself to describing what he actually saw and suffered. He hints that other people, doctors and laymen alike, would do well to follow his example. The doctors would see in the plague the operation of something 'divine'; laymen would more definitely ascribe it to the onslaught of malignant spirits or offended gods. Some undoubtedly connected it with the curse which attached to the Alcmaeonid Pericles. Others again would murmur that they had always said harm would come of allowing the homeless peasants to camp out in the Pelargikon, against the warning of an ancient oracle.

In the former passage, likewise, Thucydides is not thinking of 'necessary and permanent laws' in the sequence of events. He is merely reflecting that other wars will happen in the future. Other 'events of the same, or *much the*

---

3. Croiset, [*Histoire de la littérature grecque*], iv. 113 [translated from the French by Jennifer Roberts].
4. We may note, by the way, that if Thucydides thought this, he had discovered a truth of which Aristotle was ignorant. The whole Aristotelian doctrine of Possibility rests on the logical thesis that propositions which refer to future events (e.g. 'there will be a battle to-morrow') are neither true nor false, because, unless the future were undetermined, 'nothing could happen by chance' (*apo tychēs*) and all deliberation would be futile.
5. i. 22. 4.
6. ii. 48. 3.

same sort' will occur, 'according to the course of human things'. This last phrase is ambiguous. It might mean 'so far as man can foresee', 'in all human proba-bility'—a phrase which is least likely to be on our lips when we have in our thoughts a clear conception of non-human 'inexorable causality'.

We are too apt to take the few sound observations of nature, made by the Greeks at that date, as a proof that they conceived nature as universally ruled by law. Thucydides notes, for instance, that 'it seems (or, is thought) to be possible for an eclipse of the sun to happen only at the time of a new moon'[7]; and again, that when the moon is eclipsed, it is full.[8] He inferred, moreover, that eclipses could not, as superstitious men like Nikias supposed, give prognostications of coming events. But between an isolated observation and inference of this sort and a general conception of law in nature there was a gulf which many centuries of labour had yet to fill. In the case of earthquakes, Thucydides had no sufficient series of observations on which to base an inference. Consequently, with admirable good sense, he records, without expressing or implying any belief or disbelief of his own, the one fact of which he was certain, namely, that 'they were said and thought to be signs of coming events'.[9]

Again, when he is insisting in his introduction that the Peloponnesian War was the greatest in recorded history, he thinks it worth while to point out that it was not inferior to previous wars in the number of earthquakes, eclipses, droughts, famines, plagues, and other such convulsions of nature which accompanied it. Similar phenomena had been reported of previous wars, but this hearsay was too scantily confirmed by ascertained facts. '*It now became not incredible,*' he says, '*for all these things came upon the Greeks at the same time with this war.*'[1] An unprejudiced reader of this passage must draw several conclusions. In the first place Thucydides feels no distinction between famines and plagues on the one hand, and eclipses, earthquakes, and droughts on the other. To us it seems easy to connect the former class with a state of war, and absolutely impossible to connect the latter. Second, he saw no reason in the nature of things why events of either class should not be more frequent at times of war in Greece, and he thought the evi-dence pointed to the fact that they were. Third, if he was thinking at all of any sort of *causal connexion* between wars and (for instance) droughts, he must have attributed droughts to causes of a sort which find no place in modern science. Fourth, he shows his usual good sense in merely recording that these occurrences apparently came *at the same time (hama)*, without committing himself to any specific connexion between them. In fine, he shows a completely scientific spirit, and also an equally complete destitution of a scientific view of nature. In the former respect he is superior to the man who sacrifices to a volcano or prays for rain. In the latter he is not so far ad-vanced as a modern peasant who is just educated enough to feel that there *can* be no connexion between his seeing four magpies and some one else having a child. Thucydides will not *worship* the inscrutable agencies re-sponsible for convulsions of Nature; but he cannot rule out the hypothesis that such agencies exist and may 'acquire power' to produce the convul-

7. ii. 28.
8. vii. 50.
9. ii. 8.3.
1. His putting in 'eclipses' shows that he did not understand why the sun is not eclipsed at *every* new moon, or the moon *every* time it is full. He thought eclipses were *more frequent* at times of war and did not know why.

sions coincidently with a war in Greece. He refrains from dogmatizing on either side; regarding, we may suppose, the current belief that malevolent spirits were responsible for such outbreaks, as an incautious and unverified explanation.

M. Croiset has, in our opinion, slipped into a fallacy which is so common in the written history of thought that it seems to deserve a name of its own. We will call it the Modernist Fallacy. It takes several kindred shapes. In the present case, its formula is as follows: 'If a man in the remote past believed a certain proposition, he also believed all that we have since discovered to be implied in that proposition.' Thucydides believed—who ever did not?—that events of 'the same, or much the same, sort' recur. Therefore, he must have had a full and conscious belief in permanent and necessary laws of cause and effect, conceived as we conceive them.

What were the possible alternatives in an age which lacked the true conception of universal causality? There were two, and only two: Fate and Providence. But both of these were mythical, and associated with superstition. Fate, the older, vaguer, and less personal of the two, was conceived under the aspect of veiled and awful figures: the three Moirai, Ananke, Adrasteia.[2] It was thus that man had his first dim apprehension of that element in the world outside which opposes the will of men and even of gods, thwarts their purpose, and beats down their passion. Later ages have at least resolved this inexorable phantom into nothing more—if nothing less—mysterious than the causal sequences of Law. But this solution lay far in the future; Thucydides' contemporaries could conceive it only as a non-human will—a purely mythical entity.

The other alternative was Providence; but any conception of Providence less anthropomorphic than the will of Zeus or the agency of spirits was not possible as yet. The notion of a supreme Mind intervening once, and only once, to bring order into chaos had been reached by Anaxagoras; but this suggestion, so disastrous to the progress of thought, was not developed till Plato took it up. In any case this Mind was merely credited with an initial act of creation; it did not rule the world which it had ordered. Thucydides, moreover, as we saw, had probably considered and rejected Anaxagoras' philosophy. And, after all, the 'Mind' was just as mythical as Fate.

The word 'Chance' suggests to the modern educated intelligence something utterly impersonal; we think at once of the mathematical theory of probability, of the odds at a gambling table, and so on. But we must remember that the current name for 'Chance' in Greek was the name of a mythical Person, Tychē, a spirit who was actually worshipped by the superstitious, and placated by magical means. The religious spoke of 'the Fortune that comes from the divine', and believed that God's will was manifest in the striking turns of chance, and in spite of appearances was working for the righteous.

* * *

The recognition of non-human agencies—however undefined—as responsible for observed phenomena is, so far as it goes, a metaphysical belief. It

---

2. The Moirai (sometimes called Clotho, Lachesis, and Atropos) were goddesses of fate. Ananke, necessity or compulsion, was sometimes personified by the poets. Adrasteia was another name for Nemesis, the goddess of retribution, who visited those who become presumptuous through good fortune. She also punished extraordinary crimes [Editor].

is not a scientific belief, though perfectly consistent with the scientific spirit in the then state of physical knowledge. It is not a religious belief; for Thucydides does not imply that these powers ought to be worshipped or placated. Nothing remains but to call it mythical.

To recur now to the story of Pylos. We noticed that the series of lucky accidents on the Athenian side was paralleled by a series of extraordinary blunders on the Spartan side. In the former series Fortune is prominent to the exclusion of foresight (*gnōmē*); in the latter we see successive failures of foresight rather than the intervention of Fortune. These count as pieces of luck from the Athenian standpoint; but from the Spartans' they are simply errors of judgement. This point is clearly made in the subsequent speech of the Spartan envoys, who are careful to remark: 'We have not come to this from want of power, nor yet from the pride that comes when power is unduly increased; but *without any change in our position, we failed in judgement*—a point in which the position of all men is alike.'[3] Thus the whole narrative of the occupation illustrates the contrast of fortune and foresight. Fortune, not foresight, has exalted the Athenians; want of foresight, not of fortune, has depressed the Spartans.

It was in this light that Thucydides saw a series of events which began with a striking accident, the storm. The element of real luck was sufficient to suggest a belief that Fortune was active to a mind predisposed by superstition or some other cause to look for her agency just here. Thucydides was not superstitious; and he was both careful and acute. The belief accounts for the peculiarities of the narrative; but we have further to account for his having the belief *at just this moment in his story* so strongly upon him as to miss the clues in his informant's report. There must have been something which positively predisposed him to see Fortune at work. * * * Here we need only add that the psychological phenomenon we are supposing to have occurred in his mind is closely analogous to what might occur in a Christian historian, narrating from incomplete oral information a critical incident in Church history, which *began with a miracle*. Looking from the outset for the divine purpose, he might easily fail to bring his mind to bear critically on the indications which showed that the whole series of events could be explained as the effect of purely natural causes; for we know from daily experience that a belief in occasional interferences on the part of Providence can co-exist in the same educated mind with a conception of natural causality immeasurably clearer than any that Thucydides could have possessed.

CHARLES N. COCHRANE

Charles Norris Cochrane (1889–1946) was professor of Greek and Roman history at University College, Toronto. Cochrane saw no reason why history could not or should not be scientific. His book *Thucydides and the Science of History*, from which the following excerpts are taken, challenged Cornford's *Thucydides Mythistoricus* directly and sought to place Thucydides firmly in the tradition of fifth-century science and medicine. The Thucydides of Cochrane is a far cry from the Thucydides of Cornford. The greatness of Thucydides, Cochrane insisted, lay precisely in his role as a pioneer in scientific method.

3. iv. 18.2.

[Thucydides, Cornford, and History][†]

I

Introduction

Critics of Thucydides have been almost unanimous in associating him with the period of enlightenment of the fifth century B.C. With one notable exception,[1] the English commentators have agreed that the *Histories* reflect not a 'mythological conception of the world of human acts and passions . . . derived from an early education consisting almost exclusively in the study of the poets'[2] but rather the rationalist and humanist atmosphere of the days of Anaxagoras and Protagoras.[3]

In one respect, however, Cornford and his critics appear to be in agreement. 'The want of scientific categories, and above all of the cardinal conception of law as applying to human actions, makes a gulf between Thucydides and ourselves immensely greater than any which his want of superstitious beliefs makes between him and Herodotus.' This statement of Cornford (p. 74) finds a parallel in the judgement of Bury that 'with the Greeks, historical study never acquired the scientific character which it was reserved for the nineteenth century to impress upon it'.[4]

* * *

Gomperz, while denying by implication that Thucydides was affected by any metaphysical presuppositions, nevertheless supports the charge that he possessed no scientific categories to replace them. 'In so far, then', he says,[5] 'the sympathies of Thucydides tended to the physicists and the meteorologists. But we can scarcely assume that he was satisfied for any length of time with either of the attempts then hanging in the balance to solve the great riddle of the universe, whether with that of Leucippus or with that of Anaxagoras. His repugnance to both would probably have been due not so much to their divergence from the tenets of popular religion as to their intrinsic boldness and undemonstrableness.'

But scepticism in regard to the whole is not incompatible with a firm belief in the value of inquiries into the parts. Philosophy may continue her vain attempt to storm the bastions of heaven; but positive science, like warfare, proceeds by the method of limited objectives; and indeed often scores her greatest advances at those moments in human history when religious and philosophic doubt are most acute. In the case of Thucydides, it would seem clear that, while the sceptical rationalism of his age accounts sufficiently for his critical attitude regarding the phenomena of nature, something akin to the positive faith of the modern scientist is needed to explain the note of calm assurance with which he commends his *Histories* to the world as a possession for ever. Whatever else may be questionable, it is perfectly evident that he has no doubt of the value and usefulness of his own work.

† Charles Norris Cochrane, *Thucydides and the Science of History* (Oxford: Oxford University Press, 1929). Reprinted by permission of Oxford University Press. Greek words or phrases have been deleted when preceded or succeeded by an English translation.

1. F. M. Cornford, *Thucydides Mythistoricus* [excerpted in this volume, pp. 412–23].

2. Op. cit., p. ix.

3. Anaxagoras of Clazomenae and Protagoras of Abdera spent time in Athens when Thucydides was young; both were thinkers who used the tools of reason to examine the universe (Anaxagoras) and the human community (Protagoras) [*Editor*].

4. [J.B. Bury,] *Ancient Greek Historians* (New York, 1909), p. 147.

5. *Greek Thinkers*, i. 512 [excerpted in this volume, pp. 407–12; this passage appears on p. 412].

This self-assurance has often been noticed as a characteristic of Thucydides; and has been ascribed partly to the literary convention existing among ancient historians, that each should pose as in some way superior to his predecessors, and partly also to the lack of that modesty (or mock-modesty) which is supposed to be a product of modern times. It is the purpose of this essay to maintain that at least in Thucydides, there is another explanation than that of mere vanity, or literary good form; and at the same time to suggest an hypothesis better calculated to explain this and other characteristic features of his work than any which has come to the attention of the writer.

The truth is that Thucydides had the assured faith of a scientist because he was a scientist, because, in fact, he was inspired by contact with a department of positive science which in his day had succeeded in extricating itself from the coils of cosmology, and which by means of a method adequate to the most rigid modern demands was already advancing to conclusions which were recognized as valid and immensely significant for human life. From the remarks of Plato it may be inferred that mathematics had in his day reached this point, and was esteemed by some of the Sophists at least by reason of its practical value, but mathematics has at best a remote connexion with human life. On the other hand, biological and medical science deals directly with humanity in its normal and pathological conditions. And, in the second half of the fifth century, biology and medicine were already established as fruitful sciences in the hands of the Hippocratic school.[6] The intellectual and spiritual affiliations of Thucydides were with this school. The general philosophic background, so far as this is discernible, is the thought of Democritus[7] rather than of Anaxagoras, his alleged tutor. Specifically, however, his inspiration comes from Hippocrates, along with the principles of method which determined the character of his work. The *Histories* of Thucydides represent an attempt to apply to the study of social life the methods which Hippocrates employed in the art of healing, and constitute an exact parallel to the attempts of modern scientific historians to apply evolutionary canons of interpretation derived from Darwinian science.

II

The Background

INFLUENCE OF THE ATOMISTIC PHILOSOPHY

'I came to Athens, and nobody knew me!' Thus did Democritus give expression to the surprise and indignation which he felt at his reception in Athens, when he visited the imperial city. He had cause to be annoyed, but should not have been astonished, that the Athenians were ignorant both of his name and of his work. The Athens which he visited was the Athens of Anaxagoras and Pericles, and in such an atmosphere there was no possible welcome for the man who had deposed the fashionable *nous* (mind) from its position at the head of the cosmos, and explained the *genesis* (coming into being) and *phthora* (erosion) of all phenomenal things as the result of

---

6. The disciples of the fifth-century physician Hippocrates, who had a medical school on the Greek island of Cos [*Editor*].
7. Thucydides' contemporary Democritus of Abdera developed the ideas attributed to Leucippus into the full-blown "atomic" theory of matter that saw the world shaped by natural forces rather than divine will, whereas Anaxagoras stressed the power of *nous* (mind). According to Democritus, even the soul was made of atoms. In the Democritean system, the behavior of atoms accounts for the variety of substances and textures in the universe as well as for the phenomenon of change. The materialist orientation of Democritus formed the basis of the philosophy of Epicurus (341–270) [*Editor*].

a fortuitous concourse of atoms moving according to the law of their own nature. Yet at Abdera, it is said, the name of Democritus was one to conjure with, and the very characteristics of his thought which made him *persona non grata* in Athens supplied a congenial background for the ideas of what one may perhaps, without being too fanciful, characterize as the School of Abdera, a school to which Thucydides the sociologist, no less than Hippocrates the physician, probably belonged.

The principles of the atomists which affected the physician and the sociologist, so far as these were affected by philosophic principles, may be briefly summarized as follows. First in importance was the doctrine of causality, *ex nihilo nihil fit*,[8] formulated by Leucippus and adopted by his successor. It is superfluous to explain that the uniformity of nature is presupposed by all positive science. To Hippocrates and Thucydides therefore this doctrine was of fundamental importance * * * . But Democritean theory pointed to a world which was explicable without reference to extraneous conceptions such as the *nous* of Anaxagoras, or the Empedoclean 'Love and Strife',[9] no less than to the naive personifications of popular religion current in Aeschylean tragedy—a world moreover in which *tychē* reigned supreme, and from which final causes were rigidly excluded.

The 'atmosphere' of philosophic thought is no less significant than its positive achievements. It is generally admitted, for instance, that the atmosphere of Platonism has at all times been unfavourable to positive science, because of its insistence upon the exclusive significance of the abstract universals of thought, as opposed to the concrete particulars of the phenomenal world. In the fifth century there were powerful influences abroad analogous to Platonism, such as the doctrines of the Eleatic school,[1] which either imposed an effective barrier to all thought about mundane things, or at any rate diverted thought to bypaths such as grammar and rhetoric. The exact reverse, however, was true of the speculation of the atomist school, which was dominated by the keenest respect for the world of *genesis* and *phthora*, and which aimed at all costs to 'save the appearances'. Such an atmosphere is vital to the life of the human sciences, whether biological or social.

The phenomenal world, according to the atomists, is to be apprehended by experience, and in no other way; but to emphasize the significance of experience is to emphasize the significance of history, which is nothing more or less than the record of human experience in relation to the external world.

Without entering upon the vexed question of the quality of the experience in relation to the 'outside' world, one may conclude by reminding the reader that 'the atomists', to quote the words of Gomperz,[2] 'were, in common with the rest of their predecessors and contemporaries in natural philosophy, with the sole exception of Anaxagoras, materialists inasmuch as they looked for the only causes or conditions of the states and qualities of consciousness in the material world alone'. This is not to say that they excluded from their purview the concept of mind. It remained for twentieth-century America to discover and desig-

---

8. Nothing can be created from nothing [*Editor*].
9. The Sicilian philosopher (c. 492–432) saw the world as made up of four elements (earth, water, fire, and air) acted upon by the opposing dynamic forces of Love and Strife. The tension between Love and Strife, then, accounts for change and motion, while the elements represent the fixed and immutable [*Editor*].
1. Parmenides of Elea and his followers foreshadowed Plato in their discounting of the idea of change. They claimed that motion, for example, was impossible and the appearance of motion merely an illusion. They contrasted sharply with the atomists in seeing the world as unchanging and indivisible and in discounting the value of sense perception [*Editor*].
2. *Greek Thinkers*, i. 355.

nate 'behaviourism'.[3] All that is implied of the atomists is the limitation of knowledge to scientific analysis, and the doctrine that all psychical processes bear an ordered, and therefore ascertainable, relationship to their respective stimuli; or, in other words, are relative to the circumstances that provoke them.

Enough has been said to suggest that the atomistic philosophy of the fifth century B.C. was not merely congenial to, but the necessary preliminary of, the growth of the special sciences of human behaviour. The question remains: to what extent did the speculations of the atomists actually serve to stimulate the beginnings of these sciences? Democritus himself may be said to have initiated scientific (as opposed to philosophic) research; * * * there is an intrinsic probability that Hippocrates made the acquaintance of Democritus during his years of practice at Abdera and the neighbouring island of Thasos. This probability is confirmed by the close correspondence between their respective points of view.

Hippocrates was, of course, a practical man, engaged first and foremost in the art of healing. Accordingly, it is vain to look in his works for any explicit discussion of the purely theoretical topics which came within the purview of the Father of Physics, whom Aristotle described as 'the great Democritus', and of whom he remarked that 'no one before him had dealt with growth and change except in the most superficial way—and he seems to have thought of everything'. Yet, without the confidence inspired by an acquaintance with Democritean logic and physics, how could Hippocrates have proceeded to delimit the scope of biological and medical science, detaching it on the one hand from religion and philosophy, and on the other raising it from a condition of mere empiricism and quackery to the assured status of positive science? This, however, was the task essayed by the author of *Ancient Medicine*, whom the critics agree in regarding as a fifth-century representative of the Hippocratic school, if not indeed Hippocrates himself.

The treatise, *Ancient Medicine*, stands out for all time as the first clear statement of the principles of rational empiricism. Medicine had existed as an empirical art from the days of Homer; and * * * had come within measurable distance of being a science. Empedocles, however, and the philosophers generally had attempted to bind medicine to the cart-wheel of philosophy. This, says the author of the treatise, is their fundamental error. The riddle of the universe may remain unsolved; and yet physical science both can and ought to progress independently. 'I consider that in regard to natural science clear knowledge is derived from no other source whatsoever than from medical science. The knowledge of nature can be grasped, if and when one properly comprehends the science of medicine, but until then, it is in my opinion utterly impossible. It is this field of research which I claim for my own; viz. the nature of man and an accurate knowledge of causation in this field' (ch.xx).

On the other hand, the defect of primitive medicine was apparent. Hit or miss empiricism had carried it a goodly distance, as, for instance, in the knowledge of diet. It stopped short, however, of classification (*to eidos*) and of penetrating by induction (*gnōmē*) to the principle (*logos*) of health and disease. The knowledge so acquired is doubtless relative, but none the less 'useful' on that

3. The school of psychology developed in the early twentieth century by Americans J. B. Watson and B. F. Skinner. Behaviorists seek to explain animal and human behavior entirely in terms of measurable responses to stimuli and deny the value of theories that cannot be scientifically tested, discouraging philosophical approaches to the human psyche and introspective speculation. Behaviorism was in fact based on the work of Democritus and his followers [*Editor*].

account. For instance, it enables the physician to forecast, and it is an excellent thing for the physician to practise forecasting. The ability to *predict* is thus laid down as the essence of science.

How is such prediction possible? By experience and experience alone. 'If a man intends to predict with assurance (*progignōskein*) who will survive, who will succumb, and who will be subject to the disease for a longer time and who for a shorter, he must first familiarize himself completely with all the symptoms. He will then be in a position to judge, estimating their relative importance. He must have a clear appreciation of the symptoms and other indications, because at all times and places bad symptoms have the same bad significance and good symptoms the reverse. In Africa, Greece, and Scythia, it is evident that the symptoms which have been previously noted give truthful indications. He must therefore realize that in the same localities it is not surprising if he usually hits upon the right diagnosis provided that he knows how to judge and estimate them aright. All the diseases that reach a climax at the aforesaid times may be recognized by the same symptoms.

This important passage has been quoted in full because it illustrates so beautifully the specific qualities of Hippocratic science. There are, he says, certain uniformities of pathological condition, and these may be ascertained by the competent observer. But such uniformities are ascertainable only by close attention to the symptoms. In other words, the possibility of prediction depends on close attention to facts (the *erga* of Thucydides), coupled with intelligent appreciation of the significance of the facts (the Thucydidean *logoi*); and this, in short, is science.

But what applies to pathological applies equally to normal conditions. In the treatise, *Airs, Waters, Places* (well described as the first exposition of the fundamental principles of public health), the author examines at length normal as well as abnormal conditions of human beings in relation to their environment, with a view to forecasting what will *probably* happen when changes in environment occur.[4] In this treatise also, the factors to be considered are but two, viz. (1) a human nature (*hē anthropeia physis*), relatively stable but possessing various potentialities (*dynamies*), and (2) the environmental conditions, differing according to geography, but in each district relatively uniform from year to year. It is further assumed that the physical environment determines in general not merely the bodily characteristics of the inhabitants but their mental characteristics as well. Thus, speaking of Asiatics, he says the inhabitants are well nourished, of great beauty of appearance, and of immense size and, furthermore, uniform in their beauty and size. Asia is tamer than Europe and the inhabitants are characteristically milder and more good tempered.[5] On the other hand, the bravery, endurance, industry, and high spirit of Europeans are accounted for in just the same way.

Questions of profound interest and importance for science are raised, if not settled, in the same treatise. Thus, in connexion with the so-called Longheads,[6] there is raised the question of heredity[7] and environment, in which the clichés of contemporary speculation are employed in perhaps a fresh and more significant sense. 'Originally custom (i.e. the custom of binding the head) was

---

4. Ch. xi.
5. Ch. xii.
6. The Macrocephali or "Longheads" lived in what is today Ukraine. The author of the treatise contends that the Longheads' original practice of squeezing and binding the heads of children resulted in the creation of an inherited characteristic of long-headedness.
7. Heredity is also discussed in chapter v of [the Hippocratic treatise on epilepsy known as] the *Sacred Disease* and there made responsible for all diseases.

chiefly responsible for the length of the head, but now nature also comes to the assistance of custom.[8] Here it is asserted that there is inherent in custom (the external) an element of compulsion, while nature (the integral) acts with spontaneity. The passage also emphasizes the significance and reality of the time factor in transforming the customary into the natural.

The word *nomos* has been translated 'custom', but, as may be seen from a subsequent passage, it carries an immensely richer significance than the English word. As employed in the treatise, it really means the habit that is induced by the necessity of conforming to conditions, and so equals the whole institutional environment, which is here given its due importance.[9] Geographical environment comes first, as the stage-setting of human life. But the institutional environment with which men surround themselves is no less significant, and, while in the main it cannot but correspond to external conditions, it nevertheless admits of and indeed includes that kind of motivation which we consider psychical.[1] Apart from the effects of climate and soil, so runs the argument, the Asiatics as a rule are unmanly because they are unwilling to risk their lives and fortunes on behalf of their despotic kings; while those few inhabitants of Asia, whether Greek or non-Greek, who are not ruled by despots, but are independent, toiling for their own advantage, are exceptionally warlike. On the other hand, the aggressive and independent disposition of Europeans is due not only to the greater variety of geographical conditions prevalent in Europe, but also to the political and social environment that has evolved in correspondence with those conditions.[2]

A further observation of great significance occurs in the same passage, namely, that change (or, as we should say, evolution) is the result of shock, which rouses the temper of man and prevents its stagnation. Accordingly, there is no progress possible in the uniform conditions of Asiatic life, except, perhaps, such as may be brought about by contacts with the more aggressive peoples who are produced in other climes. For in Asia nothing occurs to occasion violent mental shocks (*ekplēxeis tēs gnōmēs*) or bodily disturbances, and yet these shocks are more likely to inflame the temper and impart to it an element of brute courage than is an unvaried monotony. Thus both the classical notion that degeneracy, and the modern notion that progress develops as the result of purely internal and spontaneous changes of the human spirit, are rigidly excluded.

This great generalization put the Hippocratics in a position to criticize current notions of causation in the field of human activity, and in particular those derived from the popular religion. As an example of such criticism may be cited the passage[3] in which the author discusses the prevalence of impotence among males of Scythia. The natives, he says, attribute the cause of this impotence to God and worship the wretched victims, each fearing for himself. 'In my opinion also these afflictions are divine, and all others likewise. There is none of them which is more divine or more human than another, but all are alike and all divine. Each one of them has its own nature and none occurs except naturally.' Proceeding, he attributes the cause of this particular affliction to Scythian habits of life in the saddle. The discussion also throws light on a characteristic feature of Greek theology, common to Roman theology as well, namely, that the gods are thought of as responsive to prayers, supplications, and gifts, and ex-

8. *Airs, Waters, Places*, Ch. xiv.
9. Ch. xvi.
1. Ch. xvi.
2. Ch. xxiii.
3. Ch. xxii.

pected to return the favours which their worshippers bestow upon them, in the concrete forms of health, wealth, and happiness. We are not concerned to bring out the shallowness of this notion, although one is irresistibly reminded by contrast of the cry of the Hebrew: 'Though he slay me, yet will I trust him.' But the author notes the vanity of the attempt to buy the favour of heaven, and, in this, as in other passages, takes religious feeling into account, but only as a subjective manifestation of the human spirit. From the standpoint of science, this is all that he or any one is entitled to do.

The subject of divine intervention in human affairs is renewed in the treatise on the *Sacred Disease* or epilepsy * * *. This treatise may be, as some think, a thesis set by the master to a pupil on the theme of 'Superstition and Medicine'. At any rate, the seizures which popular thought ascribed to possession by a god or a devil are therein referred, like the Scythian disease, to natural causes alone, and a vigorous and ironical attack is launched against the unscientific dualism which accounted for some such phenomena as 'natural', while referring others to the 'divine'. In chapter iv may be noted the attitude of genuine Greek science towards purifications (*katharmoi*). These are examined in a spirit which, though it might have appealed to Thucydides, would hardly have done so even to Plato. Chapter xv describes the mental reaction of the victims, in the same spirit though not with the same vividness of detail as Thucydides employs in his account of the conduct of those who suffered from the plague.

One more consideration will complete, for present purposes, the analysis of Hippocratic thought. Throughout, it has been assumed that scientific knowledge is relative, and that the 'absolute' truths of philosophy have nothing to do with science. It follows from this that successful prediction is possible only in the main and generally; or, in other words, that scientific penetration (*gnōmē*) yields nothing more than probability (*to eikos*). 'Chance' or 'Fortune' therefore is depersonalized and, at the same time, the word (*tychē*) is emptied of metaphysical significance. The term is used to describe that which does not yield to scientific analysis, or simply the incalculable element in human affairs.

III

Thucydides

* * *

It has been thought necessary to depict at some length the background of Thucydides' thought for two reasons. Firstly, Cornford, in his brilliant and powerful argument, has referred the *Histories* to quite another setting. Secondly, the critics of Cornford, while they have put their fingers on what are without doubt the genuine characteristics of Thucydides, do not seem to have accounted adequately for the fact that those characteristics emerge in his work. Thus, in their hands, Thucydides himself appears as a portent, an 'uncaused' phenomenon in the stream of European thought. Bury, for instance speaks of his 'powerful and original mind'; and a recent writer[4] says: 'It is all the more to the credit of Thucydides that, living in an age when scientists still occupied themselves with problems altogether beyond the reach of scientific investigation, he did not allow his mind to wander into barren speculations, but kept it with unswerving steadfastness to those lines of thought upon which experience or deduction from experience could be brought to bear profitably. Upon these lines he concentrates his whole at-

4. G.F. Abbott, *Thucydides, A Study in Historical Reality*, Routledge, 1925, p. 76.

tention; and for the rest he has nothing to do but to take the universe as he finds it.' These critics go too far. In the fifth century B.C., at least in the one department of medicine, genuine science had emerged among the Greeks; and the power and originality of Thucydides lies in his having attempted to adapt the principles and methods of that science to the study of society.

There is no doubt that Thucydides, through his well-known connexion with the Thrace-ward regions, had at least the opportunity of meeting the Father of Medicine and becoming familiar with his work. That he actually did so is a probable inference from the close and, in some cases, startling analogies of style between the *Histories* and the *Corpus Hippocraticum*.

* * *

It is our contention, however, that the analogy goes much deeper than mere style: that, in fact, Thucydides adapted the principles and methods of Hippocratic medicine to the interpretation of history; and to the demonstration of this the rest of this chapter must be devoted.

The commentators have noted that Thucydides was keenly interested in natural phenomena, and have collected examples of his observations, e.g. of eclipses, tidal waves, the whirlpool of Charybdis, the silting up of the Acheloüs mouth, volcanic action at Stromboli and Aetna, forest fires, and the effects of the plague on flora and fauna at Athens. They have further observed that in each and every case he sought a natural explanation of the phenomenon in question. But Herodotus had already, in his disquisition on the topography of the Thessalian plain, provided a model for the rational explanation of natural phenomena, when he remarked (vii. 129) that the gap at the mouth of the Peneius river is the work of an earthquake and consequently that those who like to call earthquakes the work of Poseidon may do so. Thucydides, therefore, cannot be credited with originality in this field; although one may notice in passing that his grip on the principle of the uniformity of nature is firmer than that of his predecessor. Herodotus, in default of a plausible natural explanation, may sometimes be tempted to take refuge in supernaturalism. Thucydides never yields to superstition. Ignorant, for example, though he be of the real causes of the solar eclipse, he is content to state the observable facts, that this phenomenon occurs only at the beginning of the lunar month; confident that the eclipse has no supernatural significance, and that in due course will be made the generalization which will explain the phenomenon to the satisfaction of scientific minds (ii. 28).

The originality of Thucydides lies rather in his attempt to bring *all human action* within the realm of natural causes. In this connexion should be noticed the peculiar word *prophasis* which he uses to designate a 'natural cause'. This word, which in Homer, Herodotus, and later writers unquestionably connotes 'formulated reason' or 'pretext', means in Thucydides 'exciting cause' or the 'physical antecedent of a physical state'. To Cornford *prophasis* has proved a stumbling-block; it is one of the foundation stones upon which he builds his theory of Thucydides *Myth*-historicus. Other commentators, impressed with its apparently obvious meaning in Thucydides, have argued that, in this as in other cases, etymology must give way to common sense. The fact is that the word, as used by the historian, is in the highest degree technical. It is uniformly used by Hippocrates in the sense of 'exciting cause', and has been taken over directly by Thucydides in his attempt to apply the methods of medicine to history; the adaptation of methods involving, as is usual, the adoption of terminology.

In Thucydides, then, as in Hippocrates, it is assumed that all human actions and sufferings are subject to natural causes, and by these are meant the causes that are proper to human nature. In other words, both writers accept *men* no less than *things* as ultimates for the purposes of historical as of medical science. To Cornford this appears as a grave defect. He says:[5] 'If we would understand Thucydides we must not regard a human action as partly caused by innumerable influences of environment, and by events that happened before the agent was born, right back into an immeasurable past. . . . The world upon which the Greek looked presented no such spectacle as this. Human affairs—the subject-matter of history—were not to him a single strand in the illimitable web of natural evolution; their course was shaped solely by one or both of two factors: immediate human motives and the will of gods and spirits, of Fortune, or of Fate. The rationalist who rejected the second class was left with the first alone—the original and uncaused acts of human wills.' The modern passion for reducing history to mechanics could hardly go farther than this. But surely Hippocrates and Thucydides are entitled, for the purposes of their science, to lay down their own postulates; and to admit if they so desire, specifically 'psychical' alongside of 'material' causes as ultimate factors for history. Again Cornford[6] appears to go too far when he remarks that the ancients 'looked simply and solely to the feelings, motives, characters of individuals or of cities. These and (apart from supernatural agencies) these only, appeared to them to shape the course of human history.' The observations, quoted above from *Airs, Waters, Places* effectually dispose of such a view. To Hippocrates the ultimate factors were human motives in relation to environment, institutional as well as geographical. In his study of the evolution of Greek society at the beginning of the first book, Thucydides takes the cue and applies the Hippocratean principle to the elucidation of past as well as present, with such brilliance that the passage may truly be described as one of the greatest, as it is one of the earliest studies in human geography to be found in European literature.

To embark on a detailed examination of Thucydides' psychology would take us too far afield. It is sufficient to say that, like Hippocrates, Thucydides regards human nature as a relatively uniform and stable entity, in which, for purposes of analysis, one may distinguish *gnōmē*, the intelligence which affords direction to the activities of the organism, and the various potentialities (*dynameis*) which unfold in response to their respective stimuli; and result in various changes (*metabolai*) which make for the well-being of the organism or otherwise. Here may be noted how modern is the psychology of Thucydides in contrast with the classical or 'faculty' psychology which was derived from Platonism, in that he stresses the unity of the organism in the response which it makes to any particular stimulus (iii.45.7). 'In a word then, it is impossible and absurd to suppose that, when human nature is subjected to a powerful urge in any direction, it can be diverted either by force of law, or by any other terror.' Again (iii.45.1), 'Yet carried away by hope, they take the risk of [rebelling against Athens]. No one ever condemns himself to death in advance, when he embarks on a dangerous enterprise'. This last passage illustrates how, according to Thucydidean psychology, judgement tends to reinforce desire, so that the resultant act is an act of the whole personality.

Thus personality counts as a factor in human history, and has to be taken into account in the explanation of events. Spontaneous combustion may ac-

5. P. 67.
6. P. 66.

count for forest fires (ii.77.4), but to explain the downfall of the Athenian Empire are needed the personalities of Cleon, Nicias, and Alcibiades, each of whom, in his own way, made his unwitting contribution to that catastrophe. Thucydides therefore parades them across the stage, not in order to abuse them or praise them, still less to gratify the idle curiosity of the casual reader with a mirror of statesmen, but simply in order that he may bring out the facts and ideas connected with them which are relevant to the analysis upon which his eye is steadily fixed.

On the other hand, the growth of society is no more spontaneous than its destruction. As Hippocrates had said, growth is the result of shock which stimulates the mind and awakens it from stagnation. Such shocks, Thucydides observes, as though developing the Hippocratean thesis, are those that come from the struggle for control of the valleys, resulting in the successive organizations of power which culminate in the *polis*, or the clash of cultures resulting from invasion, or the fusion of immigrant with native as in the case of Thesean Athens. No less significant are the accumulations of capital, which suggest to their possessors all sorts of possibilities hitherto undreamed of; and the invention of ships and the art of navigation, which constitute the foundations of historical Greece. In all cases, where new ideas are involved, it is assumed that these ideas were born in somebody's brain. Thus Ameinocles of Corinth appears as the man who invented the trireme and later introduced it into Samos. Similarly with the idea of consolidation (*synoikismos*). In Athens this did not come about spontaneously, but was the work of Theseus, a man of power as well as wisdom. Theseus, stimulated by the existence of perils which arose not merely from foreign incursions but also from mutual quarrels among the village communities in Attica, and working by means of persuasion mingled with force, imposed on the inhabitants of the peninsula a unitary organization which afterwards got the sanction of religion; and deserved it, because indeed it saved the Athenians not only from foreigners but also from themselves. One is reminded of the observation of Hippocrates, quoted above, that there is an element of compulsion connected with *nomos*, but the *nature* ultimately comes in to reinforce it, so that it becomes indeed a sort of second nature itself. And one may suppose that consolidation, which was in Athens brought about as the response to certain conditions, came about in Argos and elsewhere, if not in response to the same conditions, at least to conditions equally compelling, or was introduced according to the self-same law of imitation which led the Samians to copy the naval architecture of the people of Corinth, and which to this day prompts progressive individuals and nations to import and adopt the advanced ideas of their rivals.

The power of innovation or 'invention' is one of the subjects which most engage the attention of Thucydides, and one which he discusses in various passages. In their speech at Sparta (i.68-71), the Corinthians charge the Spartans with apathy and stagnation, and apparently attribute these defects of character to the peculiarity of the environment of Lycurgan institutions. On the other hand (70.2) the Athenians are represented as innovators, quick to conceive an idea and to execute the plans which they conceive, beyond their powers daring, prepared to gamble beyond their judgement, in the moment of peril sustained by hope, venturing fearlessly abroad, etc.; so that (70.9) in short, if one said that they were born neither to take any rest themselves nor to allow it to other men, one would speak the mere truth. These characteristics, which constituted such a menace to the conservative states of Greece, are (71.2) referred to the atmosphere and institutions of Athens. 'Your institutions,' the Corinthians say, 'compared with those of the Athenians, are out of date.'

* * *

Thucydides either shared with Pericles or was prepared to attribute to him a point of view substantially the same as that which he puts into the mouth of the Corinthians in the passage just quoted. In the *Funeral Speech* Pericles accounts for the unique qualities of his fellow citizens in precisely the same way, viz. as a result of the spiritual atmosphere created in Athens by the great generation to which Themistocles belonged, and maintained in ever increasing power and volume by their successors. The specific points which he makes, reminding one again of *Airs, Waters, Places,* are worth noting:

(1) The Athenians are autochthonous, and the natural product of the peculiar geographical conditions in the Attic peninsula.[7]

(2) The shock of the Persian War gave Athens the first great impulse towards her imperial destiny. While Sparta and other conservative Greek states failed to rise to the occasion, and to effect those adaptations necessary to meet the new conditions created by the war, the empire-builders of Athens seized their opportunity and created the empire, which not without toil and stress they handed on to the succeeding generation.[8]

(3) The empire, as they possessed it, was the consequence of the atmosphere, social and political, of Athens.[9]

With regard to the question of innovation—the capacity for conceiving and applying new ideas in human life—Thucydides in two passages, speaking in his own person, reveals his opinion. The first passage is in the estimate of Themistocles (i.138.3–6), the second, in the estimate of Pericles (ii.65); and, of these, the former is the more significant. In the *Funeral Speech* also (ii.37) it is argued that the spirit of equality in Athens is not inimical to distinction, that, in fact, so far from implying a cult of mediocrity, it actually makes provision for the employment of talent (*aretē*) wherever it may be found. The existence of talent—special endowment—Thucydides was prepared to recognize; whether it was the peculiar abilities of an Antiphon, or an Alcibiades, or even a Cleon,[1] or the more normal qualities of a Demosthenes or a Brasidas, each of whom played his part in weaving the web of history, so that account has to be taken of him by the judicious historian. Accordingly, in the contribution of formative ideas to the life of the community, some men, such as Pericles and Themistocles, stood preeminently above their fellows. The latter, in whose fertile brain the idea of empire was first conceived, seems to have fascinated Thucydides. In estimating his contribution to Athenian life, he protested against the somewhat unfavourable verdict of Herodotus. Employing the current formulae of sophistic analysis, nature and nurture * * *, he reveals his belief that while nurture may save men from mediocrity, it can never account for genius. For the significance of Themistocles lay precisely in the revelation which he gave of the strength of natural genius. Without the advantages of a protracted education, but by the sheer force of his genius, he was in fact supreme in his ability to extemporize expedients to meet the necessities of the day.[2] This is the answer

7. Cf. i.2.6 and ii.14–17, where the social evolution of the countryside is more fully described.
8. ii.36.2.
9. [ii.36.]4.
1. iii.36.6.
2. i.138.3.

which Thucydides makes to those (like Cornford) who complain that he makes too much of the 'uncaused actions of human will'. For history, talent—especially insight and penetration (*gnōmē*)—is, like human nature itself, original and ultimately inexplicable, a postulate in fact necessary to the science. Thus did Thucydides dispose of the question of mind in evolution; and his authority survived to create the psychological interpretation of history common to the greatest of subsequent classical historians. For us in our day it has remained to essay the task of dehumanizing the history of humanity.

* * *

The scientific historian, as such, limits himself to the semeiology and prognosis of society; leaving to the political philosopher the task of constructing, on the basis of this prognosis, an adequate system of social therapeutics. This, then, is the real reason for many of the peculiarities of Thucydides which the commentators have noted and for which they have tried to account. His 'objectivity' and 'detachment' are results of the scientific method which he consciously adopts, and seeks conscientiously to apply. This, rather than the circumstances of his birth and life—his mixed descent, his affiliation with the conservatives, his exile by the democrats—enables him to characterize his native country, and put his finger with unerring precision on both the strength and weakness of imperial democracy. Moreover, his reticence is the reticence of relevancy. His duty is to consider the significance of personalities and events, in strict relation to his purpose. Hence those silences in regard to what happened, if the events had no bearing on the particular issue under discussion, which after all distinguish history from annals. Hence also those partial portraits or sketches of personalities, so vivid as far as they go, but yet so irritating to the modern, with his habit of discursive reading and of discursive writing. These, also, are in strict keeping with scientific method, and serve to distinguish history from biography. Finally, it is vain to look in the pages of Thucydides for any systematic statement of his beliefs. The good social physician will, in prognosis, keep strictly to the task of writing the 'history' of his patients, and he will reserve his schemes of social therapeutics for special treatment later, if he himself essays the task of treatment.

Yet, to all who accept the method of science, i.e. the view that life itself is the real teacher of mankind, so that it is necessary to consider how men do as a fact behave, before considering how they should, the one task is the necessary preliminary of the other. Such a conviction may without doubt be attributed to Thucydides; therein lies for him and for those who think with him the usefulness of history.

R. G. COLLINGWOOD

R. G. Collingwood (1989–1943) was one of the most important twentieth-century students of the philosophy of history. He was professor of metaphysical philosophy at Oxford and the author of many books, including *Roman Britain* (1923) and *The Philosophy of History* (1930). In his well-known book *The Idea of History*, from which the following selection is taken, Collingwood argues that the thrust of Greek thinking about the world was fundamentally anti-historical.

[Greek Thought and the Writing of History][†]

I should like to point out how remarkable a thing is this creation of scientific history by Herodotus, for he was an ancient Greek, and ancient Greek thought as a whole has a very definite prevailing tendency not only uncongenial to the growth of historical thought but actually based, one might say, on a rigorously anti-historical metaphysics. History is a science of human action: what the historian puts before himself is things that men have done in the past, and these belong to a world of change, a world where things come to be and cease to be. Such things, according to the prevalent Greek metaphysical view, ought not to be knowable, and therefore history ought to be impossible.

For the Greeks, the same difficulty arose with the world of nature since it too was a world of this kind. If everything in the world changes, they asked, what is there in such a world for the mind to grasp? They were quite sure that anything which can be an object of genuine knowledge must be permanent; for it must have some definite character of its own, and therefore cannot contain in itself the seeds of its own destruction. If it is to be knowable it must be determinate; if it is determinate, it must be so completely and exclusively what it is that no internal change and no external force can ever set about making it into something else. Greek thought achieved its first triumph when it discovered in the objects of mathematical knowledge something that satisfied these conditions. A straight bar of iron may be bent into a curve, a flat surface of water may be broken into waves, but the straight line and the plane surface, as the mathematician thinks of them, are eternal objects that cannot change their characteristics.

Following the line of argument thus opened up, Greek thought worked out a distinction between two types of thought, knowledge proper (*epistēmē*) and what we translate by 'opinion', *doxa*. Opinion is the empirical semi-knowledge we have of matters of fact, which are always changing. It is our fleeting acquaintance with the fleeting actualities of the world; it thus only holds good for its own proper duration, for the here and now; and it is immediate, ungrounded in reasons, incapable of demonstration. True knowledge, on the contrary, holds good not only here and now but everywhere and always, and it is based on demonstrative reasoning and thus capable of meeting and overthrowing error by the weapon of dialectical criticism.

Thus, for the Greeks, process could be known only so far as it was perceived, and the knowledge of it could never be demonstrative. An exaggerated statement of this view, as we get it in the Eleatics,[1] would misuse the weapon of dialectic, which is really valid only against error in the sphere of knowledge strictly so called, to prove that change does not exist and that the 'opinions' we have about the changing are really not even opinions but sheer illusions. Plato rejects that doctrine and sees in the world of change something not indeed intelligible but real to the extent of being perceptible, something intermediate between the nullity with which the Eleatics had identified it and the complete reality and intelligibility of the eternal.[2] On such a theory, history ought to be impossible. For history must have these two characteristics: first it must be about

---

† From R. G. Collingwood, *The Idea of History* (Oxford: Oxford University Press, 1946). Reprinted by permission of Oxford University Press.

1. The Eleatic school was evidently founded by Parmenides around the end of the sixth century. These pre-Socratic philosophers denied the existence of change and contended that motion, for example, was an illusion [*Editor*].

2. A key element in Plato's world view was the primacy of the eternal and unchanging. For Plato, what was most abstract and immutable was also most real [*Editor*].

what is transitory, and secondly it must be scientific or demonstrative. But on this theory what is transitory cannot be demonstratively known; it cannot be the object of science; it can only be a matter of *aisthēsis*, perception, whereby human sensibility catches the fleeting moment as it flies. And it is essential to the Greek point of view that this momentary sensuous perception of momentary changing things cannot be a science or the basis of a science.

Greek conception of history's nature and value

The ardour with which the Greeks pursued the ideal of an unchanging and eternal object of knowledge might easily mislead us as to their historical interests. It might, if we read them carelessly, make us think them uninterested in history, somewhat as Plato's attack on the poets[3] might make an unintelligent reader fancy that Plato cared little for poetry. In order to interpret such things correctly we must remember that no competent thinker or writer wastes his time attacking a man of straw. An intense polemic against a certain doctrine is an infallible sign that the doctrine in question figures largely in the writer's environment and even has a strong attraction for himself. The Greek pursuit of the eternal was as eager as it was, precisely because the Greeks themselves had an unusually vivid sense of the temporal. They lived in a time when history was moving with extraordinary rapidity, and in a country where earthquake and erosion change the face of the land with a violence hardly to be seen elsewhere. They saw all nature as a spectacle of incessant change, and human life as changing more violently than anything else. Unlike the Chinese, or the medieval civilization of Europe, whose conception of human society was anchored in the hope of retaining the chief features of its structure unchanged, they made it their first aim to face and reconcile themselves to the fact that such permanence is impossible. This recognition of the necessity of change in human affairs gave to the Greeks a peculiar sensitiveness to history.

Knowing that nothing in life can persist unchanged, they came habitually to ask themselves what exactly the changes had been which, they knew, must have come about in order to bring the present into existence. Their historical consciousness was thus not a consciousness of agelong tradition moulding the life of one generation after another into a uniform pattern; it was a consciousness of violent *peripeteiai*, catastrophic changes from one state of things to its opposite, from smallness to greatness, from pride to abasement, from happiness to misery. This was how they interpreted the general character of human life in their dramas, and this was how they narrated the particular parts of it in their history. The only thing that a shrewd and critical Greek like Herodotus would say about the divine power that ordains the course of history is that it is *phthoneron kai tarachōdes*: it rejoices in upsetting and disturbing things. He was only repeating (i. 32) what every Greek knew: that the power of Zeus is manifested in the thunderbolt, that of Poseidon in the earthquake, that of Apollo in the pestilence, and that of Aphrodite in the passion that destroyed at once the pride of Phaedra and the chastity of Hippolytus.[4]

3. In *The Republic*, for example, in Books 2 and 3 when he is discussing the dangerous role of poetry in Greek education, and in Book 10, when he argues that poetry should be banned from the ideal state (606e–608b). Elsewhere Plato speaks more positively of poetry (in the *Phaedrus*, for example, at 245a) [*Editor*].
4. Greek gods were notoriously destructive and punitive. Zeus, the patriarch of the Greek pantheon, often hurled thunderbolts at those who displeased him. His brother the sea god Poseidon was also in charge of earthquakes. Zeus' son Apollo was associated with such pleasant phenomena as poetry, music, and healing, but he also had responsibility for plagues (such as the one that attacked the Greek army in Book 1 of Homer's *Iliad*). Havoc could also be wreaked by Aphrodite, goddess of sex and love, who had fomented the Trojan War by encouraging Paris to snatch Helen from her Greek husband. When Aphrodite was

It is true that these catastrophic changes in the condition of human life, which to the Greeks were the proper theme of history, were unintelligible. There could be no *epistēmē* of them, no demonstrative scientific knowledge. But all the same history had for the Greeks a definite value. Plato himself laid it down[5] that right opinion (which is the sort of pseudo-knowledge that perception gives us of what changes) was no less useful for the conduct of life than scientific knowledge, and the poets maintained their traditional place in Greek life as the teachers of sound principles by showing that in the general pattern of these changes certain antecedents normally led to certain consequents. Notably, an excess in any one direction led to a violent change into its own opposite. Why this was so they could not tell; but they thought it a matter of observation that it was so; that people who became extremely rich or extremely powerful were thereby brought into special danger of being reduced to a condition of extreme poverty or weakness. There is here no theory of causation; the thought does not resemble that of seventeenth-century inductive science with its metaphysical basis in the axiom of cause and effect; the riches of Croesus are not the cause of his downfall, they are merely a symptom, to the intelligent observer, that something is happening in the rhythm of his life which is likely to lead to a downfall.[6] Still less is the downfall a punishment for anything that, in an intelligible moral sense, could be called wrongdoing. When Amasis in Herodotus (iii. 43) broke off his alliance with Polycrates, he did it simply on the ground that Polycrates was too prosperous: the pendulum had swung too far one way and was likely to swing as far in the other. Such examples have their value to the person who can make use of them; for he can use his own will to arrest these rhythms in his life before they reach the danger-point, and check the thirst for power and wealth instead of allowing it to drive him to excess. Thus history has a value; its teachings are useful for human life; simply because the rhythm of its changes is likely to repeat itself, similar antecedents leading to similar consequents; the history of notable events is worth remembering in order to serve as a basis for prognostic judgements, not demonstrable but probable, laying down not what will happen but what is likely to happen, indicating the points of danger in rhythms now going on.

This conception of history was the very opposite of deterministic, because the Greeks regarded the course of history as flexible and open to salutary modification by the well-instructed human will. Nothing that happens is inevitable. The person who is about to be involved in a tragedy is actually overwhelmed by it only because he is too blind to see his danger. If he saw it, he could guard against it. Thus the Greeks had a lively and indeed a naive sense of the power of man to control his own destiny, and thought of this power as limited only by the limitations of his knowledge. The fate that broods over human life is, from this Greek point of view, a destructive power only because man is blind to its workings. Granted that he cannot understand these workings, he can yet have right opinions about them, and in so far as he acquires such opinions he becomes able to put himself in a position where the blows of fate will miss him.

On the other hand, valuable as the teachings of history are, their value is limited by the unintelligibility of its subject-matter; and that is why Aristotle

---

slighted by young Hippolytus in favor of the huntress deity Artemis, she resolved to destroy him by making his stepmother Phaedra fall in love with him. The terrible consequences of Phaedra's passion were treated in several Greek tragedies in Thucydides' lifetime; the only one that survives is Euripides' *Hippolytus*, which was produced in 428, three years after the outbreak of the Peloponnesian War [*Editor*].

5. *Meno*, 97 a–b.

6. Herodotus (1.46–91) tells at some length the story of Croesus, king of Lydia, whose material prosperity blinded him to the fragility of the human condition [*Editor*].

said[7] that poetry is more scientific than history, for history is a mere collection of empirical facts, whereas poetry extracts from such facts a universal judgement. History tells us that Croesus fell and that Polycrates fell; poetry, according to Aristotle's idea of it, makes not these singular judgements but the universal judgement that very rich men, as such, fall. Even this is, in Aristotle's view, only a partially scientific judgement, for no one can see why rich men should fall; the universal cannot be syllogistically demonstrated; but it approaches the status of a true universal because we can use it as the major premises for a new syllogism applying this generalization to fresh cases. Thus poetry is for Aristotle the distilled essence of the teaching of history. In poetry the lessons of history do not become any more intelligible and they remain undemonstrated and therefore merely probable, but they become more compendious and therefore more useful.

Such was the way in which the Greeks conceived the nature and value of history. They could not, consistently with their general philosophical attitude, regard it as scientific. They had to consider it as, at bottom, not a science but a mere aggregate of perceptions. What, then, was their conception of historical evidence? The answer is that, conformably with this view, they identified historical evidence with the reports of facts given by eyewitnesses of those facts. Evidence consists of eyewitnesses' narratives, and historical method consists of eliciting these.

Greek historical method and its limitations

Quite clearly, it was in this way that Herodotus conceived of evidence and method. This does not mean that he uncritically believed whatever eyewitnesses told him. On the contrary, he is in practice highly critical of their narratives. And here again he is typically Greek. The Greeks as a whole were skilled in the practice of the law courts, and a Greek would find no difficulty in applying to historical testimony the same kind of criticism which he was accustomed to direct upon witnesses in court. The work of Herodotus or Thucydides depends in the main on the testimony of eyewitnesses with whom the historian had personal contact. And his skill as a researcher consisted in the fact that he must have cross-questioned an eyewitness of past events until he had called up in the informant's own mind an historical picture of those events far fuller and more coherent than any he could have volunteered for himself. The result of this process was to create in the informant's mind for the first time a genuine knowledge of the past events which he had perceived but of which up till then he had *doxa* only, not *epistēmē*.

This conception of the way in which a Greek historian collected his material makes it a very different thing from the way in which a modern historian may use printed memoirs. Instead of the easy-going belief on the informant's part that his prima facie recollection was adequate to the facts, there could grow up in his mind a chastened and criticized recollection which had stood the fire of such questions as 'Are you quite sure that you remember it just like that? Have you not now contradicted what you were saying yesterday? How do you reconcile your account of that event with the very different account given by so-and-so?' This method of using the testimony of eyewitnesses is undoubtedly the method which underlies the extraordinary solidity and consistency of the nar-

7. *Poetics*, 1451[b]5 ff.

ratives which Herodotus and Thucydides finally wrote about fifth-century Greece.

No other method deserving the name scientific was available to the fifth-century historians, but it had three limitations:

First, it inevitably imposed on its users a shortness of historical perspective. The modern historian knows that if only he had the capacity he could become the interpreter of the whole past of mankind; but whatever Greek historians might have thought of Plato's description of the philosopher as the spectator of all time, they would never have ventured to claim Plato's words as a description of themselves. Their method tied them on a tether whose length was the length of living memory: the only source they could criticize was an eyewitness with whom they could converse face to face. It is true that they relate events from a remoter past, but as soon as Greek historical writing tries to go beyond its tether, it becomes a far weaker and more precarious thing. For instance, we must not deceive ourselves into thinking that any scientific value attaches to what Herodotus tells us about the sixth century or to what Thucydides tells us about events before the Pentecontaetia. From our twentieth-century point of view, these early stories in Herodotus and Thucydides are very interesting, but they are mere logography and not scientific. They are traditions which the author who hands them down to us has not been able to raise to the level of history because he has not been able to pass them through the crucible of the only critical method he knew. Nevertheless, this contrast in Herodotus and Thucydides between the unreliability of everything farther back than living memory and the critical precision of what comes within living memory is a mark not of the failure of fifth-century historiography but of its success. The point about Herodotus and Thucydides is not that the remote past is for them still outside the scope of scientific history but that the recent past is within that scope. Scientific history has been invented. Its field is still narrow; but within that field it is secure. Moreover, this narrowness of field did not matter much to the Greeks, because the extreme rapidity with which their own civilization was developing and changing afforded plenty of first-class historical material within the confines set by their method, and for the same reason they could produce first-rate historical work without developing what in fact they never did develop, any lively curiosity concerning the remote past.

Secondly, the Greek historian's method precludes him from choosing his subject. He cannot, like Gibbon,[8] begin by wishing to write a great historical work and go on to ask himself what he shall write about. The only thing he can write about is the events which have happened within living memory to people with whom he can have personal contact. Instead of the historian choosing the subject, the subject chooses the historian; I mean that history is written only because memorable things have happened which call for a chronicler among the contemporaries of the people who have seen them. One might almost say that in ancient Greece there were no historians in the sense in which there were artists and philosophers; there were no people who devoted their lives to the study of history; the historian was only the autobiographer of his generation and autobiography is not a profession.

Thirdly, Greek historical method made it impossible for the various particular histories to be gathered up into one all-embracing history. Nowadays we think of monographs on various subjects as ideally forming parts of a universal

---

8. The eighteenth-century author of the *History of the Decline and Fall of the Roman Empire* was believed to have followed this line of thought in choosing the topic of his monumental work [*Editor*].

history, so that if their subjects are carefully chosen and their scale and treatment carefully controlled they might serve as chapters in a single historical work; and this is the way in which a writer like Grote[9] actually treated Herodotus' account of the Persian War and Thucydides' of the Peloponnesian. But if any given history is the autobiography of a generation, it cannot be rewritten when that generation has passed away, because the evidence on which it was based will have perished. The work that a contemporary based on that evidence can thus never be improved upon or criticized, and it can never be absorbed into a larger whole, because it is like a work of art, something having the uniqueness and individuality of a statue or a poem. Thucydides' work is a *ktēma es aiei*,[1] that of Herodotus was written to rescue glorious deeds from the oblivion of time, precisely because when their generation was dead and gone the work could never be done again. The rewriting of their histories, or their incorporation into the history of a longer period, would have seemed to them an absurdity. To the Greek historians, therefore, there could never be any such thing as a history of Greece. There could be a history of a fairly extensive complex of events, like the Persian War or the Peloponnesian War; but only on two conditions. First, this complex of events must be complete in itself: it must have a beginning, a middle, and an end, like the plot of an Aristotelian tragedy. Secondly, it must be *eusynoptos*,[2] like an Aristotelian city-state. As Aristotle thought[3] that no community of civilized men under a single government could exceed in size the number of citizens that could be within earshot of a single herald, the dimensions of the political organism being thus limited by a purely physical fact, so the Greek theory of history implies that no historical narrative could exceed in length the years of a man's lifetime, within which alone the critical methods at its disposal could be applied.

Herodotus and Thucydides

The greatness of Herodotus stands out in the sharpest relief when, as the father of history, he is set against a background consisting of the general tendencies of Greek thought. The most dominant of these was anti-historical, as I have argued, because it involved the position that only what is unchanging can be known. Therefore history is a forlorn hope, an attempt to know what, being transitory, is unknowable. But we have already seen that, by skilful questioning, Herodotus was able to elicit *epistēmē* from his informant's doxa and thus to attain knowledge in a field where Greeks had thought it impossible.

His success must remind us of one of his contemporaries, a man who was not afraid, either in war or in philosophy, to embark on forlorn hopes. Socrates brought philosophy down from heaven to earth by insisting that he himself knew nothing, and inventing a technique whereby, through skilful questioning, knowledge could be generated in the minds of others as ignorant as himself. Knowledge of what? Knowledge of human affairs: in particular, of the moral ideas that guide human conduct.

The parallel between the work of the two men is so striking that I put Herodotus side by side with Socrates as one of the great innovating geniuses of the fifth century. But his achievement ran so strongly counter to the current of Greek thought that it did not long survive its creator. Socrates was after all in

9. The Victorian George Grote (1794–1871) wrote in several volumes the first modern history of ancient Greece that is still cited today with any frequency [*Editor*].
1. A possession for all time [*Editor*].
2. Literally, "easily seen all together"; easily grasped in a glance [*Editor*].
3. *Politics*, 1326ᵇ2–26.

the direct line of the Greek intellectual tradition, and that is why his work was taken up and developed by Plato and many other disciples. Not so Herodotus. Herodotus had no successors.

Even if I conceded to an objector that Thucydides worthily carried on the Herodotean tradition, the question would still remain: Who carried it on when Thucydides had finished with it? And the only answer is: Nobody carried it on. These fifth-century giants had no fourth-century successors anything like equal in stature to themselves. The decay of Greek art from the late fifth century onwards is undeniable; but it did not entail a decay of Greek science. Greek philosophy still had Plato and Aristotle to come. The natural sciences were still to have a long and brilliant life. If history is a science, why did history share the fate of the arts and not the fate of the other sciences? Why does Plato write as if Herodotus had never lived?

The answer is that the Greek mind tended to harden and narrow itself in its anti-historical tendency. The genius of Herodotus triumphed over that tendency, but after him the search for unchangeable and eternal objects of knowledge gradually stiffed the historical consciousness, and forced men to abandon the Herodotean hope of achieving a scientific knowledge of past human actions.

This is not a mere conjecture. We can see the thing happening. The man in whom it happened was Thucydides.

The difference between the scientific outlook of Herodotus and that of Thucydides is hardly less remarkable than the difference between their literary styles. The style of Herodotus is easy, spontaneous, convincing. That of Thucydides is harsh, artificial, repellent. In reading Thucydides I ask myself, What is the matter with the man, that he writes like that? I answer: he has a bad conscience. He is trying to justify himself for writing history at all by turning it into something that is not history. Mr. C. N. Cochrane, in his *Thucydides and the Science of History* (London, 1929)[4] has argued, I think rightly, that the dominant influence on Thucydides is the influence of Hippocratic medicine. Hippocrates was not only the father of medicine, he was also the father of psychology, and his influence is evident not only in such things as the Thucydidean description of the plague, but in such studies in morbid psychology as the description of war-neurosis in general and the special instances of it in the Corcyrean revolution and the Melian dialogue. Herodotus may be the father of history, but Thucydides is the father of psychological history.

Now what is psychological history? It is not history at all, but natural science of a special kind. It does not narrate facts for the sake of narrating facts. Its chief purpose is to affirm laws, psychological laws. A psychological law is not an event nor yet a complex of events: it is an unchanging rule which governs the relations between events. I think that every one who knows both authors will agree with me when I say that what chiefly interests Herodotus is the events themselves; what chiefly interests Thucydides is the laws according to which they happen. But these laws are precisely such eternal and unchanging forms as, according to the main trend of Greek thought, are the only knowable things.

Thucydides is not the successor of Herodotus in historical thought but the man in whom the historical thought of Herodotus was overlaid and smothered beneath anti-historical motives. This is a thesis which may be illustrated by mentioning one familiar feature of Thucydides' method. Consider his speeches. Custom has dulled our susceptibilities; but let us ask ourselves for a

4. Excerpted in this volume, pp. 423–35 [*Editor*].

moment: could a just man who had a really historical mind have permitted himself the use of such a convention? Think first of their style. Is it not, historically speaking, an outrage to make all these very different characters talk in one and the same fashion, and that a fashion in which no one can ever have spoken when addressing troops before a battle or when pleading for the lives of the conquered? Is it not clear that the style betrays a lack of interest in the question what such and such a man really said on such and such an occasion? Secondly, think of their contents. Can we say that, however unhistorical their style may be, their substance is historical? The question has been variously answered. Thucydides does say (i. 22) that he kept 'as closely as possible' to the general sense of what was actually said; but how close was this? He does not claim that it was very close, because he adds that he has given the speeches roughly as he thought the speakers would have said what was appropriate to the occasion; and when we consider the speeches themselves in their context, it is difficult to resist the conclusion that the judge of 'what was appropriate' was Thucydides himself. Grote argued long ago[5] that the Melian dialogue contains more imagination than history, and I have seen no convincing refutation of his argument. The speeches seem to me to be in substance not history but Thucydidean comments upon the acts of the speakers, Thucydidean reconstructions of their motives and intentions. Even if this be denied, the very controversy on this question may be regarded as evidence that the Thucydidean speech is both in style and in content a convention characteristic of an author whose mind cannot be fully concentrated on the events themselves, but is constantly being drawn away from the events to some lesson that lurks behind them, some unchanging and eternal truth of which the events are, Platonically speaking, *paradeigmata* or *mimēmata*.[6]

ALBERT COOK

Albert Cook is Ford Foundation Professor of Comparative Literature, English, and Classics at Brown University. He has written widely on modes of expression and is the author of poems and plays as well as scholarly works. In his book *History/Writing*, from which this excerpt is taken, he explores the ways in which authors' attempts to give true accounts of the past as historians are shaped by their rhetorical practices as writers.

Particular and General in Thucydides[†]

The elusive factors bear impersonally on states, but it is men who personally make the decisions that activate them. The contrast between factors and persons, brought to a head in Thucydides' method, carries within it at once a permanent disparity and a perilous resolution. Such a contrast is another aspect of the oscillation between clarity and its opposite, an oscillation that operates in any successful historiography between explanatory subsumptions and selected ongoing events. Men are generalizing particulars in

5. *History of Greece* (London, 1862), vol. v, p. 95.
6. Examples or imitations [*Editor*].
† From Albert Cook, *History/Writing* (Cambridge: Cambridge University Press, 1988) 46–54. Reprinted with the permission of Cambridge University Press.

a particular situation that is governed by general factors reshuffled through time. Thus is a comparable interaction in Herodotus made dynamic. Resolution into clarity, in a sense, always bears on any specific situation Thucydides depicts, since the factors can only be activated, and thereby raised, as it were, to the second degree, by being taken up in the calculations of participants. After the peace of Nicias, and on the heels of a calculated rapprochement with Argos, the Spartan ambassadors who go to Boeotia decide to return the Athenian prisoners they have been given and to announce the razing of Panactum to the Athenians, who had been promised it back (5.43). The different interpretations put by the Athenians and by the Spartan envoys upon this double announcement, and the different weight given to each event, precipitate a hostility that immediately opens a path for Alicibiades and his rivalry with Nicias (5.44).

Events, by their very nature as crystallizations of decisions, lead to persons, and to particular kinds of persons. The Spartans may be slow and the Athenians swift, as the Corinthians tell the Spartans (1.70). However, the clarity, the resignation, and even the particular brand of selfishness in Nicias, transcend national boundaries and heavily qualify the notion that he is weak. Thucydides rarely expresses estimates of his persons directly and when he does so, he is, as it were, assessing the man as by himself an extraordinary factor, as in the praises of Themistocles (1.138) or the cautionary words about Alcibiades (6.15).

Leaders, in fact, under whatever form of government, are clearly shown in Thucydides to determine initiatives. They manage the forces to which, in turn, they cannot help being subject. These factors include other leaders; Nicias loses to Alcibiades the debate over the Sicilian expedition, and he reconciles himself to it, leading the expedition. But then he is subject to another constraint on the lives of statesmen. Unless they have the precocious gifts of an Alcibiades, they will be along in years when at the helm. And war itself increases the risks of mortality. Nicias suffers through the Sicilian expedition and dies there, as Pericles had died and Archidamus, Demosthenes, and Brasidas, Phormio and Kleon.

Precocity brings with it another risk, which Alcibiades has come to stand for more than anyone else, the risk of brilliant narcissism. He might trick the Spartan envoys, but over the long run a man's character shows. It was inevitable, whatever his guilt, that he would be accused of the sacrilege against the herms and the Mysteries. Thucydides underscores this inevitability by giving us insufficient evidence to decide his guilt either way, where usually it is accuracy in just this sort of affair that he seeks. The fact that Alcibiades is accused, as he inevitably would have been, impels this rapid and adaptive politician to avoid probable death by fleeing when the Athenians send to have him returned for trial. Other Athenians had fled to avoid prosecution, not always so successfully. Later, Alcibiades repeats this success, slipping away from a Spartan death sentence to the entourage of Tissaphernes. He would inevitably be using his talents to intrigue with the Persians and with the Spartans. Through the irony of developments, he escapes the disastrous Sicilian campaign he had urged, contriving his way back finally into the good graces of the Athenians.

The forces, at every point, are there to be managed, and the very change of their configuration from present moment to present moment provides a clever man with the opportunity to take them up without necessarily being impaired by the way he had done so before. Finally Alcibiades' selfishness and skill at diplomacy come into their own under the conditions that prevail after the Sicilian disaster, in the eighth book. This, as Westlake reminds us, is "packed with reports of secret negotiations and intrigues."[1]

The disintegration of the Athenian empire entails a decentralization of forces that permits playing one force against another without effective checks. In this way the person of Alcibiades, at this moment in the war, functions doubly as an agent upon the factors and as a mirror of where they stand. Indeed, the very mode by which agency combines with mirroring will differ. Pericles' particular bearing on the general situation is resumed into the speeches that exhibit him. These speeches exemplify a particular phase of the war and serve as agencies to influence a particular kind of policy—or not to influence it, since they are partially unheeded. "When he died his foresight about the war was still further recognized" (2.65). For Nicias, and for the dark events around Syracuse, the man and the time are characterized first by a reasoned speech not forceful enough to prevail, and finally by the relative silence of desperate defensive maneuvers. The individual in this instance would seem to have developed under the pressure of circumstances, since at an earlier moment Thucydides has asserted that Nicias urged the peace "to leave a name to later time" (5.16).

Thucydides' managed silences too, * * * preserve a neutrality. "What [your] nature always willed has been tested to the point of truth" (3.64). Literally "the things (ta) which your nature always wished" are plural and particular. The wish is general, and the truth is singular, a generalizing abstraction (to alēthes). So the Boeotians say to the Plataeans, but the notion will apply to the whole History. Most of Thucydides' uses of "nature" (physis) mean "human nature." Of the twenty times he uses physis, "human," or its equivalent is attached in nine. This quality, however, is not taken for granted, nor does it operate on the surface. It must be "tested to the truth" by the participants, and overridingly by Thucydides himself, whose History constitutes such a testing.

Nor is war a special case. "Many difficulties (polla kai khalepa) fell upon the cities in the uprising," he says of the Corcyrean revolution, "Occurring and always bound to occur so long as the nature of man is the same, though more peaceful and changing in their forms according to how the particular transformations of events (xuntuchiōn) may impinge (ephistōntai)" (3.82). "For all things by their nature (pephuke) do indeed diminish" (2.64), Pericles reminds the Athenians at the moment when he is assuring them that the glory of their empire will survive in memory. Nature, necessity (anankē), and customary behavior (to eiōthos) are linked in his presentation.

Thucydides' neutrality extends even to the presentation of himself in the third person both as a writer and as a participant (4.104). And it is significant that in his "second preface"[2] Thucydides adopts for a few sentences the grammatical sleight of an imagined, neutral observer. "If someone should not consider the intervening truce to be accounted war, he would not judge rightly. Let him look to the events as to how they are discriminated, and he will find it not a likely thing (ouk eikos on) to assess it peace" (5.26). The elaborate negatives here, and the six different verbs for mental sifting, establish, as though through syntactic struggle, the neutrality of viewpoint that Thucydides everywhere aims at. A sense of the severity with which he maintains this steadiness of view impends upon this neutrality, and a sparkling clarity of presentation holds his de-

---

1. [H.D. Westlake, *Individuals in Thucydides* (Cambridge, 1968)], 231.
2. Chapter 26 in Book 5 in which Thucydides stands back from his work and reflects on the entire war as he had done in Book 1 [*Editor*].

tails in unwavering coordination. The neutrality heightens the relational inter-action between general and particular.

Many constraints bear on the historian's task generally, and some obliga-tion to preserve neutrality is one of them. Neutrality is the attitudinal aspect of the obligation to narrate events *"wie es eigentlich gewesen."*[3] Another constraint obliges him to report only facts he can be reasonably sure were the case, Thucy-dides' "accuracy" (*akribeia*). Still another constraint obliges him to select them for some kind of congruence to his purpose, as Thucydides is a military histo-rian. Another constraint inhibits the historian from avoiding a mediation of his events, inducing him to adjudicate between general and particular in any case. He is obliged to steer somewhat clear of what could be taken for bare reportage. On the one hand he must suspend judgment while suspending his long-range connections. On the other hand mediation requires that he not give just a flat summary of events; he must not simply offer a chronicle. The balance of me-diation obliges the historian to steer a constant middle course between tract and chronicle. Thucydides not only understood this requirement, as Herodotus had. The speeches offer him an indirect, "doubled" mode of introducing in-terpretation while maintaining neutrality.

In this sense he must hold to the narrative, and his skillful management of all these constraints strengthens his narrative, allowing it to take on details for which the necessity cannot be argued on any logical framework. In the case of Thucydides, these details sometimes stun through similarity; particulars worked on by a coordinating intellection evolve into generality. The narrative of the Si-cilian campaign would presumably carry a comparable sense of the action if it were divested of half its details, and yet the extra details do not diffuse the nar-rative, but rather sharpen it; the particulars function as cumulative demonstra-tion, and in the narrative mode a sense of their necessity does not vanish once a general view is sensed.

Any historian is thus pulled in two directions by the particular and by the general. The mystery of his task resides in striking a balance between them that will operate along a narrative line. To quote Paul Ricoeur * * *, "it is the place of universals in a science of the singular that is at issue," though even the word "science" is misleading here, since in the historical narrative hypothesis and conclusion are fused together. There is a mix of the two in the ongoing narra-tive that the historian mediates, and may mediate differently within a given work. Particular and general have different relationships in the speeches of Thucydides and in the more directly narrative portions. The speeches have a double role as explanatory pauses establishing a general case, and as subsumed particulars globally aligned with details of action, along the lines of Thucydides' constant distinction between *logoi* and *erga*, words and deeds. A whole speech, composed of words, is itself a sort of deed.

Thucydides' statements about persons or events are briefer than his narra-tive presentation of them. This seeming disproportion or spareness of interpre-tation actually creates, together with the management of other constraints, a sense that a general view is being gradually furthered. It permits Thucydides sharply to enunciate what all successful historians must, the partial synecdoche[4] that constitutes his *ktēma eis aei*. Particular events have to have been selected

---

3. "As it actually happened," the famous formula of the German historian Leopold von Ranke (1795–1886), father of the modern objective historical school. Von Ranke believed it was possible and indeed essen-tial to reconstruct the past in its uniqueness ("as it actually happened"); distortions and misunderstand-ings, he believed, crept in when the past was injected with the spirit of the present [Editor].

4. The figure of speech (or thought) in which the part (or the specific) stands for the whole (or the general) [Editor].

for some general aim for them not to be a chaotic mass. The selection is partial even of those the historian can know; for Thucydides these are only the events that have not been inescapably lost in the dimness of time. As particulars they suggest a generality to which they relate; they are inescapably synecdochic. But the synecdoche does not operate the way it does in poetry; there is no whole for which the parts can stand. The whole is only adumbrated, and the synecdoche remains only partial, mediating perpetually between general and particular.

This mediation entails a sense of irony, and for Thucydides, as for all or nearly all successful historians, one event is bound to throw another into an ironic light. The overlooking of Pericles' advice, the escape of Alcibiades from the war we had urged, the fruitlessness of the articulations of the Melians to save their lives, the failure of the overweening Athenians in Sicily—the ironies of event multiply in Thucydides, who rarely makes an out-and-out ironic remark. Some irony in the historical narrative is unavoidable through the initial chaos of the referent, and yet an overall irony is impossible if the historian retains the order of the referent as a goal. The ironies play over the work as a sort of multiple running check against sliding back to mere particulars or against wholly backing some oversimplifying generality that would undo the tension of the narrative. The interpretative touch of ironic statement in later historians like Tacitus or Gibbon or Burckhardt will jog the narrative along.[5] Thucydides, we may say, shows his earliness in the intensity by which he stiffly refrains, by and large, from such touches.

The speeches, again, serve to double the ironic possibilities, not only between event and event, but between what is said and what happens, between *logos* and *ergon*. Any speech, as a complex of ratiocinative recommendations aimed at the immediate future, is bound to be tested by that future, and bound to miss its mark somewhat, generating the implied irony of contrast. And even if the speech hits its mark, there is the irony that still the speech may not be heeded, as Nicias' apt speech is not. There is generally an impelling onward movement toward conquest through the whole *History*, against which any speech, or any sequence of speeches, protests in vain. So there may be said to obtain a further, deeper irony between momentary if tensely reasoned arguments and silent, overriding motives. The Athenians do not listen to Pericles when he recommends restraint about campaigns, at his point of maximum prestige and maximum social authority. "Our knowledge (*epistēmē*) is better than any other force that has good fortune (*eutuchosēs*)" (7.63). So Nicias says to troops whose morale is low as the Sicilians are pressing them hard. Not only does the disastrous outcome render these words ironic. Thucydides' own principles do, since "knowledge," here meaning military skill, ought to be sufficient to know that it will be a decisive factor only if other factors are equal. This is what Pericles had insisted long before, weighing up the whole balance of factors. There is also the irony that Nicias, who seems to be imitating Pericles, is inadequate to his model. Of the factors that count, it is precisely strength or force (*rhōmē*) and happenstance (*tuchē*) that figure large.

So particular is the narrative of Thucydides that it often stays close to the maximum point of particularity. In its onward flow, however, it pauses most notably for the speeches, which do not halt the action but poise on the brink of fu-

---

5. Tacitus (c. A.D. 55–117) is often considered the greatest of the ancient Roman historians and wrote the history of the early Roman empire; the Englishman Edward Gibbon (1737–94) wrote a long and sweeping *History of the Decline and Fall of the Roman Empire* that historians still regard as a monument of style; the Swiss Jacob Burckhardt (1818–97) studied with Ranke and wrote a number of works, of which the most famous is *The Civilization of the Renaissance in Italy* [Editor].

turity and decision. They themselves, seen not as ruminations over the events but as themselves an event, particularize still further. They are given not word by word as uttered, but word by word to delineate the arguments presented. This summarizing function makes each clause, and sometimes each word, a microscopic encapsulation of dialectical relations between particular and general. Their reference is to a moment in an idea, and as such the terms in the speeches present a double face. With respect to their referents they are reconstructively concrete, and their character as signs must work more actively just because the individual words are constructive rather than reported. But the actual words tend to be abstract with respect to their lexical origin, and also with respect to their syntactic function.

Because of his onward flow, and his intermittent nervous adduction of qualifying abstraction, Thucydides is not felt to be slipping from particular to general, or from concrete to abstract. He can get back again very fast. * * * [T]he coordinates on which he operates permit of the occasional combination of these two styles, but not for their discrimination. His partial synecdoche makes him always potentially a subordinator, but the stringing of one event onto another in the narrative line pulls against this tendency.

To use G. E. L. Lloyd's terms for persistent tendencies in Greek thought,[6] Thucydides implicitly subsumes both the polarity that would make him subordinate his particulars under a general heading and the analogy that would make him coordinate them. Polarity and analogy are readapted to the constantly testing linearity of his presentation. * * * The feeling given by Thucydides' wrenching style is of too much pressing upon the sentence to be distributed out in even clauses. Only in the tendentious argumentation of an advocate uttering a speech will they be pressed into balance, or in the high piety and enthusiasm of Pericles' Funeral Oration. And even in such instances the abstractions brought into balance are themselves terms not usually polarized.

The compression of thinking into these terms individually shows in their somewhat unusual contrast collectively. Dionysius of Halicarnassus takes Thucydides to task for a number of stylistic sleights. All of these could be redescribed as distortions of language into imbalance under pressure: the substitution of noun for verb and of verb for noun; of active for passive and of passive for active; the change of tenses; the frequent use of parentheses and involution; the substitution of person for thing and thing for person. Dionysius speaks, too, of Thucydides' enthymemes. These logical proofs with one term left out will serve well to indicate the onward "slippage" of Thucydides' demonstration.

As Wille says of Thucydides, "Formal analogies can cover actual differences, while actual analogies are concealed in formal variations."[7] This happens especially when he is moving from more particular to somewhat less, and from concrete description to abstract reflection, as spectacularly in his transition to general observations after the Corcyrean rebellion:

> Every form of death occurred, and as is wont to happen in such cases, there was nothing that did not transpire and yet more extremely. Yes, and father slew child, and people were dragged from the altars and killed upon them, and some were walled up and died in the temple of Dionysus.
> So the raw strife proceeded, and, because this was the first example of it, it seemed even worse than it was; later, practically the whole of the

6. G. E. L. Lloyd, *Polarity and Analogy: Two Types of Argumentation in Early Greek Thought* (Cambridge, 1966).
7. Günter Wille, "Zu Stil und Methode des Thukydides" (1963) in Hans Herter, ed., *Thukydides* (Darmstadt, 1968), 691.

Greek world was stirred up, because in every state quarrels gave occasion
to the democratic leaders to ask for aid from Athens, to the oligarchs to ask
Sparta. In peace, without the excuse and indeed without the readiness to
summon them; but in war and with an alliance at hand for either side, to
injury for their enemies and to advantage for themselves, inducements
were easily furnished by those wishing to innovate. Many were the calamities that befell the Greek states through this civil strife.

(3.82; Gomme, revised)

Intermediate abstraction has already begun in the sentence about the father
killing the son. This is not one instance but a type case of which there could have
been more than one instance, though one single salient instance of horror, the
walling up of supplicants in the temple of Dionysus, brings the sentence to its climax. The typification of the first instance modifies the horror of the last, while the
actuality of the last instance concretizes the whole passage even further. There is also
a shift between singular and plural for the verbs here, and for "temple" (*hieron*),
though the cases are suspended differently between particular and general.

The jump to much higher generalization in "raw strife" (*ōmē stasis*) reveals, and incorporates, the horror. Thucydides controls and compresses his
diction while his syntax forces itself into extreme torsions here. He goes on
to describe another kind of slippage than the one his mastery is enlisting, a
slippage of diction:

So as the affairs of the cities kept going into revolt, the later outbreaks, by knowledge of what had gone before, were marked by ever-
increasing novelty of rationales, shown both in the ingenuity of attack
and the enormity of revenge. They changed the customary validation
of terms as men claimed the right to use them to suit the deeds: unreasoning daring was termed loyal courage; prudent delay specious cowardice; moderation the cloak of timidity; an understanding of the whole
to be in everything inactive.

(Gomme, revised)

"As men claimed the right to use them," translates the single term *dikaiōsis*
"adjudication," a term usually applied to court actions, and sometimes to the
punishment assigned after judgment. All these senses tinge Thucydides' use
without modifying it. *This* word refuses to refer to that which it describes and
unwittingly exemplifies—the "judgers" are "judged" by Thucydides; indeed,
they are even effectually self-punished by destroying the use of the language to
get them out of such later enterprises as the Sicilian expedition or the rule of
the Four Hundred. Under such stress, however, the language must respond by
a corresponding compactness and agility, as in this extraordinary case Thucydides is exemplifying when he takes the fairly unimportant Corcyrean rebellion
as a typifying instance. When he gets to still bigger and more crucial events, he
cannot digress for so long.

The increasing pressure not to digress confines Thucydides' presenta-
tional variation simply to relativizing his linear detail. Sometimes he offers
a great deal of detail, in campaigns important for the war or for their em-
blematic force. Less often he scales down the amount of detail he gives. We
cannot be sure that his omission of speeches in Book 8 indicates incompleteness and not the writer's decision to foreshorten from this point on. It

could be said that, having been initiated to the argumentative processes of speeches, the informed reader is in a position to make do with summaries so as to move forward more cogently.

The principle of relevance in the *History* operates simply at first; every detail must relate to the one all-embracing war. But the *History* starts out at a higher level of complexity and generality than the one it maintains, since Thucydides delays his prefatory theoretical remarks till after the Archaeology[8] and delays the Pentēkontaetia ("Fifty Years History") till after the beginnings of conflict. The shifts from one to another of these four initial units might tempt a critic to provide schematizations, but the onward pressure of events will undo such large-scale structural deductions. Thucydides cannot be found to have invented a structure more complex than his implied rule of explaining only what time has brought new to the condition of the war. He could have built the *History*, after all, on a version of Herodotus' more complex pattern, the intertwining of distant with close time-frames, and of ethnographic monographs with narratives. As it is, his narrative almost mimetically changes course as the war changes course. The Olympian viewpoint of the Archaeology and the Pentēkontaetia cannot be brought in to provide a Herodotus-like expansive disquisition about Persian politics in Book 8.

By that point Thucydides has established his theoretical control over the factors governing the narrative. Those come as a gradual revelation, and their increasing explicitness reinforces the simple but elusive near-pattern he is single-mindedly elaborating. The synecdoche can only be partial, but its theoretical force holds.

Plato, and later Aristotle, devised categories that would solve problems about the relation of general and particular. In the *History*, Thucydides offers an ongoing instantiation of how one kind of relation evolves between general and particular through a complex temporal sequence.

CYNTHIA FARRAR

After studying political science and ancient history at Yale and Cambridge, Cynthia Farrar wrote *The Origins of Democratic Thinking: The Invention of Politics in Classical Athens*, the book from which this excerpt is taken. She currently teaches courses at Yale on cities, including both Athens and New Haven, and works with the Yale administration on partnerships with New Haven. *The Origins of Democratic Thinking* explores the beginnings of democratic political theory in three Greek intellectuals: the atomist Democritus, the historian Thucydides, and a character Farrar calls Platagoras, the sophist Protagoras as he appears in the dialogue Plato named after him. Farrar sees Thucydides as passionately committed to the belief that historical understanding could help people make better lives in a better community.

[Historical Understanding and the Polis][†]

Thucydides' ambition to discover truths which would inform the future, as well as to render accurately (1.22.2) facts about the past, has earned him ep-

8. The name by which scholars identify the section at the outset of Thucydides' work (1.2–22) in which he presents the early history of Greece [*Editor*].
† From Cynthia Farrar, *The Origins of Democratic Thinking* (Cambridge: Cambridge University Press, 1988) 128-37, 176-91. Reprinted with the permission of Cambridge University Press.

ithets ranging from pseudo-dramatist (Cornford) through moralist (Finley) and scientific historian (Cochrane) to pseudo (or social) scientist (Collingwood).[1] Again, such generic classifications fail to capture the distinctiveness of the Thucydidean project, which is shaped by the assumption that understanding of human nature and human interests is possible only through an accurate narrative embodiment of human experience. An interpreted, analytical history both expresses and embodies an understanding of the way men tend to behave, and the way they in fact have behaved, in particular circumstances. Thucydidean history combines and surpasses the virtues, as imaginative portrayals of ethical life, of drama and the philosophic fable. It demands both participation and reflection, and participation in and reflection on real experience, not a plausible or hypothetical tale. History could only serve as a form of political analysis and a way of living politically in so far as it was good history; for Thucydidean history appealed to what man is actually like, and the way the world actually is.

To what kinds of political developments was Thucydidean history a response? The challenge was posed by the experience of democracy; the task was to reconcile order with the exercise of autonomy and the elaboration of reflectiveness over time. In the latter years of the fifth century, politics was no longer seen to be a means of self-expression and tutor of self-restraint; nomos seemed an artificial constraint and political deliberation a matter of showmanship and manipulation, of self-promotion and self-indulgence.[2] Under these conditions, reflection on human nature and human interests threatened on the one hand to sever man's self-understanding from and on the other to dissolve it in the realm of need and desire. From the point of view of Socrates, for example, politics at Athens simply was the indulgence of desire; he abandoned conventional politics as too vicious and dangerous, but boasted that 'of the men of our time I alone do politics' (Gorgias 521d). What he meant was that he persistently questioned individual Athenians, in order to show that reasoned sifting of a man's beliefs commits him to certain behavioral principles (e.g. it is better to suffer harm than to do it). * * * [E]thics was gradually distinguished from politics and was entrusted with the task of securing social order. The interaction characteristic of the polis was no longer conceived as itself providing citizens with good reason to act in such a way as to contribute to communal well-being; to prevent men from taking advantage of their circumstances to gratify themselves, an external conception of man's good was proposed, a teleological vision of man as a rational creature. By contrast, the view of man which submerged him in the depths of need and desire portrayed him as the creature of his passions. Thus Callicles:[3] the rules of society are designed to constrain men from indulging their desires to the full and thus realizing their true natures. Thucydides' History embodies the belief that neither account of human good will do. The desire of all men, or even members of the elite, to be tyrant cannot, in the world as it is, be sustained. However, as Socrates' confrontation with Callicles in Plato's Gorgias makes clear, an appeal to reason cannot in itself stifle such desires so long as individual men believe they can realize them.

Thucydides assumes, against both Socrates and Callicles, that reason and passion will often, particularly under certain circumstances and certainly in the world as it now is, come into conflict. No appeal to one or the other which fails

1. The works of Cornford, Cochrane, and Collingwood are excerpted in this volume, pp. 412–23, 423–35, 435–43. Finley's essay "Thucydides the Moralist" appears in Moses Finley, Aspects of Antiquity: Discoveries and Controversies (London, 1968), 44–47 [Editor].
2. The nature and value of nomos (custom, law) and its relationship to physis (nature) were hotly debated in fifth-century Greece [Editor].
3. In Plato's Gorgias; see pp. 383–90 [Editor].

452   Cynthia Farrar

to take into account the potential for conflict between them can define man's real interests, because it will blind him to significant aspects of his situation. The Socratic account, founded on the claim that man's only real concern should be the well-being of his soul, ignores basic human aspirations such as the desire to survive or the ambition to win power or glory. In large part motivated by the disintegration of socially-defined values, the Socratic appeal to principles of abstract reason is doubly unrealistic in that context. The Calliclean account of human interests and human freedom, apparently a realistic response to the perception that politics is merely a battle of interests for power, ignores the real constraints on any man's capacity to dominate others. Both accounts are conceived in response to conditions of ethical disarray, but both fail to—indeed, are too rigid to—grasp the real character and import of existing circumstances; in particular, Socrates and Callicles fail to appreciate the significance of social forces, which are stigmatized by both as corrupt and debilitating. Thucydides recognizes, and his *History* portrays, the effects of social and ethical disintegration; he observes the demise of the 'noble simplicity'[4] which secured social harmony and the advent, in conditions of insecurity and conflict, of constant suspicious calculations of advantage, which led to greater insecurity and more damaging conflict. Under such conditions, man's nature and his interests can no longer be conceived or defined strictly functionally, in terms of his place or role in society. A political understanding of man's interests must give way to a construal of the interests of men as individuals in particular circumstances. The teleological theories of man *qua* man, as essentially a rational soul or natural instinct, cannot meet this need because they increase man's reflective distance from experience and thus further undermine his capacity to act prudently to secure his real interests.

    Thucydides' historical construal of man's nature and his interests acknowledges that men are now, irrevocably, reflective judges of their own well-being and suspicious of social constraints; and his history shows that under such circumstances well-being can be secured only in a political context and only by deploying principles of historical understanding. The problem is how, in a fractured society, to make men alert and responsive to the fact that their good is tied to acting responsibly, with a view to the well-being of the political community. Historical interpretation reveals that the behavior of the political community as a whole, as a unit in the world of communities of the late fifth century B.C., is an essential constituent of the well-being of its members. To have genuine force for men whose capacity for judgement or prudence[5] is obstructed by passions, such interpretation should ideally take the form of political interaction. Leadership which functions by offering and promoting historical understanding can reveal how men are constrained, and how their real interests are defined, by the way the world actually is, now. And it can foster the self-control which, as historical interpretation shows, is essential now to the realization of those interests. Leadership founded on principles of historical interpretation can thus secure both autonomy and order: the reflective agent is guided by political interactions, but a form of interaction responsive to and expressive of the agent's own reflection on his experience and his interests. Although history is most effective as a guide to prudence when it is deployed politically, over time, yet a particu-

---

4. The term appears in the analysis of factional strife at Corcyra in Thuc. 3.82. Unless otherwise specified, translations in this essay are from the Loeb Classical Library edition, trans, C. C. Smith (London and Cambridge, Mass., 1919–1923) [*Editor*].
5. By 'prudence' I mean the quality of taking thought for the future and for the consequences of one's actions.

lar history could also, Thucydides believed, serve to teach individual men how to assess their own circumstances and identify their real interests. His own history is a 'possession for all time' not because history can be expected to repeat itself but because, presented in a certain way, history prompts identification and participation, and extends and sharpens the reader's ability to assess experience. Thucydides' analytical, reflective history of the Peloponnesian War is an answer to the challenge of his time both in content and form. It showed that the Athenians, powerful as they were, had good reason to exercise self-control. And it did so in a way which took into account both the force of human desires and the influence of context, circumstance and experience. The *History* constituted a way of thinking about the good for men—prudence—compatible with each man's constant reflection on his interests under changing conditions, and thus a way of thinking useful to all readers.

How does Thucydides achieve his aims?

How can an accurate rendering of particular events be useful, and useful not merely to those who experienced the immediate aftermath of those events, but to future readers? Thucydides' *History* is an argument: it both justifies itself (that is, shows that history is the proper way to think about—and in—politics, and that it makes historical judgement possible) and justifies also a particular set of actions in a particular context. For Thucydides, what there is to know about human nature can be known only historically. There are no static truths about men, only experience of them and understanding of particular situations. The *History* itself recounts the effects of reflectiveness on social order in circumstances which aroused doubts about the relation between the individual and the political good. This analysis shows that man should not construe who he is and what he should do in terms of social conventions or a static conception of human nature both of which are vulnerable because inflexibl and unable to identify the good under changing circumstances. The reflective revision of human behavior is necessary for prudence. As a mode both of political action and of analysis, history cultivates social prudence and collective judgement, and shows the need for such cultivation. Thucydides did not seek to close off reflectiveness or the collective exercise of judgement, but to shape it.

How does Thucydides' argument work? How is the *History* structured as an argument? Thucydides offers a story of the actual experiences of persons placed in a context which, properly interpreted, reveals the connection between their actions and the reality of the situation. The power of such an account to cultivate prudence and self-control can be illuminated by comparison with the process of moral education and the goals of psychotherapy. Children learn what kinds of behavior are appropriate by being guided through a succession of experiences. They infer, over time, what principles of analysis are relevant and how to apply them in particular cases. Although experience yields no universally applicable abstract lessons and no precise parallels, children learn to exercise independent judgment of new circumstances. In psychotherapy, patients learn to interpret their own behavior, to perceive deeply-ingrained patterns of response to particular circumstances, i.e. to understand why their life keeps happening to them. In the process they come to see their personality and character, their 'nature,' as a historical artefact. Thus understanding reveals certain limitations on what is now possible, given who it is one has become, but it can also enable one to act with greater self-consciousness and to modulate if not avoid habitual, instinctive reactions. In an analogous way, Thucydides' *History* invites the reader to participate in a set of interpreted experiences which guide assessment of what is appropriate (prudent) under various circumstances and of how men tend to behave, so that he may learn how to judge for himself: how to understand his own situation and anticipate his own situation and anticipate his own likely responses to it.

The utility of the *History* thus depends on a synthesis of accurate reporting and interpretation. Thucydides integrates the interpretive tasks of the historian, the historical agents whose experience he records, and the readers who are expected to learn from that experience. The reader observes agents attempting to understand and interpret their situation in a context accurately rendered and rigorously interpreted by the historian and he learns how to interpret. Thucydides is not offering a realistic story or an argument about ideas imbedded in a realistic setting; he is making historical reality itself intelligible and illuminating. He selects from, condenses, organizes, simplifies, juxtaposes and synthesizes what (to the best of his knowledge, after thorough investigation) actually happened. His principles of historical interpretation and presentation are precisely those which an agent should use to make sense of his experience and to determine his actions. The *History* does not merely express such principles; it embodies them. Thucydides does not invent. This claim may seem implausible in view of the fact that Thucydides incorporates speeches which are written in his own style and which are said to express 'that which most befitted the occasion,' what was appropriate (*ta deonta*) (1.22.1). Even in the speeches, however, Thucydides adheres to standards of accuracy as well as truth; his project requires that he do so. Unlike Homer and Herodotus, both of whom enlivened their narratives with speeches, Thucydides committed himself to keeping as close as possible to the general sense of what was actually said (1.22.1) and to trying to meet an objective criterion of appropriateness to context. The structure and content of 1.22 make it clear that for Thucydides reconstruction of a speech was always a last resort. Where reliable information was not available, or memory failed, reconstruction proceeded not on the basis of whim or prejudice but according to the historian's rounded and informed assessment of what the situation demanded (*ta deonta*) where 'situation' includes historical circumstances, intellectual and emotional climate and a particular speaker's need to persuade a particular audience of a particular view under particular conditions.

It is Thucydides' accurate and responsible presentation of a speech to bring out its significance, sometimes supplementing what he has heard in accordance with the criterion of appropriateness, which gives force to the speeches as interpretations and guides to it. For the speeches are useful to the reader in so far as they show men responding to real situations and reveal how — and how well — they manage to interpret events and exercise prudence. The actors and speakers in the *History* are interpreters: they do and say what they believe to be appropriate (*ta deonta*, in the complex sense adumbrated above) under the circumstances as they understand them. (Appropriateness does not entail rationality, but merely response to a perceived context.) They continually assess the likely course of events and the probable consequences of their actions. Like the historian, the agent reasons on the basis of the information he possesses and what he believes about the regularities of human experience, from what is or has been to what is likely to be. He may, again like the historian, seek to discover the truth (*to saphes*, see 6.33, 6.93). Thucydides selects and disposes antithetical speeches in such a way as to illuminate various — often the most general — aspects of particular decisions or circumstances; and the considerations raised in the debates are seen to be relevant (or not) to the outcome of events. Contrasting interpretations are presented as attempts to persuade others, and as such they appeal to what is usual, plausible, likely. Each speaker offers an assessment of a situation and its implications and of the motivation for and cogency of the other speaker's assessment. (See, for example, the speeches of Hermocrates and Athenagoras of Syracuse concerning the reported Athenian preparations to attack Sicily—6.33, 6.36.) They in turn are part of a broader assessment by the historian, who places the conflicting and successive interpretations of historical agents in a context which reveals their adequacy or inadequacy. The relevant context is not simply the sum of actual events—what does happen, by way of contrast to the interpreter's assessment of what was likely to happen—but rather the historian's interpretation of what was actually possible for the agent at the time. Through his characterization of the context, the historian suggests an interpretation as a foil to the agent's. The *History* is not a series of predictions which are more or less accurate, but of interpretations which are more or less realistic, not a moral tale which teaches a universal lesson about behavior proper to all circumstances, but a realistic interpretation of a particular period of history which demonstrates what it is to be realistic. The reader of the *History*, at two removes, gains access to a reality which has been interpreted by historical agents and by the historian. He learns from a history of interpreted interactions and interacting interpretations.

What the historian offers in the narrative (speeches and actions) as a whole is precisely what the historical agent needs: an understanding of what is required in or appropriate to particular historical situations and the related ability to discern what events are likely to be associated with what others in accordance with the way men tend to behave, itself an inference from the history of human experience and a regularity which underlies the existence of resemblances between one historical situation and another. Certain general features of man's nature remain constant, and are (in general) affected in the same or similar ways by similar events (1.22.4).[6] In his analysis of the civic strife in Corcyra provoked by the war between Athens and Sparta, Thucydides invokes the concept of human nature to explain the ferocious battles and the resulting calamities which 'happen and always will happen while human nature remains the same' (3.82.2). He observes that the stress of war and want tend to undermine man's judgement (*gnomē*) and strengthen his passions (*orgē*). Not everyone is affected in this way and the consequences of this general tendency 'are severer or milder, and different in their manifestations, according as the variations in circumstances present themselves in each case' (3.82.2). Human nature for Thucydides is not a fixed set of characteristics, neither basic, instinctual drives nor what man is at his best, but rather a psychological structure which underlies man's experience of the constant interaction of reason and desire. This interactions tends to be affected in regular ways by events. Thucydides' narrative not only provides illustrations of these regularities and variations in human response; it also provides experience of them. The reader is told, for example, of the degenerate way in which Athenian politicians after Pericles sought to manipulate the feelings of the masses; he also feels the power of their rhetoric. Or, in recounting the events which led in 425 to the Athenian fortification of a site on the Peloponnesian coast and the subsequent blockade of the troops sent from Sparta, Thucydides structures the narrative so as to arouse in the reader the

---

6. Thucydides' use of the concept of human nature does not imply a belief in or a desire to affirm 'psychological laws,' as Collingwood * * * alleges [excerpted in this volume, pp. 435–43].

surprise, confusion and alterations of feeling occasioned by these develop-ments. Thucydides draws the reader into the emotional and intellectual re-sponses which the *History* as a whole seeks to render intelligible. The reader is challenged to reflect on his[7] own reactions and helped to do so. The many echoes and recurrent patterns in the *History* are not meant to lull the reader into complacent certainty that he has grasped the inner workings of history; on the contrary, they challenge him to assess the genuine differences and similarities between two contexts, to think historically. An interpreted history, which itself depends upon and deploys judgments about appropriateness and likelihood, both supplements the reader's experience and sharpens his or her judgement.

By enabling us to experience and interpret a portion of human history. Thucydidean history cultivates judgement and fosters self-consciousness and self-control. Historical understanding of human psychological response pre-pares us to confront certain kinds of conditions in awareness of their likely con-sequences. The plague that ravaged Athens just after the outbreak of the war is a prime example of an unpredictable event. It fell upon Athens unexpectedly (2.48.2), and the doctors were helpless because of ignorance (2.47.4; cf.2.48.3). The plague was unlike anything the Athenians had heretofore experienced (note 2.50.1): no human art or skill was of any use (2.47.4). 'The character of the disease,' Thucydides reports, 'was such as to baffle description; it attacked each person more harshly than was compatible with human nature' (2.50.1). That is, the severity and indiscriminateness of the plague contravened what men thought they knew about the effects of disease on human beings (see 2.51.3). Thucydides' account analyzes how this kind of calamity affected human relations in the city. Like war, and particularly in conjunction with it, the plague promotes indulgence in instinct and impulse, and shreds the fabric of society. But he also gave a detailed description of the disease itself, 'to enable men, if it should break out again, above all to have some knowledge in advance and not be ignorant about it' (2.48.3). For the plague was an utterly baffling and unfamiliar disease, and terrifying in part because it was so alien. It afflicted the healthy and strong as well as the weak, and no single remedy could be counted upon to bring relief to most sufferers: what helped one man harmed another (2.51). To have knowledge of the character of the disease would not enable fu-ture generations to prevent it or even perhaps to mitigate its violence, only to recognize it and anticipate its likely course; but even this level of understand-ing would help to stave off the terror which had so demoralized the Athenians, and perhaps diminish the devastating social consequences of despair. Through-out the *History*, in a variety of different contexts, Thucydides brings out the im-portance of mastering oneself psychologically in circumstances that tend to be undermining, and indicates that understanding of the nature of the situation and its likely effects can help to make self-mastery possible. (See, e.g., 6.34.6, 6.49.2.) Awareness of the range of conditions that men and women have en-dured, and how they have endured them, heightens the reader's self-conscious understanding of human—and, at a general level, his or her own—nature, and thus, in a way analogous to the awareness achieved through therapy, enhances the capacity for self-control. A historical understanding of human nature is also essential to the historical interpretations that underlie and cultivate judgment. In the process of reading Thucydides' *History*, as in the process of moral edu-cation, one picks up relevant principles of analysis, including how to under-

7. Or, now, 'her.'

stand human behavior under various conditions, and learns how to apply and, when appropriate, revise them in particular cases. An interpreted history shows us that certain elements of our experience may well imply others which we have not yet experienced or recognized and indicates where we should look for relevant considerations in assessing the particular reality in which we participate.

*   *   *

The dangers of freedom: Athens versus Sparta

Thucydides' exploration and analysis of the capacity to respond realistically and prudently to historical circumstance takes the form not only of a characterization of Athenian politics during and after the hegemony of Pericles, but also of a portrayal of Athenians and Spartans. The contrast between the two poses concretely the question left hanging at the end of the Archaeology:[8] is it possible to achieve or to preserve both safety and greatness, in the world as it now is? In the *History*, Thucydides dramatized and interpreted the confrontation of two radically different military and political systems, temperaments and views of the world. This dramatic contrast is evident in the counterpoint of speeches and narrative, as well as in Thucydides' own comments and the overall framework of the *History*, which is the tale of two great cities at war, each playing a distinctive role. The attitudes, way of life and behavior of the Spartans point up the weaknesses, and the strengths, of the Athenians. Thucydides' analysis of the confrontation between the two provides both a conceptual framework for interpreting the behavior of political communities in response to experience and a historical context for assessing the reality to which each city had to respond. The speeches indicate the terms in which Thucydides analyzed the conflict: the words and concepts are Thucydides' own, and they express what was appropriate (*ta deonta*). They echo and derive added meaning from the use of the same ideas in other contexts in the *History*. Moreover, the terms of analysis are justified in the event; they make sense of the behavior of the two communities in the course of the war, as Thucydides perceived it.

The speeches provide a picture of the difference between Athenians and Spartans cast in terms of those factors which are shown in the *History* to be decisive for human behavior and well-being, namely *gnomē*, *orgē* and *tuchē*. In 432 B.C. after the Athenians had laid siege to Potidaea, the Spartan allies gathered in Laconia. Various cities voiced their complaints, but Thucydides reports only the speech of the Corinthians, who urged Sparta to take up arms against Athens. Corinth portrayed the Athenians as insatiable imperialists and the Spartans, who alone could prevent Athens from subjugating Greece, as ineffectual stay-at-homes. The Athenians, they said, were 'bold beyond their power, daring beyond their judgment (*gnomē*) and sanguine in the presence of dangers.' The Spartans, on the other hand, 'do less than [their] power justifies, do not trust even the certainties of judgment (*gnomē*) and despair of deliverance from dangers' (1.70.3). This comparison incorporates the major themes of Thucydides' narrative: power, chance and judgment. The Corinthians refer indirectly to the interaction of *gnomē* and *tuchē* when they assert that the Athenians remain 'sanguine in the presence of dangers,' while the Spartans 'despair of deliverance.'

The contrast between Spartan and Athenian perceptions of *tuchē* emerges in greater detail from a comparison of the Athenian speech at Sparta in 432 with

---

8. The title by which scholars identify the section at the outset of Thucydides' work (1.2–22) in which he presents the history of early Greece [*Editor*].

the Spartan peace mission to Athens after the Athenians had blockaded the men
on Sphacteria in 425. In 432, a group of Athenians in Sparta on other business,
Thucydides reports, requested an opportunity to address the assembled Peloponnesians; they warned the Spartans to 'take counsel slowly' and to use their
own judgment rather than allow themselves to be persuaded by the judgments
of others (1.78.1). In seeking to persuade the Spartans, who were renowned for
their caution and unwillingness to take risks, the Athenians stress the overwhelming power of chance: 'Understand thoroughly before you become involved in it how great is the role of the incalculable in war,' they advised the
Spartans. 'For when war is prolonged, it usually becomes a mere matter of
chance (*tuchē*) and from chance neither side is exempt, and what the outcome
will be is unknown and hazardous' (1.78.1–2). In making this argument, however, the Athenians reveal their own attitudes: it is precisely because chance affects both cities and is unpredictable that man must rely upon his intelligence.
According to the Athenians,

> Most men go to war and resort to deeds first . . . and then, when they
> are suffering, at length engage in words. But [they said] since we ourselves
> are not as yet involved in any such error and see that you are not we bid
> you, while good counsel is still a matter of free choice to both of us . . . to
> let our differences be settled by arbitration according to our agreement.
> (1.78.3–4)

The Athenians acknowledge the role of chance, particularly in military
conflicts, but emphasize that human reason can be effective in avoiding the unknowable, risky consequences of war. And since neither side can control
chance, superiority will be determined in the realm of human intelligence:
wise counsel and free choice.

Similarly, the Spartan envoys sent to Athens in 425, after the capture of the
men on Sphacteria, both speak to Athenian values and reveal their own. They
urge the Athenians to choose peace, and to regard their speech 'as a reminder
about how to come to a good decision, addressed to intelligent men.' By turning their 'present favorable fortune to good account' the Athenians would leave
'to posterity an unendangered reputation for both strength and wisdom' instead
of being 'credited with having won even [their] present advantages by means of
fortune (*tuchē*)' (4.17.3–4, 4.18.5). Yet, in contrast to the way in which the Athenians at Sparta described the power of chance in order to define the influential
role of human reason, the Spartans at Athens manipulated the concept of the
power of human reason in order to clarify the influential role of chance. The
Spartans warned the Athenians to use their intelligence and thereby recognize
that intelligence is of no use. Describing their own bad luck, they claim 'it was
neither through lack of power that [they] experienced this misfortune, nor because [their] power became too great and [they] became reckless.' Rather, their
resources were what they had always been and '[they] simply erred in judgment
(*gnomē*)—a thing to which all are alike liable' (4.18.2–3). *gnomē* for the Spartans, like *tuchē* for the Athenians, is a factor which affects all states equally, and
is therefore *not* a critical element in assessing the prudence of a policy. The
Spartans argue that fortune, not intelligence, determines superiority. Even
Athenian strength cannot ensure that '*tuchē* will always be with [her].' In war,
men must 'follow where [their] fortunes (*tuchē*) lead' (4.18.2–4).

Together, these three speeches not only articulate the contrast between
the temperaments, as well as the values, of the two powers, but also serve as
a commentary upon this contrast, placing it in context and revealing its am-

biguities. Before the war, in an attempt to calm Spartan fear of what the Corinthians had portrayed as innate aggressiveness, the Athenians emphasize the reassuring aspect of their reliance on intelligence, namely their capacity for self-control and deliberation. By 425 B.C. the Athenians themselves, encouraged by the self-seeking Cleon (4.21, 5.16) have been seduced by *tuchē* into insatiable greed (4.21.2, 5.14.1; cf. 4.17.4) and are deaf to the Spartan invocation of the value of exploiting *tuchē* through intelligence. For their part, the Spartans were deaf to the Athenian appeal to the riskiness of war. Having departed, under the influence of fear and Corinthian pressure, from their characteristic risk-aversion, the Spartans lived up to the Corinthian portrayal once the conditions predicted by the Athenians had come about: the unexpected, the fortification of Pylos, cowed them into suing for peace. In the early years of the war, under the influence of Pericles, the Athenians exhibited self-control not envisioned in the Corinthian portrait. As the years passed, they became intoxicated by success and lived up to the Corinthian characterization (note 1.70.3 with 4.17.4, 1.70.8 with 4.21.2). Thucydides thus exhibits the weaknesses of the Spartan character while presenting them as a necessary corrective, under certain circumstances, to Athenian self-confidence. Athenian inventiveness and self-reliance were the sources of greatness; in the form of recklessness, they were the cause of devastation. By refusing the Spartan peace offer, the Athenians abandoned the limited aims which were, in Pericles' view, necessary and sufficient for the maintenance of a balance of power in Greece, and committed Hellas to the destructive, bitter spiral of conflict (see 4.19.20).

Thucydides' account of Spartan and Athenian behavior under the stress of war confirms the ambiguities implicit in the speeches. The qualities characteristic of each could be construed either positively or negatively, depending on the context in which they were expressed and shaped. Sparta could be regarded as stable and cautious, or stolid and rigid; Athens as rash and undisciplined, or enterprising and intelligent. The qualities of the Spartans were a function of the training and discipline characteristic of their way of life. Reliance on discipline was the source both of Sparta's strengths and of her weaknesses. At Mantinea, Thucydides relates, the Spartans 'proved inferior with respect to experienced skilfullness (*empeiria*).' Sparta triumphed by means of courage (*andreia*) (5.72.2–3). They were trained to be brave rather than resourceful, stalwart rather than enterprising. This lack of resourcefulness emerges in Thucydides' account of the naval confrontation at Rhium in 429. The Spartans, in their initial departure from the tradition of land warfare, lost the sea fight to a few Athenian ships. They could not comprehend their defeat (this incomprehension was itself due, says Thucydides, to lack of experience) and 'thought that there had been cowardice somewhere, failing to consider the long experience (*empeiria*) of the Athenians as compared to their own brief practice' (2.85.2–3). In their speech to the troops, the Peloponnesian commanders argued that they ought not to be afraid of further naval encounters: there were reasons why they had been defeated in the first battle. These reasons—lack of preparation, the purpose of the expedition (namely to fight on land rather than at sea), the vagaries of war and inexperience—are adduced not primarily because the Spartans can hope to alter these factors significantly (though note 2.85.3, 2.87.5) but rather as evidence that it was at any rate not cowardice that caused their defeat (2.87.2). It was not right, the commanders continued, that the *gnomē* which was not then beaten [in the previous battle], but has some answer yet within its power,[9] should be blunted by the outcome of the event; rather [they] ought to consider that although men may suffer reverses in fortune (*tuchē*) yet brave men are always the same in judgment (*gnomē*). (2.87.3)

gnomē, in the sense of the self-control which resists demoralization—determination—was essential to courage, and could, according to the Spartan generals, be divorced from experience or skill. Courage, they argued, was far more important to success than skill, knowledge or experience; as Phormio, the Athenian general, remarked to his men, the Spartans relied chiefly on courage in their encounters with the Athenians, 'as if it were their peculiar province to be brave' (2.89.2). The Spartans were proud to declare that their discipline and courage, and not the cleverness and resourcefulness characteristic of the Athenians (see 2.87.4) were the source of their strength.

The bravery and wisdom of the Spartans, King Archidamus argued, sprang from their 'well-ordered temper.' They were brave in war 'because self-control (*sophrosunē*) is the chief element in a sense of shame and a sense of shame, in turn, is the chief element in courage' (1.84.3). The Spartan 'temper' was not founded on intelligent self-reliance, but on training. In fact, the Spartans were wise in counsel, according to Archidamus, because of ignorance, having been 'educated too rudely to have contempt for the laws and with too much rigorous self-control to disobey them' (1.84.3). Spartan power, courage and confidence rested on education and training. The Spartans did not 'believe that man differs much from man, but that he is best who is trained most severely' (1.84.4). Archidamus encouraged his fellow-citizens not to be ashamed of their reputation for slowness and dilatoriness: 'This trait in us may well be in the truest sense sensible self-control (*sophrosunē*). For by reason of it we alone do not become insolent in prosperity or succumb to adversity as much as others do' (1.84.1–2). Spartan resistance to the oscillations of *tuchē*, as the commanders at Rhium also noted, depended not on intelligent resourcefulness but on stolid self-control. Thucydides himself confirms at least part of Archidamus' claim: in praise of the Chians, he likens them to the Spartans, who are 'at once prosperous and self-controlled, and the greater their city grew the more securely they ordered it' (8.24.4). *sophrosunē* is the quintessential Spartan virtue, and it persists through good times and bad; in this sense, Sparta is invulnerable to *tuchē*.

But Spartan discipline not only fostered fortitude and bravery; it also, under changing conditions, rendered Spartan courage, policy and well-being vulnerable to *tuchē*. For Spartan *sophrosunē* is self-control in its most restrictive sense: an unchanging, static way of life. Spartan inwardness, isolation and caution limit exposure to extremes of *tuchē* and make *sophrosunē* possible. When forced by circumstances to expose themselves to risk, the Spartans were therefore extremely vulnerable. According to Thucydides' commentary on the Spartan state of mind after the Athenian capture of Sphacteria,

> The reverses of fortune (*tuchē*) which had befallen them unexpectedly in such numbers and in so short a time, caused very great consternation and they were afraid that some time a calamity might again chance to happen like that which had happened on the island; and on this account they showed less spirit in their fighting, and whatever move they might make they thought would be a failure, because their *gnomē* had become

9. Translation relies on formulations suggested by Gomme, [*Historical Commentary on Thucydides* (Vol. II: Oxford, 1956), 224)].

unsure as a result of having been hitherto inexperienced in adversity. (4.55.1–4)

The Spartan response to the threat of Athenian invasions is not to send forces to meet them but to post garrisons for fear that some innovation may undermine their institutions (4.55.1; cf. 1.70.4, 1.102.3). Implicit in this comment on Spartan behavior is Thucydides' awareness that preserving the shape of Spartan life requires constant vigilance on the part of the Spartiates; when the deadliest enemy is internal, defensiveness takes precedence over initiative (cf. 5.14.3, 1.118.2). Dependent as her way of life is on the continued subjugation of the helots, Sparta is permanently polarized internally. Like the tyrants mentioned in the Archaeology, she is intent on safety. As the Athenians remark to the Melians, 'advantage goes with security (*asphaleia*), while justice and the noble are practiced with danger, a danger which the Lacedaemonians are in general the least disposed to risk' (5.107). The Spartans, as all acknowledge (see 1.68, 5.105.3), exhibit great nobility and excellence in their relations with one another; these relations are both made possible by and directed to control of the helots. In their external relations, as a result, the Spartans (like the tyrants) are suspicious of entanglement, leery of taking risks, and, as the Athenians observe, 'consider what is agreeable to be honorable, and what is advantageous just' (5.105; cf. 1.68.1–2). The peculiarities of Spartan society—its remarkable internal orderliness and discipline, and externally, its unwillingness to take action and its vulnerability to the unexpected—are all due to the fundamental instability created by Spartiate domination of the non-Spartans who make their way of life possible. *sophrosunē* cannot enable the Spartans to respond and adapt to changing external circumstances, for it is precisely change and adaptation which *sophrosunē* is intended to prevent.

The portrayal of the Athenian character and its manifestations in internal and external relations also has two aspects. In contrast to Spartan stability—which the Corinthians, in their desire to prod their ally into action, interpret as stolid passivity—the Athenians are 'given to innovation and quick to form plans and to execute their decisions' (1.70.2). Spartan practices, the Corinthians insisted, are

> old-fashioned as compared with theirs . . . It is true that when a *polis* is at peace unaltered customary practices are best, but when men are compelled to enter into many undertakings there is need of much improvement in method. It is for this reason—because of their great experience—that the practices of the Athenians have undergone greater change than yours.(1.71.2–3)

The Athenians deliberately seek the experience and activity which require that they constantly alter their practices: 'They regard untroubled peace as a far greater calamity than laborious activity . . . They were born neither to have peace themselves nor to let other men have it' (1.70.8–9). Despite the Corinthians' evident—and instrumental—respect for Athenian attributes, their characterization reveals the negative aspect of the Athenian personality: the desire for constant innovation and activity has led them to prey upon other Greek cities. They are 'always seeking more' (1.70.8). The Athenians are daring 'beyond their strength,' venturesome 'beyond their better judgment' (*para gnomēn*) and 'sanguine in the face of dangers' (1.70.3)—all dangerously destabilizing qualities, as Thucydides' account of post-Periclean Athens reveals. Rashness and lack of discipline constituted the weak profile of qualities which, viewed from another angle, were Athens' best features: self-reliance, energy, resourcefulness and the spirit of enterprise founded on a system which expressed the collective interest. Contrast Thucydides' account of the Spartan response to the occupation of Cythera and the capture of Sphacteria with his description of the Athenians' reaction when they realized that the entire expeditionary force to Sicily had been destroyed (8.1.1–4). Like the Spartans, the Athenians experienced fear and consternation. But they recovered themselves and acted assertively to meet the impending crisis. They were not, it seems, cowed or demoralized, nor did they retreat within themselves, guard against internal disorder, and batten the hatches, as the Spartans instinctively did: 'In the panic of the moment they were ready, as is the way with the *demos*, to observe discipline in everything. And as they had determined, so they proceeded to act' (8.1.4). Democratic rule was erratic; but the citizens of a democratic *polis* were capable of appreciating the need for discipline and of acting to secure it.

The ambivalence about Athenian power manifested in the Archaeology re-emerges in the contrast between Athenians and Spartans. *Sophrosunē*, for which the Spartans were renowned, was not an attribute of Athenian democracy, even as it is portrayed by Pericles in the Funeral Oration, and Thucydides evidently admired *sophrosunē*. *Sophrosunē* could hardly be said to characterize the citizens of democratic Athens as a whole, since it was a way of life as much as a quality of character, and a way of life associated with oligarchy. The contrast between Athenians and Spartans implies that the choice is a unified and complete one: *sophrosunē* is associated with a particular kind of social system and foreign policy, and so, too, is intelligence (*xunesis*). Thucydides' ambivalence, implicit in the static contrast between the temperaments of Athenians and Lacedaemonians, is to be construed historically. Before the period of which Thucydides is the historian, the qualities described by the Corinthians enabled the Athenians, on the one hand, to secure and consolidate imperial power, and the Spartans, on the other, to extend and preserve control of their own sphere of influence while avoiding internal disruption. By the time of the Peloponnesian War, however, the maintenance of an equilibrium between the traditionally stable internal order and the demands of power depended upon limiting external responsibilities to whatever was necessary to defend and consolidate Sparta's existing strength. Sparta's lack of experience, and her inflexibility, crippled her capacity to initiate glorious enterprises or to respond to the eventual encroachments of an active, innovative power. And Athens' very success created a tension between active and free-ranging ambition and the necessity of taking into account the existence and aims of other *poleis* in a world polarized by Athens' own power and strength. The Athenians retained in a new context the attributes which had brought about their rise to power. The combination of an energetic, ambitious citizen body and the demands of the increasing power secured by its activities make the achievement of stable political equilibrium in a city like Athens extremely difficult. The risks are far greater for Athens, but so is the potential.

Thucydides' ambivalence points to the need to control Athenian desires and unify and stabilize its policies without smothering the energy, intelligence and capacity to respond creatively to experience which had built Athenian power and remained its greatest resource. Yet the inflexibility and ignorance evinced by the Spartans is evidently not the answer. The Spartan virtues were invoked at Athens by Cleon (3.37.3; cf.2.87.3). From the perspective of the historian Cleon can be seen to be aggravating the weaknesses of Athenian society and stifling its strengths. A different kind of institutional structure could perhaps provide more consistent discipline. Thucydides seems to have regarded the institutions associated with the Five Thousand at Athens, the moderate oligarchy or conservative democracy which paved the way for a return to full democracy after the oligarchic revolution of 411, as an improvement over the radical democracy (8.97.2). However, institutional answers—like the extreme case of the Spartan social system—risked blunting the self-reliance of the citizens and their adaptability. Thucydides did not in the first instance look to institutions, but to leadership: Pericles led the *polis* moderately (2.65.5). The moderate blending achieved by the Five Thousand was, I would argue, an institutional approximation to this virtue, to the power of aristocratic leadership in a democracy. When he says that Athens 'though in name *demokratia* was in fact becoming rule by the foremost man' (2.65.9–10), Thucydides is not praising monarchy, but rather a singular kind of aristocracy whose force is not institutional but psychological. Equality in the sense of the absence of a guiding *gnomē* was, in Thucydides' view, no virtue. Yet the triumph of Periclean leadership was *not* replicating *sophrosunē* in a democracy, but guiding and channeling the quintessential Athenian virtues, epitomized by the capacity to act both boldly and reflectively. As Pericles declares in the Funeral Oration:

> In the same men are united a concern for both domestic and political matters, and notwithstanding our various occupations there is no lack of insight into politics. For we alone regard the man who takes no part in public affairs not as one who minds his own business, but as good for nothing; and the same individuals [i.e. the Athenians generally] either decide on or originate public proposals, in the belief that it is not discussion that hinders action, but rather not to be instructed by discussion beforehand. We have this point also of superiority over other men, that the same group of individuals is at once most daring in action and most given to reflection on the ventures we undertake; among others, boldness implies ignorance, and reflectiveness produces hesitation. (2.40.2–3)

The point being stressed in this passage is that the Athenian populace does not rely on a division of labor: each citizen is competent publicly as well as privately, each acts as well as judges. The ability of every individual Athenian to be bold and reflective in serving the ends of the whole *polis* as well as his own is the source of the city's greatness (2.41.1–2).

The historian's ambivalence—self-control or intelligence, safety or greatness—which emerges in the contrast between Athenians and Spartans and is deepened by Thucydides' historical understanding of these characteristics and aims under changing conditions, is resolved in his interpretation of Periclean Athens. The more a *polis* resembles a collectivity, the riskier, and—if it succeeds in acting as an entity—the better. The Athenian democracy represented the possibility of the free exercise of intelligence, freed from and indeed superior to the power of *tuchē* and *orgē*. Under Pericles, the Athenians were as bold as their power warranted, venturesome in accordance with *gnomē* and hopeful when it was reasonable to be so: 'Intelligence . . . trusts not so much in hope, which is strongest in times of perplexity, as in *gnomē* based on existing circumstances, which gives a more certain perception of the future' (2.62.5). By means of his ability to determine what was appropriate (*ta deonta*) and to persuade the Athenians of the wisdom of his determinations, and through his capacity to moderate and unify their behavior in accordance with those determinations, Pericles made possible intelligent self-control and thereby preserved for a time both the security and the greatness of Athens. Thus, says Thucydides, 'he kept the *polis* in safety and it was under him that it became greatest' (2.65.5). The

Athenians should not yield; neither should they expand. They had attained the height of their power. In a world shaped by the existence of that power, greatness consisted in preserving it.

* * *

Thucydides' belief that history, or more specifically the kind of history that exhibits and fosters judgment, is the way to understand who we are and what we have reason to do, rests on the assumption that we can understand life as we live it, by viewing it historically. * * * Because it faces the future in construing the past, Thucydidean history clearly points beyond itself. Thucydides recognized that the need for history, including his own history and the historically-minded leadership of Pericles, was a cultural artefact, although he also seems to have believed that some men, including himself and Pericles, possess a capacity for judgment not vulnerable to the pressures of circumstance. Thucydides also recognized that the *polis* itself and the polarization of the world of Greek communities were the product of historical forces. It seems to me unlikely that he believed that this polarization was the end-state of history, and could only be alleviated or exacerbated, that the Greek world was for all intents and purposes the only world to which prudence would ever have to attend. The likely shape of the future is implicit in Thucydides' history of past and present. Polarization was certainly the salient fact of experience. But Thucydides' portrayal of the transformation of Sicily under the pressures of war, while it fits the analysis of the effects of polarization, also hints at the possibility of changes in the structure of power within Greece, namely challenges to the hegemony of Athens and Sparta. As a move outside Athens' traditional sphere of influence, the attack on Syracuse also suggests the possibility of even wider Athenian ambitions, for example designs on Carthage.[1] And the emphasis in the Archaeology and throughout the *History* on action in common could be extrapolated to an eventuality certainly contemplated by others in the fourth century, namely a campaign by a united Hellas against Persia.

As a way of thinking about human interests, Thucydidean history, unlike the purportedly more stable kinds of theories explored by Democritus and advanced by Plato and Aristotle, discourages both cynicism and complacency. As a way of living politically, it encourages reflection within a social context, and facilitates the achievement of both autonomy and order: it binds men to a political understanding of their own good and challenges them constantly to revise and extend that understanding by examining the world and themselves. Thucydides' successors as political analysts, like Pericles' political successors, lost their nerve and succumbed to the degenerative force of circumstances; they turned away from the demands of leadership and history.

ADAM PARRY

Adam Parry was a distinguished Hellenist who wrote widely on Greek thought. In 1971, when he was chair of the Department of Classics at Yale, he was killed in a motorcycle accident at the age of 43. At the time of his death he was planning a book entitled *The Mind of Thucydides*, an outgrowth of his 1957 Harvard doctoral dissertation, *Logos and Ergon in Thucydides*. In this essay he construes Thucydides' his-

---

1. See the comments of Alcibiades, Thuc. 6.34.

torical perspective as organized around the opposition between *logos*—word, thought, argument—and *ergon*—deed, fact, action.

Thucydides' Historical Perspective[†]

The sense of the tragic, which exists as a fine suffusion in parts of Herodotus' work, dominates the whole *History* of Thucydides. This sense of the tragic is something quite different from the clinical objectivity which has been so often, and often so thoughtlessly, ascribed to him.[1] His very reluctance to speak of himself, his way of stating all as an ultimate truth, is, if we must use the word, one of his most *subjective* aspects. When you can say, 'so-and-so gave me this account of what happened, and it seems a likely version', you are objective about your relation to history. But when, without discussing sources, you present everything as *auta ta erga* (I.21.2), the way it really happened, you are forcing the reader to look through your eyes, imposing your own assumptions and interpretations of events. To say all this is of course not to cast doubts on Thucydides' veracity or on the validity of his method of inquiry, little as we know of them.

The reasons for Thucydides' personal involvement are evident enough. He was a passionate admirer of Periclean Athens.* * * When he has Pericles say (II.43.1) 'You must each day actually contemplate the power of the city and fall in love with her, and when you grasp the vision of her greatness—'and so on; when he has Pericles speak in this vein, can we doubt that he was, and as he writes is in retrospect, one of those who heard Pericles' words with willing ears? Now compare this passage with a famous one from the *Archaeology*.[2] This is in I.10.2, where Thucydides interrupts his account to speculate on the possibility of utter destruction of Athens and Sparta. Later generations would not guess, from her meager foundations, how powerful Sparta has once been; and if the same thing were to happen to Athens, her power would be judged to be twice what it is, from the evident appearance of the city. Once again we have a vision of Athens—but in how very different a perspective. If Thucydides, as I believe, wrote I.10.2 along with the rest of the *Archaeology*, after 404, or if he wrote it earlier but let it stand in his final version, he is not only making a good logical point: he is also indicating the perspective from which he is writing the *History*. Although not in the literal sense envisaged in I.10.2, Athens has been destroyed, her greatness has vanished. The transition from the first passage, Pericles' words in II.43.1, to the vision of destruction in I.10.2 marks Thucydides' experience of the Peloponnesian War. For him it was the end of the world, after the world had reached its high point. This experience must be seen as the basis both of his dramatic presentation and of his theory of history as he had worked these out in the text we have.

† From Adam Parry, *Studies in 5th Century Thought and Literature* (Cambridge: Cambridge University Press, 1972) 47–61. Reprinted with the permission of Cambridge University Press. Greek words or phrases have been deleted when preceded or succeeded by an English translation
1. The notion of Thucydides as the passionless scientific gatherer of facts goes back to the positivistic interpreters of the nineteenth century (e.g., Gomperz [*Greek Thinkers*, excerpted in this volume]), and, despite protests like those of F.M. Cornford [in *Thucydides Mysthistoricus*, also excerpted here], has become the standard handbook view, much enforced by the double and doubly dubious equation Thucydides = ancient medical writer minus modern medical research methods. See A. Parry, 'The Language of Thucydides' Description of the Plague,' *University of London Institute of Classical Studies Bulletin* 16 (1969), 106–17.
2. The title by which scholars identify the section at the outset of Thucydides' work (1.2–22) in which he presents the early history of Greece [*Editor*].

Thucydides' final theory of history is one which he can only have evolved after the defeat of Athens. This is evident enough if we read I.23.1-3, where he sums up the conclusions of the *Archaeology*.

Of former actions, the greatest was the Persian, and yet this in two bat-tles by land and two by sea had a swift conclusion. But of this war the du-ration was great, and disasters to Greece took place in it such as no others in an equal space of time. Never were so many cities captured and made empty of their inhabitants, some by the barbarians, some by the Greeks themselves as they fought against each other; and there were those that changed their populations on being captured. Never were there so many exiles and so much slaughter, slaughter in battle, slaughter in civil war. Things which formerly had been known by story only, but had been rarely attested in fact, now ceased to be incredible, earthquakes, which were at once the most extensive and the most violent of all history, and eclipses of the sun, which came with a frequency beyond any recorded in earlier times, and in some places droughts, and from them famine, and that not least worker of harm and in part utter destroyer, the death-dealing Plague. And all these things were the accompaniments of this War.

Thucydides' vision of history is of greatness measured by war, and great-ness of war measured by destruction, or *pathos*.[3] This vision is a product of Thucydides' own experience. Unlike all the other great historians of the ancient world, he writes of the events of his own lifetime. He is so strongly concerned with this experience, that he has by modern scholars been accused of having no understanding of the past, or of regarding it with contempt.[4] To some degree, that is so; but we can conjecture from the *History* itself that he did not begin with this perspective.

It is likely, on the contrary, that Thucydides, as a young man, began with a genuine interest in the past, and did researches in the Herodotean manner. Witness the vestiges of these researches in the Cylon, Themistocles and Pausa-nias episodes and in the excursus on Harmodius and Aristogeiton.[5] When the War breaks out, he decides to devote the time he can spare from the affairs of the City either largely or wholly to recording its progress. He does so because he sees that it will be a great war or the greatest of wars, but he does not yet see it in terms purely of destruction. On the contrary, he must have been hopeful of its outcome—or at least that is the mood of 431 as he dramatizes it in the *His-tory*. We may even go so far as to suppose that he includes himself in the wry comment in II.8.1 about the many young men both in the Peloponnese and in Athens who because they had no experience of it were not reluctant to make themselves part of the War. He was young, he believed Pericles, and he was a keen professional soldier. The long course of the War changes his mind. By its end he has become convinced that this war is so final a version of the historical process as to supersede all preceding events, and that the greatness of historical events is measured by their power to destroy. He might have said of it, as he does of the Plague, 'all earlier disasters ended in, were subsumed by, this one'. He therefore can see its structure only when it is past, when all there is to lose is al-

---

3. The end of book VII illustrates this principle again. 'The Sicilian *ergon* [action] [87.5] was the greatest of this war, and of Greek history, most glorious to the victors, most unfortunate to the defeated.' The two poles of glory and suffering seem balanced, for a moment, and we might have a Herodotean view. But Syracusan triumph has throughout book VII been pale next to Athenian grief; and here in the splendid final sentence that follows the one quoted, he talks only of the extent of the disaster for the vanquished.
4. Cf. Collingwood, *The Idea of History* [excerpted in this volume].
5. A series of scholars have suggested that these portions of Thucydides' work were originally independent essays [*Editor*].

ready lost. Then he can write of the loss and of what was lost for the benefit not of his contemporaries, but of men of some later civilization who will thereby be better enabled to understand the destruction of their own (I.22.4). So he does write about the past, but his own, the experienced past; and he has no great interest in earlier events, because they after all only led up to this one.

The purpose of the *Archaeology*, that is, of chs.1–22 and their summary in ch. 23 of book I, is to state and develop his theory of history and thereby to justify his exclusive concern with the Peloponnesian War. For all his famous obscurity, Thucydides' style is such as to make the patterns of his thought very evident. Taking over the devices of the Sophists and turning them to an individual use, he writes an exposition in which ideas and events are strongly marked by key terms. These key terms are semi-abstract nouns and verbs designed to distill the elements of experience into an articulate pattern. He establishes the relation between judgement and fact in the first sentence, a first example of that pervasive contrast of *logos* and *ergon* which dominates his work and is what we might call its central metaphor. The great fact is the War, *ton polemon*. It is the supreme *ergon*; as in I.23.1, Thucydides often uses the word *ergon* as a synonym of war or battle. The other side is the judging intellect, the intellect that can give a conceptual shape to events, and that is expressed in the word *axiologon*: I expected this war to be *axiologōtaton tōn progegenemenōn* (most worthy the telling of all the wars that had taken place so far). This contrast is maintained throughout the *Archaeology. Ek de tekmēriōn hōn epi makrotaton skopounti moi pisteusai xumbainei* (on the basis of the most reliable evidence I could find after the most painstaking examination (I.1.2). The facts are now the evidence and the intellectual judgment is expressed by *skopounti* (to me as I was looking into things), *skopein* (to look into something, investigate, examine) being one of Thucydides' favorite terms. Analogous terms of intellectual discernment occur twenty-three times through the end of ch. 21. The historical facts which make up the object of intellection appear primarily as words meaning *power*. History in fact is movements of power. Thus forms of the word *dynamis* (power, potency, capacity) occur ten times to the end of ch. 21 and if we include synonymous expressions * * * , we have a count of thirty-five.

* * *

He argues that the earlier Greeks—meaning by this I believe all earlier generations down to the Peloponnesian War—did not have comparable greatness, 'either in wars or in other matters' (I.3). Note that in this sentence greatness in every other sphere of life is made subordinate to greatness in war. There was no greatness because there was no power, and it soon becomes apparent that power means order, because he at once begins a description of earlier times, 2.2, where with disconcertingly inconsistent syntax he described the disorganization of that period. He dramatizes this state by his style, moving rapidly from genitive absolute to a series of nominative plural participles, to a nominative absolute to another genitive absolute, with subordinate clauses of varying kinds in between, before he finally comes to the main verb, *apanistanto*, the imperfect of *histasthai* to mark the frequency of change of historical situation which prevented any order from being established.[6] The sentence contains sev-

---

6. The genitive absolute was a construction that enabled Greeks to set the background conditions for the action of a sentence by putting a noun and a participle together in what loosely corresponded to the possessive case in English. This made it possible to have long, complex sentences without piling up finite verbs. The imperfect tense of a verb indicated the ongoing past, something that happened continuously or repeatedly over a period of time [*Editor*].

eral key terms. There was no *communication*, no *capital*, 'so men *shifted* their dwellings easily, and so had *strength* neither in the size of their cities nor in other *material means*'.

This is the beginning of history; one might almost say, man in a state of nature. Thucydides describes it in negative fashion, listing those appurtenances of civilization which were lacking, things deriving from, and adding up to, power. The effect of power and resource (*paraskeuē*) is first to create order. Minos was first to *get a navy* (4.1) and thereby he *got power* in the Aegean Sea; he *established* his sons as rulers in the islands, and set about clearing piracy off the seas so that he could get *revenue*. This establishment of order by removing piracy made possible the accumulation of *capital*: 'The establishment of Minos' navy made it possible for those living close to the sea to *amass money* and achieve security, and some began to surround themselves by *walls*.'

The missing elements of civilization begin to be filled in. And so on through the *Archaeology* a series of civilizations, as power, are established, each with its element of ships, capital, walled cities—the features, obviously, of Athens in 431—and, the final transformation, war. Thus Agamemnon (9.1) is superior in power, and this, not the legendary oath to Tyndareus, enabled him to gather the expedition against Troy.[7] The way in which the Mycenaean rule came to be inherited by Agamemnon is then described in 9.2. The foundations of that rule were laid by Pelops, who by having a *supply of money built up power for himself*. In 9.3 we read that Agamemnon took over this rule, acquired more *naval power* than anyone else, and so was able to make the attack on Troy.

And the Tyrants (13.1): 'As Greece became more powerful and more and more engaged in the acquisition of money, tyrannies began to be established in the Cities; revenues increased; and Greece began to provide herself with navies.'

And finally, Sparta and Athens (18.1–2): 'The Spartans, having power, established governments in other cities; while the Athenians equipped themselves, took to their ships and became a sea power. Then after the Persian Wars (18.2) all of Greece ranges itself on one side and the other. 'For these were greatest in power; the might of the one was on land, the other in ships.'

Thucydides sees these establishments of order and power as admirable, and his style communicates this admiration to his readers. The severe impetus of that style, where words for *power* and *force* continually spring up to dominate the order of the sentence, enforces the sense that the creation of this sort of dynamic sovereignty is the most serious pursuit of man. I say *creation*, because each of these civilizations, these complexes of power, is seen as an order imposed by human intelligence. The notion that civilization is a product of the human mind, rather than of institutions and laws vouchsafed to man by the gods, is a characteristic Sophistic concept, and no one expresses it more clearly than Thucydides. Sea-power in particular, as we shall see, is an aspect of the intelligence, and the growth of this, culminating in the Athenians' becoming entirely nautical, parallels the development of civilization in general.

But there is so far one essential point missing in Thucydides' account of history. That is, destruction, *pathos*. The reason lies in the importance he attributes to Athens and to the Peloponnesian War. He presents us, in the *Archaeology* as a whole—that is, including ch. 23—with two historical curves, two lines of historical development. One is the rise and fall of a series of civiliza-

---

7. This famous interpretation of Homer is often cited to illustrate the historian's critical powers. It shows the boldness of his thought, but also how limited a reader of Homer he was. Homer does not mention the Oath to Tyndareus; and the *Iliad* makes it clear that the Greek warrior-princes fought primarily for booty and to maintain their position in society.

tions. The Empire of Minos had to dissolve before the Empire of Agamemnon could be established, and Agamemnon's had ceased to exist by the time of the Tyrannies, while these in turn were variously undone to make way for fifth-century Athens and Sparta. In terms of this historical curve, which could be represented as a periodic curve on the graph of history, the Empire of Athens (let us for the moment forget, as Thucydides often does, about Sparta) is but one term in an endless series, perhaps the largest term so far, but still not a unique point, not the convergence of all history. The second historical curve is a line of continuous development, ignoring minor ups and downs, from earliest times—I.2.2—to Athens in 431 B.C., when, with what has been blamed as exaggeration,[8] Thucydides says that her individual power exceeded that of Athens and Sparta together when their alliance at the time of the Persian Wars was at its height. It is this second curve which makes Athens and the fall of Athens into what I have called the final version of the historical process. The rise and fall of earlier empires must accordingly be seen as steps upward, and so he stresses their rise only, casually alluding to such matters as the confusion and faction attendant on the return of the Greeks from Troy, which could have been presented as the calamitous dissolution of Agamemnon's realm. Rather than this he stresses the creativeness of the early empires, presenting all history as a single trajectory, reaching a height in Periclean Athens, and coming to an end with the close of the 27-years War. The ruin of all empires is subsumed under that of Athens.

I.23.1-3 is the inevitable and fitting summary of the scheme of history which Thucydides has developed throughout the *Archaeology*. Civilization is the creation of power and is splendid and admirable, but it inevitably ends in its own destruction, so much so that this destruction is virtually the measure of its greatness. And all this is a pattern which Thucydides finally worked out *after* the defeat of Athens in 404, and it expresses his personal experience.

But some questions remain. Is the process absolutely inevitable? And if so, how are we to regard the historian's presentation of Pericles and Pericles' policy? And how does Sparta fit into the scheme?

The answer to the first question seems to be *yes*. For one thing, Thucydides has Pericles himself say so in a beautiful passage from his last speech, II.64.3:

> Know that Athens has the greatest name among all men because she does not yield to disasters, because she has expended most labor and lost most lives in war, because she has acquired the greatest power in all history; and the memory of that power will be left eternally to succeeding generations, even if we should now sometime give way; it is the nature of all things to decline. They will remember that as Greeks we ruled over most Greeks, that we fought against others singly and all together in the greatest wars, and that we had the city richest in all things, and the greatest.

* * * [H]ere we have all the essential elements of the Thucydidean scheme, and expressed by the statesman who, Thucydides tells us in the next chapter, had such justified confidence in victory.

Other considerations too enforce this sense of inevitability. First the comparison with the Plague. Strong verbal echoes confirm our sense that the Plague is presented as a kind of concentrated image of the War.

The word *epipesein, to fall upon violently*, which is used of the Plague (II.48.3) is used again of the inevitable effects of war in the description of the revolution in Corcyra; 'things many and terrible befell the cities of Greece in

---

8. Cf. Gomme, *Historical Commentary on Thucydides*, I (Oxford 1945), p. 134.

the course of revolutions, things which happen and always will happen as long
as the nature of man remains what it is' (III.82.2). And he uses in his description of the Plague the same word *skopein, to discern*, that he had used in I.22.4
of his description of the whole War, where he expresses the hope that his work
will be judged useful 'by those who shall want *to see clearly* what happened in
the past and will by human necessity happen in the same or in similar fashion
in the future'. Of the Plague he says, in II.84.3, 'I shall confine myself to describing what it was like [instead of offering either explanation or cure], and to
putting down such things as a man may use, if it should strike again, to *see it
clearly*, and to recognize it for what it is.'

Finally, the connotations of Thucydides' basic terms imply the inevitability of the process his *History* describes. I have spoken already of his use of *logos*
and *ergon* and of equivalent terms as a kind of fundamental metaphor in his historical presentation. * * * Following out his notion that the course of civilization and thereby of all history is man's imposing an intellectual order on the
world outside him, Thucydides continually makes a division in his presentation
of history between words meaning judgement or speech or intention, etc., and
others meaning fact, thing, resource, power, etc.

* * * The point of this whole terminological system is to present history as
man's constant attempt to order the world about him by his intelligence. Each
actor within the historical drama attempts to formulate, present and enforce his
own interpretation of external events and situations. This is done in speeches,
and accordingly Thucydides, in I.22.1–2, divides his whole work into 'what [the
participants in the War] said *in speech* [in *logos*] and 'the reality of what was
done' [in *erga*]. But both of these as seen from Thucydides' own point of view
are past actions and hence both fall under the heading of *auta ta erga* (the very
deeds themselves) of the War at the end of the preceding chapter. And the *logos*
that matches *auta ta erga*, in its widest sense of all actions and speeches in the
War, is, of course, Thucydides' own *History*.

Of all the words on the fact–external reality side of the opposition, *ergon* is
by far the most common and has the widest range of meaning. It is a fundamental Greek word and means anything *wrought* or *done*, *work* being its obvious cognate. * * *

But then there is a slightly different direction in the meaning of *ergon*,
whereby it stands for *fact, reality*, the thing that was *actually done*. This is the
nuance of meaning that makes it appropriate for the common fifth-century
idiom wherein *logos* and *ergon* are distinguished: "He *says* such and such, but
actually. . . ' Some of this stretch of meaning is in the English word *deed*. We
can speak of 'deeds of war' and at the same time have an adverb *indeed* * * *.

So Thucydides, by using the word *ergon* in a great variety of contexts, and
in associating with it, by a series of antitheses, other words such as *dynamis*
(power, potentiality) and *polemos* (war), is indicating, building the notion into
the structure of his language, that power and war are simply aspects of reality.
War is the final reality. There can be no civilization, no complex of power without war, because the one word implies the other.

If it be objected that I am playing a word-game here, the answer is that it
is Thucydides' own word-game, and that he uses it to express an interpretation
of history that he makes explicit in other ways as well.

The other unanswered questions are the role of Pericles and that of
Sparta. They can be answered together. Throughout the *History*, Thucydides
presents the Athenian character as dominated by *logos* and the Spartan character as dominated by *ergon*. In two Spartan speeches, those of Archidamus and

Sthenelaidas in book 1 (80–5 and 86) and in one Corinthian speech, that at the Second Congress in Lacedaemon, also in Book I (120–4), the Spartans and their allies are characterized as distrusting the intellect and putting their faith in fact. 'We are trained to believe', Archidamus says in 84.3, 'that the chances of war are not accessible to, cannot be predicted by, human reason.' * * * 'And so,' he goes on, 'we put our faith in strict discipline' (85.1). Sthenelaidas is more brutal: *tous men logous tous pollous tōn Athenaiōn ou gignōskō* ('I don't understand the many *logoi* of the Athenians'), he begins in 86.1. He means (*a*) 'I choose to ignore the protracted speech of the Athenians in defense of their Empire', and (*b*) 'As a Spartan I reject the use of speech and reason and urge immediate recourse to fact; that is, to war.'

By contrast the Athenians and Pericles in particular urge that reason is the indispensable preliminary to action. 'We differ from other men', Pericles says in II.40.2, in the Funeral Speech, 'by not believing words harmful to action, but rather that harm lies in not working out beforehand in words what must actually be carried out.' * * *

The implications of this much-elaborated opposition between the two national characters are something like this. Inasmuch as civilization is the successful imposition of intelligence on the brute matter of the outside world, Athens, not Sparta, represents civilization. The Athenians in fact are the moving force throughout the *History*. They, from the moment they followed Themistocles at the time of the Persian Wars and took to their ships—this itself an act of the creative intelligence (I.18)—from that moment on it is they who have created an Empire far greater than those of Minos and Agamemnon. It is they who have changed the map and the character of Greece * * *. They are that incommensurate, irrational factor in reality which makes it sure that ultimately you can never win; what corresponds in the large scheme of history to what Thucydides calls *paralogos* (beyond reason), that which the keenest intelligence cannot foresee.

In Thucydides' scheme therefore, there is only one civilization in 431 B.C., that of Athens. Its power, created by intelligence, inevitably becomes war: 'As the Athenians became great, the Spartans were compelled to war' (I.23.6), and eventually this war destroys the civilization that brought it about. The Spartans are merely the external agents of this destruction. Pericles is the essence of Athenian intelligence. The word constantly attached to him is *gnōmē*. He is that aspect of intelligence which will not yield to the pressures of external reality. The reason the Athenians could have won the war if they had followed his judgement throughout is that this judgement is presented as transcending the vicissitudes of actual events. 'I continue to hold to the same conception (*gnōmē*), citizens of Athens, not to yield to the Peloponnesians . . .' So begins his first speech, the first words he speaks in the *History*.

The same assertion of unwavering judgement in the face of the *paralogoi* (unexpected events, miscalculations) of reality dominates Pericles' last speech after the Plague. In general, men's conceptions, and the words they use to express them, vary with events, and alter with every alteration they find. Pericles alone is above this, and hence Thucydides attributes to him an almost superhuman judgement, which he asserts could have carried the Empire through to victory if the Athenians, who to Pericles are part of the recalcitrant matter of history, had been to follow it.

It may fairly be objected that Thucydides has no right to insist on the inevitability of the fall of empire on the one hand and on the invincibility of Periclean policy on the other. It is the great paradox of his work and a point where his system seems to break down. Two considerations should modify this criticism. One is the peculiar nature of the Athenian Empire as Thucydides has Pericles conceive it. The Athenians do not merely use sea-power to build their realm: they become almost entirely identified with sea-power: they 'became nautical'. Inasmuch as sea-power is especially the creation of the intelligence, we have here a vision of the Athenian Empire as pure product of the mind, and consequently inaccessible to those elements in the world which the mind cannot control. 'Consider', Pericles tells his countrymen in his First Speech (I.143.5), 'if we were islanders, who could be more safe from the enemy?. . . You must *approach this conception* as close as possible, and let your homes and lands go'. This vision of Athens as a power so completely created by the intellect as to be proof against the waywardness of reality is almost fantastic; and yet perhaps true to the historical Pericles' own imagination.

The second consideration is deeper. It is the foreknowledge of Athens' defeat which Thucydides attributes to Pericles in his Last Speech. There the historian suggests that there is a valid sense in which it does not matter whether Athens falls or not, because the quality of her memory will remain; and that Pericles was clearly aware of this sense. As conception in the present becomes fact in the past, so fact in the past, in this case the uniqueness of Athenian power at one moment of history, stays alive in the present as concept. In this way, Periclean Athens does escape the grim system which Thucydides develops as the intellectual foundation of his narrative. Because Athens under Pericles remains an ineffaceable image in the mind, the city is truly invincible, and to fix this image is precisely the purpose of Thucydides' account.

GLEN BOWERSOCK

Glen Bowersock taught for many years at Harvard and has since 1980 been a Senior Member of the School of Historical Studies at the Institute for Advanced Study in Princeton. He has written widely about the intellectual history of both Greece and Rome. In this essay he conceives Thucydides' work as informed by the personality of the individual historian, a sensitive author intensely pained by the events of the war he has chosen to recount.

The Personality of Thucydides[†]

The austerity of a cold and detached intellect, it is often alleged, characterizes that massive prose fragment, the *History* of Thucydides. Contrasts are drawn between the amiable Herodotus and his younger contemporary, an innovatory practitioner of scientific historiography. Eschewing personal reminiscences, Thucydides did not even attempt to justify his own military failure at Amphipolis, a failure which led to twenty years in exile. A lecture series on "master minds" recently found a place for Thucydides,[1] and rightly; it was a stupendous mind, subtle and relentless. But a mind or an intellect cannot exist without a man, and austerity is rarely total. In the case of Thucydides it is much less than convenient generalizations would suggest.

† Glen Bowersock, "The Personality of Thucydides." Copyright © 1965 by the *Antioch Review*, Inc. First appeared in the *Antioch Review*, Vol. 25, No. 1 (Spring 1965). Reprinted by permission of the editors.
1. In 1960: the lectures in this series appear in the *Proceedings* of the British Academy.

An illustration will show this at once. In the summer of 413 a band of Thracian mercenaries, arriving in Athens too late for service in Sicily, returned home under the leadership of a certain Dieitrephes. Thucydides recorded their journey north: when they came into Boeotia, they fell upon the unprotected town of Mycalessus, which had never anticipated this chance arrival of barbarous soldiers. In the words of Thucydides:

> They sacked the homes and temples, and they slaughtered the people, sparing neither old nor young but killing all indiscriminately, women and children, even beasts of burden and whatever they saw alive . . . There was great turmoil and every form of ruin: they fell upon a children's school, which was the largest there and into which the children had just come, and they cut down every one of them. No city suffered any disaster worse that this, unexpected as it was and horrible.

This final comment is that of a man who had recorded the hideous fates of Scione, Hysiae, and Melos, and who was in his narrative moving toward the Athenian catastrophe at Syracuse. Some measure of horror is inevitable in war, but the acts of the Thracians at Mycalessus were unnecessary and not a part of the struggle between Athens and Sparta. Innocent children, normally spared, perished. This is surely the explanation of that compassionate utterance of Thucydides, who stands revealed without austerity.

The personality of the man calls for attention. A recent writer, in the preface to an excellent paperback volume,[2] has stated that in his view Thucydides agreed fundamentally with the Athenians' brutal doctrine of power as expounded in the Melian Dialogue. That is going too far, and perhaps some reconsiderations would be helpful to our understanding. For one thing, an assessment of personality will provide some control over the vexed question of the speeches. As every conscientious reader of the *History* is aware, Thucydides' own pronouncement about its composition is oddly at variance with his practice. Such a discrepancy is disturbing in an author deemed austere, rigorously scientific, not to say infallible — there would be less cause for alarm in a writer more human.

Little enough is known of Thucydides' life, but what there is ought not to be neglected. The information he gives us himself is briefly assembled: When the Peloponnesian War broke out in 431 he was sufficiently old to comprehend it, and he began then to take notes, for he realized that the war would be the greatest upheaval yet to disturb the Greek world. In the following year he fell victim to the plague which devastated Athens; fortunately he recovered and was able to observe with care the symptoms in others. In 424 he served as general at Amphipolis, which lay in a part of Thrace where he had inherited certain mining interests from his father, Olorus. Because of his tardiness at a crucial moment, Thucydides was responsible for the capitulation of Amphipolis to the enemy, and shortly afterwards he was exiled from Athens for twenty years.

These meager details, which suggest Thucydides' intimate involvement in the affairs about which he wrote, can be supplemented with a few scraps from elsewhere, notably some late biographies. The tomb of Thucydides at Athens (just possibly a cenotaph) was to be found among graves of the family of Cimon, the great fifth-century conservative political leader. This fact coheres neatly with Thucydides' own testimony that his father's name was Olorus; for Cimon on his mother's side was the grandson of a Thracian monarch of that name, and the name, as was the custom, had probably descended in the dynasty. There is no reason to question the Cimonian attachments of the historian; nor was he the only Thucydides in that family. As we know from the pamphlet on the Athenian constitution which has been transmitted under the name of Aristotle, Cimon's role as leader of the upper class conservatives was taken over at his death by a kinsman, one Thucydides the son of Melesias. This Thucydides was the principal opponent of Pericles until an ostracism in 443 removed him from Athens for at least ten years, possibly forever.

Such is the information available about the background of Thucydides the historian. Clearly the milieu from which he emerged was aristocratic and conservative, or, rather, what hostile Athenians would have called oligarchic. He belonged to a family which could be fairly described as anti-Periclean and provided not surprisingly Pericles' greatest antagonist. Yet, as any reader of the *History* can never forget, Thucydides the historian was, for posterity at least, Pericles' greatest panegyrist.

Here is a case of political conversion, of breaking with family tradition. Thucydides was young when Pericles was at his zenith, the decade in which the Parthenon was completed, and in which Athens was led with masterly resolution and electrifying oratory into war. There is a fine indication of Pericles' impact in Aristophanes' *Acharnians*, "Then in rage Pericles the Olympian with thunder and lightning confounded Greece" (530–531). The youth of the city flocked to this *stupor mundi* as he persuaded the Athenians not to yield on any point to the insistent demands of the enemy. Thucydides observed that many young men in Athens were eager for war because they did not know what it was like, and it is probable that he was speaking for himself.

The conversion to Pericles' views does not mean that Thucydides became an outright democrat. In his eulogy of Pericles in Book II, the democracy of the 430's is described as "a democracy in name, but in fact the rule of the first man." And he makes no secret in that passage of his hostility to the political successors of Pericles, demagogues who subverted his policies and undermined the fortunes of the city. The truth is that the form of democracy for which Thucydides abandoned his family politics was distinguished by its conservatism. Although he could not bear the radical democracy, one should not conclude that he was therefore an oligarch. In fact, there is no reason to think that he returned to his family's politics. The matter is much more delicate. After Pericles, the only other government which Thucydides deemed worthy of praise was the Constitution of the Five Thousand, excogitated by Theramenes in 411. This was "a moderate mixture of democracy and oligarchy," under which, says Thucydides, the Athenians for the first time in his day had a good constitution. In the 430's Pericles had made the constitution work by running things himself, but in 411 the constitution was good. Or so Thucydides opined. What best explains his opinion is a perhaps the political uncertainty which inevitably resulted from the conversion of a born conservative to a democracy which lost its attraction after the death of the leader who had impressed him. From 429 he was, so to speak, an "independent," thoughtful but unsure.

Small wonder that Thucydides' account of internal politics at Athens shows neither that objectivity nor austerity with which he is so often credited. He was convinced that the demagogues who followed Pericles contributed through their self-seeking to the collapse of the wise policies that marked the opening of the war. Something of those demagogues is known, including their names: Lysicles, Cleonymus, Cleon, Hyperbolus, and Androcles—to mention persons active within the period covered by Thucydides' *History* as it survives. Yet of these five, only one actually appears in the work as subverting the Periclean plan, and that is, Cleon. By contrast, Lysicles and Androcles are both mentioned briefly and without particular feeling, while Cleonymus, that notorious target of Aristophanes, is not mentioned at all. A passing allusion to Hyperbolus makes it plain that Thucydides did not like him, but nothing more; a reader of Thucydides would find it hard to comprehend why Hyperbolus went into exile as the victim of the last ostracism to take place at Athens.

Although it has occasionally been fashionable to deny it, Thucydides loathed Cleon. This was the man who made the "insane promise" to finish off the Pylos business in twenty days—sensible people would have been glad to be rid of him. This was the man considered a compound of ignorance and cowardice by his own soldiers, it was said—the man who preferred war to peace so that his wickedness might not be so conspicuous. Such is Thucydides' portrait of Cleon; and it is the product of strong prejudice. When an objective reader encounters Thucydides' explanation of Cleon's preference for war, he will be reminded of a parallel which Thucydides takes care nowhere to mention: Pericles himself was said by his detractors to have brought on the Peloponnesian War to conceal his own embarrassments and those of his friends. An explanation of Thucydides' animus against Cleon may be found in a note of a late biographer (Marcellinus)[3] to the effect that Cleon was responsible for Thucydides' exile. It is certain at least that Thucydides was banished in 424, a year in which Cleon was still enjoying the success of Pylos. Cleon was for Thucydides an anti-Pericles, representing the kind of democracy he disliked, the democracy which exiled him. In the Mytilenean Debate the speech of Cleon contains precise verbal echoes of Thucydides' Pericles, but very different is the sentiment that government is best left in the hands of inferior and unintelligent people.

Alcibiades, no less than Pericles and Cleon, aroused in Thucydides emotions that betray his political uncertainty. Thucydides' attitude to Alcibiades was thoroughly ambiguous; it is as if Alcibiades could have been a second Pericles but was not. Intelligent, aristocratic and beautiful, he might have been numbered among the *kaloi kagathoi*,[4] yet his private life was extravagant, his ambitions colossal. All this was well known to Thucydides, as he made plain in Book VI; but he went on to observe that as a statesman Alcibiades acted well, indeed that the fortunes of Athens might have been salvaged if Alcibiades had not been deprived of his authority. It appears, therefore, that in those latter years of the war the democracy could have been managed in a way Thucydides approved of, but the democracy in its worst aspect—in its suspicion and fickleness—prevented this from happening. Alcibiades was driven to treason and subversion, in Sparta and Ionia, before his return to Athens in 407 and second dismissal in the following year. For Thucydides, born a Cimonian and converted to Periclean democracy, the failure of Alcibiades meant the failure of Athens. One might profitably recall the melancholy question on which hangs the outcome of the competition between Aeschylus and Euripides in Aristophanes' *Frogs*: "What do you think of Alcibiades?" (1422–23) This play was produced in 405, the year of Aegospotami. Such a question at such a time would not have aroused much mirth.

The political sentiments of Thucydides were thus delicately balanced. In view of this, an item in Book VIII about Antiphon the oligarch can be properly

---

3. The biography composed by Marcellinus (probably shortly before 600 A.D.) appears largely inferential and is not generally taken as authoritative [*Editor*].
4. *Kalos kagathos* ("beautiful and good") was a standard Greek term for a cultivated man of the elite class, a "gentleman," revealing the common Greek equation of wealth, good looks, and moral excellence [*Editor*].

appreciated, for it has too often been adduced out of context to prove that Thucydides favored oligarchy. Thucydides described Antiphon as second to none of his day in virtue (*arete*) and exceptional in his ability to form plans and give expression to them. Thucydides' political commitments were, as has been shown, sufficiently independent for him to admire quality in a superior oligarch quite as much as in a superior democrat. It would be salutary to notice in Book IV Thucydides' ascription to Brasidas of virtue (*arete*) and intelligence (*xunesis*), essentially the same two characteristics that Antiphon had; again, in Book IV the words *arete* and *xunesis* are used of the Peisistratid tyrants. No sane reader would infer from these passages that Thucydides was either pro-Spartan or pro-tyrant. Why then should his remark about Antiphon prove him an oligarch?

The foregoing inquiry into the political attitudes of Thucydides reveals how personal they were and to what extent both conservative and liberal opinions impinged upon them. Herein lies the explanation of Thucydides' preoccupation with civil conflict (*stasis*). It has been observed before that he was the Western world's first historian of the class struggle, and there is scarcely anyone to dispute that his account of revolution at Corcyra is the most profound and searching analysis of *stasis* ever written. Throughout his *History* Thucydides was constantly aware of the presence of factions and the potential danger of their clashes. The actual narrative of the Peloponnesian War begins with the clash at Epidamnus between the "few" (*oligoi*) and the "many" (*polloi*), or, as they were sometimes called, the "powerful" (*dunatoi*) and the "people" (*demos*). Similar clashes are described at Thebes, Plataea, Colophon, Mytilene, Samos, to name only some. The clash at Syracuse is dramatized in the confrontation of Hermocrates and Athenagoras in Book VI; at Athens the struggles between the few and the many erupted in the oligarchic revolution of 411, so vividly described in Book VIII. When one considers Thucydides' experience of both sides and the ambiguous and uncertain political position in which he found himself, it becomes at once clear why *stasis* dominated his view of history.

In the course of time democracy and oligarchy alike had impressed and disillusioned Thucydides. Yet quite apart from their intrinsic merits as constitutions, they had become established, for good or ill, as instruments of empire. In the cities of the Greek world the many looked to Athens for support and the few to Sparta, and on the whole those two cities saw to it that the appropriate constitution in each case was imposed upon their allies. And so *stasis* at Athens had, by virtue of her vast empire, far-ranging repercussions.

Thucydides sought to understand. As he must have learned from his own experience, the answers lay with the men who made history: it was human nature which had to be understood. The medical writers of the school of Hippocrates had been analyzing the workings of the body and its diseases. Adapting their techniques and using the force of his own genius, Thucydides analyzed the workings of men in society and of society's diseases. In short, he applied the Hippocratic method to human nature, and the reason he did so was ultimately personal.

Thucydides analyzed the causes of the war in two parts: the complaints which precipitated it and the true underlying cause. This analysis was an attempt to see beyond the facts; the real cause of war, he tells us, was Spartan fear of the growing power of Athens, although men did not speak of it openly at the time. Thucydides is here a psychologist, a reader of minds. So is he again when in Book II he deals with the plague and its impact upon the character of the Athenians: those who recovered acquired false confidence that no disease would ever carry them away, while those who were dying abandoned every scruple and indulged in those pleasures which they had hitherto professed they abjured. Thucydides' terrifying account of the state of men's souls in the summer of 430 occurs together with a description of the plague symptoms, a clear indication of Hippocratic techniques applied psychologically as well as physiologically. And the social collapse of Athens in 430 was matched by the situation at Corcyra a few years later. In the celebrated passage on the Corcyraean *stasis*, Thucydides the psychologist was again at work, probing and reading minds. He noted the vanishing of all scruples, before human laws and before the gods, and he unravelled the new senses of old words used in a time of crisis. In Books IV and V, with a prejudiced passion, Thucydides can be seen reading the mind of Cleon: he had not expected that Nicias would turn over the command to him; he wanted war instead of peace so that his own baseness would be less obvious. In these expository passages, and others like them, Thucydides shows himself eager to penetrate the surface of actual events.

The effort to discern and analyze inner truth is apparent within the speeches in Thucydides as well as outside them. If Thucydides was an author less objective than is often alleged, he might well be expected to intrude something of his own thought into the speeches. And so indeed he seems to have done if one ignores his own description of his practice as given in Book I, chapter 22. That single chapter has provoked controversy for a long time. Much has been said about the chronology of the *History*'s composition; and inconsistencies, omissions, and changes of emphasis have been explained away by assumptions of different dates of composition. Yet, in the midst of this controversy, the twenty-second chapter of Book I has remained sacrosanct.

In that chapter Thucydides mentions the difficulty of recalling precisely what was said in speeches that he himself had heard and of obtaining from others a reliable report of speeches which he had not heard. However, he asserts that when he composed the speeches in his *History*, he "kept as close as possible to the general purport (*gnome*) of what was actually said"; furthermore, his speakers were made to say what was appropriate for the occasion (*ta deonta*). No one knows the date of this obscure statement of intention, and it is by no means clear what *ta deonta* would be. The sense of *gnome* is difficult, but Thucydides' words certainly mean that the speeches in his *History* are to be taken as very close approximations of the original utterances. That can hardly be the case. Fantastic ingenuity is vainly exercised on reconciling Thucydides' statement with the speeches in his work. And it requires an even more fantastic ingenuity to maintain, as a few scholars do, that every speech in Thucydides is completely historical. Think of the Melian Dialogue. How much better it is to admit that Thucydides has not done what he intended to do. After all, in the same chapter, he lays great stress on accuracy (*akribeia*); yet he is not always accurate, and in certain instances important material is simply left out. In these matters it is essential to consider what manner of man Thucydides was, what peculiarly animated him and diverted him from his scientific aims.

Not that the speeches are all unhistorical—far from it: there were undoubtedly congresses at Sparta (although Thucydides would not have heard what was said there), and Pericles undoubtedly did address the Athenian people (on more occasions than those Thucydides mentions). The speeches probably do contain—some more than others—an admixture of genuine historical material. A contemporary pamphlet, usually ascribed to an "old oligarch," includes several of the arguments in favor of empire advanced by Pericles in his first speech in Thucydides. Pericles' exhortation in the Funeral Oration—that Athenians should become lovers (*erastai*) of their city—probably comes from

Pericles himself, to judge from several parodies of this remark in two early plays of Aristophanes. But the one quotation we possess from the actual oration is nowhere to be found in Thucydides, although it is singularly effective: "The youth has been taken from the city, as if the spring were taken from the year." It has, moreover, been ably demonstrated that certain features of sophistic argument in Thucydides' speeches may reflect contemporary rhetoric. But such historical ingredients do not suffice to support the notion that Thucydides kept *as close as possible* to the general purport of the originals.

Human nature, social disorder, the struggle for power—these are the topics that engaged Thucydides, and they occur insistently in the speeches. A culminative proof of their fundamentally Thucydidean character can be had first from the recurrence of notions to be found in Thucydides' own analyses, second from the recurrence of similar points in unrelated speeches, and third from the stylistic similarity of the speeches and the analytic digressions.

Some examples can be advanced under these several rubrics. First, commentators have often been troubled by Thucydides' assertion that the basic cause of the war, namely, Spartan fear of Athens' growing power, was not a matter openly talked about and that discussion centered upon the various pretexts for war. And yet it is precisely that basic cause which is discussed in several of the speeches in Book I. This manifest contradiction shows immediately that Thucydides used the speeches as vehicles of interpretation and analysis. There can be no objection to postulating different dates of composition for those speeches and for Thucydides' remark, although the actual dates will be forever elusive. But hypotheses about times of composition are not nearly so valuable as the simple evidence that Thucydides introduced his own views into certain speeches.

There is other evidence of the same kind. Thucydides' pre-occupation with the nature of man is amply attested in passages written in his own person. He said in his preface that his book would be useful because similar events will, human nature being what it is, occur again; and on the Corcyraean Revolution he observed that *stasis* would continue to occur in various forms "as long as human nature is the same." Compare with this the comment assigned to Diodotus that human nature is a more potent force than anything else. Later, in the Melian Dialogue, the Athenians declare that it is in the nature of man to rule wherever possible. These passages in speeches are no less Thucydidean than the others.

The folly of hope was another obsession of Thucydides. It is a motif with a long pedigree in Greek thought. Solon[5] had once written how men take pleasure in "empty hopes"; in recording the plague, Thucydides wrote that those who recovered "somehow clung to an empty hope that no other disease would destroy them." In his account of the fall of Amphipolis in Book IV, he noted that men were addicted to hoping irrationally for whatever they most wanted. Compare Diodotus on ruinous hope, or better still the Athenians at Melos on "hope, a comfort in danger," which is only recognized for what it is when the time for precaution has passed. "Hope," according to Pericles' third speech, "derives its strength from despair."

To turn to the second rubric. A glance at the speeches, taken together and without reference to Thucydides' own remarks, is instructive: there is a coherence which is not historical. In his first speech in the *History*, Pericles is seen to reply point by point to objections raised in the speech of the Corinthians at the second congress at Sparta. At Melos the Athenians enunciate their brutal doc-

5. The Athenian lawgiver Solon (c. 600), wrote poetry, much of which has survived [*Editor*].

trine that power is inevitably in the hands of the stronger, but the idea has already appeared in the Athenian speech at Sparta in Book I, quite as clearly if less fully. Observe the concept of "example" (*paradeigma*) which suggests, in a way, the whole tragic story of Athens' fall. In the Funeral Oration Pericles describes the Athenians as "themselves a *paradeigma* for the world rather than imitators of others," but in the dialogue at Melos the Melians advise the Athenians to leave them alone: "This is no less in your interest than ours, for were you ever to be defeated you would become a *paradeigma* to others in view of the enormous vengeance which would be wrought upon you." for the Athenians, however, "Hatred is a *paradeigma* of power in the eyes of the ruled." Between the Funeral Oration and the Melian Debate comes the revolt of Mytilene; in both the speech of the Mytileneans at Olympia and the antilogy at Athens a *paradeigma* for the ruled is explicitly at issue.

Finally, style too shows the speeches as vehicles of analysis. Every reader of Thucydides' Greek will have discovered that the most difficult passages are precisely the disquisitions, as on the plague or Corcyra, and the speeches. The actual narrative is generally much simpler. Analysis, with its abstractions and subtleties, demanded a tougher style. Dionysius of Halicarnassus, writing in Greek under Augustus, vehemently attacked Thucydides for (among other things) the excessive difficulty and obscurity of his language: the passages which bothered him were the speeches, but also—and especially—the account of *stasis* at Corcyra.[6]

Thus, the coherence of style and substance betrays the man Thucydides, striving with prejudice, passion, and compassion, to understand his own experience. R. G. Collingwood once stated on a much read page of *The Idea of History*: "In reading Thucydides I ask myself, what is the matter with the man that he writes like that? I answer: he has a bad conscience."[7] No, it was a superb conscience. There was much to explain: the plague-ridden Athenians hurling themselves into wells, the fathers who slaughtered their children at Corcyra, the soldiers' blood that stained the waters of the Assinarus. There was much to learn: war, as Thucydides said, is a "violent teacher."

ROBERT GILPIN

Robert Gilpin is Dwight D. Eisenhower Professor of International Affairs at Princeton. He has published widely in the field of international relations and political economy. His books include *War and Change in World Politics* and *The Political Economy of International Relations*. The present essay contributes to the ongoing debate over Thucydidean realism and places Thucydides' writing in the broad context of hegemonic rivalry.

The Theory of Hegemonic War[†]

In the introduction to his history of the great war between the Spartans and the Athenians, Thucydides wrote that he was addressing "those inquirers who

---

6. Dionysius lived from about 58 to 5 B.C. His remarks appear in his essay *On Thucydides* [Editor].
7. See this volume, p. 442 [Editor].
† Robert Gilpin, "The Theory of Hegemonic War." *Journal of Interdisciplinary History* 18 (1988): 591–613. Reprinted with the permission of the editors of *The Journal of Interdisciplinary History* and the MIT Press, Cambridge, Massachusetts. © 1988 by the Massachusetts Institute of Technology and the editors of *The Journal of Interdisciplinary History*.

desire an exact knowledge of the past as an aid to the interpretation of the future, which in the course of human things must resemble if it does not reflect it. . . . In fine, I have written my work, not as an essay which is to win the applause of the moment, but as a possession for all time." Thucydides, assuming that the behavior and phenomena that he observed would repeat themselves throughout human history, intended to reveal the underlying and unalterable nature of what is today called international relations.

In the language of contemporary social science, Thucydides believed that he had uncovered the general law of the dynamics of international relations. Although differences exist between Thucydides' conceptions of scientific law and methodology and those of present-day students of international relations, it is significant that Thucydides was the first to set forth the idea that the dynamic of international relations is provided by the differential growth of power among states. This fundamental idea—that the uneven growth of power among states is the driving force of international relations—can be identified as the theory of hegemonic war.

This essay argues that Thucydides' theory of hegemonic war constitutes one of the central organizing ideas for the study of international relations. The following pages examine and evaluate Thucydides' theory of hegemonic war and contemporary variations of that theory. To carry out this task, it is necessary to make Thucydides' ideas more systematic, expose his basic assumptions, and understand his analytical method. Subsequently, this article discusses whether or not Thucydides' conception of international relations has proved to be a "possession for all time." Does it help explain wars in the modern era? How, if at all, has it been modified by more modern scholarship? What is its relevance for the contemporary nuclear age?

Thucydides' Theory of Hegemonic War

The essential idea embodied in Thucydides' theory of hegemonic war is that fundamental changes in the international system are the basic determinants of such wars. The structure of the system or distribution of power among the states in the system can be stable or unstable. A stable system is one in which changes can take place if they do not threaten the vital interests of the dominant states and thereby cause a war among them. In his view, such a stable system has an unequivocal hierarchy of power and an unchallenged dominant or hegemonic power. An unstable system is one in which economic, technological, and other changes are eroding the international hierarchy and undermining the position of the hegemonic state. In this latter situation, untoward events and diplomatic crises can precipitate a hegemonic war among the states in the system. The outcome of such a war is a new international structure.

Three propositions are embedded in this brief summary of the theory. The first is that a hegemonic war is distinct from other categories of war; it is caused by broad changes in political, strategic, and economic affairs. The second is that the relations among individual states can be conceived as a system: the behavior of states is determined in large part by their strategic interaction. The third is that a hegemonic war threatens and transforms the structure of the international system; whether or not the participants in the conflict are initially aware of it, at stake is the hierarchy of power and relations among states in the system. Thucydides' conception and all subsequent formulations of the theory of hegemonic war emerge from these three propositions.

Such a structural theory of war can be contrasted with an escalation theory of war. According to this latter theory, as Waltz has argued in *Man, the State, and War*, war occurs because of the simple fact that there is nothing to stop it.[1] In the anarchy of the international system, statesmen make decisions and respond to the decisions of others. This action-reaction process in time can lead to situations in which statesmen deliberately provoke a war or lose control over events and eventually find themselves propelled into a war. In effect, one thing leads to another until war is the consequence of the interplay of foreign policies.

Most wars are the consequence of such an escalatory process. They are not causally related to structural features of the international system, but rather are due to the distrust and uncertainty that characterizes relations among states in what Waltz has called a self-help system.[2] Thus, the history of ancient times, which introduces Thucydides' history, is a tale of constant warring. However, the Peloponnesian War, he tells us, is different and worthy of special attention because of the massive accumulation of power in Hellas and its implications for the structure of the system. This great war and its underlying causes were the focus of his history.

Obviously, these two theories do not necessarily contradict one another; each can be used to explain different wars. But what interested Thucydides was a particular type of war, what he called a great war and what this article calls a hegemonic war—a war in which the overall structure of an international system is at issue. The structure of the international system at the outbreak of such a war is a necessary, but not a sufficient cause of the war. The theory of hegemonic war and international change that is examined below refers to those wars that arise from the specific structure of an international system and in turn transform that structure.

ASSUMPTIONS OF THE THEORY

Underlying Thucydides' view that he had discovered the basic mechanism of a great or hegemonic war was his conception of human nature. He believed that human nature was unchanging and therefore the events recounted in his history would be repeated in the future. Since human beings are driven by three fundamental passions—interest, pride, and, above all else, fear—they always seek to increase their wealth and power until other humans, driven by like passions, try to stop them. Although advances in political knowledge could contribute to an understanding of this process, they could not control or arrest it. Even advances in knowledge, technology, or economic development would not change the fundamental nature of human behavior or of international relations. On the contrary, increases in human power, wealth, and technology would serve only to intensify conflict among social groups and enhance the magnitude of war. Thucydides the realist, in contrast to Plato the idealist, believed that reason would not transform human beings, but would always remain the slave of human passions. Thus, uncontrollable passions would again generate great conflicts like the one witnessed in his history.

METHODOLOGY

One can understand Thucydides' argument and his belief that he had uncovered the underlying dynamics of international relations and the role

---

1. Kenneth N. Waltz, *Man, the State, and War: A Theoretical Analysis* (New York, 1959).
2. Idem, *Theory of International Relations* (Reading, Mass., 1979).

of hegemonic war in international change only if one comprehends his conception of science and his view of what constituted explanation. Modern students of international relations and of social science tend to put forth theoretical physics as their model of analysis and explanation; they analyze phenomena in terms of causation and models linking independent and dependent variables. In modern physics, meaningful propositions must, at least in principle, be falsifiable—that is, they must give rise to predictions that can be shown to be false.

Thucydides, by contrast, took as his model of analysis and explanation the method of Hippocrates, the great Greek physician.[3] Disease, the Hippocratic school argued, had to be understood as a consequence of the operation of natural forces and not as a manifestation of some supernatural influence. Through dispassionate observation of the symptoms and the course of a disease, one could understand its nature. Thus, one explained a disease by recognizing its characteristics and charting its development from its genesis through inevitable periods of crisis to its final resolution in recovery or death. What was central to this mode of explanation was the evolution of the symptoms and the manifestations of the disease rather than the search for the underlying causes sought by modern medicine.

Thucydides wrote his history to fulfill the same prognostic purpose, namely, to recognize that great wars were recurrent phenomena with characteristic manifestations. A great or hegemonic war, like a disease, displays discernible symptoms and follows an inevitable course. The initial phase is a relatively stable international system characterized by a hierarchical ordering of the states in the system. Over time the power of a subordinate state begins to grow disproportionately, and that rising state comes into conflict with the dominant or hegemonic state in the system. The ensuing struggle between these two states and their respective allies leads to a bipolarization of the system, to an inevitable crisis, and eventually to a hegemonic war. Finally, there is the resolution of the war in favor of one side and the establishment of a new international system that reflects the emergent distribution of power in the system.

The dialectical conception of political change implicit in his model was borrowed from contemporary Sophist thinkers. This method of analysis postulated a thesis, its contradiction or antithesis, and a resolution in the form of a synthesis. In his history this dialectic approach can be discerned as follows:

(1) The *thesis* is the hegemonic state, in this case, Sparta, which organizes the international system in terms of its political, economic, and strategic interests.
(2) The *antithesis* or contradiction in the system is the growing power of the challenging state, Athens, whose expansion and efforts to transform the international system bring it into conflict with the hegemonic state.
(3) The *synthesis* is the new international system that results from the inevitable clash between the dominant state and the rising challenger.

Similarly, Thucydides foresaw that throughout history new states like Sparta and challenging states like Athens would arise and the hegemonic cycle would repeat itself.

---

3. Thucydides' contemporary, Hippocrates had a medical school on the Aegean island of Cos. He gave his name to the statement of medical ethics known as the Hippocratic oath that is still taken by physicians today [*Editor*].

CONCEPTION OF SYSTEMIC CHANGE

Underlying this analysis and the originality of Thucydides' thought was his novel conception of classical Greece as constituting a system, the basic components of which were the great powers—Sparta and Athens. Foreshadowing later realist formulations of international relations, he believed that the structure of the system was provided by the distribution of power among states; the hierarchy of power among these states defined and maintained the system and determined the relative prestige of states, their spheres of influence, and their political relations. The hierarchy of power and related elements thus gave order and stability to the system.

Accordingly, international political change involved a transformation of the hierarchy of the states in the system and the patterns of relations dependent upon that hierarchy. Although minor changes could occur and lesser states could move up and down this hierarchy without necessarily disturbing the stability of the system, the positioning of the great powers was crucial. Thus, as he tells us, it was the increasing power of the second most powerful state in the system, Athens, that precipitated the conflict and brought about what I have elsewhere called systemic change, that is, a change in the hierarchy or control of the international political system.[4]

Searching behind appearances for the reality of international relations, Thucydides believed that he had found the true causes of the Peloponnesian War, and by implication of systematic change, in the phenomenon of the uneven growth of power among the dominant states in the system. "The real cause," he concluded in the first chapter, "I consider to be the one which was formally most kept out of sight. The growth of the power of Athens, and the alarm which this inspired in Lacedaemon [Sparta], made war inevitable." In a like fashion and in future ages, he reasoned, the differential growth of power in a state system would undermine the status quo and lead to hegemonic war between declining and rising powers.

In summary, according to Thucydides, a great or hegemonic war, like a disease, follows a discernible and recurrent course. The initial phase is a relatively stable international system characterized by a hierarchical ordering of states with a dominant or hegemonic power. Over time, the power of one subordinate state begins to grow disproportionately; as this development occurs, it comes into conflict with the hegemonic state. The struggle between these contenders for preeminence and their accumulating alliance leads to a bipolarization of the system. In the parlance of game theory, the system becomes a zero-sum situation in which one side's gain is by necessity the other side's loss. As this bipolarization occurs the system becomes increasingly unstable, and a small event can trigger a crisis and precipitate a major conflict; the resolution of that conflict will determine the new hegemon and the hierarchy of power in the system.

THE CAUSES OF HEGEMONIC WAR

Following this model, Thucydides began his history of the war between the Spartans and the Athenians by stating why, at its very inception, he believed that the war would be a great war and thus worthy of special attention. Contrasting the beginnings of the Peloponnesian War to the constant warring of the Greeks, he began in the introduction to analyze the unprecedented growth of power in Hellas from ancient times to the outbreak

---

4. Robert Gilpin, *War and Change in World Politics* (New York, 1981), 40.

of the war. Although, as we have already noted, Thucydides did not think of causes in the modern or scientific sense of the term, his analysis of the factors that altered the distribution of power in ancient Greece, and ultimately accounted for the war, is remarkably modern.

The first set of factors to explain the rise of power in Athens and the expansion of the Athenian empire contained geographical and demographic elements. Because of the poverty of its soil, Attica (the region surrounding Athens) was not envied by any other peoples; it enjoyed freedom from conflict. As a consequence, "the most powerful victims of war or faction from the rest of Hellas took refuge with the Athenians as a safe retreat," became naturalized, and swelled the population. With an increase in population Attica became too small to sustain its growing numbers, and Athens began to send out colonies to other parts of Greece. Athens itself turned to commerce to feed her expanding population and became the "workshop of ancient Greece," exporting manufactured products and commodities in exchange for grain. Thus, Athens began its imperial career from demographic pressure and economic necessity.

The second set of influences was economic and technological: the Greek, and especially the Athenian, mastery of naval power, which had facilitated the expansion of commerce among the Greek states and the establishment of the hegemony of Hellas in the Eastern Mediterranean. After the defeat of Troy, Thucydides tells us, Hellas attained "the quiet which must precede growth" as the Greeks turned to commerce and the acquisition of wealth. Although Athens and other seafaring cities grew "in revenue and in dominion," there was no great concentration of power in Hellas prior to the war with Persia: "There was no union of subject cities round a great state, no spontaneous combination of equals for confederate expeditions; what fighting there was consisted merely of local warfare between rival neighbors." The technical innovation of naval power, the introduction into Greece of fortification techniques, and the rise of financial power associated with commerce, however, made possible an unprecedented concentration of military and economic power. These developments, by transforming the basis of military power, created the conditions for the forging of substantial alliances, a profound shift in the power balance, and the creation of large seaborne empires. In this novel environment, states interacted more intimately, and an interdependent international economic and political system took shape. These military, technological, and economic changes were to favor the growth of Athenian power.

The final factor leading to the war was political: the rise of the Athenian empire at the conclusion of the war with Persia. That war and its aftermath stimulated the growth of Athenian power at the same time that the war and its aftermath encouraged Sparta, the reigning hegemon and the leader of the Greeks in their war against the Persians, to retreat into isolation. With the rise of a wealthy commercial class in Athens, the traditional form of government—a hereditary monarchy—was overthrown, and a new governing elite representing the rising and enterprising commercial class was established; its interest lay with commerce and imperial expansion. While the Athenians grew in power through commerce and empire, the Spartans fell behind and found themselves increasingly encircled by the expanding power of the Athenians.

As a consequence of these developments, the Greeks anticipated the approach of a great war and began to choose sides. In time, the international system divided into two great blocs. "At the head of the one stood Athens, at the head of the other Lacedaemon, one the first naval, the other the first military power in Hellas." The former—commercial, democratic, and expansionist—began to evoke alarm in the more conservative Spartans. In this increasingly bipolar and unstable world a series of diplomatic encounters, beginning at Epidamnus and culminating in the Megara Decree and the Spartan ultimatum, were to plunge the rival alliances into war. In order to prevent the dynamic and expanding Athenians from overturning the international balance of power and displacing them as the hegemonic state, the Spartans eventually delivered an ultimatum that forced Athens to declare war.

In brief, it was the combination of significant environmental changes and the contrasting natures of the Athenian and Spartan societies that precipitated the war. Although the underlying causes of the war can be traced to geographical, economic, and technological factors, the major determinant of the foreign policies of the two protagonists was the differing character of their domestic regimes. Athens was democracy; its people were energetic, daring, and commercially disposed; its naval power, financial resources, and empire were expanding. Sparta, the traditional hegemon of the Hellenes, was a slavocracy; its foreign policy was conservative and attentive merely to the narrow interests of preserving its domestic status quo. Having little interest in commerce or overseas empire, it gradually declined relative to its rival. In future ages, in Thucydides' judgment, situations similar to that of Athens and Sparta would arise, and this fateful process would repeat itself eternally.

The Contribution of Thucydides' Model

Thucydides' history and the pattern that it reveals have fascinated students of international relations in all eras. Individuals of every political persuasion from realist to idealist to Marxist have claimed kinship to him. At critical moments scholars and statesmen have seen their own times reflected in his account of the conflict between democratic Athens and undemocratic Sparta. The American Civil War, World War I, and the Cold War between the United States and the Soviet Union have been cast in its light. In a similar vein, Mackinder and other political geographers have interpreted world history as the recurrent struggle between landpower (Sparta, Rome, and Great Britain) and seapower (Athens, Carthage, and Germany) and have observed that a great or hegemonic war has taken place and transformed world affairs approximately every 100 years. The writings of Wright and Toynbee on general war are cast in a similar vein. The Marxist theory of intra-capitalist wars can be viewed as a subcategory of Thucydides' more general theory. More recently, a number of social scientists have revived the concept of hegemonic war. The "power transition theory" of Organski, Modelski's theory of long cycles and global war, and the present writer's book on international change are examples of elaborations of Thucydides' fundamental insights into the dynamics of international relations.[5] Although these variations and extensions of Thucydides' basic model raise many interesting issues, they are too numerous and complex to be discussed here. Instead, the emphasis will be on the contribution of Thucydides' theory, its applicability to modern history, and its continuing relevance for international relations.

5. Halford J. Mackinder, "The Geographical Pivot of History," in Anthony J. Pearce (ed.), *Democratic Ideals and Reality* (New York, 1962), 1-2; Quincy Wright, *A Study of War* (Chicago, 1942); Arnold J. Toynbee, *A Study of History* (London, 1961), III, IV; Vladimir Ilyich Lenin, *Imperialism: The Highest Stage of Capitalism* (New York, 1939). See, for example, A.F.K. Organski, *World Politics* (New York, 1968; 2nd ed.): Organski and Jacek Kugler, *The War Ledger* (Chicago, 1980); George Modelski (ed.), *Exploring Long Cycles* (Boulder, 1987); Gilpin, *War and Change.*

The theory's fundamental contribution is the conception of hegemonic war itself and the importance of hegemonic wars for the dynamics of international relations. The expression hegemonic war may have been coined by Aron; certainly he has provided an excellent definition of what Thucydides called a great war. Describing World War I as a hegemonic war, Aron writes that such a war "is characterized less by its immediate causes or its explicit purposes than by its extent and the stakes involved. It affect[s] all the political units inside one system of relations between sovereign states. Let us call it, for want of a better term, a war of hegemony, hegemony being, if not the conscious motive, at any rate the inevitable consequence of the victory of at least one of the states or groups." Thus, the outcome of a hegemonic war, according to Aron, is the transformation of the structure of the system of interstate relations.[6]

In more precise terms, one can distinguish a hegemonic war in terms of its scale, the objectives at stake, and the means employed to achieve those objectives. A hegemonic war generally involves all of the states in the system; it is a world war. Whatever the immediate and conscious motives of the combatants, as Aron points out, the fundamental issues to be decided are the leadership and structure of the international system. Its outcome also profoundly affects the internal composition of societies because, as the behavior of Athens and Sparta revealed, the victor remolds the vanquished in its image. Such wars are at once political, economic, and ideological struggles. Because of the scope of the war and the importance of the issues to be decided, the means employed are usually unlimited. In Clausewitzian[7] terms, they become pure conflicts or clashes of society rather than the pursuit of limited policy objectives.

Thus, in the Peloponnesian War the whole of Hellas became engaged in an internecine struggle to determine the economic and political future of the Greek world. Although the initial objectives of the two alliances were limited, the basic issue in the contest became the structure and leadership of the emerging international system and not merely the fate of particular city-states. Ideological disputes, that is, conflicting views over the organization of domestic societies, were also at the heart of the struggle; democratic Athens and aristocratic Sparta sought to reorder other societies in terms of their own political values and socioeconomic systems. As Thucydides tells us in his description of the leveling and decimation of Melos, there were no constraints on the means employed to reach their goals. The war released forces of which the protagonists had previously been unaware; it took a totally unanticipated course. As the Athenians had warned the Spartans in counseling them against war, "consider the vast influence of accident in war, before you are engaged in it." Furthermore, neither rival anticipated that the war would leave both sides exhausted and thereby open the way to Macedonian imperialism.

The central idea embodied in the hegemonic theory is that there is incompatibility between crucial elements of the existing international system and the changing distribution of power among the states within the system. The elements of the system—the hierarchy of prestige, the division of territory, and the international economy—became less and less compatible with the shifting distribution of power among the major states in the system. The resolution of the disequilibrium between the super-structure of the system and the underly-

---

6. Raymond Aron, "War and Industrial Society," in Leon Bramson and George W. Goethals (eds.),*War—Studies from Psychology, Sociology, Anthropology* (New York, 1964), 359.
7. Karl von Clausewitz (1780–1831), a Prussian general, was the author of an unfinished but highly influential work entitled *On War*. There he defined war as a political act constituting the continuation of diplomacy by other means and advocated a system of "total war," i.e., attacking all inhabitants and property of the enemy nation in every way possible [*Editor*].

ing distribution of power is found in the outbreak and intensification of what becomes a hegemonic war.

The theory does not necessarily concern itself with whether the declining or rising state is responsible for the war. In fact, identification of the initiator of a particular war is frequently impossible to ascertain, and authorities seldom agree. When did the war actually begin? What actions precipitated it? Who committed the first hostile act? In the case of the Peloponnesian War, for example, historians differ over whether Athens or Sparta initiated the war. Whereas most regard the Megara decree issued by Athens as the precipitating cause of the war, one can just as easily argue that the decree was the first act of a war already begun by Sparta and its allies.

Nor does the theory address the question of the explicit consequences of the war. Both the declining and rising protagonists may suffer and a third party may be the ultimate victor. Frequently, the chief beneficiary is, in fact, a rising peripheral power not directly engaged in the conflict. In the case of the Peloponnesian War, the war paved the way for Macedonian imperialism to triumph over the Greeks.[8] In brief, the theory makes no prediction regarding the consequences of the war. What the theory postulates instead is that the system is ripe for a fundamental transformation because of profound ongoing changes in the international distribution of power and the larger economic and technological environment. This is not to suggest that the historic change produced by the war must be in some sense progressive; it may, as happened in the Peloponnesian War, weaken and eventually bring an end to one of mankind's most glorious civilizations.

Underlying the outbreak of a hegemonic war is the idea that the basis of power and social order is undergoing a fundamental transformation. Halévy must have had something like this conception of political change in mind when, in analyzing the causes of World War I, he wrote that "it is thus apparent why all great convulsions in the history of the world, and more particularly in modern Europe, have been at the same time wars and revolutions. The Thirty Years' War[9] was at once a revolutionary crisis, a conflict, within Germany, between the rival parties of Protestants and Catholics, and an international war between the Holy Roman Empire, Sweden, and France.[1] Similarly, Halévy continues, the wars of the French Revolution and Napoleon as well as World War I must be seen as upheavals of the whole European social and political order.

The profound changes in political relations, economic organization, and military technology behind hegemonic war and the associated domestic upheavals undermine both the international and domestic status quo. These underlying transformations in power and social relations result in shifts in the nature and locus of power. They give rise to a search for a new basis of political and social order at both the domestic and international levels.

This conception of a hegemonic war as associated with a historic turning point in world history is exemplified by the Peloponnesian War. A basic change in the nature and hence in the location of economic and military power was taking place in Greece during the fifth century B.C. This changing economic and technological environment had differing implications for the fortunes of

---

8. Philip II of Macedon defeated a Greek coalition at the battle of Chaeronea in 338 B.C., thus laying the groundwork for terminating the system of autonomous poleis in Greece and replacing it with a larger monarchic state. His son Alexander carved out much larger domains by waging war throughout Egypt and western Asia [*Editor*].
9. Fought from 1618 to 1638, mostly in Germany [*Editor*].
1. Eli Halévy (trans. R.G. Webb), *The Era of Tyrannies* (Garden City, N.Y., 1965), 212.

the two major protagonists. The Peloponnesian War would be the midwife for the birth of the new world. This great war, like other transforming wars, would embody significant long-term changes in Greece's economy, military affairs, and political organization.

Prior to and during the Persian wars, power and wealth in the Greek world were based on agriculture and land armies; Sparta was ascendant among the Greek city-states. Its political position had a secure economic foundation, and its military power was unchallenged. The growth in the importance of naval power and the accompanying rise of commerce following the wars transformed the basis of power. Moreover, the introduction into Greece of fortification technology and the erection of walls around Athens canceled much of the Spartan military advantage. In this new environment, naval power, commerce, and finance became increasingly important components of state power. Thus, whereas in the past the nature of power had favored the Spartans, the transformed environment favored Athens and other rising commercial and naval powers.

Athens rather than Sparta benefited from this new military and economic environment. Domestically, Athens had experienced political and social changes that enabled it to take advantage of the increased importance of seapower and commerce. Its entrenched landed aristocracy, which had been associated with the former dominance of agriculture and land armies, had been overthrown and replaced by a commercial elite whose interests lay with the development of naval power and imperial expansion. In an increasingly monetized international economy, the Athenians had the financial resources to outfit a powerful navy and expand its dominion at the expense of the Spartans.

By contrast, the Spartans, largely for domestic economic and political reasons, were unable or unwilling to make the necessary adjustment to the new economic and technological environment. It was not merely because Sparta was land-locked, but also because the dominant interests of the society were committed to the maintenance of an agricultural system based on slave labor. Their foremost concern was to forestall a slave revolt, and they feared external influences that would stimulate the Helots to rebel. Such a rebellion had forced them to revert into isolation at the end of the Persian wars. It appears to have been the fear of another revolt that caused them eventually to challenge the Athenians. The Megara decree aroused the Spartans because the potential return of Megara to Athenian control would have opened up the Peloponnesus to Athenian influence and thereby enabled the Athenians to assist a Helot revolt. Thus, when Athenian expansionism threatened a vital interest of the Spartans, the latter decided that war was inevitable, and delivered an ultimatum to the Athenians.

The differing abilities of the Athenians and the Spartans to adjust to the new economic and technological environment and the changed nature of power ultimately led to the war. The development of naval power and acquisition of the financial resources to purchase ships and hire sailors necessitated a profound reordering of domestic society. Whereas the Athenians had reformed themselves in order to take advantage of new opportunities for wealth and power, the Spartans would or could not liberalize due to a constellation of domestic interests and their fear of unleashing a rebellion of the Helots. The result was the uneven growth of power among these rivals that Thucydides viewed as the real cause of the war.

The critical point arrived when the Spartans began to believe that time was moving against them and in favor of the Athenians. A tipping-point or fundamental change in the Spartan perception of the balance of power had taken place. As certain contemporary historians assert, Athenian power may have reached its zenith by the outbreak of the war and had already begun to wane, but the reality of the situation is not particularly relevant, since the Spartans believed that Athens was growing stronger. The decision facing then had become when to commence the war rather than whether to commence it. Was it better to fight while the advantage still lay with them or at some future date when the advantage might have turned? As Howard has written, similar perceptions and fears of eroding power have preceded history's other hegemonic wars.[2]

The stability of the Greek international system following the Persian wars was based on an economic and technological environment favoring Spartan hegemony. When agriculture and land armies became less vital to state power and commerce and navies became more important, the Spartans were unable to adjust. Therefore, the locus of wealth and power shifted to the Athenians. Although the Athenians lost the war when they failed to heed the prudent strategy laid down by Pericles, the basic point is not altered; the war for hegemony in Greece emerged from a profound social, economic, and technological revolution. Wars like this one are not merely contests between rival states but political watersheds that mark transitions from one historical epoch to the next.

Despite the insight that it provides in understanding and explaining the great wars of history, the theory of hegemonic war is a limited and incomplete theory. It cannot easily handle perceptions that affect behavior and predict who will initiate a hegemonic war. Nor can it forecast when a hegemonic war will occur and what the consequences will be. As in the case of the theory of biological evolution, it helps one understand and explain what has happened; but neither theory can make predictions that can be tested and thereby meet rigorous scientific standards of falsifiability. The theory of hegemonic war at best is a complement to other theories such as those of cognitive psychology and expected utility and must be integrated with them. It has, however, withstood the test of time better than any other generalization in the field of international relations and remains an important conceptual tool for understanding the dynamics of world politics.

MICHAEL DOYLE

Michael Doyle teaches in the Department of Politics at Princeton University and directs the Center of International Studies. His fields of interest include comparative history, United Nations peacekeeping, and the political philosophies of international relations. He is the author of *Empires* and *UN Peacekeeping in Cambodia*. The essay reprinted here on Thucydides' particular brand of realism grows out of his larger work on democracy, political theory, and warfare.

Thucydides: A Realist?[†]

What does it mean to think like a Realist? The question is important in the study of international politics. According to a recent survey of the

2. Michael Howard, *The Causes of War* (Cambridge, Mass., 1983), 16.
† Michael Doyle, "Thucydides: A Realist?" Reprinted from *Hegemonic Rivalry*, ed. Barry S. Strauss and Ned Lebow (Boulder: Westview Press, 1991). Reprinted by permission of Barry S. Strauss.

field, more than 90 percent of the hypotheses tested by behaviorists in international politics were Realist in conception.[1] A wider survey of the field taken in 1972 (which included those more historically inclined) identified the American Realist Hans Morgenthau as the leading scholar of international relations and his *Politics Among Nations* as the leading book.[2] The overwhelming majority of other prominent postwar general theorists have worked inside the Realist tradition.

To most scholars in international politics, to think like a Realist is to think as the philosophical historian Thucydides first thought. Realists invoke Thucydides to claim him as their founder and to say that their worldview is coeval with the actual emergence of interstate politics more than two thousand years ago. * * *

But was Thucydides a Realist? The question may seem to invite a tautology. Was Thucydides, Thucydidean? Is Realism Realist? Contemporary international Realism, however, is varied, not unified. Some of its most strenuous critics also reject the continuity thesis. They draw a line between the structural and scientific "Neorealism" of today and the interpretive and historical "classical Realism" of Morgenthau and his predecessors back to Thucydides.[3] Structural Neorealism the critics decry as statist, utilitarian, and positivistic ("an ideological move toward the economization of politics").[4] Classical Realism, on the other hand, though incomplete, respects political judgment and the politics of the historical, traditional practice of international politics, according to the same critics.

Nonetheless, I propose to defend the continuity thesis but still to reject the unity thesis. Realism does hark back to Thucydides, but it now has and has long had at least three major and significantly different variants: structuralist, fundamentalist, and minimalist. Each can trace some of its crucial elements to Thucydides' history. But only one follows Thucydides' own methods and lessons, what Thomas Hobbes translated as his "everlasting possession." If thinking like a Realist is thinking like Thucydides, which Realism can best sustain a claim to Thucydides? What sort of a Realist was Thucydides?

Modern Forms of Realism

MINIMALISM

Like all forms of Realism, minimalism portrays a worldview or explanation of interstate politics as a "state of war." It is premised on three views. First, "the international scene is properly described as an anarchy—a multiplicity of powers without a government."[5] Second, the primary actors are independent states whose domestic hierarchy (sovereignty) complements international anarchy. Third, no restraint—whether moral, social, cultural, economic, or political—is sufficiently strong or general either to eliminate or to guarantee the resolution of conflicts of interest, prestige, or value. Alternatively put, the state is at least relatively autonomous. Together these three tenets generate the "state of war," an omnipresent threat of war.

1. John A. Vasquez, *The Power of Power Politics* (New Brunswick, 1983), pp.162–70.
2. Hans Morgenthau, *Politics Among Nations*, 4th ed. (New York: Knopf, 1967); Vasquez, *Power*, pp. 43–44.
3. Richard Ashley, "The Poverty of Neorealism," in *Neorealism and Its Critics*, ed. R. O. Keohane (New York, 1986), pp.260–263.
4. Ashley, "Poverty of Neorealism," p. 297.
5. Martin Wight, *Power Politics*, introduction by Hedley Bull and Carsten Holbraad (London: RIIA, and New York: Holmes and Meier, 1978), p.101.

This view, common to a number of writers in the contemporary field, assumes nothing about the rationality of states, their pursuit of power or the "national interest," or the way they set their various goals. Indeed, it assumes that the processes and preferences of states vary and are open to choice influenced by both domestic and interstate considerations. This choice includes moral choices, but it assumes that ethical choices cannot be categorical or absolute — that is, that they must necessarily depend upon a prior consideration of strategic security. Given the lack of international security, states seeking to maintain their independence must provide for their own security, and this calls for an attention to relative power.

The dominant inference of minimalism is the continuity of the state of war. Interstate politics thus constitutes a field in which generalization, when placed in proper context, can be useful. Changing any one of the three basic assumptions changes the essence of interstate politics: world government or empire, the disintegration of states, or a very unlikely normative consensus or harmony of interest—each would remove states from the international state of war. Societies would experience instead international civil politics, a cessation of interstate politics, a universal empire, or a "security community." Failing these, the state of war persists.

FUNDAMENTALISM

Fundamentalism characterizes all social interaction as fundamentally rooted in mankind's psychological and material needs that result in a drive for power. State behavior, like all social behavior from the family through all other organizations, can thus best be understood as a reconstruction of interest-oriented, power-seeking activity. The struggle for power changes form but not substance when we move from a consideration of domestic to international politics. The drive for power produces the state of war.

The fundamentalist Realist accepts the anarchy assumption of minimalism, but questions the differentiation between domestic and interstate politics. Fundamentalism specifies both the means and preferences (both power) left open by the minimalist. Rooted in human nature itself, the drive for power leaves statesmen no choice other than power politics. Power, moreover, is fungible. Its pursuit in one endeavor readily translates into resources available for others, as "good arms make good laws; good laws, good arms."

In his first edition of *Politics Among Nations*, Morgenthau noted this theory's dominant inference that "all nations actively engaged in the struggle for power must actually aim not at a balance—that is, equality—of power, but at a superiority of power in their own behalf."[6] States can, of course, make mistakes. The need to pursue power rationally, therefore, has a prudential and not necessarily a descriptive significance.

STRUCTURALISM

Structuralism also explains the state of war. Like minimalism, structuralism assumes international anarchy and the predominance of state actors. Unlike the minimalists, structuralists assume that state actors are "functionally similar units" differing in capabilities but not ends, as Kenneth Waltz noted in *The Theory of International Politics*.[7]

6. [Morgenthau, *Politics Among Nations*,] 1st ed. (1949), p. 210.
7. [Waltz, *Theory of International Politics*, Reading, Mass., 1979], pp.96–97.

Rational process, fungibility of power resources, and a strong preference for power as a means to security form a necessary part of the model. But unlike fundamentalists, structuralists see these features not as assumptions about human nature or social organization but as derivations from the structure itself. State behavior is homogenized—made rational and power-seeking—through competition and socialization. Only the rational and power-seeking will survive the competition to dominate and thus teach their rivals.

Specific structural inferences, such as the hypothesized stability of the bipolar world, the instability of multipolarity, and the weaknesses of transnational restraints, are deduced from the model, once one specifies the number and capabilities of the states that compose the system. And scientific structuralism offers the promise of regularities that can be falsified or confirmed.

The structuralist's theory is based on assumptions and arguments best articulated in political philosophy by Hobbes and Rousseau. The closest philosophical roots of the fundamentalist interpretation lie in Machiavelli's studies of the politics of both private and public life.

Minimalism, I hope to show, can best trace its ancestry back to Thucydides. Fundamentalists and structuralists among the political scientists have claimed him too. Some classicists have discussed him employing concepts that a political scientist would associate with structuralism or fundamentalism and other classicists question the Realism of Thucydides himself.

We can best interpret Thucydides as at least a minimalist, but neither a fundamentalist nor a structuralist. Before we can know what kind of a Realist Thucydides was, we need to see whether he was a Realist at all.

Thucydides' Realism

. . . AT LEAST MINIMALIST . . .

Questioning Thucydides' Realism seems odd. Thucydides, after all, was the explicator of the "truest cause" of the great war between Athens and Sparta—the real reason that made it "inevitable"—which "was the growth of Athenian power and the fear which this caused in Sparta" (1.23).[8] Interstate relations in his view existed in a condition where war was always possible—a state of war such as that "hard school of danger" that persisted between Athens and Sparta during the "peace" that preceded the actual outbreak of hostilities (1.18). He wanted, moreover, his history to be "judged useful by those who wanted to understand clearly the events which happened in the past and which (human nature being what it is) will at some time or other and in much the same ways, be repeated in the future" (1.22). But none of the three minimal Realist tenets has gone unchallenged.

Did Thucydides have a moral theory which rejected Realism? We all recall the stark warning the Athenian officials gave the Melians: "The strong do what they have the power to do and the weak accept what they have to accept" (5.89). But a recent insightful article by David Cohen focusing on the events of Book 3 at Plataea, Corcyra, and Mytilene has rejected the standard view of Thucydides as an "amoral realist."[9]

If we define Realism as "might makes right," then we cannot interpret the debate between Cleon and Diodotus as a simple triumph of Diodotus' Realist

---

8. All translations unless otherwise noted are from Thucydides, *The History of the Peloponnesian War*, translated by Rex Warner, introduction by M. I. Finley (Harmondsworth: Penguin, 1954).
9. David Cohen, "Justice, Interest, and Political Deliberation in Thucydides," *Quaderni Urbinati* 16, 1 (1984), p. 37.

prudence over Cleon's legalistic vengeance. The Athenian assembly decided to reconsider its harsh decision to execute all the Mytileneans as a punishment for the Mytilenean rebellion against Athens. Cleon demanded that the assembly stick to its harsh sentence as a just punishment for the rebellious criminals he claimed the Mytileneans were. Diodotus then told the Athenians that their assembly was a political body, not a court of law (3.44). Athenian self-interest—the stable acceptance of their imperial rule by their colonies—required moderation.

Although it was probably true that, as Cohen argued, Diodotus had to speak deceptively in order to persuade the war-weary Athenians (3.43), deception did not require him to cater to the assembly's self-interest, disguising his moral repugnance at Cleon's "monstrous" but legalistic defense of vengeance. The Athenian populace itself had already come to feel regret for the harshness of their previous decision. Prudent self-interest can thus be read as an authentic and not merely a rhetorical tactic in Thucydidean morality, when self-help was all that could sustain independence and survival.

At the outset of the war, Thucydides appeared to approve of the Athenian assembly's rejection of Corinth's legalistic condemnation of Corcyra's actions and to endorse the strategic reasons the Corcyreans offered for why the Athenians should support their cause against Corinth (1.31-4). Indeed, the speeches of the Corinthians and Corcyreans at Athens, the Corinthians and Athenians at Sparta, and Cleon and Diodotus at Athens all include a combination of moral-legal and prudential reasoning.

Thucydides seemed to disapprove of all the simple formulas. He rejected those who like Cleon and the Corinthians argued that "right makes might" (that the moral course of action inherently builds strategic support or strength). Thucydides equally rejected the "might makes right" doctrine—a massacre is a massacre, whether it be of the Mycalessians by the Athenian mercenaries (who wantonly slaughtered the city's inhabitants, including a school full of children) (7.29); Thebans by Plataeans (3.63-7); Plataeans by Spartans (3.68); or Athenians by Sicilians, such as occurred in the killing of Nicias, "who least deserved to come to so miserable an end, since the whole of his life had been devoted to the study and practice of virtue" (7.86). But "right makes right" (the categorical moral and legal view) cannot govern state behavior when necessity speaks clearly. Safety required Athenian imperialism and none can be blamed for this self-interest, Thucydides has the Athenian ambassadors say (1.75). But neither does he endorse the untrammeled pursuit of "might makes might." Let us infer that Thucydides thought that Euphemus' failure to persuade the Sicilians of Athens' moderate intentions during Athens' Sicilian intervention (6.82–87) could be attributed to the Sicilians' awareness of the barbarous treatment of the Melians, whom the Athenians had mercilessly slaughtered and enslaved (5.116). Then the Athenian defeat in Sicily is the strategic lesson of the massacre at Melos.

Instead, Thucydides seemed to have said, as did the Athenians at Sparta, that "Those who really deserve praise are the people who, while human enough to enjoy power, nevertheless pay more attention to justice than they are required to do by the situation" (1.76). Great statesmanship and virtuous citizenship consisted of finding ways to reduce the conflict between the good and the prudent, as Pericles explained when he described how Athenians had "organized our State in such a way that it is perfectly well able to look after itself both in peace and war" (2.36) and could therefore "make friends by doing good to others" (2.40). These can be the words of a Realist.

Minimalist Realism has also been challenged by scholars who dispute the state-as-actor assumption underlying Realist considerations of foreign policy. Francis Cornford[1] has challenged the Realist emphasis on state-as-actor in favor of an interpretation of the war stressing that an aggressive policy had been forced on Pericles by the domestic commercial faction within Athens that sought to promote its private business prospects overseas. The merchants were the group with most to benefit from an imperialist policy in the West and from the destruction of their Megarian commercial rivals—and both these actions were the ones that embroiled Athens with Corinth and thus with Corinth's ally Sparta.

Cornford rejected the strategic rivalry between Athens and Sparta as a sufficient explanation because neither state was best served by an aggressive policy. But for a Realist—for Thucydides—the failure to achieve what would be the best outcome for each state considered separately is hardly a sufficient indication that the states were not acting according to their strategic interest or were instead being manipulated by particularistic domestic factions. Athens may well have preferred continued peace with its empire intact; Sparta, continued peace with its equality guaranteed. But if continued peace involved the steady increase in Athens' imperial power and Sparta preferred war to inferiority (as its assembly in fact chose), then Thucydides is offering a strategic analysis and a Realist explanation of why Sparta chose war over peace, since no arrangement of international anarchy could lead to a stable peace other than the balanced power resources of the two sides.

Thucydides personified ("Athens . . .") somewhat less than modern scholars do (he more frequently used "Athenians . . ."), and he referred to factions within the state (Archidamus' peace party at Sparta, the rural versus the urban inhabitants of Athens, the demos and the oligarchy). But with the striking exception of Alcibiades, individual leaders throughout the Peloponnesian War acted in the name of and through their influence over states. And domestic factions were not fixed in their influence or preferences.

Still other scholars have challenged the analysis of changing interstate power underlying Thucydides' explanation of the war. In making this challenge, these scholars attacked a primary tenet of Realist explanation. The continuity of interstate anarchy for the Realist provides the grounds for a comparative explanation of international events. The influence of changes in relative interstate power gives evidence of the underlying symmetry of interstate anarchy.

Thucydides may assert a Realist, power-oriented "truest cause" for the war found in the growth in Athenian power and Sparta's fear of that power (1.23, 1.44, and 1.118), but he failed to offer a truly Realist explanation for the origins of the war. According to the critics, this is because he never fully explained as would a Realist the growth of Athenian power; instead he described a crisis in which allies embroiled the two antagonists, and fear led one of them (Sparta) to declare war. The charge was first made by Meyer, Schwartz, Momigliano, and others[2] and recently by Garst.[3]

---

1. Francis M. Cornford, *Thucydides Mythistoricus* (London: Routledge and Kegan Paul, 1965) [excerpted in this volume], chaps. 2–3.
2. Eduard Meyer, *Forschungen zur alten Geschichte* II (Halle: M. Niemeyer, 1989); E. Schwartz, *Das Geschichtswerk des Thukydides* (Hildesheim: G. Olms, 1960); and Arnaldo Momigliano, *Studies in Historiography* (London: Weidenfeld and Nicolson, 1966), as described in Donald Kagan's account of these views in *The Outbreak of the Peloponnesian War* (Ithaca, NY: Cornell University Press, 1969), pp. 357–364.
3. Daniel Garst, "Thucydides and NeoRealism," *International Studies Quarterly* 33 (March, 1989), pp. 3–27.

The critics focused on two particulars, the core items of Realist explanation: explicability ("inevitability") and the force of relative power ("what made the war inevitable was the growth of Athenian power and the fear which this caused in Sparta," 1.23). G.F. Hudson captured the compellingness of the Realist view of power dynamics when he discussed Far Eastern politics in the 1930s: "There is perhaps no factor which drives a state into war so inexorably as a steady loss of relative power. Sooner or later a desperate now-or-never mood overcomes the calculations of prudence, and the belief that a war may be won today, but cannot be won tomorrow, becomes the most convincing of all arguments for an appeal to the sword."[4]

The critics have accused Thucydides of having asserted the importance of power dynamics but never having demonstrated the growth of Athenian power. Instead, they have argued that his history showed that Corinth, not Athens, forced Sparta into war or that it showed the significance of differences in political institutions, rules, and conventions.

Clearly, the critics are identifying something important. Thucydides' history showed that differences in political culture between Athens and Sparta as well as Corinth's incitement to action exacerbated Spartan fear. But he did not think they were the predominant, or truest, cause of the war, which was the growth in Athenian power. Furthermore, he attempted to demonstrate this quite carefully.

The Archaeology (1.1–19) with which Book 1 begins is a long account of why the Peloponnesian War was the greatest of all wars. Suffering and other prodigies made it noteworthy, of course, but the more important reason was that its two leaders were at the height of their power and their potential power was greater than that ever before exercised in Greece. "We have no right," Thucydides claimed, "to judge cities by their appearances rather than by their actual power . . ." (1.10). He consequently explained the growth of power among the city-states, noting in particular the emergence of states in place of tribal societies, the development of shipping and the increase in money (which together led to colonization), the growth in size of territory, and the replacement of unstable and personalistic tyrannical rule by more unified public rule. These were the general sources of interstate power among the Greeks.

Differences in just those dimensions of power—ships, money, and size—identified the growth in Athenian power relative to that of Sparta. Neither the great majority (prowar) nor the minority (antiwar) of the Spartans disagreed with that proposition. King Archidamus, arguing for negotiation and peace, urged caution in the face of the already superior power of Athens and delay in the hope that foreign financial and naval aid would in a few years tilt the balance of power to Sparta's advantage (1.80–85). (But as a patriotic Greek, he could not bring himself to utter the name of Persia—the only significant prospective source of aid). The ephor Sthenelaidas, arguing for war, harangued his audience, playing upon their military honor and sense of military superiority, and warned them that it was better to have a war now, joining with their allies, against Athens than a war later, after having lost their allies, against an even stronger Athens (1.86).

---

4. G. F. Hudson, *The Far East in World Politics* (New York: Oxford University Press, 1937), p. 198. Adam Parry, *Logos and Ergon in Thucydides* (New York: Arno Press, 1981 [1957]); Peter Pouncey in *The Necessities of War* (New York: Columbia Press, 1980), p.10; and Peter Fliess, *Thucydides and the Politics of Bipolarity* (Baton Rouge, LA: Louisiana State University Press, 1966) defend the power-oriented interpretation of Thucydides' history.

Thucydides then said that it was not the allies who persuaded or forced the Spartans but the Spartans who made up their own minds deciding on war "because they were afraid of the further growth of Athenian power" (1.88). So Thucydides in the Pentecontaetia (1.89–117) next showed how it was that Athenian power grew, again stressing the same crucial sources of power the Archaeology revealed.

The growth in the relative power of Athens was a function both of its own success and of Spartan stagnation. Despite Sparta's traditional military preeminence among the Greeks, neither its institutions, economy, or culture was conducive to a growth in power following the defeat of Persia. Its conservative, subsistence agriculture precluded the commerce needed to sustain seafaring and thus naval power. Its leaders, such as was Pausanias, were too boorish and overbearing to lead the pan-Greek coalition then liberating Ionia from the weakened Persian empire (1.94–5). Its helots were prone to revolt, thereby tying down Spartan forces for domestic security. Athens, conversely, had the commerce to undergird naval power, the sophistication to lead the other Greeks, and all the domestic security that a well-walled maritime city could enjoy. Taking over the lead from Sparta in liberating the Ionians, Athens expanded its commerce, established the leadership of a league of other states which it transformed into an empire, and imposed a tribute on its "allies" (1.96–7). The increase in Athenian ships, money, and imperial expansion—the dimensions of power stressed in the Archaeology—now made for the growth in power that alarmed Sparta (see Thucydides' summary, 1.118).

Differences in institutions and culture exacerbated tension and contributed to the failure of postwar cooperation. Athenian conflicts with Sparta's most significant ally, Corinth, and Athenian ties to Sparta's traditional enemy, Argos, also increased tension. And the growth in Athenian power was not continuous. Athens sustained setbacks during the rash expedition to Egypt and in the loss of Boeotia following the First Peloponnesian War. But the fundamental sources of Athenian power that Thucydides stressed—commerce, the navy, and the empire—remained intact and continued to grow until, in Thucydides' own words, Sparta felt its position "to be no longer tolerable" (1.118).

What then should we make of "inevitability"? Donald Kagan has introduced persuasive reasons for us to believe that each of the major participants—Sparta, Athens, Corinth—had a significant range of choice which was in part domestically determined.[5] But a Realist, to be a Realist, need not endorse "growth in power; therefore, inevitability." A minimalist could accept a splitting of the two propositions. The growth in Athenian power was not in itself sufficient to make the war "inevitable." It merely made it Realistically explicable.

Supporting both Kagan's history and Thucydides' interpretation, Erich Gruen has suggested that the proper translation of Thucydides' passage is "forced them to go to war," which is less mechanical a compulsion than is suggested by "inevitable."[6] As importantly, we can stress a Thucydidean contrast not between the underlying or remote as against surface or immediate causes, but between the real reasons or truest causes actually compelling Sparta as against the expressed complaints. Athens' power grew (a real and an underlying cause), and this caused fear in Sparta (also real but an immediate cause). Together they caused the war.

5. Kagan, *Outbreak*, pp. 351–56.
6. Erich Gruen, p.32 in "Thucydides, His Critics, and Interpreters," *The Journal of Interdisciplinary History* 1, 2 (1971), pp. 327–37.

The growth in power was not sufficient to compel. The trend toward an increase in Athenian power made a war rationally preferable now rather than later. But if Archidamus' rationalistic analysis (1.80–1) was correct, Athens was already more powerful than Sparta. War thus was not clearly the rational response. The addition of Sthenelaidas' persuasive harangue against Athenian power and his evocation of Spartan hatred and fear overwhelmed Archidamus' rational discourse on Athenian power and Spartan prudence. Athenian power did not compel or produce an inevitable result without Spartan (Sthenelaidas') fear. This fear was produced not merely by Athenian power but also by domestic choices in Sparta and the threatened loss of leadership should Corinth defect, which in its turn draws us into all the contingent crises and complaints from Epidamnus onward.

If Spartan fear developed independently of the actual growth of Athenian power or was the predominant cause of Spartan's decision, Thucydides' explanation would not be Realist—it would not be constrained by the continuity of international anarchy and the logic of self-help security. If the war occurred inevitably through power dynamics and without the addition of Spartan fear, Thucydides' explanation would be Realist but purely structuralist and not minimalist. It would also, if Kagan and Gruen are correct, be much less persuasive.

How then can a Realist draw everlasting lessons expressing the actual continuity of international anarchy if inevitably is explicability and heavily contingent both on international structure (shifting balances) and domestic politics? The answer, if this analysis is persuasive, is "the way Thucydides did."

According to Hobbes, one should interpret Thucydides in the "narration."[7] Thucydides himself did not formulate general laws, though the speakers whose words he recounts often did. He did, however, seek truest causes and the exact truth, "an accurate view" (5.26). He reported competing explanations, but he only offered multiple interpretations of the same event in his own voice when he could offer nothing better and suffered from lack of information. His own method was a combination of direct explanations of the "truest cause" variety and indirect explanations implied by his placing events in multiple contexts— interstate, domestic, and personal.

George Kateb has described some of our interpretive options.[8] We find general observations made by speakers whose words we must place in their context and then try to translate into ours. We find warnings in extreme situations. And we are shown typical, generalizable situations that confront statesmen in interstate politics.

Thucydides provided direct warnings of the need to avoid the common and uncritical acceptance of popular stories (1.20) and of how parallels out of context could be abused. This was what the Athenians did when they applied their memory of the conspiracy of Harmodius and Aristogiton to Alcibiades (6.53–9).[9] He also showed how the history could be properly used. His lengthy demonstration of the comparative pettiness of previous Greek wars taught the importance of the Peloponnesian War (1.1–21). Lessons learned from recognizing the plague and its social effects might warn us of what to expect in a reoccurrence (2.48). Together, these methods made the history as a whole "useful" to "those who want to understand clearly the events which happened

7. Richard Schlatter (ed.), *Hobbes' Thucydides* (New Brunswick, NJ: Rutgers University Press, 1975), p. 18.
8. George Kateb, "Thucydides' *History*: A Manual of Statecraft," *Political Science Quarterly* 69, 4 (1964), pp. 481–503.
9. Hunter R. Rawlings, *The Structure of Thucydides' History* (Princeton, NJ: Princeton University Press, 1981), pp. 103–17.

in the past and which (human nature being what it is) will, at some time or other and in much the same ways, be repeated in the future" (1.22).

Thucydides held, just as the minimalist Realists have assumed, that no government existed above the sovereign city-states. Interstate anarchy made interstate relations explicable. Anarchy produced mutual mistrust. Even with the best will in the world, no power would surrender any part of its security or liberty to another. Shifts in relative power together with fears susceptible to provocation made mistrusts into wars.

. . . BUT NEITHER FUNDAMENTALIST . . .

If Thucydides was at least a minimalist, was he also something more, a fundamentalist? The question is complicated, but despite important similarities between the fundamentalist perspective and that of Thucydides, we can distinguish his views from the core tenet of the fundamentalist interpretation of Realism.

Fundamentalist scholars of Realism see all society, all politics, domestic as well as interstate, as being rooted in human nature and its contests of competing interests, struggles for power, and drives toward domination. For them, life is, so to speak, power all the way down.

An essential aspect of Thucydidean thought is the continuity of politics which rests on the continuity of human nature. It is "human nature being what it is" that makes it possible to understand clearly the past and the future (by its similarities to the past) (1.22).

Classical political thought, Cornford has further claimed, was almost exclusively concerned with psychological causation.[1] In this respect, Thucydides' famous trinity of interest, fear, and glory applied fundamentally to both human and political motivation. Commentators on Thucydides have employed the connection between the two motivations to construct general theories of international change. Peter Pouncey[2] and William Bluhm[3] have shown how much of a contribution to our understanding of the Thucydidean state of war can be achieved with this method. Their theories of Athenian imperialism work through a "progress of pessimism": from fundamental human aggressiveness through political organization to imperial conquest to interstate resistance to domestic strain to civil war and to collapse into a war of all against all.

But there is a significant difference for Thucydides between intrastate and interstate politics that does not allow us to assimilate the two into one continuous struggle for power as the fundamentalists would have us do. Leo Strauss's discussion of Machiavelli's princely politics highlighted part of the contrast: "Contemporary readers find in both authors (Thucydides and Machiavelli) the same 'realism,' that is to say, the same denial of the power of the gods or of justice and the same sensitivity to harsh necessity and elusive chance. Yet Thucydides never calls into question the intrinsic superiority of nobility to baseness."[4]

Part of the difference between Machiavellian and Thucydidean Realism lies in their different views of interstate and intrastate "baseness" and its opposite, virtue. Thucydides showed that ethical or legal standards were not sufficient in interstate politics. However ethical and law-abiding a citizen Nicias was, he was also a disastrously poor general (7.86). The Melians suffered the fate

1. Cornford, *Mythistoricus*, pp. 64–65.
2. Pouncey, *Necessities of War*, p. xii.
3. William T. Bluhm, "Causal Theory in Thucydides' *Peloponnesian War*," *Political Studies* 10, 1 (1962), pp. 15–35.
4. Leo Strauss, *Thoughts on Machiavelli* (Chicago, IL: University of Chicago Press, 1958), p. 292.

of the weak in interstate politics, and their appeals to law and justice fell on deaf ears. But in the *polis*, laws could make the weak equal. Domestic security made moral virtues, justice, and legality, praiseworthy. Thus Pericles in the Funeral Oration (2.37) told the Athenians to be proud and to honor the Athenian dead for their virtues and sacrifices, to which, he added, the present citizens owed their lives, welfare, and freedom.

It was not true that interstate politics were the absolute realm of necessity, with intrastate politics the ethical realm of choice. Mycalessus would have been a butchery wherever it occurred. Still, there was a striking difference in the opportunities for ethical behavior and therefore in the ethical responsibility and also in the actual practice of politicians in the two realms. Civil war (the Corcyrean *stasis*) made a state of war of domestic politics. Ethical restraint dissolved as trust and even language lost their meanings (3.82). During the plague at Athens, natural disease destroyed social security. Those who tried to help others died first (2.51). Empire, conversely, could make a nearly secure state of peace out of "interstate" politics, thereby increasing the prospect of justice. And that, together with necessity, was the justification the Athenians at the conference at Sparta could offer for their empire.

. . . NOR STRUCTURALIST

If Thucydides was at least a minimalist but not a fundamentalist, was he also something else, a structuralist? Like minimalism and fundamentalism, structuralism explains the state of war through international anarchy. But structuralism finds the complexity and contingency of minimalism (and the reductionism of fundamentalism) unnecessary. For the structuralist, the important questions can be explained parsimoniously through international structure. Thucydides respected parsimony—that is what the "truest cause" was all about. But structure was not enough to explain the origins or the end of the war, the Athenian empire, or the Spartan hegemony.

According to the proponents of structuralism, structure selects for power-seeking ends and rational decision-making processes. But Thucydides held that neither a state's ends nor its means nor its choices could be adequately determined through an analysis of international structure.

Sparta's fear was a product not just of Athenian power but also of the domestically shaped choice that Sthenelaidas extracted from the Spartan assembly. So, too, Thucydides found that the end of the war—Athens' mistakes, and its final defeat—could not be attributed to a simple decline in Athens' relative power resources. Athens' ends and choices had changed.

Thucydides would have agreed that states should, as Pericles did, calculate their security with close attention to the threats posed by other states and to the domestic and allied resources available to meet them. But states could become corrupted as Athens was by the strains of war, plague, and resultant factionalism. In the debate over the disastrous decision to send an expedition to Sicily, private interests, not public security, governed policy. The old thought the expedition would be safe; the young that it would be fun; the masses anticipated booty and steady military pay; and Alcibiades sought political power and Nicias was afraid to oppose him. "A passion for the enterprise affected everyone" (6.24). So Athens sent its largest expedition off to defeat and utter destruction. Factionalism intensified, and soon Athenians fought Athenians, making the eventual Spartan victory a product more of Athenian disunity than Spartan superiority, for "in the end it was only because they had destroyed themselves by their own internal strife that finally they were forced to surrender" (2.65).

Nor were the states that Thucydides observed functionally equivalent in the exercise of their means and choices—while differing only in the quantity of fungible capabilities. Thucydides agreed that "We have no right, therefore, to judge cities by their appearances rather than by their actual power" (1.11). But their actualized power, also according to Thucydides, was not merely a function of similar categories of power, differently distributed in quantity across the interstate system.

For Thucydides, Athens differed from Sparta not only in quantity of power but also in differences in the nonequivalent functions of power. Athens' army could no more invade and occupy Sparta than the Spartan navy could blockade Piraeus. The Athenian empire (*arkhe*) rested on the far-flung outposts and material benefits that a commercial society could readily provide to its collaborating subordinates. Sparta's anticommercial society could not sustain an empire. Spartan hegemony (*hegemonia*), conversely, rested on its military prowess.

Some polities, like the Ionian remnants of the Persian empire liberated after Salamis by Athens in the 470s B.C., were wracked by deep social fissures. Their democrats became a transstatal faction favoring Athens, just as their oligarchs favored Sparta. Each faction preferred to collaborate with foreigners in order to balance against domestic rivals rather than to adhere to domestic unity in order to balance against external threats and preserve state independence. Indeed, this was just Alcibiades' insightful point when he assured the Athenians before the expedition to Sicily that no one should overestimate Sicilian power. Despite Sicilian numbers and wealth, their factionalism meant that they were "scarcely likely either to pay attention to one consistent policy or to join together in concerted action" (6.17). The mistake of Alcibiades and Athens was not in failing to estimate the numbers of the Sicilians but in failing to realize that the Sicilian polities under Hermocrates' brilliant leadership were states much more like Athens than the weak and divided islands Athens had absorbed from the Persian empire.

For Thucydides, rational unitary action was a goal and a key to survival in an anarchic world. It was not a structurally determined attribute. Rational strategic action relied on both domestically and internationally determined circumstances.

Conclusion

The importance of Thucydides' history extends beyond Realism. Marxists have been intrigued by the little that Thucydides says about class conflict. And what political society has ever been so subordinate to its mode of production as Sparta was to the need to suppress the helot labor force? But Marxism does not rest its analysis of social development on the slave mode of production.

Liberal democrats cannot fail to consider Thucydides' indictment of the Athenian democrats for the irresponsible rashness of their decision to launch and then mismanage the expedition to Sicily, which contributed to the eventual defeat and collapse of Athenian democracy. But liberalism, however much it concerns itself with the democratic determinants of foreign policy, has as its central and distinctive contribution a view of the moral equality of all human beings. Liberals are concerned with whether the interests of the majority become public policy, whether foreign or domestic. They are equally concerned that the rights of individuals shape the definition of the public's interests, whether at home or abroad. By those criteria, few societies have been more democratic and less liberal than Thucydides' Athens. The public triumph of the liberal ideal postdates Thucydides and his contemporaries.

Realism embraces the continuity of interstate anarchy. Thucydides belongs to the Realists. They belong to him. His Realism was weighed well by Martin Wight: "One of the supreme books on power politics is the history by Thucydides of the great war between Athens and Sparta, commonly called the Peloponnesian War."[5]

Although Thucydides is at least a minimalist, he is neither a fundamentalist nor a structuralist. Paternity suits tend to be messy. The argument of this chapter may seem similarly involved. Each version of Realism can identify its views in Thucydides' history. Fundamentalists and structuralists can of course use Thucydides' history to analyze the Peloponnesian War. But to borrow Thucydides' judgments in order to support their conclusions, they will need to put their conclusions in his context—both domestic and international.

A Thucydides writing today would see the importance of the changes a Gorbachev or a Reagan has made, but would also not assume that leaders can transform their polities according to their own interests and goals. Rejecting the fundamentalist view, a contemporary Thucydides would recognize the constraint on choice maintained by the historical compromises that have shaped the institutions and culture of particular states and the international anarchy that makes national security and effective national independence go hand in hand. A modern philosophic historian with Thucydidean views, while noting the structuralist trend toward multipolarity in the international system, would not assume that those changes in international structure would be either necessary or sufficient to end the historical hostility of the Cold War. At the same time, this historian would reject the view shared by many modern liberals and Marxists that changes in the domestic structure (e.g., toward democratization or social equality) of the two superpowers could be sufficient to end the insecurity they share.

To be a Thucydidean today is thus to see that states are not structurally equivalent and that the differences are consequential. It is to recognize that interstate and intrastate politics are not fundamentally the same even though human beings play out their hopes and fears in both. Yet it is also to realize that the continuity of the "state of war" is based on the persistence of interstate anarchy, just as the chance of either peace or war is contingent on domestic choice and international opportunity.

GREGORY CRANE

Gregory Crane teaches classics at Tufts University and is the editor of *Perseus: Interactive Sources and Studies on Ancient Greece*, an electronic database for the study of Greek civilization designed both for scholarship and for teaching. Much of his recent work is on Thucydides, including *The Blinded Eye: Thucydides and the New Written Word*. The following excerpt adapted from his new book, *Thucydides and the Ancient Simplicity: The Limits of Political Realism*, explores the boundaries of Thucydidean realism.

5. Wight, *Power Politics*, p. 24.

Truest Causes and Thucydidean Realisms[†]

In concluding the introductory section of his history (1.23.6), Thucydides purports to cut through the details and to lay bare the major forces behind the Peloponnesian War:

> [5] To the question why they broke the treaty, I answer by placing first an account of their grounds of complaint and points of difference, that no one may ever have to seek out that from which the Hellenes plunged into a war of such magnitude. [6] The truest cause (*alēthestatē prophasis*) I consider to be the one which was least evident in public discussion (*logos*). I believe that the Athenians, because they had grown in power and terrified the Spartans, *made* war *inevitable* (*anankasai*). Thuc. 1.23.5–6

No one familiar with the practice of scholarship will be surprised that Thucydides' serene analysis has provoked at least as much debate as it has silenced. In particular, students of ancient history have probed almost every nuance of 1.23.6. Monographs have been devoted to individual terms such as *prophasis*, "cause" and *anankē*, "necessity" (which shows up in the verbal form *anankasai*, translated "made . . . inevitable").[1] Controversy about the actual causes of the war and even about Thucydides' reliability as a source lives on.

Nevertheless, the idea contained in this passage continues to influence students and practitioners of foreign affairs. Thucydides' explanation for the Peloponnesian War has been cited to support the general thesis that war arises when power begins to shift. Thucydides provides the basis for the "balance of power" politics which Western diplomats from the nineteenth-century German statesman Bismarck to Henry Kissinger have explicitly pursued. Academic theorists of international relations still cite Thucydides' judgment on the Peloponnesian war. Even when he has not convinced others that his particular explanation was the best, Thucydides defined "the origins of war" as a topic for academic analysis. In particular, the most recent commentator on Thucydides concludes that his brief quotation of Thucydides reflects a fundamental contribution to the study of history: "the explicit formulation of a distinction between profound and superficial causes is arguably Thucydides' greatest single contribution to later history-writing."[2]

I have rendered the phrase *alēthestatē prophasis* as "the truest cause" because I wanted to stress the Greek superlative—if there are "truest" causes, then there presumably exist other causes which are true to a lesser degree, and indeed no single cause may even provide a single, comprehensive account.[3] Thucydides was obsessed with the need to probe beyond deceptive appearances and to reveal forces that, though often hidden, nevertheless drove events. Thucydides was hardly the first Greek to express this general idea: the late sixth-century thinker Herakleitos remarked that (fr. 54) "the hidden relationship (*harmonia*) is stronger than the obvious one" and (fr. 123) "nature (*physis*) tends to conceal itself." Thucydides wanted to study the "real world" and was thus a "realist."

---

† Gregory Crane, *Thucydides and the Ancient Simplicity*. Forthcoming spring 1998 from the University of California Press. Reprinted by permission of the University of California Press.
1. Hunter R. Rawlings, *A Semantic Study of Prophasis to 400 B.C.* (Wiesbaden, 1975); Martin Ostwald, *Ananke in Thucydides* (Atlanta, 1988).
2. So Simon Hornblower, *A Commentary on Thucydides: Books 1–3* (Oxford, 1991), 65 (on Thuc. 1.23.6).
3. The superlative is not a Thucydidean idiosyncrasy: cf., for example, Hdt. 7.233, where both *anankē* and the truest *logos* appear.

Few would then deny that Thucydides was, in some sense, a "realist"—indeed, perhaps the first such author whose work survives in the tradition of European writing. But reality is elusive, and there are many kinds of realism. Of course, Thucydides can be viewed as part of a "realist" tradition in the academic analysis and practical conduct of international affairs, and I will return to this crucial aspect of Thucydides' influence. First, however, I want to investigate Thucydides' relationship to a number of more general elements of realisms past and present. Ultimately, I will return to political realism as a particular, if often amorphous, school of thought, but in the meantime I wish to stress that the same balance of theory with practice that makes realism influential in the modern world finds its counterpart in Thucydides' history. Every element of realism which Thucydides claims for himself as an historian he also attributes to Perikles. The practices of historian and statesman run parallel to one another.

The Realisms of Thucydides

Thucydides' history exhibits four characteristics common to many "realist" schools of thought—not only political, but literary, artistic and scientific. The four realisms which I will examine are "procedural" (getting the facts straight), "scientific " (believing that there really are objective facts 'out there' somewhere that can be gotten straight), "ideological" (using your claim to privileged knowledge as a stick to beat your opponents), and "paradigmatic" (seeing some phenomena more clearly and perhaps gaining a better view of the whole, but at the expense of simultaneously minimizing or ignoring other factors on which your predecessors had laid great emphasis). This list is hardly exhaustive, but these elements, though complementary and intertwined, need to be distinguished like the varying forces that interact with any object.

First, and above all, Thucydides was a realist insofar as he insisted upon a high level of observational accuracy—I will, for present purposes, call this his "procedural realism." One can argue about how successful Thucydides was in this regard, and, since Thucydides never finished the History, there are plenty of loose ends in the text. Nevertheless, Thucydides is famous for his insistence upon the importance of careful observation and precise reporting. Consider, for example, one famous passage in which Thucydides sheds some light on his methological expectations. After he has sketched his own idiosyncratic vision of ancient times, Thucydides castigates the slovenliness of his predecessors:

> [1] Having now given the result of my inquiries into early times, I grant that there will be a difficulty in believing every particular detail. The way that most men deal with traditions, even traditions of their own country, is to receive them all alike as they are delivered, without applying any critical test whatever. [2] The general Athenian public fancy that Hipparchos was tyrant when he fell by the hands of Harmodios and Aristogeiton; not knowing that Hippias, the eldest of the sons of Peisistratos, was really supreme, and that Hipparchos and Thessalos were his brothers; and that Harmodios and Aristogeiton suspecting, on the very day, nay at the very moment fixed on for the deed, that information had been conveyed to Hippias by their accomplices, concluded that he had been warned, and did not attack him, yet, not liking to be apprehended and risk their lives for nothing, fell upon Hipparchos near the temple of the daughters of Leos, and slew him as he was arranging the Panathenaic procession.

Thuc. 1.20.1–2

The Athenians are so uncritical that they have utterly misconstrued a central event in their own history, the ouster of the Peisistratids. Thucydides would later return to the Peisistratids and his own reconstruction of their departure with a famous digression in book six, but here he does not content himself with public opinion.

The statesman also bases his authority on such procedural realism. Perikles does not so much criticize individual opponents as stress his own unparalleled ability "to recognize and articulate those things which are necessary" (e.g. Thuc. 2.60.5). He is for Thucydides a model of accuracy: when the historian chooses to detail Athenian resources at the beginning of the war, he puts the detailed list of facts and figures in Perikles' mouth (2.13).

Observational accuracy depends upon the existence of a stable, objective reality separate from, and in theory identical to, observers. If equally accurate observers of the same phenomenon produce different results, then procedural realism becomes problematic. The term "scientific realism," popular among philosophers of science, describes Thucydides' second realism.

In the twentieth century, even the physicists—champions of observation, analysis and prediction—have had to abandon their implicit confidence in a deterministic, predictable world. Einstein showed that time was not absolute but relative to the speed and position of the observer, while quantum mechanics—which Einstein helped to establish—scandalized Einstein himself by suggesting that it was impossible to predict the position and velocity of particles on a very small scale. The label "scientific realist" has been developed for those who retain their confidence in an objective world independent of the observer.

The objectivity of human experience was, however, as contested in the fifth century as it is now. The early Greek philosophers Parmenides and Herakleitos had each in his very different way challenged the validity of our perceptions and posited that the ultimate reality was hidden from our view. Experience with alien cultures brought with it the recognition that at least some common assumptions were simply conventions that had no inherent truth. Herodotus, conservative as he may in some ways have been, was acutely aware that people of differing cultures extracted different meanings from the same events.[4] Fifth-century thinkers like Herodotus began to contrast "nature" (*physis*) and "culture" (*nomos*).[5] The philosopher Protagoras' most famous saying— "man is the measure of all things"—was used by some to undercut the authority of traditional ideas and beliefs. Nor was the argument confined solely to such obviously subjective (to us, at any rate) areas as religion and culture: Thucydides' contemporary, Demokritos, questioned the validity of any observation: "sweet by convention (*nomos*), bitter by convention, hot by convention, cold by convention." Demokritos labelled all sensory information—sight, hearing, smell, taste, touch—"illegitimate." Not all fifth-century thinkers shared this degree of skepticism—Empedocles, for example, urges that we exploit our senses to the full—but no one familiar with the mainstream intellectual controversies of the fifth century could take for granted the "common-sense" view that careful observation uncovered an unproblematic "real world."

---

4. The classic example is Hdt. 3.38, where Dareios [Darius] confronts Greeks, who burned their dead, with Indians, who supposedly ate theirs. Each side found the practice of the other abhorrent.
5. For a survey of the main passages, see still F. Heinimann, *Nomos und Physis: Herkunft und Bedeutung einer Antithese im griechischen Denken des 5. Jahrhunderts* (Darmstadt, 1945).

55505

Even when Thucydides explicitly stresses the importance of observational
accuracy, his goals presuppose considerable confidence in the validity of observation. Thus, Thucydides describes the care with which he constructed his
idealized accounts of events (1.22.2–3). Thucydides is acutely sensitive to the
problems of observational inadequacy and error: he thus insists that he took
nothing for granted, refusing even to trust his own observations without cor-
roboration and stressing the time and labor which he lavished on clearing up
problems. But when Thucydides deplores the inconsistent descriptions of his
informants, and promises, without qualification, to deliver in writing an accurate report, he implies that a single, true account of events is possible.[6] The
major obstacle for such accuracy is human weakness. Thus, Thucydides defends his conclusion that the Peloponnesian War was the greatest in Greek history by contrasting his reasoning with the fickle judgments of others (1.21.2). If
observers can rise above the pressures of the moment and observe the "facts
themselves" (*auta ta erga*), a true picture of events will emerge. Our intellectual powers are limited, our expectations biased, but if the disciplined observer
can rise above such limitations, a single truth does exist.

But for Thucydides, undisturbed observation is not simply an attribute
for the historian. The first words that he gives to his Perikles point in the
same direction:

> I always hold fast to the same intellectual resolve (*gnōmē*), Athenians,
> and that is the principle of no concession to the Peloponnesians. I know
> that the spirit which inspires men while they are being persuaded to make
> war, is not always retained in action; that as circumstances change, reso-
> lutions change. Yet I see that now as before the same, almost literally the
> same, counsel is demanded of me; and I put it to those of you, who are al-
> lowing yourselves to be persuaded, to support the national resolves even in
> the case of reverses, or to forfeit all credit for their wisdom in the event of
> success. For sometimes the course of things is as arbitrary as the plans of
> man; indeed this is why we usually blame chance for whatever does not
> happen as we expected.

> Thuc. 1.140.1

Perikles boasts that, whatever the circumstances, he maintains the same
gnōmē, a complex term that implies both an intellectual decision and moral resolve. This proves to be no idle boast: even after the plague has devastated
Athens and undermined the moral structure of Athenian society, Perikles fearlessly repeats this claim:

> I am the same man and do not alter, it is you who change, since in
> fact you took my advice while unhurt, and waited for misfortune to repent
> of it; and the apparent error of my policy lies in the infirmity of your in-
> tellectual resolve (*gnōmē*), since the suffering that it entails is being felt by
> every one among you, while its advantage is still remote and obscure to all,
> and a great and sudden reverse having befallen you, your mind is too much
> depressed to persevere in your resolves.

> Thuc. 2.61.2

6. It is admittedly hard to gauge the extent to which Thucydides has thought through the implications of
this 1.21.2. Lowell Edmunds ("Thucydides in the Act of Writing," in R. Pretagostini, *Tradizione e Inno-
vazione nella Cultura Greca* [Rome, GEI. 2: 831–852]) and Loraux ("Thucydides a écrit la guerre du
Péloponnèse," *Metis* 1 [1986], 139–161) have argued that Thucydides felt that writing could almost perfectly encode experience. I have elsewhere sought to qualify Thucydides' assumptions and to suggest that
they are not quite so strong: see "Thucydidean Claims of Authority" in G. Crane, *The Blinded Eye:
Thucydides and the New Written Word* (Lanham, MD, 1996).

A few chapters later, Thucydides, expressing his own reflections on the career of Perikles, gives further emphasis to Perikles' unflappable intellectual resolve. The Athenians first fine Perikles but soon restore him to power, changing their minds quickly. These Athenians thus prove Perikles' charge (1.140) that his fellow Athenians are unable to maintain a single course of action. Thucydides too says that such fickle behavior is (2.65.4) "what the masses (*ho homilos*) are wont to do." Thucydides labels Perikles' "public esteem" (2.65.8: *axiōma*) and his "intellectual power" (*gnōmē*) as the two foundations of his authority. He never flattered the people (2.65.8). Above all, he had the power to dampen their gross swings of mood, instilling fear in them when they had become too elated and restoring their confidence when they gave way to despair (2.65.9). At the center of it all stood Perikles, motionless, beyond passion and personal concerns.[7]

It is almost impossible to stress too much the fascinations which such a detached vantage point exerted in the classical period. Ultimately, geometry flourished in large part because it constituted a logically consistent system with explicit rules and assumptions in which all rational observers had to draw identical conclusions. "Give me a place to stand and I will move the world," the Greek mathematician Archimedes is reported to have said, and it is towards such an idealized position, separate from the world and its passions, that Thucydides and his Perikles strive. The achievements in mathematics were immense. Archimedes continues to occupy a position as one of the great mathematicians from any age. Euclid's *Elements* include almost five hundred theorems which Greek mathematicians had proved with great rigor in little more than a century, a task which the Greeks of Thucydides' generation had begun in earnest. This Euclidean geometry remained unchallenged until the nineteenth century, and it continues to occupy a solid position in the teaching of mathematics. Had Thucydides been born thirty years later, the great strides in this field might have attracted him in this direction rather than towards history.

The importance of scientific realism comes out when Thucydides describes the collapse of society at Corcyra. One of the most terrible consequences of this warfare was, according to Thucydides, to shift in the meanings of words:

> Words had to change their ordinary meaning and to take that which
> was now given them. Reckless audacity came to be considered the courage
> of a loyal ally; prudent hesitation, specious cowardice; moderation was
> held to be a cloak for unmanliness; ability to see all sides of a question in-
> aptness to act on any. Frantic violence became the attribute of manliness;
> cautious plotting, a justifiable means of self-defence.

> Thuc. 3.82.4

Of course, the change in language reinforces the brutalization of life, and Thucydides clearly invites (although he does not explicitly suggest) his audience to see this phenomenon in moral terms, but the degeneration of language has purely practical consequences as well. If words have no stable meaning, then communication breaks down, and with it the tasks of historian and statesmen alike both become impossible.

The undisturbed observer stands in the ideal, "Archimedean" position from which the fullness of an event can be seen and appreciated. We are, of

---

7. When Kleon seeks—and without success—to make himself a second Perikles, he echoes Perikles' claim to intellectual constancy (compare Kleon's unchanging *gnōmē* at 3.38.1 with Perikles at 1.140.1 and 2.61.2).

course, a good deal more skeptical about the possibility for such detached observation now than we were more than sixty years ago—the rejection of such "objectivity" has evolved into a dominant theme of late twentieth-century academic thought.

Furthermore, Thucydides was himself painfully aware that the same events may have very different meanings for different observers. A sudden wind, for example, begins to blow during a naval engagement, throwing the Peloponnesian ships into disorder and providing the Athenians with an opportunity to attack (Thuc. 2.84.3). This represents an "objective" phenomenon—all careful observers on both sides would have detected the same wind from the same quarter at the same time—but each side endows the same event with a very different meaning. Phormio, the Athenian commander, knew that this wind regularly began to blow shortly after dawn, and he delayed battle as he waited for it to disturb the Peloponnesian ships (2.84.2). The Peloponnesians, however, did not know Phormio's plans and did not understand that they had been maneuvered into this adverse position: when their commanders attribute their poor showing to "chance" (2.87.2: *ta apo tēs tuchēs*), they seem to interpret as accidental the wind on which Phormio had counted.

In this case, the differing interpretations reflect differing levels of knowledge: the Spartan commanders, if they could have read Phormio's mind, might have changed their view of that unfortunate wind. But the meaning of this Athenian battle as a whole is contested. Thucydides clearly sees in Athenian superior naval skill the decisive factor, but the Spartans at home find the whole thing "inexplicable" (2.85.2: *paralogos*) and assume that "some weakness" (*tis malakia*) must have caused the defeat. The Spartans clearly misread the situation (at least as Thucydides sees it), but it is not clear whether more information about the battle would have changed their minds. They were not yet prepared to accept technical matters as an explanation for military events.

Even if Thucydides successfully described who led what force to a particular place, how many men died in the subsequent battle, and what the immediate consequences were, he knew that such data did not, in themselves, necessarily mean the same thing to all parties. Rather, his history provides accurate data to serve the interpretations of readers in the future. Thucydides is more than a simple materialist, for he understands the impact of ideas upon the events. Thucydides includes in his History speeches (despite the fact that he cannot even pretend to have more than general sources for them) at least in part because they dramatize the degree to which a subject's position shapes perception.

Thucydides' scientific realism had an enormous impact upon his practice as an historian. Thucydides' predecessor, Herodotus, had cultivated an ambivalent relationship towards the events that actually took place. Although he seems to have provided us with a reasonably accurate account of the Persian wars and other fairly recent events, he frequently expresses an agnosticism towards the events which he relates. The verb form *legetai*, "it is said," is, for example, a favorite Herodotean term and crops up more than one hundred times in the *Histories*. Herodotus uses this term to distance himself from many reports, ranging from Kroisos' [Croesus'] behavior on his funeral pyre (Hdt. 1.87.1) to dried fish miraculously returning to life as they were being cooked (9.120.1). Herodotus, however, does not simply refuse to endorse many of the stories. He seems to relish elaborating events that never happened. Perhaps the most famous single episode in his history is a meeting that could never have taken place: Herodotus has the Athenian statesman and sage Solon visit Kroisos, the proverbially wealthy king of Lydia, even though Solon's travels took place at least twenty years before Kroisos became king. Solon warns the skeptical Kroisos about the fragility of human fortune—a warning that Kroisos later recalls when his empire has fallen and he faces the prospect of being burned alive. The conversation between Solon and Kroisos is "true" not because it took place (which it didn't) but because it lets us understand better the parabolic careers which Kroisos, Kyros [Cyrus], Kambyses [Cambyses], Dareios [Darius] and Xerxes will all pursue, as each in turn rises and falls. Herodotus refused to let the details of what actually happened distract him from the larger picture. He was an "idealist" for whom stories of the past constituted a means with which to study higher truths.

Thucydides was just as determined as Herodotus to extract the general from the particular, but their methods moved in opposite directions. Rather than rearranging the past so that data would better reflect his understanding of the world, Thucydidean history stressed greater rigor and subordination to the facts of the case. Thus, Thucydides felt that, once he had worked his way through the evidence, he could provide clean and well-digested descriptions of many events. On the level of individual campaigns or episodes, Thucydides seems to have been confident in his method. Nevertheless, this method did not "scale up." On the macroscopic level, contradictions and unresolved tensions pull at Thucydides' history. Herodotus' world is, for all its willfulness, a far more ordered place, almost Newtonian in its predictability, than the messy picture that we find in Thucydides: the Plague, Melos, and the Sicilian expedition all undermine the vision offered by Perikles in his funeral oration; in Herodotus, by contrast, Solon's analysis of prosperity, which contradicts present phenomena (such as the then good fortune of Kroisos) finds itself validated throughout the Histories, as not only Kroisos, but Kyros, Kambyses, Dareios and Xerxes—all the most powerful figures in the text—all to some extent fit the same Herodotean parabolic curve of rise and decline (cf. Hdt. 1.5.4). In the beginning of the twentieth century, Francis Cornford's Thucydides Mythistoricus[8] brilliantly showed that Thucydides saw the rise and fall of Athens in terms very similar to those at work in Herodotus and even Aeschylus—at some level, Herodotean forces operate in Thucydides' history, just as Newtonian mechanics work perfectly well in virtually all day-to-day circumstances. Nevertheless, it is equally true that, if we follow Thucydides' own historical logic as it plays out in the opening of book one, Sparta was an archaic, obsolescent power that should have given way to Athens, with its sea-power, its money and its dynamism. The accuracy and precision which Thucydides demanded made it impossible for his work to approach the intellectual or moral closure of Herodotus' Histories. Perhaps this is why Thucydides' work is, at least in contrast to that of Herodotus, so humorless, its ironies so harsh.[9] Herodotus could poke fun at his subjects as well himself (as he does, for example, when he draws attention to the implausibility of the Constitutional Debate at 3.80.1), because his world, for all its vagaries and contingencies, ultimately made sense.

Third, Thucydides and Perikles both exploit their procedural accuracy to further a third, subtle, often insidious, project, which I will call "ideological realism." On this point, Mark Twain's remarks on James Fenimore Cooper are helpful, for they make explicit a point which neither Thucydides nor his Perik-

8. Cornford, Thucydides Mythistoricus (London, 1907) [excerpted in this volume, pp. 412–23].
9. There are relatively few traces of humor in Thucydides: Kleon's embarrassment at 4.28 is probably the clearest. The stratagem by which the people of Egesta staged for the Athenians an exaggerated estimate of their resources has great comic potential, but it is not clear, given the grim outcome of the Sicilian expedition, whether Thucydides intends for us to find this story funny.

les had any motivation to highlight. Twain castigated Cooper's inaccuracies for purely practical reasons:

> If Cooper had been an observer, his inventive faculty would have worked better, not more interestingly, but more rationally, more plausibly. Cooper's proudest creations in the way of 'situations' suffer noticeably from the absence of the observer's protecting gift. Cooper's eye was splendidly inaccurate. Cooper seldom saw anything correctly. He saw nearly all things as through a glass eye, darkly. Of course, a man who cannot see the commonest little everyday matters accurately is working at a disadvantage when he is constructing a 'situation.'[1]

Twain goes on to develop his famous critique of a scene from Cooper's *Deerslayer*, in which five Indians in succession, attempting to jump from a overhanging tree towards a very slowly moving barge a few feet below, all manage to fall into the water astern. The reason behind Twain's outrage is clear: his *Huckleberry Finn* and "Jumping Frog of Calaveras County," fantastic as they may be taken as a whole, were believable because Twain labored to construct them out of smaller details which were in themselves plausible and because, to the extent that Twain departed from such a strict canon of objective plausibility, he knew precisely what he was doing. He understood the Hesiodic trick of mixing true things with false (cf. Hesiod, *Theogony* 26–28)[2] so that he could blur the realistic and the fantastic, making each reinforce the other. His procedural realism was fundamental to his success at creating idealized characters or situations that were at once incredible and convincing, and hence powerful.

Twain's realism is, for the most part, an explicit literary device. It lends power to his prose, but Huckleberry Finn and the Jumping Frog are manifestly literary creations. Thucydides wrote a history that purported to be a true account, while the Thucydidean Perikles claimed always to have the best advice for the state. Ideological realism claims for itself a monopoly on truth and opposes itself to "idealism," the pursuit of an attractive, but ultimately ill-founded, vision of the world. This ideological realism itself partakes of two dimensions. The first is, or more properly represents itself as being emotionally detached. Not only does Thucydides assume that a single objective reality does exist and that he is the man to observe it, but he uses these two assumptions to help assert a special authority for himself and his text. As the careful observer, Thucydides claims impartiality and the moral authority that comes with it.

The Thucydidean Perikles plays the same game in his three speeches on the war (1.140–144, 2.60–64 and esp. the account of Athenian resources at 2.13), where he claims a more detailed vision of the situation than any of his (unquoted) rivals. The same assumptions of direct knowledge shape the Funeral Oration, where an idealized Athens exploits the tension between the state and the individual, drawing on every strength inherent in Athenian democracy. Of course, the Athens of the Funeral Oration never existed, but, while such a rosy view of the community belongs to the genre of state funeral orations, the Athens which the Thucydidean Perikles conjures up is an extraordinary creation that maintains to this day a place in the general curriculum.[3] The Thucy-

---

1. Mark Twain, *Collected Tales, Sketches, Speeches and Essays 1891–1910* (New York, 1992), 184.
2. Hesiod was an early Greek epic poet c. 700. His *Theogony* is about the origins and genealogies of the gods [*Editor*].
3. Edward Everett, who, at a very young age, served as the first Eliot Professor of Greek at Harvard, and later became the most famous orator of his day, had Thucydides in mind when he delivered the "real" Gettysburg address. Lincoln had been invited to deliver a few remarks that would follow the featured speech by Everett. On the influence of the Athenian Funeral Oration in nineteenth-century America, see Garry Wills, *Lincoln at Gettysburg: The Words That Remade America* (New York, 1992).

didean Perikles dismisses many conventions of the genre (giving, for example, short shrift to Athens' ancient history and even the Persian Wars), while basing itself on several of the more compelling traits that shape Thucydides' Athenians. The energy which Perikles attributes to the Athenians (e.g. 2.39, 40.2, 41.1) helps account for, and give depth to, the horrified Corinthian vision of Athenian dynamism which preceded the war (1.68–71). At the same time, the energy and dynamism of the Funeral Oration gives Alcibiades his opening when he urges the risky Sicilian expedition, which ran against Perikles' strategy (1.144.1, 2.65.11). Above all, the Thucydidean Perikles bases Athenian patriotism on the one motivation which Thucydides always acknowledges: Perikles calls upon the Athenians to gaze upon the "power" (*dunamis*) of their city and thus let themselves be carried away with passion, becoming "lovers" of the city (2.43). The admiration for power—whether hypostasized as profit (1.8.3) or as empire (e.g., 6.13.1)—is, with fear (its complement), the only factor that can reliably inspire Thucydides' humans.

The plague follows immediately after the idealistic Funeral Oration, and the implied contrast is harsh: Athenian democracy wilts before the pressure of this disease, and the social virtues which Perikles praises collapse (2.53) as the corpses begin literally to pile up (see 2.52.4). Nevertheless, Funeral Oration and Plague are not a self-contained doublet but the opening sections of a three-part sequence: shortly after the Plague account, Thucydides brings Perikles back into the narrative so that the statesman can deliver his response to events. Perikles thus speaks before *and* after the plague. He has the last word, and events, terrible as they may be, do not cow him. His speech at 2.60–64 brilliantly synthesizes his own "realistic" assessment of the situation (which Thucydides endorses at 2.65) with the "idealizing" heroic values of the old Greek elite. This final speech is a masterpiece of ideological realism.

On the one hand, Perikles appeals to the pride of his listeners. They inhabit a "great city" and thus constitute a collective aristocracy that must live up to its status (2.61.4). The Athenians have achieved so much and they are so much superior to their enemies that they deserve to feel disdain (2.62.4) for their adversaries. Athens has earned the "greatest name" (2.64.1) because it would not yield to misfortunes. Even if Athens should fall now (as, Perikles concedes, it surely will sooner or later), the achievements of the present will ensure that "memory" of their deeds will survive (2.64.3). Perikles thus appeals to the same "eternal fame" as does Achilles—except that, of course, Athenian fame will rest upon genuine achievements, for which the mendacious poets are unnecessary (2.41.5)—and to which, of course, the plainspoken Thucydides is ideally suited (1.22.4).

At the same time, the heroic exhortation rests upon an appeal to cool judgment and a sound appreciation of the world as it really is. Perikles demands respect on the grounds that (2.60.5) he "is second to none at recognizing what things need doing and at explaining these things." If the Athenians have lost confidence in his strategy for the war, then they have only their own "infirmity of intellect" (2.61.2) to blame. Pain is obvious to the Athenians, while their intellects fail to perceive the advantage which is not immediately before them. Their intellect is prostrate. Fears about the ultimate outcome of the war are groundless and arise only because the Athenians do not see things as they really are (2.61). "Rational analysis based on what really exists" (2.62.5), which provides the most secure foundation for "foresight" (*pronoia*), justifies Athenian confidence. If the Athenians will only concentrate their minds upon "the future good and present honor" (2.64.6), they will hold out. The speech goes back and forth, playing the "real" and the "ideal" off against one another so that cold calculation appears to call for the pursuit of glory.

Yet the historian Thucydides is a good deal less disingenuous than the author and essayist Twain. Twain makes it clear that procedural realism is important because it lends a text greater credibility. Thucydides even turns the difficult and quirky nature of his text to his own advantage. Readers may find the history slow going or at times somewhat dry in comparison to Homer or (presumably) the unnamed Herodotus, but only because Thucydides has subjected himself to strict intellectual discipline and refused to compromise truth for charm. If Thucydides loses readers in the present, the greater purity of his account will nevertheless strengthen his case in the long run (1.22.4). While Thucydides concedes that his history may not win any prizes at first or enjoy wide popularity, he argues that it will nevertheless constitute a permanent heirloom that will be treasured and will even increase in value over time. But, of course, such disclaimers are self-serving. While directing our attention to his concessions about charm, Thucydides invites us to concede the far greater point of accuracy and even practical value.

The impact of Thucydides' claim to an austere, but authentic, account would be immense, for it helped lay the foundations for that rhetorical posture by which so-called technocrats justify their position in society. At the same time, Thucydides is simply varying the hackneyed court-room persona familiar to all contemporary Athenians. Just as speakers regularly contrast their own inexperience with rhetoric and necessary reliance on the plain, but unpolished, truth, Thucydides distinguishes himself from others. The protestations of stylistic simplicity culminate a few sentences later when Thucydides delivers his explanation for the outbreak of the Peloponnesian War (Thuc. 1.23.5–6). Everything that precedes in the *History* is calculated to lend this judgment greater weight, and much of Thucydides' subsequent narrative inevitably serves to reinforce this initial judgment.[4] Thucydides exploits to the full the ideological dimension implicit in the very term "realism," for Thucydides claims to portray the "real" world while his counterparts struggle to provoke pleasing, but potentially mendacious, effects.

Thucydides' ideological realism extends, however, beyond the claims of scientific accuracy. It includes an extra dimension that appeals more openly to the emotions and bullies its audience into submission. The famous passage from Thucydides' analysis of civil war and its horrifying moral consequences on Corcyra contains an illustration of ideological realism at its most brutal and its consequences (Thuc. 3.83). Thucydides makes little attempt to conceal his dismay at the collapse of moral society. The breakdown in trust not only poisons human relations but creates a nightmarish world in which "blunter wits" cut down their cleverer fellows. The practices of intelligence—calm observation and rational analysis—become liabilities, and thus the very conditions necessary for Thucydides as historian disappear. When the "ancient simplicity was laughed down and annihilated" (Thuc. 3.83), it took with it anyone who shared Thucydides' intellectual values and left behind a world antithetical to those values which Thucydides championed.

But if Thucydides invites his readers to share in his horror at this debased condition, he nevertheless contributes to this corrosive process as well.

---

4. In particular, the restless and insatiably acquisitive character that Thucydides attributes to his Athenians (see esp. the Corinthian speech at 1.68–71 and Alcibiades' speech at 6.16–18) makes Athenian attempts at expansion inevitable and thus strengthens the judgment (see Crane, *The Blinded Eye*).

Thucydides' *History*, like Machiavelli's *Prince* and Hobbes' *Leviathan*, does much to undermine conventional pieties. Thucydides' Athenians regularly subordinate power to justice, and their example has ever since served to justify hard-nosed power politics. Perikles' Funeral Oration remains one of the great visions of democratic freedom, but Thucydides' account of the plague, which inverts Perikles' values, undercuts his idealization of Athens and forces him to construct a new argument at 2.60–64. Thucydides only allows "the ancient simplicity" to appear in his text when it can cast discredit upon someone or when events show the weakness of such traditional values. Even as Thucydides' *History* champions the rational analysis which became untenable at Corcyra, it adopts the cynicism which helped cause the very condition he deplores.

This cynicism constitutes a second ideological element commonly claimed by realists. Not only does realism claim for itself the "real world," but it adds an emotional charge to this claim and implies that those who do not share its vision are naive. Realism of this kind relies for much of its effect upon intimidation, but it is both effective and self-fulfilling, for it justifies in the name of self-defense the most ruthless measures. Thus, Machiavelli expresses the "realist" position in a celebrated passage of *The Prince*:

> I shall depart from the methods of other people. It being my intention to write a thing which shall be useful to him who apprehends it, it appears to me more appropriate to follow up the real truth of a matter than the imagination of it; for many have pictured republics and principalities which in fact have never been known or seen, because how one lives is so far distant from how one ought to live, that he who neglects what is done for what ought to be done, sooner effects his ruin than his preservation; for a man who wishes to act entirely up to his professions of goodness soon meets with what destroys him among so many who are not good. Hence it is necessary for a prince wishing to hold his own to know how not to be good, and to make use of it or not according to necessity.

Machiavelli, *The Prince* 15[5]

According to Machiavelli, because not all men are good, the ruler, who is responsible for the fate of others, *must* learn how not to be good. Machiavelli cleverly plays upon the responsibility of the prince, asserting a moral imperative to amorality and espousing an altruism of power politics, whereby the individual gives up something of his personal goodness to further the good of the community. Machiavelli goes on to repeat his distinction between the "real world" and the "imaginary" one: he will speak of those "issues with regards to which an imaginary prince" might be praised and concentrate on those issues that are "real" (*vere*). In this way, 'realists,' from Thucydides to Machiavelli and Hobbes and on through to modern academic theorists such as Hans Morgenthau, John Herz, Kenneth Waltz and Robert Gilpin, traditionally claim not only for themselves a superior perspective and proprietary vision of the world "as it really is."[6] They undermine the authority of their intellectual adversaries, in modern times applying to them the dismissive label "idealists."

---

5. Translation after Machiavelli, *The Prince* (London, 1911).
6. Hans Morgenthau, *Politics among Nations* (New York, 1948); J. H. Hertz, *Political Realism and Political Idealism* (Chicago, 1951); K. N. Waltz, *Theory of International Relations* (Reading, MA, 1979); Robert Gilpin, *War and Change in World Politics* (Cambridge, 1981).

Thucydides' relationship to the bullying ideological realism which he alternately deplores and practices emerges with particular force in the Mytilenean debate. If Thucydides reserves his strongest praise for Perikles (2.65), Kleon, the would-be Perikles, receives equally explicit condemnation, receiving the term "most violent of the citizens" (3.36.6). Kleon opens his speech calling for the liquidation of the Mytileneans with an extended exercise in realist intimidation. When Kleon lashes out at speakers who indulge in intellectual virtuosity at the expense of practical considerations and to the tangible harm of the state (3.37–38), he anticipates countless realist condemnations of idealism. At the same time, in equating the cultivation of anger and the indulgence in retribution with *sōphrosunē*, the "self-control" or "restraint" which Greek aristocrats claimed for themselves (3.37.2–38.1), he illustrates the perversion of language that Thucydides would deplore at 3.82.4. Kleon's critique of specious intellectualism, however, recalls the charges which Thucydides levels at his own specious predecessors, both poetic and prose.

Thucydides struggled to establish synthesis that would answer the valid criticisms of Kleon while avoiding violence and brutality. He attempted to constitute the old aristocratic world view, but in such a way as to render it impervious to charges of naiveté. Thus, Thucydides gives to his Diodotos, an otherwise unknown figure who answers Kleon and argues for clemency, one of the most admired speeches in Greek literature. Faced with a bitter and venomous diatribe from Kleon, Diodotos concedes to his opponent the rules of debate. He refuses to seek mercy on the grounds of either justice or compassion. He argues instead that mercy is simply more expedient and (Thuc. 3.44) thus manages to give the restive Athenians justification to resist Kleon. But brilliant as Diodotos' speech may be, the Athenians would show no such mercy a decade later when they annihilate the population of Melos. Plato understood the limits of this clearly: in book one of the *Republic*, he accepts the same rules of debate as does Diodotos, restricting himself to arguments based upon advantage, but he introduces advantage only to set it aside. The real argument begins in book two, when Plato's interlocutors insist that justice be defended not because of the advantages it confers but because it is good in and of itself. Plato thus leapt beyond that logic of advantage in which Thucydides remained. But if Plato achieved an intellectual eminence that few thinkers in any culture could equal, Thucydides' disciplined restraint has also attracted its admiration.

Finally, I wish to examine as a fourth trend what I will term "paradigmatic realism": new ways of looking at the world may bring overall advantages, but the advance must often be balanced against its cost. Even in the sciences, new schemata that all agree are superior may have serious drawbacks: no one would dispute the superiority of Einsteinian relativity over Newtonian views of time and space, but the increase in understanding came at the price of an enormous increase in complexity, and even now no physicist uses general relativity when, as in most day-to-day circumstances, the old-fashioned view of time and space will do. In the humanities and social sciences, where intellectual progress is far more ambiguous, the benefits of a new realism are almost always problematic. If realists drag new phenomena into the light, they also push other phenomena back into the shadows. The disciplined observer learns not only what to see but also what it ignore—this is as true for the painters, novelists and experimental physicists as it is for political philosophers and historians. No outlook is ever neutral: scientists and scholars alike see what they expect to see. The historian of science, Thomas Kuhn, popularized the term "paradigm" as a label for the formalized perspectives of professional scientists,[7] but his concept arguably applies beyond the sciences. It certainly applies to Thucydides.

Kuhn, for example, distinguished "pre-paradigm" science from its more mature counterpart. "In the absence of a paradigm or some candidate for paradigm, all of the facts that could possibly pertain to the development of a given science are likely to seem equally relevant. As a result, early fact-gathering is a far more nearly random activity than the one that subsequent scientific development makes familiar."[8] Kuhn cites Pliny's *Natural History*, with its wide scope and lack of precise focus, as typical of "pre-paradigm" science. Herodotus was no Pliny, nor did Thucydides shape history at all so decisively as did Newton physics or Darwin biology, but the change which Thucydides imposed upon history—for better or for worse—reflects in some degree the sudden narrowing of focus that Kuhn identifies with the rise of paradigm. Herodotus constructed a brilliant and heterogeneous book—in all probability, the first full-length prose work ever constructed—but, although Herodotus was well known and widely read throughout antiquity, and although Herodotus was, in some ways, arguably more scientific than Thucydides, it was Thucydides—willful, obscure, idiosyncratic but brilliant—who established the ideal canons of the historian. This influence was a mixed blessing, for Thucydides helped limit history to the political and military, while marginalizing social factors and oversimplifying events. Thucydides excluded women from his work to a degree unmatched by virtually any classical Greek author:[9] his was a masculine vision and he did much to establish the gendered vision which almost all realists would share for the subsequent two thousand years.[1] He did more than simply compose a history of the Peloponnesian war. He also established the starting point for ancient historians. And while few of those who followed lived up to the standards which Thucydides espoused, Thucydides did much more than Herodotus to define ancient historiography.[2]

This is not the place to go into Twain-like detail about Thucydides' historical offenses. Much of what follows in this book will examine those elements of traditional Greek culture which Thucydides disdained or which modern readers, going beyond even Thucydides, have overlooked. I will turn to political realism as a particular paradigm which Thucydides in some measure founded and which, in one form or another, seems destined to flourish. First, however, I wish to consider the degree to which Thucydides felt that he had established what historians of science might now term a scientific paradigm.

Successful paradigms, at least within the sciences, allow their users to predict events with greater certainty. Certainly, Thucydides makes it clear that he

7. The classic explanation remains T. S. Kuhn, *The Structure of Scientific Revolutions* (Chicago, 1970); R. Boyd's Introductory Essay in Boyd, P. Gasper and J. D. Trout, edd., *The Philosophy of Science* (Cambridge, 1991), 12–14 briefly summarizes Kuhn while placing his work within the broader framework of the philosophy of science. Kuhn was criticized for using the term "paradigm" inconsistently and he tried in later work to define this concept more narrowly, but many practicing historians of science find the original exposition to be the most useful, perhaps because of its ambiguities and flexibility: e.g., I. B. Cohen, *Revolution in Science* (Cambridge, 1985), xvi–xvii.
8. Kuhn, *Structure*, 15.
9. Perhaps the most enduring change which Thucydides helped establish was the astounding decline in the role assigned to women as we move from Herodotus to Thucydides: numerically, women appear only about one tenth as often in Thucydides as in Herodotus. Even then these few Thucydidean women appear mainly as victims or relatives, whereas Herodotus' women play a far more active role. I have explored these topics at length in Crane, *The Blinded Eye*, where I point out that Thucydides excludes not only women, but all family relationships—male and female alike. Thucydidean misogyny (if that is the correct term) contributes to the large project of reducing the world to individuals and states.
1. J. A. Tickner, "Hans Morgenthau's Principles of Political Realism," *International Theory: Critical Investigations*, ed. J. D. Derian (New York, 1995), 53–71.
2. On the "failure and success of Herodotus," see Donald Lateiner, *The Historical Method of Herodotus* (Toronto, 1989), 211–227.

looked for the ability to foresee future events in his statesmen. Consider, for example, his praise for the early fifth-century Athenian statesman Themistokles (Thuc. 1.138.3). The fact that Themistokles himself ended his days as a wanted man, an exile from Athens and client of the Persian king (Thuc. 1.135–138), did not diminish Thucydides' admiration for him. Similarly, Thucydides takes care to inscribe within the history his own judgment that Perikles' strategy for Athens was correct. Perikles' own mortality constituted the only flaw in his reasoning, for no one after Perikles' death was able to provide the leadership necessary to keep Periklean strategy on track (2.65.7–12).

The idea that human intelligence could accurately manage the future did, in fact, find expression in the fifth century. Demokritos reportedly said that "human beings invented the image of chance (*tuchē*) as a pretext for their own foolishness, for only rarely does chance conflict with intelligence. Intelligent careful observation make most things in life run smoothly." Other texts, such as *Prometheus Bound* 436–510 and the "Ode to Man" in Sophokles' *Antigone* attest that, in the fifth-century, a certain pride in human achievements had at least leavened traditional archaic pessimism about the human condition. Some intellectuals gave full weight to the power of technology and emphasized the possibilities which human intelligence opened up. The optimism visible in the fifth century clearly influenced Thucydides: his "archaeology"[3] dismisses early human history and even the heroic age, stressing that modern society had progressed far and that untrustworthy poets such as Homer had grossly exaggerated events of the past (such as the magnitude of the Trojan war).

Thucydides struggled to establish history as what we would now call a scientific discipline, and if he was unsuccessful in this, it is not clear how much farther we have really progressed in the intervening two thousand years. Nevertheless, if history is supposed to generate scientific laws by which we may accurately predict future events, Thucydides was not successful. I have already alluded to the irresolved problems within Thucydides analysis of the past (for example, the 'archaic' Sparta's defeat of the 'modern' Athens). If Thucydides could not even 'predict' the past, it is hardly surprising that his history ultimately presents a bleak picture of mortal capacity to cope with the future. He begins his history with the boast that (1.22.4) he wrote so that future generations could scrutinize his account and "judge it useful," but this confidence seems to evaporate as the narrative progresses. He approaches his superb account of the plague at Athens with marked diffidence (Thuc. 2.48.3). Thucydides can claim a great deal of intellectual authority, since he lived through the plague and suffered from it himself, but his account, however accurate, has few pretensions. He can offer no treatment, much less explanations, for the plague. At most he hopes that others will recognize this disease from his account if it ever crops up again.[4]

By the time Thucydides describes civil war on Corcyra, knowledge of the past becomes even more problematic. On the one hand, he includes in this analysis perhaps his strongest assertion about the predictive power of good observation (Thuc. 3.82.2). Grim as the subject matter may be, the savagery of the Corcyreans provides us with a case study in which we see human behavior that is typical for such circumstances. Given the conditions that obtain in Corcyra, human beings anywhere will pursue the same harsh measures. Indeed, Thucy-

---

3. The title by which scholars identify the section at the outset of Thucydides' work (1.2–22) in which he presents the history of early Greece [*Editor*].

4. Even here, Thucydides has enjoyed little success: identifying the plague with a modern disease remains a perennial source for scholarly speculation, but no explanation has ever won wide support.

dides justifies his analysis of Corcyra as a case study on the grounds that what happened at Corcyra repeated itself throughout the Greek world and that Corcyra is a general, not a special, phenomenon, Certainly, every continent, including Europe and North America, has in the past decade produced its own Corcyras, and it would be all too easy to establish case studies eerily similar to Thucydides' analysis of Corcyra.

And yet, even if the Corcyrean excursus constitutes a high-water mark for Thucydidean exposition, the triumph of accurate history proves double-edged. The memory of atrocities is not simply a neutral finding but, like the process of war, takes on a life of its own and begins to exert its own force upon events (Thuc. 3.82.3). The participants in civil war become students of factional fighting, and by learning of previous struggles they perfect and intensify their own ruthlessness. Memory becomes an incitement to murder and betrayal, as the reputation of past crimes undermines confidence for the future. The self-fulfilling nature of ideological realism finds its way into the history.

Thucydides and Political Realism

If historians, ancient and modern alike, have generally found that their work, however rigorous and "scientific" in method, does not constitute a science, Thucydides' aspirations have taken root in the "social" or "human sciences." In particular, Thucydides has earned a remarkable position as an acknowledged creator of the paradigm for political realism. Although more recently "post-modernist" and feminist scholars have subjected realism to searching new analyses, the quest to establish a scientific discipline has remained strong. While Thucydides did not work with the categories of late twentieth-century criticism and while I believe that his work has close affinities with the project of social science, nevertheless the history is remarkable in that it both anticipates a number of elements widely shared by realists and reflects a sense, however imperfectly conceptualized at times, of the weaknesses in political realism.

Thucydides' direct influence on modern political thought begins already with Thomas Hobbes, whose first major work was a translation of Thucydides, and on whose thought Thucydidean influence was substantial. The famous "Athenian thesis" of Thuc. 1.76—that honour, fear, and profit" (as Hobbes translates *timē, deos,* and *ōfelia* drive all men—reappears in the most influential passage that Hobbes ever wrote. The thirteenth chapter of *Leviathan* varies the language, but not the substance, of Thucydides, citing "competition," "diffidence" and "glory" as the three forces which drive man. Hobbes attributes to this triad his famous "warre . . . of every man, against every man" which is the natural state of mankind. If anything, however, Hobbes oversimplifies the picture that we find in Thucydides, presenting us with a much more mechanistic and less nuanced model of human behavior.[5]

In the twentieth century, Thucydides' history enjoys a firm position, for better and for worse, as an exemplary analysis of power politics. The struggle between "the expedient "(*to sumpheron*) and "the just" (*to dikaion*) which plays itself out from the opening debate of the history anticipates such later concepts as the *raison d'état* of Richelieu in seventeenth-century France, the *Realpolitik* of Bismarck in nineteenth-century Germany, the "big stick" of Theodore Roosevelt in early twentieth-century America and the cold-war balance of power for

---

5. [Chapter 13 of *Leviathan* appears in this volume, pp. 397–400.] On the relationship between Hobbes' thought, with particular emphasis on the differences that modern observers often overlook, see Laurie Johnson, *Thucydides, Hobbes, and the Interpretation of Realism* (DeKalb, Illinois, 1993) and Laurie Johnson-Bagby, "The Use and Abuse of Thucydides," *International Organization* 48 (1994), 131–152.

which George Marshall was a primary architect.[6] Robert Tucker, writing in the 1960s, explicitly compared Kennedy's July 1961 address to the nation with Perikles' first speech in Thucydides.[7] Thucydides' analysis of the causes of the Peloponnesian War, despite the criticisms of classicists, has remained compelling to many students of international affairs as "the prototype statement of how we usually express the causes of war.[8] Another recent history of International Relations Theory stresses Thucydides' crucial position for this field: "Thucydides depicts a condition in which power wields the ultimate authority in relations among states, so that 'the strong do what they have the power to do and the weak accept what they have to accept.' "[9] At the same time, the ancient historian Donald Kagan, who published a four-volume history of the Peloponnesian War, used his decades of experience with Thucydides as a foundation for broader work. His 1995 *On the Origins of War*, which moves from the Peloponnesian War and Thucydides to the Cuban Missile Crisis, drew advance praise from, among others, George Shulz, former U.S. Secretary of State.[1]

Thucydides has, however, not only attracted considerable attention as a general analyst. He has also become recognized as the first representative of a specific "realist" paradigm for international relations. These realists, in turn, tend to divide into two groups. The "classical realists," such as E. H. Carr, Hans Morgenthau, and John Herz, emerged when Fascism, the second world war, and the subsequent confrontation with the Soviet Union made the harsh Thucydidean outlook particularly attractive. These writers tended, like Hobbes, to concentrate upon constants of human nature to explain state behavior. Subsequently, "neorealists," including Robert Gilpin, Kenneth Waltz, and Robert Keohane, shifted their emphasis away from human nature and towards the overall structure of the international system. They argued that "unit level factors" (such as individual states) were less important than the overall system, and that the overall system of interstate relations defined the constraints which individual states must follow. More recently, scholars such as Richard Ashley, James Der Derian, Jean Bethke Elshtain, J. Ann Tickner, and Alexander Wendt have begun to subject realism to a searching critique from a variety of theoretical perspectives,[2] but even in this revisionist debate Thucydides continues to play a role.[3]

6. On Richelieu, see H. Kissinger, *Diplomacy* (New York, 1994), 58–59; W. F. Church, *Richelieu and Reason of State* (Princeton, 1973), 495–504; George Marshall explicitly pointed out the resemblance between the emerging Cold War and the tensions between Athens and Sparta (see his speech delivered at Princeton on Feb. 22, 1947: Dept. of State Bulletin vol. 16, 391). His reading of Thucydides shaped his view of the contemporary affairs on which he exercised tremendous influence.
7. Tucker in R. E. Osgood and R. W. Tucker, *Force, Order, and Justice* (Baltimore, 1967), 201 recalls Perikles at 1.140–4–5 when he insists that the real issue is not the Megarian dispute but Athenian independence. "Substitute the surrender of West Berlin for revoking the Megarian decree and Pericles' words [at Thuc. 1.140.4–5] seem entirely analogous to the words of President Kennedy in the summer of 1961: 'West Berlin is more than a showcase of liberty, a symbol, an isle of freedom in a communist sea . . . above all it has now become, as never before, the great testing place of Western courage and will, a focal point where our solemn commitments . . . and Soviet ambitions now meet in basic confrontation. . . . If we do not meet our commitments to Berlin, where will we later stand? If we are not true to our word there, all that we have achieved will mean nothing.'" (Address to the Nation on July 25, 1961, Department of State bulletin 45: 268, 273.)
8. Martin Wight, *Power Politics* (New York, 1978), 138.
9. T. L. Knutsen, *A History of International Relations Theory* (New York, 1992), 32.
1. Donald Kagan, *On the Origins of War and the Preservation of Peace* (New York, 1995).
2. Contributions by these authors are collected in Der Derian, *International Theory: Critical Investigations*; to evaluate some of the developments underway, compare this collection (which includes pieces by Hans Morgenthau and Robert Keohane) with Keohane, *Neorealism and Its Critics* (New York, 1986), where Ashley's contribution plays a far more marginal role. Realism has come under increasing attack: the director for one major university press informed me that it had considered three separate manuscripts critiquing realism within the previous three-month period in early 1995.
3. E.g. Jean Bethke Elshtain, "Feminist Themes and International Relations," in Der Derian, *International Theory: Critical Investigations*, 345–346, who stresses "texts as contested terrain"; see also Der Derian's essay in the same volume, 382–385.

Writers within and about political realism take pleasure in determining which assumptions define realist thought. These assumptions, although they vary slightly, remain fairly consistent from author to author. They are important both because they help contemporary realists focus their own intellectual practice and because Thucydides is often cited as a source for one or more of them.

First, political realists, even if they concede to civic life a measure of order and morality, tend to stress the amoral nature of interstate relations. Whatever the religious or political ideology of the time, when nations compete with one another, the powerful dominate the weak. Expressions such as *raison d'état* and *Realpolitik* serve to describe the harsh decisions which actors make when they place the interests of the state over conventional morality. The Melian dialogue and the "Athenian thesis" propounded at Thuc. 1.76 are commonly cited as examples of this brutal Hobbesian war of all against all. Whatever Thucydides' personal preferences may have been,[4] he makes clear in his analysis of early Greek history that fear (*deos*), honor (*timē*), and advantage (*ōfelia*) (the three qualities which the Athenians cite twice at 1.76) are fundamental, even dominant, forces that drive international affairs. Even some ancient historians who express frustration with Thucydides admire him for this: as Paul Cartledge remarks, "Thucydides has a claim to both originality of thought and permanency of value in his unswerving insistence, for purposes of historical interpretation, on the amorality of interstate relations."[5] While Thucydides' history brings out the brutality of, and does not endorse, such behavior, it stresses the gap between conventional morality and actual practice. Thucydides' insistent demystification of motives and rejection of conventional pieties is a major leitmotif of this book.

Second, the quest for power—power with which to provide security and power for its own sake, as a good in and of itself—drives this international free-for-all. For Thucydides, money and power are closely linked. Thus, he represents the accumulation of wealth as a fundamental engine for the growth of power and prosperity alike. Writing of Greek experiences under the domination of Minos, he outlines his model for the development of power and power relations (1.8.3). Here Thucydides projects backwards into the distant past an association of money with power that had gained particular force in his own time. When Perikles analyzes Athenian strength at the opening of the war, he locates Athens' primary strength in its financial reserves and in the ongoing revenues from its empire (1.141; 2.13). In the Mytilenean debate, Kleon and Diodotos each stress the importance of keeping the allied cities in good condition lest they become unable to pay tribute and thus useless to Athens (3.39.8, 46).

Other figures in Thucydides express a sophisticated awareness that power involves perception as well as material force. Thus, Perikles insists that the Athenians must never "yield to the Peloponnesians" on any point (1.140.1). The particular dispute is less important than the act of yielding (1.140.5). The famous Mytilenean debate turns upon the question of how Athens can best use its material force to make the allies fulfill its own needs. Diodotos, whose opinion carries the day, argues that, if the Athenians spare most of the Mytileneans and thus do not exploit their material force to the fullest, they will immediately gain access to more tribute from Mytilene and will in the future waste less of their re-

---

4. Few students of Thucydides, whether from classics, political philosophy or international relations, would deny that Thucydides, despite his pose as a detached observer, structured his narrative in such a way as to provoke our horror at the extremes of power politics.
5. Paul Cartledge, *Sparta and Lakonia: A Regional History: 1300–362 B.C.* (London and Boston, 1979), 255; see also G. E. M. de Sainte Croix, *The Origins of the Peloponnesian War* (London, 1972), 5–34.

sources in putting down revolts (3.46). Melos was a small island with negligible resources, but the Athenians insisted on subduing it because domination of all the islands would have a powerful symbolic effect upon the rest of the allies (5.95, 97). The Thucydidean Alcibiades owes much of his reputation for brilliance to his understanding of the relationship between the appearance and reality of material power (e.g. 6.15.2).

But if all states and all individuals pursue power to some extent, ambition consumes the Athenians far more intensely than any other group. The qualitatively distinct thirst for power which shapes Athenian character is, in fact, crucial to the history. It terrifies the Corinthians, leading them to badger the Spartans into war (1.68–71), while it provides Alcibiades with a psychological argument for the Sicilian expedition (6.18). Thucydides even inserts power into the one idealizing vision of Athens that the history contains: during the Funeral Oration, Perikles urges his fellow Athenians to gaze upon the power (*dunamis*) of, and thus become infatuated with, Athens (2.43.1).

Third, realists have traditionally viewed interstate affairs as an anarchic system in which hegemony or domination alone can bring order. The quest for power, for all its problems, is at least ambiguous, because success in this quest can bring order to a chaotic world. Realism thus brings with it a certain bias towards supranational structures, even empires, as a constructive thing, and for those with more liberal values this can lead to an intellectual tension. The United Nations is only the most prominent example of the compromises that can result from this tug of war between the realist fear of anarchy and the liberal respect for multiple sovereignty and decentralized power. Thucydides fits squarely within this tradition: where Perikles' Funeral Oration articulates an almost heroic vision of individual freedom, Thucydides clearly represents human society as anarchic, almost Hobbesian: without strong imperial superstructures such as those imposed by Minos in the past or Athens in the present, individual prosperity has little chance. Even Perikles, when plague ravages the city and Athenian society starts to come unglued, shifts his focus in his final speech, stressing the primacy of state over individual and reflecting the fear that anarchy is the "state of nature" within as well as between city-states.

Fourth, realists generally view the group as the standard unit of analysis. Because for three hundred years the modern nation state has dominated international relations (by convention, since the Peace of Westphalia in 1648), it provides the focus for most realist work, but virtually all realists acknowledge the nation state to be a special case—tribes, empires, fiefdoms, or virtually any other organized group (such as city-states) would do just as well. This attitude corresponds closely to Thucydides' practice, especially in the early books, which tend to lump together "the Athenians," "the Corinthians," and "the Spartans," representing each as speaking with a single, undifferentiated voice.

Nevertheless, individual actors exercise an increasing influence on events in the later books, and the integrity of the individual city-states grows weaker. I believe not only that Thucydides' attitude genuinely shifts, but also that his attitude does more than reflect what he sees. The fragmented nature of events in book eight reflects two failures of Thucydides' intellectual expectations. First, the Periklean model of leadership ceases to function, as Thucydides himself points out (Thuc. 2.65.10–11). Even talented men such as Alcibiades and Phrynichos simply cannot place the welfare of the state above their own, and they fail to provide the kind of leadership that Thucydides attributes to Perikles. But there was a second factor at work which Thucydides does not recognize, for it occupies a blind spot in his vision. Thucydides represents the weak leadership that followed Perikles as a decline from a previous state of affairs, but this is only partially correct, for, with the possible exception of Themistokles (cf. 1.138), Perikles towered over his predecessors as well. The politics of Alcibiades, Phrynichos, and the other figures who dominate the end of the history are not so much a new phenomenon as they are a throwback to the traditional politics of the archaic and classical period, with their emphasis on the connections and alliances of individuals. Thucydides does not make this connection, because he has resolutely excluded from this narrative virtually all of the mechanics which normally governed such behavior. Here his paradigmatic vision is at its weakest, for he excludes and underestimates crucial aspects of this system. Reversion to traditional standards thus appears as a decline from Periklean standards.

Thucydides' "tragic vision" of Athenian decline has both an objective and a subjective dimension. On the one hand, there was the terrible contradiction between Athens' greatness and its fall. Even Perikles in his final speech treats the fall of Athens as inevitable. I will stress as well the distance that separates the "heroic" Athens of Marathon and Salamis from the ruthless Athens of Melos and the Sicilian expedition. The object of Thucydides' history is thus tragic.

But Thucydides' vision is also itself tragic because it is incomplete, and because this incompleteness, which blinds Thucydides to many crucial elements of history, is also intimately linked to those very strengths which define him. Thucydides has established himself as the first realist because he refused to pay court to sentimentalities and pious fictions. His Athenians in particular exhibit an extraordinary candor about their purposes and goals, and while even this candor is at times deceptive and manipulative, the degree of honesty and "self-knowledge" which these Athenians exhibit is at time astonishing. Nevertheless, that very ruthlessness of analysis and refusal to accept surface appearances—the refusal, as he puts it at 1.10.3, to "scrutinize appearances rather than powers" (*tas opseis . . . . mallon skopein ē tas dunameis*)—which so characterizes his work also rendered many factors difficult for him to assess. For, of course, appearances often are important, actors do not always cast aside their pious fictions, and the bonds of loyalty and friendship do not always break under pressure.

Fifth, realists treat human behavior, at least insofar as it governs the relations between states, as rational. If behavior is rational, then we can expect to determine, through disciplined observation, rules with which to predict what choices actors will pursue in the future. Neorealists differ somewhat in that they push the source of rationality one level up from the "unitary actors" and into the international system, while classical realists look to the psychology of the individual actors or the sociology of individual states. The assumption of rationality, to a greater or lesser extent, underlies all serious inquiry—even research into psychoses assumes that scientific analysis can isolate and lay bare the causes for actions which seem bizarre and inexplicable. Nevertheless, both classical realists and neorealists lay particular stress on rationality because they specifically intend to place the study of international relations on a sounder, more "scientific" basis.

Sixth, modern realists share Thucydides' desire for a scientific outlook that will provide tangible benefits to those who make decisions in the future. By confronting the realities of human nature, we can, it is argued, learn how to control them and thus avoid the greatest misfortunes. This is the underlying idea behind Hobbes' *Leviathan* (itself influenced by Thucydides) and much of the recent work on political realism. As Robert Gilpin puts it, "political realism is, of course, the very embodiment of this faith in reason and science. An offspring of modern science and the Enlightenment, realism holds that through calculations of power and national interest statesmen create order out of anarchy and thereby moderate the inevitable conflicts of autonomous, self-centered, and competitive states.[6]

Thucydides, as we have already seen above, is ambivalent about the progress of mankind and the possibilities of reason. He reveals in the thematic and methodological introduction to his work as a whole a sense of history as an ongoing process of development. Early humanity was primitive, life nasty, brutish and short. Basic human responses, such as greed and fear, have provided a foundation for political structures, and these political structures have, as they have grown in size and power, brought increasing order and prosperity. Against the brutalization of war, his Diodotos attempts to provide a rationalized basis for a relatively humane perspective.

But, of course, events proved almost as problematic for the wary humanism of Diodotos as for the more open idealizations of Perikles' Funeral Oration. Just as the plague undercuts Perikles' bold claims, the Athenians would a decade later use the argument of expediency to justify massacre at Melos. At the same time, no new Perikles or even Diodotos would arise. Instead, the problematic Alcibiades would emerge as the most striking personality in the latter part of the history. The tensions between public and private interest would not be resolved, and Athens, the modern sea-power, would ultimately fall to its clumsy Spartan adversaries. Thucydides' history breaks off in mid-stream, its tensions unresolved.

Seventh, realists have drawn criticism for their unconsciously gendered view of the world: realist thinkers have conceptualized international relations in terms of masculine aggression, reflecting the overwhelming predominance of men even now and especially in the governing of state behavior. To a very large extent, this bias towards the masculine and the creation of a world in which men, and men alone, are primary actors was, in fact, something that Thucydides did much to fashion: if we move from Herodotus to Thucydides, the frequency of references to women drops by an order of magnitude,[7] but the phenomenon reflects more than simple misogyny: women disappear from Thucydides' narrative along with families and households, as Thucydides tries to create a discursive world in which individual citizens and city-states are the sole actors.

To sum up, Thucydides easily meets the rather broad criteria by which political realists define themselves, and he clearly deserves his position as the honorary forerunner of a fluid paradigm for studying groups interacting together. At the same time, Thucydides presents a far darker view of the world than any of his modern academic counterparts, and his work manages to maintain, without flattening or glossing over, the tensions which he could not resolve. Thucydides was hardly the first surviving Greek author whose work gave expression to the notion that "might makes right": his Athenians at Sparta or Melos had their own antecedents whom students of realism need to consider. At the same time, the assumptions of the world into which Thucydides was born—the Greece of c. 460 BCE—were clearly different from those which prevailed as he wrote about the war's end (2.65) some time after 404 BCE. The changes were in some ways

---

6. Gilpin, *War and Change*, 226.
7. Thucydides: 34 instances; Herodotus 373. When the differing sizes of these two authors are considered, the main word for woman (*gunē*) shows up nine times more often in Herodotus than in Thucydides. On this, see Crane, *The Blinded Eye*.

as momentous as those which separate American society of the 1930s from that of the 1990s. A generation of warfare as well as many individuals contributed to this process. Thucydides, the failed general, who mixed with his aristocratic connections from all sides and brooded upon Athens over years of exile, contributed to as well as mirrored the changing times.

Chronology

Events that seem important but are not mentioned by Thucydides appear in brackets. Events mentioned out of sequence are starred. Slashed dates (e.g., 478/77) reflect the fact that the Athenian year went from summer to summer. All dates are B.C.

Before the Pentecontaetia:

> Trojan War
> consolidation of Peloponnesian League
> ancient sea battle between Corinth and Corcyra
> defeat of Persia by Greeks (479)

The Pentecontaetia (479–431):

A. From the end of the Persian Wars to the Thirty Years' Peace
> building of walls at Athens
> foundation of Delian League (478/77)
> Athenian siege of Eion
> suppression of revolt on Naxos
> ostracism and exile of Themestocles from Athens, death of Pausanias
>> in Sparta
> battle of the Eurymedon River (467)
> revolt of Thasos and Spartan promise of assistance (465/64)
> helot rebellion in Sparta; Athenian aid summoned and then rejected
> Athenian alliance with Argos (462/61)
> [ostracism of Cimon (461)]
> Megara joins Athenian League
> beginning of "first" Peloponnesian War, 461)
> beginning of Athenian military operations in Egypt
> fighting between Aegina and Athens
> Corinthian occupation of Megara; fighting between Athens and Corinth
> Long Walls built at Athens
> fighting in Boeotia (457)
>> battle of Tanagra (Athenians defeated by Spartans) (457)
>> battle of Oenophyta (Spartans defeated by Athenians) (457)
> naval attack on Peloponnesus by Tolmides of Athens
> destruction of Athenian fleet in Egypt
> naval operations of Pericles around Peloponnesus
> [peace negotiated between Athens and Persia?]
> five-year truce negotiated between Athenians and Peloponnesians (451)
> continued fighting in Boeotia (447)
>> Athenian victory at Chaeronea
>> Boeotian victory at Coronea
> revolt of Euboea from Athens (446)
>> revolt subdued by Pericles

523

Thirty Years' Peace (446/45) signed by Athens and Sparta
   exile of King Pleistoanax from Sparta
B. From the rebellion of Samos (440) to the Spartan declaration of war
   on Athens
Athenian subjugation of rebellious Samos
civil war in Epidamnus (435)
   Epidamnian appeals to Corcyra, Corinth
Corcyraeans persuade Athenians to enter a defensive alliance with them
   (433)
Athenians and Corcyraeans fight Corinthians at Sybota (433)
Potidaea revolts from Athens (432)
   Athenians besiege Potidaea
Athenian decrees against Megara?
Spartan assembly votes to declare war on Athens
Peloponnesian League votes to declare war on Athens (432/31)
Embassies sent back and forth:
   Spartan embassy seeks expulsion of Alcmaeonids (i.e., Pericles)
   Athenian counter-embassy seeks expulsion of "curse of Taenarus" and
      "curse of the Goddess of the Brass House"
   Spartan embassy asks Athenians to lift siege of Potidaea, free Aegina, and
      most especially revoke decree excluding Megara from all ports in
      Athenian Empire
   Spartan embassy asks Athenians to give up their empire
Pericles persuades Athenians to reject terms of embassies
Theban attack on Plataea by night (431)

The Peloponnesian War (431–404):

Book 2	fighting at Plataea
431–429	King Archidamus leads first Peloponnesian invasion of Attica
	Athenians commence naval harassment of Peloponnesian coast
	second Peloponnesian invasion of Attica
	plague at Athens
	Athenians try to negotiate with Spartans
	deposition of Pericles
	capitulation of Potidaea
	reinstatement of Pericles
	Spartans invest Plataea
	death of Pericles (429)
Book 3	revolt and surrender of Mytilene
429–426	debate in Athenian assembly over Mytilene
	Spartans destroy Plataea
	civil war in Corcyra
	Athenians try to force Melos into empire
	Athenians send ships to Sicily to assist allies Rhegium and
Leontini
	unsuccessful operations of Demosthenes in Aetolia
	successes of Demosthenes in Ambracia
Book 4	[Aristophanes' *Acharnians* produced at Athens]
425–422	Athenians under Demosthenes fortify Pylos

Cleon and Demosthenes force surrender of Spartans on Sphacteria (425)
Spartans cease invasions of Attica
[raising of tribute in Athenian empire]
civil war in Megara, fighting in Megarid
Brasidas saves Megara for Peloponnesian League
trial of generals who had been sent to Sicily
Boeotians defeat Athenians at Delium (424/23)
Brasidas assisted by King Perdiccas of Macedonia
Acanthus, Stagirus, Scione, Mende revolt from Athens
Brasidas gains control of Amphipolis
*Thucydides exiled (mentioned 5.26)
armistice concluded between Athens and Sparta
fighting continues in Chalcidice
Perdiccas of Macedonia switches to Athenian side

Book 5   422–416
Brasidas and Cleon killed at battle of Amphipolis (422)
Peace of Nicias, 421
execution and enslavement of people of Scione
treaty of Sparta and Argos expires
Corinth, Elis, Mantinea ally with Argos
Boeotians destroy Panactum
rivalry of Alcibiades and Nicias at Athens
Athens allies with Argos, Mantinea, Elis
Sparta defeats Argive coalition at battle of Mantinea (418)
*ostracism of Hyperbolus (mentioned 8.73)
Perdiccas returns to Spartan side
debate between Athenians and Melians (416)
Athenians execute Melian men, enslave women and children

Book 6   416–414
[Euripides' Trojan Women produced at Athens]
Athenians determine to invade Sicily
herms vandalized at Athens
accusations at Athens regarding parody of mystery religions of Eleusis
Athenian fleet sails for Sicily (415)
Alcibiades recalled for trial, jumps ship, defects to Sparta
Nicias and Lamachus seize Epipolae, prepare to attack Syracuse

Book 7   414–413
Gylippus arrives in Sicily, prepares defense of Syracuse
Nicias asks the Athenians to relieve him of his command because of illness, advises they either recall expedition or send reinforcements (414/13)
Athenians send reinforcements with Eurymedon, Demosthenes
King Agis fortifies Decelea (414/13)
Syracusans defeat Athenians in naval battle in Great Harbor (413)
surrender and execution of Demosthenes and Nicias (413)

Book 8   413–411
news of defeat in Sicily arrives at Athens (413)
Council of Elders appointed at Athens

entry of Persia into the war on Spartan side
Pharnabazus and Tissaphernes, coastal satraps,
   offer assistance
Spartans exchange freedom of Asiatic Greeks for Persian
   support in war
revolt of Chios, Erythrae, Clazomenae, then Miletus
Persia begins paying Peloponnesian crews
Sparta gains possession of Rhodes
Alcibiades forced to leave Sparta
tries to engineer return to Athens by promising to deliver
   Persian support
oligarchic revolution in Athens (411)
   government of Four Hundred established
   democracy established at Samos
Athenians recall Alcibiades
some of Four Hundred try to admit Sparta into Athens
Spartans spark revolt of Euboea (411)
Four Hundred replaced by Five Thousand
restoration of democracy in Athens (411)
Athenian victory at battle of Cynossema
Thucydides' narrative breaks off (411)

The following derives primarily from the *Hellenica* of Xenophon, with some interpolations from other sources as marked:

Athenian victory at Cyzicus under Alcibiades (410)
Mindarus killed
Spartan offer of peace rejected on advice of Cleophon [Diodorus 13.52ff.]
Alcibiades returns to Athens (407)
Alcibiades' fleet defeated at Notium (406)
Alcibiades deposed, goes into exile in Chersonese
battle of Arginusae (406)
heavy casualties on both sides
Callicratidas killed
execution of victorious generals at Athens for failing to retrieve
   sailors from water after battle (406)
Spartan terms again rejected on advice of Cleophon [Lysias 13.8–12]
Spartan victory at Aegospotami (405)
Lysander executes three thousand Athenian prisoners
Lysander lays siege to Piraeus while kings Agis and Pausanias
   besiege Athens (405)
Cleophon executed
Lysander dictates terms to Athenians
   declines to kill all men and enslave all women and children
Long Walls destroyed (404)
   establishes Spartan puppet government ('Thirty Tyrants') (404)

The Principal Combatants at the Outbreak of the War, as listed in Thucydides (2.9)

The Kings of Sparta
during the Peloponnesian War

A. the Eurypontid house
    Archidamus II, c. 469-427
    Agis II, 427–c. 399

B. the Agiad house
    Pausanias, 445–426 (filling in for his temporarily deposed father Pleistoanax)
        and again 408–394
    Pleistoanax, 426–408

The Kings of Persia during the
Fifth Century

Darius I, 521–486
Xerxes I, 486–465
Artaxerxes I, 465–424
Darius II, 424–404

Glossary

Starred entries appear only in Xenophon and are mentioned casually or not at all in Thucydides' text. All dates are B.C. unless otherwise noted.

Acropolis   the fortified hill of a Greek city. The acropolis of Athens was home to important temples such as the Parthenon, dedicated to Athena.

*Aegospotami   site of the decisive Spartan victory in the Hellespont in 405 that effectively ended the Peloponnesian War. The Spartan forces were commanded by Lysander. There is good reason to believe the Athenians were betrayed by pro-Spartans. Alcibiades apparently attempted to warn the Athenians of the vulnerability of their position, but his cautions were disregarded.

Agis II   Eurypontid king of Sparta, 427–c. 399. Agis commanded at the battle of Mantinea in 418 and fortified Decelea in northern Attica in 413 at the suggestion of Alcibiades. He was also involved in the siege of Athens in 405–404, though the chief role in the eventual reduction of Athens was played by Lysander.

agora   the civic center and marketplace of a Greek polis. The agora was the focus of a wide variety of activities—economic, social, and judicial.

Alcibiades   rogue Athenian "hawk" aristocrat (c. 450–404) and rival of the older and more cautious Nicias. Alcibiades advocated a provocative foreign policy and then defected to Sparta in 415 when he was arrested on charges of impiety. Driven out of Sparta under suspicion of seducing and impregnating the wife of King Agis, he was eventually recalled to Athens, exiled once again, and was finally murdered in Asia Minor by unknown assailants.

Alcidas   Spartan admiral during the Archidamian war. He failed to relieve Mytilene in 427 and was one of the founders of the colony of Heraclea Trachinia in 426.

Amorges   illegitimate son of the satrap Pissuthnes. The Spartans helped Tissaphernes to quash Amorges' rebellion from Persia in 412.

Antiphon   Athenian aristocrat, one of the leaders of the oligarchy of the Four Hundred established in 411.

Apollo   the strong-willed and often capricious Greek god of arts, sciences, and intellect. His oracle at Delphi was renowned throughout the Greek world.

Archidamus   Agiad king of Sparta, c. 469–427, after whom the first decade of the Peloponnesian War is known, even though he died before it was half over.

archon   one of nine judicial officials at Athens.

*Arginusae Islands   site of an Athenian naval victory off the coast of Asia Minor in 406. The eight Athenian generals in command were subsequently recalled to Athens and prosecuted for failing to retrieve sailors from the water after the battle. The six who returned were executed. The account of Xenophon must be compared with that of Diodorus of Sicily (13.101–2).

Aristides respected Athenian politician who was charged with allocating tribute payments when the Delian League was established in 478.

Arrhabaeus king of Lyncestis, and an enemy of Perdiccas. Brasidas and Perdiccas disagreed on the best way to deal with Arrhabaeus, causing a rupture between Macedonia and Sparta.

Artaxerxes king of Persia, 465–424. Artaxerxes was the grandson of Darius I and the son of Xerxes.

assembly the principal organ of Athenian government. Membership was restricted to adult male citizens. Both rich and poor attended. During the fifth century, the assembly normally met several times a month, although the long war with Sparta disrupted the regularity of these meetings. Debate was vigorous, and voting was on the principle of one man, one vote.

Astyochus Spartan admiral, 412–411.

Athenagoras leader of the democratic party at Syracuse.

Attica the territory of Athens.

boeotarchs magistrates of the federal government of Boeotia. During most of the Peloponnesian War (beginning in 427) there were eleven of these; probably before that there were nine.

Brasidas charismatic Spartan military commander; from the Spartan point of view, the hero of the Archidamian War. He won over much of northern Greece (by oratory as well as by force) before being killed at Amphipolis in 422.

*Callicratidas Spartan admiral for 406/5. He died at the battle of Arginusae.

Chalcideus Spartan commander and associate of Alcibiades. He helped foment rebellion in the Athenian empire and sought Persian support for Sparta in 412 by negotiating with the satrap Tissaphernes, but he was killed shortly afterwards at Panormus.

Charicles Athenian general active in the Peloponnesus in 413.

Cimon son of the Persian War hero Miltiades and probably a relative of Thucydides the historian. An advocate of war with Persia and peace with Sparta, Cimon was a hero of Athenian conservatives and the rival of Pericles. The Spartans' rebuff of the Athenian force he had brought to assist them against the rebellious helots in 462 led to his ostracism the following year. With his pro-Spartan policy discredited, fighting broke out between the Athenian and Spartan alliances, the so-called "first" Peloponnesian War that ended in 446/45 with the Thirty Years' Peace. Cimon returned from his ostracism in 451; with his death in 449, Athenian operations against Persia ceased.

Clearidas Spartan general in command at Amphipolis along with Brasidas in 422. He assumed leadership of the Spartan forces at Amphipolis upon Brasidas' death.

Cleon brash Athenian politician who rose to prominence after Pericles' death. He advocated a strong stand against Sparta. Cleon did not belong to the old aristocracy or share their manners, and many Athenians of aristocratic descent disliked him, including Thucydides. Despite his lack of military experience, he succeeded along with the general Demosthenes in capturing the Spartan soldiers off Pylos in 425. He was killed at Amphipolis in 422 at the same battle in which Brasidas died.

Cleophon Athenian politician prominent after the democratic restoration of 410. He consistently opposed peace with Sparta. Advocates of peace arranged for his execution on a trumped-up charge of treason in 404.

Cnemus Spartan admiral active during the early years of the Archidamian War.

*Conon   Athenian commander in the Hellespontine War. Escaping from Aegospotami when he saw the impending disaster, he took refuge with King Evagoras of Cyprus and did not return to Athens until over ten years later, when he had scored a striking victory over the Spartan fleet at Cnidus in 394.

currency, Athenian   A drachma a day was the pay of a rower in the fleet. It was made up of six obols; two obols was the daily pay of an unskilled worker prior to the outbreak of the war, three by its end. A hundred drachmas (i.e., 600 obols) constituted a mna, and sixty mnas (6,000 drachmas) made a talent. Maintaining a trireme cost a talent a month.

Cyzicus   site of Athenian naval victory by the Propontis in 410. This success enhanced the precarious reputation of the Athenian commander Alcibiades.

Darius I   king of Persia, 521–486. The first phase of the Persian Wars, in which Athens and Sparta united in defense of Greece, was masterminded by Darius and ended in the defeat of the Persian army by Athenian forces at Marathon in northern Attica.

Darius II   king of Persia during most of the Peloponnesian War, from 424 to 404. Father of Cyrus the Younger.

Delian League   modern name for the naval confederacy organized in 478, after the end of the Persian Wars, under the leadership of Athens. The name comes from the island of Delos, where the league treasury was kept; contributions were assessed for each of the over 100 league members by the Athenian statesman Aristides. The league's purpose was to discourage further Persian attacks on Greek territory and to make retaliatory raids on Persia. The Athenians' refusal to permit states to withdraw from the league when they wished to do so marked the conversion of the confederacy from a voluntary association into a de facto Athenian empire.

Delphi   in central Greece, the site of the oracle of the god Apollo. Greeks (and non-Greeks) regarded its pronouncements with the greatest reverence.

democracy   a form of government in classical Greece in which free male citizens were theoretically on an equal footing in civic life regardless of wealth or family background. Athens was a democracy and encouraged democratic governments in states in her empire. Like other Greek governments, democracies denied voting rights to women and supported slavery.

Demosthenes   Athenian general, d. 413. Demosthenes came to prominence in Athens after he won stunning victories in Acarnania against Peloponnesian and Ambraciot armies. His occupation of Pylos led to the capture of the Spartan hoplites on the adjacent island of Sphacteria in 425, a project in which Cleon also played an important role. In 413 Athenians sent him to Syracuse with troops to reinforce Nicias' army. When the combined forces of the Syracusans and the Peloponnesians had defeated the invading Athenians, they executed Demosthenes and Nicias.

Diodotus   Athenian, otherwise unknown, who spoke in the assembly against Cleon's argument that all the males in Mytilene should be put to death, following the Mytilenaeans' rebellion from Athens in 428–427.

Diomedon   Athenian general active in the east in 411.

Dorians   the ethnic subgroup of Greeks to which the Spartans and other Peloponnesians belonged.

drachma   see currency, Athenian.

ephors   five high-ranking Spartan administrators chosen annually to keep a check on the kings. With the power of the monarchy also diluted by the system of dual kingship, the ephors often had the primary say in policy decisions. Every year the ephors declared war on the helots so that these slaves could be killed with impunity.

Eucles Athenian general in command in northern Greece along with Thucydides in 424 when Amphipolis and other cities were lost to Brasidas. It is uncertain whether he was exiled like Thucydides.

Eurylochus Spartan commander killed by Demosthenes' forces at Olpae in Amphilochia.

Eurymedon Athenian general implicated in the carnage at Corcyra in 425 during the civil war there. He was prosecuted along with his colleagues Sophocles (not the playwright) and Pythodorus for failing to subdue Sicily in 424; returning to Sicily a decade later, he was killed fighting in the harbor at Syracuse in 413.

Five Thousand a moderate oligarchy that succeeded the narrower Four Hundred in September of 411 and governed until September of 410. Not much is known about the government of the Five Thousand except that Thucydides admired it.

Four Hundred the name given to the short-lived oligarchy that took power in Athens and ruled during the spring and summer of 411. The Four Hundred may not have been sincere in their claim that they planned to hand power over to a larger group of Five Thousand, but they were eventually forced to do so.

Gylippus commander of the Peloponnesian forces sent to assist the Syracusans against the Athenians. According to Thucydides, he opposed the execution of Demosthenes and Nicias.

helots the state slaves essential to the running of the Spartan system. They outnumbered the citizen Spartans about ten to one. This ratio made the Spartans hesitant to undertake long or far-flung military campaigns for fear of rebellion at home, but in wartime helots sometimes fought in the Spartan armed forces. Disagreements about how to respond to a helot rebellion in the 460s led to the tensions between Athens and Sparta that sparked the outbreak of the so-called "first" Peloponnesian War of 461–446.

Hermocrates anti-Athenian statesman at Syracuse. Failing in his attempt to unify Sicily against the Athenians, he assisted Gylippus in defeating the invading forces from Athens.

herms pillars bearing the face and phallus of the god Hermes. These stood in front of Athenian homes to offer protection to the household. Mass panic erupted when a large number of them were defaced during the night in 415 just at the Athenian navy was about to set sail for Sicily.

Hipparchus younger son of the Athenian tyrant Peisistratus. Thucydides denies that he was co-tyrant along with his brother Hippias, who succeeded Peisistratus in 527, but he was certainly important enough to be murdered in 514 in a coup aimed at both brothers.

Hippias son of Peisistratus and tyrant of Athens from 527 to 510. Expelled by the forces of the Spartan king Cleomenes, he took refuge at the Persian court.

Hippocrates (Athenian) Athenian general during the Archidamian War, killed at the battle of Delium in 424. A Spartan commander by the same name was active in the Hellespontine War in 412/11.

Hippocrates (Spartan) see above.

hoplite a heavily armed soldier, the core of Greek infantry. Hoplites took their name from their shield (hoplon); they were also outfitted with helmets, shin guards, spears and thrusting swords. Hoplites moved in the closely packed phalanx formation, each man relying for protection on the shield of his comrade to the left. They were drawn from the middle class, since the poor could not afford hoplite weaponry, which soldiers had to purchase out of their own pockets.

Ionians   the ethnic subgroup of Greeks that included Athens as well as much of the coastal region of Asia Minor and many islands in the Aegean.

Lacedaemon   another name for Sparta.

Laches   Athenian general active in the Sicilian expedition of 425.

Laconia   the territory around Sparta.

Lamachus   Athenian general sent out to command the Sicilian expedition along with Alcibiades and Nicias. His plan to attack Syracuse at once was vetoed by the others, and it is impossible to calculate how the Athenian invasion might have turned out had he not been killed in battle in the summer of 414.

Long Walls   built between 461 and 456 to connect Athens with its port the Piraeus. The Long Walls made Athens proof against a siege as long as the empire was intact and could supply food via ship.

*Lysander   Spartan admiral prominent at the end of the Peloponnesian War and credited with the victory over Athens. He was in command at the decisive battle of Aegospotami and accepted the surrender of Athens. He supported the oligarchy of the Thirty Tyrants at Athens and established oligarchies in most of the states previously allied with Athens as well. Ultimately the Spartans rejected his harsh policies, assisting in the restoration of democracy at Athens and modifying the oligarchic governments he had set up elsewhere. Disappointed in his hope of making the Spartan monarchy elective, Lysander finally died fighting for Sparta in 395.

Marathon   plain in northern Attica where the Athenians defeated the invading Persians in 490.

metics   resident aliens in Athens normally involved in trade. Although they lacked citizenship, they mingled comfortably in Athenian society and contributed to the war effort.

Mindarus   Spartan admiral, 411/10. Under his command, the Spartans suffered several defeats. He died at the battle of Cyzicus, where the Athenians were led by Alcibiades.

mna   see currency, Athenian.

Nicias   conservative Athenian politician (c. 470–413) who gave his name to the Peace of Nicias that ended the Archidamian War in 421. An opponent of Alcibiades' policies, he advised against the expedition to Sicily. When the Athenians decided to go ahead with the invasion, they placed Nicias in charge along with Alcibiades and Lamachus. He never became enthusiastic about the enterprise, but his attempts to be recalled to Athens were unsuccessful. In part because religious considerations prevented him from marching during an eclipse, the Athenian forces in Sicily were captured and he was executed.

*Notium   site of an Athenian naval defeat in Ionia in 406. The debacle led to the final exile of Alcibiades.

obol   see currency, Athenian.

oligarchy   literally, the rule of the few. Government by a few families or by a clique was extremely common in Greece. Bitter civil war frequently broke out in city-states between oligarchs and democrats; the fighting in Corcyra in the 420s showed how bloody these conflicts could be.

ostracism   a curious legal and political procedure at Athens that seems to have been designed to alleviate civic tensions without bloodshed. Every spring the Athenians decided whether they wished to hold an ostracism. If so, as long as a quorum of 6,000 votes was satisfied, the man for whom the most ballots were cast was compelled to leave Attica for ten years. No crime needed to be alleged against him, and when his ten years were up, he could return to Athens and resume his civic rights. "Winners" of this inverted popularity contest included Themistocles and Hyperbolus.

Pagondas   boeotarch in 424/3, instigator of the Boeotians' successful attack on the Athenians at Delium.

Paralus   along with the *Salaminia*, one of the state triremes of Athens, used to carry official dispatches. The *Paralus* brought news of the defeat at Aegospotami to Piraeus.

Pausanias (regent)   notorious Spartan commander, regent for the minor Pleistarchus, whose father King Leonidas had been killed at Thermopylae in 480. Pausanias served with valor in the Persian Wars but alienated the Greeks by his subsequent arrogant behavior. He was accused of planning to sell Greece out to the Persians and of fomenting a helot rebellion. When he took sanctuary in a temple of the Goddess of the Brass House, the ephors walled it up to starve him to death and made sure to bring him out still breathing so that he would not die on consecrated ground. This episode opened up the Spartans to the charges of impiety regarding the "curse of the Brass House" that the Athenians hurled back at them when they had asked the Athenians to expel any members of the Alcmaeonid family, which was also under a religious curse; Pericles' mother was an Alcmaeonid. The investigations into Pausanias' alleged misdeeds also turned up evidence implicating Themistocles. Pausanias was the father of Pleistoanax.

Pausanias (nephew of the above)   Eurypontid king of Sparta in 445–426 (filling in for his temporarily deposed father Pleistoanax) and again in 408–394. He assisted the Athenian democrats in overthrowing the Spartan-inspired Thirty Tyrants in 403.

Peace of Nicias   agreement that ended the so-called Archidamian War (first phase of the Peloponnesian War) in 421, named for the Athenian statesman who played a key role in negotiating it. Ambivalence about the peace in both Athens and Sparta contributed to the its failure.

Pedaritus   Spartan commander sent to Chios in the summer of 412. He was killed fighting the following winter.

Peisander   Athenian politician. A former democrat, he became an eager supporter of the oligarchic revolution of 411. His accusations led to the deposition of the strategos Phrynichus (see below). When the democracy was restored, he fled to Sparta and was condemned for treason in absentia.

Peisistratus   tyrant of Athens intermittently from 560 to his death in 527. Upon Peisistratus' death power passed, according to some traditions, to his sons Hippias and Hipparchus, though Thucydides claims that Hippias ruled alone. After a conspiracy claimed Hipparchus's life in 514, Hippias' government became autocratic and unpopular. Spartan assistance enabled the Athenians to drive Hippias out in 510.

peltasts   lightly armed Greek soldiers who carried small round shields and light throwing spears. They functioned as skirmishers.

Perdiccas II   king of Macedonia, c. 450–413. At one time an Athenian ally, Perdiccas later turned on the Athenians in the 430s and promoted revolts at Potidaea and elsewhere. During the war, he switched alliances as convenience dictated, allying with Brasidas in 425, with Athens in 422, with Sparta and Argos in 417, and again with Athens in 415.

Pericles   the best-known statesman of fifth century Athens and a member of the distinguished Alcmaeonid family on his mother's side. Pericles was elected some thirty times to serve as one of Athens' ten strategoi, serving uninterruptedly in that capacity for the thirteen years before his death in 429. He led the democratic party in Athens, promoting innovations such as state pay for state service (such as jury duty) that enlarged the proportion of the citizen body that could afford to participate in civic life. In the 440s Pericles negotiated the Thirty Years' Peace with Pleistoanax of Sparta; in the 430s he encouraged an aggressive foreign policy and supported Athens' entry into the Peloponnesian War. He was impeached in 430 when the war was going badly and was subsequently returned to office, probably at the regular elections, but he died the following year.

phalanx   the tightly packed formation in which hoplites engaged in battle. A phalanx was normally eight men deep, but innovative tactics sometimes extended it. At the battle of Delium (424), the Thebans fought twenty-five men deep. During the fourth century, generals experimented with even deeper lines. The weight of two phalanxes pressing against each other was enormous. Hoplites had no motivation to leave the phalanx because each man relied for protection on the shield of his comrade to the right.

Pharnabazus   satrap of Dascylium. Though he first cooperated with Sparta, in 408 he sought to implement an Athenian–Persian alliance. He may have been involved with Lysander in the murder of Alcibiades.

Phormio   skilled Athenian naval commander active in mainland Greece during the Archidamian War.

Phrynichus   Athenian politician and general active in the east and in Athens in 412/11. After being accused by Peisander, he was recalled by the Athenians on the grounds that he had betrayed Iasos to the Peloponnesians; the real reason seems to have been his hostility toward Alcibiades. A democrat when he held his military command, he then shifted his allegiance to the oligarchs and went at their behest to Sparta in the hopes of making peace. Tensions culminated in his murder in the agora in 411.

Piraeus   the port of Athens, fortified in stages throughout the fifth century and linked with Athens by the Long Walls.

Pleistoanax   Eurypontid king of Sparta, son of the disgraced regent Pausanias. Pleistoanax was exiled in 445 under suspicion of taking bribes from Pericles not to attack Athens. He was recalled in 426 and ruled until his death in 408.

proxenus   a sort of inverse ambassador. A proxenus was a citizen and resident of one state who served as a liaison with another. The proxenus of polis A in polis B was a citizen of polis B who had sufficient connections in polis A that he agreed with polis A to represent their interests in polis B. Thus for example the pro-Spartan Athenian general Cimon was the Spartan proxenus at Athens and took it upon himself to represent Spartan interests in his native state. Unlike an ambassador, a proxenus lived in the city of which he was a citizen.

Pythodorus   Prosecuted along with his fellow generals Sophocles and Eurymedon in 424 because the Athenians believed they failed to subdue Sicily when they had it in their power to do so. (It is not clear whether he was recalled from exile and is the same Pythodorus who landed Athenian troops on the Peloponnesus in 414.)

Salaminia   along with the *Paralus*, one of the state triremes of Athens, used to carry official messages. The *Salaminia* was dispatched to Sicily to bring Alcibiades back to Athens for trial in connection with the religious scandals of 415.

Salamis   island off the coast of Attica where the Greeks decisively defeated the Persians during the Persian Wars in 479.

satrap   a Persian provincial governor; his territory was known as a satrapy. During the last years of the Peloponnesian War, the coastal satraps became key players in international affairs as both sides vied for their support.

Sitalces   king of Odrysian Thrace. An ally of Athens early in the war, he died in 424/3.

Sophocles   Athenian general. He and his colleagues Pythodorus and Eurymedon were prosecuted in 424 because the Athenians believed they failed to subdue Sicily when they had it in their power to do so. Not the same man who wrote the Oedipus plays.

stele (pl. stelae)   a stone slab with a text and/or decoration inscribed on it. Stelae were commonly used as markers—of graves, victories in battle, or property boundaries—or to display important texts such as legal decrees and treaties.

Sthenelaidas   Spartan ephor who advocated war with the Athenians during the congress at Sparta in 432.

talent   see currency, Athenian.

Themistocles   wily Athenian politician, engineer of the victory at Salamis over Xerxes' Persian forces. A controversial figure, Themistocles persuaded the Athenians to build a fleet in anticipation of the Persian invasion and was also instrumental in provoking the Spartans by fortifying Athens with walls after the war. During the decades after the Persian invasions, he was ostracized and ultimately exiled under suspicion of treason. Ironically, the architect of the Greek victory at Salamis spent his last years at the Persian court.

Theramenes   prominent Athenian politician and military man, active during the last decade of the war. In the civil discord of 411 and again under the Thirty Tyrants, he sought a middle ground; historians are divided as to whether he was a patriotic moderate or a self-seeking manipulator. He was also involved (as a trireme-captain) in the uproar after the battle of Arginusae that led to the execution of the six generals who returned to Athens. Not to be confused with Therimenes, below.

Therimenes   Spartan commander at Miletus in 412/11. After the Spartans and Persians had come to an agreement, he sailed away and was lost at sea. Not to be confused with Theramenes, above.

Thrasybulus   Athenian general and prominent democratic politician. Along with Thrasyllus, he led the democratic faction during the conflict at Samos. Banished by the Thirty Tyrants in 404, he marshalled a band of patriots and was the hero of the democrats' successful recapture of Athens the following year.

Thrasyllus   Athenian soldier and politician, leader along with Thrasybulus of the democratic faction at Samos in 411. He was in command at the battle of Arginusae and along with five fellow generals was executed at Athens in the aftermath.

Tissaphernes   Persian satrap who administered the coastal provinces of Asia Minor. At the instigation of Alcibiades, he intervened in the Peloponnesian War on the Spartan side in 412, but his support for the Peloponnesians was half-hearted; his real goal was to facilitate a stand-off that would exhaust both sides.

trierarch   a wealthy citizen called upon to maintain and command the Athenian warship known as the trireme. By institutions like the trierarchy, the Athenians ensured that the resources of the affluent would be used in the interest of the state; thus the trierarchy was both a military command and a form of indirect taxation.

trireme   a light, sleek ship over a hundred feet long and under twenty feet wide, with a height of under eight feet. Propelled by three banks of rowers, triremes were the mainstay of Greek navies in the fifth century.

tyrant   a strongman who came to power in a Greek state by some unconstitutional means, such as a coup d'état. Tyrants were often viewed as enlightened rulers who supplanted selfish aristocracies and ruled in the public interest, but in time the word came to have an unpleasant connotation. Sparta boasted that no tyrant had ever ruled there; Athens was ruled by Peisistratus and his sons in the sixth century.

Selected Bibliography

TEXTS OF THUCYDIDES

The original Greek text of Thucydides is available in several classical series that include all major Greek and Roman authors. These collections include not only the Oxford Classical Texts and the Biblioteca Teubneriana, which offer texts in the original languages alone, but also the Loeb Classical Library, which offers a facing English translation, and the Bibliothèque Guillaume Budé, in which a facing translation appears in French. American readers will probably draw the most profit from the Loeb Classical Library; its volumes are easily recognizable by their brightly colored covers, green for Greek and red for Latin. Thucydides appears in these valuable series as follows: Oxford: *Thucydides Historiae*, 2 vols., ed. H. S. Jones (Oxford, 1900, revised by J. E. Powell, 1942); Teubner: *Thucydides Historiae*, 2 vols, ed. K. Hude (Leipzig, 1913–1925; Books 1–2 revised by O. Luschnat, 1960); Budé: *Thucydide: La Guerre du Péloponnèse*, 6 vols., ed. J. de Romilly, R. Weil, and L. Bodin (Paris, 1958–1972); Loeb: *Thucydides*, trans. C. F. Smith (London and Cambridge, Mass., 1919–1923). The Oxford and Teubner texts include the short and not necessarily reliable biographies of Thucydides written in antiquity and the Middle Ages.

MODERN SCHOLARSHIP

A good deal of thoughtful work on Thucydides has been written in English, and we have cited works in English or in English translation wherever possible. Where reference works in foreign languages appeared to us to be particularly useful to students of Thucydides, we have included them also, but we have tried to keep citations of works not available in English to a minimum. Most of the books and journals cited here are to be found in college, university, and public libraries.

Two very useful commentaries on Thucydides are available in English. An extremely full one was composed largely by A. W. Gomme and completed after Gomme's death by A. Andrewes and K. J. Dover, *A Historical Commentary on Thucydides*, 5 vols. (Oxford, 1945–1972); the first volume includes a long introduction. S. Hornblower's more recent *Commentary on Thucydides:* vol. 1 (Oxford, 1991) and vol. 2 (Oxford, 1996) go down to 5.24. Those who read German will benefit from the standard German commentary by J. Classen and J. Steup, *Thukydides* (reprinted Berlin, 1963).

Readers who know some Greek can look up the incidence of individual words in the text in E.-A. Bétant, *Lexicon Thucydideum*, 2 vols. (Darmstadt, 1969).

A number of the most helpful standard reference works in classical studies are not in English, such as C. Daremberg and E. Saglio, ed., *Dictionnaire des antiquités grecques et romaines* (Paris, 1977–1919; reprint, Graz, 1962–63) and

A. Pauly, G. Wissowa, and W. Kroll, ed., *Realencyclopaedie der classischen Altertumswissenschaft* (Stuttgart, 1894–1980). Standard reference works in English include D. Bowder, *Who Was Who in the Greek World* (Ithaca, 1982) and S. Hornblower and A. Spawforth, eds., *The Oxford Classical Dictionary*, 3rd ed. (Oxford, 1996).

Standard histories of Greece during the fifth century include volume 5 of the second edition of the *Cambridge Ancient History, The Fifth Century* B.C., ed. D. M. Lewis et al. (Cambridge, 1992). The period is also treated in V. Ehrenberg, *From Solon to Socrates: Greek History and Civilisation during the Sixth and Fifth Centuries* B.C. (London, 1968); J. B. Bury, *A History of Greece*, 3rd ed., rev. by Russell Meiggs (London, 1967); G. W. Botsford and C. A. Robinson, *A Hellenic History*, 5th ed., rev. by D. Kagan (London, 1969); R. Sealey, *A History of the Greek City-States, 700–338* B.C. (Berkeley, 1977); and J. V. A. Fine, *The Ancient Greeks: A Critical History* (Cambridge, Mass., 1983).

Several books deal with the Peloponnesian War. The most detailed are the four volumes by D. Kagan: *The Outbreak of the Peloponnesian War, The Archidamian War, The Peace of Nicias and the Sicilian Expedition*, and *The Fall of the Athenian Empire* (Ithaca, 1969, 1974, 1981, 1987). The origins of the war are also treated in G. E. M. de Sainte Croix, *The Origins of the Peloponnesian War* (London, 1972) and E. Badian, *From Platea to Potidaea: Studies in the History and Historiography of the Pentecontaetia* (Baltimore, 1993). Aspects of the war are treated in P. A. Brunt, "Spartan Policy and Strategy in the Archidamian War," *Phoenix* 19 (1965): 255–280; P. Green, *Armada from Athens* (on the Sicilian expedition; New York, 1970); A. Andrewes, "Thucydides and the Persians," *Historia* 10 (1971): 1–18; and C. Rubincam, "Casualty Figures in the Battle Descriptions of Thucydides," *Transactions of the American Philological Association* 121 (1991): 181–188. On some of the individuals involved in the war, see H. Westlake, *Individuals in Thucydides* (Cambridge, 1968). Alcibiades forms the subject of N. Pusey, "Alcibiades and *to philopoli*," *Harvard Studies in Classical Philology* 51 (1940): 215–231; E. Bloedow, *Alcibiades Re-Examined* (*Historia* Supplement 21; Wiesbaden, 1973); W. Ellis, *Alcibiades* (London, 1989); and S. Forde, *The Ambition to Rule: Alcibiades and the Politics of Imperialism in Thucydides* (Ithaca, 1989). Pericles is treated in V. Ehrenberg, *From Solon to Socrates* (London, 1968); D. Kagan, *Pericles of Athens and the Birth of Democracy* (New York, 1991); and G. Cawkwell, "Thucydides' Judgment of Pericles' Strategy," *Yale Classical Studies* 24 (1975): 53–70. The aftermath of the war is treated in B. S. Strauss, *Athens after the Peloponnesian War* (Ithaca, 1986) and C. H. Hamilton, *Sparta's Bitter Victories: Politics and Diplomacy in the Corinthian War* (Ithaca, 1979).

Students will also draw profit from books on Athens and Sparta. These include J. W. Roberts, *City of Sokrates* (London, 1984); A. Powell, *Athens and Sparta: Constructing Greek Political and Social History from 478* B.C. (Portland, 1988); P. Cartledge, *Sparta and Lakonia: A Regional History: 1300–362* B.C. (London, 1979); and W. G. Forrest, *A History of Sparta c. 950–192* B.C. (London, 1980). The politicians active during the Peloponnesian War and the Athenians' responses to them are discussed in W. R. Connor, *The New Politicians of Fifth-Century Athens* (Indianapolis, 1992) and M. Vickers, *Pericles on Stage: Political Comedy in Aristophanes' Early Plays* (Austin, Tex., 1997).

Many valuable book-length studies of Thucydides are available in English. Students may want to begin with W. R. Connor, *Thucydides* (Princeton, 1984). Other valuable works include F. E. Adcock, *Thucydides and His History* (Cambridge, 1963, repr. Hamden, Conn., 1973); J. H. Finley, *Three Essays on Thucy-*

dides (Cambridge, Mass., 1967); V. Hunter, *Thucydides the Artful Reporter* (Toronto, 1973); L. Edmunds, *Chance and Intelligence in Thucydides* (Cambridge, Mass.,1975); P. Pouncey, *The Necessities of War: A Study of Thucydides' Pessimism* (New York, 1980); D. Proctor, *The Experience of Thucydides* (Warminster, England, 1980); H. Rawlings, *The Structure of Thucydides' History* (Princeton, 1981); S. Hornblower, *Thucydides* (Baltimore, 1986); M. Ostwald, *Ananke in Thucydides* (Atlanta, 1988); J. de Romilly, *Thucydides and Athenian Imperialism*, trans. P. Thody (Oxford; reprint Salem, N. H., 1988); J. Allison, *Power and Preparedness in Thucydides* (Baltimore, 1989); L. Kallet-Marx, *Money, Expense, and Naval Power in Thucydides' History 1–5.24* (Berkeley, 1993); and G. Crane, *The Blinded Eye: Thucydides and the New Written Word* (Lanham, Md., 1996).

Although it concentrates on the period prior to the Peloponnesian War, much can be learned about military matters in Thucydides' time from V. Hanson, *The Western Way of War: Infantry Battle in Classical Greece* (New York, 1989). A great deal of information is also contained in W. K. Pritchett, *The Greek State at War*, 4 vols. (Berkeley, 1971–1985) and M. Sage, *Warfare in Ancient Greece: A Sourcebook* (London, 1996). *The Athenian Trireme* by J. S. Morrison and J. F. Coates (Cambridge, 1986) includes valuable illustrations; the political implications of trireme warfare are explored in B. S. Strauss, "The Athenian Trireme, School of Democracy," in J. Ober and C. Hedrick, eds., *Demokratia: A Conversation on Democracies, Ancient and Modern* (Princeton, 1996), 313–325. On Thucydides and religion, see N. Marinatos, *Thucydides and Religion* (Königstein, 1981) and S. Hornblower, "The Religious Dimension of the Peloponnesian War," *Harvard Studies in Classical Philology* 94 (1992): 169–197. Gender issues in Thucydides are treated in Crane, *The Blinded Eye*, Chapter 3; T. Wiedemann, "Thucydides, Women, and the Limits of Rational Analysis," *Greece and Rome* 30 (2): 163–170; D. Harvey, "Women in Thucydides," *Arethusa* 18 (1985): 67–90; and P. Cartledge, "The Silent Women of Thucydides: 2.45.2 Re-Viewed," in R. Rosen and J. Farrell, ed., *Nomodeiktes: Greek Studies in Honor of Martin Ostwald* (Ann Arbor, 1993): 125–132.

Thucydides can profitably be studied in connection with Herodotus. Works on the writing of history in Greece include V. Hunter, *Past and Process in Herodotus and Thucydides* (Princeton, 1982) and C. Fornara, *The Nature of History in Greece and Rome* (Berkeley, 1988).

Those interested in the period Thucydides discusses will want to explore other literature written in Athens at the time—tragedies like Sophocles' *Oedipus the King* and Euripides' *Suppliants* and *The Trojan Women*, for example. The comic dramatist Aristophanes dealt directly with the war in numerous plays including *The Acharnians*, *Peace*, and *Lysistrata*. Though written several centuries later, Plutarch's *Lives* of Pericles, Nicias, and Alcibiades drew on earlier sources now lost to us and shed light on the history and mores of the war era. All these works are available in a variety of translations, including those included in the Loeb Classical Library collection. The speeches of Athenian orators, even those composed during the fourth century, often shed light on the events of the war. See, for example, the Loeb editions of *Minor Attic Orators, Vol. 1: Antiphon, Andocides*, trans. K. J. Maidment (London and Cambridge, Mass., 1941) and *Lysias*, trans. W. R. M. Lamb (London and Cambridge, Mass. 1930). The Loeb series also offers twelve volumes of Diodorus of Sicily, translated by C. H. Oldfather.

Thucydides' views of Athenian democracy are debated in M. McGregor, "The Politics of the Historian Thucydides," *Phoenix* 10 (1956): 93–102; M. Pope, "Thucydides and Democracy," *Historia* 37 (1988): 276–96; and Chapter 6 of J. P. Euben, *The Tragedy of Political Theory: The Road Not Taken* (Princeton, 1990). Particular issues regarding the oligarchy are discussed in E. Harris, "The Constitution of the Five Thousand," *Harvard Studies in Classical Philology* 93 (1990): 243–80. The treatment of power relations in Thucydides' work more broadly construed is discussed by classicists and several political scientists, such as D. Grene, *Greek Political Theory: The Image of Man in Thucydides and Plato* (Chicago, 1965); G. Kateb, "Thucydides' History: A Manual of Statecraft," *Political Science Quarterly* 79 (1964): 481–503; A. Saxonhouse, "Nature and Convention in Thucydides' History," *Polity* 10 (1978): 461–487; M. Palmer, *Love of Glory and the Common Good: Aspects of the Political Thought of Thucydides* (Lanham, Md., 1992); C. Orwin, *The Humanity of Thucydides* (Princeton, 1994); P. Rahe, "Thucydides's Critique of Realpolitik," *Security Studies* 5 (1995/96): 101–39; and D. Garst, "Thucydides and Neorealism," *International Studies Quarterly* 33 (1989): 3–27. Thucydides has been examined in the context of contemporary international relations in B. S. Strauss and R. N. Lebow, ed., *Hegemonic Rivalry: From Thucydides to the Nuclear Age* (Boulder, col., 1991). Forthcoming from _____ is B. S. Strauss and D. McGann, eds.,_____

Thucydides has been compared with both Machiavelli and Hobbes. On Machiavelli, see M. Palmer, "Machiavellian *virtù* and Thucydidean *arete*: Traditional Virtue and Political Wisdom in Thucydides," *Review of Politics* 51 (1989): 365–385; and S. Forde, "Varieties of Realism: Thucydides and Machiavelli," *Journal of Politics* 54 (1992): 372–393; comparisons with Hobbes appear in R. Schlatter, "Thomas Hobbes and Thucydides," *Journal of the History of Ideas* 6 (1945): 350–362; G. Slomp, "Hobbes, Thucydides and the Three Greatest Things," *History of Political Thought* 11 (1990): 565–585; and L. Johnson, *Thucydides, Hobbes, and the Interpretation of Realism* (DeKalb, Ill., 1993).

The much-debated popularity (or lack of it) of the Athenian empire is discussed in G. E. M. de Sainte Croix, "The Character of the Athenian Empire," *Historia* 3 (1954): 1–41 and D W. Bradeen, "The Popularity of the Athenian Empire," *Historia* 9 (1960): 257–269. Students will also draw profit from R. Meiggs, *The Athenian Empire* (Oxford, 1972).

The speeches in Thucydides' work are treated in P. Stadter, ed., *The Speeches of Thucydides* (Chapel Hill, 1973) and M. Cogan, *The Human Thing: The Speeches and Principles of Thucydides' History* (Chicago, 1981). Discussions of individual speeches appear in A. Andrewes, "The Melian Dialogue and Pericles' Last Speech," *Proceedings of the Cambridge Philological Society*, new series 6 (1960): 1–10 and "The Mytilene Debate," *Phoenix* 16 (1962): 64–85; E. Bloedow, "The Speeches of Archidamus and Sthenelaidas at Sparta," *Historia* 23 (1981): 129–143); and D. Lateiner, "Nicias' Inadequate Encouragement (Thucydides 7.69.2):" *Classical Philology* 80 (1985): 201–213. On the most famous speech in Thucydides, Pericles' Funeral Oration, see J. Ziolkowski, *Thucydides and the Tradition of Funeral Speeches at Athens* (New York, 1981) and N. Loraux, *The Invention of Athens: The Funeral Oration in the Classical City* (Cambridge, Mass., 1986).

The influence of Thucydides on modern thinking about politics and warfare is evident in B. Gildersleeve, "A Southerner in the Peloponnesian War," *Atlantic* 80 (September, 1897): 330–342; L. Lord, *Thucydides and the World War* (New York, 1945); R. Campbell, "How Democracy Died," *Life* 30 (January 1,

1951): 96–100; and G. Wills, *Lincoln at Gettysburg: The Words that Remade America* (New York, 1992), where the Periclean Funeral Oration is discussed as a model for Lincoln's speech. An assessment of changes in thinking about Thucydides in contemporary scholarship appears in W. R. Connor, "A Post-Modernist Thucydides," *Classical Journal* 72 (1977): 289–98.

FURTHER BIBLIOGRAPHY

Ample bibliographies of recent work on Thucydides appear in Hornblower, *Thucydides*, and Orwin, *The Humanity of Thucydides*.

Index of Places and Peoples

Only the text of *The Peloponnesian War* has been indexed; footnotes, headnotes to each book, and the material in "Backgrounds and Contexts" have been excluded. All place names are listed in this index, along with the name of the place's inhabitants where that is known. Page numbers in bold refer to maps. References to Athens and the Athenians, except on maps, have not been included, since they appear on almost every page.

Index of Important Figures

Thucydides named many more individuals in his history than could be included here. Only the text of *The Peloponnesian War* has been indexed; footnotes, headnotes to each book, and the material in "Backgrounds and Contexts" have been excluded. This index generally includes people who are rulers, important politicians, or major military figures. In addition, any individual who could be categorized as historical, legendary, divine, or heroic has been listed for readers who are familiar with Greek mythology and general history.

NORTON CRITICAL EDITIONS

ELIOT *Middlemarch* edited by Bert G. Hornback

ELIOT *The Mill on the Floss* edited by Carol T. Christ

ERASMUS *The Praise of Folly and Other Writings* translated and edited by Robert M. Adams

FAULKNER *The Sound and the Fury* edited by David Minter *Second Edition*

FIELDING *Joseph Andrews with Shamela and Related Writings* edited by Homer Goldberg

FIELDING *Tom Jones* edited by Sheridan Baker *Second Edition*

FLAUBERT *Madame Bovary* edited with a substantially new translation by Paul de Man

FORD *The Good Soldier* edited by Martin Stannard

FORSTER *Howards End* edited by Paul B. Armstrong

FRANKLIN *Benjamin Franklin's Autobiography* edited by J. A. Leo Lemay and P. M. Zall

FULLER *Woman in the Nineteenth Century* edited by Larry J. Reynolds

GOETHE *Faust* translated by Walter Arndt, edited by Cyrus Hamlin

GOGOL *Dead Souls* (the Reavey translation) edited by George Gibian

HARDY *Far from the Madding Crowd* edited by Robert C. Schweik

HARDY *Jude the Obscure* edited by Norman Page

HARDY *The Mayor of Casterbridge* edited by James K. Robinson

HARDY *The Return of the Native* edited by James Gindin

HARDY *Tess of the d'Urbervilles* edited by Scott Elledge *Third Edition*

HAWTHORNE *The Blithedale Romance* edited by Seymour Gross and Rosalie Murphy

HAWTHORNE *The House of the Seven Gables* edited by Seymour Gross

HAWTHORNE *Nathaniel Hawthorne's Tales* edited by James McIntosh

HAWTHORNE *The Scarlet Letter* edited by Seymour Gross, Sculley Bradley,
   Richmond Croom Beatty, and E. Hudson Long *Third Edition*

HERBERT *George Herbert and the Seventeenth-Century Religious Poets* selected and edited by
   Mario A. DiCesare

HERODOTUS *The Histories* translated and selected by Walter E. Blanco, edited by
   Walter E. Blanco and Jennifer Roberts

HOBBES *Leviathan* edited by Richard E. Flathman and David Johnston

HOMER *The Odyssey* translated and edited by Albert Cook *Second Edition*

HOWELLS *The Rise of Silas Lapham* edited by Don L. Cook

IBSEN *The Wild Duck* translated and edited by Dounia B. Christiani

JAMES *The Ambassadors* edited by S. P. Rosenbaum *Second Edition*

JAMES *The American* edited by James W. Tuttleton

JAMES *The Portrait of a Lady* edited by Robert D. Bamberg *Second Edition*

J MES *Tales of Henry James* edited by Christof Wegelin

JAMES *The Turn of the Screw* edited by Robert Kimbrough

JAMES *The Wings of the Dove* edited by J. Donald Crowley and Richard A. Hocks

JONSON *Ben Jonson and the Cavalier Poets* selected and edited by Hugh Maclean

JONSON *Ben Jonson's Plays and Masques* selected and edited by Robert M. Adams

KAFKA *The Metamorphosis* translated and edited by Stanley Corngold

LAFAYETTE *The Princess of Clèves* edited and with a revised translation by John D. Lyons

MACHIAVELLI *The Prince* translated and edited by Robert M. Adams *Second Edition*

MALTHUS *An Essay on the Principle of Population* edited by Philip Appleman

MANN *Death in Venice* translated and edited by Clayton Koelb

MARX *The Communist Manifesto* edited by Frederic L. Bender

MELVILLE *The Confidence-Man* edited by Hershel Parker

MELVILLE *Moby-Dick* edited by Harrison Hayford and Hershel Parker

MEREDITH *The Egoist* edited by Robert M. Adams

Middle English Lyrics selected and edited by Maxwell S. Luria and Richard L. Hoffman

Middle English Romances selected and edited by Stephen H. A. Shepherd

MILL *Mill: The Spirit of the Age, On Liberty, The Subjection of Women*
   selected and edited by Alan Ryan

MILTON *Paradise Lost* edited by Scott Elledge *Second Edition*

Modern Irish Drama edited by John P. Harrington

MORE *Utopia* translated and edited by Robert M. Adams *Second Edition*

NEWMAN *Apologia Pro Vita Sua* edited by David J. DeLaura

NEWTON *Newton* edited by I. Bernard Cohen and Richard S. Westfall

NORRIS *McTeague* edited by Donald Pizer *Second Edition*

Restoration and Eighteenth-Century Comedy edited by Scott McMillin *Second Edition*

CH *Adrienne Rich's Poetry and Prose* edited by Barbara Charlesworth Gelpi and
Albert Gelpi
OUSSEAU *Rousseau's Political Writings* edited by Alan Ritter and translated by
Julia Conaway Bondanella
. PAUL *The Writings of St. Paul* edited by Wayne A. Meeks
IAKESPEARE *Hamlet* edited by Cyrus Hoy *Second Edition*
IAKESPEARE *Henry IV, Part I* edited by James L. Sanderson *Second Edition*
IAW *Bernard Shaw's Plays* edited by Warren Sylvester Smith
IELLEY *Frankenstein* edited by J. Paul Hunter
IELLEY *Shelley's Poetry and Prose* selected and edited by Donald H. Reiman and
Sharon B. Powers
MOLLETT *Humphry Clinker* edited by James L. Thorson
OPHOCLES *Oedipus Tyrannus* translated and edited by Luci Berkowitz and
Theodore F. Brunner
PENSER *Edmund Spenser's Poetry* selected and edited by Hugh Maclean and
Anne Lake Prescott *Third Edition*
TENDHAL *Red and Black* translated and edited by Robert M. Adams
TERNE *Tristram Shandy* edited by Howard Anderson
OKER *Dracula* edited by Nina Auerbach and David Skal
OWE *Uncle Tom's Cabin* edited by Elizabeth Ammons
WIFT *Gulliver's Travels* edited by Robert A. Greenberg *Second Edition*
WIFT *The Writings of Jonathan Swift* edited by Robert A. Greenberg and William B. Piper
ENNYSON *In Memoriam* edited by Robert H. Ross
ENNYSON *Tennyson's Poetry* selected and edited by Robert W. Hill, Jr.
IACKERAY *Vanity Fair* edited by Peter Shillingsburg
IOREAU *Walden and Resistance to Civil Government* edited by William Rossi
Second Edition
IUCYDIDES *The Peloponnesian War* translated by Walter Blanco edited by Walter Blanco
and Jennifer Tolbert Roberts
OLSTOY *Anna Karenina* edited and with a revised translation by George Gibian
Second Edition
OLSTOY *Tolstoy's Short Fiction* edited and with revised translations by Michael R. Katz
OLSTOY *War and Peace* (the Maude translation) edited by George Gibian *Second Edition*
OOMER *Cane* edited by Darwin T. Turner
URGENEV *Fathers and Sons* translated and edited by Michael R. Katz
OLTAIRE *Candide* translated and edited by Robert M. Adams *Second Edition*
ASHINGTON *Up from Slavery* edited by William L. Andrews
ATSON *The Double Helix: A Personal Account of the Discovery of the Structure of DNA*
edited by Gunther S. Stent
HARTON *Ethan Frome* edited by Kristin O. Lauer and Cynthia Griffin Wolff
HARTON *The House of Mirth* edited by Elizabeth Ammons
HITMAN *Leaves of Grass* edited by Sculley Bradley and Harold W. Blodgett
ILDE *The Picture of Dorian Gray* edited by Donald L. Lawler
OLLSTONECRAFT *A Vindication of the Rights of Woman* edited by Carol H. Poston
Second Edition
ORDSWORTH *The Prelude: 1799, 1805, 1850* edited by Jonathan Wordsworth,
M. H. Abrams, and Stephen Gill